Inclusion in Early Childhood Programs

Children with Exceptionalities

Fourth Canadian Edition

Inclusion in Early Childhood Programs

Children with Exceptionalities

K. Eileen Allen

Carol L. Paasche

Rachel Langford

Karen Nolan

NELSON EDUCATION

NELSON EDUCATION

Inclusion in Early Childhood Programs:
Children with Exceptionalities
Fourth Canadian Edition

by K. Eileen Allen, Carol L. Paasche,
Rachel Langford, and Karen Nolan

Associate Vice President, Editorial Director:
Evelyn Veitch

Publisher:
Joanna Cotton

Marketing Manager:
Rosalind Wright

Developmental Editors:
Alwynn Pinard
Lesley Mann

Permissions Coordinator:
Lisa Best

Senior Production Editor:
Julie van Veen

Copy Editor:
Dawn Hunter

Proofreader:
Lisa Berland

Indexer:
Jin Tan

Senior Production Coordinator:
Hedy Sellers

Design Director:
Ken Phipps

Interior Design:
Tammy Gay

Cover Design:
Suzanne Peden

Cover Images:
Girl with rings: April Cornell/
Ontario Foundation for Visually
Impaired Children
Girl painting: © Ariel Skelley/
CORBIS
Boys climbing: Stone/Getty Images
Group with parachute:
© Michael Newman/PhotoEdit

Compositor:
Interactive Composition
Corporation

Printer:
Edwards Brothers

**Library and Archives Canada
Cataloguing in Publication**

Inclusion in early childhood
programs: children with
exceptionalities / K. Eileen
Allen . . . [et al.].
—4th Canadian ed.

First-2nd eds. published under
title: Exceptional children. Includes
bibliographical references and
index.
ISBN 0-17-640720-0

1. Children with disabilities—
Education (Preschool)—Canada.
2. Inclusive education—Canada.
3. Children with disabilities–
Canada—Development. 4. Early
childhood education—Canada.
5. Special education—Canada.
I. Allen, K. Eileen, 1918–

LC4019.2.I53 2006 371.9′046
C2005-904837-9

Brief Contents

Contents

Preface to the Fourth Canadian Edition

The fourth Canadian edition of *Inclusion in Early Childhood Programs* contains a number of organizational and content changes, most of which reflect the recommendations of instructors who have reviewed the book, as well as the experience of professors who have used this book as a text in a college curriculum.

Basic Approach

As in previous Canadian editions of this text, we believe that regardless of what special need a child has, he or she is still first of all a child. Therefore, whenever possible, a child with special needs should be able to attend and be included in a neighbourhood early childhood program and school. We are aware that in order for inclusion to be effective for all children within a group, additional support staff, resources, and specialized equipment may be necessary.

An inclusive approach to working with children who have exceptionalities has, at its foundation, knowledge of child development theory. In this edition of the book, we have continued to include brief synopses of theoretical child development information, recognizing that extensive development content can be acquired from other texts and is included in other courses.

Our approach to working with young children continues to focus on supporting, encouraging, and responding to the developmental needs of all children. We have tried to provide information that will enable teachers to feel comfortable teaching children with special needs and to successfully include them into their early childhood programs.

We view the early childhood teacher as a member of a dynamic team that includes the teacher, the child, the child's family, and other children in the centre, supported by consultants—such as the early childhood interventionist/resource teacher, physiotherapists, and other specialists, the personnel of the school that the child will eventually attend, and the members of the community in which the child lives.

The historical background of the treatment of children and adults with special needs has been somewhat different in Canada than it has been in the United States. Whereas the United States now has federal legislation that designates specific rights and services for young children with special needs, Canada's legislation is mainly provincial and territorial. This text describes primarily the Canadian perspective.

In most of Canada, it was only in the 1990s that a team approach toward inclusion was recognized as the most effective way of providing support and service to children with special needs and their families. At one time, programming for Canadian children with special needs took place in segregated settings. It is now recognized in most areas of Canada that an inclusive approach is most effective, providing models for those who need them, and giving all children an opportunity, through interacting with those who may be different from themselves, to develop openness, acceptance, and appreciation for individual differences. We are aware that there are circumstances in which some children need to begin their preschool or school experience in a specialized setting, with the goal of moving into an inclusive setting as soon as specific skills (behavioural or otherwise) are acquired and necessary supports are available.

New to This Edition

We have made a great many revisions in this edition. We have reorganized the order of the chapters to meet the recommendations of reviewers and reflect our own experiences in teaching.

We have updated the research throughout the book, including more Canadian-based information wherever possible, and have provided more information from Canadian sources. This edition of the text includes new photographs, charts, and data, most of which are of Canadian origin.

Significant changes include:

- Chapter 2: new sections on a social model for understanding disability and on strategies for advocacy for inclusion
- Chapter 4: additional material on the importance of teachers working in inclusive programs being aware of legislation and social changes relevant to the care and education of children with social needs and their families in their community, province or territory, and Canada at large
- Chapter 6: new information on Tay-Sachs syndrome
- Chapter 7: an updated section on children who are gifted or talented
- Chapter 8: expanded information on cochlear implants
- Chapter 9: new sections and information on AIDS and anaphylactic reaction
- Chapter 10: reorganization of the headings in the section on autism spectrum disorder, also called pervasive development disorder (PDD), to reflect current trends, as well as an updated section on Retts disorder
- Chapter 11: revision of the chapter on the developmental behavioural approach to include a more specific focus (with information and examples) on task analysis
- Chapter 12: now includes examples of screening tools
- Chapter 14: retitled "Intervention with Specific Age Groups: Infants, Toddlers, and School-Aged Children"; now includes a new section on information and programming strategies to support inclusion when working with school age children who attend before- and after-school programs
- Chapter 15: reorganization of the content in the chapter on arranging the inclusive learning environment
- Chapter 17: inclusion of new strategies for dealing with difficult or challenging behaviours
- Chapter 18: now includes a communication checklist for children from birth to age five
- Chapter 19: inclusion of additional information on brain research
- Chapter 20: reorganization so that the chapter on bilingualism and second-language development falls at the end of the text book; this change was made because children learning a second language do not have a specific "special need"; however, they often need specific interventions and require additional support

We continue to strive to present a comprehensive text that will meet the needs of those who want to learn more about ways to understand and work with infants, toddlers, preschool, and school-aged children who have developmental differences.

We have, as indicated above, tried in this edition of the text to include more helpful information for those who work with the large number of school-aged children with special needs who attend before- and after-school and summer programs. Aside from the specific information in Chapter 14, we believe that much of the material in other chapters can be adapted for use with older children. It should be noted that the section on infants and toddlers is more comprehensive than is the section on school age intervention. This reflects the lack of North American research on working with children with special needs in before- and after-school programs.

Comments

Working on this updated Canadian edition continued to be very challenging. Though research exists, much of it is published and disseminated only on a local or provincial and territorial basis. The Child Care Resource and Research Unit of the University of Toronto and the organization SpeciaLink Canada are making major efforts to obtain and publish Canada-wide research and resource materials on inclusive child care. Furthermore, though a number of innovative and interesting education and early childhood programs have been developed in Canada, we have concluded that it has been difficult for these programs to get publicity, ongoing funding, and recognition.

In summary, in this book we have sought to obtain as complete an updated record as possible of current trends in Canada and to provide useful information for teachers who will be working with young children with special needs in inclusive settings. We have contacted, wherever possible, Canadian organizations in an attempt to strengthen the Canadian content in the text by using these organizations' definitions and research. The Instructor's Manual for this new edition has been revised to include more current and Canadian material, as well as a large number of new test questions. Microsoft® PowerPoint® presentations have been created for the Fourth Canadian Edition and may be downloaded from the ECE Resource Centre.

We encourage instructors and students to visit the Thomson Nelson Early Childhood Education Resource Centre website (**http://www.ece.nelson.com**), which has links to a variety of ECE-related sites, free downloadable activities, and information about other Thomson Nelson titles. Forms and charts from the text that are available for downloading are flagged with the icon shown in the margin.

Acknowledgments

We are grateful to K. Eileen Allen and the other authors of *The Exceptional Child* for having written an excellent text, and we have sought to include here some of the new research and resource materials found in the fifth edition of that text. In addition, we are most grateful for the opportunity offered to us by Thomson Nelson to freely adapt and rework the material in this edition to reflect the Canadian experience. We feel privileged to have been able to work on a text that, we believe, will be of assistance to early childhood teachers working in inclusive early childhood settings. We were well-supported by many people at Thomson Nelson throughout this project: Joanna Cotton, Publisher, Social Sciences and Humanities; Alwynn Pinard and Lesley Mann, Developmental Editors; Rosalind Wright, Marketing Manager; Julie van Veen, Senior Production Editor; Dawn Hunter, copy editor; Lisa Berland, proofreader; Angela Cluer, Director, Media Services; Sue Peden, cover designer; Tammy Gay, interior designer; and Steven Savicky, photographer.

We want to give special thanks to all those who have supported us in writing this book. These include the many agencies and people who have contributed pictures and expertise: Adventure Place; Bloorview McMillan Children's Centre; Thomson Delmar Learning; Janet MacDougall and the staff of Yes I Can! Preschool; Moira Bell and the staff of George Brown College Casa Loma Child Care; June Williams and the staff of the Seneca College Lab School; the staff and families of Play and Learn (a program of the Bloorview McMillan Rehabilitation Centre); Ruth Fahlman, Westcoast Multicultural and Diversity Services, Vancouver; Sharon Hope Irwin of SpeciaLink; Martha Friendly and the staff of the Child Care Resource and Research Unit; the Community Living Toronto Early Childhood Education Services; April Cornell, Executive Director of the Ontario Foundation for Visually Impaired Children; Epilepsy Ontario; The Canadian Lung Association; the Asthma Society of Canada; the Spina Bifida and Hydrocephalus Association of Ontario; Toronto and Central Ontario Regional Hemophilia Society; the Muscular Dystrophy Association of Canada; the Arthritis Society; and all those others who have made their personal libraries and resources available to us.

Special thanks go to the professors in the Centre for Early Childhood Development at George Brown College, the professors in the School of Early Childhood Education at Seneca College, and Dr. Judith Bernhard, Ryerson University, for their ongoing support. We are particularly appreciative of the new contributions made by Melanie Panitch, Director, School of Disabilities Studies, Ryerson University; Najhwa Khbeis, Director of the Le Club Childhood Program; and Bernice Cipparrone, Director of the Parkdale/High Park Ontario Early Years Centre, a program of The Child Development Institute. We also want to thank April Cornell and Margaret Engel, co-authors of the first and second editions, who have continued to lend their ongoing support and expertise.

This manuscript was reviewed by a number of our peers across Canada, and we want to thank those who shared with us their insights and their constructive criticism. The people who reviewed the third edition of text in preparation for the fourth edition were Shirley Bainbridge, Mohawk College; Heather Anne Houston, Canadore College; Maxine King, St. Clair College; Leslie Kopf-Johnson, Algonquin College; Marilyn Montgomery, Niagara College; and Jane Proudlove, Red Deer College.

We also want to give special thanks to the children, families, and early childhood educators who have permitted us to use photographs of them. Many of the new photos for this edition were taken at the Ontario Foundation for Visually Impaired Children and the Parkdale/High Park Ontario Early Years Centre. We are grateful to April Cornell and Bernice Cipparrone for their assistance and support.

Carol L. Paasche, Rachel Langford, and Karen Nolan (2005)

About the Canadian Authors

Carol L. Paasche was a Professor and Coordinator of Early Childhood Education at Seneca College, Toronto, Canada for 30 years. Since taking early retirement, she has established a counselling and consultation practice, primarily focused on working with parents and children. She also consults to early childhood centres. Carol Paasche has been an executive on the board of nonprofit community-based before- and after-school program; was a founding member of a community-based, parent-participating, inclusive child care centre; and is the author of the book *Children with Special Needs in Early Childhood Settings* (New York: Delmar, 2004), a resource book for teachers of young children with special needs.

Before teaching adults, Carol Paasche taught in an integrated cooperative nursery school, worked with children with special needs, and did counselling with elementary and junior high school children. Carol Paasche has a B.A. in Psychology and Child Development from Antioch University and an M.Ed. from the Harvard Graduate School of Education. She also completed a year of doctoral studies in Educational Psychology at the University of Michigan.

Rachel Langford is a Professor and Coordinator in the Centre for Early Childhood Development at George Brown College in Toronto. She is editor of *Ideas*, a journal about the emotional well-being of young children in child care.

After receiving an elementary school teacher certificate and an early childhood education diploma, Rachel Langford worked for 18 years in a variety of primary and early childhood settings in British Columbia. She has presented many workshops on inclusive and anti-bias education, English as a second language programming, and emergent curriculum. She edited the *Checklist for Quality Inclusive Education: A Self-Assessment Tool and Manual for Early Childhood Settings* for the Early Childhood Resource Teacher Network of Ontario.

Rachel Langford has a B.A. and an M.Ed. from the University of British Columbia and a Ph.D. in Sociology and Equity Studies in Education from OISE, the University of Toronto. She received the 2005 George L. Geis Award for the most outstanding Canadian doctoral dissertation in higher education.

Karen Nolan is a Professor and Coordinator of Early Childhood Education at Seneca College in Toronto. Before 1998, Karen worked in a variety of early childhood settings, supporting children with special needs and their families. She was a teacher at Bloorview McMillan Children's Centre in two programs: Play and Learn, and Play Haven. Karen was also an Early Childhood Consultant for Adventure Place, a mental health agency in Toronto.

Karen Nolan has a Diploma in Early Childhood Education from Seneca College, a B.A.A. in Early Childhood Education from Ryerson University, and a B.Ed. from York University, Toronto. She is currently completing her Masters in Education at Brock University.

Section

Early Intervention

CHAPTER 1

An Inclusive Approach to Early Childhood Education

KEY CONCEPTS

advocacy groups

handicappism

inclusion

individual family service plan (IFSP)

individual program plan (IPP)

integration

mainstreaming

peer imitating

peer tutoring

people-first language

reverse integration

sensitive (critical) periods

teachable moments

zero reject

OBJECTIVES

After studying the material in this chapter, the student will be able to

- Define inclusion.
- Trace society's changing attitudes toward children with special needs.
- Discuss inclusion in terms of early development, critical learning periods, and teachable moments.
- Discuss the benefits of inclusion for all children in an early childhood setting.
- Identify the challenges associated with implementing inclusive early childhood programs.

Introduction

This book is about inclusion in the lives of young children. **Inclusion** means that children with special needs attend preschool, child care, educational, and recreational programs with their peers. Inclusion is about belonging, being valued, and having choices. Inclusion is about accepting and valuing human diversity and providing the necessary support so that all children and their families can successfully participate in the programs of their choice.

For the past 25 years, families and professionals have been working to provide appropriate and quality education for all children. The first attempt at implementing this goal was called **mainstreaming.** The term **integration** also has been used to describe the placement of children with special needs in education programs. Some professionals argue that there are clear-cut differences between mainstreaming and integration; others use the terms interchangeably. Currently, many early education professionals use the term *inclusion*. The difference between mainstreaming or integration and inclusion is philosophical. In mainstreaming, children with special needs have to "be ready" to be integrated into the mainstream. The emphasis is placed on helping the child with special needs meet the existing expectations of the classroom. Sometimes the child who is "integrated" is withdrawn from the regular program for part of the day and provided with separate support. However, this separation from other children can result in fewer opportunities for the development of social relationships between the child with special needs and those without special needs. In inclusive education, children with special needs are full-time members of the educational setting. The emphasis is on providing the support necessary so that the children are

Inclusion
children are included, with additional assistance and resources, regardless of ability in early childhood settings, educational environments, and community programs

Mainstreaming
children with special needs have to "be ready" to be integrated into the mainstream

Integration
children with special needs are given extra support so that they can be integrated into a regular setting and meet the existing expectations of the classroom

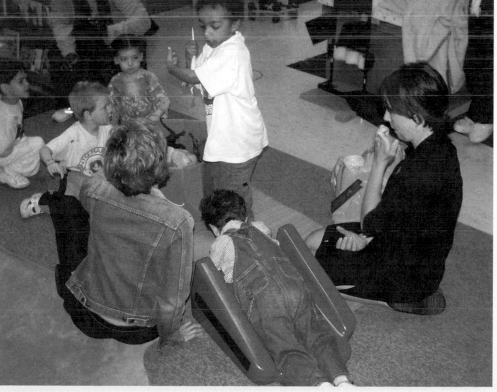

Photo 1–1
Inclusion supports the right of all children, regardless of individual abilities, to participate in early childhood programs.

accommodated and can participate in a meaningful way in ongoing social and educational activities. Support may include adaptation of the curriculum, materials, and educational practices. Support may also include additional staff, consultation, or specialized training for the existing staff. Support services, such as speech therapy and physical therapy, are carried out as part of the daily activities and routines within the early childhood program (see Photo 1–1 on the previous page).

Inclusion Defined

Ehlers (1993) describes three ways to view inclusion: through beliefs and values, through experiences, and through outcomes. We should consider all three views when planning for and implementing inclusive early childhood programs.

The *beliefs and values* that every family brings to inclusion are a reflection of their unique history, culture, and family relationships (Harry, 1998; Luera, 1993). Family choices must drive the inclusion process. The family identifies the community to which it belongs and in which the child is to be included. The concept of "goodness of fit" (Thomas & Chess, 1977) is important when developing inclusive programs. An inclusive program must consider the unique experiences of every child and family, and how the program can address the child's strengths and needs as well as family priorities.

The beliefs and values that influence inclusion occur at the levels of the family, the community, and the society (Peck, 1993). A family's belief system will have a direct impact on their views about inclusion. The sociopolitical context in which children and families live and work also affects inclusion. This includes how our society views high-quality early childhood care and education for all children. In other words, if providing high-quality child care for children of working parents is not a societal priority, providing high-quality child care for children with special needs will not be a priority either.

The *experience* of inclusion varies from child to child and from family to family. The goal is to create a match between the program and the child and family. Inclusive classrooms are caring communities that support the ongoing development of participants (Salisbury, Palombaro, & Hollowood, 1993). Inclusion requires planning, teamwork, and support: "Our values and beliefs will help define our experience with inclusion; in turn, our experience will shape future values and beliefs" (Odom et al., 1996).

The *outcomes* observed and reported by the parents and teachers of children in inclusive programs are broad based and *holistic*. The outcomes include some of the developmental changes observed in specialized (segregated) special education programs (e.g., improved communication skills, improved motor skills). They also include important changes in social behaviour and a general sense of belonging. Many parents of children in inclusive educational programs report that their child received his or her first invitation to a birthday party or to play at a friend's house after being involved in inclusive programs. Some parents report that they feel more included in the community because their child is attending a "regular" school.

Billingsley, Gallucci, Peck, Schwartz, and Staub (1996) propose a three-domain conceptualization of the outcomes of inclusive education. These three interlocking domains are membership, relationship, and development:

1. The *membership domain* includes the child's interactions with groups. This includes being a member of a class, being a member of a small group within a

class, and being a member of non-school-related groups (e.g., children's choir at church). The defining criterion of this domain is that other members of the group are willing to make accommodations for the child with special needs to support inclusion and membership.

2. The *relationship domain* describes peer relationships—that is, relationships with playmates and classmates. This domain looks at the different roles that the child plays in her or his relationships with peers. For example, in the majority of interactions with peers, is the child with special needs receiving help? Does the child have opportunities to be in a role of helping other children? Are there reciprocal or play and companionship types of interactions? Looking at relationships this way allows us to provide rich descriptions of the peers in the child's social network and the many different roles each peer plays.

3. The *development domain* looks at more traditional types of early childhood special education outcomes: changes in participation in classroom routine and rituals, changes in social-communicative behaviour, changes in functional skills, changes in pre-academic skills, and other goals that are included on a child's **individual program plan (IPP)** or **individual family service plan (IFSP)**.

Together, these three domains provide a tool for teachers and families to use to describe the unique outcomes found in inclusive educational settings. This outcome framework can be used to guide the development of goals and objectives for inclusive educational programs (see the discussion of IPPs in Chapter 12 and IFSPs in Chapter 3).

Individual program plan (IPP) an approach to providing services to individuals with special needs: the process involves developing a written plan based on the child's strengths, needs, and interests; implementation and evaluation are part of the IPP process

Individual family service plan (IFSP) similar to the IPP, the IFSP is a written plan that describes services for families with young children with special needs; it is written collaboratively with parents and describes the child's current strengths and needs

INCLUSIVE LANGUAGE: CHANGING TERMINOLOGY

In the past, the term *handicapped* was applied to individuals who were noticeably different, either physically or intellectually. Usually, they were referred to as "deaf and dumb," "blind," "crippled," or "retarded." Society provided "homes for crippled children" and "institutions for the mentally retarded" (a common term used then for individuals who were judged to be of lesser intellectual abilities). Now, we vigorously question the appropriateness of such terms, especially when describing a given individual. Later, terms that covered a broader but more individualized range of disabilities came into use: *Behaviour disordered, learning disabled, mentally deficient,* along with *handicapped, deviant,* and so on, were commonly used to describe both children and adults. Individual identities were locked into differences: "He's Down syndrome"; "She's autistic"; "These boys are mentally retarded." This language devalued people and reflected prejudice and stereotyping toward people with diverse abilities. When society and individuals act on prejudice and stereotyping, discrimination and handicappism result. **Handicappism** is "a set of assumptions and practices that promote differential and unequal treatment of people because of apparent or assumed physical, mental, or behavioral differences" (Bogdan & Biklen, 1993, p. 69).

In this text, a people-first approach to describing children who require extra support will be used (Status of Disabled Persons Secretariat, 1991). Such statements as "She is a special needs child" highlight the "problem," rather than the child; whereas "This child has special needs" puts the focus on the child. The new word order and terminology is referred to as **people-first language.** Incidentally, the people-first approach highlights a fundamental assumption of inclusion—that all children are children and our practices should reflect that reality (Wolery & Wilbers, 1994). Moreover, all children have multiple identities; identifying a child solely by his or her

Handicappism assumptions and practices based on physical, mental, or behavioural differences that foster differential and unequal treatment of people

People-first language language that focuses on the person instead of the disability

Photo 1–2
Identifying a child solely by exceptionalities overlooks the importance of home culture and language.

exceptionalities (e.g., "He is an autistic child") may overlook other aspects of the child, such as the importance of cultural and linguistic heritage in the child's life. The way a child is described may depend on the context and, in some situations, the child's special needs may not be relevant (Photo 1–2). Using people-first language consistently requires self-monitoring. For example, although we strive to use people-first language, instead of describing "the child who is gifted," we put the descriptor before the child, saying the "gifted child." This practice likely reflects different (e.g., more positive) attitudes toward giftedness in contrast to other categories of special needs.

The term *handicapped* is becoming unacceptable. The term *child with special needs* provides a better perspective. This language helps identify that some children need extra support to reach their full potential. This text avoids comparing children (e.g., atypical versus typical; abnormal versus normal) so that the range and diversity in human growth and development can be recognized as a source of enrichment rather than as divisiveness among people. However, when historical references are made, the language used to describe children with special needs at that time will be retained. The language used to describe an individual's abilities is a living language. We need to be constantly aware of changes in usage.

Best Practices for Inclusive Early Childhood Programs

Advocacy group
a group of individuals who work together for a particular cause; the Epilepsy Association works to ensure equal access, opportunity, and acceptance within society for persons with epilepsy

Researchers, professional organizations, parent organizations, and **advocacy groups** in the field of special education have put forth general principles for inclusive early childhood programs (Irwin, 1997; Irwin, Lero, & Brophy, 2000; Langford, 1997; Odom & McLean, 1996). These principles are equally useful when discussing quality early childhood education programs for *all* children. They can be used to identify the *best practices* for meeting the needs of young children with special needs in early childhood programs. Practices have to reflect or be compatible with the following principles:

- be research-based or value-based
- be family-centred
- be bias-free
- have a transdisciplinary approach to programming
- be developmentally or chronologically age-appropriate
- allow for full participation

The following is a brief description of each of these principles.

RESEARCH-BASED OR VALUE-BASED

Accountability must be a cornerstone practice for teachers working with all young children and their families. Practices, strategies, and techniques used in early child education and early childhood special education must be supported by empirical research. In some instances (e.g., the inclusion movement) practices are pushed by personal and social values rather than by research. In these cases it is necessary to work toward gathering the research evidence necessary to evaluate those practices.

FAMILY-CENTRED

In family-centred or family-focused intervention, practices are designed with, rather than for, the child and family. This view of intervention acknowledges that the child is part of a dynamic family system and that any change in the system (e.g., intervention or change in programs) affects all parts of the system. Families should have the right to choose the level of their involvement in program planning and advocacy.

BIAS-FREE

Recommended practices embrace a bias-free perspective and celebrate the concept of family uniqueness. *Family uniqueness* encompasses ethnic, racial, linguistic, and socioeconomic differences, as well as the unique structure and traditions of individual families. This is especially important as our society becomes more diverse and families may encompass unique blends of backgrounds. This bias-free perspective recognizes and respects the different needs and value systems of the children and families. A bias-free perspective must be translated into practice by developing programs that naturally integrate differences into everyday activities. Educators supporting inclusive practices question their attitudes toward differences. They acknowledge bias and prejudice in themselves and others and work effectively to intervene in situations of discrimination.

TRANSDISCIPLINARY APPROACH TO PROGRAMMING

Early childhood and early childhood special education programs should involve professionals from different disciplines working as a team on behalf of young children and their families. Disciplines, in addition to education and special education, that are often represented on early childhood teams include speech pathology, audiology, occupational therapy, physical therapy, nursing, medicine, art therapy, nutrition, psychology, music therapy, and social work. Team members share expertise in their own discipline as well as expertise in working cooperatively with other professionals. (Chapter 3 provides additional information about transdisciplinary teams.)

DEVELOPMENTALLY OR CHRONOLOGICALLY AGE-APPROPRIATE

The concept of developmentally appropriate practice can be equated with "the problem of the match" (Hunt, 1961) or "the goodness of the fit" (Thomas & Chess, 1977) between a child and an intervention technique. For children with developmental differences, the issue of chronologically age-appropriate practices is crucial. This principle challenges researchers and practitioners to consider the unique learning needs of an individual child while developing an intervention program within an environment that is chronologically age-appropriate. In other words, a five-year-old child with special needs should be using materials and exploring environments that his or her peers are using and exploring, regardless of the child's developmental levels.

FULL PARTICIPATION

Full participation refers to opportunities for individuals with special needs to go to school and participate in education experiences, as do other children and youth. For young children these experiences may include preschool, child care, swimming lessons, play groups, trips to the movies, religious training, and dance lessons. A family with a child with special needs should have the same range of activities and services available to them as any other family (Bailey & McWilliam, 1990). At the same time, extra supports (e.g., financial grants, lower staff-to-child ratios) are provided to enable children with special needs to participate in all activities. Irwin (1997) refers to the principle of **zero reject,** in which no child is ever excluded for reasons of level or type of special need from full participation in a program or service. Using this principle, children with special needs are never limited to shorter days or excluded from some types of programs (Photo 1–3).

Reverse integration is the term used to describe programs in which children without special needs participate in programs originally established for children with special needs. In reverse integration programs, the number of children who require extra support is equal to or more than the number of children who do not require extra support. In contrast, some professionals believe that the optimal situation is one in which the percentage of children with special needs in an inclusive program is the same as the percentage found within the

Photo 1–3
Inclusion increases awareness and promotes acceptance.

Zero reject
no child is ever excluded for reasons of level or type of special need from full participation in a program or service

Reverse integration
programs in which children without special needs participate in programs originally established for children with special needs

specific community. Irwin refers to this as the principle of naturally occurring proportions (Irwin, 1997).

It should be noted that all provinces and territories in Canada have their own legislation pertaining to the education of children with special needs. Children in the public education system have the right to access services under the Canadian Charter of Rights and Freedoms. Because early childhood programs are optional, equal access and participation are not guaranteed. Thus, in Canada the move toward including all children is voluntary. Funding, training, and resourcing have often followed decisions by programs to include children with special needs, but without cohesive legislation and regulatory or financial support, it can be easier to find barriers than to create opportunities for inclusion.

Though some of these problems still need to be addressed, there is fairly general agreement at this time that inclusion of children with special needs is a sound and ethical policy.

Inclusion in Perspective

EARLY ATTITUDES

The number of children with diverse abilities participating in community programs has increased steadily over the past 30 years. This is in marked contrast to the way children with special needs were viewed in the past. Caldwell (1973) describes three stages that North American society has gone through in its treatment of children with special needs, and we've included a fourth.

Forget and Hide

Until the middle of the twentieth century, families, communities, and society in general seemed to try to deny the existence of people with disabilities. As much as possible, these children were kept out of sight. Families often were advised to institutionalize immediately any infant who was born with a disability.

In 1958 the Canadian Association for Retarded Children (now called the Canadian Association for Community Living) was established. One person in Canada who contributed much to the process of changing attitudes toward those with special needs was Jean Vanier, a son of the Right Honourable Georges P. Vanier, governor general of Canada. Jean Vanier began by working with people who had intellectual impairments. He was inspired by Gandhi's love and acceptance of the underprivileged and the untouchables in India. In 1964, through Vanier's efforts, a small home known as l'Arche was opened in the village of Trosly-Breuil, France, for patients who had lived in local institutions for the mentally retarded. Supported by volunteers from Canada and other countries, the people who lived in l'Arche actively joined in village life and were accepted by its citizens. The l'Arche model became the basis for a movement that developed similar centres throughout Europe and North America. The first Canadian l'Arche community was founded in the early 1970s.

Screen and Segregate

The purpose of the "screen and segregate" period was to identify individuals with disabilities and provide them with a program separate from their peers without special needs. This movement grew partly out of the belief that individuals would be better served within the segregated or specialized group setting.

In the 1960s and early 1970s, parents, through their local advocacy associations, began pressing provincial and territorial governments for funding for early childhood programs for their children with disabilities. Legislative action was taken in some provinces.

For example, in 1972, the Day Nurseries Act in Ontario was amended to provide a funding mechanism for service for children with developmental handicaps. At this time, funding was also provided by the Ministry of Community and Social Services to open programs for school-aged children who were being excluded from local public school programs because of the severity of their intellectual impairment. As a consequence of this process, a system that was separate from the system available to other children of the same ages (therefore, segregated) was developed (Photo 1–4, p. 10). It was not until the early 1980s that educational services for all school-aged children were provided through the Ontario Ministry of Education.

Identify and Help

The "screen and segregate" period lasted for 20 years or more, at which point the rights of people with disabilities began to be recognized. The "identify and help" period began in the 1970s because of social and political activities. Wolf Wolfensberger at the National Institute on Mental Retardation (now known as the G. Allan Roeher Institute, York University, Toronto) advocated for the integration of persons with special needs into all aspects of the "normal" social system

Photo 1–4
Programs designed exclusively for children with special needs were developed in the late 1960s and early 1970s.

(Wolfensberger, 1972). This movement included advocating integration of young children with special needs into regular early childhood settings. In the mid-1970s, large institutions for intellectually impaired and emotionally disturbed children were downsized or closed and residents returned to mainstream society. The philosophy of normalization and integration at that time was broadened to include all children with special needs, not just those defined as mentally retarded. By 1982, the federal government had adopted the Charter of Rights and Freedoms; this helped to prevent discrimination on the basis of disability (see Chapter 2).

Include and Support

This stage came after Caldwell's stages. It describes our current view of people with special needs. The underlying assumption of the "include and support" period is that people with special needs should be included as full members of society and that they should be provided with appropriate supports, such as education and accessible environments, to ensure their full and meaningful participation.

Rationale for Early Intervention and Inclusion

Early childhood education has been gaining widespread acceptance in our society since the middle of the twentieth century. The formal inclusion of all young children regardless of ability is relatively new to the early education scene, though the acceptance of children with special needs has occurred informally within many programs. The rationale for early childhood inclusion will be discussed in terms of ethical issues, socialization concerns, developmental considerations, and cost-effectiveness problems.

THE ETHICAL ISSUE

The right of children with special needs to live as full a life as possible has been a major ethical force among integration and inclusion advocates. It was Dunn (1968) who first brought the unfairness of segregated education for people with disabilities into public consciousness. He asserted that special classes, for the most part, provided inadequate education for children with disabilities and developmental delays. Advocacy for the inclusion of children with special needs runs parallel to advocacy for bias-free early education. According to Derman-Sparks and the A.B.C. Task Force (1988–89), the goal these two social movements have in common is to gain acceptance in our educational system for all children—those with cultural, gender, racial, socioeconomic, intellectual, or physical differences. Until this is accomplished, ethical issues related to any kind of segregation in our child care and educational systems remain unresolved.

THE SOCIALIZATION ISSUE

Including young children with diverse abilities implies that these children will be given equal social status with all other children. Inclusion promotes awareness of human differences. Members of the community become more accustomed to children with diverse abilities; this leads to greater acceptance. It cannot be overemphasized that young children with special needs are entitled to the same kinds of enriching early experiences as all other children. As Haring and McCormick (1990, p. 102) point out, "separating young children with handicaps from normal experiences creates distance, misunderstanding, and rejection. . . . Moreover, separating these youngsters from the real world means that there must be reentry. Reentry problems can be avoided by not removing the child from normal settings."

Young children with special needs who play and interact only with other children with special needs will not learn a range of developmentally and culturally appropriate social skills. Play with all children must be an integral part of any program designed to promote healthy development in young children with special needs (Wolery & Wilbers, 1994).

All children, during their preschool years, should have the opportunity to get to know children with diverse abilities, especially children whose differences are obvious—children who are blind or deaf, those who have physical disabilities, and those who have cognitive disabilities. During their very early years, all children, unless otherwise influenced, will accept children who are developmentally different (Photo 1–5). In fact, a difference may not even figure in a child's efforts to describe a classmate. One parent tells the following story:

Andrea came back from preschool saying she wanted to invite Katie home for lunch the next day. I could not figure out who Katie was. Andrea tried to describe Katie's hair, then her new jacket, then her paintings. I still couldn't place her. Finally Andrea said, "Katie's the one who comes with shiny ribbons in her hair," and I knew immediately who Katie was. She was the child in the wheelchair who always had big colourful bows at the ends of her braids! Apparently, being confined to a wheelchair was not one of Katie's outstanding characteristics for my child.

THE DEVELOPMENTAL ISSUES

The significance of the early years in laying the foundations for lifelong learning is all but indisputable. As will be described in Chapter 5, it is then that children acquire a broad range of skills in all areas of development:

- They learn to move about, to get independently from one place to another, to explore and experiment.
- They become skilled at grasping, holding onto, releasing, and manipulating increasingly more complex objects.

Photo 1–5
Young children are usually accepting of children who are developmentally different.

- They become increasingly able to take care of their personal needs—toileting, dressing, and eating.
- They acquire their native language and use it in a variety of ways to get what they need (and prefer) from others in their environment.
- They develop the ability to think, get ideas, solve problems, make judgments, and influence others.
- They respond with increasingly sophisticated words and gestures when others speak to them or attempt to influence them.
- They discover ways of getting along with and interacting with others—some who are like themselves and others who are different.

A quality early childhood program can assist all children in acquiring the developmental skills just mentioned. The experience is of special benefit to children with developmental differences or children at risk for developmental problems. For these children, it is like opening a door to both the present and the future. An inclusive early childhood program may be their *only* access to appropriate early learning experiences. They will encounter a variety of challenging materials and equipment, as well as planned and unplanned activities. There will be interactions with all kinds of children who serve as models to imitate and to play with, children who will help and who will need help. There will be teachers who understand differences in development and will assist all children, regardless of their developmental abilities, in taking advantage of sensitive learning periods and teachable moments.

Sensitive or Critical Periods

Sensitive or critical periods
a time when a child is especially responsive and able to learn a particular skill

The majority of young children will acquire basic developmental skills on their own. Some of these skills, however, seem to come about more readily at particular times. These are referred to as developmentally **sensitive or critical periods.** During these periods, children appear to be especially responsive and able to learn from specific kinds of stimulation. The same stimulation at other times is thought to have little impact on development. It is important that all children be in an enriched and responsive learning environment during these periods. For children with developmental differences, it may be even more essential (Olswang & Bain, 1991).

A developmental disability often prevents a child from reacting in ordinary ways during a sensitive period. Parents, especially new parents, on their own in the home setting, may not recognize signals from their child that a critical learning period is at hand. By contrast, teachers in an inclusive setting, where there is a range of developmental differences among children, tend to pick up on all kinds of subtle behavioural variations and many forms of communication.

Critical learning periods that are not recognized and not utilized are common among infants and children who are visually or hearing impaired. Think of the learning experiences so readily available to most children: hearing the difference between the doorbell and the telephone; puzzling over a birdcall, a flash of lightning, or an angry face. These children turn automatically, dozens of times a day, to look and listen and learn specific things at specific times (Photo 1–6). These same

Photo 1–6
Many children turn to look and learn dozens of times each day.

cues, quite literally, are *not there* for the child with a sensory impairment. Without special assistance and opportunities to follow the lead of other children who are responding to what is going on, the child with a sensory impairment is isolated from everyday events.

Language acquisition appears to be especially linked to a critical period in development. A child with a hearing impairment may never acquire adequate communication skills if the hearing loss is not treated before what is thought to be the critical period for language development. Conversely, a child whose hearing impairment is identified early may experience fewer difficulties in language development. A combination of appropriate treatment and a special education program for the hearing impaired or an inclusive preschool (or a combination, depending on the child's age and severity of loss) allows for building on critical learning periods as they occur.

Children with physical differences are also denied critical learning opportunities, but for different reasons. Many cannot move themselves about. They cannot explore their environment. They may not be able to open doors, get into cupboards, run to the window—or learn by simply getting into mischief. Contrast this with children who are physically able and on the move from morning to night. They are touching, reaching, running, tumbling, climbing, and getting into this and that. They try adults' patience at times, especially during critical learning periods when they seem to be in constant motion, as in the following example.

The infant who is learning to walk is forever on the go. Once walking is mastered, a great cognitive advance seems to take place. Then comes another surge of motor development. The child learns to run, jump, and climb, practising these skills relentlessly, all day long. Conversely, those who do not walk until late childhood may have continuing challenges. They may never become skilled at activities that involve sustained running, jumping, and climbing. Even more serious, they may have missed other critical aspects of early learning during the sensorimotor stage when cognitive development and motor activity are so interdependent.

Teachable Moments

For teachers in an inclusive setting, another concept of developmental significance is that of **teachable moments.** These are points in time (perhaps associated with critical periods) when a child is highly motivated and better able to learn particular skills, such as walking, riding a tricycle, or learning to count. All children, including those with a severe impairment, have many such teachable moments (Photo 1–7). They can occur any time throughout daily routines and activities. It is important that teachers recognize these opportunities and ensure they lead to appropriate learning activities. Teachers also can help parents understand the significance of teachable moments and guide parents in recognizing them and finding ways of responding. The inclusive program is an especially suitable place for parents to observe teachers and try out various ways of working with their child.

The infant who is blind and getting ready to learn to walk is a good illustration of a teachable moment. First, though, think about developmental sequences and the infant who is sighted. Walking usually is preceded by a period of just standing, then holding onto furniture, and finally cruising about. Most infants do this spontaneously; no teaching is necessary, no special arrangements are needed.

Teachable moments
a specific point in time when a child's level of readiness and interest come together to create the best milieu for new teaching

Photo 1–7
Throughout the program day, all children have teachable moments.

On its own, the baby who cannot see may barely progress beyond the standing stage. What is needed is someone who recognizes pulling-to-stand as a teachable moment and helps the baby build on it. Experienced parents usually recognize the sign; inexperienced parents may not. The teacher in an infant program should be geared to such moments and ready to adapt the environment and provide specific supports. The more the infant who is visually impaired (or any other infant) moves about, the more the infant progresses in every area of development. In fact, a major reason for utilizing teachable moments as often as possible is to keep the child involved in the process of learning. Hanson and Lynch (1995, p. 210) put it this way:

> The child learns to be motivated and engaged in the environment and to seek interactions both with the social aspects of the environment— people—and with the nonsocial or physical aspects of the environment of toys, materials, and household items.

Imitation

Peer imitating
young children with special needs observe and imitate more advanced skills modelled by peers

Another important rationale for inclusion is that young children with special needs will observe and imitate more advanced skills modelled by peers (Goldstein, 1993). The logic is sound; **peer imitating** is a major avenue of learning for everyone, old and young alike (Photo 1–8).

Young children learn by doing. If children with developmental differences are to learn to play appropriately, they must have children around them who play appropriately and whom they can imitate. If children with poor social skills are to learn to share and take turns, they must have opportunities to imitate and interact with children who know how to share and take turns. If a young child who is hearing impaired is to learn to initiate conversations, there must be peers available who are interesting and appropriate conversational partners. In a segregated setting where there are only children with hearing impairments, it is unlikely that children will do much talking or modelling of appropriate language skills for one another. This is a powerful argument for inclusion of all children in group settings. Totally segregated programs can lead to even greater developmental disruption. When there are no appropriate behaviours to imitate, inappropriate and purposeless behaviours tend to dominate.

Until the late 1950s, for example, many children with Down syndrome were institutionalized soon after birth. Though they often were in an early childhood wing of a residential building, their playmates were children like themselves. The playmates, too, had been institutionalized at an early age. They, too, had never had opportunities to learn even the most basic developmental skills. And so the myth was perpetuated for generations that children with Down syndrome were unteachable.

What many of these children did learn through imitation was a variety of

Photo 1–8
Young children with special needs will observe and imitate more advanced skills.

bizarre or self-destructive behaviours. As noted, their only models were other institutionalized children who had few appropriate social behaviours. Today an infant with Down syndrome is rarely institutionalized; many are included in community early childhood programs. Most will acquire basic developmental skills and attain varying degrees of academic achievement. (See Peterson, 1987, p. 40, for a comprehensive summary of program results for children with Down syndrome.)

THE COST ISSUE

In Canada, the cost of a full-day child care space varies greatly across provinces and territories, depending on a number of variables, including the age of the child. Because of the greater number of adults required for infant group care, infant programs tend to be more costly than group care for preschool and school-aged children.

Most programs serving young children with special needs use specially trained early childhood educators or persons with parallel training, as well as consultants, such as physiotherapists, occupational therapists, speech pathologists, registered nurses, behaviour consultants, and others, including those trained in signing or orientation and mobility skills. Since the staff required for children with special needs is usually greater than regular staff requirements, the cost of operating quality inclusive programs is relatively higher. Because of government grants, the actual fee paid by parents of children with special needs should be no different from that paid by other parents.

The data in Table 1–1 were compiled by the Childcare Resource and Research Unit of the University of Toronto. The material was collected from government officials and child care organizations.

TABLE 1–1

MEDIAN MONTHLY PARENT FEES FOR FULL-TIME, CENTRE-BASED CARE (1998)

Province/Territory	Infant (0 to 17 mos.)	Toddlers (18 mos. to 3 yrs.)	Preschool (3 to 6 yrs.)
Alberta	$525	$450	$425
British Columbia	$650	$547	$460
Manitoba	$573	$383	$368
New Brunswick	$380	$360	$360
Newfoundland	N/A[1]	$380	$360
Northwest Territories	Not reportable[2]		
Nova Scotia	$470	$412	$412
Ontario	$783	$603	$541
Prince Edward Island	$440	$380	$360
Quebec	$407	$404	$328
Saskatchewan	Not reportable[2]	$405	$380
Yukon Territory	$630	$550	$514
Total	**$531**	**$477**	**$455**

[1]No infant care was provided at the time of data collection.

[2]Not reportable due to small sample size.

SOURCE: By permission of Martha Friendly, Author and Coordinator, Childcare Resource and Research Unit, University of Toronto.

The fees vary across provinces and territories, as do the program options (for example, full- or half-day, segregated or integrated programs). In Newfoundland and Labrador parents whose children require additional support to attend an integrated child care program may receive a child welfare allowance (if they meet eligibility requirements) to hire an individual to provide the support. The Child Care Inclusion Program in Saskatchewan provides funding to child care facilities to include children with varying abilities in programs. In the Northwest Territories, parents are eligible for fee assistance for their children with special needs, even if they are not employed or at school. In other provinces, the family must pay or be income tested or needs tested for a subsidy to cover the cost of the regular child care fees. In many areas throughout Canada, there are waiting lists for services for all children, including children with special needs.

Another aspect of the cost issue is the large number of children with special needs who continue to go unserved or who are cared for in unsupervised settings. Simply put, there are not enough inclusive, affordable, quality early childhood programs to go around. Investing public money in additional segregated, rather than inclusive, programs would be a setback—philosophically and financially—in meeting the developmental needs of all young children. In the case of children with special needs, it is vital to begin to support parents and begin the intervention process, as well as to provide an inclusive environment for the child, at an early age. The cost to the public of a "late start" may be substantial, as the child grows older. (See Chapter 3 regarding the role of parents.)

Supporting Inclusion: Implications for Teachers

The mere act of placing children with special needs into inclusive environments is not enough. Teachers must take the responsibility for ensuring that effective socializing and learning occur among all the children. Particular teacher skills are needed. Many of these skills stem from knowledge of child development (Photo 1–9). Effective inclusion requires

Photo 1–9
Effective inclusion requires specific planning and implementation.

- individualizing programs and activities to meet each child's specific needs and abilities (see Chapter 12)
- recognizing that there are no well-defined markers between children who require more support in their development and children who do not
- remembering that the range of development is broad and that children show many developmental differences
- avoiding the possibility of limiting children's learning by labelling, as a label often becomes a self-fulfilling prophecy
- recognizing the value of play as an avenue for learning for all children, and at the same time, recognizing that play skills often have to be taught to children with special needs, many of whom neither play spontaneously nor know how to play

- arranging a balance of large- and small-group experiences, both vigorous and quiet, so that all children, at their own levels, can be active and interactive participants
- structuring a learning environment in which children with special needs and their peers are helped to participate *together* in a variety of activities related to all areas of development
- supporting the development of all children by creating a learning environment that includes a range of materials and experiences that will enable all children, regardless of ability, to participate and learn

Photo 1–10
The learning environment should be arranged to promote social interactions between children with special needs and those without.

STRUCTURING CHILD–CHILD INTERACTION

The effectiveness of inclusion depends on the interactions between children who require extra support and those who do not. Peer interactions do not necessarily occur. Guralnick and his colleagues (Devoney, Guralnick, & Rubin, 1974; Guralnick & Neville 1997) have continued to conduct research on this issue. Their research indicates that all children play together when *the teacher structures the environment so as to promote such interaction* (Photo 1–10). (Chapters 4 and 15 discuss ways for teachers to accomplish this structure.) An interesting sidelight in the Devoney study was that when playing with their peers, children with special needs played in a more organized and mature way than had been characteristic of their earlier play.

In a recent study that focused on imitation in an inclusive classroom, Garfinkle and Schwartz (1998) demonstrated that children with autism can learn to imitate their peers during small-group activities. After the imitation training, the amount of time children with autism played together with peers in small groups during free-choice time increased. From these and other research studies, it is apparent that teacher-structuring of play activities is essential. Curriculum planning for an inclusive early childhood program must focus on activities that lead to all children in an inclusive environment working and playing together (see Chapter 15).

PLANNING CLASSROOM ACTIVITIES

Curriculum planning for inclusive classrooms also requires teachers to integrate the goals identified on the children's IPP/IFSP into ongoing classroom activities. This approach allows teachers to use learning experiences in dramatic play, art, nature walks, and water play to address specific goals and objectives across developmental domains (e.g., cognitive, social, communication, motor, self-help/care).

PROFESSIONAL COLLABORATION

In addition to classroom practices, full inclusion of all children requires integrating professional efforts. Administrators, teachers, aides, volunteers, health-care and social-services professionals, and members of the interdisciplinary team need to work

Photo 1–11
Members of the interdisciplinary team plan together.

together (Photo 1–11). Within an inclusive setting, professional growth comes with the collaborative search for ways to provide for children who have developmental differences. Part of the search has to do with looking for paths that lead to a genuine partnership with parents. As will be discussed in Chapters 3 and 11, this means listening to parents, consulting with them, and learning from them. In fact, everyone—children, parents, teachers, classroom staff, and clinicians—can learn from one another in an inclusive early childhood setting. Early childhood teachers, however, receive a special bonus: In learning to meet the needs of children who require extra support, they become more skilled at meeting the needs of all children. By learning to build on the capabilities of children with special needs, they become better attuned to the special capabilities of all children.

Benefits of Inclusion for Young Children
BENEFITS FOR CHILDREN WITH SPECIAL NEEDS

In addition to the philosophical and legal issues discussed earlier, there are a number of specific benefits of educating young children with special needs in inclusive programs. Children with developmental differences are likely to benefit from a quality inclusive early childhood environment because it provides

- more stimulating, varied, and responsive experiences than do segregated classrooms, where all the children have special needs
- developmental scaffolding for curriculum activities, rather than a *deficit curriculum model* in which the major emphasis is on children's limitations rather than their strengths
- opportunities to observe, interact with, and imitate children who have acquired higher-level motor, social, language, and cognitive skills
- implicit motivation to "try a little harder," in that more skillful children expect and encourage improved behaviours from those children with lesser skills; as Peterson (1987, p. 359) puts it, "A more demanding environment may push the child ahead to develop more appropriate behavioral repertoires"
- opportunities to learn directly from other children: It appears that certain skills are learned more easily from other children—their explanations and demonstrations are often closer to the capabilities of the child with special needs than are those of the adults

BENEFITS FOR ALL CHILDREN

Developmental Progress

Children who are developing at an expected pace benefit from inclusive programs "at least to the same degree and sometimes to a greater degree than would have been expected if they had attended nonintegrated preschools" (Thurman & Widerstrom, 1990, p. 39). There is no evidence of negative effects on any children who are in inclusive programs (Buysee & Baily, 1993; Sharpe, York, & Knight,

1994). In studies that have compared the amount of teacher attention to individual children and children's rate of engaged learning time in classrooms with and without children with special needs, there are no differences, again suggesting no negative impact on child development (Photo 1–12). Another safe conclusion to be drawn from the current research, according to these authors, is that *the developmental outcome for children in inclusive programs depends on the quality of teaching* and on how well the teacher is provided with special supports when needed, rather than on the process of inclusion itself.

Photo 1–12
Parents may wonder, "Will my child receive all the necessary attention and services required?"

Peer Tutoring

A well-documented benefit of inclusion for all children is **peer tutoring**—one child instructing another. It appears that both the child being tutored and the child doing the tutoring receive significant benefits from the experience. The common sense of this is readily apparent; most of us have discovered that given an unpressured opportunity to teach someone else something we know (or are learning), our own skill and understanding are increased. The same is true of children. As pointed out by Spodek, Saracho, and Lee (1984), voluntary peer tutoring among young children of all developmental levels can promote

- social interactions among children with and without special needs
- acceptable play behaviours
- appropriate and enhanced use of materials

Peer tutoring (a child demonstrating to another child how to do something) should not be confused with peer modelling (the unconscious process that occurs when a child observes and interacts with other children). Both peer tutoring and peer modelling enhance the development of children with special needs.

Peer tutoring
one child instructing or assisting another

Development of Sensitivity

Rafferty, Boettcher, and Griffin (2001) surveyed 244 parents of children who attended a community-based preschool in New York. Almost all parents surveyed reported that inclusion helped typically developing children to understand differences in others. The children developed sensitivity and became increasingly aware of their own strengths and weaknesses.

BENEFITS FOR FAMILIES

In general, parents' attitudes about inclusion were influenced by their experiences with inclusion (Lamorey & Bricker, 1993). Parents of children with special needs were most often positive in their responses, although they did identify some concerns. Attitudes of parents of children without special needs improved as experience with inclusion increased. In a study involving 125 parents of children who attended inclusive preschool programs, Peck, Carlson, and Helmstetter (1992) found that parents perceived their children's experience as generally positive and were supportive of inclusive education. Additionally, Peck and his colleagues found that parents reported that their children were more accepting of human differences and had less discomfort with people with developmental differences and people who looked or behaved differently from the way they did.

BENEFITS FOR SOCIETY

Not only does inclusion have positive effects on all children, but it also appears to be of long-term benefit to society. Children who grow up with opportunities to interact with children with special needs are likely to be more tolerant in later years. They tend to mature into adults with greater understanding and respect for those who have diverse abilities in our society (Kishi & Meyer, 1994). Many teachers report that most young children, unless influenced by inappropriate adult attitudes, have a natural acceptance of individual differences. They are unlikely to make negative judgments and comparisons of children who are developmentally different. When they do comment or ask questions, they are doing so because they need to learn about whatever it is that is unfamiliar about the child who requires extra support.

The Concerns and Challenges of Inclusion

As noted repeatedly, the inclusion of young children with special needs in a preschool setting appears to be of general benefit to everyone. Even so, concerns continue to be voiced. This section reviews arguments for and against the practice. Such arguments, however, must be based on the assumption that the studies were conducted in a quality program with well-trained and caring adults in a ratio appropriate to the number of children enrolled (Doherty-Derkowski, 1995). A poorly structured, poorly staffed program can have a negative effect on any child, from the most delayed to the most gifted.

In the United States, inclusion is the law. In Canada, though not required by law, the inclusion of young children with special needs into early childhood community programs is recognized as a preferred practice. The pros and cons of early inclusion continue to be raised and to be the focus of considerable research. The discussion that follows has to do with identifying the most common concerns and providing brief glimpses of research findings that address those issues.

WILL SPECIAL NEEDS BE SERVED?

Parents and teachers have expressed concern that the special needs of children with developmental differences may not be met adequately in a community early childhood program. They feel that teachers may not have the time or the skills needed. The opposite is of concern, also: If a program is meeting the special needs of some children, then what about the other children who do not require extra support? Are they going to be shortchanged?

This concern has been addressed in a number of research studies. By and large, the data indicate that most parents believe that their children benefit from inclusive programs (Photo 1–13). Again, the findings are based on well-structured programs with knowledgeable teachers. Little parent satisfaction is found in poor programs, integrated or otherwise. In a review of a number of research studies, Lamorey and Bricker (1993) state that, in general, the needs of the children were met in inclusive programming. Some parents were concerned about the quality of training received by teachers in these programs. There is a need for different types of training in early childhood education. Professionals need to work on adapting preservice training for teachers in early childhood, early childhood special education, and related therapy fields to prepare professions to work together to deliver quality service to children with special needs in inclusive programs (Odom & McEvoy, 1990; Washington, Schwartz, & Swinth, 1994).

Many researchers have documented that the parents of children without special needs report that their children are learning important social and academic lessons from their experiences in inclusive classrooms (e.g., McGregor & Vogelsberg, 1998). A similar reaction is found among parents of children with special needs. Guralnick (1994, p. 180) reported the following:

Photo 1–13
Most parents believe that inclusive programs benefit their children.

> Particular benefits to children with special needs were noted in relation to promoting the acceptance of children with disabilities in the community, preparing the child for the real world, encouraging children with special needs to learn more, and providing opportunities to participate in a wider variety of interesting and creative activities.

Another parent concern is the possible rejection of children with special needs by their peers. It appears that the children's developmental level did not influence their parents' perceptions of the inclusive programs. In other words, parents of children with severe developmental disabilities were no more positive or concerned than were the parents of children with mild disabilities.

In general, teachers' attitudes are favourable toward inclusion, once they have actually worked with children with special needs in an inclusive setting. Thurman and Widerstrom (1990, p. 40) offer the following summary statement: "There does not appear to be any basis for the fear of children being slighted, as an examination of successful programs at the preschool level demonstrates." Individual programming for children with special needs often spills over into better practices for all children. The authors then go on to talk about their personal experiences: "Teachers who thought mainly in terms of group activities learned, through their work with special children, to plan for individual differences among all children more effectively."

CONCERNS ABOUT INAPPROPRIATE BEHAVIOURS

Another frequently expressed concern is that children will learn immature or inappropriate behaviours from classmates who show less skilled behaviours. Again, this is an unfounded fear. This is not to imply that children do not imitate other children. They do. They should. As noted earlier, imitation is an important avenue for learning. But children learning new skills tend to imitate peers who have comparable or more skills. Rarely (and then only briefly) do they imitate less skilled behaviours of another child. The exceptions are those children who get undue attention from teachers and parents for imitating inappropriate behaviours.

Summary

Including young children with special needs in regular early childhood programs is the preferred practice in Canada. The degree to which a child is included in an early childhood program depends on his or her special needs and the intensity of the services that are required. The reasons for inclusion are based on ethical, social, developmental, and cost considerations. No longer is it acceptable, as it once was, to keep children with special needs out of the social and educational mainstream.

For children with and without developmental differences, the early years are critical years. A variety of learning seems to be *programmed* at particular times as a part of the developmental plan. These types of learning may never again be acquired as readily or as well. An abundance of *teachable moments* occur during infancy and the preschool period. These are best used in an inclusive setting with teachers who are trained to recognize such developmental opportunities. An inclusive early childhood program also provides opportunities for children with developmental disabilities to imitate their more skilled peers. At the same time, the peers of children with special needs are provided with significant learning experiences in helping children who are less able to acquire a variety of skills—motor, social, and intellectual. However, in inclusive settings all children do not necessarily work and play together of their own accord. Teachers should structure the program so that interactions can occur and be reinforced.

A number of concerns about the advisability of inclusion continue to be voiced. A common one, expressed by both parents and teachers, is that the special needs of children may not be adequately met in an inclusive program. Another is that other children will receive less than their share of attention if children with special needs are properly served.

There is also the concern that some children will learn inappropriate and bizarre behaviours from children with special needs. Numerous research studies conducted over the past 15 years demonstrate that these anxieties are largely unfounded. In fact, the opposite is true: The advantages of inclusion, for all children, are numerous and well documented.

RESOURCES

CANADIAN ASSOCIATION FOR COMMUNITY LIVING

http://www.cacl.ca

The Canadian Association for Community Living promotes the well-being of people with developmental disabilities and their families. Links to the various provincial and territorial chapters of this organization are available at this site.

ROEHER INSTITUTE

http://www.roeher.ca

The Roeher Institute is Canada's national organization for the study of policy affecting persons with intellectual impairments. A number of publications and videos on inclusion in community living are available. Its information services also provide current information through its library.

SPECIALINK: THE NATIONAL CENTRE FOR CHILD CARE INCLUSION
http://www.specialinkcanada.org
This organization's goal is to expand the quality and quantity of opportunities for inclusion in child care, recreation, education, and other community settings to young children with special needs and their families.

THE CIRCLE OF INCLUSION
http://www.circleofinclusion.org
This website is for early childhood service providers and families of young children. It offers demonstrations of and information about the effective practices of inclusive educational programs.

STUDENT ACTIVITIES

1. Put together a panel discussion on the pros and cons of inclusion.
2. Observe an inclusive early childhood program. Identify the benefits and challenges.
3. Talk with a teacher in an early childhood centre. Discuss the implications of inclusion for the teachers.
4. Observe an early childhood setting. Record any episodes of a child learning through observing, imitating, or peer tutoring.
5. Set up a simulated parent conference with three other students, two playing the child's parents, the other two the child's teachers. The parents' concern is that their three-year-old without special needs may not get enough attention because a child who is blind is scheduled to be included into the program. Role-play a discussion of the situation.

REFERENCES

Baily, D. B., & McWilliam, R. A. (1990). Normalizing early intervention. *Topics in Early Childhood Special Education, 10*(2), 33–47.

Billingsley, F., Gallucci, C., Peck, C. A., Schwartz, I. S., & Staub, D. (1996). But the kids can't even do math: An alternative conceptualization of outcomes for inclusive education. *Special Education Leadership Review, 3*(1), 43–55.

Bogdan, R., & Biklen, D. (1993). Handicappism. In M. Nagler (Ed.), *Perspectives on disability* (2nd ed., pp. 69–76). Palo Alto, CA: Health Market Research.

Buysee, V., & Baily, D. B. (1993). Behavioral and developmental outcomes in young children with disability in integrated and segregated settings: A review of comparative studies. *Journal of Special Education, 26,* 434–461.

Caldwell, B. M. (1973). The importance of beginning early. In J. B. Jordan and R. F. Dailey (Eds.), *Not all little wagons are red: The exceptional child's early years.* Reston, VA: Council for Exceptional Children.

Derman-Sparks, L., & the A.B.C. Task Force. (1988–89). *Anti-bias curriculum.* Washington, DC: The National Association for the Education of Young Children.

Devoney, C., Guralnick, M. J., & Rubin, H. (1974). Integrating handicapped and nonhandicapped preschool children: Effects on social play. *Childhood Education, 50,* 360–364.

Doherty-Derkowski, G. (1995). *Quality matters: Excellence in early childhood programs.* Don Mills, ON: Addison-Wesley Publishers.

Dunn, L. M. (1968). Special education for the mildly retarded—Is much of it justified? *Exceptional Children, 35,* 5–22.

Ehlers, L. (1993). Inclusion in the lives of young children with disabilities. In S. M. Rehberg (Ed.), *Starting point: A series of definition papers* (pp. 33–43). Olympia, WA: Office of the Superintendent of Public Instruction.

Friendly, M., Beach, J., & Turiano, M. (2002). *Early childhood education and care in Canada, 2001.* Toronto: Childcare Resource and Research Unit, Centre for Urban and Community Studies, University of Toronto.

Garkfinkle, A. N., & Schwartz, I. S. (1998). Observational learning in an integrated preschool: Effects on peer imitation and social interaction. Unpublished manuscript, University of Washington.

Goldstein, H. (1993). Structuring environmental input to facilitate generalized language learning by children with mental retardation. In A. P. Kaiser & D. B. Gray (Eds.), *Enhancing children's communication: Research foundations for intervention.* Baltimore, MD: Brookes.

Guralnick, M. J. (1994). Mothers' perceptions of the benefits and drawbacks of early childhood mainstreaming. *Journal of Early Intervention, 12,* 168–183.

Guralnick, M. J., & Neville, B. (1997). Designing early intervention programs to promote children's social competence. In M. J. Guralnick (Ed.), *The effectiveness of early intervention* (pp. 579–620). Baltimore, MD: Brookes.

Hanson, M. J., & Lynch, E. W. (1995). *Early intervention.* Austin, TX: Pro-Ed.

Haring, N. G., & McCormick, L. (1990). *Exceptional children and youth.* Columbus, OH: Charles E. Merrill.

Harry, B. (1998). Parental visions of "a normal life." In L. Meyer, H. Park, M. Grenot-Scheyer, I. Schwartz, & B. Harry (Eds.), *Making friends: The influence of culture and development,* (pp. 47–62). Baltimore, MD: Brookes.

Hunt, J. M. (1961). *Intelligence and experience.* New York: Ronald Press.

Irwin, S. H. (1997). Including all children. *Interaction, 4*(10), 15–16.

Irwin, S. H., Lero, D., & Brophy, K. (2000). *A matter of urgency: Including children with special needs in child care in Canada.* Wreck Cove, NS: Breton Books.

Kishi, G., & Meyer, L. (1994). What children report and remember: A six-year follow-up of the effects of social contact between peers with and without severe disabilities. *Journal of the Association for Persons with Severe Handicaps, 19*(4), 277–289.

Lamorey, S., & Bricker, D. (1993). Integrated programs: effects on young children and their programs. In C. A. Peck, S. L. Odom, & D. D. Bricker (Eds.), *Integrating young children with disabilities into community programs* (pp. 249–270). Baltimore, MD: Brookes.

Langford, R. (Ed.). 1997. *Checklist for quality inclusive education: A self-assessment tool and manual for early childhood settings.* London, ON: Early Childhood Resource Teacher Network of Ontario.

Luera, M. (1993). Honoring family uniqueness. In S. M. Rehberg (Ed.), *Starting point: A series of definition papers* (pp. 1–9). Olympia, WA: Office of the Superintendent of Public Instruction.

McGregor, G., & Vogelsberg, T. (1998). *Inclusive schooling practices: Pedagogical and research foundations.* Missoula, MT: University of Montana Rural Institute on Disabilities.

Odom, S. L., & McEvoy, M. A. (1990). Mainstreaming at the preschool level. *Topics in Early Childhood Special Education, 10*(2), 48–61.

Odom, S. L., & McLean, M. (1996). *Early intervention/early childhood special education recommended practices.* Austin TX: Pro-Ed.

Odom, S. L., Peck, C. A., Hanson, M., Beckman, P., Kaiser, A., Lieber, J., Brown, W. H., Horn, E. M., & Schwartz, I. S. (1996). Inclusion at the preschool level: An ecological systems analysis. *SRCD Social Policy Report, 10,* 18–30.

Olswang, L. B., & Bain, B. A. (1991). Intervention issues for toddlers with specific language impairments. *Topics in Language Disorders, 11*(4), 69–86.

Peck, C. A. (1993). Ecological perspectives in the implementation of integrated early childhood programs. In C. A. Peck, S. L. Odom, & D. D. Bricker (Eds.), *Integrating young children with disabilities into community programs* (pp. 3–15). Baltimore, MD: Brookes.

Peck, C. A., Carlson, P., & Helmstetter, E. (1992). Parent and teacher perceptions of outcomes for typically developing children enrolled in integrated early childhood programs: A statewide survey." *Journal of Early Intervention, 16,* 53–63.

Peterson, N. L. (1987). *Early intervention for handicapped and at-risk children.* Denver, CO: Love Publishing.

Rafferty, Y., Boettcher, C., & Griffin, K. W. (2001). Benefits and risks of reverse inclusion for preschoolers with and without disabilities: Parents' perspectives. *Journal of Early Intervention, 24,* 266–286.

Salisbury, C. L., Palombaro, M. M., & Hollowood, T. M. (1993). On the nature and change of an inclusive elementary school. *Journal of the Association for Persons with Severe Handicaps, 18,* 75–84.

Sharpe M. N., York J. L., & Knight, J. (1994). Effects of inclusion on the academic performance of classmates without disabilities. *Remedial and Special Education, 15,* 281–287.

Spodek, B., Saracho, O. N., & Lee, R. C. (1984). *Mainstreaming young children.* Belmont, CA: Wadsworth.

Status of Disabled Persons Secretariat. (1991). *A way with words: Guidelines and appropriate terminology for the portrayal of persons with disabilities.* Ottawa: Ministry of Supply and Services Canada.

Thomas, A., & Chess, S. (1977). *Temperament and development.* New York: Bruner/Mazel.

Thurman, K. S., & Widerstrom, A. H. (1990). *Infants and young children with special needs: A developmental and ecological approach.* Baltimore, MD: Brookes.

Washington, K., Schwartz, I. S., & Swinth, Y. (1994). Physical and occupational therapists in naturalistic early childhood settings: Challenge and strategies for training. *Topics in Early Childhood Special Education, 14*(3), 333–349.

Wolery, M., & Wilbers, J. S. (1994). *Including children with special needs in early childhood programs.* Washington, DC: National Association for the Education of Young Children.

Wolfensberger, W. (1972). *The principle of normalization in human services.* Toronto: National Institute on Mental Retardation.

CHAPTER 2

Canadian Legislation:

Support for Children through Early Intervention

KEY CONCEPTS

advocacy

amniocentesis

medical model

prenatal

social model

OBJECTIVES

After studying the material in this chapter, the student will be able to

- Understand the differences between legislation for children with special needs in Canada and legislation for children with special needs in the United States.
- Explain how the War Measures Act of 1942 influenced the funding of child care in Canada.
- Specify how the Medical Care Act of 1966 supported the well-being of young Canadian children.
- Describe how the Canada Assistance Plan Act influenced the growth of Canadian child care.
- Recognize the impact of the Canada Health and Social Transfer Act on child care in Canada.
- Identify key differences between a social model and a medical model for understanding disability.
- Describe the importance of advocacy.

Introduction

Public policy on behalf of infants and children with special needs (and children at risk for needing extra support during the developmental years) has been expanding steadily over the past several decades in North America. Beginning in the early 1960s, the Congress of the United States passed a number of laws that supported early identification, prevention, and treatment of developmental problems. Shortly thereafter, parallel legislative action took place in Canada.

At this time, Canadian activists—many of whom had disabilities or had children with special needs—began to question society's use of a **medical model** for understanding disabilities. They introduced a **social model** as an alternative.

To gain an appreciation of the differences that influenced the field of early childhood education in Canada and the United States, it is important to review the historical background against which Canadian early childhood legislation developed. The education and care of young Canadian children are the responsibility of provincial and territorial governments and not, as in the United States, the responsibility of the federal government. The chapter concludes with a discussion on the importance of advocacy in the field of inclusive early childhood education.

Medical model
an approach to understanding disabilities that individualizes and pathologizes a disability as a biological impairment, a deficit, or a dysfunction residing within the person

Social model
an approach to understanding disabilities that identifies the barriers that prevent the social inclusion of people with disabilities and then focuses on the capacity of people with disabilities to change these barriers, with the help of others

Federal Legislation in Canada

THE INFLUENCE OF THE BRITISH NORTH AMERICA ACT

The legislation of any young country influences the development of the services that it provides to its population. In Canada, the British North America Act of 1867 established that the provinces were to be responsible for local matters. Although the Act was silent on the role to be played in local services by the federal government, it stated that the federal government should take responsibility for those matters affecting all provinces, such as national defence (Sobsey, 1985). Education and social services are identified as "local matters." Therefore, child care and care for children with special needs (when it became available) were regarded as provincial and territorial concerns. A variety of child care centres and related services evolved in an informal manner as the need arose in each province and territory. Examples of these are the following:

- The first daycare centres were founded by Roman Catholic nuns in Quebec in the 1850s.
- The first Toronto *crèche* (daycare centre), now called Victoria Day Care Services, was founded for the benefit of needy families in the 1890s.
- Edmonton and Winnipeg started daycare centres in 1908–1909.
- Vancouver Children's Hospital opened an infant and preschool centre for children of mothers working in the hospital in 1910.
- The National Council of Women and the Young Women's Christian Association (YWCA), both advocates for women's rights, were strong advocates for the development of summer camps and child care programs.

THE WAR MEASURES ACT: ITS IMPACT ON CHILD CARE

It was not until World War II, with the passing of the War Measures Act, that the federal government provided funds for child care. The War Measures Act enabled the federal cabinet to enact specific legislation that it deemed necessary, which potentially limited some freedoms of citizens (for example, gas was rationed to ensure appropriate supply).

Since more female workers were required to replace male workers in essential industries, the provision of child care became a priority issue. The provincial governments and the federal (sometimes called "Dominion") government were asked to participate in the provision of daycare for those children whose mothers were employed in an essential industry.

Photo 2–1
The Dominion–Provincial Wartime Day Nurseries Agreement provided for the shared funding of daycare centres.

The Dominion–Provincial Wartime Day Nurseries Agreement, under the War Measures Act, provided for shared funding between the federal government and any province that was interested in developing daycare for children (Photo 2–1). Thus, in 1942, a mother working in an essential industry in Ontario paid about 33 percent of the cost of daycare for her child or children, while the remainder of the cost was shared on a 50–50 basis between the federal and provincial governments (Stapleford, 1976, p. 2). This was the first time that child care was included in Canadian legislation.

Federal funding for child care was withdrawn after World War II when the War Measures Act expired. With the termination of the War Measures Act and the return of men to the workforce, it was expected that mothers would resume caring for their children. Any continued cost sharing for child care was limited to agreements between local municipalities and provincial governments. Provincial legislation evolved as a result of pressures from women who wanted to continue to work outside the home. An example was the 1946 Day Nurseries Act in Ontario.

More than 20 years passed before the federal government would once again provide a mechanism for the funding of child care.

THE CANADA ASSISTANCE PLAN ACT (1966–1996): FEDERAL SUPPORT FOR SOCIAL SERVICES

Although there was public interest in continuing some form of cost sharing for child care services through federal legislation, it was not until the passing of the Canada Assistance Plan (CAP) Act in 1966 that certain welfare programs, including subsidized child care, entered the federal cost-sharing picture. Under this open-ended legislation, the federal government offered to share with any province or territory the cost of up to half the financial assistance required for children in child care whose families were deemed to qualify through a needs test or income test.

It should be noted that funding specifically for children with special needs was not addressed in this legislation.

The Canada Assistance Plan Act had two major sections:

1. *Assistance programs* provided funding in such categories as food, shelter, and health-care services.
2. *Welfare services* focused on reducing, removing, or preventing the causes and effects of poverty, child neglect, and dependence on public assistance. Some services included under this legislation were rehabilitative programs, adoption, and community development.

There were also other programs available under the Canada Assistance Plan:

- the Indian Welfare Services Agreement
- the Vocational Rehabilitation of Disabled Persons Agreement (VRDP)
- Family Benefits Assistance (FBA)
- General Welfare Assistance (GWA)

For many years after the introduction of the Canada Assistance Plan, there was slow but steady growth within the child care system and its related services, including specialized programming for infants and young children with special needs. Child care for low-income working families continued to be supported across Canada through federal cost sharing. The number of full-day child care spaces (daycare and home daycare) for both subsidized families and those paying the full fee rose approximately 500 percent between 1973 and 1984, going from 28 373 to 171 654 (Health and Welfare Canada, 1986).

The 1970s saw a move toward the active involvement of parents through the Parent Cooperative movement and parent associations for children who were gifted, were emotionally disturbed, or had physical and developmental disabilities (Health and Welfare Canada, 1990) (Photo 2–2).

The early 1990s saw ceilings placed on the funds available to some provinces and territories. In 1996 the Canada Assistance Plan Act was repealed and the Canada Health and Social Transfer Act was established.

Photo 2–2
Programs for children with special needs developed as a result of the advocacy of parent associations.

THE CANADA HEALTH AND SOCIAL TRANSFER ACT (CHST) OF 1996

During times of economic flux, at both the federal and provincial or territorial government levels, there is often an impact on funding formulas for health and social services for children and families, such as has been revealed in the Canada Health and Social Transfer (CHST) Act. The elimination of the Canada Assistance Plan Act and the introduction of the Canada Health and Social Transfer Act signalled that the federal government had transferred social responsibilities, such as welfare and child care, to the provinces and territories. Under the new legislation, the federal government guaranteed an annual, though shrinking, "lump sum" contribution to each province or territory, to be spent on health and social services, including welfare. Unlike the CAP, which refunded provinces and territories 50 percent of the cost for child care to families in need, there was no requirement that any of the annual lump sum under the CHST be allocated to child care. Some provincial and territorial governments with growing child care services were forced to consider transferring larger welfare costs, including those for child care, to the local governments. The local government was then responsible for determining how to obtain enough funding to meet their child care costs. Increasingly, public opinion, especially from working parents, seems to indicate the need for both provincial or territorial and federal funding for child care. This will require the introduction of a new method of federal child care funding to relieve financial pressure on provincial and territorial governments. (See the Resources section at the end of this chapter for further information on individual provinces and territories.)

THE CHARTER OF RIGHTS AND FREEDOMS: THE IMPACT ON CHILDREN WITH SPECIAL NEEDS

The Charter of Rights and Freedoms became a part of the Canadian Constitution in 1982. Section 15 of the Charter guarantees equal rights for all citizens. It has been argued that there is a right to education implicit in the Charter (MacKay, 1987). Since the responsibility for both school-age and preschool education lies with each provincial or territorial government, it is up to the provinces and territories to show that any lack of service that limits these rights (for example, lack of service to a child with special needs) is due to the child's excessive needs, which go beyond the "reasonable limits" clause as stated in section 24 of the Charter of Rights and Freedoms.

The equality rights in the Charter did not come into force until 1985, providing time for provincial and territorial ministries and local school boards to plan for the integration of children with special needs into the regular school system. Although education for school-aged children is mandatory under provincial and territorial legislation (usually starting at six years of age), early childhood education, including Kindergarten or child care, is not mandatory. Therefore, under the Charter of Rights and Freedoms, parents of school-aged children who have special needs and who are denied access to education have the right of legislative appeal (that is, they are able to take their provincial or territorial ministry of education to court and demand equal educational opportunities for their children). However, parents of a preschool child who has a special need are unable to use the power of the courts, since early childhood education is optional, not a legislated requirement. Therefore, the courts cannot regard it as a right under the Charter of Rights and Freedoms.

The phrase "least restrictive environment" became popular in the 1970s as part of the development of normalization and integration activities throughout Canada. Those who followed the normalization philosophy agreed that children or adults with special needs should not be placed in an institution but should remain in their own community, preferably in their own home. Similarly, children with special needs should not be segregated but should be included in early childhood programs in order to experience a full range of activities and to interact with their peers in the neighbourhood (MacKay, 1987) (Photo 2–3).

In January 1990, the Canadian government signed the United Nations Convention on the Rights of the

Photo 2–3
Children with special needs have the right to be included in community early childhood programs.

Child. This was interpreted as a sign that the federal government continues to be committed to recognizing the rights of all children (Castelle, 1990, p. 22), including children with special needs.

Provincial and Territorial Legislation for Child Care

Because there continued to be a lack of any federal child care legislation beyond the subsidy arrangements in the Canada Assistance Plan, most provinces and territories began developing their own child care legislation, either through separate acts or through inclusion in existing provincial or territorial laws. For example, British Columbia historically had both segregated and integrated child care programs for children with special needs. Beginning in 1993, a more inclusive approach, the *Supported Child Care* initiative, was implemented. A special needs diagnosis is required for a child to access supported child care. Contacts are negotiated either with an agency or an individual to provide the support that facilitates inclusion. In 2001 low-income parents of children with special needs were required to meet the social criteria (e.g., seeking work, attending school) as well as the financial eligibility criteria in order to be eligible for a fee subsidy.

In Saskatchewan, the Child Care Inclusion Program provides support to nonprofit child care facilities to include children with varying abilities in child care programs (Lysack, 2000). Quebec has a policy encouraging the inclusion of children with special needs in regular programs, and grants are available for this. For four-year-olds with special needs, the school board has the obligation to deliver a Kindergarten program if the parents so request. However, in general, as Irwin (1997, p. 15) notes,

> Most Canadian child care centers include *some* children with special needs *some* of the time. Generally speaking, though, this inclusion is on an *ad hoc* basis—responding on a child-by-child basis, admitting or excluding a particular child depending on the resources and skills currently available to that center.

Table 2–1 lists the child care legislation of each province and territory and notes whether the legislation contains a reference to services or funding for children with special needs (Friendly & Beach, 2005). (See the Resources section at the end of this chapter for further information on provinces and territories.)

Educational Legislation in Canada

In Canada, the responsibility for the education of school-aged students with special needs lies with the provincial and territorial governments. Although all provinces and territories recognize the right to education for all children, the legislation varies across jurisdictions.

Differences exist in provincial and territorial educational legislation with respect to the diagnostic categories of identified exceptionalities. How an individual student is designated as being eligible for special services also varies. However, in some provinces diagnostic categories, such as "orthopedically impaired," "visually impaired," and "educable mentally retarded," are used for determining program designation.

Some ministries of education assume responsibility for servicing children with special needs who are of preschool age. For example, in Ontario, children who are

TABLE 2–1

PROVINCIAL/TERRITORIAL CHILD CARE LEGISLATIVE CHART

Province/Territory	Regulatory Body	Title of Legislation	Special-Needs Funding
Alberta	Alberta Children's Services	Social Care Facilities Licensing Act; Chapter S-10, RSA 2000 Alberta Day Care Regulation 180/2000	Funding varies depending on the special needs of the child and the type of service required. Through the Inclusive Child Care Program funds are paid to contracted operators on behalf of eligible children.
British Columbia	Ministry of Children and Family Development	Child Care BC Act, SBC 2001, Chapter 4, Assented to March 29, 2001, Updated to November 5, 2001	Funding is available to assist with additional costs of caring for children with special needs in the program of parents' choice. It can cover consultation, training, and extra staffing.
Manitoba	Department of Family Services and Housing Child Day Care	The Community Child Day Care Standards Act 1983, as amended in 1986; Community Child Care Standards Act, C.C.S.M. cc158. (amended September 2004)	Staffing grants are the main grant support at facilities caring for children with special needs.
New Brunswick	Early Childhood and School-Based Services Department of Family and Community Services	Family Services Act 1980; New Brunswick Legislative Assembly, Family Services Act and Day Care Regulations 1983–85, as amended	Children with special needs attend an Integrated Day Care Centre which receives extra funding.
Newfoundland and Labrador	Department of Health and Community Services	Child Care Services Act.—SNL 1998, chapter c-11.1, amended 1999 c22 s6, 2001 c36; Child Care Services Regulation 37/99	Eligible parents receive a child welfare allowance which is paid directly to the parent who hires an individual to provide support to the child in a child care setting.
Northwest Territories	Early Childhood and School Services, Department of Education, Culture and Employment	The Northwest Territories Child Day Care Act; Child Day Care Standards and Regulations 1988	Care providers are funded to provide extra support, and parents are eligible for free assistance for their children with special needs if they demonstrate financial need and have a medical referral from a recognized health care official for the child.

TABLE 2–1 (CONT.)

PROVINCIAL/TERRITORIAL CHILD CARE LEGISLATIVE CHART (CONT.)

Province/Territory	Regulatory Body	Title of Legislation	Special-Needs Funding
Nova Scotia	Early Childhood Development Services, Department of Community Services	Day Care Regulations made under Section 15 of the Day Care Act, amended to N.S. Reg. 202/2004	Differential funding to licensed full-time non-profit centres enrolling identified children with special needs are available.
Nunavut	Adult Education, Career and Early Childhood Services, Department of Education	The Northwest Territories Child Day Care Act; Child Day Care Standards and Regulations 1994	Funding through increased daily operating grants is given to care providers. Additional funding may be provided for adaptive equipment or for a one-on-one worker.
Ontario	Early Years Programs Branch, Policy Development and Program Design Division, Ministry of Children and Youth Services	The Day Nurseries Act; Revised Statutes of Ontario, 1990 (reprinted 1998), amended by the Services Improvement Act, effective January 1, 1998, c.D-2, amended by 1997, c. 30, Sched. C; 1999, c.12, Sched. E, s.2; 1999, c.12, Sched.G, s. 21; O.Reg. 500/00; 2001, c.13, s.14	Inclusion of children with special needs is encouraged. Special needs resourcing (e.g., assistance for staffing, equipment, supplies) is provided.
Prince Edward Island	Children's Secretariat, Department of Health and Social Services	The Child Care Facilities Act, 1988; Prince Edward Island Child Care Facilities Regulations 1988; The Social Assistance Act 2003	Centres may apply for a special needs grant (often for additional staff) on behalf of a child.
Quebec	Ministère de l'Emploi, de la Solidarité sociale et de la Famille	An Act Respecting Child Care Centres and Child Care Services, R.S.Q. chapter C-8.2 , R.2., as amended June 1, 2004; Regulation Respecting Day Care Centres, C-8.2, r.5.1, as amended June 8, 2004; Regulation Respecting Reduced Contributions C-8.2, r.3, as amended June 8, 2004	Grants (one-time grant and additional daily grant per child on top of the regular operating grants) for children with identified special needs in licensed integrated child care programs.
Saskatchewan	Child Day Care Program, Department of Community Resources and Employment	The Child Care Act 1990, as amended by the Statutes of Saskatchewan, 2000; Saskatchewan Child Care Regulations 2001	Includes grants for programs serving children with special needs in licensed integrated child care programs.
Yukon	Child Care Services Unit, Department of Health and Social Services	Child Care Act 1990; Family Day-Home Regulations and Day Care Centre Regulations 1990	Funding for adaptive equipment, transportation, programming support and additional staff is available for centres and family day homes through a Supported Child Care Fund.

SOURCE: By permission of Martha Friendly, Author and Coordinator, Childcare Resource and Research Unit, University of Toronto.

hearing impaired are eligible from two years of age for special education services at no extra cost, even though they are much younger than the age at which children enter the public education system (Council of Ministers of Education, 1989).

THE IMPACT OF U.S. LEGISLATION ON CANADA

In contrast to Canada, in the United States the provision of services to young children with special needs is required by federal legislation (Photo 2–4). Many of the service components required under U.S. legislation and the extensive research used in the development of program resources and strategies have significantly influenced services and program practices across Canada. The *Portage Guide to Early Education* is an early example of the many U.S. resources now widely used in Canada. More recent programs, such as the Brigance Diagnostic Inventories, which enable ongoing record keeping of children's development, are also now widely used.

Photo 2–4
The U.S. public law clearly recognizes the importance of parent contributions to the child's progress.

Table 2–2 provides a brief overview of major U.S. legislation that has directly influenced the resources and services available to young Canadian children with

TABLE 2–2

U.S. LEGISLATION FOR THE EDUCATION OF CHILDREN WITH SPECIAL NEEDS

Year	Public Law	Title and Significance
1968	90-538	**Handicapped Children's Early Education Assistance Act (HCEEAA).** Federal funds support improvements in early intervention services for children with disabilities, at-risk children, and their families.
1972	92-424	**Head Start Amendments.** Although Head Start programs always included children with special needs, these amendments require that 10 percent of enrollment be reserved for children with special needs. In 1974, the regulations were changed to ensure service to children with more severe disabilities. In 1990 Head Start was reauthorized at its highest funding level ever through the Child and Development Block Grant.
1973		**Rehabilitation Act of 1973.** Section 504 of this act is a civil rights law that protects children and adults from discrimination.
1975	94-142	**Education for All Handicapped Children Act.** This law guarantees that all children and youth, regardless of the severity of their disability, have the right to a free and appropriate public education. The law gives specific support to early education programs. Special funds, called incentive monies, are authorized to encourage states to locate and serve preschool children in need of early intervention services (also referred to as *Child Find*). This law has a number of important rulings:

• **Zero Reject:** Local school systems must provide an appropriate free education for all children regardless of the severity of their special needs.

TABLE 2–2 (cont.)

U.S. legislation for the education of children with special needs (cont.)

Year	Public Law	Title and Significance

- **Nondiscriminatory Evaluation:** All children must be fully assessed before being placed in a special education program. Tests must be appropriate to the child's language and cultural background.
- **Appropriate Education:** Local school districts must provide educational services that are appropriate to each individual child.
- **Least Restrictive Environments/Mainstreaming:** To the greatest extent possible, children with special needs will be educated in regular programs.
- **Due Process:** This legal procedure enables parents to call a special hearing when they do not agree with the process of removal. This further ensures that a child cannot be removed from a classroom simply because of annoying or inconvenient behaviour.
- **Parent Participation:** The importance of parents' contributions to their child's progress is recognized.

1986   99-457

Education of the Handicapped Amendments. These amendments to the Education for All Handicapped Children Act are the most comprehensive legislation ever enacted on behalf of infants and young children. This law has several parts or Titles. Title I and Title II focus on the very young:

- **Title I:** A state may serve children who are experiencing developmental delays or who are at-risk from birth through two years of age if it chooses. An exception is that any state serving infants and toddlers without disabilities must serve infants and toddlers with disabilities. Very young children do not need to be labelled as having a particular kind of disability to receive services. An individualized family service plan must be provided.
- **Title II:** States receiving federal funds for early intervention programs must serve young children with developmental disabilities. Parent-support services are allowable as "related services."

1990   101-176

Individuals with Disabilities Education Act (IDEA). This amendment to PL 94-142 changes the emphasis of programs from providing segregated programs for specific conditions to providing support to individuals with special needs in community settings.

1990   101-336

Americans with Disabilities Act Law (ADA). This law gives civil rights protection to individuals in private employment, all public services and accommodations, transportation, and telecommunications.

1992   93-112

Developmental Disabilities Act (DDA). This law requires that everyone with a disability be given access to jobs, education, housing, and public buildings. This law also rules that states offering preschool services to children without disabilities must offer comparable services to those with disabilities. Schools are also required to make accommodations for children who have disabilities but do not qualify for special education.

1997   105-17

Reauthorization of the Education for All Handicapped Children. The name was changed to the **Individuals with Disabilities Act (IDEA)** to reflect people-first terminology. IDEA-1997 requires educators to deal with challenging behaviours proactively.

Box 2-1 UNDERSTANDING DISABILITY FROM A SOCIAL MODEL PERSPECTIVE

In the past two decades, people with disabilities, influenced by the civil rights and women's movements, have dramatically revised the way disability is understood. Academics and activists with disabilities shifted the focus away from the more traditional emphasis on individual deviancy and pathology, and toward an exploration of social issues, such as inaccessible buildings, exclusionary policies and practices, and prejudice, as the "real" or sociological problems of disability.

This new focus is frequently called the "social model" of disability. It is distinct from a "medical model" of disability, which individualizes and pathologizes the disability as a biological impairment, a deficit, or a dysfunction residing within the person. Disability rights activists believe that an overemphasis on the medical model has detracted from full citizenship for people with disabilities. The social model is also characterized by the identification of the barriers that prevent the social inclusion of people with disabilities. It allows for an analysis of these barriers, on the one hand, and the capacity of people with disabilities and their allies in changing them on the other. In this struggle for social justice, hundreds of activist parents launched national organizations, including the March of Dimes, Easter Seals, the Muscular Dystrophy Association, and the Associations for Community Living. Mothers of children with disabilities have been at the forefront of this activism.

For example, the social model approach turns the focus away from examining how individual families react to having a child with a disability and focuses instead on the social and historical factors that influence these reactions. It considers what resources are available to families and examines the interconnection between the organizational resources that can or cannot be accessed and the way families interpret the meaning of a child's disability. So the question becomes not "How do families respond to disability?" but rather "How does society respond to families?" It is only by asking questions from this social perspective that we can create new knowledge about disability that takes into account its various and richly textured social dimensions.

SOURCE: Melanie Panitch, Director, School of Disability Studies, Ryerson University. Prepared for this text.

special needs and to their families. Box 2–1 looks at the shift from using a medical model to understand disabilities to using a social model.

National Health Care and Prevention in Canada

Although people criticize the lack of child care legislation and educational legislation at the federal level in Canada, it is to the credit of the federal government that a national health-care system was introduced for all Canadians in 1966. The Medical Care Act offered medical care whose cost was shared between the federal and provincial governments. Services provided specifically for children included childhood immunization at the request of the child's parents. With this legislation came an increase in the provision of screening and assessment services for children (including those with special needs) at hospitals and health centres in major

Amniocentesis
a medical procedure to
determine if genetic
abnormalities are present in the
developing fetus; can be done
about the 16th week of
pregnancy (gestation)

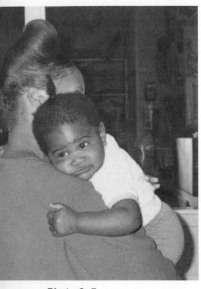

Photo 2–5
Support services for infants may be
provided through health or social
services programs.

Canadian cities. Such procedures as **amniocentesis** and other pregnancy-related health-care services became more readily available. Although a variety of funding mechanisms now exist for the provision of health care across provinces and territories, every family is entitled to receive medical assistance and care.

Efforts have been made to establish and implement community prevention programs that encourage families to use the local health services and centres. Therefore, assistance, such as support services for infants, may be provided through either provincial or territorial health or social service legislation (Photo 2–5). The source of funding, whether from the Ministry of Health or the Ministry of Social Services, influences the model of service delivery (medical versus social services) and the required educational background of the service providers (for example, nurse, early childhood educator, therapist).

THE PUSH FOR FEDERAL CHILD CARE LEGISLATION IN CANADA

During the past decade, the provinces and territories have continued to struggle to develop sufficient child care services to meet the needs of a growing population of young children and their families. Many young families have emigrated from other countries to Canada and may need more initial support. Federal and provincial or territorial agencies and many advocacy groups representing both parent users and professional staff have come together to demand that the federal government enact specific child care legislation. This legislation is needed to address universal concerns, such as the quality of child care, accessibility of care, staff training, affordability, and the full inclusion of children with special needs in child care centres.

Organizations that have Canada-wide representation through provincial or territorial and local chapters, and that are actively involved in advocating for these concerns, include the Canadian Child Care Federation, the Canadian Association for Young Children, the Canadian Council for Exceptional Children, the Canadian Rehabilitation Council for the Disabled, and the Child Care Advocacy Association of Canada. Other associations with broad membership, such as the Canadian Association for Community Living (formerly the Canadian Association for the Mentally Retarded), SpeciaLink, and the Roeher Institute, are also working on behalf of children with special needs.

Early childhood educators have always been strong advocates young children (see Box 2–2).

Several detailed reports, such as the *Canadian National Child Care Study* and the *You Bet I Care!* study (Doherty, Lero, Goelman, Tougas, & LaGrange, 2000a, 2000b; Pence et al., 1997), have confirmed that existing services do not meet the needs of many young children, including those with special needs. Therefore, the Canadian goal is to have federal legislation that would give support to all children within child care programs rather than having separate provincial and territorial legislation for children with special needs.

In the mid-1990s, the federal government began to introduce new services for early childhood development, such as Aboriginal Head Start (a targeted early intervention program) and Community Action Programs for Children (e.g., Brighter Futures). A new program to support research and developmental projects related to child care, Child Care Visions, was announced in 1995. In 1999, the federal,

Box 2-2 EARLY CHILDHOOD EDUCATORS AS ADVOCATES

Advocacy is speaking and acting in support or on behalf of people or ideas. Early childhood educators have had a long tradition of being advocates. Our commitment to providing high quality care and education for young children has compelled many educators to take action at different times in their professional career. Sometimes, the power of one educator (personal advocacy) positively changes practices in the care and education of children. Other times the power of many (collective advocacy) changes government policies. There are different levels of advocacy that vary in factors such as degree of involvement and time commitment. All levels of advocacy are courageous and important.

Low-Level Advocacy

- Intervene in situations of discrimination, speak out in opposition to bias and defend people discriminated against.
- Support the inclusion of a child and act on behalf of the family.
- Join local, provincial, national and international professional organizations concerned with the inclusion of children with special needs (See organizations at end of many chapters.)

Mid-Level Advocacy

- Initiate networking with community groups who are committed to inclusive ECE (e.g., parent groups, cultural organizations).
- Raise a concern about exclusionary practices in your setting and provide leadership in making changes.
- Share information about inclusive practices with coworkers and promote the value of them.

High-Level Advocacy

- Submit a grant proposal to fund inclusive programming in your setting.
- Present information about the benefits of inclusion to community groups, government bodies and organizations.
- Join an advocacy group lobbying governments for supportive policy, funding and social change.
- Provide a workshop about inclusive practices.

Sometimes our advocacy efforts are successful; sometimes our efforts may result in only some small measure of success. Personal and collective advocacy are long, hard processes. However, inspiring gains have been made in inclusive care and education as a result of activism and advocacy by many committed educators and groups. Fortified by the strength of our convictions, educators will continue to advocate in support of inclusion, human respect and dignity.

SOURCE: Early Childhood Resource Teacher Network of Ontario. (1997). *Resource sheet unit V: Checklist for quality inclusive education: A self-assessment tool and manual for early childhood settings.* Haliburton: ON: Early Childhood Resource Teacher Network of Ontario.

Advocacy
speaking and acting in support or on behalf of people or ideas

provincial, and territorial governments issued a National Children's Agenda that proposed a "new vision" for children in Canada. At the same time, the Social Union Framework Agreement confirmed that consensus of a majority of provinces and territories is necessary to initiate a new national social program like child care.

An indication of the future of child care in Canada came in September 2001, when the prime minister and premiers signed an Early Childhood Development

Prenatal
occurring or existing before
birth

(ECD) Accord that provides more funding for services and programs for families and children, from **prenatal** to age six. Under the ECD Accord, the federal government planned to invest $2.2 billion in early childhood development over five years through CHST. Increased services include infant screening programs, family resource programs, and early development centres. Soon after, other national policy initiatives, including the *Multilateral Framework on Early Learning and Child Care* (Federal/Provincial/Territorial Ministers Responsible for Social Services, 2003), recognized the importance of learning and care in the early years. In 2004, the Organisation for Economic Co-operation and Development's 20-nation Thematic Review of Early Childhood Education and Care reported that Canada has "fallen far behind international developments in early childhood education and care" (Friendly & Beach, 2005). In the spring of 2005, federal and provincial and territorial governments began negotiations on a national early learning and child care system based on four principles: quality, universality, accessibility, and developmentally appropriate programming.

Summary

Canadian legislation supporting the inclusion of children with special needs has been influenced by U.S. federal legislation. In the United States, a number of federal laws, specifically PL 94-142 and PL 99-457, have been passed that support the identification, prevention, and treatment of developmental differences in young children. Though there is no comparable federal legislation in Canada, a parallel development has occurred through the inclusion of children with special needs within provincial and territorial educational and child care legislation. In addition, an alternative social model for understanding disabilities has led to increased advocacy efforts to ensure social justice and inclusion for children with disabilities and their families.

The British North America Act established a structure whereby each province would be responsible for developing its own child care and educational legislation. This included responsibility for services for children with special needs. Through the Canada Assistance Plan Act, provinces and territories entered into cost-sharing agreements with the federal government for child care services. The Medical Care Act ensured health care for all Canadians, including support for the prevention and treatment of developmental disabilities. This legislation was cancelled in March 1996 and was replaced by the Canada Health and Social Transfer Act of 1996. Through this legislation, the federal government transferred responsibility for health and welfare to the provinces and territories, along with a guaranteed, but decreasing, annual monetary contribution. At the same time, agreements in recent years between the federal and provincial or territorial governments point to a new federal role in social programs and collaboration between these governments to establish joint initiatives in early childhood services. Early childhood educators must continue to advocate in a variety of ways for inclusive programs within a national early learning and child care system.

CURRENT INFORMATION ON PROVINCIAL AND TERRITORIAL SERVICES AND RESOURCES

Note: Information for this section comes from Friendly, M., & Beach, J. (2005). *Early childhood care and education in Canada 2004.* Toronto: Childcare Resource and Research Unit, University of Toronto.

Province/Territory	Contact	Statistical Information	Publications	Comments
Alberta	Children's Services 11th floor, Sterling Place 9940-106th St. Edmonton, Alberta T5K 2N2 780-427-3992	Number of licensed/ regulated spaces (2004) Infant and preschool 26 574 School-aged 17 767 Family daycare 6 554 Children with special needs N/A	• The Inclusive Child Care Program (1981): Guidelines to Assist Children with Special Needs in Inclusive Day Care Centers or Family Day Homes • Focus on Children (1990)	The Inclusive Child Care Program in Alberta provides for inclusion of children with special needs. Funds are paid to contracted operators and amounts vary depending on the needs of the child and the types of services required. Delivery of the program can vary across provincial regions. Staff members working with children with special needs are not required to have additional training.
British Columbia	Early Childhood Development and Child Care Policy Ministry of Children and Family Development P.O. Box 9778, STN Provincial Government Victoria, British Columbia V8W 9R4 250-953-4570	Number of licensed/regulated spaces (2004) Centre-based (full-time) 19 350 Family daycare 17 372 Children with special needs 5 000	• Supported Child Care: The Report of the Special Needs Day Care Review in British Columbia (1993) • The Government's Response to Supported Child Care: The Report of the Special Needs Review in British Columbia (1995) • Program Guidelines: Early Intervention Programs (1993; revised 1995) • Community Support Services Policy Manual: Services for Children with Special Needs (1996)	The Supported Child Care Initiative is British Columbia's inclusive approach to serving children with special needs in typical child care programs. Funds are provided to cover equipment and additional staffing costs.

Province/Territory	Contact	Statistical Information	Publications	Comments
British Columbia, cont.			• Supported Child Care: Enhancing Accessibility— A Resource Manual for Communities, Child-Care Settings and Child Care Providers (1997) • Building a Better Future for British Columbia's Kids (1999)	
Manitoba	Child Day Care Manitoba Family Services and Housing 219–114 Garry Street Winnipeg, Manitoba R3C 4V6 204-945-2668	Number of licensed/regulated spaces (2004) Full-day infant/toddler/ preschool 11 226 School-age 6 126 Family daycare 4 209 Children with special needs 1 341	• The Community Child Day Care Standards Act, Manitoba Regulation 69/86 updated in 1993, contains definitions of "child with disabilities" and "special needs" • Children with Disabilities Program Guide (1990) • The Manitoba Children First Plan: A Status Report (1999) • A Vision for Child Care and Development in Manitoba (2001)	Funding for children with disabilities is provided through the Children with Disabilities Program. Children with special needs are integrated into many nonprofit child care centres. Staffing grants are provided at facilities caring for children with special needs. No special training is required for staff working with children with special needs.
New Brunswick	Early Childhood and School-Based Services Program Development and Monitoring Department of Family and Community Services P.O. Box 6000 551 King St. 2nd floor Fredericton, New Brunswick E3B 1E7 506-869-6878	Number of licensed/regulated spaces (2004) Centre-based 11 747 Family daycare 150 Children with special needs in integrated daycare services 589	• Day Care Regulations 83 to 85 (1983) • Day Care Facilities Standards (1983) • Standards of Early Intervention Programs (1992) • A Policy Framework for Child Care Services in New Brunswick (1994) • Greater Opportunities for New Brunswick Children: An Early Childhood Development Agenda (2001) • Opening the Door to Quality Childcare and Development Phase I (2002)	The Early Childhood Initiative (ECI) provides prevention-focused childhood services. Screening is conducted to identify "priority" infants and preschool children and their families. Priority preschool children are those at risk of a delay in school readiness. They may have a physical or intellectual challenge or may live in families facing multiple social risk factors. Identified children are placed in integrated child care settings, which receive additional funding. Staff members do not need additional training.

Newfoundland and Labrador	Child Care Services Child, Youth and Families Services Division Department of Health and Community Services Government of Newfoundland and Labrador P.O. Box 8700, Confederation Building, West Block St. John's, Newfoundland A1B 4J6 709-729-4055	Number of licensed/regulated spaces (2004) Centre-based infant 48 Centre-based full-time 3499 Centre-based part-time 556 Centre-based school-age 578 Children with special needs 273	• The Family and Rehabilitative Services Policy Manual • The Direct Home Services Program Procedures Manual • Direct Home Services Program Intervention Description Brochure • People, Partners and Prosperity: A Strategic Social Plan for Newfoundland and Labrador (1998)	There is no written policy regarding children with special needs, but parents may receive a child welfare allowance, if they meet eligibility requirements, to hire an individual to provide support to the child in a child care setting. Staff members working with children with special needs do not require any special training.
Northwest Territories	Early Childhood and School Services Department of Education, Culture and Employment Government of the Northwest Territories Lahm Ridge Tower, 3rd floor, P.O. Box 1320 Yellowknife, Northwest Territories X1A 2L9 867-920-3491	Number of licensed/regulated spaces (2004) Total regulated spaces 1219 Children with special needs N/A	• Child Day Care Act and Regulations 1988 • Early Childhood Development Framework for Action and Action Plan (2001)	Funding through higher operating grants is provided to care providers. Families are eligible for fee assistance if financial need is established and a medical referral for the child is obtained.
Nova Scotia	Early Childhood Development Services Department of Community Services P.O. Box 696 Halifax, Nova Scotia B3J 2T7 902-424-5489	Number of licensed/regulated spaces (2004) Full-time 9318 Part-time 3282 Family daycare 159 Children with special needs 376	• Integration of Children with Special Needs in Day Care (1989) • Our Children: Today's Investments—Tomorrow's Promise (2001) • Partnerships for Inclusion (2002/03)	Registered child care centres can receive Supported Child Care funding (for additional staff, materials, and equipment) if they enroll children with special needs. Eligibility is based on evidence of the child's disability.

Province/Territory	Contact	Statistical Information	Publications	Comments
Nunavut	Adult Education, Career and Early Childhood Services Department of Education, Government of Nunavut Box 1000, Station 980 Iqaluit, Nunavut X0A 0H0 867-975-5600	Number of licensed/regulated spaces (2004) Infant 158 Preschool 547 After school 95 Children with special needs N/A	• The Territory of Nunavut was created in April 1999. Nunavut initially adopted the child care legislation and regulations of the Northwest Territories. • Responsibility for child care programs moved from the Early Childhood and School Services Division to the Adult Education, Career and Early Childhood Services Division of the Department of Education (2002).	Care providers are funded with an increased daily operating grant to provide extra support for children with special needs. To receive additional funding, children with special needs must be identified by a health-care professional.
Ontario	Early Years Programs Branch Policy Development and Program Design Division Ministry of Children and Youth Services Hepburn Block, 4th Floor 80 Grosvenor Street Toronto, Ontario M7A 1E9 416-327-0326	Number of licensed/regulated spaces (2004) Centre-based 206 743 Family daycare 19 838 Children with special needs 21 305	• Day Nurseries Act (1978) • Ontario Child Care Review (1996) • How to Improve Ontario's Child Care (working paper, 1997) • Making Services Work for People: A Framework for Children and People with Developmental Disabilities (April, 1997) • Report of Early Years Study (1999) • The Early Childhood Developmental Initiative: A Vision for Early Childhood Development Services in Ontario (2000)	Although Ontario does not have a written policy regarding children with special needs, integration of children with special needs into community child care services is encouraged and funding for staffing and equipment, for example, is provided.
Prince Edward Island	Children's Secretariat Department of Health and Social Services PO Box 2000, 16 Garfield Street Charlottetown, Prince Edward Island C1A 6A5 902-368-6517	Number of licensed/regulated spaces (2004) Infant (full-time) 40 Preschool (full-time) 1918 School-age (part-time) 695 Special needs 215	• Resource Manual for Case Conferences • For Our Children: A Strategy for Healthy Development (2000)	Prince Edward Island has all integrated child care programs for children with special needs. Funding is available for programs to provide individualized programming. No additional training is required for staff working with children with special needs.

44

Quebec	Ministère de l'Emploi, de la Solidarité sociale et de la Famille 425 rue Saint-Amable Quebec City, Quebec G1R 4Z1 514-873-2323	Number of licensed/regulated spaces (2004) Infant/toddler/preschool centre-based 93 995 Family daycare 82 044 Children with special needs 2 274	• Nouvelles dispositions de la politque familiale: Les infants au coeur de nos choix (1997)	Quebec's policy on special needs encourages the inclusion of children in regular programs. Funds are provided for equipment and individual programming.
Saskatchewan	Child Day Care Program Saskatchewan Department of Community Resources and Employment 1920 Broad Street Regina, Saskatchewan S4P 3V6 306-787-3855	Number of licensed/regulated spaces (2004) Infant 452 Toddler 1 129 Preschool 3 085 School-age 874 Family daycare 2 370 Children with special needs 370	• The Child Care Act 1989–90, Chapter c-7.3 • The Saskatchewan Child Care Regulations, June 1995 • Saskatchewan's Action Plan for Children: Building on Community Success: Creating a Long-Term Plan for Saskatchewan's Youngest Children and Their Families (Working paper, 1996)	The Child Care Inclusion Program provides support to families, nonprofit child care centres and licensed family daycare homes to include children with special needs. Three types of grants, varying in amount of funding, are provided.
Yukon Territory	Early Childhood and Prevention Department of Health and Social Services Government of the Yukon P.O. Box 2703 Whitehorse, Yukon Territory Y1A 2C6 867-393-7082	Number of licensed/regulated spaces (2004) Infant/toddler 345 Preschool 398 School-age 243 Family daycare 383 Children with special needs approx. 45	• New Child Care Regulations (regulations implemented in 1995)	Children with special needs must be integrated into mainstream child care programs as stated in the 1995 Child Care Regulations. After a child care professional assesses a child as having special needs, an individual program plan must be developed. Funding for adaptive equipment, transportation, programming support, and additional support is available for centres through a Supported Child Care fund.

STUDENT ACTIVITIES

1. Write to the early childhood branch of your provincial or territorial department of education or social services and ask how you might obtain information regarding early childhood education programs for children with special needs in your area.
2. Locate the office of a local advocacy group, and arrange to talk to the person working on behalf of children with special needs about his or her work and the challenges it presents.
3. Choose one piece of legislation mentioned in this unit. Do a detailed, research-oriented report on the history and current status of the legislation.
4. Obtain and study a copy of the 2003 Multilateral Framework on Early Learning and Child Care. Give reasons for the importance of this document.
5. Form several small groups. Have each group select one piece of legislation described in this chapter or describe legislation that the group feels should be enacted. See if you can successfully advocate for this law: Convince others in the class that this law should be enacted.

REFERENCES

Castelle, K. (1990). *Children have rights too! A primer on the U.N. convention on the rights of the child*. Etobicoke, ON: Defence for Children International.

Council of Ministers of Education. (1989). *Special education information sharing project: Summary of responses*. Toronto: Council of Ministers of Education, Canada.

Doherty, G., Lero. D., Goelman, H., Tougas, J., & LaGrange, A. (2000a). *You bet I care! Report 2: Caring and learning environments: Quality in child care centres across Canada*. Guelph, ON: University of Guelph, Centre for Families, Work and Well-Being.

Doherty, G., Lero. D., Goelman, H., Tougas, J., & LaGrange, A. (2000b). *You bet I care! Report 3: Quality in regulated family child care across Canada*. Guelph, ON: University of Guelph, Centre for Families, Work and Well-Being.

Friendly, M., & Beach J. (2005). *Early childhood education and care in Canada 2004* (6th ed.). Toronto: University of Toronto, Childcare Resource and Research Unit, Centre for Urban and Community Studies.

Health and Welfare Canada. (1986). *Status of Day Care in Canada 1985*. Ottawa: Author.

Health and Welfare Canada. (1990). *Status of Day Care in Canada 1989*. Ottawa: Author.

Irwin, S. H. (1997). Including all children. *Interaction, 4*(10), 15–16.

Lysack, M. (2000). Partnerships for inclusion: Saskatchewan's special needs child care review. In E. Lowe (Ed.), *Linking research to practice* (pp. 80–86). Ottawa: Child Care Federation.

MacKay, A. W. (1987). The Charter of Rights and special education: Blessing or curse? *Canadian Journal for Exceptional Children, 3*(4), 118–127.

Federal/Provincial/Territorial Ministers Responsible for Social Services. (2003). *Multilateral Framework on Early Learning and Child Care.* Ottawa: Government of Canada.

Pence, A., Griffins, S., McDonnell, L., Goelman, H., Lero, D., & Brockman, L. (1997). *Shared diversity: An interprovincial report on child care in Canada. Canadian national child care study.* Ottawa: Statistics Canada and Human Resources Development Canada.

Stapleford, E. M. (1976). *History of the day nurseries branch—A personal record.* Toronto: Ministry of Community and Social Services, Ontario.

CHAPTER 3 | Partnership with Families

KEY CONCEPTS

case manager

culturally sensitive

empowerment

failure to thrive

family uniqueness

individual family service plan (IFSP)

nonintrusive

reciprocal relationships

resource teacher/
early interventionist

service coordinator

transdisciplinary team

OBJECTIVES

After studying the material in this chapter, the student will be able to

- Identify issues that are common among families of children with developmental differences.
- Outline the major components of an individual family service plan (IFSP).
- Define the concepts "enabling" and "empowering" as related to families of children with developmental differences, and explain the social significance of the concepts.
- List a number of ways for teachers to communicate with parents.
- Draw up a format for holding a conference with parents that includes follow-up.

Introduction

Family involvement has long been a tradition in early childhood education. With the advent of intervention programs for young children with developmental disabilities, family involvement now is viewed as essential (Photo 3–1). Contrast this with earlier times when parents were advised, almost routinely, to institutionalize a child who had a disability. Professionals and parents alike agreed that institutions could not offer the individualized support and nurturing that were needed to facilitate early development. Today, relatively few children are institutionalized: Most live in their family's home; others may live in residential or group homes within their family's community. However, it was not until the 1970s that family support and involvement in their children's special education programs and intervention services were aided through provincial and territorial funding.

Turnbull and Turnbull (1988, p. 21) describe the shift:

> The pendulum has swung in many ways: from viewing parents as part of the problem to viewing them as a primary solution to the problem, from expecting passive roles to expecting active roles, from viewing families as a mother–child dyad to recognizing the presence and needs of all members, and from assigning generalized expectations from the professionals' perspective to allowing for individual priorities defined from each family's perspective.

Photo 3–1
Family involvement is essential in early childhood intervention programs.

The major trends examined in this chapter are the following:

- involvement of families in planning and implementing intervention services and educational programs for their infants and young children with developmental differences
- the rights and options of families
- avoidance of professional intrusion into family affairs
- **empowerment** of the family
- family roles and responsibilities in case management

As background, various aspects of family living will be touched on, starting with the many types of families in today's society. Having an infant with a disability and the impact this has on parents and on the family as a whole will be described. The rationale and justification for family involvement will follow, with emphasis on the family as a system of interactive, **reciprocal relationships.** Strategies that early childhood teachers engage in when working with parents of children with special needs will conclude the chapter. (Throughout the chapter, primary caregivers will be referred to as "parents," even though it is not always the case that a parent is the primary caregiver.)

Empowerment
planning and carrying out intervention activities in ways that pass as much control and decision making as possible on to the family

Reciprocal relationships
interactions between individuals in which each person gives and receives in response to the giving and receiving of the other

Family Patterns and Expectations

The makeup of families, and their expectations regarding the behaviour of family members, varies from family to family and from culture to culture. The emotional climate within families varies, too. Often it is characterized by the way parents interact with their children (which is not a one-way street, as we shall see later in the chapter). As we develop strategies and programs to facilitate family involvement, it is important to understand the families with whom we work. Our society is becoming increasingly diverse, and the families with whom we work come from different cultures and speak different languages. There may also be cultural differences in what people know and believe about disabilities and child-rearing. We must understand and respect these differences as we work to build **culturally sensitive,** reciprocal, and responsive programs (Kalyanpur & Harry, 1999).

The concept of **family uniqueness** recognizes that every family is a distinct collection of individuals who have come together to create a new whole. Although many families may share similar characteristics, it is important not to assume that these families share common beliefs and practices. For example, not all Jamaican-Canadian families share common views on child-rearing, nor do all Jewish families have the same priorities when it comes to early intervention goals, nor do all families headed by lesbian couples express their spirituality in similar ways. The concept of family uniqueness requires that practitioners learn how to work with families as individuals, how to communicate with families effectively, and how to develop cultural self-awareness to understand the ways our own beliefs influence our work (Harry, 1992).

FAMILIES OF CHILDREN WITH EXCEPTIONALITIES

Whatever the makeup of a family, those with children who have special needs will feel the impact on family life. Some families say that they become closer as they learn to adapt to a child's disability and that the child's disability has enhanced the existing strengths of their family (Turnbull & Turnbull, 1993). Others are less able to cope; still others are pulled apart. At one point, it was thought that the divorce rate was greatly increased among families with a child with disabilities. Research (Wikler, Haack, & Intagliata, p. 1984), however, suggests that there are no differences in the divorce rate when social and economic factors are held constant.

The vast majority of research about families is actually research about mothers of children with disabilities. Yet there has been some research that shows fathers demonstrate feelings similar to those of mothers, although fathers often are more concerned about long-term care issues and less concerned about day-to-day issues (Meyer, 1995).

When we talk about families, we usually mean parents. However, it is important to consider the needs of other family members in adapting to a child with special needs. Often grandparents have a very difficult time accepting and understanding a child's disability (Meyer & Vadasy, 1986). Although early childhood teachers may have limited contact with grandparents, teachers may serve as a support and resource to families who who are dealing with difficult reactions from family members, including the child's grandparents (Photo 3–2).

Another important group that must be considered is siblings. Siblings will have a lifelong relationship with their brother or sister with special needs, and they can benefit from special support and honest information about the special need. As Tozer (2001, p. 35) points out, "certain issues often arise for a sibling of a child with special needs, although each sibling, even in the same family, will be different." According to Tozer, there are typical stressors for siblings:

- jealousy about the time and attention the child with special needs gets from parents or caregivers
- guilt about being angry with a sibling with a special need

Culturally sensitive
classroom activities, materials, and curricula that acknowledge and respect the different ethnicities that are represented in the classroom and community

Family uniqueness
a perspective that recognizes that every family is different

Photo 3–2
Grandparents are major caregivers in the families of many children.

- embarrassment about a brother or sister
- stress at home
- worry about bringing friends home
- restrictions of family activities
- teasing or bullying about a brother or sister
- protectiveness about a dependent or ill brother or sister
- concerns about the future

FAMILY ABUSE AND THE CHILD WITH SPECIAL NEEDS

There is evidence that suggests children with disabilities are more likely to be abused than are other children (Sobsey 1995; Sobsey & Varnhagen, 1988). One explanation is that infants and young children with developmental differences, through no fault of their own, often behave in ways that upset their parents. For example, some infants who have special needs have high-pitched, inconsolable crying that seems to go on night and day. Such crying appears to put healthy parent–infant interaction in jeopardy (Frodi & Senchak, 1990). Other infant behaviours can have adverse effects, too. Consider these examples:

There may be difficulty with feeding, in which the parent gets food into the child only after much time and effort and then, repeatedly, the child fails to keep it down.

Lack of responsiveness is sometimes seen in infants with sensory impairments. In many instances, it is difficult to tell whether the child's disability and resulting behaviours led to parental abuse or if the abuse caused the child's disability.

Peterson (1987, p. 424) describes this dilemma:

> A normal child living in a stressful environment with an abuse-prone parent can become handicapped as a result of injury from abuse. On the other hand, a family with a handicapped child and without adequate support systems may incur enough stress to cause parents without abusive tendencies to abuse the child. In either case, the awareness of the potential problem of child abuse is crucial for educators who deal with young handicapped children and their families.

Although we are still learning about the complex interactions between family violence and children with special needs, several facts have been well documented:

- Children with developmental delays are more likely to experience abuse than are those children without development delays (Brown & Schormans, 2003).
- Children with intellectual disabilities are 3.7 times as likely to experience neglect, 3.8 times as likely to experience physical and emotional abuse, and 4 times as likely to be sexually abused as are children without intellectual disabilities (Sullivan & Knutson, 2000).
- Many childhood disabilities result from child abuse (e.g., traumatic brain injury as a result of shaking an infant or violence during pregnancy).

Adequate and appropriate support systems are a key factor in ensuring the well-being of families of children with developmental disabilities (Janko, 1994). Support is often taken for granted when a family has regular income, extended health insurance, adequate housing, and caring family and friends. Even so, additional support is usually required as soon as a newborn is identified as having serious developmental issues. Families do not plan to have a child with a disability. They expect a healthy infant who will grow, slowly but surely, into an independent and productive adult. From the start, parents of children with disabilities are often faced with disappointments and adjustments. These will affect every member of the family and every aspect of the family's life together.

FAMILY ADJUSTMENT

Grief is the usual reaction when parents first realize that they have an infant with disabilities. Even when an older child comes to be diagnosed as having a disabling condition, grieving is the normal response of most parents. It is almost as if their child had died. In a way, it is so. Ken Moses (1987) suggests that parents of children with disabilities experience a grieving process that is strikingly similar to that of people who experience a death. Working with groups of parents, Moses saw anxiety, anger, denial, guilt, depression, and fear expressed over and over again. Gradually he came to understand that the parents were grieving the *loss of the dream* of what their child was to have been for them. Emily Perl Kingsley's (1987) *Welcome to Holland* (Box 3–1) illustrates this sense of loss and points out what Moses believes is essential in the recovery process—to separate from the lost dream and to generate new, more attainable dreams.

Families who are dealing with the kind of loss associated with a child who has disabilities have complex and often conflicting feelings that surface and resurface throughout the years (Photo 3–3). As early childhood educators, we will find ourselves listening and responding to this type of grief as our centres and classrooms become inclusive. If we listen and respond to family needs, we will recognize the dynamics that affect all members.

Families need to begin the process of adapting to the realities of caring for a child with special needs. Almost immediately, they will have to begin to make urgent decisions and solve complicated issues affecting the family unit. These might include the following:

- extensive (and perhaps painful or life-threatening) medical treatment and surgery; hospitalization that may occur repeatedly and for extended periods
- heavy expenses and financial burdens other than medical ones, such as the cost of special foods and equipment
- frightening and energy-draining crises, often recurring, as when the child stops breathing, turns blue, or has a major seizure
- transportation problems; baby-sitting needs for the other children; time away from jobs to get the child with a disability to consultation and treatment appointments
- lack of affordable, available, or appropriate child care for families with children who have developmental differences
- continuous day-and-night demands on parents to provide what are routine but difficult caregiving tasks (e.g., it may take an hour or more, five to six times during a single day and night, to feed an infant with a severe cleft palate condition)
- constant fatigue, lack of sleep, and little or no time to meet the needs of other family members
- little or no opportunity for recreational or leisure activities; difficulty (and additional expense) of locating baby sitters who are both qualified and willing to

Photo 3–3
Families need to adapt to the realities of caring for a child with special needs.

Box 3–1   WELCOME TO HOLLAND

BY EMILY PERL KINGSLEY

I am often asked to describe the experience of raising a child with a disability—to try to help people who have not shared that unique experience to understand it, to imagine how it would feel. It's like this. . . .

When you're going to have a baby, it's like planning a fabulous vacation trip—to Italy. You buy a bunch of guide books and make your wonderful plans. The Coliseum. The Michelangelo David. The gondolas in Venice. You may learn some handy phrases in Italian. It's all very exciting.

After months of eager anticipation, the day finally arrives. You pack your bags and off you go. Several hours later, the plane lands. The stewardess comes in and says, "Welcome to Holland."

"*Holland?!?*" you say. "What do you mean Holland?? I signed up for Italy! I'm supposed to be in Italy. All my life I've dreamed of going to Italy."

But there's been a change in the flight plan. They've landed in Holland and there you must stay.

The important thing is that they haven't taken you to a horrible, disgusting, filthy place, full of pestilence, famine and disease. It's just a different place.

So you must go out and buy new guide books. And you must learn a whole new language. And you will meet a whole new group of people you would never have met.

It's just a *different* place. It's slower-paced than Italy, less flashy than Italy. But after you've been there for a while and you catch your breath, you look around . . . and you begin to notice that Holland has windmills . . . and Holland has tulips. Holland even has Rembrandts.

But everyone you know is busy coming and going from Italy . . . and they're all bragging about what a wonderful time they had there. And for the rest of your life, you will say "Yes, that's where I was supposed to go. That's what I had planned."

And the pain of that will never, ever, ever, *ever* go away . . . because the loss of that dream is a very very significant loss.

But . . . if you spend your life mourning the fact that you didn't get to Italy, you may never be free to enjoy the very special, the very lovely things . . . about Holland.

care for a child with a disability, especially if the child has severe problems (medical or behavioural)

- lack of, limited, or restricted respite care facilities
- jealousy or feelings of rejection among brothers and sisters who may feel that the child with special needs gets all the family's attention and resources
- marital problems arising from finances, fatigue, differences about management of the child's disability, or feelings of rejection by husband (or wife) who feels passed over in favour of the child

When these problems are further compounded by the social and economic effects of poverty, the subsequent development of the child with a disability and the growth and well-being of the rest of the family are doubly jeopardized.

Such problems suggest how nearly impossible it would be to provide effective intervention for a young child with a disability without including the child's family (Photo 3–4).

Photo 3–4
Truly effective early intervention includes the parents.

It was Bronfenbrenner (1974) who convinced developmentalists of the range of environmental (and family) influences on a young child's development. The mother–child relationship, once thought to be the major determining factor, has proven to be but one of many. Innumerable strands of reciprocal relationships, both cultural and personal, are at work. They form the system, or *ecological niche,* into which the child is born and in which the child is reared. A child's ability to cope or adapt depends on understanding his or her larger social system, made up of family functioning, support of friends and community, and cultural beliefs.

The Individual Family Service Plan (IFSP)

Many early intervention programs in Canada have begun to put into place a service focused on the family. This is modelled after the requirements of the U.S. law PL 99-457, which amended the Education for All Handicapped Children Act (see Chapter 2). This U.S. legislation emphasizes family support, thereby recognizing that infants and young children are best served in the context of a strong and healthy family. Frankel (1997) describes family-centred care in Canada as occurring when early childhood educators are aware of and sensitive to the family's beliefs, values, and expectations. Cultural customs, along with social values and family lifestyles, shape family expectations about a child's development and about child-rearing practices. It is essential for effective teachers to invest time in understanding each family's background to gain insight into how it affects the family's goals and aspirations for the child. For example, different cultures have varied perspectives on beliefs and feelings about children with special needs. Perceptions of what constitutes a special need may vary widely among different cultures, as well as within the same culture. It is important for educators to become aware of these differences and use these understandings about the family to individualize their program for the child and to support the family with an **individual family service plan (IFSP).** Family-centred care empowers the family to set priorities for care and intervention and to determine what the professional can do to support them in their parenting role (Frankel, 1997). The entire IFSP process—developing, implementing, and evaluating—must be conducted in a culturally sensitive manner, including the use of an interpreter whenever needed.

Woods and McCormick (2002) offer the following recommendations for supporting the family's role in the assessment process:

- Provide the family with choices in the assessment process.
- Conduct the assessment in the child's natural environment, with everyday materials and activities.
- Avoid professional jargon and acronyms.
- Present results in a strengths-based and a family-friendly manner, using interpreters as needed.
- Provide time for questions.
- Provide information to parents on such things as development, the child's disability, or legislation.
- Provide information on resources, such as respite.
- Encourage participation of the extended family or other family supports in the assessment and team meetings.

individual family service plan (IFSP)
a written plan that describes services for families with young children with special needs; it is written collaboratively with parents and describes the child's current strengths and needs

INDIVIDUAL FAMILY SERVICE PLAN COMPONENTS

The purpose of an IFSP—a term that some service providers use interchangeably with individual program plan (IPP)—is to identify and organize resources to assist families in raising their children who have developmental disabilities (see Chapter 12). These are some of its major features:

1. Help should be provided in a form that meets the unique needs of each child and family.
2. The IFSP should be an ongoing process that supports but *does not take the place of* parents' natural caregiving roles.
3. Family-centred as well as child-centred services should be provided through a **transdisciplinary team** approach.
4. Family members must be equal participants in the team (Photo 3–5).
5. A **case manager** should be identified and assigned the task of coordinating services and keeping the program moving.
6. Specific steps ensuring a smooth transition to the next intervention program should be described.

Identification of Needs

Each infant and toddler with special needs should first receive a transdisciplinary assessment. In addition, the family should be asked to participate voluntarily in a transdisciplinary identification of its strengths and unique needs. Families should receive the necessary services for their child even if they are unable to participate, or choose not to participate, in the identification process. Services designed to meet the assessed needs of the child and the identified needs of the family should be organized into an IFSP by the transdisciplinary team. The parents, other family members (grandparents, aunts, uncles, etc.), or an appointed guardian should be represented on the team. The family should be encouraged to invite an advocate, counsellor, or friend to assist or support them in presenting their position.

An important point, to be stressed again and again, is that the initial step in preparing an IFSP is *not* an assessment of the family. It is the family's *voluntary identification* of its strengths, resources, needs, and concerns, as these relate to *enhancing the development* of their child. Those who make up the intervention team need to recognize family issues that are beyond the scope of an early intervention program and advise the parents of appropriate resources.

Nonintrusiveness

Constant care is needed to ensure that families are benefited, rather than weakened or demeaned, by participation in the IFSP. Professionals involved in the IFSP process should be **nonintrusive:** that is, they should not intrude into a family's life or lifestyle without the family's invitation to do so. Family members are not to be prodded into discussing private or sensitive matters. Personal information gleaned from professional probing usually has little or no bearing on the special needs of the child.

The out-of-family perception of a family's needs often misses the mark (Harry, 1992). Instead, it is likely to represent the professionals' own biases and values. Emphasis in the IFSP should be on helping families identify their own needs and recognize their own abilities. Only when early intervention programs recognize and build on the diverse and unique strengths of each family will the IFSP concept fulfill its promise as a positive force in the lives of children with disabilities and their families (Dunst & Trivette, 1989).

Photo 3–5
Family members are essential members of the child's IFSP team.

Transdisciplinary team
team that shares the responsibilities for assessment, program planning, implementation, and evaluation across members

Case manager
the member of the IPP team who assumes responsibility for coordination of the program and services for the child

Nonintrusive
professionals respecting the privacy of families and not intruding into families' lives or lifestyles without an invitation to do so

IFSP Evaluation

The IFSP should be evaluated at regular intervals by the team. The purpose of the evaluation and review is to appraise the progress made by the child and family toward the objectives identified in the IFSP. If progress is unsatisfactory, program revisions are in order.

Service Coordination (Case Management)

A transdisciplinary team approach to early intervention implies that a number of professionals are dealing with the same child and family. It is strongly recommended that one particular person be designated as **service coordinator** (case manager). The service coordinator may be chosen because of his or her professional expertise in the child's exceptionality or because it is anticipated that the service coordinator will have longer contact and more frequent involvement with the family. The communications specialist might be the service coordinator when the main concern revolves around speech and hearing, the physiotherapist when there are evident motor delays, and the nutritionist in cases of **failure to thrive.** In addition to providing clinical skill, the service coordinator needs to be a sensitive listener, a child and family advocate, and a linkage agent (getting families linked to needed services). In many areas, the resource consultant/**resource teacher/early interventionist** serves as the service coordinator.

    The service coordinator is essential to team functioning as well as to family functioning. Without a liaison or go-between, both the team and the family tend to become confused. When there is a duplication of efforts (the family may be put through three or four intake interviews, for example), intervention services lose continuity and coherence, and whole programs can fall into chaos and disintegration.

    Generally speaking, the duties of the service coordinator/case manager are decided by each team. Assigned tasks might include these:

- coordinating the individual child's assessments and identification of family needs with prescribed services
- chairing team and family conferences
- making sure that records are kept up to date, paperwork gets done, and appointments are made (and kept)
- arranging the child's transitions to other programs and providing follow-up services
- serving continually as a source of contact, interpretation, and support for the family

Families, to the maximum extent possible, should have the opportunity to select their own case manager/coordinator. In some instances, family choice cannot be an option and a service coordinator must be assigned. A family that feels that its needs are not met adequately by the assigned case manager must be helped to find a more acceptable one.

Family Member as Case Manager/Coordinator

A family member who may want to serve as case manager should be encouraged and supported by other members of the IFSP or IPP team. Training should be provided for family members in how the system and how the network of backup services operate (Bailey, 1989). Gathering the necessary resources and assistance should not add to the family's burdens. Instead, the family should reap positive benefits and become stronger and more capable through the case-management process.

Service coordinator
the member of the IPP team who assumes responsibility for coordination of the program and services for the child

Failure to thrive
refers to undersized infants whose bodies, for various reasons (organic, genetic, or environmental) either do not receive or cannot use the nurturance necessary for proper growth and development

Resource teacher/early interventionist
a professional with special training and expertise in planning and implementing developmentally appropriate programs for children who have developmental problems

Learning to take the responsibility for getting needed assistance is seen as one approach to reducing overdependency on the team service system. Parent associations for specific disabilities will often help parents to locate resources that will prepare them for their role in case management.

Program-to-Program Transitions

The transdisciplinary team should provide support for the child and the family during transitions from one program to another. The hallmark of effective early intervention is the child's graduation into a more challenging program—frequently a program that is in a different setting. The transition between programs calls for special kinds of planning and support. The focus of Chapter 13 is on planning and implementing transitions.

ENABLING AND EMPOWERING FAMILIES

A major public concern about the individual family service planning process was that it would promote increased dependency. Many feared that families would become less able to function independently. Out of this public concern grew the major philosophical thrust of IFSP, the *enabling* and *empowering* of families. Deal, Dunst, and Trivette (1989, p. 33) suggest the following definitions of the terms:

> Enabling families means creating opportunities for family members to become more competent and self-sustaining with respect to their abilities to mobilize their social networks to get needs met and attain goals.

> Empowering families means carrying out interventions in a manner in which family members acquire a sense of control over their own developmental course as a result of their own efforts to meet needs.

The intent of the *enabling* and *empowering* concepts is to strengthen families without taking away their ability to cope. The IFSP aims to support and build on those things the family already does well. Professionals believe that this can be accomplished by providing families with the information and skills that will enable them to try to solve their own problems and meet their own needs. The case manager should play the pivotal role in fostering and overseeing the empowerment of families. According to Dunst and Trivette (1989, p. 99), "Case management may be considered effective only to the extent that families become more capable, competent, and empowered as a result of the help-giving acts of case managers."

The Family–Teacher Partnership

Families and teachers should be partners in facilitating children's development. It is important to recognize that families must maintain the right to have the final word. They bear the ongoing and primary responsibility during the long years of their child's growth and development (frequently, many additional years when a child has a disability). Numerous research studies describe the benefits of active parent involvement in a child's early intervention program (Photo 3–6). Without it, children tended to regress or slip back once the program ended (Simeonsson & Bailey, 1990). Parent involvement has two major functions: (1) it provides an ongoing reinforcement system that supports the efforts of the program while it is underway, and (2) after the program ends, the child's gains are maintained and expanded on as a result of the family's increased knowledge and confidence in their ability to support the changing developmental needs of their child.

Photo 3–6
There are many benefits to active parent involvement in their child's intervention program.

Photo 3–7
Truly effective early intervention includes parents.

RATIONALE FOR PARENT PARTICIPATION

Many reasons can be given for encouraging parents' involvement in their child's early education and intervention program (Photo 3–7):

- Families are the major socializing agents for their child, as transmitters of cultural values, beliefs, and traditions.
- Families know their child better than teachers or clinicians do; thus, families have a source of information that is available from no one else.
- Family members can help the child transfer knowledge from school to home and neighbourhood: Only a few hours a day are spent in school; many more hours are spent at home.
- Consistency of adult expectations can be maintained. Young children become anxious when important adults do not agree on expectations. Confusion and even resistance may result if, for example, teachers expect a child to put on his or her own coat while parents always do it for the child.
- Pleasing parents is important to young children in that the parents are the source of many pleasant and necessary reinforcers for their young child—food, warmth, comfort, outings, playthings, and so forth.
- Children with disabilities acquire developmental skills more quickly when parents learn to participate in home teaching (Shearer & Shearer, 1977).
- Involvement in an early intervention program offers families access to support from other families and a better perspective on their own child's strengths and needs.

DEGREE OF PARTICIPATION

The extent to which parents can be actively involved in their child's program depends on a number of factors:

- work schedule and job constraints
- additional young children at home who need care
- availability of transportation
- parental health (both physical and psychological)
- parental maturity and understanding of the child's needs
- attitudes and comfort level of the parent with medical personnel, teachers, and authority figures
- the program's ability to accommodate to the primary language of the family

It is important to recognize that simply *maintaining a child's enrollment in a program is a form of parent involvement*. Lack of active participation does not imply lack of interest in the child or the program. Instead, as noted by Barber, Turnbull, Behr, & Kerns (1988, p. 197), it may be a form of energy conservation:

> Family life with a child who has a disability is a marathon rather than a sprint. A crucial aspect of supporting families during the early years is to empower them with coping strategies that can help them to run the full course with their son or daughter and to avoid the trap of investing their energies heavily for a short period of time and then burning out.

COMMUNICATING WITH FAMILIES

The teachers' approach to parents should be the same as the teachers' approach to children: respect and appreciation for individual differences in culture, values, attitudes, and learning styles. When mutual understanding can be established between parents and teachers, children are more likely to experience a good learning environment. When communicating with parents, it is important to do the following:

- Establish two-way communication.
- Talk *with*—rather than *to*—parents.
- Simultaneously try to share knowledge and obtain feedback.
- Share information that may address the expressed and unexpressed concerns of the parents. Unexpressed concerns may be one of the biggest obstacles to communication. With some parents, it may be a long while, for example, before they are able to talk about their child's exceptionality or even to express openly that a concern exists.

The following sections describe the various ways that teachers can communicate with families.

Informal Exchanges

A tremendous amount of information can be exchanged during informal encounters (Photo 3–8). The quick conversations that occur in programs where parents pick up and deliver children are especially fruitful. Positive comments made by teachers to parents in the presence of the child, are important when working with any family. This is especially true when working with families who have a child with special needs. Often people focus on the negative or inappropriate behaviour of the child, so parents come to realize that seemingly small events have developmental significance. Children learn that their accomplishments have merit; otherwise, why would the teacher pass on the news? And why would both of these important adults, parent and teacher, look so pleased? Appreciative comments have another function, too. They serve as models for parents. Hearing them helps parents learn to put into words their own recognition and appreciation of their children's efforts.

Photo 3–8
Arrival and departure times are not the time to discuss concerns about the child.

Parent Observations

In all programs for young children, parents should be welcome at any time. Since parents are the primary partners in their child's development, they have the right to see and question every-thing that goes on in the classroom. This is especially true when we are working with families who have children with special needs. Firsthand observations offer one of the best ways of providing indirect parent education. Watching their child inter-acting with other children and adults, with materials and activities, provides insights that can be obtained in no other way. The following ideas should be kept in mind when parents are observing:

- Every parent observation is followed by at least a brief discussion with a teacher.
- If possible, the teacher should be the one who was in the activity area where the parent had observed for the longest period.
- When a conversation cannot take place on the spot, a follow-up telephone call is important to
  - answer questions parents might have or share information regarding why certain play or group situations were handled as they were
  - help parents recognize the positive aspects of their own child's uniqueness and developmental progress
  - describe the appropriateness of individualized curriculum activities in enhancing the child's development and meeting their child's special needs
- Parent observations may be regularly scheduled or held on the spur of the moment (Photo 3–9).
- When a formal observation is planned, it is best for teachers to provide some type of structure. A clipboard with a simple observation form works well. Parents are asked to note the child's activities, playmates, and special interests, as well as avoidances, if relevant.
- Focused observation helps parents note what is actually going on with their child. Taking notes helps parents see the subtleties of their child's involvement. This enables the parents to be a part of the programming process while not inter-fering in their child's activities. A parent engaged in close observation and note taking tends to discourage the child from staying too close to his or her side.
- Videotaped observations may be used in place of on-site parent observations. Videotapes are also useful when parents need to turn to translators for interpre-tation. Follow-up discussions can then take place afterward.

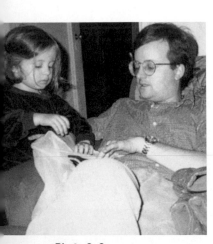

Photo 3–9
Parent observations may be regularly scheduled events.

Telephone Calls

Telephone calls help keep communication going between teachers and parents. When children arrive by bus and parents work, the telephone may become the chief means of maintaining contact. Telephone calls may be used for the same kinds of casual reporting as arrival and departure contacts. Many parents prefer that a con-venient day and time of day be arranged in advance so that they can plan to have a few minutes to talk freely. When teachers' calls become a regular event, most par-ents welcome them—a call from school no longer signals trouble. Usually, the focus is on routine matters, such as the outcome of a visit to the audiologist, the progress of an illness, or the reason for an absence of several days. For children who are not picked up by their own parents, the teacher should phone to report any unusual happening at school: torn or soiled clothing; a scrape, fall, or rash; or an unex-plained change in a child's behaviour. The teacher should always try to reach the parent before the child arrives home. The advance call can allow parents time to think of the best way to handle the situation before they see their child.

Written Notes

If immediate reporting and feedback are not essential, written notes sent home with the child can be useful. Once a relationship has been established between a teacher and parent, a written note often is preferred to a telephone call. Parents can read the note at a convenient time. Written notes can be used to request items from home, such as extra clothing, beautiful junk, and so on. Notes home can also provide parents with exciting news of a child's progress (Photo 3–10). Notes of this kind give parents something specific and positive to talk about with their child. In addition, notes are one more way for teachers to help parents recognize the developmental significance of a child's seemingly routine accomplishments.

Audiotapes and Videotapes

For some families, written materials are not an effective way to communicate. Since English may be a second language for many families, audiotape reports can be used as a substitute for written reports. These can then be interpreted by an individual of the family's choice, thus respecting the family's right to privacy.

For other families, an audiotape log may be an option. This system should be negotiated individually with a family because of the equipment involved. The family and the centre both need to have a tape recorder on which to listen to the message and then record a response. The tape, and in some cases the tape player, would be carried back and forth between school and home. Similarly, many centres are now using videotapes to communicate with families. Videotapes are especially useful when trying to demonstrate a new program, skill, or sign that the child is learning. Again, this system needs to be negotiated individually with families to make sure that the family has access to a VCR and is comfortable having their child videotaped.

E-mail

Communicating via e-mail may be very convenient for many parents and teachers. It is important to discuss with parents the type of information they want to receive by e-mail. Because of security implications, highly confidential information should neither be composed nor sent through e-mail.

The Two-Way Journal (or Communication Book)

Some settings take the brief written note idea a step further and use a journal system. Parents and teachers both write in the journal. It travels back and forth between school and home on a frequent and fairly regular basis. Once such a system becomes established, it seems a relatively effortless but rewarding method for keeping the communication lines open between home and school.

Newsletters

Most parents appreciate having newsletters sent home. One of the major purposes of a newsletter is to describe the everyday events and learning experiences that go on at school. A newsletter can also serve as a reminder to parents of upcoming events or situations that involve all families (e.g., cold weather and the need for warm clothing). Newly enrolled children and families, teachers, and volunteers can be introduced in the newsletter. Whenever possible, try to include children in the process. They can dictate special events or provide drawings for the newsletter.

A newsletter must be written at the reading level of the families receiving it. In many programs, newsletters need to be written in two or more languages.

Photo 3–10
A written note sent home with the child might say, "Your child managed to eat by herself today."

PARENT–TEACHER MEETINGS

Meeting together has been the traditional form of parent–teacher interactions. Usually held on the premises of the school or program, the meetings provide opportunities for parents to see their children's work, interact with teachers, and compare notes with other parents.

Large-Group Meetings

Group meetings can be very beneficial to families. Group meetings usually focus on issues of general interest or concern to the parents, such as aspects of child development, curriculum, or behavioural challenges. A recognized expert in a particular area may be invited to speak. Time for questions and open discussion is an important part of any family–teacher get-together. An informal social time or open house often precedes or follows the group discussion. Casual socializing helps parents to get to know teachers and other parents better. Parents should have many opportunities to visit their child's classroom, where paintings, clay work, woodworking, or other projects are on display. Parents of children with an identified special need should also be encouraged to attend workshops or meetings offered by disability-specific organizations.

Parent Conferences

In addition to IFSP planning, regular parent conferences should be scheduled two or three times a year, more often in some instances. Conferences should have the purpose of building parent–teacher communications. A positive note must be established at the onset. Conferences with parents require a quiet place with comfortable seating. After greeting the parents cordially and exchanging social pleasantries, conversation should focus on a review of the purpose of the conference. This should be followed by a brief progress report. The report should combine both parent and teacher observations, interspersed with many examples of how the child is gaining (or has mastered) particular developmental skills, both at home and at school. Throughout, parents should have ample opportunity to comment, ask questions, and express their concerns. Strategies that work at home and school should also be discussed. The conference should close with a brief summary of the discussion, a restatement of long- and short-term learning goals for the child, and a restatement of the child's unique and valuable qualities. A date for the next conference should be set.

In every parent conference, the focus must be on issues related to the child's development and learning. Teachers should avoid counselling parents on deeply personal concerns but still attempt to help the family find an appropriate resource.

Ethical issues are a concern of many teachers in their work with parents (Feeney & Kipnis, 1992). What should be done, for example, when a child has serious health problems that the parent appears to neglect? or behaviour problems that parents apparently do not recognize? Before going into such a conference, the teacher must make extensive observations and, when appropriate, take frequency counts of the behaviour in question. The teacher should also consult with other teachers. This will ensure staff agreement that a serious problem exists and that it cannot be handled through rearrangement of particular aspects of the program. No matter how carefully the teacher sets a positive note at the outset of such a conference, or how tactfully he or she brings up the problem, parents may feel threatened. Inevitably, they

Photo 3–11
Teachers need parents' input to help the child.

feel that whatever is "wrong" with their child is their fault (or is perceived by teachers as the parents' fault). At first mention of their child's shortcomings, parents may feel alienated, defensive, and even angry. Little can be accomplished in that kind of an emotional climate. Teachers, therefore, should bring up difficult problems only when the child's present or future well-being is at stake and teachers cannot help the child without the parents' help (Photo 3–11).

It would be unconscionable for teachers not to bring up certain problems—for example, ongoing excessive drowsiness. The teacher must discuss this with the parents immediately. After brief greetings, the opening statements should have to do with the frequency of the problem as observed and documented. It should be pointed out to the parents how much the child is missing because of his or her lethargic state. At no point should the teacher back down. The teacher should advise the parent to consult immediately with the child's doctor. Should the condition continue, the teacher should contact the public health nurse or the case manager for support.

PARENT FEEDBACK

Most feedback from parents is obtained indirectly. Much of it comes from incidental comments during informal parent–teacher exchanges. Parents' responses are most useful if questions relate to specific aspects of the program. In addition, questions should be designed so that parents can rate the degree of satisfaction of each item, rather than having to give a yes or no answer. Suggestion boxes can also be helpful. Parents can make their comments anonymously if they are supplied with the form. Teachers' responses to parents' suggestions can be posted on the bulletin board. If parents are given acknowledgment that comments are not only wanted, but acted on, they are more likely to continue to contribute their ideas and suggestions.

Photo 3–12
Much can be learned from a home visit.

Home Visits

Home visits have a long tradition of bridging the gap between school and home. Getting to know a family in its own setting enables teachers to work more effectively with children in the school setting (Photo 3–12).

During home visits, teachers can discover the interests, concerns, and needs of new children, and prepare the environment and curriculum to reflect these needs. Through home visits, the process of establishing a positive connection with each child begins. Educators will also benefit from meeting different family members and learning something about their roles within the family.

During home visits, personal biases may influence the impressions and judgments about diverse socioeconomic conditions, child-rearing practices, and child behaviour. It is important to question personal assumptions and reflect on how they can affect interactions with children and families. When discussing home visits with other staff members, be sure to focus on family strengths and the benefits of visits. Home visits provide teachers with an initial understanding of a child and family; as the relationship with them deepens, understanding will change and broaden.

In conducting home visits, spend time playing with children and looking at the toys and books they value. Follow the child's lead in play. Bringing a special book or toy from the classroom setting (particularly one that reflects diversity and inclusion) to share with the children may add to the home visit. However, children may prefer to show their teacher every single toy or book they posses! Ask children, using different communication strategies, what they like to do and indicate how activities in the classroom setting are like the ones they enjoy. By doing so, teachers show the children that they are people who care about and value what children think and feel.

Teachers should always remember the parents' role in their child's learning. Not only are parents the child's first teachers, but they are also the child's most frequent teachers. With appropriate support, parents can make their home a significant learning environment for their children. "The goal is to find ways to build on what the family is already contributing to their child's learning and growth" (ERIC/OSEP, 2001). Home is the place where all developmental skills can be practised over and over, in a real-life setting, with those who have a personal stake in the child's development.

Summary

The family, regardless of its makeup, is a young child's most important teacher. Although early childhood teachers are partners with parents in the teaching process, parents are always the primary partners. With children who have developmental differences, parents' involvement in their child's early intervention program is especially important. Involvement takes many forms. Simply keeping their child in the intervention program may be the only involvement some parents can manage.

An ecological approach to understanding early development is fundamental to the individual family service plan. The first underlying assumption is that children who are young and special can be helped best in the context of their family and culture. The second is that family members, including grandparents and siblings, are as likely to be in need of special services as is the child. The IFSP is to be an interdisciplinary team effort that includes parents as team members. A case manager is to be appointed to keep the program organized and running. The emphasis is on helping families become stronger and more able through the IFSP process.

The teacher–parent partnership is fostered in a variety of ways. A relationship that will benefit children is based on open communication and teachers' respect of the range of individual differences among parents. Many of the most effective teacher–parent exchanges are brief and informal chats—for instance, when a parent brings the child to school or observes in the classroom. Telephone calls, written notes sent home with children, e-mails, newsletters, and group meetings keep the lines open between teachers and parents. Formal conferences are another means of communicating with parents, as are home visits. Teachers may also seek parent feedback about the program itself through questionnaires and suggestion boxes.

RESOURCES

w w w

CHILD AND FAMILY CANADA
http://www.cfc-efc.ca
The site offers information on 800 toy libraries, parent resource centres, and related services.

VANIER INSTITUTE OF THE FAMILY
http://www.vifamily.ca
The Vanier Institute is an acknowledged leader on issues affecting families.

CONTACT A FAMILY
http://www.cafamily.org.uk
This British charitable organization helps families who care for children with any disability or special need.

SPECIALINK CANADA
http://www.specialinkcanada.org
This is a Canada-wide mainstream network whose goal is to promote high-quality daycare for every child in the country, regardless of abilities.

STUDENT ACTIVITIES

1. Select several classmates to role-play parent–child pairs during a program's arrival time. Take the role of teacher and initiate brief exchanges with the individual parents concerning a sleep problem, a child's new leg braces, a special painting a child has done, or a child's reluctance to play outdoors.
2. Prepare a one-page newsletter based on events that occurred in the classroom where you observe or practise-teach.
3. If possible, interview a family with a child who has special needs to identify any special circumstances and caregiving arrangements they have had to deal with.
4. Select a partner to play the role of a parent who has a child with a special need. Demonstrate the kinds of nonintrusive questions you would ask to assist the family in identifying their needs and strengths.

5. Select the one best match for each item in column I from column II and place that letter in the appropriate space in column I.

I		II
___	1. interaction with the family	A. newsletter
___	2. respite care	B. reconstituted family
___	3. blended family	C. reciprocal interactions
___	4. case manager	D. major socializing agents
___	5. parent feedback	E. relief caregiving
___	6. ethical issue	F. child abuse
___	7. parents and family	G. questionnaire
___	8. classroom activities report	H. IFSP organizer

REFERENCES

Bailey, D. (1989). Case management in early intervention." *Journal of Early Intervention, 13*(2), 120–134.

Barber, P. A., Turnbull, A. P., Behr, S. K., & Kerns, G. M. (1988). A family systems perspective on early childhood special education. In S. L. Odom & M. B. Karnes (Eds.), *Early intervention for infants and children with handicaps.* Baltimore, MD: Brookes.

Bronfenbrenner, U. (1974). *A report on longitudinal evaluations of preschool programs, vol. 2: Is early intervention effective?* (DHEW Publication No. OHD 76 30025). Washington, DC: U.S. Department of Health, Education, and Welfare.

Brown, I., & Schormans, A. (2003). Maltreatment and life stressors in single mothers who have children with developmental delay. *Journal on Developmental Disabilities, 10*(1), 61–66.

Deal, A. G., Dunst, C. J., & Trivette, C. M. (1989). A flexible and functional approach to developing individualized family service plans. *Infants and Young Children, 1*(4), 32–43.

Dunst, C. J., & Trivette, C. M. (1989). An enablement and empowerment perspective of case management. *Topics in Early Childhood Special Education, 8*(4), 87–102.

ERIC/OSEP Special Project. (Fall 2001). *Family involvement in special education. Research Connections in Special Education, 9.* Arlington, VA: The ERIC Clearinghouse on Disabilities and Gifted Education.

Feeney, S., & Kipnis, K. (1992). *Code of ethical conduct and statement of commitment.* Washington, DC: National Association for the Education of Young Children.

Frankel, E. (1997). *Resource sheet unit III, checklist for quality inclusive education.* Haliburton, ON: Early Childhood Resource Teacher Network of Ontario.

Frodi, A., & Senchak, M. (1990). Verbal and behavioral responsiveness to the cries of atypical infants. *Child Development, 61*(1), 76–84.

Harry, B. (1992). Developing cultural self-awareness: The first step in values clarification for early interventionists. *Topics in Early Childhood Special Education, 12*(4), 333–350.

Janko, S. (1994). *Vulnerable children, vulnerable lives.* New York: Teachers College Press.

Kalyanpur, M., & Harry, B. (1999). *Culture in special education.* Baltimore, MD: Brookes.

Meyer, D. (1995). *Uncommon fathers.* New York: Woodbine House.

Meyer, D. J., & Vadasy, P. F. (1986). *Grandparent workshops: How to organize workshops for grandparents of children with handicaps.* Seattle, WA: University of Washington Press.

Moses, K. (1987). The impact of childhood disability: The parents' struggle. *Ways Magazine,* Spring.

Peterson, N. L. (1987). *Early intervention for handicapped and at-risk children.* Denver, CO: Love Publishing.

Shearer, M., & Shearer, D. E. (1977). Parent involvement. In J. B. Jordan, A. H. Hayden, M. B. Karnes, & M. M. Wood (Eds.), *Early childhood education for exceptional children: A handbook of ideas and exemplary practices.* Reston, VA: Council for Exceptional Children.

Simeonsson, R. J., & Bailey, D. B. (1990). Family dimensions in early intervention. In S. J. Meisels & J. P. Shonkoff (Eds.), *Handbook of early childhood intervention* (pp. 428–444). Cambridge (UK): Cambridge University Press.

Sobsey, D. (1995). Violence against children with disabilities, An overview. *Connection: Newsletter of the Institute for Prevention of Child Abuse, 4,* 1–5.

Sobsey, D., & Varnhagen, C. (1988). *Sexual abuse and exploitation of people with disabilities, final report.* Ottawa: Department of National Health and Welfare (ERDS No. ED346620).

Sullivan, P. M., & Knutson, J. F. (2000). Maltreatment and disabilities: A population-based study. *Child Abuse & Neglect, 24*(10), 1257–1273.

Tozer, R. (2001). Spotlight on siblings. *Interactions, 15*(1).

Turnbull, A. P., & Turnbull, H. R. (1988). *Families, professionals, and exceptionality: A special partnership.* Columbus, OH: Charles E. Merrill.

Turnbull, A. P., & Turnbull, H. R. (1993). Participatory research on cognitive coping: From concepts to research planning. In A. P. Turnbull, J. M. Patterson, S. K. Behr, D. L. Murphy, J. G. Marquis, & M. J. Blue-Banning (Eds.), *Cognitive coping, families, and disabilities* (pp. 1–14). Baltimore, MD: Brookes.

Wikler, L., Haack, J., & Intagliata, J. (1984). Bearing the burden alone? Helping divorced mothers of children with developmental disabilities. In J. C. Hansen & E. I. Coopersmith (Eds.), *Families with handicapped members: The family therapy collections* (pp. 44–63). Rockville, MD: Aspen Systems.

Wood, J. J., & McCormick, K. M. (2002). Toward an integration of child-and family-centered practices of assessment in preschool children: Welcoming the family. *Young Exceptional Children, 5*(3), 2–11.

CHAPTER 4

Preparing Teachers for Inclusive Programs

KEY CONCEPTS

contingent stimulation
coordinated teaching
developmental disequilibrium
dual placements
facilitative teacher
incidental teaching

mediated learning model
readiness
scaffolding
teachable moments
transactional aspect of
    development

OBJECTIVES

After studying the material in this chapter, the student will be able to

- Describe the knowledge and training needed to work in early childhood inclusive programs with children who are developmentally different.
- Define developmentally appropriate learning experiences and justify the statement that all young children, regardless of their abilities, need such experiences.
- Discuss early education arrangements for children who have severe and multiple disabilities.
- Compare contingent stimulation, teachable moments, spontaneous teaching, and incidental teaching; and identify developmental principles they have in common and their significance to children's learning.
- List 10 or more characteristics demonstrated by effective teachers working in inclusive environments.

Introduction

Qualified early childhood teachers should be the central element in programs for infants, toddlers, preschool-aged, and school-aged children. These teachers should be supported by assistants who are trained or who are in the process of being trained, or by caregivers who have had on-the-job experience. Qualified early childhood education personnel should supervise caregivers providing child care in family-home daycare settings. Program quality is determined by the teachers' skills in managing the learning environment. Quality is further determined by teachers' personal attitudes about children and themselves, and by their beliefs regarding how children learn. In the inclusive classroom, the need for quality teaching is critical. The developmental diversity among children calls for skilled and sensitive teachers who will respond to children's special needs with a range of individualized programs. At the same time, inclusive classrooms call for teachers who recognize that young children with developmental disabilities are more like other children than they are different from them.

All children need learning activities and experiences geared to their level of development and interests. Children who are meeting developmental expectations within their particular culture need such experiences; children who are gifted need them; children with developmental differences need them. Effective early childhood teachers use a developmental approach as the basis for every aspect of their teaching. They recognize that all children have basic needs and all children have special needs. They recognize further that special needs cannot be met unless basic developmental needs also are met.

This chapter focuses on those general teaching skills and general developmental and behavioural principles that apply to all young children and all early childhood teachers. The point to be emphasized is this: *If children with developmental differences are to benefit from special approaches, learning experiences must take place within a developmental framework.* In other words, teachers must make particular adaptations. These adaptations are then incorporated into each child's individual developmental program.

The Teacher Experience in an Inclusive Setting

Teaching in an inclusive early childhood program is both challenging and rewarding. In these settings, teachers encounter the richest and widest range of developmental likenesses and differences among children. Skilled teachers enjoy this diversity, once they are convinced of the underlying developmental similarities among children of varying abilities (Photo 4–1).

No one professional can meet the needs of all the diverse learners in an inclusive early childhood program. Teachers in an inclusive classroom are members of a team of professionals who work together to meet the needs of all the children in the program. Each member of the team brings specialized knowledge to planning and implementing an appropriate developmental program for a child with special needs. Teamwork is especially important in providing the systematic and specialized instruction that is necessary to meet the needs of children with challenging behaviour or severe disabilities. The expertise that the early childhood educator brings to

Photo 4–1
Skilled teachers enjoy the diversity found in working with children of varying abilities.

the team is in creating a classroom environment and learning activities that are fun, motivating, safe, interesting, responsive, and supportive.

To ensure successful inclusion, the challenge for early childhood teachers is to make adaptations that accommodate the developmental needs of the range of children in the group. Program adaptation is not a new or unusual challenge for early childhood teachers. Adjusting curriculum and teaching strategies to individual differences and developmental variations has long been the heart of early childhood education. The full implications of this philosophy tend to be overlooked, however, where children with special needs are concerned.

A study conducted by several Canadian researchers (Lero, Irwin, & Brophy, 2000) found that most of the frontline staff and directors who participated in the study showed positive attitudes toward the inclusion of children with special needs. Factors that enabled teachers to be most successful with inclusion were support from resource teachers and consultants, external therapists, emotional support, and assistance from coworkers. The researchers suggest that these ongoing resources strengthen team efforts within centres and built on staff strengths and motivation (Lero, Irwin, & Brophy, 2000). Directors of child care centres identified several factors that made it more difficult to develop inclusive programs, such as reduced general funding for child care programs, reduced funding or subsidies for children with special needs, and reduced access to specialists.

TRAINING PROGRAMS FOR EARLY CHILDHOOD TEACHERS

People who want to prepare themselves to work with children with developmental differences will find a range of training options:

- Some provinces and territories have early childhood departments, child development and public health agencies, and university- or college-based institutes or centres that offer in-service and on-the-job training.

- Universities, two-year colleges, and vocational/technical schools are sources of early childhood training and basic courses on special needs. Also offered are specialized, post-diploma courses for those wanting to receive more advanced training in special needs and in inclusive programming strategies.
- Some provinces and territories have colleges and universities that offer distance education and Internet courses in early childhood education and related areas.
- Workshops and seminars sponsored by agencies, such as the Learning Disabilities Association of Canada (formerly the Association for Children with Learning Disabilities) and the Association for Community Living (formerly the Association for the Mentally Retarded), are available in many communities.

SPECIALIZED TRAINING FOR EARLY CHILDHOOD TEACHERS

Post-diploma and degree programs offering specialized training for work with a range of developmental differences are available in a number of provinces and territories. The resource teacher/early interventionist post-diploma certificate program provides specialized training for early childhood education teachers in working with children with special needs and their families. With the expansion of the number of children included in community programs, the need for persons with additional knowledge and specialized training has greatly increased. If we are to be successful in accomplishing inclusion as an option for *all* children, regardless of ability, greater recognition of the need for specially trained personnel as well as greater financial support must be forthcoming from all levels of government.

All early childhood educators should undertake ongoing professional development. Workshops that provide additional knowledge about the specific developmental disability of each child who is about to be enrolled are necessary for effective teaching (Photo 4–2).

Teachers also need on-the-job experience with children with special needs, but they should always have support from specially trained staff, such as resource/early interventionist teachers, resource consultants, and program advisers. Teachers must also work in close partnership with the parents of each child with special needs. The kinds of information offered in this text will provide a useful and comprehensive starting point for working in inclusive settings with children who have special needs.

DUAL PLACEMENTS AND COORDINATED TEACHING

A child with severe impairments should be provided with various kinds of inclusive experiences whenever possible and appropriate for the child and the child's family. For some children in specialized programs, this may mean frequently scheduled visits to inclusive settings. Other children may spend a part of each preschool or child care day in an inclusive setting. With careful

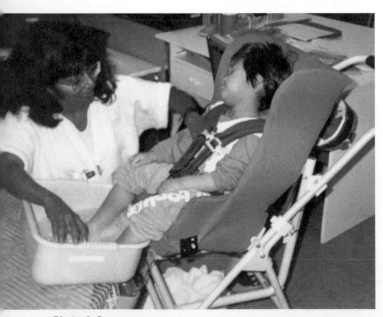

Photo 4–2

To provide effectively for children with developmental differences, teachers need additional knowledge about the child's specific disability.

coordinated teaching between the two staffs—those from the specialized program and those from the inclusive early childhood setting—these **dual placements** can be of benefit to all children. It is important that early childhood teachers become aware of the special community support services available to families and child care staff in their area. With written permission from the child's parents and the centre's supervisor, the child's teacher may find it helpful to contact one or more local services for a child needing special support. For example, if a three-year-old is observed as having no verbal communication skills, the local hospital might be asked for an assessment by the speech pathologist. The speech pathologist might recommend a language-stimulation program.

In rural areas where specific agencies and organizations are often not yet established, it is helpful to contact a national organization and ask to be referred to the nearest local agency in that province or territory. Local elementary school principals and public health nurses are usually good sources of information on the availability of social services or special consultants in a given area. Some remote regions are visited once a year by a travelling clinic or team of consultants. Most of these consultants will give support if requested in writing before their visit. Retired specialists may also be willing to volunteer or offer support and advice. The child care centre should consult any services that are involved with the child's family in his or her home.

Agencies and service organizations that focus on specific developmental differences can recommend or provide videos, DVDs, articles, books, and other kinds of information. (See the Resources at the end of each chapter for the websites of many of these organizations.) These materials describe the disabilities and the challenges that confront the child and family. If a child who has a vision impairment, for example, is to be included in a program, it is imperative that teachers begin immediately to find out about blindness and how it affects early development. The Canadian National Institute for the Blind or any of several other organizations with expertise in the area of vision impairments, such as departments of health, are best able to provide helpful materials. To be truly effective, such materials should be used along with background information provided by the family. It should not be forgotten that parents are the most important source of information about their children and their children's disabilities. No amount of special coursework or special training can take the place of the unique information that parents have to offer about their child with a developmental disability.

The Applied Developmental Approach

A CHILD IS A CHILD

In an inclusive early childhood setting, teachers need a particular mindset: seeing each child as a child, rather than as a "stutterer" or an "epileptic" or a "Down syndrome child" (Photo 4–3). By viewing every child first as a child, teachers come to realize that many behaviours are not necessarily related to a child's disability. Blaming a child's tantrums or excessive shyness or aggressiveness on his or her disability is commonplace but seldom justifiable. More accurate and certainly more helpful to the child is to view behaviours from the developmental perspective: as developmental commonalities, developmental irregularities, or cultural differences that are seen in all children to a greater or lesser degree. Children's speech is a prime example. Individual children speak differently, just as communities speak differently.

Coordinated teaching
When a child with special needs is in dual placements, staff from the specialized program and those from the inclusive early childhood setting provide coordinated programming for the child

Dual placements
When children with special needs spend a part of the day in a specialized program and part in an inclusive child care setting

Photo 4–3
A child is first of all a child.

Consider the many ways the English language is used in this country; obviously, a difference in language use does not necessarily imply a developmental disorder.

REVIEW OF DEVELOPMENTAL PRINCIPLES AND PRACTICES

Teachers who work with children with developmental differences need, first and foremost, a thorough foundation in child development. It is nearly impossible to recognize or evaluate many developmental differences without an understanding of the range and variations of behaviours and skill levels found among all children.

Developmental Sequences

Noting sequences of developmental accomplishments rather than of chronological age is a key factor in working with young children. Effective teachers have learned that it is more useful to know that a child is moving steadily forward than to know that the child is above or below the so-called norm.

Example:

A 39-month-old child with Down syndrome is just beginning to pull up to a standing position. The child's teachers are predicting that she soon will be walking and are planning her program accordingly. How can the teachers be so confident? It's easy; they know this child has passed, in order (though later), each of the preceding large gross motor skills milestones.

Interrelationships among Developmental Areas

Understanding the interrelatedness of developmental areas is important, too. Recognizing that each area of development affects and is affected by every other area is essential when teaching young children (Photo 4–4).

Example:

A four-and-a-half-year-old boy with a developmental delay had refused solid foods throughout his life. Clinical findings indicated that the prolonged soft diet, requiring little chewing, had contributed to poorly developed muscle tone, hence poorly controlled movement of the mouth and tongue. The result was almost unintelligible speech, which in turn played a part in the child's cognitive and social development. Teachers and clinicians agreed that the child needed help in acquiring speech, social, and cognitive skills. They also agreed that even with treatment it was unlikely that there would be much improvement in any of the developmental delays unless the child learned to eat solid foods. That probably would not happen until the parents could be supported in modifying their child's diet.

Developmental Inconsistencies

Though not all children go through exactly the same sequence of development, there is a sequential pattern that children can follow: Typically, they go from lying on

Photo 4–4
Each area of development affects and is affected by every other area.

their back or stomach to turning over, to sitting, to crawling, to pulling up, to standing, to walking. However, development is an irregularly paced process—even among children developing within cultural expectations. A period of rapid development often is followed by an unsettled period known as a time of **developmental disequilibrium.** During such periods, children seem to be developmentally disorganized: calm and capable one moment, screamingly frustrated (and frustrating) the next. Some children may even regress, or appear to go backward, for a while.

Example:

A three-year-old with a nine-month-old sister competing for attention may revert to babyish ways. He displays tantrums for no apparent reason, loses the bladder control that seemed to be well established, and demands the bedtime bottle that had been given up months ago. Teachers can help parents understand that their child is continuing to progress well in every other aspect of development and, therefore, it is unlikely that the current problems will persist. They might recommend that the parents attempt to give some individual time to this child, away from the baby who is perceived as getting so much attention. It may be agreed that there is no need for a clinical assessment of the child for the time being, that the situation is likely to be but a temporary regression to earlier behaviours. It is further agreed that both parents and teachers will continue to observe the child carefully, in the event that the situation does not change within a reasonable period.

Transactional Aspects of Development

Continual interplay goes on between children and their environment. The process is referred to as the **transactional aspect of development.** The concept recognizes the young child as a dynamic individual who is affected by, and has an effect on, almost everyone and everything that he or she comes in contact with (Horowitz, 1987). Learning can be both positive and negative, reflecting the consequence of both direct and indirect or unintended teaching. It is easy for teachers to recognize their role in promoting intentional learning: They set up appropriate curriculum experiences, respond to children positively, and allow children to explore and experiment. Seldom, however, are teachers aware of inappropriate learning that may be promoted unintentionally. For example, the experience of having a single wagon or a single pegboard for a large group of three- and four-year-olds may teach more about shoving, pushing, waiting endlessly, and doing without than about the fine and gross motor skills the materials were intended to promote.

A summary of a case study (Allen & Goetz, 1982) that illustrates efforts to help a child expand his attention span is given below. The situation demonstrates how an inappropriate behaviour may be learned from the way teachers' well-intentioned efforts combine with the transactional nature of teacher–child interactions. In other words, the very behaviour a teacher wants to eliminate may be unintentionally reinforced by the way the teacher responds to the child:

James was a five-year-old who seldom stayed with an activity more than a moment or two. Teachers were constantly intercepting him, trying to settle him down, get him interested in something. As the weeks went by James continued to flit, more than ever, it seemed. What was he learning from the teachers' efforts? Certainly not to focus his attention, which was their goal. Instead, he was learning, at some unrecognized level, that flitting about was a sure way to get the teacher attention he needed and could not seem to get in any other way. Unfortunately, this constant flitting maintained a short attention span that interfered with James's acquiring other developmental skills.

Developmental disequilibrium
a period of inconsistent behaviour, which often follows a spurt of rapid development

Transactional aspect of development
the understanding that children and adults influence each other in their ongoing relationships and that both children and adults learn from these interactions

Photo 4–5
Adult–child transactions have powerful potential for promoting healthy development.

Contingent stimulation
responding to a child in a way that prompts further learning

Readiness
the point when a child has the necessary prerequisite skills to engage in specific new learning

Fascinating accounts of this transactional process are found in a number of research studies. One example is Fraiberg's (1974) comments on unsettling transactions between infants who are blind and their mothers. The infant's inability to see its mother's face interferes with its ability to respond to her smiles. The unresponsiveness often is perceived by the mother as rejection. Without her realizing it, her behaviour changes: She smiles less and less because her infant provides her with less delight. Both mother and baby, through no fault of their own, promote a mutual unresponsiveness. This comes at a critical developmental period when both need to be engaging in mutually reinforcing behaviours that lead to a strong parent–child attachment.

Conversely, adult–child transactions have an equally powerful potential for promoting *healthy* development (Photo 4–5). Negative examples were cited here because of a general tendency for adults to overlook or underappreciate their everyday responses to children. Many of these responses carry the unsuspected potential for inappropriate learning emerging from routine interactions between children and adults. It must be remembered that children are learning *something*, for better or worse, from every environmental encounter.

Contingent Stimulation

Closely related to transactional processes is the principle of **contingent stimulation.** In the context of child development, *contingent* implies a kind of dependency or conditioning in which new learning comes about because of the prompt responses of another. With young children, in particular, it refers to the ways in which parents and other significant adults respond to cues from the child. Adults who react to an infant's cooing, gurgling, and babbling stimulate the infant's continuing efforts to communicate (Goulet & Schroeder, 1998). Contingent stimulation is readily observable in the simple give-and-take games that both parents and their babies initiate and take such delight in: peek-a-boo, pat-a-cake, chase-and-hide, and toss-the-toy-out-of-the-crib. When adults make their responses at least partially contingent on what the infant or child says and does, specific developmental benefits result:

- Language development is earlier and better.
- Cognitive development is accelerated and richer.
- Self-esteem is much more evident.
- Attachments are more secure.

Readiness and Teachable Moments

Readiness is a useful concept when appropriately defined as a combination of genetic and environmental factors: *maturation, motivation,* and *opportunity.* When these three come together, the child is often *ready* to learn a new skill and a *teachable* *moment* is likely to occur. **Teachable moments** are those naturally occurring opportunities when a child is most likely to learn a new skill. Consider the following two examples:

An infant reaches for the spoon while being fed, a cue that he or she is ready—that is, mature enough and has acquired the necessary perceptual motor skills—to reach for and hold a spoon (though not always right-side up). The reaching also indicates readiness to begin to explore the difficult business of self-feeding. What is needed now is opportunity. Opportunity tends to come in the form of a patient adult who is willing, for many meals running, to scrub the floor, the high chair, and the child after every meal.

Toddlers often get to the point where they demand to be changed, or they pull off their wet diapers by themselves. These children are giving clear cues that they are moving toward the idea of learning to use the toilet.

Observant teachers attuned to developmental differences among children easily translate the concepts of readiness and teachable moments into practice. Every day, children show interest in exploring and acquiring new knowledge and skills (Photo 4–6).

Examples:

- *A two-year-old trying to put on a shoe heel-to-toe.*
- *A three-year-old struggling to make an upside-down coat stay on the hook.*
- *A four-year-old asking, "Where did the ice go?"*
- *A five-year-old trying to balance a teetering block structure.*

In each case, based on knowledge of the individual child, the teacher makes decisions about how to use the moment to a child's best advantage.

INCIDENTAL TEACHING OPPORTUNITIES

In many ways, **incidental teaching** is similar to contingent stimulation and teachable moments. All three depend on child-initiated contacts. An incidental teaching episode, however, is *always* initiated by the child. The child approaches the teacher, asking for help, materials, or information. Because the contact is child initiated, the teacher knows that the child is interested and therefore likely to be receptive to a brief learning experience about whatever it is that prompted the contact.

Incidental teaching moments represent the systematic application of principles compatible with both a developmental and a behavioural approach to early learning (Warren & Kaiser, 1988). It also exemplifies quality teaching practices that include

- meeting a child where his or her interests lie
- responding in a way that matches the child's skill level
- introducing the bit of novelty that provides challenge for the child

From the behavioural perspective, the incidental teaching process is a combination of the shaping, prompting, and reinforcement procedures, central to effective

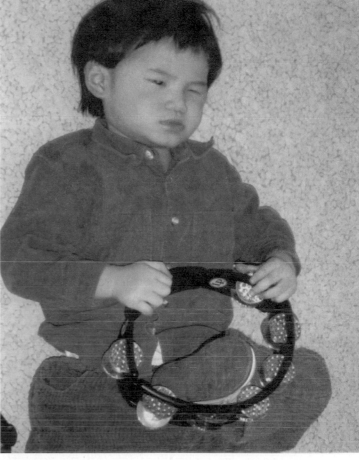

Photo 4–6
Every day, children show interest in exploring and acquiring new knowledge.

Teachable moments
specific points when a child's level of readiness and interest come together to create the best milieu for new teaching

Incidental teaching
using a spontaneous teaching opportunity, which is always initiated by the child when he or she asks for help, materials, or information

teaching. (Reinforcement procedures, including shaping and prompting, will be discussed in Chapter 11.) In spite of being child initiated, every incidental teaching episode occurs in a planned environment, one that teachers have arranged so as to make good use of children's contacts.

The effectiveness of incidental teaching depends on teachers' efforts at

- providing an interesting classroom environment in which children can be busy, active, and inquiring
- selecting appropriate objectives for each child that match his or her skill levels and interests
- answering a child's initiation of contact with a request for a response from the child related to a developmental objective for that particular child
- responding to the child with whatever is most appropriate in terms of his or her initial contact

These practices are illustrated in the following example having to do with a child with muscular dysfunction. One of the individual program plan (IPP) objectives for André was to increase his ability to reach:

Teachers had observed André over several days and had identified a number of his play interests. On the physical therapist's recommendation, his preferred toys were put in full view but out of reach. Whenever André asked for, or otherwise indicated interest in, a toy or material, a teacher held it out to him slightly out of reach, but close enough so that he could get it with a little effort. When he got his hands on the object, his efforts were applauded: "You reached for the truck and now you are going to play with it." As André's reach improved, teachers gradually increased the distance. Later, to facilitate the development of overhead reaching, teachers held things just a bit above André's eye level. This, too, they increased gradually.

Incidental teaching opportunities are particularly evident in a curriculum approach referred to as emergent curriculum, because one source of curriculum emerges out of the child's contacts and interests and what adults know is necessary for the child's education and development. Gestwicki (1999, p. 55) describes emergent curriculum as "a very organic process, growing from real actions and interactions" between adults and children. In Chapter 15, emergent curriculum as an approach for teaching children with special needs will be explored further. In Chapters 16 and 18, the specific use of the process of incidental teaching to promote social and language development will be described.

Characteristics of Effective Teachers in Inclusive Settings

In addition to a thorough knowledge of child development, several other traits characterize effective teachers in an inclusive setting. True, teaching styles and interactions with children reflect a teacher's own unique personality; nevertheless, effective teachers seem to have a number of characteristics in common. These are described in the following eight points.

AWARENESS OF THE BIG PICTURE

Effective teachers of young children have an interest and a social view that extends beyond just the early childhood setting (Gestwicki & Bertrand, 2003). These teachers are linked professionally in many ways to a community, city, province or territory, and country. Teachers who are aware of the "big picture" know about community, municipal, and provincial or territorial services for children with special needs and their families. They value their role as advocates for the inclusion of children with special needs in society and see themselves as part of a larger movement toward social change.

ENTHUSIASM THAT SUPPORTS LEARNING

Teachers of young children need unlimited enthusiasm to support children's progress and accomplishments, great and small (Photo 4–7). This is especially important for children with developmental disabilities, who may learn at a slower rate and in smaller steps. A teacher's enthusiastic support becomes a major motivation to wanting to learn more. Every child, regardless of his or her abilities, is quick to catch enthusiasm for almost any activity from a patient, skillful teacher who rejoices with the child over each step or partial step forward.

Photo 4–7
Teachers must have unlimited enthusiasm.

Enthusiasm is a reciprocal or mutually supportive process. The teacher's enthusiasm stems from the child's accomplishments, small as they sometimes are. The child's accomplishments, in turn, are supported by the teacher's skills and enthusiasm in promoting the child's learning. It is imperative, therefore, that teachers of young children know how to carry out task analysis, the process of sequencing developmental tasks into small, incremental steps. Small-step successes give both child and teacher many opportunities to enjoy their work together. (Task analysis will be discussed in Chapter 11.)

CONSISTENCY THAT PROVIDES SECURITY

The effective teacher is consistent and can be depended on to provide a predictable and stable environment. In addition, expectations need to be communicated in ways that all children can understand. The teacher then can be confident about keeping to expectations, knowing that they are culturally, developmentally, and individually realistic and understood by all. Consistency provides children with security, an especially important factor for children with challenging behaviours. Children who feel secure tend to be more self-confident. They learn to make sound judgments when they are sure of what is expected of them and know that things will remain the same unless teachers give fair warning of a change.

Consistency does not rule out change. Children change throughout their developmental years. Teachers' expectations also must change. What remains consistent are the developmental and cultural appropriateness of the changing expectations and the teachers' care in communicating the changes to the children. Consistency, however, must never be confused with rigidity or inflexibility. An inflexible teacher is not an effective teacher.

FLEXIBILITY FOR SUPPORTING INDIVIDUALITY

The ability to be flexible, to improvise, to adapt an activity to individual or group needs at any given moment is a hallmark of effective teaching (Photo 4–8, p. 80). A flexible teacher knows when to cut an activity short if it turns out to be too difficult or if it fails to hold children's interest. The opposite is also true. A flexible teacher knows how and when to extend and elaborate on an activity that has developed into an especially absorbing and worthwhile experience for one or more children.

Photo 4–8
Teachers need to be flexible enough to allow children to improvise and initiate.

Flexibility does not rule out consistency. Truly effective teachers are a blend of consistency and flexibility. They are good judges of when to *bend the rules.* They know when to overlook a minor transgression when a child is trying to handle frustration or work through any other kind of learning experience, as in the following examples:

Jana's physical attacks on other children were frequent. Never had she been heard to tell anyone what she wanted; instead, she hit, grabbed, or shoved. One day, however, she stunned teachers by shrieking, "Get out, you stupid!" The rudely shouted command and name-calling were directed at an approaching child who obviously meant no harm. The teacher, though regretting the verbal assault on a well-intentioned child, ignored the inappropriateness of Jana's response. Instead, the teacher supported Jana for talking, not hitting. This was done in the presence of the other child, to promote the child's understanding that Jana was learning to replace hitting with talking.

The teacher's flexibility indicated responsiveness to the most urgent priority for Jana as well as to the child who had been rebuffed. It let the child know that classroom expectations were operating, in spite of occasional exceptions. As for the unacceptable verbal behaviour, even if it should accelerate for a while, teachers should not be unduly concerned. When verbal requests dependably replace physical assaults, a new goal, polite requesting, can be written into Jana's IPP.

The second example focuses on a five-year-old who is gifted and a block-building activity:

The classroom rule was that block structures could be built only as high as the builder's head. Toward the end of the school year, a capable five-year-old had discovered a balancing principle that enabled her to build the tower she was working on higher and higher. At one point she stood on a stool so as to continue building. (Technically, when she was standing on the stool, the blocks were not as high as the child's head.) The teacher's decision to be flexible about the height of the block structure was based on the purposefulness of the child's experimentation. The teacher's continuing presence conveyed consistency about classroom rules: that one child may not endanger another.

ABILITY TO BUILD TRUSTWORTHINESS

The more that children can trust the consistency of teachers' expectations, the more trustworthy children themselves become; hence, the more flexible teachers can be. Teachers who respect children and their need to develop initiative can give children even greater freedom to explore and experiment with their own behaviour. The consistent teacher knows that children know what is expected of them. The teacher knows, too, that children usually can be trusted to stop themselves before a situation gets dangerously out of bounds. Consistency on the part of the teacher allows mutual trust to flourish as a teacher–child relationship grows.

PROVISION OF POSITIVE CHILD-GUIDANCE TECHNIQUES

Everyone needs limits, especially young children who are trying so hard to learn the many things expected of them. Limits, in the form of culturally appropriate expectations, allow children to relax, to know that they can depend on someone else to make some of the decisions. Expectations, in general, should be limited to health and safety issues and stated positively as much as possible.

Limits should be established to cover situations in which

- a child is likely to hurt himself or herself
- a child is likely to hurt another person
- a child is likely to damage or destroy property

Whatever expectations there are *must be enforced*. Therefore, the number of rules should be kept to a minimum because enforcing rules is not an especially productive role for teachers.

A typical set of rules, designed to clearly govern teachers' decisions about situations in which children must be redirected, might include the following:

- Children are not allowed to push other children when in high places.
- Children are not to hit other children.
- Children may not throw sand, toys, books, or other hard objects.
- Teachers' cupboards (out of children's reach, we hope) are to be opened only by teachers.
- Children are not to leave the classroom or play yard without a teacher or other authorized adult.

Rules should be stated to clarify the desired outcome behaviour, for example:

- "The sand stays in the sandbox."
- "Books are to read and look at."
- "Those are the teacher's cupboards; children's cupboards are down there."

Only when a child fails to heed a reminder or redirection should the teacher give negative and emphatic commands: "Kelly, I can't let you throw sand." Rules apply to every child in the group. "No sand throwing" means *NO sand throwing*. This includes children with developmental differences.

There should be no double standards. Double standards do the child with a special need a disservice by not helping him or her learn acceptable behaviour. Furthermore, double standards can lead to resentment and dislike among children who try to abide by the rules. Fortunately, there is no need for double standards. Every child can learn to abide by the few safety rules that are necessary in an early childhood setting.

On many occasions, children truly do not understand what is expected of them from teachers' efforts at positive redirection. When a teacher advises, "The sand stays in the sandbox," a child may continue to throw sand about while carefully keeping within the boundaries of the sandbox. Clearly, the child does not understand the message the teacher had intended; neither are the other children in the sandbox receiving the protection they deserve. In these instances, specific statements of expectations may be more appropriate right from the start. Clear and indisputable limits offer security to children who may not grasp the subtleties of positive redirection or who may be disciplined differently in their home environment.

ABILITY TO FACILITATE AND SUPPORT CHILDREN'S EFFORTS

Though teachers must set limits and hold to them, their major role is that of *facilitator*, a person who makes things happen. Therefore, the **facilitative teacher**

- provides a range of interesting and appropriate materials and activities
- presents these in ways that are attractive and conducive to children's learning
- offers the right amount and kind of assistance—not too much, but never refusing to assist
- is aware of what the next step is for each child on each developmental task
- responds to each child with ample feedback as to the effectiveness of his or her efforts (Photo 4–9)

Facilitation and support, in just the right degree, are especially important during children's play. As Gordon and Browne (2000) point out, it can be difficult for teachers to decide when to join children at play and when to remain outside the activity. The important question is "whether their presence will support what is happening or whether it will inhibit the play." In an inclusive classroom, teachers tend to find it appropriate to join in more frequently but as unobtrusively as possible. Supportive teacher participation can go a long way toward fostering play relationships among children with or without disabilities, especially when the teacher quietly fades in and out, depending on the progress of the activity (Kontos & Wilcox-Herzog, 1997). Children with special needs tend to have lower self-esteem; it is important for the teacher to work on supporting the building of self-worth and to offer opportunities for independence.

Photo 4–9
Provide encouragement and support for the child's efforts.

Facilitative teacher
a teacher who makes things happen by planning, implementing, and evaluating a range of teaching strategies

ABILITY TO INTEGRATE THERAPEUTIC RECOMMENDATIONS INTO EVERYDAY LEARNING EXPERIENCES

Supporting a child with special needs in an inclusive early childhood program includes environmental arrangement, curricular adaptation, and systematic use of teaching strategies to help the child be as effective as possible in interactions with the environment.

Example:

The speech therapist was working with a five-year-old on beginning B, M, and P sounds. At the small-group breakfast table, the teacher improvised a riddle game based on the therapist's objectives. The teacher described and gave the beginning sounds of various foods the children had encountered over the year. Children supplied the words or labels. The cues for the child in speech therapy had to do with such things as bananas, milk, and pears; butter, muffins, and plums. Everyone at the table participated and learned from the game and had fun with it. No one was the wiser (including the child with special needs) that speech therapy was going on.

Everyday activities of this kind actualize and integrate the therapy sessions; in other words, they provide a bridge that allows the child to practise, generalize, and consolidate what is learned in therapy sessions to functional, everyday situations.

The Teacher as Mediator

According to Vygotsky (1978) and Feuerstein, Rand, Hoffman, & Miller (1980), it is essential that teachers of young children serve as mediators between the child and the learning environment. These social-constructivist theorists emphasize the role of the adult in helping children learn to solve cognitive and social problems. The strategy is to provide decreasing levels of support while placing higher demands as the child progresses toward the goal of independent problem solving. Vygotsky refers to this part of the teaching/learning process as **scaffolding.**

Example:

An objective written into Maya's IPP was that she learn to talk to other children. She had the prerequisite language skills but was not using these with peers. The teacher began the scaffolding process by bringing children together in a group and asking Maya to say "Hi" to each child (high support, low demand). When Maya became successful in this kind of interaction, the teachers arranged opportunities away from group time for Maya to greet peers (higher demand). Gradually, the teacher reduced the amount of assistance and support. Before long, Maya was spontaneously saying "Hi" (and a good deal more!) when she encountered other children.

The **mediated learning model** theorizes that cognitive and social development are intertwined. The teacher's role is to foster children's awareness of their own thought processes by asking them to predict outcomes, test reality, and communicate their thoughts. Most importantly, the teacher emphasizes generalization by encouraging children to think about how a given skill could be used in a different situation: for example, "What might you say to Julie when she doesn't want to play with you?" According to Mills and Cole (1999), teachers who practise mediated teaching create an environment that is conducive to learning by

- thinking through the purpose of an activity
- assessing the current skill levels of each child
- providing support and placing demands that reflect the appropriate developmental goals for a child
- demonstrating intentionally; that is, organizing the experience in ways that clearly communicate what is to be learned
- helping children generalize new learning to situations beyond the immediate setting
- taking cues from children's interest and responding to child-initiated learning situations
- providing activities that have meaning or function in the everyday life of the child

In other words, the role of the teacher as mediator is to highlight significant aspects of the environment, emphasize social context, and encourage the child to explore the options.

The foregoing discussion of the attitudes and attributes of effective teachers in an inclusive early childhood program is by no means complete. Teachers also need to know how to do these things:

- integrate behavioural and developmental principles when teaching young children
- work with parents and members of other disciplines

Scaffolding
a teaching and learning process in which the teacher provides decreasing levels of support while placing higher demands as the child progresses toward the goal of independent problem solving

Mediated learning model
based on the teaching premise that cognitive and social processes are interdependent factors in all learning

- arrange and present materials and equipment
- schedule the daily program to provide children with an appropriate balance of child-initiated and teacher-structured learning experiences

Summary

In the inclusive classroom the need for quality teaching and appropriate learning experiences is critical. Effective teachers make ongoing adaptations to the learning environment to meet the developmental needs of all children. Teachers who work with young children who have severe impairments should have the support of a resource consultant available to them. Many children with special needs may initially benefit from dual placements, with one program highly specialized to ensure the intensive treatment the child requires and the other providing opportunities to use newly learned skills as spontaneous opportunities occur.

Early childhood teachers in inclusive classrooms need ongoing professional training. Knowledge about particular disabilities is available, as needed, through various workshops, training programs, organizations, resource centres, and resource teachers/specialists who can assess children and consult with early childhood teachers, as well as from the parents of children with particular developmental differences. What teachers in an inclusive preschool or child care setting need most is knowledge and experience in working with young children in general. To this end, this chapter briefly reviewed significant developmental principles and practices: developmental sequences, the interrelatedness of developmental areas, inconsistencies in development, the transactional aspects of the developmental process, and contingent stimulation.

Special mention was made of readiness and incidental teaching opportunities. Use of incidental teaching moments is effective in teaching all children. It is especially effective when working with children with developmental differences. Because an incidental teaching opportunity is child initiated, it signals to a teacher that the child is ready and interested in learning whatever he or she has contacted the teacher about. The teacher's responsibility is to be *ready* to take advantage of this teachable moment. Other characteristics of effective teachers in an inclusive early childhood program are awareness of the "big picture," enthusiasm, consistency, flexibility, trustworthiness, the ability to limit children as necessary, the capability to integrate therapy-prescribed activities into the regular curriculum, and the skill to mediate children's learning opportunities.

RESOURCES

SpeciaLink Canada
http://www.specialinkcanada.org
SpeciaLink produces newsletters, papers, reports (e.g., *A matter of urgency*), and videos about inclusive practices.

Canadian Abilities Foundation
http://www.enablelink.org
This site provides access to a wide range of disability information and resources, including provincial and territorial advocacy and support groups.

STUDENT ACTIVITIES

1. Locate and record the names and locations of several agencies in your community that provide resources for children and their families who need extra support. Select one and report on the kinds of materials they have available for teachers and for parents. Obtain samples, if possible.
2. Talk with teachers in an inclusive early childhood or child care centre about their children with developmental differences and their families. Record their comments, concerns, and general attitudes about the children and their parents.
3. Observe a preschool session. Count the number of child-to-teacher contacts. Briefly describe those the teacher turned into a spontaneous teaching or incidental teaching episode.
4. Locate a program that serves children who have severe disabilities. Ask your instructor to arrange an observation. While observing, list the special equipment and services provided for the children.
5. Think about a situation when you were a child and
   a. a teacher did something you felt was unjust
   b. a teacher did something that really met your needs
   For each of these situations:
   i.   briefly describe the situation, identifying what characteristics of the teacher's behaviour had an effect on you
   ii. indicate how it affected how you felt and responded
   iii. state what you think the teacher should have done

REFERENCES

Allen, K. E., & Goetz, F. M. (1982). *Early childhood education: Special problems, special solutions*. Rockville, MD: Aspen Systems.

Feuerstein, R., Rand, Y., Hoffman, M., & Miller, R. (1980). *Instrumental enrichment: Redevelopment of cognitive functions of retarded performers*. Baltimore, MD: University Park Press.

Fraiberg, S. (1974). Blind infants and their mothers: An examination of the sign system. In M. Lewis & L. A. Rosenblum (Eds.), *The effect of the infant on its caregiver* (pp. 215–232). New York: Wiley.

Gestwicki, C. (1999). *Developmentally appropriate practice: Curriculum and development in early education*. New York: Delmar.

Gestwicki, C., & Bertrand, J. (2003). *Essentials of early childhood education*. Toronto: Nelson Thomson.

Gordon, A. M., & Browne, K. W. (2000). *Beginnings and beyond. Foundations in early childhood education* (5th ed.). Albany, NY: Delmar.

Goulet, M., & Schroeder, R. (1998). *How caring relationships support self-regulation: Video and video guide*. Toronto: George Brown College.

Horowitz, F. D. (1987). *Exploring developmental theories: Toward a structural/behavioral model of development*. Hillsdale, NJ: Erlbaum.

Lero, D., Irwin, S. H., & Brophy, K. (2000). *A matter of urgency: Including children with special needs in child care in Canada*. Cape Breton, NS: Breton Books.

Mills, P. E., & Cole, K. N. (1999, June). *Mediated learning: Developmentally appropriate early childhood methods designed to facilitate inclusion*. Paper presented at the Early Childhood Special Education Summer Institute, Wenatchee, WA.

Vygotsky, L. (1978). *Mind in society: The development of higher psychological processes*. Cambridge, MA: Harvard University Press.

Warren, S. F., & Kaiser, A. P. (1988). Research in early language intervention. In S. L. Odom & M. B. Karnes (Eds.), *Early intervention for infants and children with handicaps* (pp. 89–108). Baltimore, MD: Brookes.

Section II

Developmental Differences

CHAPTER 5

An Overview of Developmental Differences

KEY CONCEPTS

adventitious deafness

auditory

biological risk

blindness

chronic

communication and language disorders

congenital deafness

developmental delay

developmental deviation

developmental disability

developmental milestones

developmental sequences

dysgraphia

dyslexia

emotional disturbance

environmental risk

handicap

health impairments

hearing impairment

multiple disabling conditions

orthopedic impairments

resilience

special needs

specific learning disabilities (SLD)

tactile

traumatic brain injury

visual impairment

vulnerability

OBJECTIVES

After studying the material in this chapter, the student will be able to

- Describe characteristics of children who are meeting developmental and cultural expectations and those who are not.
- Provide three reasons to justify this statement: "To work effectively with children with special needs, teachers need to have a thorough knowledge of the range of individual and cultural differences in development."
- Distinguish between developmental sequences and developmental milestones, recognizing the impact of a child's culture on these aspects of development.
- Describe biological and environmental factors that can put infants and young children at developmental risk.
- Discuss the arguments both for and against labelling young children as having developmental differences and support each argument with examples.
- Recognize the major categories of developmental differences that are likely to affect children.

Introduction

Young children are alike in many ways. They also are different in just as many ways. Too often, the strengths of children with special needs are overlooked. The focus is on remediation of their delays or differences. Remember:

- A child is first of all a child, regardless of his or her individual difference.
- Every child is unique and therefore exceptional in one or more ways.

In small, closely knit societies, the fact that some children are different is not an issue. This seldom holds true in complex societies, such as ours. Setting some children apart, even excluding them from society, seems to have been built into our system almost from the start. As we have seen, however, change is happening. Inclusive educational programs are a major step in the right direction. The underlying issue of classification is still with us. Having to distinguish between those children said to be developing within developmental and cultural expectations, and those who are developing differently, continues to plague us. Policymakers, early childhood teachers, early childhood consultants, and special education administrators often use categories of exceptionality that vary from area to area and across province and territories.

Definitions of normalcy and of developmental differences vary among physicians, psychologists, educators, and many other professionals associated with the growth and development of young children (Bee, 1999). The variations come from each professional's training, clinical practices, and traditions. Government policymakers, for example, may use their own specific guidelines to identify particular disabilities, whereas educators may use different guidelines. In other words, there is little consensus as to which children are to be classified as developmentally disabled, which are classified as gifted and talented, and which are classified as developmentally normal (Photo 5–1). The result is confusion for everyone and especially for students and newcomers to the field of early childhood education and early intervention.

This chapter will provide an overview of characteristics of children who are meeting developmental and cultural expectations and those children who show exceptionalities within these expectations. In this book, children who are at risk, who have disabilities, and are gifted, and children of different language backgrounds, will be included in the term exceptional. Recent research on brain development and the concept of *normal development* will be discussed first, as background. The rationale is obvious: To work effectively with infants and children with special needs, teachers must have a thorough knowledge of growth and development within particular cultural norms. All early intervention programs should have as a main goal the facilitation of a child's overall development. A parallel goal is to implement strategies that promote the inclusion of all children. This chapter will also include and identify categories of developmental differences.

Photo 5–1
The child with special needs may or may not be easy to recognize.

RECENT RESEARCH ON BRAIN DEVELOPMENT

Recent research on the brain has important implications for learning and development. Only one-quarter of its potential size at birth, the brain is particularly sponge-like in the first few years. It is during this time that the brain forms a "network of neural pathways" (Shore, 1997).

A major developmental task in the first three years of life is to form and reinforce these links (called synapses) so that they become a permanent part of the brain's "wiring." These synapses occur through continual and repeated use, primarily as a child experiences "the surrounding world and forms attachments to parents, family members and other caregivers" (Shore, 1997, p. 17). By the time the child is a year old, there are trillions of synapses. The pathways they form make up the wiring of the brain. The number and organization of these connections influences all the individual's intellectual and social functioning. Neurons develop rapidly before birth. After birth, brain development consists of "wiring and rewiring" the connections. Within each brain millions of neurons (nerve cells) form and are connected to one another by synapses. After a child's first birthday, new synapses continue to form, while unused synapses are discarded more quickly. By 10 years of age, a child has nearly five hundred trillion synapses, which is the same as the average adult. The brain maintains flexibility for future learning, continually discarding those synapses that have not been used. Simply stated, the growth of the brain operates on a use-it-or-lose it principle. Thus children's brains need to be stimulated in order to be protected from this process of elimination. (See Chapter 19 for further discussion of brain research.)

What Is Normal or Typical Development?

As noted above, there are many interpretations of terms used to describe the developing child. One of the most common and frequently used terms, *normal development,* has long been the subject of dispute. What is normal for one child may be quite different for another. For example, most early childhood teachers expect children to make eye contact when spoken to. Teachers tend to be concerned if a child fails to do so. Yet, in certain other cultures, such as some Canadian First Nations groups and some areas in the West Indies, children are considered disrespectful if they look directly at the adult who is speaking to them. Drawing on the works of Vygotsky (1978) and Rogoff (1990), Bernhard (1995, p. 415) states that it is important for early childhood professionals to question theories and assumptions of human development because cross-cultural evidence suggests that there may be more than one pathway of normal development. In North American culture, a growing independence during the preschool years is expected from a child, whereas in Latin American cultures, what is valued is the child's demonstration of affection and strong ties to parents. Without this understanding of multiple pathways of normal development, Bernhard (2000, p. 89) argues, professionals may consider a preschool child from a Latin American culture delayed if the child does not demonstrate autonomy.

One goal for professionals is to distinguish between behaviour that is typical for the culture in which the child and family live and behaviour that is atypical for that culture and suggests a disability that will alter development. Trent, Artiles, and Englert (1999, pp. 299–300) summarize this goal in another way: A theory that takes into account sociocultural contexts "affords us the possibility to also view 'competence,' 'ability,' and 'disability' . . . in new ways."

In addition to culturally defined differences within what is considered normal, there are individual differences among children. No two children grow and develop at the same rate, even within the same culture. Some children walk at eight months; others do not walk until 18 months. Most children begin walking somewhere in between. All children within this range, and even a bit on either side of it, are normal with respect to walking. The same is true for every other area of development. In summary, broad variations and significant differences in child development are evident within every culture.

DEVELOPMENTAL SEQUENCES

Some principles of human development can serve as guidelines for describing characteristics of children who are progressing in their development and those who are progressing differently. One is that the **developmental sequences** of child growth and development within particular cultures are predictable. Well-trained early childhood teachers (and experienced parents) know that each normally/typically developing child can be expected to move step by step toward mastery of each developmental skill in every area of development. Normal/typical development in this sense implies an ongoing process of growing, changing, and acquiring a range of complex skills. As children develop, individual differences begin to show. Each child will accomplish a specific step but will do so at his or her own rate. Furthermore, no matter how quickly or slowly a child is developing, in most instances, each preceding step occurs before practice on the next step begins. A child rolls over before learning to sit, sits before standing, and stands before walking (Photo 5–2).

> **Developmental sequences**
> an ongoing process of moving step by step toward mastery of each developmental skill in every area of development

Exceptions are common, even to this basic principle of developmental sequencing. For example, most infants crawl before they walk, but some do not. A few infants move about by sitting up and hitching forward with one foot. Others lie flat on their back and push with both feet. Such self-propelling methods of getting about are quite appropriate, even though less common. In some cultures, children are carried on the mother's back all day, and when children are expected to walk, they do so without crawling before walking.

It must be remembered, too, that no two children grow uniformly and at the same rate. Nor do they move forward in all developmental areas at the same time. Rarely is developmental progress smooth and flowing; irregularities and slowdowns are typical. In fact, progress in one skill may actually stop when the child is attempting to learn a new skill in a different area of development. A common example is the infant who talked early and then quit talking for a time, while learning to walk. Some children even regress, that is, slide backward, under certain conditions—for example, the three-year-old who temporarily loses bladder control with the arrival of the new

Photo 5–2
A child must be able to sit before learning to stand.

Photo 5–3
In the North American culture, learning to feed ourselves is a major milestone.

baby. Almost all children experience **"special needs"** on a short-term basis at one time or another.

It may appear that the toddler who walks or talks early is somehow "better" than those who walk or talk several months later. We now know that a developmental lead is not necessarily retained. By Grade 1, the later walkers and talkers are often equally skilled in both language and motor performance.

DEVELOPMENTAL MILESTONES

Regardless of variations that may occur, certain behaviours or skill sequences can be seen in a fairly predictable order in almost every child who is developing normally. These significant points or events at certain ages often are referred to as **developmental milestones** (Photo 5–3). If we take into consideration "cultural context," we may find in various developmental pathways different milestones at different ages (Bernhard, 2000). However, a child who does not reach or is seriously delayed in reaching one or more developmental milestones needs attention. It could be a warning signal that something may be amiss in the child's development. Thus, it is necessary for everyone working with very young children to have a thorough knowledge of different cultural and developmental milestones and sequences in each area of development.

Special needs
challenges in learning and functioning in one or more areas of development and increased vulnerability to environmental and non-environmental stresses

Developmental milestones
points at which specific skills are acquired in a fairly predictable order

If all goes well, the developing child passes milestone after milestone in every area of development. Nevertheless, the question posed at the start, "What is normal?" has not been given a truly complete answer. What about a child who is developing normally in some areas but is delayed, even disabled, in others? What about children with severe orthopedic disabilities, for example, who cannot walk, let alone run and jump and climb as other children do? Many children with orthopedic impairments are developing normally otherwise and can be gifted in language, intellectual, or artistic development. The opposite may also be true: Children who are delayed in language or cognitive development may have well-developed motor skills. It is helpful to look more closely and examine why some children would be identified as having exceptionalities.

Who Are Children with Exceptionalities?

Efforts to decide which children have exceptionalities have been going on for decades. At times, the term has been all-inclusive. Its use has ranged from children with the mildest of speech differences to those who were outstandingly brilliant (but different). The term has been used most frequently in the field of education.

Other terms that are frequently used to identify children who are in need of additional support services include the following:

- *Special or challenging needs.* These are the preferred terms used by early childhood educators, service providers, and advocates for children who

1. face barriers in their learning and functioning in one or more of the following areas of development: physical, social, emotional, communication, intellectual, behavioural

2. have "increased vulnerability to environmental and non-environmental stresses, including those related to family, social, economic and cultural circumstances" (Ontario Ministry of Community and Social Services, 1984).

- *Handicap.* This relates to environmental or functional demands that, when placed on a person with a disability, are not met (Winzer, 1997).

- *Impairment.* This refers to incapacities or injuries, especially those having to do with the sensory and neural systems; thus, we speak of children with visual impairments, orthopedic impairments, and speech and hearing impairments.

- *Atypical.* This is a much broader term that covers almost any variation from what is considered normal; often it is a matter of degree: how different or how far behind must a child be to be considered atypical? Seldom is this term used in reference to children who are gifted.

- *Developmental disability.* This term usually refers to a variety of conditions that interfere with the child's physical, sensory, or cognitive development and originate between conception and 18 years of age.

It can be useful to think of developmental disabilities as taking two basic forms: delays and deviations. What is the difference? A **developmental delay** is present when a child is performing like a developing child of a younger age. As an example, consider Josh, a three-year-old just beginning to put together two-word sentences. Josh has moved steadily through each earlier milestone in language development. It is evident that this three-year-old is experiencing a language delay; normal language will come, though later than for other children his age. By the age of eight or ten, it is unlikely there will be any hint of Josh's earlier delay. A **developmental deviation** is present when some aspect of a child's development is different from what is seen in other developing children. Another language example will be used—this time, a three-year-old with severe oromuscular dysfunction because of cerebral palsy (Photo 5–4). The child makes many sounds and tries very hard to talk but cannot be understood. This is a deviation. It is likely that this child will continue to have speech problems.

Developmental deviations, however, are not necessarily handicapping. Individuals with six toes on each foot have a physical deviation; yet they most surely would not be thought of as having a handicap. Conversely, what may seem to be an equally nondisabling deviation can be a handicap if it is a source of anxiety for the person. Such things as a large birthmark on the cheek, missing fingers, or a short-ened leg might be a handicap for some but of little concern to others. The impact depends on how well the child, especially in the early years, is helped to adapt to and accept the deviation.

Recognizing a child with a developmental disability is not always easy to do. Whereas a severe spinal cord malformation, present at birth, is easily identified, other disabilities, such as a severe hearing loss in a newborn, may be nearly impos-sible to recognize unless the infant is receiving high-quality medical screening or is in an intensive neonatal health-care facility.

We must also consider whether a child who speaks a language other than English or French in either an English or French classroom is "exceptional." Haring and McCormick (1990) refer to this as an "environmentally related limitation." It

Handicap
relates to environmental or functional demands that, when placed on an individual with a disability, cannot be met

Developmental disability
one of a range of conditions that interfere with any aspect of the normal development of the child

Developmental delay
development of a skill progresses at a slower rate so that a child demonstrates the skill as a younger child would

Developmental deviation
some aspect of a child's development is different from what is seen in other developing children

Photo 5–4
Oromuscular dysfunction often leads to difficulties with speech.

Photo 5–5
At one time a child who did not speak English or French was considered to have a "handicap."

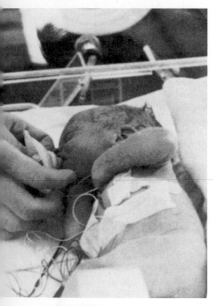

Photo 5–6
Infants may be high risk at the time of birth.

Biological risk
infants and children whose systems have undergone some kind of biological insult, such as an accident, injury, or severe stress, are at risk for developmental disabilities

Environmental risk
factors in a child's environment, such as poverty, child abuse, family beliefs, and inaccessibility of medical care, that put the child at risk for developmental disabilities

should be noted that the same child may well be highly capable in the language of his or her home environment (Photo 5–5; see also Chapter 20). Note, too, that the child's preschool teacher might be considered to have a handicap in the child's own community if the teacher speaks only English or French. Therefore, in this textbook, the child who speaks a language other than English or French in either an English or French classroom is not considered to have a developmental disability. Rather this child has a special need that may require extra support until he or she has mastered the necessary linguistic skills to function in the classroom.

CHILDREN AT RISK

Many infants and young children are said to be at risk or at high risk. This means there is reason to believe that serious problems are likely to develop. For example, mothers who were heavy drinkers or chemically addicted during pregnancy often bear children who are at risk developmentally (Photo 5–6). Their newborns may or may not show immediate special needs. Infants who are born addicted and at a very low birthweight are likely to be considered children with high-risk needs; they may be in grave developmental danger. These children are more likely than are others to exhibit learning disabilities, emotional disorders, and attention deficits. Another less dramatic, but all too frequent, example of children at risk are those born into serious poverty. Developmental risk is likely to occur in cases of malnutrition, inadequate shelter, and poor health care.

An important characteristic of children who are at risk is that the potential for healthy development is there. The majority of infants and children at risk have a good chance of overcoming initial setbacks. What are required are early and comprehensive intervention services: medical treatment, ample nurturance, and in many cases, family support services (see Chapter 3). Risk factors, including those already discussed, can be grouped into two major categories: biological risk and environmental risk.

Biological Risk

The term **biological risk** applies to infants and children whose systems have undergone some kind of biological insult, such as an accident, an injury, or severe stress. The incident may have occurred before birth (prenatal), at birth (perinatal), or following birth (postnatal). For example, a newborn with respiratory distress syndrome (RDS) is at risk but likely to recover if given immediate treatment. Premature birth or low birthweight (5.5 pounds or 2500 grams or less) are risk factors that require immediate, intensive intervention. Without it, many infants suffer severe developmental complications.

Environmental Risk

Poverty is the greatest single factor associated with **environmental risk.** As noted earlier, families who live in severe poverty are often seriously undernourished and may lack adequate shelter. In addition, they may have little or no way to learn about caring for their infants and may not know how to obtain appropriate social services and medical care. At the same time, Polakow (1992, p. 144) reminds us, as well, that as early childhood educators "we need to recognize that the lack of entitlement to health care, housing, nutrition, and childcare create stressful and powerless lives; that the problems that are often diagnosed as emotional impairments and learning disabilities are very real reactions to concrete conditions of want." As will become evident in Chapter 6, the effects of poverty produce many biological risk conditions. However, poverty is not the only environmental factor that puts infants and young children at risk. Other factors include

- child abuse and unfit living conditions because of addicted or dysfunctional family members
- family beliefs that prohibit urgently needed medication, medical treatment, or surgery
- the inaccessibility of medical care when families live in remote areas

RESILIENCE AND VULNERABILITY

Biology and environment (nature/nurture) may not interact in the same way for every child. The degree of inborn and learned **resilience** and **vulnerability** appear to make a difference (Steinhauer, 1998). Horowitz (1996) has concluded that given a facilitative environment, vulnerable children often have a good developmental outcome and that resilient families and children in a poor environment also may do quite well, because they learn to utilize whatever resources are available to them. Child care professionals who interact with children daily are in a unique position to promote optimism and resiliency (Kordich Hall, 2000). However, the vulnerable child raised in an unfavourable environment is in greater jeopardy to be at developmental risk.

Resilience
the ability to "come back" after a damaging or traumatic experience

Vulnerability
lack of resistance to or ability to recover from a damaging or traumatic experience

THE DISADVANTAGES OF LABELLING

Convincing arguments can be made for not putting a specific diagnostic label on infants, toddlers, and preschoolers who are developmentally different. Many young children who are developmentally different in one way or another resemble their peers far more than they differ from them. With the exception of children with severe impairments, children with developmental disabilities go through the same sequences of development as do other children, though at different rates. It should not be assumed that a disability in one area of development means that special programming is required in all areas (Photo 5–7, p. 96). Furthermore, many infants and young children start out with serious challenges that they are able to overcome if they receive appropriate early intervention services. Premature infants are a good example. Often they are delayed in acquiring early developmental skills. Yet by age two or three, many of these children, with adequate care and nutrition, are catching up. Freedom from developmental delay does not hold true for all low-birthweight babies, but many show no long-term disability. This is in contrast to those born a generation ago, when treatment of premature infants was less advanced (Bee, 1999).

Some impairments, even though serious, may never be handicapping if the child receives appropriate support and intervention services. The condition may continue to exist, but the child finds ways to compensate and so learns to function in spite of it.

Example:

Bret was a child born with one short arm and a malformed hand. The family, from the start, had referred to this as his "little hand." At preschool, there was nothing Bret could not do as well as any other child, be it puzzles, form boards, or block building. In Kindergarten, he was among the first to learn to tie shoes. By Grade 7 he was a champion soccer player.

Photo 5–7

Special needs in one area of development do not mean that special programming is required in other areas.

Individuals like Bret seldom consider themselves to have a handicap, nor do their families view themselves as having a child with a handicap. It is unlikely that this positive attitude could be maintained if the label "handicapped" (with the inevitable differences in attitude that accompany the term) had been attached to this child in infancy.

Those opposed to labelling or categorizing argue that it can be harmful. The harm may be especially great when young children are concerned. The very young may get locked into categories that are developmentally unsuitable or put into programs that compound their delay, as in the following example.

Example:

At three, Jodie was talking very little, seemed incapable of following simple directions, and had few play skills. She scored low on an IQ test and was placed in a preschool for children who had intellectual impairments. It was not until age seven that a severe hearing loss was discovered. Between three and seven, crucial developmental years, Jodie functioned as a child with an intellectual impairment. Why? Because she had been labelled as having an intellectual impairment and consequently had not been identified as a candidate for deaf education services; she was not receiving the stimulation needed to develop language and cognitive skills.

THE ADVANTAGES OF LABELLING

Labelling is useful and at times necessary for

- enhancing public awareness of developmental differences
- gaining access to public funds from provincial, territorial, and federal governments
- advocating for support services and changes
- clarifying and facilitating communication between professionals (for example, in research)
- identifying specific medical conditions (such as hemophilia and anaphylaxis)

Classification of Developmental Differences

Disagreement has long revolved around classifying individuals with developmental differences. Should we label children who are developmentally different according to categories, such as *deaf, blind, emotionally disturbed,* or *intellectually impaired*? In the United States, there is government legislation (PL 99-457) that recognizes the potential harm of prematurely classifying children under the age of six. For this reason, funding by categories has been discontinued in this legislation for children under age six. Instead, the more flexible concept of *developmental delay* is used to cover all developmental differences. Such an approach is more in keeping with the tremendous variability of development among young children.

There is no comparable federal legislation in Canada. At this time, some provinces and territories are developing and others are adapting legislation that provides for young children with special needs. The current direction in Canada is to focus on providing funding for all children who are experiencing developmental challenges during the early years. However, to qualify for specific treatment programs and services, some policymakers believe that young children need to be assessed and in many instances categorized. In their view, it is in such instances that having a classification system becomes important. Classification, labelling, and categorization are also necessary in situations where medical doctors and other professionals communicate with others by using research and sharing case information. Those doing research into various disabilities need to have a common vocabulary. To make important decisions, those in favour of categorizing argue that questions, such as the following, need to be raised:

- How many individuals have a particular disability? (Is it widespread? increasing? decreasing?)
- Does it occur mostly in particular areas or among certain groups (urban, rural, immigrant, itinerant farm worker)?
- How many teachers, clinicians, and facilities are needed to provide services for children in this category?
- What proportion of public money should be allocated to serve each of the different groups of developmental disabilities?
- Which individuals are eligible for government financial assistance?

DEFINITIONS OF CATEGORIES

In spite of disagreements, categorization does exist. A major problem is that the systems vary. The medical profession may group the individuals with disabilities

Photo 5–8
Difficulties with speech and language vary greatly.

Communication and language disorders
difficulties with speaking or learning language, which can lead to serious disruptions in cognitive and social development

Specific learning disabilities (SLD)
a difficulty in any of the following areas: attention, memory, reasoning, coordination, communicating, reading, writing, spelling, calculation, social competence, and emotional maturation

Dyslexia
an impaired ability to read and understand written language

Dysgraphia
difficulty with or inability to express thoughts in writing, and/or to identify the written symbols of language

one way, special education programs another way, and government agencies still another way.

Brief descriptions of each category are given in the following discussion. In later chapters, developmental differences will be regrouped and discussed in greater detail, focusing on early identification, assessment, and intervention.

Communication and Language Disorders

Communication and language disorders among young children vary greatly (Photo 5–8). It is difficult to define clearly what is and what is not a disorder because so many factors affect language development:

- individual differences in temperament
- rate of development
- cultural expectations
- general health and well-being
- opportunity to hear language and talk to others

Also, a number of typical or frequently experienced irregularities are common in the course of language development. These need not become problems unless the child is unduly pressured.

Communication and language disorders are likely to accompany other developmental disorders. Children with cerebral palsy often have serious speech disorders, as do children with hearing impairments and severe emotional disturbances. Whatever the cause, it is important that communication and language disorders receive attention as early as possible. Problems in this area can lead to serious disruptions in cognitive and social development. (Note: Do not confuse a child with a language disorder with a child who is learning English as a second language. See Chapter 20.)

Specific Learning Disabilities

Like communication and speech disorders, **specific learning disabilities (SLD)** or learning disabilities (LD) are difficult to define satisfactorily. In the school-aged child, the label is often one of exclusion—what the child does *not* have:

- an intellectual impairment
- a hearing impairment
- a visual impairment
- an identifiable neurological problem, such as cerebral palsy

In spite of no observable or identifiable disabilities, these children have trouble acquiring basic academic skills. The Learning Disabilities Association of Canada's (LDAC) definition states that school-aged children with learning disabilities include those with potentially average, average, or above-average intelligence. Nevertheless, these children may have difficulties in any of the following areas: attention, memory, reasoning, coordination, communicating, reading, writing, spelling, calculation, social competence, and emotional maturation (LDAC, 2002). The largest group of children characterized as having a learning disability are those having difficulty with reading. The problem is often referred to as **dyslexia.** Other children may have trouble learning to print and write. This may be referred to as **dysgraphia.** More than 100 different labels have been assigned to children whose learning problems baffle clinicians and educators. The labels, it should be noted, do little to help children with their learning disability.

Cognitive Delays

Generally speaking, it is unwise to assign the label of cognitive delay to a young child. Children change; they evolve. The younger the child, the more likely it is that changes will occur. The range of "normal" intellectual functioning is enormous. Furthermore, a child's family circumstances may change, health problems may clear up, or the child may enter an early intervention program. Any one of these has the potential to produce dramatic change in a child's cognitive skills. Issues related to cognitive development and mental functioning will be addressed in Chapters 6 and 19.

Gifted

Children described as gifted or talented do exceptionally well in one or more areas of development. They often are a good fit with the concept of multiple intelligences. Gardner (1993) theorized six types of intelligence: linguistic, logical-mathematical, musical, spatial, bodily kinesthetic, and personal-social. Children who are gifted show accomplishments that seem to appear spontaneously, as part of their own unique developmental process. It is unlikely that these early and outstanding abilities emerge because of special training or parental pressure. Parents of especially bright or talented children often are surprised when told of their child's remarkable abilities (Robinson, 1981).

Multiple Disabling Conditions

A number of children have **multiple disabling conditions,** meaning more than one disability (Photo 5–9). It has been estimated that 20 percent to 50 percent of children with serious hearing deficits have additional disabilities. The same is true of children with cerebral palsy. Many of the syndromes are also characterized by several disabilities occurring together. It is not uncommon, for example, for a child with Down syndrome to have a heart defect, respiratory problems, a marked hearing loss, and hard-to-understand speech.

Multiple disabling conditions
the condition of having more than one disability

The number of children with multiple disabilities is rising. Three possible reasons for the increase are as follows:

1. Excessive use is being made of drugs and alcohol by increasing numbers of pregnant women.
2. Many of the diseases that cause both prenatal and postnatal disabilities in infants and young children have not yet come under modern medical control. In other words, we do not yet know how to treat a number of the medical problems that occur at the same time.
3. Advanced medical practices now allow us to keep babies who have serious disabilities or have a very low birthweight alive. A major concern is that we do not know how to treat many of the disabilities with which these children are born.

Photo 5–9
Some children may have multiple special needs.

Orthopedic Impairments

Developmental differences that interfere with walking or other body movement are considered **orthopedic impairments.** In many instances, orthopedic and neurological impairments are closely related, one example being cerebral palsy (Photo 5–10).

Orthopedic impairments
developmental differences that interfere with walking or other body movements

Photo 5–10
Cerebral palsy is an example of an orthopedic impairment.

The term *orthopedic impairments* includes

- impairments caused by congenital anomalies and structural deformities, such as club foot, absence of a limb, or paralysis
- impairments caused by diseases, such as polio
- neurological and spinal cord damage resulting in problems, such as paralysis of major muscles
- impairments from other causes, such as incidents that result in severely fractured bones, amputations, or burns

It is commonly thought that neurological problems are evident at birth. Often the opposite is true. It may be weeks or months (even well into the first year) before the infant gives evidence of a neurological impairment. The problem may become noticeable only when certain of the very early reflexive (primitive) behaviours do not drop out on schedule and so interfere with the acquisition of new and more mature responses. For example, most newborns automatically grasp a finger placed in their hand. However, unless this primitive grasp reflex disappears between one and four months of age, infants will not be able to learn to release objects at will.

Emotional Disturbance

Emotional disturbance
characterized by behavioural or emotional responses so different from appropriate age, cultural, and community norms that the responses adversely affect educational performance

Emotional disturbance has no formally agreed on definition and is thus subject to much controversy. One proposed definition is that the disability is characterized by behavioural or emotional responses so different from appropriate age, ethnic, and community norms that the responses adversely affect educational performance, including academic, social, vocational, or personal skills. Whatever the definition, emotional disturbance is a label that *should not be assigned to young children*. The reasons are similar to those given earlier for avoiding the label of intellectual impairment with young children. Alternative terms for emotional disturbance (which are more appropriate, developmentally) might be *behaviour disorders, behaviour problems,* or *behaviour challenges*. The term *social adjustment problems* is also used. These terms will be used interchangeably in this text. Even so, they are used with caution. Why? One reason is that children's behaviour during the early years is heavily influenced by child-rearing practices, cultural values, and expectations of the family and community. Parents who are aggressive, for example, tend to have children who also behave aggressively (Hetherington & Martin, 1979). Thus, the child's aggressiveness is perfectly "normal" in the light of the family environment.

The social and emotional characteristics of young children also are highly influenced by particular stages of development. (In times gone by, early childhood educators and pediatricians even used such terms as "the terrible twos" to describe the toddler's struggle for independence.) Behaviour difficulties often arise out of the frustrations a young child experiences in trying to master basic developmental skills, such as learning to feed himself or herself, learning culturally acceptable bowel and bladder practices, and learning what to fear and what not to fear. In most cases, therefore, a child's behaviour should be judged by what is developmentally appropriate for his or her particular age range and cultural background. The majority of behaviour problems occurring in early childhood do not carry over into adult life. Note: There are other developmental disorders that have symptoms that involve severe behaviour disorders. These include pervasive developmental disorder (PDD) and attention deficit hyperactivity disorder (ADHD). These conditions will be discussed in Chapter 10.

Deafness and Hearing Impairments

As defined by U.S. legislation (PL 94-142), the deaf are individuals whose hearing loss is so severe they cannot process spoken language, even with hearing aids or other forms of amplification. Children with a **hearing impairment** are those whose loss has a negative effect on their education, but not to the same degree as it does on children who are deaf. Hearing impairments have a delaying effect on a young child's cognitive, social, and language development (Photo 5–11). The degree of developmental damage is determined by the severity of the hearing loss and the age of the child when the hearing problem developed.

Generally speaking, the greater the loss, the greater the disabling effects; the earlier in life the loss, the greater the developmental damage. Because of the age factor, deafness and hearing impairments often are labelled according to when the damage occurred:

- **Congenital deafness** is experienced by individuals who have been deaf since birth.
- **Adventitious deafness** is experienced by individuals who are born with normal hearing but lose it through injury or disease.

If the loss occurs after a child has acquired some language, the developmental problems tend to be less damaging. In fact, children who have even a short exposure to language before they lose their hearing do a great deal better in developing language skills than do children who are born deaf. Nevertheless, even a mild hearing loss can have negative effects on all aspects of development unless the child receives appropriate early intervention.

Health Impairments

Young children with severe **health impairments** often have limited strength, vitality, and alertness. They also may experience pain and discomfort much of the time. A regular childhood may be nearly impossible because of frequent hospitalizations or intensive medical treatment.

Health disorders can take many forms, including

- heart problems (weak or damaged heart)
- leukemia (cancer of the bone marrow)
- asthma (disorder of the respiratory system)
- sickle-cell disease (red blood cell malformation)
- hemophilia (a bleeding disorder)
- diabetes (faulty metabolism of sugar and starch)
- cystic fibrosis (lung and digestive problems)

Health disorders may be described as **chronic** or acute (although a chronic problem can develop into an acute state). In either case, the child's overall development is threatened. Although poor health problems may not be the actual cause of other developmental differences, they can create situations that lead to other concerns.

Photo 5–11
Deafness has an impact on every aspect of a child's life.

Hearing impairment
a hearing loss that can have a delaying effect on a child's cognitive, social, and language development

Congenital deafness
deafness present at the time of birth

Adventitious deafness
deafness acquired through injury or disease after birth

Health impairments
chronic or acute disorders, such as heart problems, leukemia, and asthma, that threaten a child's overall development

Chronic
a health problem of long duration and frequent recurrence

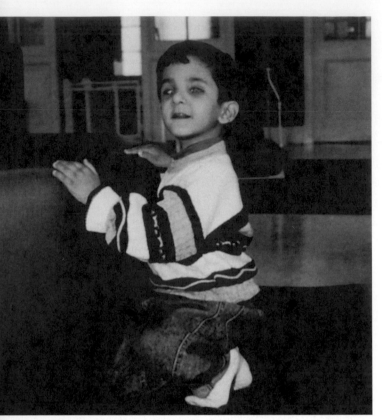

Photo 5–12
Legal blindness is defined as visual acuity of 20/200 or less in the better eye after correction or a much reduced field of vision.

Visual impairment
vision loss that include the following conditions: blind, partially sighted, blindness, and low vision

Tactile
refers to that which is learned or perceived through touch

Auditory
refers to what is experienced through hearing

Blindness
vision loss severe enough that it is not possible to read print, requiring the child to be educated through the use of Braille and other tactile and auditory materials

Example:

A child who is physically weak and unable to run and jump and play with children of the same age may be socially isolated. Brothers and sisters may resent having to play with the child instead of their own playmates. They also may resent that so much of the parents' attention and resources seem to be focused on the sick child. This may lead to the sick child feeling lonely, rejected, anxious, guilty, and even more isolated.

Blindness and Visual Impairments

There is no clear-cut definition of **visual impairment** (Photo 5–12). A legal-medical definition proposed by the U.S. National Society for the Prevention of Blindness is currently accepted in Canada, and it includes the following:

- *Blind.* Visual acuity of 20/200 or less in the better eye with the best possible correction; or a much reduced field of vision (at its widest diameter, a visual arc of 20° or less).
- *Partially sighted.* Visual acuity between 20/70 and 20/200 in the better eye with the best possible correction.

The American Foundation for the Blind offers these educational definitions:

- *Blindness.* Visual loss is severe enough that it is not possible to read print, requiring the child to be educated through the use of Braille and other **tactile** and **auditory** materials.
- *Low vision (partially seeing).* Residual vision is sufficient to allow the child to read large print or possibly regular print under special conditions and to use other visual materials for educational purposes.

Total **blindness,** whether congenital or occurring after birth, is readily identified. The baby simply does not respond to people or objects within its range of vision. Less severe visual disorders may be more difficult to identify. Frequently, the difference does not show up until it is time to learn to read and write. By this time the child may have developed a number of other problems in trying to compensate for the undiagnosed vision loss.

Combined Deafness and Blindness

Children who are described as being both deaf and blind have a combination of vision and hearing problems so severe that they require highly specialized intervention programs. Two such serious sensory deficits in combination usually result in a number of other differences in language, cognitive, and social development.

Pervasive Development Disorders

Pervasive development disorders are serious disturbances evident in the first three years that affect a child's verbal and nonverbal communication skills, reciprocal social interaction, or ability to engage in imaginative play. Pervasive developmental disorders include autism, Rett's disorder, childhood disintegrative disorder, Asperger's disorder, and childhood schizophrenia (see Chapter 10).

Traumatic Brain Injury

The category **traumatic brain injury** includes injuries (either open- or closed-wound) to the head that cause tearing of the nerve fibres, bruising of the brain against the skull, or bruising of the brain stem. The most common consequences as far as learning is concerned are

- confusion in spatial orientation and directionality
- marked distractibility and short attention span
- problems in both short- and long-term memory
- impulsivity and, sometimes, aggressiveness

Traumatic brain injury includes injuries to the head that cause tearing of the nerve fibres, bruising of the brain against the skull, or bruising of the brain stem

Summary

Decisions as to which children are developing normally and which children have exceptional development vary among child development theorists, government agencies, and the various professions involved with young children. The terminology used to refer to children who are exceptional has gone through a series of changes over time, reflecting changes in societal attitudes. Normal development is difficult to define because it is so complex a process, particularly in light of recent brain research. Normal development includes a range of developmental skills and may take a different developmental pathway within cultural environments. Certain guidelines are available, based on knowledge of developmental sequences and developmental milestones. Because young children are in a constant state of change, it is preferable to think of them as having a developmental delay or difference—not a handicap.

Children at developmental risk are those who are likely to develop a developmental delay if they do not receive special services as early as possible. Risk factors—biological, environmental, or both—may occur prenatally, at the time of birth, or during the early developmental years.

Classifying or categorizing children in terms of particular developmental differences is a common educational and administrative practice. Most professionals argue against categorizing, especially for young children, because infants and children change rapidly during the early years. Nevertheless, a classification system seems necessary from both the funding and the professional training standpoint.

RESOURCES

LEARNING DISABILITIES ASSOCIATION OF CANADA
http://www.ldac-taac.ca
This website provides LDAC's official definition of learning disabilities as well as links to related sites.

COUNCIL OF MINISTERS OF EDUCATION, CANADA
http://www.cmec.ca
This site provides a link to the Ministry of Education in each province and territory, with access to information on special education.

SPARROW LAKE ALLIANCE
http://www.sparrowlake.org
This organization is dedicated to promoting the optimal development of all children and youth. Some publications focus on fostering resiliency in young children.

STUDENT ACTIVITIES

1. Meet with an advocacy group for children with special needs and find out how and why it was established and what changes have resulted from its actions.
2. Select a specific developmental difference and identify how social attitudes and treatments have changed over the past hundred years.
3. Research legislation in your province or territory and summarize definitions of developmental disabilities.
4. Study a copy of your province's or territory's guidelines, regulations, or legislation for funding services to preschool children with disabilities. Chart your findings.
5. Participate in a panel discussion on the inappropriateness and disadvantages of labelling young children as having learning disabilities, cognitive impairments, or emotional disturbances.

REFERENCES

Bee, H. (1999). *The developing child* (8th ed.). Needham Heights, MA: Allyn & Bacon.

Bernhard, J. K. (1995). The changing field of child development: Cultural diversity and the professional training of early childhood educators. *Canadian Journal of Education, 20*(4), 415–436.

Bernhard, J. K. (2000, March). Reconceptualizing ECE: Questioning theories and assumptions in human development. In E. Lowe (Ed.), *Linking research to practice, second Canadian forum*. Ottawa: Canadian Child Care Federation Publication.

Gardner, H. (1993). *Frames of mind: The theory of multiple intelligences*. New York: Basic Books.

Haring, N. G., & McCormick, L. (1990). *Exceptional children and youth*. Columbus, OH: Charles E. Merrill.

Hetherington, F. M., & Martin, B. (1979). Family interaction. In H. C. Quay & J. S. Werry (Eds.), *Psychopathological disorders of childhood* (pp. 247–302). New York: Wiley.

Learning Disabilities Association of Canada (LDAC). (2002). *LD defined*. Retrieved August 15, 2005, from http://www.ldac-taac.ca/Defined/defined-e.asp.

Kordich Hall, D. 2000. Fostering optimism in young children. *Ideas/Interaction, 14*(3), 19–23.

Ontario Ministry of Community and Social Services. (1984). *Metro report. Services for special needs preschool children in Metropolitan Toronto.* Toronto: Ontario Ministry of Community and Social Services.

Polakow, V. (1992). Deconstructing the discourse of care: Young children in the shadows of democracy. In S. Kessler & B. B. Swadener (Eds.), *Reconceptualizing the early childhood curriculum* (pp. 123–148). New York: Teachers College Press.

Robinson, H. B. (1981). The uncommonly bright child. In M. Lewis & L. A. Rosenblum (Eds.), *The uncommon child* (pp. 57–81). New York: Plenum.

Rogoff, B. (1990). *Apprenticeship in thinking: Cognitive development in social context.* New York: Oxford University Press.

Shore, R. (1997). *Rethinking the brain.* New York: Families and Work Institute

Steinhauer, P. D. (1998). Developing resiliency in children from disadvantaged populations. In *Canada health action: Building on the legacy volume I, Determinants of health: Children and youth* (pp. 47–102). Catalogue No. H21-126/6-1-1997E. Ottawa: National Forum on Health, Health Canada.

Trent, S., Artiles, A., & Englert, C. S. (1999). From deficit thinking to social constructivism: A review of theory, research, and practice in special education. *Review of Research in Education, 23,* 277–307.

Vygotsky. L. S. (1978). *Mind in society: The development of higher psychological processes.* Cambridge, MA: Harvard University Press.

Winzer, M. A. (1997). *Children with exceptionalities: A Canadian perspective.* Scarborough, ON: Prentice-Hall Canada.

CHAPTER 6 | Children with Cognitive Delays

KEY CONCEPTS

amino acid

anemia

anoxia

asymptomatic

at risk/high risk

autosomal recessive disorder

biological insult

biological risk

cognitive delay

congenital

first trimester

metabolic disorders

muscle tone

neurological

perinatally

postnatally

prenatally

protein deficiency

respiratory distress
   syndrome (RDS)

standardized IQ test

standardized tests

stigmata (stigma)

syndrome

OBJECTIVES

After studying the material in this chapter, the student will be able to

- Explain why it is especially inappropriate to label a young child as "mentally retarded."
- Specify several possible underlying causes of cognitive delays and give examples.
- Discuss the correlation between poverty and cognitive delays in young children.
- Identify major conditions that are likely to affect the development of the young child.
- Discuss basic programming considerations for a child with developmental delays.

Introduction

Determining the cause of any developmental difference is a complex process. The cause of a **cognitive delay** is at times difficult to recognize; at other times, the reasons may be clearly evident. Cognitive delays may have their origins in the prenatal, perinatal, or postnatal period of development. Furthermore, it is important to try to determine the extent of the delay and whether or not, or in what ways, it is likely to permanently affect a child's life.

Cognitive delay
intellectual growth that does not follow the expected rate of development due to genetic or environmental conditions or a combination of both

Consider the following examples of questions that might arise when we attempt to determine the cause of a cognitive delay in a child:

1. Two three-year-old boys display hearing impairments: One is talking well; the other is not talking at all. Why?
   - Do they have different kinds of hearing losses?
   - Has one child had more frequent or more severe ear infections?
   - Is one child in a better early childhood program?
   - Do cultural and family differences account for the developmental differences?
2. What might account for performance differences among three preschool children who have been labelled as "cognitively delayed" but who have no recognizable physical disabilities?

Questions such as these are common among child developmentalists, clinicians, and educators. Though the issues are not new, there are no ready answers. The best response, so far, is that the causes of cognitive delays appear to be a combination of factors: heredity, biology (physical makeup), temperament (personality style), and a long list of environmental factors that interact in complex ways.

The range of both normalcy and individual differences is broad. Furthermore, all children develop at slightly different rates, excelling more quickly in some areas of development than others. It is important to observe children fully and refer them for professional assessments before jumping to the conclusion that an observed deviation from normal growth and development is serious or permanent. One thing is certain: More harm than good comes from prematurely labelling a child.

The term "mental retardation" is used primarily by the medical community. Early childhood professionals are urged to use the term "cognitive delays" because of the historical negative connotations associated with the term "mental retardation."

Because a child has a cognitive delay does not mean that the child cannot learn. Every child has the potential to learn, and the base point at which learning starts depends on the degree of delay. Some children may acquire cognitive skills more slowly than others do. Some may never acquire higher-level thinking skills. What we need to keep in mind is that none of us can fully know the potential of any child.

Assessment tools and tests can guide us in determining an appropriate level at which to start programming to support cognitive development. In spite of the difficulties associated with assigning categories to—and specifying the causes of—cognitive delays, some guidelines are available. Practical knowledge about the causes of developmental irregularities is accumulating rapidly. In addition, classification systems have been designed that can be used under prescribed conditions with some infants and young children. These issues—causes and characteristics of cognitive delays—are the focus of this chapter.

Characteristics of Cognitive Delays

According to Deiner, Dyke, and Hardacre (1999, p. 239),

> Delayed cognitive development is intellectual growth that does not follow the expected rate of cognitive development because of genetic or environmental conditions or a combination of these. Most children with developmental delays follow the same sequence of cognitive skill acquisition as other children, but the rate of acquisition is slower. Some children will not reach the higher level of abstract thinking skills if the brain is not fully developed or is injured. . . . Cognitive delay is a broad term that can refer to children of all ages and with differing degrees of delayed cognitive development. Within this are two broad categories of children: those who are classified as developmentally delayed (children 0 to 9 years) and those who are classified as mentally retarded.

Children with cognitive delays may display the following characteristics:

- difficulty learning new skills
- poor **muscle tone**
- slowness to become involved in an activity
- difficulty comprehending verbal directions
- immature or developmentally inappropriate social behaviour
- delays in fine motor skills, gross motor skills, or language
- difficulty in using self-help/care skills without assistance

Muscle tone
the interaction between the central nervous system and motor activity; the term does not mean the same thing as muscle strength; without muscle tone there is no voluntary movement

In Canada, as well as the United States, people working with children of any age should be aware of the American Association of Mental Retardation's definition of cognitive delay or, as it is still at times referred to, "mental retardation":

> Mental retardation refers to substantial limitations in present functioning. It is characterized by significantly subaverage intellectual functioning, existing concurrently with related limitations in two or more of the following applicable adaptive skill areas: communication, self-care, home living, social skills, community use, self-direction, health and safety, functional academics, leisure, and work. Mental retardation manifests before the age of 18. (American Association of Mental Retardation [AAMR], 1992)

This statement includes several additional important points:

- *Intellectual functioning* usually refers to the score an individual gets on a **standardized IQ test,** such as the Stanford-Binet or the Wechsler Intelligence Scales.
- *Significantly subaverage* is a score of 70 or below obtained by an individual in one of the **standardized tests.**
- *Adaptive skill areas* refers to an individual's ability to communicate verbally or nonverbally, to take care of personal needs (bathing, dressing, feeding self, toileting), and to carry out simple basic social responsibilities expected of individuals of similar age and culture.
- *Mental retardation begins before the age of 18.*

Standardized IQ test
a measure of intellectual performance based on averages that have been established by testing large numbers of individuals of the same age (ideally of the same socioeconomic background, too)

Standardized tests
assessment instruments that include precise directions for administration and scoring

The AAMR definition is an important and much-needed advancement in social and educational policy. It changes the way we view those who, in earlier times, might have been placed in an institution or assigned to classes for the mentally retarded. No longer can any individual be labelled as "mentally retarded" solely on the basis of a low IQ score. Individuals who are functioning well in their home and in the community, regardless of their inability to read or write or do well on IQ tests, are not to be labelled as "mentally retarded" (AAMR, 1992).

Causes of Cognitive Delays

Causes of a cognitive delay can occur at any stage of development: before the child is born (**prenatally**), during the birth process (**perinatally**), or any time following birth (**postnatally**). Any condition present at the time of birth is referred to as **congenital.** Congenital problems may or may not be genetically related. Deafness, for example, can be caused in one child by an infection the mother had during early pregnancy; in another child it may be genetically linked to parents who are deaf. Some of these differences can be recognized at birth; others may not be detected or do not manifest until much later. Generally speaking, the more severe the disabling condition, the earlier it is recognized. There are, however, many exceptions. For example, a serious hearing loss may not be identified until the child enters group care.

Research indicates that biology and environment each have an equal impact on human development. Without exception, environmental factors have an impact on a child's biological foundation, influencing the developmental outcome. Environment affects and is affected by heredity in two ways. Parents with high IQs tend to produce children with high IQs and also tend to provide a rich and stimulating environment for their children. In addition to this, behaviour geneticists state that children are born with particular types of temperaments that affect the way the environment responds to them. Thus, some children may actually create for themselves a more responsive learning environment because of their more responsive temperaments. A healthy infant, as we will see, "hooks" parents into responding (Photo 6–1). Strong, early bonding is the usual result. An ill, low-birthweight infant

Prenatally
occurring or existing before birth

Perinatally
occurring or existing at the time of birth

Postnatally
occurring or existing after birth

Congenital
refers to a physical condition that originates during the prenatal period

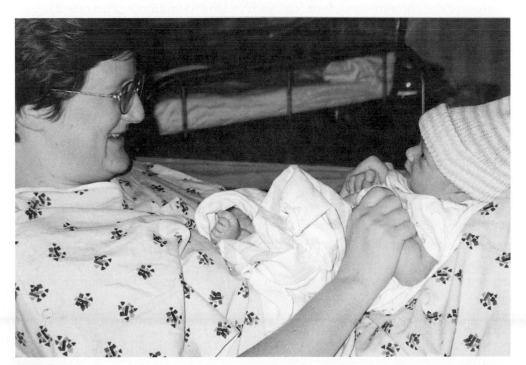

Photo 6–1
A healthy infant "hooks" parents into responding.

may have little or no energy to expend on any activity and so the outcome may be less positive. These complex interactions and transactions, with the child as the pivot point, need to be kept in mind in the discussions that follow.

Risk Factors

Risk factors, including those already discussed, can be grouped into two major categories: *biological* and *environmental*.

BIOLOGICAL RISK

Biological Insult

Biology plays a major role in determining both healthy and at-risk development. **Biological insult** refers to interference with or damage to an individual's physical structure or functioning. The biological insult may occur at the time of conception, during pregnancy (often within the **first trimester,** because of health problems in the mother), during the birth process (from complications, such as the umbilical cord becoming wrapped around the baby's neck), or following birth (from respiratory distress, viral infections, and so on). All of these, singly or in combination, together with environmental factors, can lead to cognitive delays.

Some examples of a **biological risk** are the following:

- A newborn with **respiratory distress syndrome (RDS)** is **at risk**—in serious trouble medically—but likely to recover if given immediate and appropriate treatment.
- Premature birth or low birthweight (5 pounds [2500 grams] or less) are risk factors that require immediate, intensive intervention. Without it, many of the infants affected will suffer irreversible developmental damage.
- Other biological risk factors include genetic disorders, such as Tay-Sachs syndrome, and chromosomal disorders, such as Down syndrome (Photo 6–2), which may have accompanying physiological problems, putting the child at greater risk developmentally.

Genetic Disorders

The genetic makeup of every individual is determined at the moment of conception. Each parent contributes 23 chromosomes on which there are thousands of genes. In a process called cell division (involving two processes, *meiosis* and *mitosis*), the chromosomes from each parent divide and recombine. Physical characteristics, such as size, body build, eye and skin colour, sex, and even the shape of the nose, are determined at that moment. Genetically determined abnormalities also become evident at this time. They may be caused by deviations in chromosomal structure or by abnormal single genes. Chromosomal abnormalities are usually biological accidents that occur one time and do not affect future pregnancies.

Most single-gene disorders are found in healthy carriers. When both parents have the same recessive abnormal gene, statistically, one in four of their children will be affected by the disorder.

Syndromes

Various syndromes make up a major class of genetic abnormalities. The term **syndrome** refers to a grouping of similar physical characteristics called **stigmata (stigma).** When several stigmata are found in a recognizable pattern (having a

---

Biological insult
interference with or damage to an individual's physical structure or functioning

First trimester
the first three months of prenatal development

Biological risk
infants and children whose systems have undergone some kind of biological insult, such as an accident, injury, or severe stress, are at risk for developmental disabilities

Respiratory distress syndrome (RDS):
a problem commonly found among premature infants because of the immature development of their lungs; it may also occur in about 1 percent of full-term infants during the first days of life

At risk
indications (either physical or environmental) that an infant or child may develop serious problems

Photo 6–2
The most readily recognized chromosomal disorder is Down syndrome.

Syndrome
a grouping of similar physical characteristics

Stigmata (stigma)
an identifying mark or characteristic; a diagnostic sign of a disease or disability

similar chromosomal error), the child is said to have the syndrome. In many instances, children with a given syndrome have similar physical characteristics, which may make them look somewhat alike.

Down syndrome. The most widely recognized chromosomal disorder is Down syndrome (Trisomy 21). It occurs approximately once in every seven hundred births, with the risk slightly higher among young teenage mothers and greatly increased in women over 45. The cause (oversimplified) is an addition to the 21st chromosome pair (hence the term Trisomy 21). In about 25 percent of cases, the problem originates in the sperm of the father.

Children with Down syndrome are often easy to identify because of the following physical characteristics:

- a small, round head that appears somewhat flattened in the back
- a low-set bridge of the nose, giving a flat mid-face appearance
- low-set, small ears with unusually shaped earlobes
- a protruding tongue due to poor muscle tone
- short fingers and toes with the little fingers and little toes curving inward
- a simian crease (a single, almost straight line across the upper part of one or both palms, instead of the usual pair of parallel lines)
- curving folds of skin at the inner corners of the eyes, which give an almond shape to the eyes

About 50 percent of children with Down syndrome have congenital heart defects and intestinal abnormalities. Hearing impairments, often from severe cases of ear infections, such as otitis media, are also common. Some degree of cognitive delay, ranging from mild to severe, becomes increasingly apparent as these children grow older.

Fragile X syndrome. Fragile X syndrome is caused by a marker on the X chromosome of some males. Because boys inherit their X chromosome from their mothers (and the Y chromosome from their fathers), this disorder often shows a sex-linked pattern with one mother having more than one affected son, even if the sons have different fathers. The consequences of this condition are cognitive deficiencies varying from mild to severe, repetitive speech, and autistic-like behaviours. Fragile X syndrome can cause some disability in both sexes, but boys tend to be more seriously effected physically, mentally, and behaviourally (Zigler & Hodapp, 1991).

Metabolic disorders
single-gene defects that cause a breakdown somewhere in the complex chemical activities needed to metabolize food

Metabolic Disorders

Metabolic disorders (Photo 6–3) cause a breakdown somewhere in the complex chemical activities needed to metabolize food. The breakdown can destroy, damage, or alter cells. Metabolic disorders are single-gene defects.

Two of the more common genetically related metabolic disorders are phenylketonuria and galactosemia.

Phenylketonuria (PKU). Phenylketonuria occurs in infants born without the liver enzymes needed to digest

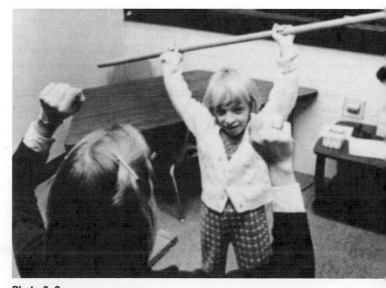

Photo 6–3
Metabolic disorders account for some developmental irregularities.

Amino acid
one of the chief components of proteins; amino acids are obtained from the individual's diet or are manufactured by living cells

the **amino acid** known as phenylalanine. Phenylalanine is present in milk, wheat, eggs, fish, and meat. The mother's normal metabolism protects the infant before birth, but as soon as the infant is fed milk, toxic (poisonous) substances build up, leading to irreversible brain damage. Today, blood tests are available and all newborns should be routinely screened for this disorder. If placed immediately on a highly restricted diet, the child can usually be saved from serious intellectual impairment. The diet, low in phenylalanine, must be continued during most of the child's developmental years. It is also recommended that a woman who has PKU stay on the diet throughout her childbearing years. If an affected woman does not, any baby she carries will be severely brain damaged because it will be exposed to an abnormal metabolic environment in utero. The control of PKU demonstrates how environmental manipulation can modify genetic disorders successfully.

Galactosemia. Galactosemia is a metabolic disorder in which milk cannot be digested. Infants with galactosemia tend to appear normal at birth. The moment milk is introduced, vomiting, diarrhea, and enlargement of the liver begin. Without treatment, death usually occurs within the first few months of life. Should the infant live, intellectual impairment is inescapable. Again, the problems can be avoided with screening of the newborn. If milk intolerance is detected in the early days of life, a special diet, started immediately, will prevent intellectual impairment.

Abnormal Gene Disorders

Autosomal recessive disorder
a gene carried by healthy parents on any one chromosome except the sex chromosomes that, if inherited from both parents, results in a child with a medical condition not present in the parents

Tay-Sachs disease. Tay-Sachs disease is a rare **autosomal recessive disorder** occurring most commonly in children of Eastern European Jewish descent. This disorder is caused by a faulty enzyme of fat metabolism. Fatty accumulations in the brain interfere with neurological processes. The result is a rapid degeneration of the nervous system from birth on, with death usually occurring around three or four years of age.

Some other gene disorders do not affect the brain directly, but result in frequent absences from school, affecting the child's learning (see Chapter 9). These include cystic fibrosis, sickle-cell disease, and muscular dystrophy.

Prenatal Conditions, Infections, and Intoxicants

Most developmental abnormalities, especially those that occur prenatally, cannot be explained by genetics. Less than 3 percent of all birth defects are thought to be purely genetic in origin. Factors that have a negative effect on a mother's health during pregnancy are responsible for 25 percent or more of all developmental deviations.

A few of the conditions and infections that can occur in utero are described below.

Rubella. Rubella (also known as German or three-day measles) can have a devastating effect on the fetus (unborn infant). If contracted during the first trimester, rubella can lead to severe and lifelong disabilities. Fortunately, childhood immunizations have now drastically reduced the incidence of congenital rubella.

Asymptomatic
showing no signs of a disease or impairment, which nevertheless may be present

CMV virus. CMV virus (cytomegalic inclusion disease), which can be contracted by the mother through intimate contact, is a frequent cause of severe damage to infants. Often, the pregnant woman has no symptoms. Ninety percent of infants with CMV are **asymptomatic** at birth; that is, they show no problems. It is only later that intellectual impairment, deafness, diseases of the eyes, and other disabilities begin to show up.

Herpes simplex. Herpes simplex is an incurable viral disorder that can cause recurring severe to mild genital sores. Even when it is in remission, a woman can pass it on to her unborn infant. The results can be devastating, even fatal, as in cases of inflammation of the infant's brain and spinal cord. Less damaging results include periodic attacks of genital sores.

AIDS (acquired immune deficiency syndrome). AIDS is a condition that interferes with the body's ability to ward off disease. An infected mother can pass AIDS on to her unborn infant (see Chapter 9.)

Diabetes. Diabetes in the mother puts the infant at **high risk** for serious developmental problems, even death. Today, a woman with diabetes has a better chance of bearing a healthy baby because of medical advances. Nevertheless, maternal diabetes must be monitored throughout pregnancy.

High risk
a high probability of developing serious problems

Toxemia. Toxemia is a frequent complication of pregnancy, which produces a variety of symptoms, including swelling of the mother's arms and legs, poorly functioning kidneys, and high blood pressure. Women with toxemia often deliver babies who are premature or of low birthweight and at medical risk.

Drugs, alcohol, and other chemical substances. Maternal use of any chemical substance during pregnancy, whether for medicinal purposes or as a "recreational" substance (for example, crack cocaine, alcohol, and some prescription drugs) often results in serious abnormalities in the unborn infant. These range from deformed arms and legs to mild to severe intellectual impairment. Estimates for the United States "run as high as 375 000 newborns a year who are born hooked due to maternal drug use" (Bliley, 1989). Similar problems can be the result of alcohol intake during pregnancy. Alcohol consumption, even in moderate amounts, has been linked to a variety of developmental problems now grouped under two headings: *fetal alcohol syndrome (FAS)* and *fetal alcohol effect (FAE)*. Research by Streissguth, Barr, and Sampson (1990) indicates that the potential for subnormal IQ is three times greater among children whose mothers drink during pregnancy. They also report that even occasional "binge" drinking can be extremely damaging to the fetus. In addition to some degree of intellectual impairment, the physical abnormalities associated with FAS include a small head, droopy eyes, a wide space between the nose and upper lip, the occasional cleft palate, and heart problems. It is not known whether there is a "safe" amount of maternal alcohol consumption. In light of this, the only safe course is for women to refrain from drinking during pregnancy.

A number of drugs used by pregnant women for medicinal purposes also can cause serious birth defects. *Pregnant women should not take medications without consulting a physician.* This is particularly important in terms of over-the-counter drugs.

Illegal drugs—cocaine, for example, and its many variations—used during pregnancy can put the unborn infant at high risk for both short-term and long-term developmental problems. Many such infants are born prematurely, have very low birthweight, or are stillborn; others die of SIDS (sudden infant death syndrome), otherwise known as "crib death," during the first year. Many more suffer neurological damage that may not show up until years later as a serious learning disability (Keith et al., 1989). It is not known how much drug use is too much. It is known, however, that "even a single hit can have a devastating effect at any time during pregnancy. In some cases, it appears to cause strokes in the fetus" (Bee, 1992, p. 73). As indicated above, no drug is safe for a developing fetus. Children who are exposed to cocaine prenatally are often underweight, have smaller head circumferences, and are at greater risk for developmental delays than are children who have not been exposed. Current research suggests that risk is cumulative: Children who have more risk factors (such as drug exposure, low birthweight, poor prenatal care, and poor nutrition) are more likely to have developmental delays than are children with fewer risk factors, even if one of those risk factors is prenatal drug exposure (Hanson & Carta, 1996). Thus, as with alcohol, the best thing a woman can do for her baby is to completely abstain from drug use during pregnancy.

Rh blood incompatibility. In Rh blood incompatibility, the mix of the mother's blood type and the father's causes serious problems. The mother's body may reject the fetus, or the fetus's red blood cells may be destroyed. The danger of Rh incompatibility can be controlled with early medical treatment. Rarely does the problem occur with a first child.

Poor nutrition. Poor diet (maternal malnutrition and **protein deficiency** due to lack of milk, cheese, grains, eggs, fish, chicken, and meat) can result in premature and seriously low-birthweight babies. These infants are at high risk for a number of developmental problems, including limited brain cell development, illness, and a higher risk of death during the first year. Stunted growth throughout childhood is often another consequence. (Note, however, that many reasons other than poor nutrition also are responsible for premature and low-birthweight infants.) The effects of poor diet are particularly damaging during the last trimester of pregnancy, when significant maturing of the brain and nervous system take place. It is now recommended that a pregnant woman gain 25 to 30 pounds (10 to 15 kilograms) during pregnancy—and more if she is underweight to begin with.

Birth Complications

Birth itself can result in trauma—that is, injury or shock. An infant, perfectly healthy until the moment of birth, can experience damage during the birth process. For example, **anoxia,** lack of oxygen available to the brain cells, can occur because of labour complications. Brain damage or severe **neurological** problems, such as cerebral palsy or intellectual impairment, may result. Recent evidence, however, indicates that a healthy newborn may be able to withstand a fairly substantial shortage of oxygen without suffering major damage. When damage does occur, it may not come from a newborn's inability to breathe immediately. Instead, the failure to start breathing may have been caused by earlier, perhaps unsuspected, damage in utero. This is one example of how difficult it is to be certain about the cause of a developmental problem.

Premature infants, especially, are subject to another kind of trauma: hemorrhaging or bleeding into the brain. These immature newborns are also at higher risk for breathing problems, heart failure, and infections (Photo 6–4). Even less severe problems at birth can result in later trouble. It is now thought that some school-age learning disabilities may be associated with

Protein deficiency
a factor in maternal malnutrition when the mother's diet is lacking in milk, cheese, eggs, meats, and so on, which can result in premature or seriously low-birthweight babies

Anoxia
a shortage of oxygen to the brain that can cause physical damage to the brain before, during, or at any time after birth; anoxia is one of the major causes of physical and cognitive dysfunction

Neurological
refers to the functioning of the nervous system

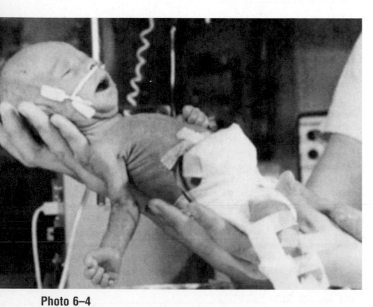

Photo 6–4
Premature and low-birthweight infants are often in need of intensive care.

low birthweight or seemingly minor disturbances at the time of birth (Hittleman, Parekh, & Glass, 1987).

Complications after Birth

Following the birth process, other events can lead to developmental problems. Among these are meningitis, encephalitis, lead poisoning, and poor nutrition.

Meningitis. Meningitis is a viral or bacterial infection that causes inflammation of the protective covering of the brain and the spinal cord. When meningitis-related death occurs in newborns, the cause usually is organisms found in the intestines or birth canal of the mother. The results of meningitis are unpredictable. Some children show no serious effects; others experience major neurological damage.

Encephalitis. Encephalitis is an infection that attacks the brain itself. The symptoms are so many and so varied that the infection often is not diagnosed correctly. A range of aftereffects are possible, from no damage to identifiable neurological damage and later learning problems.

Lead poisoning. Lead poisoning can cause grave damage to young children whose bodies and nervous systems are still developing. The Canadian Paediatric Society (1996, p. 781) states:

> Since lead may be present in soil, air, water or food, it cannot be avoided. Levels of lead in the body which are not high enough to cause outward symptoms of lead poisoning may nevertheless be associated with developmental and behavioural abnormalities in children. Lead can certainly cause intellectual and behavioural changes in children if they are exposed to it over long periods.

The chief risk to preschool-aged children is from the ingestion of lead-based paint, which can be found in older (those built before World War II) homes and buildings. If paint or plaster is peeling or chipped, it should be tested for lead content. To do so, caregivers are advised to contact the local public health agency.

Children who eat well-balanced diets are at less risk of lead poisoning than are children who are malnourished or have calcium or iron deficiencies.

Further sources of lead cited by the Canadian Paediatric Society (1996, pp. 793–794) include

- lead-glazed ceramics (utensils and pots made of lead-glazed ceramics should not be used for cooking or serving food or beverages, especially acidic ones, such as tomatoes, fruit juice, and so on)
- old painted toys and furniture (Photo 6–5)
- folk medicines
- cosmetics from Asia
- imported earthenware toys

ENVIRONMENTAL FACTORS

Many cognitive delays, regardless of when they occur—before, during, or after the birth of the baby—can be directly or indirectly related to poverty. Families living in poverty experience the highest rates of infant death, failure to thrive, and birth defects. The same holds true for subsequent developmental problems, including intellectual impairment, learning disabilities, and social and emotional deviations.

Photo 6–5
The lead-based paint used on this radiator would be dangerous to a young child if ingested.

The Impact of Poverty

The link between poverty and developmental delays cannot be denied. Consider the following:

- Poor nutrition during pregnancy, as indicated previously, as well as during infancy and early childhood, can have a major impact on the overall development of the child.
- Pimento and Kernested (2000) cite information from Statistics Canada in the Canadian Institute of Health report, stating that 21 percent of all children in Canada under age 7 and 18 percent of those under age 18 live in poverty: "These living conditions result in a higher incidence of disease, hospitalization, and deaths due to injuries" (p. 112).
- Children who are poor are likely to be living in unhealthy environments that are beyond their control to change. Poverty usually means having food insecurity, living in housing that is often substandard (cold, damp, drafty, or crowded) and in unsafe areas, having inadequate clothing, and not having access to safe play and recreation opportunities (Pimento & Kernested, 2000).
- About 30 percent of women and young children living in poverty suffer from **anemia.** In these instances, family diet tends to be nutritionally inadequate.
- Though health care is available for all Canadian residents, and families in poverty are eligible for health-care services, they may not know how to, or be able to, obtain them. Therefore, women from these families may have more health-related complications during pregnancy, which can lead to developmental problems in their infants before, during, and following birth.
- Families living in poverty tend to be larger, with more unplanned pregnancies.
- Living space for those in poverty is usually smaller, and there are fewer play materials to promote learning and language development.
- Women living in poverty are often the sole support of the family. While mothers are at work (often in jobs paying the minimum wage), children are often cared for in substandard and unlicensed daycare homes or centres where learning opportunities and nurturing care are limited.
- "Between 1989 and 1994 the rate of child poverty in Canada climbed from 14.5 percent to 19.5 percent. Although the rate of infant mortality has decreased, children in poor neighbourhoods are still twice as likely to die as infants in non-poor neighbourhoods" (Canadian Council on Social Development, 1996). Furthermore, in their publication *The Determinants of Health,* Fraser Mustard and John Frank (1991) cite the research of David Barker, who notes the importance of the childhood environment in determining responses (intellectual and other) throughout life.

Anemia
a reduced number of red blood cells usually resulting from inadequate nutrition; often characterized by listlessness and pale appearance of the skin

Strategies and Ideas for Programming

Because of the range of differences in cognitive delays, there is no set "program" to recommend. However, the following general guidelines should be helpful:

- Break down tasks into small steps, focusing on one step at a time.
- Use repetition until a child accomplishes the desired response.
- Support the child's efforts by verbally reinforcing positive steps.
- Use a variety of resources, such as music, movement, and sensory materials, to support exploration and stimulate learning.

- Guide the child's actions, using hand over hand when appropriate.
- Support the child's involvement in music and movement by modelling or, when necessary, by sitting behind the child and guiding his or her arms, legs, and so on, with your own motions and touch.
- Work from simple to complex, and concrete to abstract, when teaching a new idea. Use physical or concrete examples whenever possible.
- In group games and activities, try to find a role that is developmentally appropriate and can enable a child with cognitive delays to participate actively with his or her classmates. This role might include distributing equipment, helping to rearrange furniture, erasing a blackboard, and so on.
- Use predictable schedules and routines. When changes are pending, try to prepare the child in advance.

While implementing the above recommendations, it is important to keep in mind the importance of inclusion, of enabling the child with a special need to participate in the ongoing curriculum and to be as much a part of it as possible.

Summary

In summary, for the purposes of this text, the term "cognitive delays" is used to refer to a continuum of cognitive differences, ranging from those children who have a mild delay to those who have a severe impairment in their cognitive functioning.

A cognitive delay may or may not be permanent, depending on the cause, level of severity, and the timing and effectiveness of intervention.

There are a range of factors that may influence the cognitive development of a child, including the following:

- Conditions that occur prenatally, usually caused by problems during the first trimester, as well as some conditions that may be caused by an as yet unidentified deviation in the child's genes or chromosomes
- Certain viral and bacterial infections, as well as parasitic organisms
- Environmental conditions affecting the diet and living environment of the mother or child or both

Programming for a child with a developmental delay must be based on individual needs and should be implemented in a way that supports the inclusion of the child within the preschool program of his or her class.

RESOURCES

CANADIAN ASSOCIATION FOR COMMUNITY LIVING
http://www.cacl.ca
The Canadian Association for Community Living offers a range of resources for information on developmental delays. This site also provides links to all the provincial and territorial chapters of the CACL.

ROEHER INSTITUTE
http://www.roeher.ca
The Roeher Institute is Canada's national organization for the study of policy affecting people with intellectual impairments.

INDEPENDENT LIFE RESOURCES
http://www.ilresources.com
This site provides a wide range of links to North American resources and organizations concerned with developmental delays.

DOWN SYNDROME ASSOCIATION OF TORONTO
http://www.dsat.ca
This site provides information and support to families who have children with Down syndrome.

STUDENT ACTIVITIES

1. Take a poll among the female members of your class to determine how many of them are protected against rubella. Consult your public health department for information on preventing prenatal infections.
2. Discuss with your mother your own birth and that of your brothers and sisters to determine the kinds of problems, if any, that she or the infants experienced. (Feel free to carry out this activity with any woman who has given birth and is willing to discuss the issues with you.)
3. Study a copy of your province's or territory's guidelines, regulations, or legislation for funding services to preschool children with cognitive delays. Chart your findings.
4. Serve as a discussion leader: Invite three or four other students to discuss, before the class, the issue of not labelling a young child as "cognitively delayed."
5. Make a listing of the kinds of services available in your community for pregnant teenage girls. Make a similar list of the services available for pregnant women with alcohol problems or drug-related problems.
6. Select the one best match for each item in column I from column II and place that letter in the appropriate space in column I.

	I		**II**
____	1. bacterial or viral infection	A.	maternal diet
____	2. mitosis	B.	lack of oxygen
____	3. amino acid	C.	Down syndrome
____	4. rubella	D.	Stanford-Binet
____	5. first trimester	E.	early gestation period
____	6. anoxia	F.	chromosome activity
____	7. chromosomal disorder	G.	condition present at birth
____	8. standardized IQ test	H.	phenylalanine
____	9. low-birthweight babies	I.	meningitis
____	10. congenital	J.	German measles

REFERENCES

American Association of Mental Retardation (AAMR). (1992). *Mental retardation* (4th ed.). Washington, DC: AAMR.

Bee, H. (1992). *The developing child.* New York: Holt, Rinehart & Winston.

Bliley, T. J. (1989). Born hooked: Confronting the impact of perinatal substance abuse. Opening statement at the Hearing before the Select Committee on Children, Youth, and Families. Washington, DC: U.S. Government Printing Office.

Canadian Council on Social Development. (1996). *Child poverty in Canada, report card 1996, Campaign 2000.* Toronto: Author.

Canadian Paediatric Society. (1996). *Well beings: A guide to promote the physical health, safety and emotional well-being of children in child care centres and family day care homes.* Toronto: Creative Premises.

Deiner, P. L., Dyke, L., & Hardacre, L. (1999). *Resources for educating young children with diverse abilities.* Toronto: Harcourt Brace, Canada.

Hanson, M. J., & Carta, J. J. (1996). Addressing the challenges of families with multiple risks. *Exceptional Children, 62*(3), 201–212.

Hittleman, J., Parekh, A., & Glass, L. (1987, April). *Developmental outcome of extremely low birth weight infants.* Paper presented at the biennial meeting of the Society for Research in Child Development, Baltimore.

Keith, L. G., MacGregor, S., Freidell, S., Rosner, M., Chasnoff, I. J., & Sciarra, J. J. (1989). Substance abuse in pregnant women: Recent experiences at the Perinatal Center for Chemical Dependence of Northwestern Memorial Hospital. *Obstetrics and Gynecology, 73,* 715–720.

Mustard, J. F., & Frank, J. (1991). *The determinants of health.* The Canadian Institute for Advanced Research, Population Health Publication #5, Toronto: Canadian Institute for Advanced Research, 1991.

Pimento, B., & Kernested, D. (2000). *Healthy foundations in child care.* Toronto: Nelson Thomson Learning.

Streissguth, A. P., Barr, H. M., & Sampson, P. D. (1990). Moderate prenatal alcohol exposure: Effects on child IQ and learning problems at age 7½ years. *Alcoholism: Clinical and Experimental Research, 14,* 662–669.

Zigler, E., & Hodapp, R. M. (1991). Behavioral functioning in individuals with mental retardation. *Annual Review of Psychology, 42,* 29–50.

CHAPTER 7

Advanced Cognitive and Developmental Abilities:

Children Who Are Gifted

KEY CONCEPTS

advanced psychomotor ability
emergent curriculum
environmental influences
genetic predisposition
gifted and have ADHD

giftedness
potentially gifted
precocious
special ability in art
special ability in music

OBJECTIVES

After studying the material in this chapter, the student will be able to

- Define giftedness in young children and explain the factors that contribute to giftedness.
- Identity the characteristics of young children who are gifted.
- Give reasons why potential giftedness and talents may not be identified in young children with disabilities and children from different cultural backgrounds.
- Develop programming strategies that support children who are gifted as well as all children in the class.

Introduction

Children who have advanced cognitive and developmental abilities are usually referred to as *gifted* or *talented*. These children demonstrate abilities that are advanced in one or more areas of development when compared with their peers of the same age, maintain this advanced state throughout their developmental years, and continue to outperform children of the same age and socioeconomic status. Other children neither catch up to them nor overtake them.

Preschool children who are gifted are often not recognized as requiring specialized individual programming. However, when specialized programming is not provided, these children may become bored and disinterested, at times creating behaviour challenges for their teachers. In the United States, some states now require the development of a formal Individual Education Plan (IEP) for children who are gifted, similar to that required for children with disabilities (Wolf, 1994). Unlike the United States, Canada does not have a formal identified process for evaluating giftedness in the preschool years.

Origins of Giftedness

What is the source of **giftedness,** especially when it takes the form of a high IQ and general intellectual competence? The child's **environmental influences** seem to be a major factor; however, of equal importance is the genetic makeup of the child. It is when a child with the **genetic predisposition** for giftedness enters an enriched environment that giftedness is more clearly identified and encouraged. In general, better-educated families are better off financially. This enables them to provide the daily, taken for granted enrichment that is a key element in their children's performance. Given two children with equal genetic endowment, the child in the enriched environment almost surely would be observed as and labelled as "brighter" than the poorly nourished child raised in a nonstimulating environment. In other words, giftedness, most likely, is a combination of "good genes" and a stimulating environment. Unfortunately, standard methods used to identify children who are gifted are often culture- and class-bound, and not sufficiently sensitive to recognize future performance potential.

Giftedness
evidence of superior or unusual ability in areas such as intellect, creativity, artistic talent, physical agility, or leadership

Environmental influences
the impact of environment on the development of the child

Genetic predisposition
a child is born with a genetic makeup that will enable him or her to function at an intellectually high level

Characteristics of Young Children Who Are Gifted and Talented

Precocious is a term often used to describe young children who appear to be remarkably bright or unusually verbal. Precocious children tend to demonstrate outstanding talents, far beyond what would be expected for their age. The precocity may show up in some specialized areas, such as painting or music or math. In the child who is truly gifted, the accomplishments seem to appear spontaneously, as a part of the child's own unique developmental process. They appear to occur without special training or parental pressure. It should be noted that some children are extremely bright—but not gifted (see Table 7–1, p. 122).

In general, the characteristics that identify young children who may be potentially gifted appear to be a combination of advanced verbal skills, high levels of curiosity, and the ability to concentrate and remember. Many children who are cognitively advanced also seem to learn rapidly and to enjoy problem solving. The following list

Precocious
the term used to describe young children who appear remarkably bright or unusually verbal and who may demonstrate outstanding talents in some specialized area, such as art, music, math

TABLE 7–1

CHARACTERISTICS OF A BRIGHT CHILD VERSUS A GIFTED LEARNER

Bright Child	Gifted Learner
Knows the answers.	Asks the questions.
Is interested.	Is highly curious.
Is attentive.	Is mentally and physically involved.
Has good ideas.	Has wild, silly ideas.
Works hard.	Plays around, yet tests well.
Answers the questions.	Discusses in detail, elaborates.
[Is at the] top [of the] group.	[Is] beyond the group.
Listens with interest.	Shows strong feelings and opinions.
Learns with ease.	Already knows.
[Needs] 6–8 repetitions for mastery.	[Needs] 1–2 repetitions for mastery.
Understands ideas.	Constructs abstractions.
Enjoys peers.	Prefers adults.
Grasps the meaning.	Draws inferences.
Completes assignments.	Initiates projects.
Is receptive.	Is intense.
Copies accurately.	Creates a new design.
Enjoys school.	Enjoys learning.
Absorbs information.	Manipulates information.
[Is a] technician.	[Is an] inventor.
[Is a] good memorizer.	[Is a] good guesser.
Enjoys straightforward, sequential presentation.	Thrives on complexity.
	Is keenly observant.
Is alert.	Is highly self-critical.
Is pleased with own learning.	

SOURCE: Characteristics of a Bright Child vs. a Gifted Learner by Janice Szabos, *Challenge 34.*

of specific clues to potential giftedness in a young child is adapted from Roedell, Jackson, and Robinson (1981) and Karnes and Johnson (1989).

The child who is **potentially gifted**

Potentially gifted refers to a child who has advanced vocabulary and oral language ability, understands abstract concepts, uses play materials in creative ways, catches on quickly to new ideas and concepts, memorizes easily, and has a long attention span

- has a large vocabulary that he or she uses appropriately, has an interest in words, and enjoys practising new words
- uses language to give suggestions, express ideas, pass on information, and ask content questions: "How did the fox know the baby rabbit was there?"
- uses metaphors and analogies: "The moss on the tree is like an old man's beard"
- makes up songs and stories, invents rhymes, plays with the sound and rhythm of words
- modifies his or her language to meet the comprehension level of younger children, and uses language to handle conflicts and aggression in play situations
- appears to understand abstract concepts, such as time, family relationships (that father can be both a husband and a brother), cause and effect (why the ice has melted), and connections between past and present experiences (Photo 7–1)
- uses blocks, play dough, or drawing materials to make interesting patterns; creates unusual and well-thought-out designs; thinks through the steps in what he or she is creating ahead of time

- demonstrates unusual speed in mastering new concepts, songs, and rhymes
- is able to follow easily the steps in a task (for example, replicating a boat or hat that a teacher has demonstrated how to make)
- maintains, over time, absorption in particular topics (for example, dinosaurs: pores over books and pictures about dinosaurs, memorizes their names and characteristics, learns to pronounce the difficult names)
- demonstrates complex classification and discrimination skills: spontaneously groups items, such as toy cars, boats, airplanes, and trucks; arranges objects according to size and colour
- is skilled in putting together new and difficult puzzles; appears to examine puzzle pieces first and then put them in place, rather than depending on trial and error
- seems to have good orientation skills and a sense of spatial relationships: has some idea of how to get back to school when on a walk, manoeuvres wheel toys so as to avoid obstacles, keeps to his or her own space during dance and rhythmic activities

Photo 7–1
Preplanning is one characteristic of children who are gifted.

- notices what is new and different in the environment (for example, rearrangement of equipment, a teacher's new hairstyle or new dress, a new drying rack)
- shows a sense of humour (tells about the new kitten falling in the fruit bowl), makes up jokes and riddles
- indicates awareness of the feelings of others, both children and adults; may comment when a teacher is not feeling well or another child appears withdrawn or especially happy

Needless to say, no child is likely to show all of these traits; many, however, will show two, three, or more, in various combinations. What is also important is to note the child's ability to

- process abstract concepts (for example, comprehending the humour in a situation or understanding the quantity that a numeral stands for)
- comprehend the consequences of actions
- solve problems (for example, how to make a series of blocks balance, how to fit the pieces of a difficult puzzle together)
- learn new songs quickly

- use a new toy, game, or computer program appropriately, with little learning time
- show curiosity in new situations, asking questions that show insight

Some children demonstrate special talent in a specific area, such as art, music, or psychomotor coordination. The following information, adapted from Saunders and Espeland's *Bringing Out the Best* (1991), identifies a number of behaviour patterns in children that may indicate special talents in these areas. By recognizing special talent or ability, a teacher of young children may be able to develop and provide appropriately challenging and stimulating learning opportunities, ones that can be enjoyed by all the children but that will enable the inclusion of those who are more advanced.

Special ability in art
an indication that a child may be potentially gifted in this area

Children who have **special ability in art**

- demonstrate eye–hand coordination that is developmentally advanced
- are able to include fine detail in pictures, clay, or play dough objects
- are able to remember and replicate detail in objects, pictures, and scenes they have seen
- recognize and respond to differences in textures and colours (hues and tones)
- show an interest in and respond to photos, paintings, and sculptures
- express their feelings, emotions, and moods in their drawings, paintings, and sculpted creations, such as in play dough, collages, and so on

Special ability in music
an indication that a child may be potentially gifted in this area

Children who have **special ability in music**

- often request and initiate music-related activities and show the ability to respond emotionally to different pieces or types of music
- can label the name of a familiar song from hearing the tune or beat
- can carry a tune when singing
- can sing in key with a song that is within their range
- can recognize the sounds of particular instruments within a group instrumental performance and can label the familiar instruments by name
- can dance, move, clap, and tap in time with music and rhythms
- can respond to poetry that has a rhythmical flow and rhyming words
- may spontaneously make up their own tunes, songs, or rhythmical chants

Advanced psychomotor ability
eye–hand or eye–foot coordination is at the level of a much older child, as found in some children who are gifted

Children with **advanced psychomotor ability**

- demonstrate a well-developed sense of balance: hopping; climbing on a jungle gym; showing early ability in gymnastics, skating, and so on
- show advanced abilities in sport-related activities: can throw and catch a ball, dribble a basketball, skate, and so on
- have advanced coordination as is evident in their running, jumping, climbing, and tumbling skills
- compete easily with older children in sport-related activities
- are able to create vigorous dances involving active coordinated movement: rolling, jumping, hopping, twisting, and so on

CHILDREN FROM MINORITY BACKGROUNDS WHO ARE GIFTED

Many of the characteristics of children who are recognized as gifted relate to high-level language skills. Bright children from minority cultures and different ethnic backgrounds often are not recognized because they lack the language skills of the dominant culture (Photo 7–2). This difference should never be interpreted to mean that a child has less potential. Rather, it is usually due to the fact that the child has had less opportunity to acquire sophisticated language. Often, the child's home-language skills, which are not observed, may be advanced (see Chapter 20).

In reviewing the work of a number of researchers, Karnes and Johnson (1989) note other influences that tend to work against the identification of preschoolers from minority backgrounds who may be gifted:

- having the attitude that giftedness does not exist among children from low-income backgrounds
- defining giftedness in ways that reflect only the majority culture's values
- using identification procedures that are unfavourable to children from low-income and minority groups (as will be discussed in Chapter 12)
- providing few environmental opportunities for enhancing intellectual or artistic achievement in children from a minority culture who are young and bright (no one can excel at anything without the opportunity to try)

Clearly, there are children who are gifted in every ethnic and racial group at all socioeconomic levels. Thus, early identification and appropriate preschool education for children without economic advantages is critical as a means of identifying and nurturing those with special gifts and talents (Stile & Kitano, 1991).

Photo 7–2
Children from different backgrounds often are not recognized as gifted because of the teachers' inability to understand the child's home language.

CHILDREN WITH DISABILITIES WHO ARE GIFTED AND/OR TALENTED

The fact that a child with a disability also may be a child who is gifted and/or talented is often overlooked (Photo 7–3, p. 126). For example, a child with a learning disability may have superior intelligence or outstanding artistic or mechanical talents. The same is true of children who are deaf, children with cerebral palsy, or those with almost any other kind of developmental disability. The potential for intellectual or artistic giftedness in these children seldom receives much attention. Educational emphasis and energy tends to be narrowly focused on helping children overcome physical or sensory "deficits." As Gallagher (1988) points out, rarely do we even search for potential giftedness in special populations.

Identifying children who are gifted among children with disabilities may be difficult. Conventional assessment instruments often fail to pick up on these children's strengths, let alone their giftedness. Wolfle (1989) suggests using direct observation in a natural setting as a valuable way of discovering the special talents that a child with special needs may have. The importance of this recommendation is borne out by the following story of a situation that occurred with a four-year-old in an inclusive preschool:

Benjamin, blind since birth, had developed a number of unusual and repetitive behaviours, typical of those that sometimes are observed in young children who cannot see. His

Photo 7–3
The special talents of a child with special needs often go unnoticed.

preschool teachers noted, however, that the strange behaviours stopped whenever there was music in the classroom. Benjamin appeared to listen intently and always asked for more. One teacher began sitting down with Benjamin with musical instruments. One time it was a ukulele, then an autoharp, another time a recorder. After a brief period of experimentation, Benjamin would "find" tunes he could play on any one of the instruments. Next the teacher took him to a classroom that had a piano. Again, with only limited exploration of the instrument, Benjamin began to improvise recognizable tunes. The teacher shared these experiences with Benjamin's parents, who were able to buy a piano. Benjamin spent hours at the piano and became an eager piano student. By the age of 16, he was regarded as a gifted young pianist.

Many young children with disabilities and sensory impairments have high potential for both intellectual and creative achievement. Attention needs to be directed toward these children in early childhood programs so that their curiosity and eagerness to learn are encouraged rather than allowed to wither. Karnes and Johnson (1987) argue that it is important to fund early intervention demonstration programs that focus on all young children who are gifted. These programs could provide training in identifying and nurturing the young gifted child from every socioeconomic level. With early intervention and appropriate learning opportunities, children from minority groups and children with all kinds of disabilities—like all other children who are gifted—could be helped to realize their potential.

Children who are **gifted and have ADHD** differ in cognitive, social, and emotional ways from children who are of average intelligence and have ADHD. Lovecky (1999) states that on intelligence and achievement tests, children who are gifted and have ADHD show a greater degree of inter- and intra-test variability, with greater amounts of scatter in their performance scores. They miss many easier items and are correct on much more difficult items. Children who are gifted and have ADHD, although deficient in many of the supporting work skills needed to succeed in

Gifted and have ADHD
unlike most children who are gifted, these children have trouble effectively using the strategies and skills they have, and their giftedness is not recognized

school (note taking, outlining, organization of ideas, writing skills), are often more proficient at learning things rapidly when compared with other same-aged peers with ADHD.

Furthermore, children who are gifted and have ADHD are more proficient in such things as grouping by category, using mnemonic devices, using recall of one thing to trigger another, and organizing by pattern or spatial characteristics. However, unlike most children who are gifted, children who are gifted and have ADHD have trouble effectively using these strategies. They know them and forget to use them. When they remember to use the strategies they know, their work is superior. As with many children who are gifted, children who are gifted and have ADHD are highly sensitive to both the external environment and their internal feelings. Because of the ADHD, children who are gifted and have ADHD can have more extreme reactions, because they do not have the emotional resilience to cope with fearful or upsetting situations (Lovecky, 1999).

Strategies for Supporting Young Children Who Are Gifted and/or Talented

It is important to *support* and *challenge* children who are gifted, while at the same time not draw attention in such a way as to give the children a false sense of importance or the message that they are expected always to achieve at the highest level. Too much "emphasis on success may result in children avoiding situations that may lead to failure" (Elkind, 1981).

We must not forget the importance of supporting *all* areas of the young child's development. It should not be assumed that advancement in one area of development (for example, cognitive or language skills) necessarily precludes the need for support in another (such as gross or fine motor abilities).

Yewchuk and Jobagy (1991), in an article about the importance of recognizing the emotional needs of children who are gifted, state:

> Pressure to succeed, personal expectations, emotional sensitivity, lack of support from parents and peers—all may have a detrimental effect on the emotional development of the gifted child. Educators are finally becoming aware of the advanced academic needs of the gifted child, and programming is finally taking place. What is now required is that teachers and counsellors become aware of the social and emotional needs of the gifted child, as these can have a profound effect on the academic ability of the child.

Recent research seems to indicate that *truly* gifted children develop best in an environment that *recognizes* and *responds* to their special needs. Thus, very young children who show an interest in ideas and concepts beyond those of other children the same age should be encouraged and given opportunities to explore and expand their particular area of interest. Providing greater access to libraries, museums, and computer programs may enable these children to find answers to their questions and motivate them to further inquiry. Children who excel in psychomotor, music, and creative art abilities may need challenging and varied opportunities for expanding their particular talent. The child care setting might provide obstacle courses, opportunities for creative dance, time for music improvisation, and materials for sculpting, constructing, and handicraft work. (For more extensive research information on children who are gifted and talented, see Klein & Tannenbaum, 1992.)

In our experience, the following techniques and methods have worked successfully with young gifted and/or talented children:

1. Observe *all* children, especially those with identified special needs, for their unique strengths, abilities, and talents.

2. Plan small-group activities that may require all children, including the child who is gifted, to work as a team and to help one another reach a shared goal—for example, a cooking activity that requires eye–hand coordination for pouring and stirring, physical strength for beating and mixing, intellectual ability for interpreting a recipe, social skills for sharing, and language skills for reporting. Through such activities as this, all children take part and support one another.

3. Make sure stimulating activities and materials are always available in the classroom. These may include
   - a terrarium-building activity
   - new tapes or CDs to listen to
   - a range of taped or recorded music and props for creative movement
   - tape recorders for children to use for their own compositions
   - computer programs that challenge creative thinking and problem solving, abilities that do not simply require "yes/no" or "right/wrong" answers, and do not preclude opportunities for the child to play interactively with other children
   - different types of creative art materials (frequently augmented and changed) that allow opportunities to explore colour, form, and texture
   - a range of different types of building blocks, unit blocks, Legos, and so on, that require balance, form spatial relations, and stimulate creative construction and play
   - new props that will stimulate creative role-playing—for example, new hats, makeup, jewellery, uniforms, and supplies for "community helper" play—as well as props that can be used to expand building projects: farm and forest animals, family figures, electrical (battery and bulb) hookups, and so on
   - opportunities for trips supported by specific preparation and follow-up: scrapbooking, drawing things they saw, and recording or writing (with teacher support) about the trip

Children who are gifted are creative thinkers and often make connections between what appear to be dissimilar topics or ideas. Therefore, it is important that teachers be responsive and follow the child's lead. Planning curriculum that builds on children's interests and involves them in developing and planning long-term projects is critical (Photo 7–4). It is often a good idea to begin by working with the children to draw a web of the knowledge that the children have, and then to set up a process for investigating new information, documenting the process and the children's findings with photographs,

Photo 7–4
Planning curriculum that builds on children's interests and involves them in developing and planning long-term projects is critical.

pictures, videos, audiotapes, and so on. Gestwicki (1999) refers to this kind of programming strategy as **emergent curriculum.**

4. Use volunteers who can provide unique learning experiences; often, they can help keep the gifted child intellectually stimulated and involved.

5. Help parents recognize ways in which they can support their child's abilities, interests, and talents. Teachers might suggest
   • trips to exhibits, museums, street festivals, and building sites
   • hands-on experiences, such as fixing broken things, creating three-dimensional structures, and exploring new media

   As Wolfle (1989) points out, "The gifted child is a child who should be treated like a child. . . . Like their peers, [gifted children] love drawing, going on field trips, playing in the housekeeping area, but [they] seem to want to delve into everything deeper." For this reason, it is important for teachers to provide time, often over a number of days or weeks, for children to fully explore and expand on their interests and projects.

6. Develop interesting and enriching special program opportunities—for example, arranging for visitors with special skills (musicians, scientists, artists/sculptors, chefs, tailors, etc.), taking trips to interesting places and events, and locating people who will donate time or materials that will enhance learning opportunities for the whole class. Be sure to call on the children's parents for contributions. Kitano (1989) stresses that "offering learning activities at a range of levels hurts no one and helps gifted children, as well as many others." She urges teachers to be flexible and offer choices that will appeal to all children.

7. Provide specific guidance to the children to help them pursue and expand on special interests. Teachers might try to find times in which they can cluster children who share similar interests and who are able to do more extensive work on a specific interest or group project. Teachers can then guide them in how to do basic research to find answers to their questions, challenge them with new and interesting questions and ideas, and give them opportunities to discuss their insights.

In conclusion, when programming for young children, it is important to support the development needs of all the children in the group. The breadth of needs that teachers must accommodate varies from group to group. The process of inclusion, whether it is with a child who is developmentally delayed, has specific physical needs, or is developmentally accelerated in one or more areas, challenges the teacher to plan program and learning opportunities in which all the children can participate and from which all can benefit. The teacher should work to facilitate the inclusion of the child who is cognitively and developmentally advanced as a member of his or her peer group. Teachers need to be flexible and willing to consider and respond to the questions and observations of the children in their group, especially those of young children who are cognitively advanced and who may need more pervasive challenges and cognitive stimulation.

Emergent curriculum curriculum that is developed from a variety of sources, including children's play activities and questions, and that is personally meaningful, intellectually engaging, and socially relevant

Summary

Young children who are gifted and/or talented are those with exceptionally advanced skills in one or more areas of development. Characteristics that identify young potentially gifted children are a combination of advanced verbal skills, high levels of curiosity, and the ability to concentrate and remember. Many potentially gifted children from culturally different backgrounds and low-income families are not identified because of restricted learning opportunities and culturally biased identification procedures. Many children with developmental disabilities are gifted; however, their potential often goes unrecognized because of the focus placed on overcoming their deficit areas.

It is of prime importance that teachers plan daily programs that meet the needs of all the children in their group, providing a broad range and variety of intellectually challenging and creative opportunities for play and learning.

RESOURCES

ALBERTA ASSOCIATION FOR BRIGHT CHILDREN
http://www.albertaabc.org
This organization provides information and advocacy for gifted and talented children, their families, and their teachers.

GIFTED EDUCATION IN ALBERTA
http://www.educ.ucalgary.ca/altagift
This site provides resources and links to information on gifted education programs.

ASSOCIATION FOR BRIGHT CHILDREN OF ONTARIO
http://www.abcontario.ca/
Numerous links and resources on gifted and talented children are available at this site.

CENTRE FOR GIFTED EDUCATION (CANADA)
http://www.ucalgary.ca/~gifteduc
This site provides relevant information on academic programs and school services for gifted and talented children.

GIFTED DEVELOPMENT CENTER (DENVER, COLORADO)
http://www.gifteddevelopment.com
A great deal of statistical data is available at this American website.

THE NATIONAL FOUNDATION FOR GIFTED AND CREATIVE CHILDREN
http://www.nfgcc.org
This is another good American website for finding data about gifted children.

STUDENT ACTIVITIES

1. Contact your provincial, territorial, or local association for bright (or gifted) children. Find out what types of programs and resources this association offers.
2. Meet with a parent of a child who has been identified as gifted. Ask the parent to describe the skills and abilities that the child demonstrated when he or she was young. Indicate how this child was different from his or her playmates.

3. Observe a group of preschool children. List any instances of behaviour that you feel are signs of potential giftedness. Discuss your observations with the classroom teacher.

4. Have you or one of your brothers, sisters, or friends been described as gifted or talented? Describe the exceptional characteristics that led to such a label.

5. Contact your local association for learning disabilities to find out how they would identify children who are gifted or talented within the population they serve.

REFERENCES

Elkind, D. (1981). *The hurried child*. Reading, MA: Addison-Wesley.

Gallagher, J. J. (1988). National agenda for educating gifted students: statement of priorities. *Exceptional Children, 55*(2), 107–114.

Gestwicki, C. (1999). *Developmentally appropriate practice, curriculum in early education* (2nd ed.). New York: Delmar.

Karnes, M., & Johnson, L. (1987). An imperative: programming for the young gifted/talented. *Journal for the Education of the Gifted, 10*(3), 195–214.

Karnes, M., & Johnson, L. (1989). Training for staff, parents and volunteers working with gifted young children, especially those with disabilities and from low-income homes. *Young Children, 44*(3), 49–56.

Kitano, M. K. (1989). The K–3 teacher's role in recognizing and supporting young gifted children. *Young Children, 44*(3), 57–63.

Klein, P., & Tannenbaum, A. (1992). *To be young and gifted*. Norwood, NJ: Ablex.

Lovecky, D. V. (1999). *Gifted children with AD/HD*. Providence, RI: Gifted Resource Center of New England.

Roedell, W. C., Jackson, N. E., & Robinson, H. B. (1980). *Gifted young children*. New York: Teachers College Press.

Saunders, J., & Espeland, P. (1991). *Bringing out the best: A resource guide for parents of young and gifted children*. Minneapolis, MN: Free Spirit Publishing.

Stile, S., & Kitano, M. (1991). Preschool-age gifted children. *DEC Communicator, 17*(3), 4.

Szabos, J. (1989). Bright child, gifted learner. *Challenge, 34.*

Wolf, J. S. (1994). The gifted and talented. In N. G. Haring, L. McCormick, & T. G. Haring (Eds.), *Exceptional children and youth* (pp. 456–500). New York: Merrill.

Wolfle, J. (1989). The gifted preschooler: Developmentally different, but still 3 or 4 year olds. *Young Children, 44*(3), 41–48.

Yewchuk, C., & Jobagy, S. (1991). The neglected minority: The emotional needs of gifted children. *Education Canada,* Winter.

CHAPTER 8

Sensory Impairments:

Vision and Hearing

KEY CONCEPTS

amplification device
auditory brainstem response (ABR)
auditory nerve
cochlea
cochlear implant
conductive hearing loss
cortical/cerebral visual impairment
deaf
earmould
intermittent hearing loss
multisensory deprived (MSD)
occlusion
peripheral vision

postlingual hearing loss
prelingual hearing loss
preorientation and mobility skills
refractive errors
residual hearing
residual vision
sensorineural hearing loss
sensory impairments
signing
speech reading
strabismus
total communication
visual acuity problems

OBJECTIVES

After studying the material in this chapter, the student will be able to

- Discuss hearing and vision impairments and their impact on the development of young children.
- Identify warning signs indicating an infant may have a hearing loss.
- Identify signs of a possible hearing loss for a child with language.
- Indicate some strategies useful in helping a child make the transition into an inclusive program.
- Discuss the possible effects of a visual impairment on a child's language, cognitive, motor, and social development.
- Describe strategies that teachers may use in preschool activities to facilitate the learning of children with visual impairments who are in an inclusive environment.

Introduction

From the moment of birth, almost everything that children learn about themselves and their world comes through their five senses—hearing, vision, touch, taste, and smell. In healthy newborns, the five senses are functioning from birth. Every aspect of development depends on these systems being in good working order. The most serious and most prevalent **sensory impairments** are hearing and vision losses. Most of what infants and children are expected to learn is acquired through these two senses. A child who is both blind and deaf (also referred to as **multisensory deprived** or **MSD**) is at extreme developmental risk (Malatchi, 1995).

The normal activity level of an early childhood program may be both confusing and frightening for children with MSD. For successful inclusion to occur, highly specialized support services and teaching staff may be necessary.

A hearing loss almost always has an impact on language acquisition (Photo 8–1). This, in turn, often has an effect on cognitive functioning. Cognitive learning, after the first year-and-a-half of age (regardless of the potential level of intelligence), is tied closely to both receptive and expressive language. As noted in earlier chapters, development of cognitive skills is nearly inseparable from development of language skills.

Children who are blind learn language with considerably less difficulty than do children who are deaf. Children who are blind can benefit from the many incidental learning opportunities available every day. They hear environmental sounds, footsteps, doors closing, and other sounds that, when tied to the child's concrete experiences, provide the basis for cognitive insight. All of this gives children who are blind a greater potential for academic success. Because of the far-reaching influence of language in forming and maintaining relationships, children who are blind may have more options for social learning than do children who are deaf.

Infants and young children with severe hearing or vision impairments require teachers and support people who are trained to meet their special needs. Sometimes this special care may be necessary in an intensive, highly specialized program. Other times, a regular early childhood centre, supported by specialized intervention, may meet the child's needs. The developmental needs of children who are blind or deaf are the same as those for all children. Therefore, it is important to try, whenever possible, to ensure that they are in inclusive early childhood programs and are involved in all the social, physical, and cognitive experiences available.

Sensory impairments
difficulties in the ability to sense the environment through a specific sensory modality, such as hearing or sight

Multisensory deprived (MSD)
refers to a child who is both blind and deaf

Photo 8–1
A hearing loss almost always has an effect on language acquisition.

Causes of Hearing Impairments

Hearing impairments may be caused by prenatal, perinatal, or postnatal factors. Prenatal causes include those that are genetic in origin, as well as viral infections the mother experienced during the first trimester of pregnancy, such as rubella. Perinatal (at birth) causes are mainly due to a lack of oxygen at birth. Postnatal causes of hearing deficits include accidents, prolonged high fevers, measles, rubella, mumps, meningitis, and, sometimes, reactions to medication. Injuries that affect the ear drum, ear and sinus infections, and any other circumstances that result in blockage of the eustachian tubes also cause impairment to hearing. Fluid buildup in the middle ear is a major cause of temporary hearing loss.

Definitions and Types of Deafness and Hearing Loss

The Canadian Hearing Society (MacKenzie, 1999, p. 15) defines hearing loss as follows:

- *Congenital:* A hearing loss occurring before or at birth.
- *Prelingual:* A hearing loss occurring before speech and spoken language have been acquired.
- *Unilateral:* A hearing loss involving one ear.
- *Bilateral:* A hearing loss involving both ears.
- *Conductive:* Loss of hearing sensitivity caused by the inability of sound to pass from the outer ear and through the middle ear. Common causes of conductive losses are holes in the ear drum, an infection in the middle ear, a buildup of ear wax, problems with the three little bones in the middle ear, atresia, and stenosis. Many of these problems can be treated by medication or surgery, and hearing can be restored.
- *Sensorineural:* A loss of hearing sensitivity caused by damage to the hair cells in the inner ear or along nerve pathways to the brain. This results in permanent loss.

Children with hearing impairments may also be classified in two ways, as deaf or as hard-of-hearing. Children who are **deaf** are those whose hearing loss is so severe that they cannot process spoken language even with hearing aids or other amplification devices. Children who are classified as *hard-of-hearing* have a lesser loss but enough to have a definite effect on their social, cognitive, and language development.

Hearing losses may be thought of as **prelingual** (occurring before speech and language have had a chance to develop) and **postlingual** (occurring after the onset of language). Lowenbraun and Thompson (1994) corroborate that children with a prelingual loss have greater difficulties in all areas of development throughout their growing-up years. The impact on development is greatest when a hearing loss is *congenital*—that is, the infant is born with little or no hearing. Generally speaking, there are fewer developmental consequences when the hearing loss occurs *after* the child has begun to learn language.

Types of Hearing Loss

Hearing losses are categorized in various ways, through various kinds of assessments. To ensure valid results, both screening and testing should be done by audiologists who are specially trained to work with infants and young children. The results of hearing tests usually are plotted on what is called an audiogram. A hearing loss is classified according to where the loss occurs:

- Problems in the outer or middle ear produce a **conductive hearing loss.**
- Problems in the inner ear (in the **cochlea** or the **auditory nerve**) produce a **sensorineural hearing loss.**
- Problems in the higher auditory cortex produce central deafness.
- A combined loss involves two or more of the above.

In most instances, a conductive hearing loss interferes with audibility, not understanding. If the sound is loud enough to be heard, the child can understand the message. In many instances, this type of loss can be corrected or greatly reduced with appropriate medical treatment.

Deaf
having a hearing loss so severe that the individual cannot process spoken language even with amplification

Prelingual hearing loss
hearing loss occurring before the child has acquired speech

Postlingual hearing loss
hearing loss occurring after the child has acquired speech

Conductive hearing loss
refers to problems in the mechanical transmission of sounds through the outer or middle ear, which in turn reduce the intensity of sound vibrations reaching the auditory nerve in the inner ear

Cochlea
a snail-shaped structure in the inner ear that allows hearing to occur

Auditory nerve
the nerve along which the sensory cells (the hair cells) of the inner ear transmit information to the brain

Sensorineural hearing loss
a hearing loss that involves a malfunctioning of the cochlea or auditory nerve

A young child with chronic ear infections, such as *otitis media,* may suffer a hearing loss that comes and goes a number of times in the course of a year, as the infection flares up and clears up. These infections often cause a buildup of fluid, which leads to what is called an **intermittent hearing loss.** Because of reoccurring hearing losses, children's language development and learning abilities may be delayed. Once the infection is cleared up permanently, language is likely to improve. It is important to observe children closely and impress on the parents the importance of seeking medical treatment if the condition persists, in order to prevent long-term developmental delays. It should be remembered that even after an ear infection has been eliminated, residual fluid may remain, resulting in distorted hearing.

Intermittent hearing loss
hearing comes and goes because of a buildup of fluid caused by repeated ear infections

Identifying an intermittent hearing loss is difficult. The condition is often missed entirely in routine screening tests because the child is hearing adequately and therefore responding appropriately at the time of testing. These children may be diagnosed as having speech problems or categorized as having a learning disability. On careful study of their health records, most of the children have histories of chronic otitis media, yet the resulting hearing loss *was not identified* in general screening procedures. Recently, some schools have begun providing screening programs that check for both conductive hearing loss and sensorineural hearing loss. This testing has been effective in identifying hearing loss (Roeser, 2000). Once a hearing loss is identified, it is important that the child is immediately referred for further diagnosis and appropriate treatment.

Unlike conductive hearing problems, sensorineural and central deafness do not respond readily to medical intervention. Sensorineural hearing losses can cause inaudibility and sound distortion. With a sensorineural loss, even if sound is made loud enough to be heard, the child may still have difficulty understanding speech. A child whose loss is too severe to be helped by a hearing aid may benefit from a cochlear implant (Discolo & Hirose, 2002).

WARNING SIGNS

Soon after birth, most infants make a variety of responses to various noises. The whole body may move in a *startle response,* eyes may blink, or a rapid increase in sucking may occur. At about three to four months, infants begin to *localize*—that is, turn their heads in the direction of sounds. Over the next several months, they get better and better at localizing. Early use of hearing becomes refined to the point that infants can discriminate among voices and indicate a preference for their mother's voice, as contrasted to that of a stranger (Allen & Marotz, 2003).

When infants do not make such responses, hearing loss is a definite possibility. However, all infants make so many random movements that the infant who is hearing impaired may be difficult to identify. Furthermore, if the infant has some **residual hearing,** the loss may be all the more difficult to identify. This infant may be hearing just enough to be able to respond appropriately *some of the time,* giving the appearance of normal hearing. Another complication is that even infants who are profoundly deaf babble, at least for a while. It is interesting to note that studies have found that infants who are deaf and who are exposed to sign language also babble—with their hands (Petitto & Maramette, 1991).

Residual hearing
the degree of hearing of a person who is deaf or hearing impaired

Though hearing losses are one of the most common disabilities present at birth, they are often not detected until a child is between one and three years old (Mason &

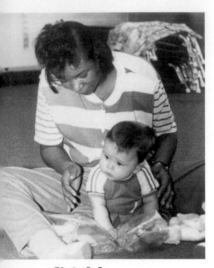

Photo 8–2
Teachers and caregivers are in a strategic position to note possible hearing problems.

Amplification device
devices, such as hearing aids, that make sound louder and clearer for a child with a hearing impairment

Herrmann, 1998). Parents are usually the first to sense that *something* is wrong, but they may not suspect a hearing loss. Physicians and health-care workers are often slow to diagnose a hearing impairment—yet the earlier an impairment is detected, the earlier intervention can begin. Early intervention and appropriate treatment can minimize the negative effects of hearing loss on all aspects of a child's development. It is now possible to screen hearing shortly after birth, using an automated auditory brainstem response measurement (Mason & Hermann, 1998).

Infant caregivers and early childhood teachers are in a strategic position to notice possible hearing impairments and risk conditions (Photo 8–2). Persistent ear infections, discharge from the ears, or constant poking or pulling at the ears often indicate a possible impairment. If a parent or teacher suspects a hearing loss, it should be checked by a medical specialist immediately. The earlier a hearing deficit is recognized, the earlier the child can be treated and, if need be, fitted with **amplification devices** (hearing aids). It should be emphasized that most children with hearing impairments have some residual hearing. To maximize the use of residual hearing for future language development, it is important that intervention by a trained specialist occur as early as possible. Remember, it is only when the child begins to hear, or to learn to use whatever residual hearing he or she has, that speech will begin to develop.

Children with a conductive hearing loss may drop certain initial consonants (the ones that are described as voiceless: p, h, s, f). They simply do not hear these sounds and so they do not reproduce them. With sensorineural hearing loss, a marked delay in speech and language development is a major warning sign.

With children who have acquired some language, teachers need to be alert to a child who displays these behaviours:

- does not respond when spoken to
- does not understand, or looks puzzled, when addressed directly with a simple question or request
- cocks his or her head to one side, studies the speaker's face, or watches the speaker's mouth
- asks for frequent repetitions ("Huh?" "What?")
- turns one ear to the source of sound or speech
- seems overly shy, avoids children and teachers
- is inattentive
- makes inconsistent or irrelevant responses
- complains of ringing or buzzing in the ears
- has an articulation or voice-quality problem
- speaks too loudly or too softly

Further signs of a potential hearing impairment are shown by a child who

- has a speech delay or slow response to usual sounds
- does not participate or concentrate or both during activities based on speech (for example, story time, show-and-tell), especially if the child is not directly facing the speaker
- persistently withdraws from the other children and is moody
- has an unexplained personality change, especially during a cold or following an ear infection
- always wants the radio, TV, or tape or CD player on high volume
- pulls at his or her ear(s)

When teachers become aware of a possible hearing loss, the first step is to speak with parents about seeking clinical help. Because any degree of hearing loss has an impact on speech and language development, early detection is extremely important. For this reason, it is also a good idea to have annual screening of every child's hearing.

AUDITORY BRAINSTEM RESPONSE (ABR)

A frequently used procedure called **auditory brainstem response (ABR)** is now being used effectively to provide an objective measure of the degree of hearing in infants and young children suspected of hearing impairment. This procedure involves placing surface electrodes on the child's forehead, as far back as the ear. It is most effective in determining high-frequency impairment. Whereas other screening devices require a child to respond to stimuli, this process, by monitoring involuntary brain activity, is independent of the child's participation and is, therefore, extremely useful in identifying high-frequency hearing deficits in infants and preverbal children.

Auditory brainstem response (ABR)
a procedure that measures the brain's response to high-frequency sound

THE IMPACT OF HEARING LOSS

"All hearing losses are serious" (Cook & Klein, 2004). The cumulative effects of a severe hearing loss on children's cognitive, social, and language development are clearly evident. Many children who are deaf are educationally delayed as much as three to five years. In addition, many have significant social and behavioural problems. As children who have hearing impairments grow older, some fall even further behind due to the increasing complexity of school and community expectations.

Later developmental delays in children with impaired hearing may be related to restricted play opportunities during the early years (Photo 8–3). Play skills seem to

Photo 8–3
Hearing problems often restrict children's play opportunities.

develop quite normally up until about two years of age. At this point, hearing children begin to use words symbolically. They begin to attach words to play materials and activities.

Effects on Language Development

The most serious and far-reaching effect of a hearing impairment is on early speech and language development. Language acquisition appears to be tied to certain periods in a child's development (the *critical period* idea, as discussed in Chapter 1). According to this theory, a child who cannot hear sounds and verbal stimulation at certain points in development may never fully master language. Inadequate auditory input during early development almost always leads to serious delays in language acquisition and in speech production. Faulty early language development may also be caused by a lack of responsiveness from family and teachers. Unwittingly, they may fall into the habit of not talking to the young child who has impaired hearing. It is easy to see how this happens. The child's range of responses is limited, thus providing inadequate feedback for family and friends. Consequently, the child's language skills become even more delayed.

Effects on Cognitive Development

Once the typically developing child is beyond the sensorimotor stage, cognitive skills, as mentioned at the outset, become inseparably intertwined with language skills. In turn, language skills (including the ability to communicate thoughts) continue to be inseparably related to adequate hearing. Thus, children with hearing loss often perform less effectively than do hearing children when it comes to cognitive activities. As noted earlier, many children with severe hearing impairments are often several years behind in their education. Their educational delay, however, is seldom due to poor cognitive potential. Usually, the cause is the inadequate auditory input; in other words, the child has been denied a major channel for cognitive development.

Effects on Social Development

Children with hearing impairments often experience some degree of social isolation in a hearing world. They may begin to be left out of things, even within the family, at a very early age. The child with a hearing impairment may be in the room where a family activity is going on, but nevertheless, he or she is often unintentionally excluded, for a very simple reason: The child is not able to enter into the verbal give-and-take and so has no way of figuring out what is going on. Unless someone takes responsibility for helping the child understand everyday family and school events (Photo 8–4), the child will often remain a passive and silent observer. Poor communication between the child and others frequently leads to social adjustment difficulties. Reports of impulsivity, aggressiveness, or low self-esteem begin during the preschool years. This social immaturity may increase with age as communication demands increase (Martin & Clark, 1996).

As they get older, many children with severe hearing deficits tend to be less mature socially. Often they have a low frustration threshold. This may be related to an earlier inability to make their preferences known. At times, children with hearing impairments also may seem to be uncaring and unaware of the needs and feelings of others. It is unlikely that they are truly indifferent. It is more likely that they have not heard, and therefore not learned, the language of sympathizing, a language that most young children acquire almost spontaneously.

Photo 8–4
Someone needs to help the child who has a hearing impairment to understand everyday family and school events.

Effects on Family Life

Having a child with a hearing loss can dramatically change the tenor of family life. The more severe the loss, the greater the impact. A young child's inability to accurately process the communicative efforts of others makes it frustrating and difficult for family members, especially when they have to establish behaviour limits for the child (Steinberg & Knightly, 1997). It is also challenging for families to spend the time and effort required to carry out the recommended intervention procedures that will help the child learn to function in a hearing world. Families often need a great deal of support, including behaviour management and family therapy, to help them to adapt to their child's deafness (Greenberg & Kusche, 1993).

Methods of Communication

With the help of a trained teacher of the deaf, children with hearing impairments, even those with a severe loss of hearing, can be taught to speak and to understand speech. In recent years, more and more infants and toddlers have been fitted with special hearing aids as soon as their impairment is identified.

Once a hearing loss is identified, the child, regardless of age, immediately should be fitted for hearing aids and other equipment that will maximize the use of any residual hearing. (This may also involve having the child's teachers and caregivers wear special microphones that enhance the sound the child receives through his or her hearing aid.) Speech will begin to develop spontaneously only at the point when a child hears and makes sense out of what he or she hears. It has been found that many children learn by lip reading, more accurately called **speech reading.** They learn to read what another individual is saying by watching his or her face, mouth, tongue, and throat movements. Other forms of communication are also available to children who are hearing impaired. McCormick and Schiefelbusch (1990) describe the various systems as follows:

Speech reading
the more accurate term for lip-reading

Total communication
a system for teaching children who have severe hearing impairments that combines speech reading and a sign system

- *American Sign Language* (ASL) is the language of the majority of deaf people in the United States and Canada. It is a language with its own words and grammar.
- *Signed English* is a sign language that parallels the English language. For every word there is a sign. Word order is the same as in spoken English.
- *Finger spelling* is a system made up of an alphabet of 26 hand-formed letters that correspond to the regular alphabet. One hand is held in front of the chest and the other hand spells out the words, letter by letter.
- *Total (or simultaneous) communication* is, as the name implies, a system in which communication combines both speech and a sign system (Photo 8–5).
- *Informal systems* include pantomime, gestures, and body movements that accompany speech and are used naturally by most speakers. Amer-Ind, or American Indian Hand Talk (Skelly & Schinsky, 1979), is a more formalized system that nevertheless is flexible and free of grammatical complications.

Photo 8–5
Total communication is a system that combines both speech and a sign system.

Signing
manual communication systems
such as finger-spelling or ASL
(American Sign Language)

Which Method?

There is a longstanding controversy concerning which system to use in teaching language to a young child. Questions include the following: Is there a best way? Should the child be held to oral communication exclusively and allowed to do no **signing** of any kind? Is a combination method, such as total communication, the most effective? The total communication approach is favoured by those who have studied families in which there are hearing impairments. Each method has its own philosophy, methodology, and expectations (Martin & Clark, 1996). Many professionals have formed particular biases, but there is no definitive research that shows that one method of training is distinctly superior to any other.

One thing to consider is the fact that sign language is the primary form of communication when people with minimal or no hearing want to communicate with one another.

The final decision about signing, speaking, or combining the two must be made by the parents. Teachers need to accept the parents' decision and work with them and with specialists to provide the child with the best learning environment possible.

Early Intervention with Children with Hearing Impairments

The importance of early language stimulation and training for infants and young children who are hearing impaired cannot be overemphasized. Language deficits among older children with hearing impairments may be the result of failure to begin language learning activities during the infant and toddler years. The longer the delay in starting language intervention, the less likely it is that the child will develop fully functional language skills. Without preventive measures, even a mild hearing loss can result in a permanent loss in language ability.

Guidelines for Teachers

Throughout the years, early childhood teachers have worked successfully with children with hearing impairments. Effective programming usually incorporates the skills of a specially trained early childhood consultant for the hearing impaired. The specialist should assist both teachers and parents in providing children who have hearing impairments with an education tailored to their special hearing loss. The following guidelines from specialists are often recommended for working with children with hearing impairments:

1. Sit, kneel, or bend down to the child's level to talk. Look directly at the child when talking or communicating with him or her. Children with hearing impairments need to be talked to face to face.
2. Talk in a normal voice. Avoid an overly loud voice and do not overenunciate. Overenunciation makes speech reading difficult.
3. Use a clear voice and talk at a slightly slower pace.
4. Use gestures when appropriate, but avoid overgesturing. Too many gestures interfere with the child's efforts to speech read.
5. Use brief, but complete, sentences when the child who is hearing impaired has reached that stage of language development. As with hearing children, *holophrastic* and *telegraphic* language (Chapter 18) belong to particular stages of language development.

6. Always try to seat the child directly across from the teacher. This gives the child the best possible position for speech reading.

7. Face the light when talking to a child who has a hearing impairment. The light needs to be on the speaker's face, not on the child's. Glaring light in the child's eyes interferes with bringing the speaker's face and mouth into full focus.

8. To get the child's attention, gently touch or tap a child on the shoulder or hand. Always be aware of the possibility of startling a person who does not hear.

9. When talking about something in the room, point to it, touch it, hold it up. (If the teacher picks up the scissors and demonstrates the cutting task while giving the instructions, the child has a better chance of understanding what is expected.)

10. Include children who are hearing impaired in all music activities. Provide many opportunities for them to participate by
    • putting their hands on various instruments so they can feel the vibrations
    • allowing them to play the instruments
    • having frequent rhythmic activities, such as clapping, jumping, rolling, and twirling
    • pairing a child who has normal hearing with a child who is hearing impaired for various musical games

11. Involve children with hearing impairments in story time. Choose books with bright, clear pictures that tell the story. Gesture when telling the story, and use facial expressions that give clues to the moods in the story.

12. Keep to a regular schedule of activities each day. To feel secure, young children, and especially children with hearing impairments (who often do not pick up on environmental signals), need to know what comes next.

13. Some children with impaired hearing make strange noises. They do not hear themselves but the noises often bother other children. Teachers must find subtle ways to help these children be quiet when necessary (perhaps gently putting a finger on the child's lips, and on the teacher's, in a "sh" gesture).

14. When a manual interpreter is present (unusual in an early childhood setting), allow the child who is hearing impaired and the interpreter to choose the most favourable seating.

Though many of the preceding guidelines focus on the child who has a hearing impairment, the early childhood teacher should constantly be working toward full inclusion—planning for group activities that will enable the full and equal participation of *all* children. Special adaptations can and should be planned, if necessary, so that a child who has a disability can participate in group activities as fully as he or she is able.

Amplification Devices (Hearing Aids)

Electronic hearing aids are a great help, especially for people with a conductive hearing loss. A hearing aid has three basic parts: a microphone, an amplifier, and a receiver (Figure 8–1, p. 142). Most young children are fitted with hearing aids that are placed on the bone directly behind the ear or inserted into the ear canal. In most cases, plastic tubing carries the amplified sound to an **earmould** made especially for each child.

Earmould
that part of an amplification device (hearing aid) that is fitted to the individual's ear

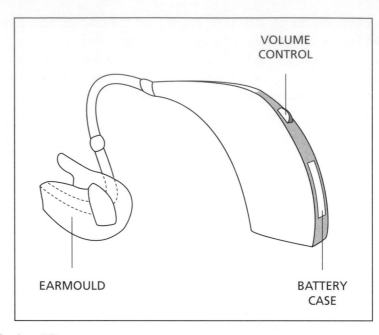

VOLUME
CONTROL

EARMOULD

BATTERY
CASE

Figure 8–1   Hearing aid that fits behind the ear

In spite of the great benefits of hearing aids, problems occur. The fact that a child is wearing a hearing aid does not guarantee that the child is hearing. Teachers and parents need to be aware of possible minor breakdowns in the system:

- *Improperly fitting or damaged earmould.* If the earmould does not fit properly, it can cause irritation and discomfort. The same holds true if the earmould becomes chipped or cracked. A cracked or poorly fitted earmould also can make a squealing feedback sound, which can be extremely annoying.
- *Feedback.* This irritating, high-pitched squealing sound can be caused by an earmould that is cracked or improperly seated in the ear.
- *Dead or feeble batteries.* Batteries die with amazing frequency. Teachers and parents should know when batteries are dead because the child will stop responding. However, batteries should be replaced well before they are dead so that children do not have to cope with periods of diminishing sound.
- *Switched-off device.* Teachers must check regularly to make sure a child's hearing aid is turned on. Young children tend to turn the devices off, sometimes repeatedly. This happens most frequently when they are first learning to wear their aid. Eventually, most children become accustomed to wearing the device and leave it turned on all the time. At this point, children can begin to check its working order for themselves. Nevertheless, adults should continue to spot-check at least once a day (Photo 8–6).
- *Sore ears.* The earmould should never be inserted into a sore, cracked, or infected ear. At the first sign of irritation, the child should see a health-care provider.

Photo 8–6
Teachers should check children's hearing aids at least once a day, more often with young children.

FM SYSTEMS

Many children can use an additional amplifying system that helps reduce background noise. These devices work like miniature radio stations. They can be connected directly to hearing aids, or the child may wear a small plastic neckloop. Teachers clip a microphone and transmitter to their clothing and transmit their voices directly to the receiver, which is worn by the child.

Because so many things can go wrong with hearing aids and FM systems, it is important that teachers, in conjunction with parents, make sure that all hearing devices are tested on a daily basis. They should receive special instructions from an audiologist on how to examine the devices to make sure that they are functioning properly.

COCHLEAR IMPLANT

With **cochlear implants** an electrode (computerized device) is surgically inserted into the inner ear (cochlear). Cochlear implants are expensive, but they appear to be the most effective means of bringing some form of hearing to children who have a profound hearing loss because of damage to the cochlea and who are unable to benefit from the use of other hearing devices. A cochlear implant bypasses the damaged hair cells in the inner ear and directly stimulates the auditory nerve (National Institute on Deafness and Other Communication Disorders, 2002).

Cochlear implants can now be used in children under a year old. Children who are deaf at birth are the best candidates for early implantation. The earlier the implanting of the device takes place, the sooner some form of hearing is experienced and the less delayed the child's language, socialization, and cognitive development are likely to be (Tanner, 2004).

In conclusion, whether a child has a cochlear implant or is prescribed hearing aids, it is important to remember that the earlier some form of remediation takes place, the earlier the child will begin to develop language.

Cochlear implant
a device, surgically placed by opening the mastoid structure of the skull, that allows electrical impulses (sound) to be carried directly to the brain

Blindness and Vision Impairments

TYPES OF VISION IMPAIRMENTS

Vision impairments vary as to cause, type, and severity. They are usually grouped in terms of physical abnormalities, visual acuity, and muscular imbalances. (For definitions see Chapter 5.)

Physical Abnormalities

Physical problems resulting in impaired vision are fairly common. These may develop prenatally, or the damage can occur at birth or any time thereafter. The cause may be diseases, such as maternal rubella, inherited disorders, injury, or drugs taken by the mother during pregnancy. Even some medically prescribed drugs, such as Accutane (used to treat acne), may produce toxic reactions in the fetus. Some of the disorders that teachers are most likely to encounter include the following.

Cataracts. Cataracts cause progressive clouding of the lens of one or both eyes. This is a prenatal disorder.

Glaucoma. Also a prenatal disorder, glaucoma is caused by a gradual destruction of the optic nerve because of the buildup of pressure caused by poor circulation of the fluids of the eye.

Retinopathy of prematurity (ROP) or retrolental fibroplasia. This disorder occurs at birth and is due to the formation of a kind of scar tissue on the retina of one or both eyes. This used to occur more frequently as it is caused by an excessive concentration of oxygen administered to premature infants. At present, ROP is mainly found in extremely low-birthweight infants, even if the oxygen concentration has been ideal. Treatment is available if the condition is identified early. Ophthalmological screening of the premature infant is essential.

Retinal blastoma. Retinal blastoma is a type of cancer of the eye. Infants may have an eye removed to prevent the spread of cancer. A prosthetic eye can usually be fitted.

Physical problems within the brain. Some types of visual impairments are caused by physical problems within the brain. Infections or injuries that occur before, during, or following birth may damage the optic nerve or the visual cortex (portion of the brain where messages from the eyes are processed). Although vision is altered, the eyes appear normal.

Cortical/cerebral visual impairment
visual impairments originating in the brain

Cortical/cerebral visual impairment. Cortical/cerebral visual impairment is vision loss that is due to damage to the parts of the brain that receive and interpret the visual information from the eye. This type of impairment is often accompanied by other developmental disabilities.

Visual Acuity

Visual acuity problems
problems in how well an individual is able to see

Refractive errors
problems, such as astigmatism, hyperopia, and myopia, are caused by a minor malformation of the eye that influences the bending of light rays

Visual acuity problems usually are caused by **refractive errors** (Figure 8–2). Eyes that appear normal may have refraction errors. Refraction is the bending of light rays. When there is even a minor malformation of the eye or certain parts of it, refractive errors can occur. The most common refractive errors are discussed below. Refractive errors are correctable with eyeglasses.

Astigmatism. Astigmatism is a defect of the lens that is caused by uneven refractions in different planes of the eye, causing blurred vision.

Figure 8–2 STRUCTURE OF THE EYE: REFRACTORY ERRORS ARE COMMON

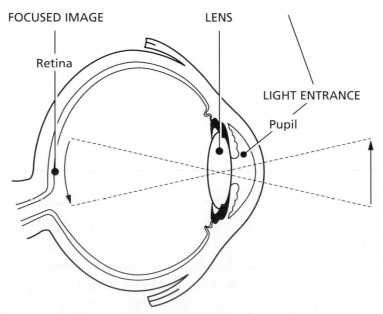

Hyperopia. Hyperopia is also known as farsightedness. With this disorder, objects that are close-up are seen less clearly.

Myopia. Myopia is commonly known as nearsightedness. With this condition, far-away objects are seen less clearly.

Muscular Imbalances

When the major eye muscles are not working together, double vision as well as other problems may result. The following are among the most common.

Amblyopia. A common term for amblyopia is lazy eye. In an older person, amblyopia causes double vision. In young children, the brain may choose to develop the eye that can see more clearly and repress the image received from the other eye, eventually destroying that eye's ability to function. This condition also causes a lack of depth perception.

Strabismus. When **strabismus** exists, the two eyes are unable to focus together on the same image. There are several forms of strabismus: cross-eyed, wandering eye, or one eye that turns in or outward (wall-eyed). To avoid seeing double, the brain in young children shuts off the nondominant eye, which will not develop if it is not being used to see, gradually leading to permanent loss of vision if not corrected. If the child sometimes focuses with the left eye, sometimes with the right eye (alternate strabismus), both eyes may continue to work well.

Strabismus
eye muscle imbalance problems, which are correctable with eyeglasses

Nystagmus. Nystagmus is characterized by quick, involuntary, jerky up-and-down or back-and-forth eye movements as the child tries to obtain a single image. These movements seriously interfere with the ability to see. This condition is usually caused by neurological abnormalities and not by problems with the eye muscles. This condition improves with age.

Muscle imbalances are usually correctible by eyeglasses, patching, or surgery.

Identifying Vision Impairments

Congenital blindness and severe low vision can be identified in the first year of life. It is usually the parents who first become aware that their infant does not look at them or at objects that they wave or offer to their child. Partial vision losses are more difficult to recognize. Often they go undetected until the child is in school. Even then, there are children with vision impairments who are not identified until Grade 3 or 4, when the print in schoolbooks gets smaller, pictures are fewer, the print becomes more densely packed, and the children become aware that they cannot see what is being written on the chalkboard.

Accurately assessing the visual function of a young child with disabilities is essential in determining appropriate intervention and educational strategies (Koenig et al., 2000). Many children with visual impairments are identified through routine screening in preschool and child care settings or by their parents, who suspect a possible vision problem. The *Snellen Illiterate E Test* for identifying visual acuity and muscle imbalance (e.g., amblyopia) is widely used for young children, beginning at about two years of age. Teller Acuity Cards, a preferential-looking procedure (Teller, McDonald, Preston, Sebris, & Dobson, 1986) can be used in younger children and low-functioning older children. The *Denver Eye Screen Test* is an instrument that can be used with even younger children (as young as six months).

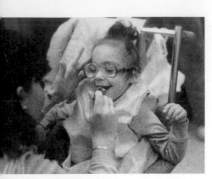

Photo 8–7
Children with early and severe vision loss have little idea of what they are supposed to be seeing. They require guidance and support in how to explore objects.

Photoscreening is a relatively new technique being used to detect amblyopia, strabismus, cataracts, and significant acuity conditions in infants, toddlers, and children with developmental delays in situations that were previously difficult to screen (American Academy of Pediatrics, 2002).

A major problem in trying to assess vision is that children with visual impairments have no idea what they are supposed to be seeing (Photo 8–7). In other words, they really do not know that what they see is imperfect and different from what others are seeing.

Warning Signs

The following list of warning signs, or alerts, is adapted from material published by the U.S. National Society to Prevent Blindness. The alerts are grouped according to children's behaviour, appearance, or verbal complaints:

- rubs eyes excessively
- shuts or covers one eye
- tilts head, thrusts it forward
- has difficulty doing work or playing games that require close use of the eyes
- blinks excessively or becomes irritable when doing close work
- is unable to see distant things clearly
- squints, squeezes eyelids together, frowns
- has crossed eyes or eyes that turn outward
- has red-rimmed, encrusted, or swollen eyelids
- has inflamed, infected, or watery eyes
- has recurring sties
- has itchy, burning, or scratchy-feeling eyes
- is unable to see well—holds objects close to the eyes or trips easily
- experiences dizziness, headaches, or nausea following close work
- has blurred or double vision

Occlusion
an obstruction; as used here, something to prevent vision; an occluder is the object the examiner uses to prevent a child from seeing (usually one eye at a time)

If parents' and teachers' observations or a vision screening suggests an impairment, the next step is for parents to obtain medical assistance. The best qualified consultant is a pediatric ophthalmologist. The ophthalmologist can arrange for the child to receive a visual evoked potential test. This procedure involves placing surface electrodes on the child's scalp and then showing the child different visual patterns. This evaluation process measures involuntary brain activity and is very useful in identifying visual impairments in infants and young children. The ophthalmologist may also prescribe eyeglasses, medication, surgery, eye exercises, **occlusion** (covering) of one eye, or some combination of these (Photo 8–8).

A note of caution: If a screening test does not reveal an impairment but the symptoms continue, it is wise to refer a child for a medical checkup anyway. A

Photo 8–8
An ophthalmologist may prescribe eyeglasses for a child with visual problems.

child with a vision impairment (or any other kind of impairment) may still pass a general screening test. In the case of vision screening, there may have been unintended coaching by the examiner, or the child may have peeked around the occluder during testing. Test results (of all kinds) should always be regarded with caution, especially when a teacher or parent has reason to believe that a child's behaviours indicate a potential impairment.

Children with severe visual impairments, especially school age children with weak **residual vision,** may be referred to a low-vision clinic. The clinic can determine if the child will benefit from using magnifiers, telescopic lenses, specific electronic devices, or closed-circuit greatly magnified television. As children advance in the elementary grades, a number of other sophisticated reading and writing devices are available. (Sacks and Rosen, 1994, provide interesting descriptions of many truly amazing vision-support devices.)

Residual vision
vision remaining after disease or damage occurs to a person's visual system

THE IMPACT OF VISION IMPAIRMENTS ON DEVELOPMENT

Poor vision has an impact on overall development. The more severe the visual impairment, the greater the developmental delay. A lot of what a young child learns comes from scanning the environment, then focusing and pondering on what is occurring. Learning also comes from watching others, imitating them, and observing what follows. For these reasons, poor vision affects a child's language development, large and small motor development, and cognitive and social development. Why? Because the child's ability to interact with people, objects, and activities is seriously curtailed. For example, the child with vision impairments may fail to recognize the presence of amusing events, such as a kitten scampering about. Children with vision impairments may be oblivious to the consequences of their behaviour (such as spilled juice staining a bedspread). They may be unable to enter into new experiences because they have no visual sense of what is going on. A card game, such as Go Fish, for example, cannot be understood just by listening to it being played.

It is likely that the inability to play freely will hinder the development of a child who has a vision impairment. Whereas babies who are sighted begin deliberately reaching for and playing with nearby objects, infants who are blind remain passive. They continue to hold their hands at shoulder height, a posture typical of very young children. Babies with vision impairments play alone a lot of the time because they are not able to be visually stimulated by seeing play activities and other stimuli in the environment (Photo 8–9). In addition, they may receive fewer invitations to play and so have fewer of the play challenges that children who are sighted exchange among themselves. Therefore,

Photo 8–9
Tactile exploration of the environment is essential for children with severe vision loss. Using real objects supports this exploration.

parents and teachers have to create structured play opportunities for children who are visually impaired in order to provide opportunities for them to acquire the cognitive, social, language, and adaptation skills that are repeatedly practised in play and are necessary preparation for higher-order skills.

Effects on Language Development

Language acquisition depends on discovering and identifying objects and actions. This is difficult for children who cannot see the objects and the actions. They must depend almost entirely on what can be touched or heard, which reduces their learning opportunities. Once the child with a visual impairment begins to understand how to explore objects and formulate ideas about them, language proceeds more rapidly. It takes a child who is visually impaired at least a year longer to develop a full range of language skills. By school age, most are using language within developmental and cultural norms.

Effects on Cognitive Development

Children who are blind or have low vision generally lag behind children who are sighted in cognitive development and concept formation. For example, an infant who is sighted, in play with adults, will learn quickly that everyone has a nose. The toddler who is blind can learn to identify his own nose and those of his parents, but may not be aware, unless taught, that all people have noses. Delays are more noticeable during the first three or four years of life (Teplin, 1995). However, with adequate nurturing and early intervention, the preschool child who is blind can develop the functional skills for academic learning.

Effects on Motor Development

Although a vision impairment is not the cause of differences (delays or deviations) in motor development, it can exert an influence. The greater the vision loss, the greater the delays in reaching, crawling, and walking. In fact, a child who is blind does not develop the ability to localize sound and move toward it until the end of the first year (Fraiberg, 1977). Many children who are blind do not walk until they are two years old. Motor development is further delayed by the child's difficulty in learning skills related to judging distance, direction, body position, and objects' positions in space. Children who are blind often develop strange ways of walking and positioning themselves, because they have no visual reference points or models. It is therefore very important that children who are blind receive appropriate programming to facilitate developmentally normal body posturing and movement patterns.

Effects on Social Development

Young children with vision impairments frequently are unable to participate in the interactions that build good social skills and interpersonal relationships. They may, because they are often focusing on listening to sounds in the environment, appear to be quiet and passive as infants. Parents, as noted earlier, must be helped to both stimulate and respond to their infant's developmentally different ways of interacting. Play skills, as previously mentioned, develop more slowly in children who are visually impaired. Toys, for example, are used less creatively and play is often stereotyped because of the lack of visual models necessary for expanding the imagination.

Furthermore, the young child with a vision impairment will often find it more challenging to interact with peers because he or she is unable to pick up on the non-verbal cues in interactive play. For this reason, adult support in interpreting play, giving a running verbal commentary of what is happening, available alternatives in the environment, and so on, is extremely important for the young child with a visual impairment.

INTERVENTION PROGRAMS

Intervention programs serving infants and toddlers who are blind and visually impaired often focus on the parent as teacher. During the first year of life, as with many early intervention programs for children with other special needs, programs for children with visual impairments are often home-based. A specially trained person visits the home on a regular basis. Throughout Canada, the Canadian National Institute for the Blind (CNIB) provides ongoing support to families of young children with severe visual impairments *as long as they are registered as visually impaired*. The visiting specialist provides information about the effects of vision impairment on all aspects of development and coaches parents in special techniques for interacting with their infant or toddler (Photo 8–10). The specialist also is likely to provide instructional play materials, demonstrate teaching strategies, and help parents record their child's progress.

Photo 8–10
Specialists need to guide the child with a visual impairment in exploring new objects.

In some areas there are intervention programs for older toddlers and preschoolers. The toddler program often includes parents. Older preschool children are likely to stay at school without a parent. Even so, parents should continue to be an integral part of their child's learning activities. Many school-aged children, depending on the severity of the vision impairment and their progress, will be able to make the transition from a segregated early childhood or kindergarten classroom (if available) to an inclusive setting. Other children, needing further specialized training, may continue in the segregated setting part-time, and for the remainder of the school day participate in an inclusive classroom.

Norma Kelly (personal communication, 1993), founder of the Ontario Foundation for Visually Impaired Children, stated that before considering integrating a child with a visual impairment into a group setting, it is also important to determine

- the child's ability to track sounds; that is, can the child identify the teacher's voice and other voices?
- the child's level of **preorientation and mobility skills;** that is, can the child "map out" and travel the room safely?
- the child's comfort level and self-confidence in asking for help and questioning to seek clarification.

Preorientation and mobility skills
the ability of a child who has a visual impairment to map out and travel in a room safely

Many children who are blind or visually impaired learn to function well in an adequately staffed inclusive program. When teachers model appropriate ways to interact with a child who is visually impaired, supporting their activity to build feelings of competence and independence, other children learn to do the same. They learn to call the child's name or touch the child's shoulder to attract his or her attention. They learn to put things directly into a child's hands, naming each object at the moment. They learn to help the child get about by describing things specifically: "Here are the lockers. Jenny's locker is the second one. You can put her truck on the bottom shelf." However, assisting a classmate who has a vision impairment must never be a burden for the other children. Children who serve as helpers need to enjoy the job and feel positive about being able to provide assistance.

GENERAL GUIDELINES FOR TEACHERS

A number of conditions causing vision impairments are responsive to treatment procedures. It is important that teachers be alert to any signs that might indicate a change in a child's vision. It is the teachers' responsibility to alert parents and professionals if they note any changes.

A resource teacher/early interventionist or a specially trained consultant can help early childhood teachers arrange the classroom and develop curriculum activities that support the inclusion of a child with a visual impairment. This will ensure good learning experiences throughout the program for the child with a visual impairment. The broad goal of early education for children with vision impairments is to strengthen their intact sensory channels and provide activities that require hearing, touch, taste, and smell.

The hardest part, for many adults, is to refrain from overprotecting a child who has little or no vision. Like all young children, children who have vision impairments need to explore their environment if they are to learn. In the process, they may bump into a wall, fall down, get up, start out again, have another mishap, and another, and another. To make sure the child does not come to unnecessary harm, the classroom and play yard must be kept safe and orderly. Pathways need to be clear of toys and misplaced equipment that the child with a visual impairment (and the teachers and the other children) may trip over. Most importantly, children with impaired vision need to continue to be helped with their mobility skills throughout the day (Photo 8–11).

Learning to get about efficiently and safely on their own will be of prime importance throughout life. If furniture is to be rearranged, the child with a visual impairment should be alerted ahead of time and then physically guided over the new pathways. This enables the child to avoid the frustration of not knowing his or her way around and the embarrassment of bumping into things.

Teachers must also avoid the tendency to deny the child's right to learn self-defence and the right of possession. One way is to refrain from speaking out prematurely on behalf of the child. On many occasions, however, the teacher may need to supply the words: "Melinda, say, 'No! My eggbeater!'" Another time it may be necessary to tell the child who is visually impaired that he or she is about to lose a turn. For example: "Marcie, Khalil has been waiting for a turn on that swing. He is next. Khalil, tell Marcie, 'My turn.'" At this point, the teacher must be sure to follow through. It is important that the child who is sighted yield the swing, give back the eggbeater, or respond to any other reasonable request made by the child who is visually impaired.

WORKING WITH CHILDREN WHO HAVE VISION IMPAIRMENTS

It is important to determine the degree of residual vision. Find out from the child's parents and the vision specialist what the child can see. Many children with visual impairments see shadows, colour, and large pictures or objects. Some children's **peripheral vision** may be their best vision. For this reason, a turned-away head does not necessarily signal inattention.

Photo 8–11
A child with a visual impairment requires ongoing support in the development of orientation and mobility skills.

Peripheral vision
that degree of vision available at the outer edges of the eyes

Orientation and mobility skills should be a major initial teaching priority. The following suggestions should support children with vision impairments in adjusting to an early childhood program:

- Familiarize the child with the classroom layout and storage of materials, placing as many toys as possible on low shelves where they can be easily touched. Harrison and Crow (1993) suggest introducing the child to the room at a time when other children are not present. This allows the child to explore at his or her own pace.

- Be sure to reorient the child whenever changes in the room occur (e.g., moved furniture, shift of toys from one shelf to another, or a change in schedule).

- Put identifying material or subtle noisemakers on the floor, doors, room dividers, and lockers, such as
  - a wind chime near the door to the play yard
  - tile in the creative arts and sensory play areas
  - carpeting in the blocks area and large-group area
  - rough matting by doors to the outside
  - a patch of velveteen glued to the child's locker
  - cork or raised tape along certain walls or furniture to guide the child by touch

- Use specific words when giving directions, to tell the child what to do: "Put the book on the table"; or "I'm sitting by the piano. Bring your shoes to me." Avoid nonspecific phrases, such as "Come here," "Put it there," or "Be careful."

- Talk to the child about everything in the immediate environment. Give the names, over and over, for everyday objects, such as ball, dog, cup, and brush. Naming the object is not enough. For a child who is visually impaired to understand the meaning of "watering can," for example, the child must hold one, feel what is inside, pour from it, and handle it empty and filled with water.

- Give the child action words. Tell the child many times over what he or she is doing (Photo 8–12): "You are *running* on the grass." "You are *brushing* your teeth." "You are *drinking* juice."

- Help the child localize and sort out sounds. Tell the child what the classroom sounds are and where they are coming from: the guinea pig squeaking *by the window*; the faucet dripping *in the sink*; the fan whirring *on the ceiling*. Help children learn to identify the sound of an eggbeater, the tick of a timer, the swishing of sandpaper blocks rubbing together. Play sound-guessing games. The teacher (or another child) can make the sound of one of several objects on a tray (tearing paper, closing a book, dropping a marble in a cup). The child who is visually impaired then must locate the correct object(s) by touch. To make the game challenging for children without visual impairments as well, the teacher can turn away from the children while making the sound, or can make the sound under a cloth or in a large box open only on the teacher's side.

- Teach sounds that may signal danger in contrast to those that are simply frightening. The sound of the power mower in the playing field is something to stay away from. The drone of the vacuum cleaner signals something the child can help push. The fire alarm indicates STOP whatever is going on and stand by the door. The squeak of chains warns children to stay back because the swings are in motion.

Photo 8–12
Facilitating self-help/care skills in children with serious vision impairments is a challenge for parents and teachers.

The teacher's goal should be to plan activities that involve all children and incidentally are of specific benefit to the child with a visual impairment:

- Offer several opportunities each day to learn through smelling, touching, and tasting.
- Vary the consistency of paint by adding sand, soap, cornstarch, and so on. Introduce different sizes and weights of paintbrushes, rollers, or markers; different types of paper; textures; and so on.
- Use actual objects, rather than plastic replicas, for teaching—for example, in a session on fruit, a real banana and orange should be used for feeling, cutting, peeling, smelling, tasting, and comparing. (Be sure to check whether any children have food allergies.)
- Plan cooking or baking experiences that involve measuring, smelling, tasting, touching, before-and-after cutting, mixing, and so on.
- Offer sorting activities that support learning categorizations—for example, same versus different, or seriation from small to large, cold to hot, smooth to rough, and so on.
- Use touch, hearing, smell, or taste to tell the difference between shapes, sizes, textures, and odours.
- Provide left-to-right training. Informal practice in working from left to right is a skill all preschool children need in preparation for reading English. The child who is visually impaired is no exception; Braille and other academic activities follow the same format. When using pegboards, for example, there can be teacher-initiated activities in which the child is encouraged to fill the board systematically by placing pegs in left-to-right and top-to-bottom progression.

Special considerations for children with visual impairments include the following:

- Use the child's name before speaking to the child, thus signalling that the statement is directed to him or her.
- Ensure your tone of voice communicates the tone and mood of the message. Many verbal statements are accompanied by nonverbal gestures, facial expressions, and other types of body language the child cannot see.
- Encourage as much active participation as possible, as this will ensure the greatest amount of opportunity for obtaining sensory information.
- Seat the child close to the teacher in situations where support may be necessary—such as circles.
- Provide real objects as often as possible. Many toys "share only visible representation of the real object" (Stewart & Cornell, 2004).
- Provide many physical prompts. This is especially important in music times when the child may need to be physically guided in hand or body gestures. Having the child place his or her hands on yours during hand movements will also support learning.
- Help the child with a visual impairment to feel more secure by ensuring that during gross motor circle activities, certain parts—such as marching, jumping, and so on—can be done in one place.
- Make sure that teacher demonstrations take the form of subtle physical assistance and hand-over-hand guidance.

- Have the teacher guide and support the child from behind, gradually reducing assistance as the child masters the successive steps required to accomplish the task (see the section on "Task Analysis" in Chapter 11).
- Make sure that whenever possible materials are introduced that have high contrast in colours—this will help the child with low vision.
- Explain ahead of time to the child any new ideas or experiences being planned for a group or circle time.
- Keep an eye on the child when he or she is playing with other children, making sure that they are including the child who is visually impaired in their play in as equally important roles as those they take for themselves.
- Help the child with basic social skills; for example, the child should learn to turn his or her face toward people when talking, use appropriate physical posture, and so on.

In addition, teachers may find it useful to consult a resource person, who can assist them in arranging the classroom and developing cirriculum activities. A resource person can also assist parents and teachers in achieving the broader goal of strengthening children's intact sensory abilities through touch and sound (Pogrund, Fazzi, & Hess, 2002).

MANNERISMS OF CHILDREN WHO ARE BLIND

Rhythmic, seemingly purposeless, mannerisms may occur almost continually among some children who are blind, especially when they are left too long on their own (Photo 8–13). They may rock back and forth for long periods, poke their eyes, flip their hands about in front of their face, or spin around and around. These movements may be accompanied by strange noises or high-pitched squeals. It is speculated that these behaviours develop because of reduced stimulation. Lacking vision, infants receive less motivation and challenge from their environment. In turn, they do not learn to explore their environment the way infants who are sighted do. It is almost as if the strange behaviours were the infants' efforts to create their own stimulation and so have something to which to respond.

Whatever their causes, these behaviours can interfere with the development of social skills. They make the child stand out as uncomfortably different. As teachers help children who have severe vision impairments learn appropriate play skills, the children will spend less of their developmentally valuable early learning time in unproductive spinning, poking, and twirling. Other children can be of help, too, especially with prompts from the teacher. For example: "Come, Sarah, let's go and get Mila and I'll pull you both in the wagon."

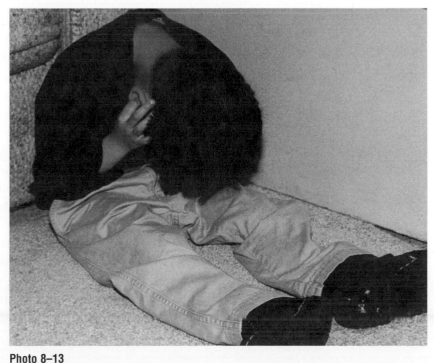

Photo 8–13
Children with severe vision impairments often have ritualistic behaviours.

Summary

Hearing or vision impairments greatly interfere with overall development. Infants who are blind or have an identified hearing loss should receive early intervention services and programming in the first months of life. In fact, early intervention planning and programming should begin as soon as the condition is identified. It is important to include parents in this process. Some children with vision and hearing impairments need to be educated in the most stimulating and enhancing environment possible. This may require a specialized setting, at least in the very early years, if these children are to develop the basic skills necessary and prerequisite to adapting effectively to a group setting.

Hearing losses are classified in three ways: conductive hearing loss, sensorineural hearing loss, and problems originating in the higher auditory cortex. (Combined losses can also occur.) The most serious result of a severe hearing loss is interference with early speech and language development. Chronic ear infections, especially otitis media, which may come and go, are responsible for impairments in both hearing and language. Infants who do not startle or blink their eyes in response to loud noises may be hearing impaired. A hearing loss may be suspected in children who have acquired some language, especially if they begin asking to have things repeated or behave in ways that suggest difficulty with understanding.

Specially trained teachers can teach speech to children with hearing impairments; also available are a variety of language systems, including American Sign Language (ASL). However, the long-standing controversy continues: Should the child be taught to communicate only through speech? Or should the child be allowed to use all forms of communication? Regardless of the child's special program, early childhood teachers are important agents in facilitating language development and cognitive learning in young children with hearing impairments. Part of the teacher's responsibility is to make sure each day that a young child's hearing aid is working effectively.

Children classified as educationally blind do not have functional vision. For educational placement, children who are low-visioned or are partially sighted will often be able to learn by using specially presented printed or other visual materials. In the preschool child, identification of a vision impairment may be difficult, because screening tests cannot be relied on to identify all vision impairments. Therefore, parents and teachers need to be alert to behavioural signs that a child may have a vision impairment. If not identified and treated, poor vision affects all areas of development.

Learning for children with vision impairments requires more time, more practice, more verbal mediation, and more encouragement from adults. Many early intervention programs serving infants and toddlers are home-based and focus on training parents as teachers. Young children, even those who are visually impaired, are more readily included in an early childhood setting if a specially trained consultant is available to assist the teacher. It is important that teachers and parents restrain themselves from overprotecting the young child who is visually impaired, because children with vision impairments need to learn how to be self-reliant in order to cope with daily challenges.

RESOURCES

The following resources have been compiled as the most useful sites on which to find relevant research and information related to children with vision and hearing disabilities. Those that are specific to Canada have been noted with an asterisk (*). The resources from the United States have material that was not found on the Canadian sites or are sites that were recommended by Canadian sources.

CANADIAN ASSOCIATION OF THE DEAF*
http://www.cad.ca

CANADIAN HARD OF HEARING ASSOCIATION*
http://www.chha.ca

DEAF CHILDREN'S SOCIETY OF BC*
http://www.deafchildren.bc.ca

DEAFNESS RESEARCH FOUNDATION
http://www.drf.org

MSN ENCARTA
http://cncarta.msn.com

NATIONAL ASSOCIATION FOR PARENTS OF CHILDREN WITH VISUAL IMPAIRMENTS (NAPVI)
http://www.spedex.com/napvi

NATIONAL INSTITUTE ON DEAFNESS AND OTHER COMMUNICATION DISORDERS
http://www.nidcd.nih.gov

THE CANADIAN HEARING SOCIETY*
http://www.chs.ca

ASSOCIATION FOR EDUCATION AND REHABILITATION OF THE BLIND AND VISUALLY IMPAIRED (AER)
http://www.aerbvi.org

AMERICAN FOUNDATION FOR THE BLIND (AFB)
http://www.afb.org

AMERICAN PRINTING HOUSE FOR THE BLIND (APH)
http://www.aph.org

BLIND BABIES FOUNDATION
http://www.blindbabies.org

BLIND CHILDRENS CENTER
http://www.blindcntr.org

CANADIAN NATIONAL INSTITUTE FOR THE BLIND (CNIB)*
http://www.cnib.ca

FOUNDATION FOR BLIND CHILDREN (ARIZONA)
http://www.the-fbc.org

Hospital for Sick Children*
http://www.sickkids.on.ca

National Organization of Albinism and Hypopigmentation (NOAH)
http://www.albinism.org

Perkins School for the Blind
http://www.perkins.pvt.k12.ma.us

Special Education Technology (BC)*
http://www.setbc.org

Texas School for the Blind and Visually Impaired
http://www.tsbvi.edu

STUDENT ACTIVITIES

1. Locate a person with a hearing or vision loss (friend, schoolmate, grandparent, etc.). Talk with that person about the impact of the loss on everyday life.
2. Invite several of the people from activity 1 to come to class and demonstrate the use of their amplification or magnification devices. If appropriate, ask whether members of the class can try the devices.
3. Simulate greatly impaired vision by playing blindfold games in class, such as moving about the classroom without mishap. Try moving toward one particular person based on recognizing that person's voice among several. Have several students blindfolded at one time and ask them to guess the source of sounds that you provide (closing a door, lowering a window shade, sharpening a pencil, and so on).
4. Prepare an identify-by-touch guessing game that children, both sighted and visually impaired, could enjoy together. Try it out with your classmates and have them critique it. Alter your game to include appropriate recommendations. Now try the game out with young children.
5. Select the one best match for each item in column I from column II, and place that letter in the appropriate space in column I.

	I	II
___	1. otitis media	A. scar-tissue formation
___	2. amplification device	B. hearing aid
___	3. cochlea	C. vision screening
___	4. strabismus	D. blind at birth
___	5. American Sign Language	E. children's eye doctor
___	6. residual vision	F. crossed eyes
___	7. retinopathy of prematurity	G. partial sight
___	8. pediatric ophthalmologist	H. inner ear structure
___	9. Snellen Illiterate E Test	I. may cause intermittent hearing loss

REFERENCES

Allen, K. E., & Marotz, L. R. (2003). *Developmental profiles: Pre-birth through twelve* (4th ed.). Clifton Park, NY: Delmar Learning.

American Academy of Pediatrics. (2002). Use of photo screening for children's vision screening. *Pediatrics, 109,* 524–525.

Cook, R. E., & Klein, L. S. (2004). *Adapting early childhood curricula for children in inclusive settings.* Upper Saddle River, NJ: Prentice Hall.

Discolo, C. M., & Hirose, K. (2002). Pediatric cochlear implants. *American Journal of Audiology, 11*(2), 114–118.

Fraiberg, S. (1977). *Insights from the blind.* New York: Basic Books.

Greenberg, M. T., & Kusche, C. A. (1993). *Promoting social and emotional development in deaf children: The PATHS project.* Seattle, WA: University of Washington Press.

Harrison, F., & Crow, M. (1993). *Living and learning with blind children: A guide for parents and teachers of visually impaired children.* Toronto: University of Toronto Press.

Koenig, A. J., Holbrook, M. C., Corn, A. L., DePriest, L. B., Erin, J. N., & Priestly, I. (2000). Specialized assessment for students with visual impairments. In A. J. Koenig & M. C. Holbrook (Eds.), *Foundations of education: Instructional strategies for teaching children and youths with visual impairments* (Vol. 2, pp. 103–172). New York: American Foundation for the Blind.

Lowenbraun, S., & Thompson, M. D. (1994). Hearing impairments. In N. G. Haring, L. McCormick, & T. G. Harry (Eds.), *Exceptional children and youth* (pp. 355 395). New York: Merrill.

MacKenzie, K. (Ed.). (1999). *Starting point: A resource for parents of deaf or hard of hearing children.* Toronto: The Canadian Hearing Society.

Malatchi, A. (1995). *Together We Can: The Virginia Project for the integration of children with deaf-blindness—Final report.* Richmond, VA: Virginia Institute for Developmental Disabilities.

Martin, F., & Clark, J. (1996). *Hearing care for children.* Needham Heights, MA: Allyn and Bacon.

Mason, J. A., & Herrmann, K. R. (1998). Universal infant hearing screening by automated auditory brainstem response measurement. *Pediatrics, 101,* 221–228.

McCormick, L., & Schiefelbusch, R. L. (1990). *Early language intervention.* Needham Heights, MA: Allyn & Bacon.

National Institute on Deafness and Other Communication Disorders. (2002). *Cochlear implants.* National Institute of Health Publication No. 00-4798, Bethesda, MD: NIDCD. Retrieved August 17, 2005, http://www.nidcd .nih.gov/health/hearing/coch.asp.

Petitto, L. A., & Maramette, P. F. (1991). Babbling in the manual mode. *Science, 251,* 1493–1496.

Pogrund, R. L., Fazzi, D. L., & Hess, C. L. (Eds.). (2002). *Early focus: Working with young children who are lind or visually impaired and their families.* New York: American Foundation for the Blind.

Roeser, R. J. (2000). *Auditory diagnosis.* New York: Thieme Medical.

Sacks, S. Z., & Rosen, S. (1994). Visual impairment. In N. G. Haring, L. McCormick, & T. G. Haring (Eds.), *Exceptional children and youth.* New York: Merrill.

Skelly, M., & Schinsky, L. (1979). *Amer-Ind gestural code based on universal American Indian hand talk.* New York: Elsevier North Holland.

Steinberg, A. G., & Knightly, C. A. (1997). Hearing: Sounds of silences. In M. L. Batshaw (Ed.), *Children with disabilities* (4th ed., pp. 241–274). Baltimore, MD: Brooks.

Stewart, K. A., & Cornell, A. (2004). Learning through the senses. In D. Gold & A. Tait (Eds.), *A strong beginning, a sourcebook for health and education professionals working with young children who are visually impaired or blind.* Toronto: The Canadian National Institute for the Blind.

Tanner, L. (2004, May). Ear implants work best when started young. *Personal Health,* May 15–21. Retrieved August 17, 2005, from http://www.americanvoiceinstitute.org/PHHealth71.htm#3.

Teller, D. Y., McDonald, M. A., Preston, K., Sebris, S. L., & Dobson, V. (1986). Assessment of visual acuity in infants and children: The acuity card procedure. *Developmental Medicine and Child Neurology, 28,* 779–789.

Teplin, S. W. (1995). Visual impairment in infants and young children. *Infants and Young Children, 8*(1), 8–51.

CHAPTER 9 | Orthopedic and Health Problems

KEY CONCEPTS

adaptive equipment
anaphylactic shock
anoxia
athetosis
ataxia
cerebral palsy
chemotherapy
contractures
genetic mutation
health conditions
hydrocephalus
hypertonicity
hypotonicity
immune system

incontinence
metabolize
orthopedic conditions
Prader-Willi syndrome
primitive reflexes
prostheses/prosthetic devices
radiation
regeneration
seizures
shunting
spasticity
spina bifida
wedges, bolsters,
   and prone-boards

OBJECTIVES

After studying the material in this chapter, the student will be able to

- Define and give examples of orthopedic and health impairments.
- Explain the general effects of orthopedic and health impairments on overall development.
- Describe the role of the early childhood teacher in working with children with orthopedic and health conditions.
- Discuss the implications of both obesity and undernourishment in young children in general and in young children who have health concerns.
- Outline classroom procedures to consider in preparation for emergency situations related to orthopedic and health impairments.

Introduction

Physical activity and general good health are critical to early development. Infants and young children who eat well, sleep well, and move about freely are likely to acquire a well-integrated range of cognitive, language, social, and physical skills. Problems with health and motor control, however, tend to interfere with everything a child tries to do or learn. Since young children's learning is activity based, a physical impairment may affect overall development because it interferes with the ability to move about, explore, rearrange play materials, and seek out play things and playmates. Even casual observation indicates that innumerable times a day, children who are able-bodied will move about, rearranging their own learning environment.

Example:

A nine-month-old tires of playing with familiar toys. She crawls to the bookcase and soon discovers the fun of taking books off the shelf. This infant has found a challenge for herself and a match for her rapidly developing motor skills. Of course, pulling books off the shelf may be viewed as mischievous by parents or caregivers. If so, they need to challenge themselves to find new play materials that both stimulate the child and meet their adult standards of appropriateness.

In this chapter, the discussion will focus on the two broad categories of physiological disabilities: orthopedic challenges and health conditions. Their definitions, given below, have helped reduce confusion about the meaning of the term *physical disability.*

Orthopedic conditions involve the skeleton, joints, and muscles. Included are the following:

- missing or malformed limbs, or paralysis
- structural problems, such as clubfeet
- congenital hip dislocations
- damage caused by diseases, such as polio and bone tuberculosis
- neurological disorders, such as **cerebral palsy** and **spina bifida,** resulting in such problems as paralysis of major muscles
- **contractures** (muscular tightening) caused by fractures, burns, or amputations

Health conditions are defined generally as limited strength, vitality, or alertness due to chronic or acute health problems. Among them are the following:

- heart conditions
- epilepsy
- asthma
- leukemia
- sickle-cell disease
- diabetes
- hemophilia
- cystic fibrosis
- HIV/AIDS
- nutritional problems

Actual boundaries between physical disabilities and serious health impairments frequently overlap. Furthermore, neurological problems may complicate both. Orthopedic, health, and neurological impairments may all be present, as in cerebral palsy, spina bifida, and other childhood conditions.

Orthopedic conditions
conditions involving the bones and joints

Cerebral palsy
a condition that affects muscular control; it is caused by damage to various parts of the brain. Its effects range from very mild (nonincapacitating) to moderate (involving fine or gross motor skills, or both), to pervasive (involving almost all areas of the body's physical activity)

Spina bifida
the imperfect development of the spinal cord and spinal column that occurs during the first 30 days of fetal development; it can cause severe disabilities

Contractures
permanent tightening of muscles and joints

Health conditions
refers to the range of health problems a child might have and how these affect their growth, development, and everyday lives

This chapter will also consider the impact of nutritional problems on the development of young children.

Orthopedic Conditions

Orthopedic conditions cover a wide range of impairments. In general, they include any condition that interferes with the normal functioning of bones, joints, and muscles (Photo 9–1). The conditions may be evident at birth, as with cerebral palsy, hip dysplasia, and clubfoot, or they may be identifiable later in childhood, as in the case of muscular dystrophy.

CEREBRAL PALSY

Cerebral palsy (CP) is a neurological condition that involves the inability to coordinate muscle action, as well as limited ability to sustain normal posture, achieve balance, and to control normal movements and skills. CP is the most common source of physical disabilities among infants and young children. The basic cause is damage to the brain occurring before, during, or after the infant's birth. Cerebral palsy is a nonprogressive disorder resulting from oxygen deprivation (**anoxia**), injury, infection, hemorrhage (excessive bleeding), or malformation of the brain. Seldom can the exact cause be specified. The extent of the damage to the brain, and the corresponding impact on the child's ability to control physical movement, will determine how well the child will function. One way of classifying cerebral palsy is by the type of abnormal muscle tone displayed; the other is by how the various parts of the body are affected.

It is frequently thought that neurological conditions are evident at birth. Often the opposite is true. It may be weeks, months, or well into the first year before the infant gives evidence of a neurological impairment. The condition may become noticeable only when certain very early reflexive (primitive) behaviours do not disappear on schedule and so interfere with the acquisition of new and more mature responses. For example, most newborns automatically grasp a finger placed in their hand. However, unless this primitive grasp reflex disappears between one and four months of age, infants will not be able to learn to release objects at will. Early identification of any behavioural dysfunction or developmental difference is extremely important, because the sooner a disability is identified, the sooner therapeutic remediation and special programming can begin.

Classifications Based on Muscle Tone

Muscle tone may be described in terms of *hyper* (high) or *hypo* (low) muscle tension. The child who displays **hypotonicity** is one who has too little muscle tone. The result is an inability to move about or maintain postural control (the rag doll syndrome). Infants with this type of condition are often referred to as "floppy babies." Many have difficulty simply holding up their heads. This deprives them of the learning experiences that most infants get from being held in an upright position. The child with **hypertonicity** is one who has taut muscle activity, preventing fluid movements. The following conditions, which often accompany cerebral palsy, are associated with muscle tone.

Spasticity. Most children with cerebral palsy fall into the category of **spasticity.** They usually are considered to be hypertonic. Without early intervention, a child may

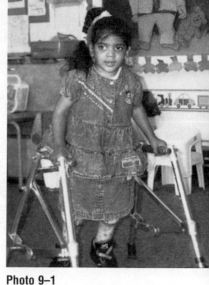

Photo 9–1
Children with orthopedic impairments can participate when provided with specialized equipment.

Anoxia
a shortage of oxygen to the brain that can cause physical damage to the brain before, during, or at any time after birth; anoxia is one of the major causes of physical and cognitive dysfunction

Hypotonicity
too little muscle tone; "floppiness"

Hypertonicity
abnormally high muscle tone

Spasticity
abnormal muscle tone—evident in taut muscle activity or too little muscle tone, both of which prevent fluid movements, as seen in cerebral palsy

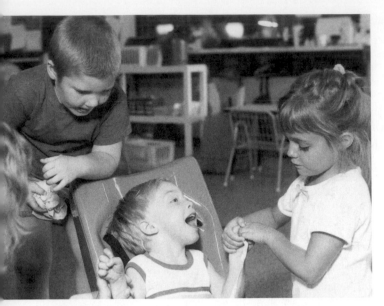

Photo 9–2
Hypertonicity causes muscles to tighten, as seen in this child's clenched fist and grasp.

Athetosis
fluctuating or uneven muscle tone; muscle control that goes from one extreme to the other (either too low or too high) is typical

Primitive reflexes
the responses the infant is born with, such as grasping, stepping, rooting, and sucking. Most of these disappear around four months of age and are replaced by similar but voluntary behaviours, as in the sucking response

Ataxia
a lack of motor coordination, ataxia is characterized by poor balance and a lurching kind of walk, reflecting a lack of voluntary muscle control

become locked into certain positions because muscles become permanently contracted. These muscle contractures occur frequently in the hips, knees, ankles, elbows, and wrists, as well as in the child's fingers and toes, which may become irreversibly curled or clenched (Photo 9–2).

Athetosis. Fluctuating or uneven muscle tone is called **athetosis.** Muscle control that goes from one extreme to the other (either too low or too high) is typical. Children with this condition tend to retain **primitive reflexes** past the normal time. This interferes with the development of voluntary motor responses.

Ataxia. A lack of motor coordination, **ataxia** is characterized by poor balance and a lurching kind of walk, reflecting a lack of voluntary muscle control. Purposeful activity is extremely difficult. For example, a teacher's carefully organized collage materials are swept off the table as a result of involuntary muscle responses as the child strives to participate.

Mixed. Approximately 30 percent of children with cerebral palsy have a mixture of spasticity and athetosis or ataxia.

Classifications Based on Body Parts

A second way of classifying cerebral palsy is according to the parts of the body that are affected. The following terms describe the location of the involvement:

- *Diplegia.* Involvement of all four extremities (legs and arms); the legs are usually more severely affected.
- *Hemiplegia.* Only one side of the body is involved.
- *Paraplegia.* Involvement of the legs only.
- *Quadriplegia.* Involvement of both arms, both legs, trunk, and the muscles that provide head control.

The extent of motor impairment varies in children with cerebral palsy. Some children have disabilities so severe they cannot hold their heads still or straighten their arms or legs. Others have control problems so slight as to be scarcely noticeable. Many children with cerebral palsy, like children with other developmental disabilities, fail to meet major motor milestones at expected times. A distinction must be made, however. Children with general developmental differences usually have delays in all areas. In contrast, children with cerebral palsy may have developmentally appropriate cognitive and receptive language ability (Photo 9–3), but their motor skills, including those affecting speech production, may be poorly developed.

Young children with cerebral palsy, especially those with mild to moderate involvement, usually benefit from an inclusive early childhood classroom experience. All children with a motor dysfunction should receive ongoing evaluation. The parents and early childhood teachers should participate in developing a program for the child, while at the same time receiving appropriate training on physical management techniques and special programming strategies. The success of the early childhood program experience will depend on the teachers and child receiving adequate assistance and support from the interdisciplinary team, which should include a resource teacher, a pediatric physiotherapist, and an occupational therapist, as well as a speech and language therapeutic consultant.

SPINAL CORD INJURIES/DAMAGE

Spinal cord damage presents motor problems quite different from those associated with cerebral palsy. When the spinal cord is injured or severed, muscles below the point of damage become useless or severely impaired. Put simply, the muscles no longer receive messages from the brain. Sensations normally experienced below the point of injury no longer are transmitted back to the brain. It is important to note that the brain itself is not affected. However, because of interruption in neural communication between the brain and certain parts of the body, there are no sensations as to where the limbs are or what is happening to them. A child may suffer serious burns, cuts, or broken bones without knowing it. Parents, teachers, and caregivers of young children must be aware of this and constantly be alert to protecting a child who has nonfeeling extremities and trunk. It should be noted that **regeneration** (repair or renewal) of the spinal cord is not possible at this time, but huge scientific advances are being made in this area. The use of stem cells to regenerate injured or repair congenitally malformed spinal cords is currently being researched in a number of different countries. Initial findings are very positive (Stem Cell Research Foundation, 2004).

The most familiar of the spinal cord injuries is spina bifida (**myelomeningocele** and **meningocele**). The damage comes from imperfect development of the spinal cord and spinal column during the first 30 days of fetal development. Children with spina bifida experience a number of problems in addition to paralysis of the affected limbs (Photo 9–4, p. 164). The two most common problems are hydrocephalus and incontinence.

1. **Hydrocephalus.** Blockage of the circulation of the spinal fluid in the cranial (brain) cavity. This is usually corrected through **shunting,** whereby tubes are surgically inserted in the back of the neck to drain spinal fluid from the brain to another area of the body, often the abdominal cavity (Canadian Paediatric Society, 1992, p. 590). Without shunting, the spinal fluid will accumulate in the head cavity, enlarging the head and damaging the brain.

   Occasionally, shunts may become blocked. It is important that teachers be aware of the symptoms related to blocked shunts. These symptoms involve dizzy spells, nausea, sleepiness, and vomiting. The child's parents are the most appropriate resource for identifying their child's specific symptoms. Parents should also indicate to the teacher what action should be taken if any of these signs should occur.

2. **Incontinence.** Lack of bladder or bowel control. Many children with myelomeningocele cannot feel the urge to urinate. Often they are unable to receive messages from the urinary sphincter muscles. The result is that the child has little or no control of urinary functioning. The same may be true of bowel activity. Although these problems are difficult to overcome, many

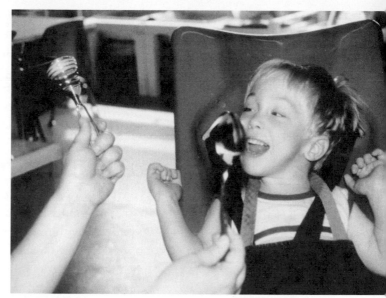

Photo 9–3
Children with cerebral palsy often have excellent cognitive and receptive language abilities.

Regeneration
the regrowth, repair, or renewal of the spinal cord or other parts of the body

Myelomeningocele
a congenital protrusion of the spinal cord through the vertebrae; paralysis and lack of sensation below the protrusion (usually the lower trunk and legs) are often the result

Meningocele
a congenital protrusion of the spinal cord through the vertebrae; it is limited to the covering of the spinal cord and usually causes little or no neurological impairment

Hydrocephalus
a condition that occurs as the result of a buildup of cranial spinal fluid in the head; if not corrected (shunted), can lead to an enlargement of the head and, ultimately, pressure on and deterioration of the brain

Shunting
a process for implanting a tube (shunt) into the brain to allow proper circulation and drainage of fluids from within the skull into one of the body cavities

Incontinence
a lack of bladder or bowel control

Photo 9–4
Children with spina bifida experience paralysis of the limbs below the area of spinal damage.

Photo 9–5
Progressive weakness of the muscle structure characterizes several early childhood disabilities.

children who experience them can be helped to learn techniques for managing their own bowel and bladder needs. Liptak (1997) points out that competence in toileting is necessary for social growth toward independence and that prevention of soiling, wetting, and odour enhances the child's self-esteem (p. 544). As the team evaluates the child's developmental skills, adaptive behaviours, and emotional strengths, they can also begin to determine the child's readiness to learn toilet skills and other everyday tasks.

MUSCULAR DYSTROPHY

Progressive weakening of the muscles is the major characteristic of muscular dystrophy—a neurological condition—and related muscular disorders (Photo 9–5). As children with muscular dystrophy get older, they lose their large motor skills first. Loss of fine motor skills comes later. Several types of muscular dystrophy exist; each type involves specific muscle groups. The most common is Duchenne muscular dystrophy, a sex-linked disorder that affects only boys. In Duchenne, progressive muscle weakness begins at the hips and shoulders and gradually moves out to the arms and legs. Children with this condition often walk on tiptoes and have large calf muscles but weak legs. Children with muscular dystrophy tend to move slowly and become easily tired (Muscular Dystrophy Association of Canada, 1997). Hand skills are often retained, even when the limbs are severely impaired. One child, for example, was able to string small wooden beads in complicated patterns if the beads were placed in a basket in his lap. However, when he ran out of beads he was unable to lift his arms to get more beads from the nearby table. While still mobile and able to get around, a child with muscular dystrophy must be encouraged to move about the classroom frequently. Prevention of muscle contractures is a major goal of both therapy and classroom activity for these children.

OSTEOGENESIS IMPERFECTA

Brittle bones is the common term for this congenital condition. The child's bones do not grow normally in length or thickness and they break easily. Joints, too, are involved and may show excessive range of motion, as in children who can bend their thumb backward to touch the wrist. Dwarfism, dental defects, and hearing problems also may be associated with this bone disease. Often, the child's hearing gets progressively worse, adding another dimension to teachers' planning. Generally, the child's cognitive skills are not affected, but a child may seem to be "behind" because of frequent hospitalization and absences from school.

OSTEOMYELITIS

Infection of the bones is the simple definition of osteomyelitis. It can be a physically disabling disease if not treated promptly and properly. Medication (antibiotics) and surgery are used to treat this condition in children.

HIP DYSPLASIA

This condition, also known as *congenital dislocation of the hip* (CDH), is the result of abnormal development of the hip joint. The head of the thigh bone (femur) may be out of the hip socket or may move in and out at random. This condition is found much more often in females than in males. Hip displacement is usually diagnosed soon after birth and treated nonsurgically, frequently through the use of casts and braces. Without treatment, the child will usually not be able to walk normally and will usually develop a waddling kind of gait.

JUVENILE ARTHRITIS (JA)

Juvenile arthritis is characterized by continuous inflammation of one or more joints. It may last for as little as several months to a year; however, many children experience it for a number of years. Most children will go through periods of flare-ups and then remissions. A major symptom is chronic and painful inflammation of the joints and tissue surrounding the joints. Some children also develop a fever and rash. At no time is this condition contagious. Severe inflammation of some joints may effect the growth of some children. Physiotherapy and occupational therapy, as well as medication to ease pain and reduce inflammation, are major parts of the treatment for this condition (Laxer, Shore, & Boone, 1996, pp. 2–6). Sitting for long periods (though often less painful for the child than movement is) causes further stiffening of the joints. Therefore, children with juvenile arthritis need both the freedom and the encouragement to move about a great deal, at home and at school. Symptoms often disappear by the time a child is 18 years old. The teacher's major goal must be to help the child keep his or her motor skills functional and to be aware of providing alternative group activities, if the activities being provided are too painful for the child to participate in.

Program Implications of Orthopedic Conditions

It is generally agreed that early and appropriate intervention has a positive effect on the acquisition of motor skills in young children with developmental concerns (Photo 9–6). Children with orthopedic disabilities, in spite of great individual differences, have basic classroom needs in common:

- the service of allied health professionals working as a team with classroom teachers
- **adaptive equipment** designed to meet each child's physical needs
- environmental adaptations to facilitate and support each child's learning efforts

TEAM EFFORT

The teacher's need for input from various health professionals in carrying out individualized early intervention programs has been discussed elsewhere in several contexts. A brief review, related to orthopedic and neurological conditions, is presented here.

As noted repeatedly, good motor skills are critical to every aspect of children's development. The pediatric physiotherapist or occupational therapist, trained to focus on early motor skills, is often selected as case coordinator/manager. The early interventionist/resource teacher, however, may be the key person in developing a specific program for the child. The early interventionist needs to work closely with parents, teachers, and others involved in the care of the child, establishing and adapting goals and specific objectives as the child's skills and behaviours change. The early interventionist often is the person who must coordinate the roles and

Photo 9–6
Children may need adult support in learning how to handle their orthopedic equipment.

Adaptive equipment
mobility devices, prostheses, and prescribed alterations of standard furnishings to meet the needs of children with special needs

responsibilities of various members of the team involved in meeting the ongoing needs of the child. For example, in drawing up an intervention program for a child with cerebral palsy who also has a feeding problem, the early interventionist may make use of a nutritionist, a social worker, and, perhaps, a dentist to provide consultation or direct assistance. If the child also has a speech or language problem, the services of a speech and language pathologist, an audiologist, and a psychologist are likely to be enlisted.

The pediatric physiotherapist or occupational therapist needs to understand the goals of early childhood education and also needs to help teachers understand the goals of developmental therapy. As therapists and teachers share the knowledge base of their respective professions, there is "shared implementation and integration of children's daily therapy programs into the everyday format of the home and classroom structure" (Mather & Weinstein, 1988, p. 7).

The ways in which a child who has a physically disability is positioned and helped to move about, at home and at school, are crucial to the child's development. Depending on the therapists' assessments, individual remediation activities are mapped out for each child. The classroom teacher should never be expected to put a child through stressful exercises. In fact, current practice tends to consider such exercises counterproductive for most children. Activities that are pleasant for both the child and the teacher (and often fun for other children as well) are the usual recommendations. *Under no circumstances should teachers initiate positioning exercises or remedial motor activities without specific guidance from a certified therapist.*

ADAPTIVE EQUIPMENT

The pediatric therapist also guides teachers in the use of special mobility devices (Photo 9–7), demonstrates how **prostheses** are used, and shows ways in which to adapt regular play equipment. Some of the more common prostheses are discussed below.

Prostheses
artificial devices replacing body parts that are damaged or missing at birth or later removed

Photo 9–7
Adapting the pedals of the tricycle, with straps and a frame to hold the child's foot in place, enables the child to join her peers.

Mobility Devices

Braces, crutches, walkers, and wheelchairs are among the mobility devices prescribed for children who cannot move about easily. Young children with paraplegia may use a low, small-wheeled flat cart. They lie "tummy-down" on the cart and propel themselves from one activity to another by pushing with their hands and arms. These devices are frequently referred to as scooter-boards or tummy-boards. Power wheelchairs are increasingly in use even by two- and three-year-olds. For stand-up activities, children with poor balance are often fastened into a standing board—also known as prone-standers. Children with uncertain motor skills, even though they are able to walk, tend to fall more frequently than do other preschoolers. The falls are likely to distress adults more than they do the child. Usually, the child has become quite accustomed to falling down. Many children with conditions that impair their physical functioning are given training in how to fall as well as in how to get themselves up again. The latter is especially important. Adults must restrain themselves from "rushing to the rescue," picking the child up before he or she has a chance to get up independently. Adults who restrain themselves save the child from being unnecessarily and additionally disabled through *learned helplessness.* Children who fall frequently are often fitted with a helmet to prevent serious head injury.

Children with poor balance and poor motor control sometimes can hold on to and push a piece of play equipment as a means of getting about. A doll carriage or stroller or a large wooden box with a handle bar attached works well. If the box does not slide readily, wooden slats can be attached to the bottom. If the piece of equipment is too light, it can be loaded with bags of sand or large unopened juice cans, thus providing a feeling of greater security.

Teachers should never take the initiative in encouraging a child to walk without specific guidance from a pediatric therapist. Neurological and medical factors first must be evaluated by a physician or other accredited specialist before walking becomes part of the developmental programming for this child (Fallen & Umansky, 1985).

Some children who lack precise hand control may need **prosthetic devices,** such as on-head sticks to enable them to operate computers and battery-operated toys. These devices enable children who are unable to communicate by other means to communicate.

Prosthetic devices
artificial devices replacing body parts that are damaged or missing at birth or later removed

Positioning Devices

Motor and neurological problems are often accompanied by muscular weakness that interferes with head and trunk control. Maintaining a sitting position becomes difficult, as does grasping and hanging on to objects. The pediatric therapist can help teachers reduce the hampering effects of motor problems by recommending (or even procuring) specially designed equipment, such as **wedges, bolsters, and prone-boards** (Photo 9–8). *Cautionary note:* The inappropriate use of adaptive

Wedges, bolsters, and prone-boards
therapeutic positioning devices prescribed for use by physiotherapists and occupational therapists in treating children with impaired motor skills

Photo 9–8
It is important to consider floor coverings when working with children with mobility problems.

equipment may do *more harm* than good. It is essential that therapists and early interventionists/resource teachers explain to teachers of young children the purpose of each piece of equipment and guide the teachers in the proper use of the equipment for each individual child. Specialists must also help early childhood teachers be aware of situations that might arise and suggest precautions that should be taken while a child is using the equipment.

ADAPTING MATERIALS

Ingenious teachers have adapted almost every ordinary preschool material to fit the needs of children with motor impairments. A sampling of ideas follows.

Manipulative Materials

For children who must spend a lot of their time standing or in a wheelchair, interesting materials can be mounted on a board fastened to the wall. Wall displays allow children to grasp and manipulate objects they otherwise might not be able to manage. (These arrangements also give a new dimension to materials for normally developing children.) Items that can be mounted on a playboard include the following:

- bolts, such as those used to lock doors
- bicycle bells
- light switches
- old-fashioned telephone dials
- touch-tone phones
- doorknobs that turn
- clothes pins
- metal boards with magnetic pieces
- large-holed pegboards with large pegs
- felt boards with pockets for storing felt pieces
- Velcro tabs on which the child can place Velcro-tabbed sequential story pictures or other Velcro-backed pictures or items

Creative Materials

For children with impaired fine motor skills, creative materials can be adapted in a variety of ways:

- Large crayons, chalk, and paintbrushes should be available. Even these may be too small for some children to hang on to. If so, a section can be wrapped with layers of securely taped-down plastic material, enabling the child to get a firmer grip.
- Pencils, crayons, and coloured markers can be pushed through a small sponge-rubber ball or pencil grip, or wrapped in sponge material. These will enable the child to have a firm enough grasp to scribble or draw.
- Paper can be taped to the table. This prevents it from sliding away when a child is colouring, painting, or pasting.
- Magic markers or thick-tipped felt pens can be provided for children with weak hand and wrist control. They require less pressure than crayons but result in the rich, bright colours that please children.
- Finger-paint, potter's clay, and water-play can be made available more frequently. These materials require a minimum of fine motor control but make a major contribution in the improvement and strengthening of small-muscle function.

Self-Help/Care Devices

Many devices (available through special education catalogues) assist children in feeding, grooming, and dressing themselves. In addition, low-cost adaptations can be devised:

- Put a small suction device under a child's plate to keep it from sliding out of reach or off the table.
- Build up a spoon handle by taping a hair roller or piece of foam rubber in place to give the child better control of the spoon.
- For a child who cannot hold a spoon, make a cuff that keeps the spoon in the palm of the hand. The cuff is a wide strap that has a pocket for the spoon and is fastened around the hand with a Velcro closure.
- Use Velcro to replace buttons, zippers, and snaps. In many cases, the Velcro can be put on over existing buttons and buttonholes.
- Hang other devices for feeling, touching, smelling, examining, and manipulating at the child's level from fixtures like those used in hanging mobiles. These fixtures can also be adapted so that they can be lowered or raised depending on the appropriate height for the individual child.

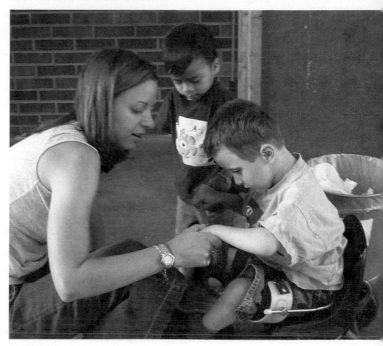

Photo 9–9
Easily accessible equipment supports children's independence.

ADAPTATIONS OF THE CLASSROOM

Alterations may be needed in the classroom and play yard if children with motor problems are to have a safe and appropriate learning environment (Photo 9–9).

WHEELCHAIR ACCOMMODATION

Space to manoeuvre a wheelchair in and out of activities and to turn it around is essential. Toileting areas must be clear so that a child can wheel in and out of the bathroom easily and pull up parallel to the toilet. Handrails mounted on the wall are needed so that the child can learn to swing from the wheelchair onto the toilet seat. Ramps can be constructed to facilitate movement in and out of the building and the classroom.

Railings

Attached in strategic places, indoors and out, railings help children with poor balance and inadequate coordination move about more independently. Railings can serve all children. They can also be used as exercise and ballet bars.

Floor Coverings

Carpeting, if it is well stretched and securely fastened down, is good for children with mobility problems. It also provides a warm and comfortable play surface for the many activities that all children engage in on the floor. When carpeting is not possible, crutches must have nonskid tips and the shoes of a child with a motor impairment should have nonskid soles. Nonskid soles can be devised by gluing textured rubber onto the soles of a child's shoes.

Eye-Level Materials

Teachers need to ask themselves, "How does this room appear at a child's level?" Are there interesting things (such as manipulative wall hangings) for all children to watch, touch, and work with? What is available at eye level for a child on a scooter-board or in a wheelchair, or one who gets about only by crawling?

Orderliness and Visibility

These concepts, and a number of others related to environmental arrangements, are discussed in considerable detail in Chapter 14. All are of major importance when designing learning environments for young children and especially so when the program includes children with motor problems.

Health Conditions

Most children experience a variety of health problems during infancy and early childhood. For the most part, these are relatively mild and do not interfere appreciably with growth and development. However, there are children who are chronically ill and have to live their everyday lives with serious health conditions. These present the child and his or her parents and teachers with ongoing problems that must be dealt with throughout the developmental years.

ASTHMA

Asthma is among the most common chronic health problem in children. It is a "condition that affects the airways to the lungs. . . . [I]n asthma the inside lining of the bronchial tubes of the lung is super sensitive . . . the bronchial tubes of children with asthma react to certain . . . triggers (smoke and dust, for example) and become narrowed and partly blocked" (Canny & Levinson, 1996, p. 3). During an attack, the child has discomfort and tightness in the chest. Breathing may be laboured and may turn to wheezing. Depending on the child, attacks may also be triggered by certain foods, pollens, animal furs (dander), air moulds, smoking, and other environmental pollutants, as well as overexertion, emotional stress, and head and chest colds. When a child is having an asthma attack (wheezing and shortness of breath), stress will usually increase the severity of the condition. It is therefore important that the teacher respond to the child's needs, but not overreact.

Before the actual onset of an attack, the child may begin to have a runny nose and/or a dry, hacking cough. Breathing (wheezing) may become loud and laboured. Lips and fingertips may take on a bluish look because of a lack of air. When a child begins to have an attack in the classroom, he or she should be encouraged to follow these steps:

1. Relax, rest, try to stay calm, and breathe easily.
2. Remain sitting in an upright position.
3. Sip warm water (avoid cold liquids)—this may help to prevent a full-blown episode.

Furthermore, if medication or special equipment, such as a Ventolin mask or inhaler, is available for the child, this should be used as soon as it becomes apparent that the condition is increasing in severity (Photo 9–10). The Asthma Society of Canada (n.d.) recommends removing the child from any possible triggers (e.g., stopping exercise, coming in from the cold, taking away pets) and administering the child's bronchodilator medication. If the child's condition does not improve after two treatments of medication, medical attention should be sought immediately. It is further recommended that on enrollment of a child with asthma, the teachers meet with the parents and obtain specific instructions as to how to recognize and respond to that child's condition. Consultation with the child's physician or community public health nurse is also advisable. If no special medication or equipment is available and a child appears to be having an asthma attack, it is important to quiet the child and follow the three steps above. If the symptoms seem to be increasing in severity, the child should be taken without delay to the nearest medical facility and the parents and physician notified immediately. Teachers should not hesitate to call in paramedics if a medical facility is not near. A child can die from a combination of oxygen deprivation and exhaustion (Marotz, Cross, & Rush, 2001).

CYSTIC FIBROSIS

Among Caucasian children, cystic fibrosis (Photo 9–11) is the most common inherited single-gene disorder (in contrast to other racial groups, among whom it occurs infrequently). The disease is incurable, but with modern medical care, many people with this disorder live into their 30s and 40s. From earliest infancy, children with cystic fibrosis are at high risk for severe respiratory infections (Gallico & Lewis, 1992).

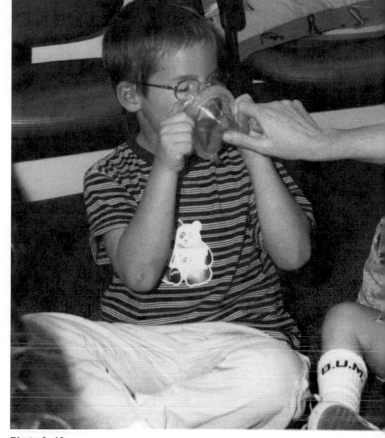

Photo 9–10
Administration of asthma medication should become part of the daily routine.

Cystic fibrosis is characterized by excessive mucus, progressive lung damage, and the body's inability to absorb fats and proteins appropriately. Children have trouble gaining weight and tend to have chronic coughs, an excessive appetite (even though they do not gain weight), frequent foul-smelling bowel movements, and unusually salty perspiration. It is this excessively salty perspiration, detected through a medical sweat test, that confirms the diagnosis of cystic fibrosis. In recent years, new knowledge has been gained through research. Scientists at the Hospital for Sick Children in Toronto have identified a region on chromosome 19 that contains a gene that modifies the severity of cystic fibrosis (Hospital for Sick Children, 1999). Though there is still no known cure for cystic fibrosis, advances in treatment continue to take place:

- In 1991, significant progress in CF treatment was made with successful experiments in the aerosol administration of Dnase, an enzyme that breaks down human genetic material. When Dnase was administered to CF lungs, it acted to break down "junk" DNA in lung secretions and reduce the thickness of these secretions, which otherwise plugged the airways and encouraged infection (Canadian Cystic Fibrosis Foundation, 2000).
- The transplanting of single lung lobes into a person with CF, from live donors (we have five lobes in each lung), is also prolonging the lives of children with CF (Canadian Cystic Fibrosis Foundation, 2000, p. 17).

Photo 9–11
Cystic fibrosis occurs most frequently in Caucasian children.

The rate of deterioration in children with CF varies from child to child. Symptoms may be minimal in one five-year-old and severe in another. In general, teachers should encourage physical activity as long as the child is reasonably well. As the child gets older, health problems tend to worsen and more frequent hospitalizations are sometimes required. Both the child and the family are likely to need considerable emotional support from teachers.

HEMOPHILIA

Another inherited disorder is hemophilia, which is experienced primarily by males. Females usually do not have the disease; they are the carriers or transmitters. Hemophilia occurs when the blood clots too slowly or not at all. As described by Apgar and Beck (1973, p. 295),

> the chief danger is not bleeding to death from accidental injury. . . . It is internal bleeding that poses the greatest threat to life and health. Bleeding into the joints, especially knees, ankles, and elbows can cause severe and constant pain, and eventually permanent crippling. . . . Internal bleeding episodes, particularly in children, can be triggered by what seem to be trivial bumps, falls and minor injuries. Often they occur without any known injury at all.

It is important that young children with hemophilia be encouraged to be as active as possible without exposing them to unnecessary risks. If a teacher suspects a joint bleed, the child's doctor should be contacted because clotting factor therapy is often the only effective treatment. It is important to know that joint bleeds do not necessarily cause bruising. A physician should be consulted immediately if a child

- is irritable or appears to be in pain
- favours one limb over another
- has a warm feeling around a joint
- walks with a limp or refuses to walk or crawl
- has one joint that appears swollen when compared with the same joint on the other limb

Ice should be applied to relieve pain, the child's activity should be limited, and the affected joint should be elevated until the swelling goes down (Hemophilia Society, 1997).

Active children with hemophilia who are in good physical condition seem to have fewer episodes of bleeding than do inactive youngsters with a similar degree of clotting deficiency. Sometimes, an increase in physical activity results in a decrease in bleeding.

Despite some increased risk, most children with hemophilia grow up to lead normal adult lives. To ensure this outcome, teachers and parents must avoid treating an affected child as overly special or so fragile that the child becomes excessively dependent or excessively concerned about personal health and well-being. Padding corners of furniture as well as the knees and elbows of the child's clothing will enable the child to move more actively without fear of personal harm from bumping into things.

LEUKEMIA

Leukemia is one of several forms of cancer to be found among young children. It is a disease that destroys bone marrow through an overproduction of white blood cells. It was viewed as a fatal disease up until a few years ago; now, **chemotherapy**

Chemotherapy
the treatment of cancer by using drug therapy used to kill cancer cells

and **radiation** have proved very effective in the treatment of this condition in children. Fatigue, consistent aching of joints, and easy bruising are symptoms related to leukemia. They should be checked by a physician if they are observed in a child.

A child with leukemia, whether treatment for the leukemia is administered in a hospital or at home, is likely to have associated physical discomfort and may be experiencing emotional upset because of both the disorder and the stresses associated with the treatment. Teachers must be sensitive to what the child may be experiencing.

Radiation
the use of high-energy penetrating rays to damage cancer cells, stopping them from growing and dividing

SICKLE-CELL DISEASE

Sickle-cell disease, another genetically transmitted, recessive condition, is found almost entirely among black children and in varying degrees of severity (Photo 9–12). Whereas in Africa the **genetic mutation** was probably an advantage—offering protection against malaria, in North America, many generations later, this once-useful sickle-shaped red blood cell has led to a chronic, painful, health problem that can result in death during childhood. A crisis is said to occur when a number of the "sickled" cells stick together and cause a blockage. The result is severe pain in the abdomen, legs, and arms; swollen joints; fainting; and overall fatigue. Special therapy can help a child to adapt and have a fairly normal existence, but there is no cure for this disorder. Research indicates that because malaria is not a threat in North America, the number of children with this condition is steadily decreasing, and it is felt that this genetic mutation has almost died out through natural selection (Jorde, Carey, & Whiter, 1995).

Children with sickle-cell disease are often particularly vulnerable to infection. The decision to enroll the child in an early childhood program is a delicate one that should be reached jointly by parents, physician, and staff (Kendrick, Kaufman, & Messenger, 1988). A child with a mild case of sickle-cell disease should continue to participate in regular preschool activities. Teachers should cooperate with the parents and the physician in preventing a sickle-cell crisis by helping the child avoid fatigue, stress, and exposure to cold, and by making sure the child has *adequate fluid intake*.

Genetic mutation
an alteration in the chromosomal materials (genes) that control inherited characteristics

Photo 9–12
Sickle-cell disease occurs mostly in black children.

CARDIAC DISORDERS

Heart disease is a common term for cardiac disorders. Many heart defects result in death during the infant's first year. Other defects can be surgically repaired, allowing the child to lead a normal life. Causes of congenital heart problems range from genetic abnormalities, to the mother's exposure to rubella during the first trimester of pregnancy, to maternal alcoholism. Children with heart disease may complain of shortness of breath, and physical activity may be more tiring than it is for other preschoolers. Some children experience cyanosis, a blueness of the skin, lips, and fingernails, that is due to poor oxygenation of the blood. The child with chronic heart problems should not be pressed to participate in activities that bring on excessive fatigue. Most children with cardiac problems are fairly reliable monitors of their own exertion tolerance. Children who have had complete surgical correction should be able to participate in all preschool activities. Teachers, parents, and health-care providers, however, need to exchange information on a continuing basis. Based on the current status of a child's condition, they should jointly work together to plan activity levels for home and school.

JUVENILE DIABETES (MELLITUS)

Also known as insulin-dependent diabetes or Type I diabetes, this form of diabetes is the type most often found in young children. Diabetes is a genetic disease, regarded as the most common of the inborn errors of metabolism. The problem arises because the pancreas (a gland located behind the stomach) fails to produce enough of a natural chemical called *insulin*. Insulin is required if the body is to **metabolize** glucose (a form of sugar). Without insulin, cells cannot use the glucose already in the bloodstream. The result is insufficient nourishment to carry on the body's functions. Children with diabetes must receive insulin on a regular basis. However, adverse reactions to insulin are a constant threat. One such threat is *hypoglycemia,* or excessively low levels of sugar circulating in the blood. Another is *hyperglycemia,* or too much sugar circulating in the bloodstream. Hypoglycemia can result in a diabetic coma (unconsciousness). According to the Canadian Diabetes Association (1997), the person experiencing hypoglycemia will exhibit some of the following signs:

Metabolize
the chemical process within living cells by which energy is manufactured so that the body systems can carry out their functions

- cold, clammy, or sweaty skin
- pallor
- shakiness or lack of coordination
- irritability
- hostility and poor behaviour
- staggering gait
- fatigue
- eventually fainting and unconsciousness

Furthermore, "the child may complain of: nervousness, excessive hunger, headache, blurred vision and dizziness, abdominal pain or nausea" (Canadian Diabetes Association, 1997). "It is important to immediately (as long as the child is conscious) get the child to eat sugar, or drink fruit juice, regular pop ... anything that will get some sugar into his or her system. The administration of sugar can cause no harm, *while withholding sugar could have serious consequences.*"

Teachers and caregivers will need to be involved in other ways too, including

- carefully regulating food intake
- monitoring the child's exercise and activity level
- observing the child for changes in behaviour and signs of infection
- occasional urine testing

It is important that teachers, parents, and health-care providers be in partnership and communicate regularly. This ensures the best possible care, with the fewest complications, for the child (Canadian Diabetes Association, 1997).

SEIZURE DISORDERS

Seizures
bursts of electrical energy in the brain that cause uncontrolled muscular movement and reduced or total loss of consciousness, as in epilepsy

The terms *epilepsy, seizure,* and *convulsion* are used somewhat interchangeably to describe disturbances in the normal electrical discharges in the brain. **Seizures** may be *focal* (partial), localized to one muscle group (or sensory system), or they may be *generalized* with loss of consciousness. Sometimes focal seizures may spread and become generalized. What happens, in simple terms, are *bursts* of electrical energy that result in reduced or total loss of consciousness. Uncontrolled muscular movements, ranging from brief twitching of the eyelids to massive shaking of the entire body, accompany these bursts or episodes. These random motor movements have been categorized in various ways:

- *Febrile seizures.* Febrile seizures are the most common. They occur in 5 percent to 20 percent of children under the age of five. In general, the seizure is brought on by a high fever. Usually, it lasts less than 15 minutes and stops by itself. Rarely are these seizures harmful, and children who experience them do not develop epilepsy.
- *Absence (petit mal) seizures.* Absence (petit mal) seizures are those in which there is momentary loss of consciousness. This may occur many times a day with some children. The lapses are so brief that they may go unnoticed, even though there could be slight twitching of the eyelids, neck, or hands. The child is often accused of *daydreaming.*
- *Tonic-clonic (grand mal) seizures.* Tonic-clonic (grand mal) seizures usually cause children to lose consciousness and fall to the floor with violently jerking muscles. They may stop breathing temporarily, lose bowel or bladder control, and bubble saliva about the mouth.
- *Partial or psychomotor seizures.* Partial or psychomotor seizures, found only rarely in young children, sometimes resemble a temper tantrum or an episode of bizarre behaviour characterized by lip-smacking, repetitive arm and hand movements, or aimless running about. Though there is the appearance of consciousness, the child is usually unaware of behaving strangely.

A variety of medications are used to control seizures in children. The medication may have an adverse effect, causing the child to be drowsy or inattentive. An important role for teachers is to *observe* and *record* changes in the child's behaviour. Behavioural observations assist the child's physician in altering the medication or dosage as needed. In general, the anticonvulsant medications prescribed for a child are effective in preventing seizures (Photo 9–13). Rarely does the early childhood teacher encounter a tonic-clonic (grand mal) seizure. However, it is important to know what to do should there be an episode. The following recommendations are adapted from material published by Epilepsy Ontario (1989):

Photo 9–13
If seizures are not well controlled, a helmet may be recommended to protect the child from injury.

- Remain calm. Children will react the same way as teachers do. The seizure itself is painless.
- Do not try to restrain the child. Nothing can be done to stop a seizure once it has begun. It must run its course.
- Clear the space around the child so that no injury from hard objects occurs and there is no interference with the child's movements.
- *Do not try to force anything between the teeth.*
- Loosen tight clothing, especially at the neck; turn the child's head to the side, and wipe away discharge from the mouth and nose to aid breathing.
- When the seizure is over, allow the child to rest.
- Generally, it is not necessary to call for medical assistance unless the seizure lasts more than 10 minutes or is followed by another major seizure.
- The child's parents must always be informed of a seizure. Teachers and parents should plan together on how best to handle future seizures for that particular child.

The child with epilepsy should not be restricted from participating in the full program, unless specific limitations are imposed by the child's physician. It would be useful for the child's teacher to know what may trigger a seizure for this particular child (e.g., flashing lights, fatigue).

A seizure episode can be turned into a learning experience for the children in the class. Teachers can explain in simple terms what a seizure is. They can assure children that it is *not catching* and that children need not fear for themselves or for the child who had the seizure. Epilepsy Ontario suggests that it is important for teachers to help other children understand, but *not pity*, the child who has seizures so that he or she remains "one of the gang." It is important that the child not feel self-conscious on regaining consciousness. Other children in the class should be encouraged to continue in their ongoing activities.

Making sure that the child receives the prescribed medication regularly and in the proper amounts is the best approach to preventing seizures. Teachers who are asked to administer medication must follow the guidelines described later in this chapter.

In concluding this section on epilepsy, it seems important to reiterate two points. The first is a repeat of the cautionary note: *Never attempt to force anything between the child's upper and lower teeth.* This procedure, once thought necessary, was discontinued years ago. Children's teeth can be damaged and adults' fingers severely bitten. The second point that bears repeating is that *teachers should remain calm.* In the interests of everyone, a teacher must not panic. Young children rarely become unduly alarmed about anything if their teachers do not appear anxious or upset. Children's anxieties over a seizure episode are reduced almost immediately if adults are confident and matter-of-fact in assuring them that the child soon will be all right. In fact, the teacher's quiet care of the child having the seizure can be a valuable experience in human concern that is of benefit to all children.

TOURETTE SYNDROME AND BEHAVIOURAL TICS

"Tourette Syndrome is a neurological disorder in which the individual experiences involuntary, multiple tics (muscular jerking), effecting the head, arms, legs, and at times vocalization" (Paasche, Gorrill, & Strom, 2004). Tourette syndrome is often not recognized until the child is five years old or older. It is found more frequently in boys. Typical symptoms include involuntary (not controllable) head jerking, facial grimacing, repetitive eye blinking or squinting, repetitive nose movement, tongue clicking, body scratching, leg jerking, foot tapping, and focal sounds. The tic behaviour is likely to become more pronounced during times of excitement. The movement and noises that a child with Tourette syndrome makes can be disturbing to other children. It is up to the teachers to try to redirect the child with Tourette syndrome into a new activity, while at the same time communicating to other children that this child has no control over this part of his or her behaviour. Often, using an example that other children are familiar with—such as coughing or sneezing, over which they have no control—will help them to be more understanding and accepting of the child with Tourette syndrome. There are now some medications available that can help a child to control the symptoms.

AIDS (ACQUIRED IMMUNE DEFICIENCY SYNDROME)

AIDS stands for acquired immune deficiency syndrome. It is a disease that leaves a person open to contracting illnesses that a healthy **immune system** might otherwise

Immune system
that aspect of body functioning responsible for warding off diseases

overcome. It is caused by the human immunodeficiency virus (HIV). Individuals may be infected without knowing it and without showing symptoms of the infection. Children who are infected may seem delayed or small for their age, or they may display neurological problems, *before they display visible symptoms.*

AIDS is transmitted primarily through intimate sexual contact, blood-to-blood contact (as through shared hypodermic needles), or from an infected mother to her baby (prenatally or through beast milk). It is estimated that one-third to one-half of the infants born to infected mothers will be infected. However, all infants of HIV-infected mothers will test positive for the disease in the first year or so of life. Why? Because the infant is still operating on its mother's antibody system, while its own is gearing up and getting ready to function.

There is no evidence of casual transmission by sitting near, living in the same household with, or playing with a person with clinical AIDS (American Academy of Pediatrics, 1990). According to the National Association for the Education of Young Children (NAEYC) Information Service (personal communication, 1991), HIV is not transmitted through urine, stool (diarrhea), vomit, saliva (mouthing of toys and other objects), mucus, sweat, or any other body fluid that does not contain blood. All children with HIV infection or AIDS should be admitted to the program as long as their own health and developmental status allow them to benefit from the program. "No case of person-to-person transmission has been documented in child care centres or schools. Because the risk of transmission through school contact is thought to be negligible, there is no justification for excluding a child with HIV infection if the child's health permits" (Rutstein, Conlon, & Batshaw, 1997).

Typically, however, many children who have AIDS are quite ill and unable to be in a child care program or a preschool classroom. Also, children with AIDS are highly vulnerable to all of the many childhood infectious illnesses; enrollment in an early childhood group of any kind may be against their best interest. For those children who are well enough to be in a program, universal hygiene precautions are required of caregivers:

- thorough handwashing
- wearing disposable gloves when dealing with bodily secretions
- cleaning caregiving surfaces with bleach and water solution

According to Best, Bigge, and Sirvis (1994), "because these precautions constitute good hygiene for anyone who requires physical care, their universal adoption allows protection for care providers while preserving the privacy of the student with AIDS" (p. 314).

In an early childhood centre, no children or adults should be attending or working in the program if they have open, oozing sores that cannot be covered or kept under control with medication. Nor should they be in the program if there is any bloody discharge accompanying diarrhea. This applies to everyone, those with and those without known HIV infection. The foregoing recommendations are in accord with medical, technical, and legislative findings as reviewed by Dokecki, Baumeister, and Kupstas (1989) and the NAEYC Information Service (personal communication, 1991). Once again, a reminder: Information on AIDS/HIV is changing continuously. Therefore, it is essential that everyone working with infants, young children, and families keep abreast of current findings.

Nutritional Problems

OBESITY (OVERWEIGHT)

Obesity is not necessarily a handicapping condition. It is a developmental health disorder that affects 15 percent to 20 percent of the children and youth in North America. Unchecked, obesity may lead to significant long-term health problems, as well as social and psychological problems. Overweight children are often unable to keep up physically with their peers and may be teased by others or excluded from play activities. This may lead to a poor self-image, decreasing physical fitness, and fewer opportunities to build satisfying social relationships (Marotz, Cross, & Rush, 2001).

Fat babies do not necessarily become fat adults; substantial evidence exists, however, that overweight preschoolers are not likely to *outgrow* the problem. As weight increases, children move less vigorously and so continue to put on more weight. This further compounds both their physical and their psychological problems. The increase of obesity in children has risen dramatically in the past few decades. According to Brizee, Sophos, and McLaughlin (1990), the increase is thought to be associated with reduced physical activity and increased consumption of convenience foods and fast foods, which tend to be high in fat. Research indicates that genetics plays a major role in predisposing a person to obesity. Two controllable factors contribute to excessive weight gain that teachers can help to prevent:

- *Overeating*. The consumption of too many calories, or at least too many calories from the wrong kind of food. Often, an overweight person eats excessive amounts of foods with poor nutritional content, popularly known as junk food.
- *Underexercising*. Lack of physical activity often is given as a major reason for obesity.

Photo 9–14
Some children may need their food intake planned by a dietary specialist.

All children, including those who are obese, need an adequate number of calories each day, but the calories need to come from the right kinds of foods—fruits, vegetables, grains, lean meats, fish, milk, and cheese. Through responsible menu planning, early childhood educators can introduce children to a variety of nutritionally sound foods.

Strangely enough, many children who are overweight are undernourished. The early childhood teacher should work closely with parents and a nutritionist or health-care nurse to make sure that a child with a weight problem is getting a daily intake of appropriate foods in appropriate amounts. Teachers can also focus parts of the early childhood curriculum on helping children understand the role of good nutrition and exercise in everyday life.

Some children may require the concentrated supervision of a nutritionist or dietary specialist (Photo 9–14). Situations requiring intensive nutritional intervention vary. Sometimes patterns of excessive food intake may have been established unintentionally by parents and caregivers. By providing an abundance of food, parents may seek to compensate for the many ordinary life experiences they are unable to provide for the child. For example, a parent who works long hours may lack the energy to interact with the child in the evening. Providing the child with a sugary treat not only pleases the child but alleviates the parent's feelings of guilt.

Physical activity is of major importance for all children (Photo 9–15). This is especially true for children who have a tendency to put on extra weight. These children should be monitored daily to ensure that they are encouraged to participate in gross motor activity. It is the responsibility of the early childhood teacher to make sure that the daily curriculum provides for ample outdoor activity.

Photo 9–15
Physical activity is important for all children.

Frequently, children with conditions that limit regular physical activity may require a diet with fewer calories. Children with other conditions, such as the genetic syndrome *Prader-Willi*, engage in uncontrolled and obsessive food consumption. Refrigerators must be kept locked. Food cannot be left out, even in a pet's dish. Teachers must keep uneaten food, even leftovers on other children's plates, securely out of the way of the child with **Prader-Willi syndrome.**

Prader-Willi syndrome
a genetic disorder characterized by obesity, short stature, disorders in sexual development, and a tendency toward behavioural and cognitive disabilities

UNDERNOURISHMENT

Consuming too few calories is as damaging to a growing child as taking in too many. Many children with physical impairments burn far more calories each day than they are able to take in. One example is children with severe cerebral palsy. They use up tremendous amounts of energy on the unwelcome but constant and uncontrollable muscular reactions characteristic of their disability. Often these children are far below ideal body weight. The same disability and muscle impairment that burns so many calories can also lead to other nutritional problems. Some affected children have trouble holding food in their mouth or chewing and swallowing. Parents, teachers, and caregivers need specialized help in learning to provide easy-to-swallow foods that are high in nutritional value (Photo 9–16).

Although young children with physical disabilities may be undernourished due to eating difficulties, poor children also may be malnourished because their parents cannot afford to buy and prepare nutritious food on a daily basis. It is imperative, therefore, that meals provided by child care staff and parents, whether in centres or in private homes, follow Canada's Food Guide (Health

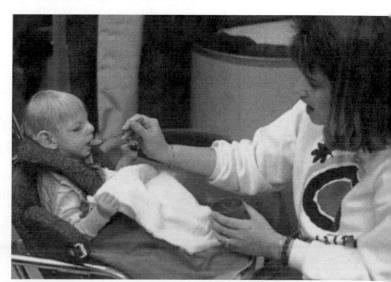

Photo 9–16
Feeding a child with a physical disability can be a long and difficult process.

Canada, 2005) in detail. Many centres now offer breakfasts as well as hot lunches and snacks. Elementary schools in impoverished areas may also provide breakfast and lunch for schoolchildren.

ANAPHYLACTIC SHOCK

Anaphylactic shock
a rapid allergic reaction that can be life-threatening if not treated immediately; it is caused by an intense overreaction of the body's immune system to a trigger

Anaphylactic shock is a rapid allergic reaction that can be life-threatening if not treated immediately. It is caused by an intense overreaction of the body's immune system to a trigger. The usual triggers are nuts, bee or wasp stings, and in some cases fish, penicillin, spices, or latex. Not every case has an obvious trigger and specific triggers don't produce specific reactions. The symptoms of anaphylactic shock include

- tingling, itching, swelling
- throat tightness, swelling
- difficulty swallowing
- wheezing, coughing, difficulty breathing
- chest tightness
- sense of fear
- flushing of face and body
- weakness or dizziness
- hives or a nettle-like rash
- stomach cramping, vomiting, diarrhea
- feeling faint

Coma or death may result if treatment does not occur.

Current treatment for an anaphylactic shock reaction is adrenaline (epinephrine). This is supplied in the form of an EpiPen. It is important that teachers are taught how to use the EpiPen properly. When teachers have a child with a known anaphylactic trigger in the class, it is essential that the EpiPen be kept on the premises at all times and brought along on any trips, walks, and so on. The EpiPen should be administered as soon as there is evidence of a reaction and before there is a lot of deterioration. Do not hesitate to administer epinephrine if any anaphylactic symptoms appear. Always go to the hospital, even if symptoms seem to go away after the first injection. The effects of epinephrine can wear off 10 to 20 minutes after the injection. Determine how long it will take to get to a hospital and be sure there is enough epinephrine to get to an emergency room. If the child appears to be okay after exposure to a known trigger, monitoring of the child must continue for at least six hours, as there may be a delayed reaction. The child's parents and doctor must be notified right away (Paasche, Gorrill, & Strom, 2004).

Health Problems and Classroom Practices

Early childhood teachers sometimes feel anxious, inadequate, even threatened, when first asked to include a child with a serious health problem or a disabling physical condition in their class. However, teachers find that the more they work with children with disabilities, the more natural it seems. The NAEYC *Health Manual* (1991, p. 14) advises teachers:

> Having good information is one of the best ways to feel confident and in control. When you know what to do—whether it is taking a temperature, giving first aid, or keeping a child relaxed during an asthma attack—both

you and the child are going to benefit from your knowledge. Lack of information often leads to panic in emergencies or improper care, such as spreading disease by not washing hands when necessary. You can provide the necessary care, remain calm, and maintain control.

Useful information for teachers comes from many sources in addition to parents and the interdisciplinary team members who are involved in the child's intervention program. The most important are up-to-date health records on each child and complete knowledge about a child's medication program. Teachers also must be sure they know what they will do in both routine and emergency situations related to specific health problems among the children in their class. Every time a child with a health condition is to be enrolled, teachers must have a careful briefing by both the child's parents and a health-care professional before the child enters the program.

HEALTH RECORDS

A complete and frequently updated health record must be maintained on every child in the group. To provide the best possible support to the child and family, the health record should contain the following essential information:

- telephone numbers where parents and other emergency contacts can be reached at all times
- name of the child's regular physician, health-care provider, or clinic, with address and telephone numbers
- permission slips authorizing emergency health care and transportation, and the administration of prescribed medications
- health insurance information, where relevant
- child and relevant family health history
- immunization information with dates
- results of medical assessment or physical and dental examinations and treatment
- results of special testing, such as vision or hearing assessments
- dated reports, signed by the attending teacher, on all injuries or illnesses that occur while the child is in the classroom, playground, or on a school-sponsored excursion
- notations on allergies, special diets, treatment procedures, medications, prosthetic devices, or other health concerns
- notations on health-related communications with parents and health-care providers, including referral recommendations and follow-up
- ongoing records of medications given to the child while at school

ADMINISTERING MEDICATION

Regulations regarding the administration of medication by teachers should follow provincial guidelines. These guidelines, as well as those for recording this procedure, differ across provinces and territories. It is important that teachers familiarize themselves with the regulations in their specific area.

Teachers may be required to administer medication during program hours. All medication should be stored in a child-resistant container and labelled with the following information:

- child's name
- physician's name and phone number

- name of the medicine
- dosage to be given to the child
- schedule for administering dosages

Requests for the administration of medication should be *put in writing and signed* by the parents. Each time medicine is given, *the time and date must be recorded* on the child's record sheet and initialled by the person who did the medicating. *Medication must be kept in a locked cupboard or refrigerator and out of reach of all children.*

EMERGENCY CONSIDERATIONS

All programs serving young children should have carefully laid-out plans for emergency situations. When children with health problems and physical disabilities are enrolled, individual plans need to be formulated for each child:

- Confer with parents (or the child's doctor) to plan in advance for an emergency health crisis.
- Understand the cause of a crisis and how often it is likely to occur.
- Learn how a child may behave before as well as during and after a crisis.
- Know what to do during and following the crisis, and understand when to call for additional help.

Preventing a health crisis is important, too. For example, it is wise to prepare a list of classroom activities. Give this list to the child's parents or physician and ask them to indicate activities that should be avoided or modified. In addition, the other children need to be prepared for possible health crises of classmates. Teachers can give simple explanations. They also can assure children that the teachers will be able to take care of all the children, not just the child who has the problem.

Summary

Physical disabilities in children include a wide range of orthopedic and health impairments. Neurological involvement often accompanies both types of problems. The physical disabilities that teachers are most likely to encounter were described briefly in this chapter in terms of characteristics, causes, program recommendations, and the responsibilities of teachers, including crisis management, as needed.

Children with both orthopedic and health problems are likely to benefit from being enrolled in a regular early childhood classroom if the staff has adequate support. Early interventionist/resource teachers and other specialists must be used to support teachers in planning and implementing a range of appropriate activities. The specially trained interventionist/resource teacher or physiotherapist is essential in cases of orthopedic involvement, though a variety of other disciplines also play significant roles, depending on the nature of the child's condition.

Early childhood educators and other members of the transdisciplinary team should work together to integrate therapeutic recommendations into everyday activities.

Regular classroom activities, materials, and equipment often can be adapted to meet the needs of children with physical disabilities. A major responsibility of teachers is to help the child with a physical disability keep active and involved to the maximum extent possible. Teachers need to help children with physically handicapping conditions or disabilities learn how to do as much as possible for themselves so that their medical condition or disability does not take over their lives. Another responsibility of teachers is to prepare themselves to meet emergency situations. When teachers remain calm and quietly in charge, young children do not panic.

RESOURCES

The following organizations provide information as well as written and physical resources for parents, professionals, and children. Canadian resources are identified with a (*).

ANAPHYLAXIS CANADA*
http://www.anaphylaxis.org

THE FOOD ALLERGY AND ANAPHYLAXIS NETWORK
http://www.foodallergy.org

ARTHRITIS SOCIETY OF CANADA*
http://www.arthritis.ca

ASTHMA SOCIETY OF CANADA*
http://www.asthma.ca

CANADIAN CYSTIC FIBROSIS FOUNDATION*
http://www.cysticfibrosis.ca

CANADIAN DIABETES ASSOCIATION*
http://www.diabetes.ca

CANADIAN HEMOPHILIA SOCIETY*
http://www.hemophilia.ca

EPILEPSY CANADA*
http://www.epilepsy.ca

MUSCULAR DYSTROPHY CANADA*
http://www.mdac.ca

NATIONAL HEMOPHILIA FOUNDATION
http://www.hemophilia.org

SPINA BIFIDA AND HYDROCEPHALUS ASSOCIATION OF CANADA*
http://www.sbhac.ca

VIRTUAL CHILDREN'S HOSPITAL
http://www.vh.org/pediatric/index.html

STUDENT ACTIVITIES

1. Divide into groups of six or seven students. Select one person as a discussion leader and talk about disabilities or serious health problems that members have experienced firsthand or through living with a sibling, close relative, spouse, or friend who has a disability. Discuss common experiences and attitudes.

2. Work with three or four other students in preparing a manipulative board to mount on the wall. Expand on the ideas suggested in this chapter. Be creative. Arrange for a tryout of the creation in one or more preschool classrooms.

3. Select a common preschool manipulative material and demonstrate ways in which it might be adapted so that a child with impaired fine motor skills could use it successfully.

4. Devise a game with beanbags, suitable for four- and five-year-olds, that would allow a child in a wheelchair to participate.

5. Select a possible crisis situation, such as an asthma attack, insulin shock, or tonic-clonic (grand mal) seizure. Describe what you would say to a group of four- and five-year-olds who had witnessed such an episode for the first time.

REFERENCES

American Academy of Pediatrics. (1990). Lack of transmission of human immunodeficiency virus from infected children to household contacts. *Pediatrics, 85*(2), 1115–1119.

Apgar, V. C., & Beck, J. (1973). *Is my baby alright?* New York: Trident.

Asthma Society of Canada. (n.d.). *Managing asthma at school.* Toronto: Asthma Society of Canada.

Best, S. J., Bigge, J. L., & Sirvis, B. P. (1994). Physical and health impairments. In N. G. Haring, L. McCormick, & T. G. Haring (Eds.), *Exceptional children and youth* (6th ed.). New York: Merrill.

Brizee, L. S., Sophos, C. M., & McLaughlin, J. F. (1990). Nutrition issues in developmental disabilities. *Infants and Young Children, 2*(3), 10–22.

Canadian Cystic Fibrosis Foundation. (2000). *1960–2000, forty. Proud of our progress. Confident of our future.* Toronto: Author.

Canadian Diabetes Association. (1997). *Kids with diabetes in your care.* Toronto: Author.

Canadian Paediatric Society. 1992. *Well beings: A guide to promote the physical health, safety, and emotional well-being of children in care centres and family day care centres.* Toronto: Creative Premises.

Canny, G. J., & Levinson, H. (1996). *Childhood asthma, a handbook for parents.* Toronto: Asthma Clinic, Hospital for Sick Children.

Dokecki, P. R., Baumeister, A. A., & Kupstas, F. D. (1989). Biomedical and social aspects of pediatric AIDS. *Journal of Early Intervention, 13*(2), 99–112.

Epilepsy Ontario. (1989). *Epilepsy, epilepsy, epilepsy.* Willowdale, ON: Author.

Fallen, N. H., & Umansky, W. (1985). *Young children with special needs.* Columbus, OH: Merrill.

Gallico, R., & Lewis, M. E. B. (1992). Learning disabilities. In M. L. Batshaw & Y. M. Perret (Eds.), *Children with disabilities: A medical primer* (3rd ed., pp. 471–498). Baltimore, MD: Brookes.

Health Canada. (2005). *Canada's food guide to healthy eating.* Ottawa: Minister of Supply & Services.

Hemophilia Society. (1997). *Your child's hemophilia.* Montreal: Centeon, L.L.C.

Hospital for Sick Children. 1999. "Researchers pinpoint region for cystic fibrosis modifier gene." Toronto: Hospital for Sick Children, Public Affairs. Retrieved August 17, 2005, from http://www.sickkids.on.ca/releases/cfres.asp.

Jorde, L. B., Carey, J. C., & Whiter, R. W. (1995). *Medical genetics.* St. Louis, MO: Mosby.

Kendrick, A. S., Kaufman, R., & Messenger, K. P. (Eds.). 1988. *Healthy young children.* Washington, DC: National Association for the Education of Young Children.

Laxer, R. M., Shore, A., & Boone, J. E. (1996). *You, your child and arthritis* (2nd ed.). Toronto: The Arthritis Society of Canada.

Marotz, L. R., Cross, M. Z., & Rush, J. M. (2001). *Health, safety, and nutrition for the young child* (5th ed.). Albany, NY: Delmar.

Mather, J., & Weinstein, E. (1988). Teachers and therapists: Evolution of a partnership in early intervention. *Topics in Early Childhood Special Education, 7*(4), 1–9.

Muscular Dystrophy Association of Canada. (1997). *A teacher's guide to Duchenne muscular dystrophy.* Toronto: Author.

National Association for the Education of Young Children (NAEYC). 1991. *Health manual.* Washington, DC: Author.

Paasche, C. L., Gorrill, L., & Strom, B. (2004). *Children with special needs in early childhood settings.* Albany, NY: Delmar.

Rutstein, M. R., Conlon, C. J., & Batshaw, M. L. (1997). HIV and AIDS. In M. L. Batshaw (Ed.), *Children with disabilities* (4th ed., pp. 162–182). Baltimore, MD: Brookes.

Stem Cell Research Foundation. (2004). 22512 Gateway Center Drive, Clarkesburg, Maryland 20871. Retrieved August 17, 2005, from http://www.stemcellresearchfoundation.org.

CHAPTER 10

Social, Adaptive, and Learning Disorders

KEY CONCEPTS

anxiety disorder

Asperger's disorder

attention deficit hyperactivity
   disorder (ADHD)

autism

autism spectrum disorder

behaviour disorder (BD)

echolalic

emotional disturbance

encopresis

enuresis

hyperactivity

hyperkinesis

learning disability

learning disorders

perseveration

pervasive developmental
   disorder (PDD)

phobias

pica

tangible reinforcers

OBJECTIVES

After studying the material in this chapter, the student will be able to

- Recognize the symptoms of anxiety disorders found in young children.
- Describe eating and toileting concerns sometimes associated with behavioural disorders, and discuss appropriate adult attitudes toward these types of situations.
- Provide a convincing argument against labelling or diagnosing a preschool child as having a learning disability.
- Recognize the major warning signs in a preschool child that suggest the potential for learning disabilities related to later reading, writing, and math skills.
- Discuss the use and misuse of the term hyperactivity.

Introduction

Disorders associated with behaviour and with learning have been linked to various developmental conditions. In this chapter we will discuss those that are not a result of a primary disability, such as intellectual developmental disabilities or blindness. The behaviours discussed here are qualitatively different. Behaviours such as occasionally not following directions or finding it hard to sit still for 20 minutes are common behaviours of young children.

In this chapter we will examine behaviour disorders, learning disorders, attention deficit hyperactivity disorder (ADHD), and pervasive developmental disorders. The diagnosis of all four of these types of disabilities is based on a professional's diagnosis of a child's behaviours. Although there are standard diagnostic criteria for these disabilities, based on criteria set in the *Diagnostic and Statistical Manual of Mental Disorders* (*DMS-IV-TR;* American Psychiatric Association [APA], 2000), there are several types of professionals who can diagnose these types of disabilities, including physicians, psychologists, neurologists, and psychiatrists. However, there is no blood test or other physical procedure or examination that confirms or refutes the diagnosis. For this reason, it is especially important that the family or primary caretaker is involved in the assessment process; that the assessment instruments used are culturally relevant, bias-free, and in the child's home language; and that at least part of the assessment is conducted in an environment that is familiar to the child. The terms *behaviour disorder, ADHD,* and *learning disability* should be used with extreme caution when describing a young child.

The label *behaviour disorders* is widely used to classify a variety of social and **emotional disturbances** ranging from mild to severe. Children who are identified as having a **behaviour disorder (BD)** are those whose behaviour is extreme, chronic, and unacceptable. Defining and diagnosing behaviour disorders are ongoing challenges in special education and are extremely problematic in early childhood. Sometimes drawing the distinction between developmentally and culturally appropriate behaviour and behaviour that impedes a child's development in one or more areas is difficult for even the most skilled teacher or parent.

The term **learning disorders** is often applied to children with average IQs and reasonable adaptive functioning who nevertheless have difficulty learning to read, write, or do math. A behaviour or learning disorder may be a child's major or *primary* special need, or it may be a *secondary* problem. There are some children who function successfully in most areas of development but exhibit one or more inappropriate behaviour patterns. In these cases, the behaviour disorder is the primary concern.

The inability, or lack of opportunity, to learn appropriate behaviours or to understand routine expectations may be the cause of secondary behaviour concerns. The frustrations the child experiences in trying to perform everyday developmental tasks and engage in effective social exchanges are often a factor. Children with developmental special needs tend to get relatively little positive feedback from parents, caregivers, and teachers; yet their maladaptive behaviours, such as head banging, shrill squealing, or eye-poking, draw a great deal of attention. Thus, the maladaptive behaviours become more dominant, making it even more difficult for these children to acquire necessary developmental skills.

When working with young children who present challenging or inappropriate behaviours, it is essential to keep in mind what is developmentally appropriate

Emotional disturbances
characterized by behavioural or emotional responses so different from appropriate age, cultural, and community norms that the responses adversely affect educational performance

Behaviour disorder (BD)
a chronic or pervasive challenging behaviour

Learning disorders
the name given to a group of problems that can cause children who have average IQs and reasonable adaptive functioning to nevertheless have difficulty learning to read, write, do math

within various cultures. Most four-year-olds do not follow all directions, they challenge adults occasionally, and they can go from laughter to tears in a few seconds. For this reason, the term behaviour disorder should be used with extreme caution when describing the behaviour of young children.

There is general agreement among most child developmentalists that preschool children (with few exceptions) *should not be labelled as emotionally disturbed*. Early development is characterized by constant change. Therefore, the label *emotionally disturbed* is premature, nonfunctional, and likely incorrect.

Emotional and Psychological Disorders

SEPARATION PROBLEMS

Infants and young children are frequently fearful of strangers and unwilling to separate from a parent or major caregiver (Photo 10–1). The behaviour tends to peak between 12 and 15 months of age and then to lessen gradually. Children in families in which there is general instability may be especially fearful of strangers and, throughout the preschool years and beyond, have trouble separating.

Entering preschool or a child care centre for the first time can be intimidating for young children. Young children with disabilities may experience even more anxiety. They are likely to have had fewer play experiences away from home than other children have. Also, they often have been the focus of intensive adult care and concern to a degree that may not be possible in a school situation. Separation anxiety is common. In most cases it need not become a major problem if the first days of school are carefully planned by teachers and parents.

In a few instances, a child and parent may have prolonged and severe difficulty in separating. At the least hint that the parent might leave, the child has a severe emotional reaction that may be a consequence of the parent trying to slip away without saying goodbye after agreeing to stay. In these cases, teachers must involve parents in a plan to help the child learn to separate. Discussions of the difficulties the child is experiencing should take place away from the classroom and out of the child's hearing. The separation process should focus on the parent's gradual withdrawal, usually over several days. The amount of time required depends on the child and the severity of the problem. Throughout the parent's separation efforts, teachers should encourage and appreciate the child's participation in the program. Gradually, the teacher's support will replace the parent's support.

Occasionally, a child who likes coming to the program may use protest as a way to keep the parent at school. These children often engage in every activity and play happily as long as the parent stays. As soon as the parent tries to leave, however, the child starts to cry or scream and strongly protest. Parents in these situations often complain about the child's behaviour. Yet, after saying goodbye they have a tendency to pause and look back, as if waiting for the child to begin to protest. At times, it is the parent who is having a separation problem. In these cases, the teacher may

Photo 10–1
Saying goodbye to a parent may take extra time when a child is new to a program.

have to assist the lingering parent in leaving swiftly with only a brief and matter-of-fact goodbye. The child almost always settles back into play after a token protest.

OVERDEPENDENCY

The early childhood teacher may be the target of a child's efforts to get extraordinary amounts of attention. Sometimes this is the child who has had difficulty separating from his or her parents, but not always. The child who is overly dependent may cling to a particular teacher, hang on to the teacher's clothing, and shadow the teacher's every move. Complaining, whining, and tattling may be accompanying behaviours. Working with a child who is overly dependent requires the teacher to walk a fine line between giving too much attention and too little. Too much attention is likely to increase the child's dependency problems; too little may lead the child to feel unliked or rejected, or even distrustful of the situation.

To receive the full benefit from the program, a child must be helped to relate to all teachers (Photo 10–2) and, eventually, to children. Once the child is familiar with the program and the routines, the *weaning* process can begin. It is not a question of reducing the amount of attention; it is one of making decisions as to when to give attention in order to help rather than to hinder the child's progress. Consider the following examples:

The teacher watches for those moments when the child is not clinging and immediately gives attention: "It looks as if you are enjoying that book. Let's read the pictures together. What do you suppose is going to happen to the kitten?"

When a child is pulling at the teacher's clothing or person, the teacher should resist the impulse to react or respond. Hard to do, yes; but it is to the eventual benefit of both the child and the teacher. As always, preventive measures are best: As the child approaches, the teacher can reach out and put an arm around the child or take the child's hand before the clinging or clutching starts.

Teachers should support the child in taking personal responsibility, beginning with non-threatening situations: "If you want to play in the rocking boat I'll go with you while you talk to Sherri. If you ask, I know she'll stop rocking so you can get in."

Finding ways to get the child to allow another teacher to respond to his or her needs is another step in solving a difficult situation. The teacher should choose those times when the child really wants something, as when one teacher says to another: "Ms. Singh, Charles wants the red truck. Will you get it out for him?" or to the child, "I can't read your book because I have to set up finger-painting. Let's ask Mr. John to read it to you."

Occasionally, a teacher finds it flattering to be singled out for undivided devotion and unintentionally reinforces the child's overly dependent behaviours. In these instances, both child and teacher need the help of other staff members.

Children who are overly dependent or anxious may also complain of headaches, stomach aches, or nearly

Photo 10–2
Children need to learn to relate to more than one teacher.

invisible cuts and scrapes. Though the hurt is real to the child, it also has become a sure way of getting focused attention from an important adult. Most young children can be expected to have these kinds of complaints sometimes. When the complaints go on day after day, it is cause for concern. The first step is to check with parents to make sure that there are no physical problems. Classroom procedures then become the same as for other problematic behaviours: minimum attention to the aches and scrapes, as well as additional attention when the child is actively engaged in play activities. This helps the child focus on the fun times at school.

WITHDRAWAL AND SHYNESS

Some children seem to be alone most of the time. They rarely engage in social play activities. Often, they turn away when other children approach. In structured, large-group activities, they may be there in body but are remote and not there in spirit. Teachers seldom express the degree of concern over these children that they do with children who show extreme emotional reactions and aggressive behaviour. The behaviours of the child who is withdrawn are easily overlooked; those of the child who is disruptive seldom go unnoticed. Yet the child who is withdrawn may be in greater developmental jeopardy than the child who displays disruptive behaviours.

Withdrawal problems and their causes may be so complex as to require clinical treatment and a segregated, therapeutic classroom. However, most children who show signs of withdrawal in early childhood settings are likely to have less serious problems with less obscure origins. The cause may be a recent upheaval at home, such as a parent leaving or a serious illness in the family. It may be a change of neighbourhood where the new children's ways seem strange, even frightening or bullying. It may be the first venture of an only child or a child with a disability into a play setting with other children. These children may have been overprotected unwittingly, due to the parents' efforts to keep them from getting hurt or catching a childhood disease. There are also those children who are simply shy. All children experience shyness off and on to some degree. In some children, shyness becomes a longstanding habit. Whatever the cause, teachers usually can help these children become more involved.

Careful observation is the required first step. Specific questions should be asked:

- Does the child engage in particular activities when playing alone?
- Are there materials and equipment (Photo 10–3) that the child appears to enjoy or prefer?
- Does the child spend time watching certain children or certain activities more than others?
- Is the child likely to leave an activity if certain children approach? Does the child avoid these children consistently?

Photo 10–3
Does the child have a favourite toy or piece of equipment to use as a starting point?

- Are some children less threatening for the child to sit next to in group activities or to play next to in parallel play situations?

When a child's preferences (and avoidances) have been noted, plans can be made to gradually reduce the child's isolation. The following are three examples of first approximations to social interactions for Jeanine, a child whose isolated behaviours were of concern.

On several occasions the teacher had observed Jeanine watching housekeeping play with apparent interest. The teacher arranged that he and the child together deliver additional materials to the activities in progress. The teacher announced: "Jeanine and I have brought some more birthday candles. We'll put some of them on the cake, too, okay?"

Jeanine seemed fascinated by the rocking boat. A quiet but friendly child asked the teacher for another ride. The teacher responded, "Yes, Jon, but let's give Jeanine a ride, too. Here, Jeanine, you sit across from Jon." Another time a third child is invited, who also is seated across from Jeanine, and then a fourth who sits next to Jeanine. In each of these early steps, the teacher selected quieter, less rambunctious children to share the ride.

Jeanine was watching two children working with pegboards. The teacher said, "Jeanine, I'll put a pegboard down here for you." The teacher placed the pegboard at the end of the small table near, but not between, the other children. "All three of you can reach the basket of pegs."

Having Jeanine take pegs out of a common basket was a step forward from the week before. At that time, the teacher had seated her near the other children but had given her a small basket of pegs of her own.

Sometimes, the child who is shy will focus almost exclusively on one or more of the adults in the program. Overdependency does not seem to be the problem; it is as if some children prefer the company of adults. They always find ways to sit next to the teacher. They linger during transitions to help the teacher clean up. They engage the teacher in long, one-to-one conversations. This may be pleasant for the teacher, but it does not promote the kinds of social development that come with learning to interact with other children. The teacher's job becomes one of consciously involving another child or two in the conversation or the cleanup operation. If no other children are about, the teacher should respond to the child pleasantly but briefly, and then move to an area where there are other children. Usually the child who is shy will follow. This increases the opportunity for the teacher to involve other children.

ANXIETY AND DEPRESSION

Depression, fearfulness, and anxiety occur in young children, though to a lesser degree than found in preadolescents and teenagers. Common **anxiety disorders** in the early years revolve around separation problems, overdependence, and withdrawal (Photo 10–4, p. 192) or avoidance of social contacts. Some young children are more prone to being overly anxious than are others. These children may need extra support and reassurance when entering new situations. It is important to build self-esteem in young children, to give them a strong sense of their own worthiness. Children who enter preadolescence and adolescence with low self-esteem are more likely to become depressed or anxiety ridden (Harter, 1990).

Anxiety disorder
an extreme and lasting concern and fearfulness in certain situations, which other children their age do not experience; these commonly include separation problems, overdependence, withdrawal from social interactions, and so on

Photo 10–4
Withdrawal is one form of anxiety disorder seen in young children.

Phobias
fears that result in excessive
and unrealistic anxiety about
everyday happenings

PHOBIAS

Fears that result in excessive and unrealistic anxiety about everyday happenings are called **phobias.** The individual with a phobia may go into a panic reaction at encountering a feared object or event, or at the mere thought of encountering it. For example, there are people who take unrealistic measures, such as climbing 20 flights of stairs to avoid riding an elevator; or they walk a kilometre out of the way, every day, rather than pass a well-fenced yard in which there is a small, securely tied dog that barks at passers-by. A certain amount of fear is appropriate. Fears are natural adaptive mechanisms in young children and are built in for survival purposes. No child should be laughed at or shamed for his or her fears. By the same token, children's fears should not be allowed to get blown out of proportion. As with all developmental issues, there is a fine line between too much and too little attention. Adaptive fears can become unrealistically stressful if adults are overly attentive to (thereby reinforcing) the child's fearful responses. Conversely, not receiving enough attention can make the child feel insecure and rejected. These feelings may lead to other kinds of maladaptive behaviours and stressful reactions.

Eating and Elimination Disorders

Eating problems associated with particular disorders, as well as with being overweight and underweight, were described in Chapter 9. Incontinence associated with spinal cord damage also was discussed. This section will look at several other eating and elimination disorders sometimes found among young children in group settings.

PICA

Pica
craving to eat nonfood
substances

The uncontrollable eating of nonfood substances is called **pica.** In pica, the young child eats nonfood substances, such as clay, dirt, animal feces, bits of paint, glass, hairballs, and so on, without discriminating these nonfood items from food. Early childhood teachers may encounter children who constantly *taste* substances considered inedible, such as dirt, tar, grease, chalk, paper, finger-paint, paste, play dough, or clay. Though sometimes a health threat, most young children experiment with the tasting of inedible materials. This should *not* be confused with pica. In pica, the intake of this material is frequent and at times in great quantities. It can lead to malnutrition, cuts in the mouth, and intestinal obstructions. Whether it is pica or simple experimental tasting, this random intake of nonfood substances should be discouraged, with an explanation to the child that it can make him or her sick. If the child continues, the problem usually is solved by removing the material with the simple statement: "I can't let you play with the play dough if you eat it. It will make you sick." If everything fails to work, a specialist should be consulted.

Children also may go on food jags. They insist on certain foods to the exclusion of all others. Except in extreme cases (or if too much pressure is put on the child to "eat right"), the jag usually disappears in a reasonable time. Some children eat excessive amounts of a certain food. One four-year-old was known to eat whole heads of lettuce, almost ravenously. At times this eating behaviour may indicate a nutritional deficit. Whenever a teacher is concerned about a child's eating, the parents and public health nurse should be consulted.

SOILING AND WETTING

It is not uncommon for early childhood teachers to encounter children who are not toilet-trained, or are not reliable about getting themselves to the toilet in time. The same holds true for young children with developmental disabilities, many of whom may not be toilet-trained when they reach preschool age. The reasons vary. Often, conflict has resulted in a toilet-training impasse between the child and parents. In the early childhood program, where emotional involvement is at a minimum, toilet-training usually can be accomplished quickly. Effective training guides include *Steps to Independence* by Baker and Brightman (1997). It is the rare child, even among children who are severely intellectually impaired, who cannot be trained to use the toilet.

Even after they are toilet-trained, young children, including those with disabilities, may have soiling or wetting episodes on occasion. They often give clues of an impending accident by jiggling or clutching themselves. What is needed is a quiet instruction from the teacher *before* the accident occurs: "Run in and use the toilet. I'll save the swing until you get back." When a toilet accident does occur, a child should never be ridiculed or made to feel guilty. Even the most conscientious child can slip up. Clothing should be changed matter-of-factly. Every young child should have spare clothes at school, rotated from home if possible (Photo 10–5, p. 194).

Chronic soiling or wetting sometimes occurs in an older preschool or primary-age child who has been reliably toilet-trained. It is important to be aware of the following:

* Persistent wetting, especially in girls, may be related to a chronic urinary tract infection.
* A child may have a recurring low-grade intestinal virus causing loose or runny bowels.
* Children with diabetes may have failure of urine control at times.
* Some children are anxious about using a strange bathroom or may have been trained to greater privacy than is available at school.

Once in a while, even when all physical disorders have been ruled out, a child may continue to have toileting problems. **Encopresis** (chronic soiling problem) and **enuresis** (chronic wetting problem) are the clinical names often assigned to such conditions. Though there are a number of possible reasons, earlier difficulties associated with elimination or toilet-training may have become intertwined with anxiety, fear, and other emotional reactions. These can result in a child's unpredictable and hard-to-control soiling or wetting accidents. In these cases, as in all others, the clothes should be changed matter-of-factly, without reprimand or moralizing. Working together, teachers, parents, and the appropriate team member(s) can help a child with enuresis or encopresis gain reliable control.

Encopresis
chronic soiling problem

Enuresis
chronic wetting problem

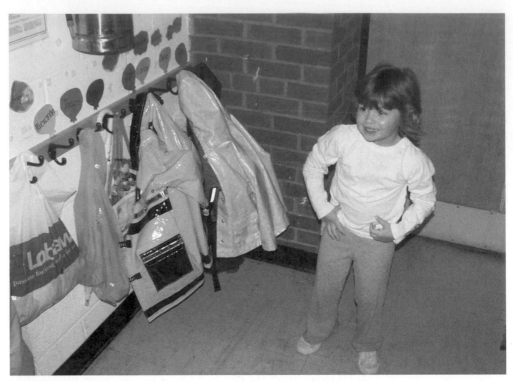

Photo 10–5
Every child needs a change of clothing at school.

Social/Learning Adaptation Disorders

Pervasive developmental disorders, attention deficit hyperactivity disorders, and schizophrenia are three conditions that, to varying degrees, interfere with the child's ability to

- initiate and maintain relationships with others
- concentrate for any length of time
- assimilate new material into his or her existing framework of knowledge

AUTISM SPECTRUM DISORDER OR PERVASIVE DEVELOPMENTAL DISORDERS

Autism spectrum disorder
or pervasive developmental
disorder (PDD)
a serious disturbance that affects a child's social-language interaction or ability to engage in imaginative play or both

Autism spectrum disorder or **pervasive developmental disorder (PDD)** refers to a group of childhood disorders usually evident by age three. These disorders have identifiable characteristics and behaviours that can be exhibited in children to extremely varying degrees. The primary characteristics include

- abnormal social interaction (poor reciprocal social interactions).
- impaired communication (verbal and nonverbal communication skills).
- peculiar interests and behaviours. Children often have a limited range of activities and interests, which are frequently stereotyped and repetitive (APA, 2000).

Autism and childhood schizophrenia are the most commonly known PDD conditions.

Autism

Autistic disorder, sometimes referred to as childhood autism or early infantile autism, is the most severe form of PDD. New research indicates that the prevalence of autism in North America has increased significantly in recent years. It has jumped from 40 to 60 cases per 10 000 people, which represents approximately 190 000 Canadians (Fombonne, 2003a, 2003b). The Autism Society of Canada (2005) has gathered "information from reporting provincial departments of education that shows an estimated 150% increase in reported cases in Canada over a six-year period (1998–2004)." Approximately 1 in 200 children born today have an autistic disorder (Fombonne, 2003a, 2003b). It is not yet clear whether this huge increase is due to a greater recognition and detection of autism, or whether environmental conditions have affected the prenatal or postnatal development of the child. Autism is four times more common in boys than in girls. Children with autistic disorder exhibit a moderate to severe range of communication, socialization, and behaviour problems.

One of the earliest signs of **autism** is resistance to being held or cuddled. The infant tends not to mould to the mother's (or caregiver's) body, as do most infants. As toddlers and little children, children with autism treat others as *inanimate* (lifeless) objects. Rarely do these children make eye contact (Photo 10–6). Following rituals to excess and maintaining rigid requirements for sameness are typical. Changing the position of a piece of furniture or offering a drink from an unfamiliar cup may trigger a violent tantrum. Self-stimulating behaviours, such as spinning, rocking, head banging, and self-biting, are common. According to a pediatric neurologist (Coleman, 1989, p. 25), these children also engage in other odd behaviours; for example, they may

Photo 10–6
Many children who are diagnosed with autism rarely make eye contact.

Autism
a pervasive developmental disorder, a social-communicative problem that emerges before a child is three years old

- line up objects or toys for hours on end
- fixate at looking at spinning objects, such as wheels of toy cars
- walk on their toes
- flap their hands or make finger motions in front or their eyes when excited
- overreact to sensory stimuli (e.g., covering their ears to shut out vacuum cleaner sounds, the sounds of crying infants, or sometimes the most ordinary of sounds)
- show unusual development of language (e.g., one child may have beautifully clear speech with complex language, but the message is so disorganized that it makes no sense, while another child may use language simply to express rote memorization; many of these children can recite many commercial jingles heard on television, but they have no communicative language)
- lack appropriate intonation in their speech
- lack social language (e.g., a child may know all the words to every stanza of more than 40 popular songs and folk ballads but have no social language except for a few stereotyped, **echolalic**—repetitive—phrases).

The *DSM-IV-TR* (2000) includes the following characteristics in describing autistic disorder[1]:

- qualitative impairment in social interaction
- qualitative impairments in communication (may have delay or total lack of development of spoken language; may have speech but be unable to hold a two-way conversation; may use stereotyped and repetitive words and phrases)
- restricted repetitive and stereotyped patterns of behaviours, interests, and activities
- delays or abnormal functioning in at least one of the following areas with onset before age three: (1) social interaction, (2) social communication, or (3) symbolic or imaginative play
- the disturbance is not better accounted for by Rett's disorder or childhood disintegrative disorder (i.e., is not degenerative)

Echolalic
describes a condition in which language is characterized by repetition of words and sentences that do not convey meaning; this condition is often associated with autism

Diagnosis is usually made before age five. Since there is currently no physical or medical test for autism, a thorough assessment completed by an interdisciplinary team is warranted. This team should include a physician, psychologist, teacher, language specialist, and the parent(s).

There are a number of successful early intervention programs for children with autism (Dawson & Osterling, 1997). The most successful programs for children with autism include predictable routines, use of effective instructional strategies, and curricular content that is developmentally appropriate for the individual child.

The following are useful strategies:

- Keep messages simple and direct.
- Use real objects and actions along with words (e.g., show the child a shoe and demonstrate how to lace it).
- Emphasize spoken language by having the child ask for things by name rather than by gesturing.
- Seek to maintain eye contact with the child, redirecting his gaze by gently turning his head, if necessary.
- Give the child opportunities to interact with younger children who are at a more comparable level in language and social development.
- For behaviour management programs, use **tangible reinforcers** (small toys, stickers, music, or favoured foods, if all else fails) and pair these with adult attention.
- Establish and maintain a predictable environment, including teacher's language and behaviours, daily schedule, and classroom furnishings and materials.

Tangible reinforcers
material things that the individual likes; in children, favourite foods and drinks, toys, stickers, and so on (older children usually like money)

Photo 10–7
Picture exchange communication systems are being used more in early childhood environments.

- Try picture exchange communication systems (PECS). These are being used in more and more early childhood environments. PECS involve using pictures with nonverbal children to facilitate communication (Photo 10–7).

In working with families of children who have autistic behaviours, it is important to support the parents in every way possible and to work with other members of the transdisciplinary team to help parents find specialized help, as well as *respite care,* as required by the family.

Another urgent need of parents is frequent assurance that the autism was not caused by a lack of love or caring on their part. Parents of children with autism have often been greatly wronged. Without valid evidence, for many years professionals implied that parents (more often than not the mother) were somehow responsible for their child's autism. According to Bee (1999, p. 557), children are born with the disorder: "Whatever the specific origin, the evidence jointly points to the conclusion that autism reflects different brain functions of some kind."

ASPERGER'S DISORDER

Asperger's disorder is a neurobiological disorder that shares many of the characteristics of autism. The difference is that children with Asperger's disorder are intellectually high functioning and their symptoms can range from mild to severe. There is a significant impairment in social development but no significant impairment in language, cognitive, or self-help skills or adaptive behaviour (APA, 2000). The *DSM-IV-TR,* under the category of "Pervasive Development Disorder," indicates the following characteristics as typical of Asperger's disorder. A child with at least two of these characteristics to be considered as falling under this classification[2]:

1. marked impairment in the use of multiple nonverbal behaviors, such as eye-to-eye gaze, facial expression, body postures, and gestures to regulate social interaction
2. failure to develop peer relationships appropriate to developmental level
3. lack of spontaneous seeking to share enjoyment, interests, or achievements with other people (e.g., by a lack of showing, bringing, or pointing out objects of interest to other people)
4. lack of social or emotional reciprocity

Further behaviours include one or more of the following:

- repetitive and stereotyped patterns of behaviour, interests, and activities
- inflexibility to, and problems adapting to, change (e.g., in routines or room arrangement)
- ritualistic behaviours
- stereotyped and repetitive motor mannerisms (e.g., hand or finger flapping, twisting)

Children who have Asperger's syndrome differ from those classified under autism in that they are high functioning and usually have well-developed language. The major emphasis in working with children with Asperger's syndrome needs to be on helping them to develop socially interactive relationships. The preschool teacher needs to plan opportunities for small-group interactions with others and should also try to find ways in which this child can participate actively in the ongoing early childhood program.

Asperger's disorder
a neurological disorder with many of the same characteristics as autism; the exception is that children with Asperger's disorder are intellectually high functioning

Rett's Disorder

This disorder, also known as Rett syndrome, has recently been identified as stemming from a rare genetic disorder (Beers, 2005). It is diagnosed primarily in females. Parents report normal development over the first 18 months followed by a loss of abilities, especially in the area of gross motor skills. This regression continues in the areas of speech and hand use. Diagnosis is often made based on the repetitive gestures and hand movements often described as hand writing. Behaviours in children with Rett's disorder are often confused with those found in autism.

CHILDHOOD SCHIZOPHRENIA

There is less scientific knowledge about childhood schizophrenia than there is about autism. Childhood schizophrenia is characterized by loss of ego boundaries and an impaired sense of reality. Major characteristics of the disorder include tantrums and repetitive or otherwise bizarre behaviours or postures. Other characteristics are rejection of and withdrawal from social contacts and unpredictable mood swings. The child frequently is described as "cut off from reality" and given to hallucinations. Children with schizophrenia usually have normal language development, though the language may be used for noncommunicative purposes. Many of these children talk to themselves in a private language that no one can decode. Children with schizophrenia tend to have more varied symptoms than do children with autism. They are also more likely to have contact and interactions with other people. Early childhood teachers rarely encounter a child with schizophrenia because the onset of the condition usually occurs after the preschool years. However, if a child with this condition were enrolled in an early childhood program, as with other conditions, a team approach involving specialists should be used in developing an intervention program for this child.

Hyperactivity or hyperkinesis refer to children who are highly active, energetic, impulsive, and distractible and who have a hard time waiting their turn or listening to instructions

Attention deficit hyperactivity disorder (ADHD) behaviour that is characterized by consistently short attention span, inattentiveness, distractibility, impulsivity, and heightened levels of movement and physical activity (hyperactivity)

ATTENTION DEFICIT HYPERACTIVITY DISORDERS (ADHD)

Hyperactivity (or **hyperkinesis**) is a catchall diagnosis and label that is much overworked. It is used to refer to children who are highly active, energetic, impulsive, and distractible and who have a hard time waiting their turn or listening to instructions (Photo 10–8). These children may be described as showing "excessive motor activity." Regardless of particular behaviours, these children have two things in common:

1. Many adults find their behaviours challenging.
2. An identifiable physical or neurological cause is seldom found for their high activity level.

    Attention deficit hyperactivity disorder (ADHD) is a term that has come into popular use over the past several years. It is classified as a subsection under "Attention Deficit and Disruptive Behavior Disorders" by the APA (2000), which uses "attention deficit hyperactivity disorder," but also recognizes that some children have ADHD without hyperactivity. ADHD includes the following behaviours (APA, 2000, pp. 65–66)[3]:

- Inattention
    a. often fails to give close attention to details or makes careless mistakes in work or other activities
    b. often has difficulty sustaining attention in tasks or play activities
    c. often does not seem to listen when spoken to directly

Photo 10–8
Hyperactivity is used as a catchall phrase to refer to children who are highly active, energetic, impulsive, and distractible.

  d. often does not follow through on instructions and fails to finish schoolwork, chores

  e. often has difficulty organizing tasks and activities

  f. often avoids, dislikes, or is reluctant to engage in tasks that require sustained mental effort

  g. often loses things necessary for tasks or activities (e.g., toys)

  h. is often easily distracted by extraneous stimuli

  i. is often forgetful in daily activities

- Hyperactivity

  a. often fidgets with hands or feet or squirms in seat

  b. often leaves seat in classroom or in situations in which remaining seated is expected

  c. often runs about or climbs excessively in situations in which it is inappropriate

  d. often has difficulty playing or engaging in leisure activities quietly

  e. is often "on the go" or often acts as if "driven by a motor"

  f. often talks excessively

- Impulsivity

  a. often blurts out answers before questions have been completed

  b. often has difficulty awaiting a turn

  c. often interrupts or intrudes on others (e.g., butts into conversations or games)

Many of these same behaviours are also characteristic of young children diagnosed as having a learning disability. The attention deficit hyperactivity disorder label, authoritative as it may sound, does little to lessen the problems associated with supporting a young child who is constantly on the move. It should also be noted that those children who have ADHD without hyperactivity have trouble focusing and may appear to be "daydreaming."

Causes of ADHD

Research has yet to reveal one specific cause of ADHD. Several hypotheses have been offered, one or two of which are backed up by fairly sound evidence. One is the possible role of genetic transmission. Bee (1999) reports a recent study in which one-fourth of the subjects with ADHD had parents with a history of hyperactivity. Studies of twins also show possible genetic implications. Among identical twins, both are more likely to have hyperactivity, which is not the case among fraternal twins (Deutsch & Kinsbourne, 1990). Researchers continue to work on the brain and its various functions, or malfunctions, to explain ADHD. A correlation has also been found between ADHD and a mother's smoking or drug and alcohol use during pregnancy. Longitudinal data published by Barkley (1998) indicate that the mean age of onset of ADHD is between three and four years of age. ADHD affects 3 percent to 5 percent of school-aged children (Barkley, 1998; Wolraich, Hannah, Pinnock, Baumgaertal, and Brown, 1996). It was once thought that children outgrew ADHD in adolescence, but it is now believed that only the hyperactivity decreases during the teen years. Many symptoms do continue into adulthood, affecting approximately 2 percent to 4 percent of adults (Murphy & Barkley, 1996).

The Hyperactive Label

The term *hyperactivity* is both misused and overused, especially when applied to young children. Among children of preschool and primary school age, there is a broad range of activity levels. Some seem to be on the move continually. Teachers often feel as if these children never settle into any activity for any length of time. Yet few of these children have any organic problems. A child who can stay with any activity for several minutes at a time is not clinically hyperactive. The child may be difficult to entertain, not interested in typical learning tasks, easily distracted by activity in other areas of the room, or perhaps worried and unhappy, but the child is *not* hyperactive as per the accepted *DSM-IV-TR* (APA, 2000) definition.

Intervention Strategies for Managing Attention Deficit Hyperactive Behaviour

Attention deficit hyperactive behaviour in young children does place them at a greater risk for accidents because they do not anticipate the consequences of their actions. Also, adults become more frustrated by excessively active, impulsive children who must be watched constantly.

There can be serious consequences for children who do not receive adequate treatment for ADHD. These may include poor self-esteem, academic failure, and poor social development and interactions. Treatment plans should be developed with the parent or caregiver to best meet the individual needs of the child and family.

The most commonly used approaches to helping children diagnosed as having ADHD are medication, special diets, and behaviour management, often most effectively used in combination with one another.

Medication. In assessing highly active children, it is argued that distinctions should be made between (1) the child whose high activity level is truly organic and (2) the child who is simply overly active. The reason for making the distinction is that some children in the organic group may benefit from prescription drugs, such as Ritalin or Dexedrine. Psychostimulants, such as Ritalin or Dexedrine, are the most widely used class of medication for the management of ADHD. When effective, these medications can lead to increased attention and concentration, and decreased levels of impulsivity and activity (Swanson & McBurnett, 1993). However, medication may have undesirable side effects, including weight loss (loss of appetite), insomnia, or increased blood pressure.

Medication should be used only under the supervision of a physician and only when there is indisputable evidence that it is the most beneficial treatment. Sometimes, it is parents and teachers who come to rely on the medication. In other words, they may become "addicted" to having the child on medication because the child is much less troublesome when medicated.

Kopelwicz (1996) reminds us clearly about the limitations of medication when he comments, "Ritalin (the most commonly prescribed drug for children with ADHD) lets a kid pay attention more. It does not force kids to do their homework, it doesn't teach social skills, it doesn't make them smart, it just makes them more accessible to perform in these areas" (p. 15).

Special diets. Special diets should be viewed with skepticism. The controversial Feingold diet (introduced during the 1970s), for example, linked artificial food colouring and food additives with hyperactivity. Dr. Feingold (1975) asserted that many children labelled as hyperactive would improve if synthetic colours and flavours and natural salicylates were removed from their diets. Research studies investigating his claims found no clinically significant differences between untreated groups of children and those on the Feingold diet (Conners, 1980). True, no harm can come from feeding children foods that are nutritious and additive-free.

However, even if a curative diet is nutritious (and some are not), looking for a diet as the sole cure for a behaviour disorder often results in ignoring challenging behaviours that require a different treatment.

Classroom management of hyperactive behaviour. Teachers must think about preparing the environment carefully, looking for positive behaviours to reward, and treating the child as one who is learning to develop self-control. Beware of the self-fulfilling prophecy: "Oh, you forgot to take your pill this morning. I guess this will be a bad day." Too many children and parents come to believe that the child's improved concentration is totally the result of medication. Without the planning of adults, and effort on the part of the child, improvement would not be possible. Each time the child feels responsible for the improved behaviour and experiences a sense of accomplishment, the more likely he or she is to continue the behaviours that lead to more self-control.

Systematic classroom observation usually reveals one or more activities that engage even the most overly active child for 3 to 20 minutes at a time, several times a week. Such observations are important. They give teachers a place to start a positive behaviour-management program designed to increase the child's span of attention. Even briefly focusing on an activity—any activity—sends a signal to teachers. Now is the time to give positive attention to the child while the child is engaged in this purposeful activity. This is in contrast to what teachers (and parents) often do—that is, giving their attention when the child is flitting about, thus reinforcing the negative behaviour.

Teachers should watch for those times when a child is appropriately involved in an activity. It is then that they should go to the child with a relevant comment, supportive interest, or a gentle challenge: "I bet you can fill that pail full of sand, all the way to the top. I'll watch while you do it." Few children can resist staying with a task when so challenged by an interested and responsive adult.

A child's span of attention often can be extended by calling attention to unexplored aspects of the activity or by asking questions. While supervising the water table, the teacher might ask, "I wonder what would happen if we put a little yellow food colouring in the blue water?" (Or some nontoxic soap powder? Or a drop or two of glycerin?) At the finger-painting table the teacher can pose questions, such as "What can your thumbs do? the tips of your fingers? the backs of your hands?" An overly active child's "stick-to-it-tiveness" may also be enhanced by offering additional but related materials: "Here are some new cookie cutters to use with the dough when you get it all rolled out. Do you want to start with the heart or the diamond?" Or, "The big doll looks as if it needs a bath, too." The key is always to offer the ideas and materials while the child is still engaged in the activity—before the child loses interest and leaves.

Overly active children, when they look as if they are getting ready to quit an activity, should be helped to plan where they will play next. Noting that a child is about to leave an area, the teacher can say, "Let's decide where you want to play now." If the child seems unable to make the decision, the teacher can offer choices: "There is room for you in the block corner or at the water table." Once a choice has been made, it is best for the teacher to accompany the child to the chosen area. If there is a teacher in the block area, for example, the first teacher can say something like: "Julie has come to work with blocks. Will you help her get started?" Otherwise, the accompanying teacher should help the child get involved (Photo 10–9, p. 202).

Impulsive behaviours are often displayed by children who are overly active. These behaviours can include

- abruptly grabbing something
- suddenly hitting a child or throwing something
- unexpectedly and suddenly leaving an activity

Anticipation and intervening before the impulsive behaviour occurs is a key element in the behaviour management of impulsive behaviours. Children need to be guided in developing prosocial alternatives.

To further reduce overactive and impulsive behaviours in young children, teachers may want to try the ideas listed below. These suggestions are readily carried out in any early childhood program:

- Observe the child in various activities over several days. If observations indicate, for example, that a child's attention begins to wander after five or six minutes of music time, plan to end that child's participation as it gets toward the five-minute mark. A second teacher can quietly draw the child away and provide another activity before the child wearies of music. The child can be given crayons or a puzzle, or might assist the teacher setting up the snack tables. It is important that a special activity not be offered if the child has already disrupted the music group.

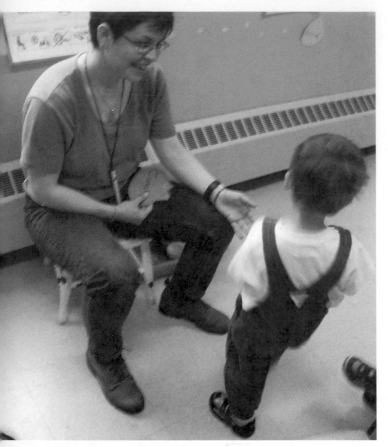

Photo 10–9
Teachers should help children plan where they will play next.

- Keep the classroom and play yard neat and orderly. Limit the quantity of materials that are out at any one time. Encourage the children to restore (tidy up) each play area before they leave it. A disorganized environment encourages nonfocused behaviour, especially with overly active children.
- Alternate active and quiet experiences, large and small groups, and teacher-initiated and child-initiated activities. Extended free-play periods can be especially difficult for overly active children. For many children who are very active or who have attention deficits, the amount of free-play time and the number of play choices usually need to be limited.
- Transition times should be as consistent as possible. Externally imposed transitions are frequently difficult for children with ADHD; therefore, forewarning a child of an impending transition is helpful in that it allows the child some time to prepare for the upcoming change.

When working with a child who is overly active, teachers frequently need to review the following questions:

- Are the classroom activities interesting, varied, attractive, and lively? In other words, are they fun and are they challenging?
- Are the activities a good match to the child's skill levels?
- Are activities and interest centres adapted on a regular basis to reflect the changing interests and developmental levels of the children?
- Is the child getting attention when focusing on an activity, or involved in prosocial behaviour, even for a moment or two, rather than for flitting about or infringing on another child's territory?

Working toward positive answers to these questions is essential in reducing hyperactivity. When behaviour-management strategies and knowledge of what is appropriate curriculum are laced together with care and concern for the child's well-being, hyperactivity inevitably lessens. The same four-pronged approach also works effectively with children who display a variety of other behaviour concerns.

It is important to consider the following: "Most children who are diagnosed by competent mental health professionals as having attention-deficit hyperactivity disorder, do; but as early childhood educators, we must always ensure that our classrooms are developmentally appropriate and that children are not being inappropriately labeled because our classroom is inappropriate" (Landau & McAninch, 1993, p. 53).

Learning Disabilities

Children with learning disabilities, to varying degrees and in varying combinations, may display the following:

- constant motion and purposeless activity
- poor perceptual motor skills
- low tolerance for frustration
- frequent mood swings
- poor coordination, in both large and fine motor activities (Photo 10–10)
- distractibility and short attention span
- poor auditory and visual memory
- a variety of language deficits

From the above list, it is obvious that learning disabilities encompass a wide range of behavioural disorders. Efforts at clinical classification are continuing. Some textbooks discuss learning disabilities in conjunction with attention deficit disorders. Others may group learning disabilities with cognitive disorders or impaired mental functioning. Other classifications are motor dysfunction and impaired motor planning (sometimes associated with the term *minimal brain damage*). In this text, learning disabilities will be discussed as a separate category. The decision is based on the extensive overlap of learning disabilities with other behaviour disorders and related developmental disabilities. Providing a separate discussion may serve to clarify some of the issues. Nevertheless, the overlaps remain, as is evident in the sections that follow.

Learning disability
one of a number of disorders that may affect the acquisition, organization, retention, understanding, or use of verbal or nonverbal information, even though the individual is of at least average intellectual ability (thinking or reasoning or both)

LEARNING DISABILITIES DEFINED

What is a **learning disability?** Two answers come immediately to mind: the first, the many things that it is; the second, the many other things that it is not. This is the official definition adopted in 2002 by the Learning Disabilities Association of Canada[4]:

> "Learning Disabilities" refer to a number of disorders which may affect the acquisition, organization, retention, understanding or use of verbal or nonverbal

Photo 10–10
Fine motor control is often more poorly developed in children suspected of having a learning disability.

information. These disorders affect learning in individuals who otherwise demonstrate at least average abilities essential for thinking and/or reasoning. As such, learning disabilities are distinct from global intellectual deficiency.

Learning disabilities result from impairments in one or more processes related to perceiving, thinking, remembering or learning. These include, but are not limited to: language processing; phonological processing; visual spatial processing; processing speed; memory and attention; and executive functions (e.g. planning and decision-making).

Learning disabilities range in severity and may interfere with the acquisition and use of one or more of the following:

- oral language (e.g. listening, speaking, understanding);
- reading (e.g. decoding, phonetic knowledge, word recognition, comprehension);
- written language (e.g. spelling and written expression); and
- mathematics (e.g. computation, problem solving).

Learning disabilities may also involve difficulties with organizational skills, social perception, social interaction and perspective taking.

Learning disabilities are lifelong. The way in which they are expressed may vary over an individual's lifetime, depending on the interaction between the demands of the environment and the individual's strengths and needs. Learning disabilities are suggested by unexpected academic under-achievement or achievement which is maintained only by unusually high levels of effort and support.

Learning disabilities are due to genetic and/or neurobiological factors or injury that alters brain functioning in a manner which affects one or more processes related to learning. These disorders are not due primarily to hearing and/or vision problems, socio-economic factors, cultural or linguistic differences, lack of motivation or ineffective teaching, although these factors may further complicate the challenges faced by individuals with learning disabilities. Learning disabilities may co-exist with various conditions including attentional, behavioural and emotional disorders, sensory impairments or other medical conditions.

For success, individuals with learning disabilities require early identification and timely specialized assessments and interventions involving home, school, community and workplace settings. The interventions need to be appropriate for each individual's learning disability subtype and, at a minimum, include the provision of:

- specific skill instruction;
- accommodations;
- compensatory strategies; and
- self-advocacy skills.

Therefore, as defined, a learning disability is *not* the result of the following list of conditions, although it may occur concurrently with any one of them:

- visual, hearing, or motor impairments
- cognitive delays
- emotional disturbance;
- environmental, cultural, or economic disadvantages
- second language learning

During the last 35 or 40 years, hundreds upon hundreds of studies have been conducted on learning disabilities. Competent researchers in the field of psychology, neurology, education, and educational psychology have attempted to come up with definitive answers to the elusive question of how to define (and diagnose) learning disabilities. Diagnosing learning disabilities in preschool children is particularly difficult (Photo 10–11).

As described in the formal definition given in U.S. law (PL 94-142), learning disabilities are related primarily to academic performance: "the imperfect ability to listen, think, speak, read, write, spell, or do mathematical calculations." Because most early childhood educators consider it developmentally inappropriate for preschool-aged children to be spending their school hours in such pursuits, we might ask whether young children should *ever* be considered to have a learning disability. "No" seems to be the logical response; yet not

Photo 10–11
What is a learning disability? There is no agreed on answer, especially where young children are concerned.

all teachers are comfortable with that and for good reason. Many young children show behaviour patterns similar to those associated with learning disabilities in older children. They may include being distractible, easily frustrated, excessively active, or poorly coordinated. These behaviours already are interfering with their everyday learning activities in a variety of ways. A number of early childhood educators believe that early intervention is in the best interest of these children, helping them to deal with their behaviours during the preschool years, before the consequences have an opportunity to compound and create additional difficulties for the child. The type and timing of such intervention is a recurring issue in early childhood education.

PREDICTING LEARNING DISABILITIES IN YOUNG CHILDREN

Is it possible that certain behaviours in a young child may be predictive of subsequent trouble with academic tasks? The answer seems to be "Yes," as long as it is understood that the judgment is based on *hunch* and educated guesswork. Teachers of young children frequently identify a child whose behaviours appear to put him or her at risk for learning disabilities and, perhaps, later academic problems. The next question: Is it possible that these worrisome behaviours can be eliminated, or at least reduced, before they have a serious impact on later academic performance? Again, the answer seems to be "Yes." During the past several years, early identification of young children who may potentially have a learning disability has gained strong support. Child developmentalists, parents, and professionals from other disciplines, such as medicine and psychology, believe that many of the learning, social–emotional, and educational concerns associated with learning disabilities can be prevented or remedied if identification and intervention are provided before the child enters school (Haring & McCormick, 1990, p. 140) (Photo 10–12, p. 206).

Exercising caution is necessary in the identification of young children at potential risk for later learning disabilities. The first step is observation of the child in a

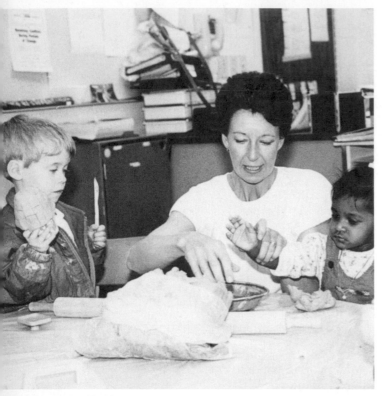

Photo 10–12
Teachers of young children frequently identify a child whose behaviours indicate risk of learning disabilities and, perhaps, later academic difficulties.

Photo 10–13
Readiness comes through appropriate early learning experiences and many unhurried opportunities to practise.

number of activities. The next step is matching the observed performance to performance expectancies in all areas of development. At the same time, it must be remembered that all young children are unique and have different rates and patterns of development; furthermore, young children often demonstrate marked differences or delays in their development. These are some of the reasons for considering learning disabilities an inappropriate diagnosis for a young child. In most instances, it is more beneficial to the child to view early differences as developmental deviations calling for learning experiences that meet individual needs. This is a more effective use of professional energy than is trying to decide whether to pin (or not to pin) the label "learning disabled" on a child.

SIGNS OF POSSIBLE FUTURE LEARNING DISABILITIES

A cue in older preschool children that learning problems may lie ahead is a lack of what are sometimes called *readiness* or prerequisite skills. As will be described in Chapter 19, these are skills thought to be necessary for academic success once the child enters grade school. However, simply waiting for the *unready* child to become ready rarely helps the child. Readiness comes through experiences, learning, and the opportunity to practise and master developmental skills (Photo 10–13). What follows are examples of particular deviations or delays in various areas of development that are thought to be related to potential learning disabilities.

1. Indicators of Visual-Sensory Gross Motor Difficulties

Many developmentalists theorize that all early learning is sensorimotor based. Children about whom teachers express concern in terms of future academic performance invariably show some kind of sensorimotor problems. In addition, they often show generalized delay in reaching basic motor milestones and exhibit one or more of the following characteristics:

- *Poor body control* results in poorly coordinated or jerky movements and trouble with running, throwing, catching, hopping, or kicking.
- *Poor balance* may cause the child to fall off play equipment, fall down, or fall into furnishings or other people. (An inability to walk a balance beam is almost always a symptom in a Kindergarten or Grade 1 child.)

- *Uncertain bilateral and cross-lateral movements* are often a telltale sign of future difficulties with academic tasks. The child with a bilateral problem may not be able to use both arms simultaneously or in synchrony, as children do when catching a ball or jumping off a wall. Or a child may not use opposite legs and arms in opposing harmony (cross-laterality), as seen in agile children climbing to the top of a jungle gym. The clearest example of cross-laterality is crawling: left leg and right arm moving forward, alternating with right leg and left arm moving forward.

- *Inability to cross body midline* has long been viewed as a possible predictor of future academic difficulty. In such cases the child has trouble using the right hand to work on a task where any part of the task lies to the left of the midpoint of the child's body or vision. The same holds true of the left hand and the right-side focus. A common example is a child painting on a large piece of paper at the easel. The child transfers the brush from the right hand to the left when painting on the left half of the paper and back again when painting on the right.

- *Faulty spatial orientation* interferes with children's ability to understand where they are in space, in relation to their physical surroundings. For example, a child may walk into a wall; poor orientation interferes with the child perceiving the wall as being *right there*. Or the child may gear up for a mighty jump only to land with frightening force because the ground was much closer than the greater height the child had anticipated. Putting clothes on inside out or backward, or having difficulty going up and down stairs, also may indicate difficulties with spatial orientation.

2. Indicators of Fine Motor Difficulties (Poor Fine Motor/Eye–Hand Coordination Skills)

Difficulties in buttoning, lacing, snapping, cutting, pasting, and stringing beads are characteristics of older preschool children thought to be at future academic risk. Often these children are unable to draw a straight line or copy simple shapes, such as a circle, cross, or square. When they manage to draw a crude imitation, the circle seldom is closed, the corners on the square are rounded or irregular, and the cross is crossed far off centre. Tasks of this kind and others, such as cutting with scissors, are virtually impossible for these children to master without extensive training and practice.

3. Visual-Perception Difficulties

Visual-perception difficulties refer to how well the child's processing mechanism handles the information that comes in visually—that is, how well the child makes sense of what is seen. Various aspects of perceptual motor skills will be described in Chapter 19; here the focus will be on other aspects related specifically to the current topic of learning disabilities, where difficulties take several forms.

Poor visual perception has nothing to do with blindness or impaired vision. In other words, there is no *physical disability*. The following issues are of concern in this area:

- *Visual discrimination* is the ability to look at objects or pictures and note how they are alike or how they are different. Children with poor visual discrimination may have trouble sorting objects according to colour, size, or shape. They may not be able to match lotto pictures, copy block designs, or tell the difference between the smiling and the frowning clown pictures. Often they can be seen trying to fit a large object into too small an opening or container.

Photo 10–14
Visual discrimination and visual orientation skills go together.

- *Visual orientation* is related to spatial orientation. The child may recognize three-dimensional objects, such as a head of lettuce, a cap, or a paint-brush, but not recognize the same items in two-dimensional pictures (Photo 10–14). Another example of visual disorientation is recognizing objects in their normal or upright positions but failing to recognize them when they are turned over or lying sideways. One child insisted that an overturned wooden armchair was a cage; the moment it was turned right-side up, he labelled it as a chair. Even when the chair was turned over while he watched, he insisted it was a cage the moment it was overturned.

- *Visual memory* involves remembering what was just seen, at least for a few seconds. Children with poor visual memory may not remember the name of the animal on their card, for example, even though the picture has been face down for only a moment. Or, in the familiar take-away game, they cannot recall what was removed even though there were only three or four articles on the tray when it was presented just a moment before.

- *Visual tracking* involves the ability to follow objects visually. Children with difficulties in tracking may have trouble keeping an eye on the ball, following the flight of a bird, or buttoning buttons in order, from top to bottom. Visual-tracking ability is likely to be associated with reading skills, in that reading requires systematic eye movements from left to right and from top to bottom.

- *Visual–motor integration* is a skill that can also be thought of as eye–hand coordination. Children with these kinds of problems may have trouble with almost every motor task that requires vision: fitting appropriately shaped pieces into a puzzle box, cutting on the line, drawing around a form, or tracing a simple shape. It is as if the child's hands cannot do what the eyes say needs to be done.

4. Auditory-Perception Difficulties

Many young children who are at risk for future learning disabilities have trouble processing what they hear (Photo 10–15). Again, this is not a physical problem; deafness or being hard-of-hearing is not the cause of the child's difficulty. Basically, the problem results from the inability to tell the difference between sounds—lack of auditory discrimination. *Hat* and *mat* may sound the same to these children. Often, they cannot tell the difference between high and low musical tones, especially as the range lessens. Localization of sound is usually a problem, too. The child may have to look in two or three directions when trying to locate a whistler or a barking dog.

5. Language Deviations

Children at risk for learning disabilities frequently have trouble with receptive or expressive language, or both (see Chapter 18). Acquiring the more advanced grammatical forms and the ability to formulate organized sentences tends to come

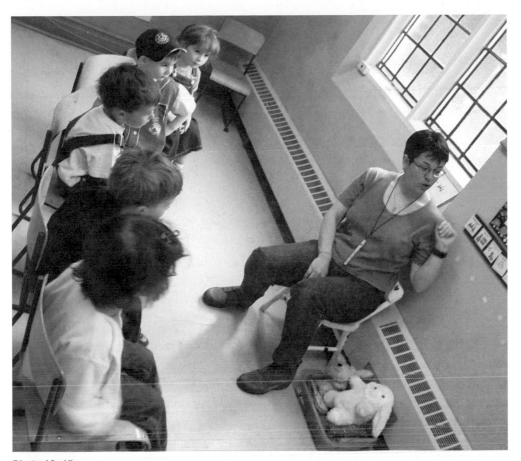

Photo 10–15
A child may have trouble making sense out of what people are saying.

considerably later for children with potential learning disabilities than for most children. Although vocabulary is not necessarily more limited, trouble can arise, for example, when the child tries to recall a well-known word to describe a familiar concept. Carrying out directions that include common prepositions such as *in, on, under,* and *over* is often baffling. If the teacher says to put the block *on top of the box,* a child may look at the teacher questioningly while putting the object *in* the box. Many of these children have trouble repeating short sentences, rhymes, and directions. In addition, they often have difficulty imitating sounds, gestures, body movements, facial expressions, and other forms of nonverbal communication.

6. Cognitive Disorders

Trouble in organizing thoughts and processing information with logic is characteristic of many young children with potential learning disabilities. They tend to operate only in the here and now, to think concretely, demonstrating little or no ability to deal with any kind of abstract thought or event. Although concrete thinking is characteristic of young children, most older preschoolers are able to deal with a certain amount of abstraction.

Cognitively disorganized children may also have trouble carrying out simple directions or remembering what it was they were supposed to do, even while they are working on the task. Trouble generalizing from one event to another is also common. A rule about no running indoors may not generalize to no running in the classroom or in the halls or in the library, even though all are indoors within the same building. Especially frustrating for adults, as well as the child, is that the same mistakes are made again and again, simply because there is no carryover from one event to the next.

7. Perseveration

Perseveration (repeating the same act over and over, seemingly endlessly) is found in some children who seem likely to develop a future learning disability. These children appear unable to stop what they are doing of their own accord. A child may scrub back and forth with the same crayon, or draw the same shape for minutes at a time, until stopped by a teacher or parent. Some children chant the same words or make the same hand gestures repeatedly until someone succeeds in diverting them to something else. It usually is difficult for the child who perseverates to change activities. Even when a change is accomplished, there may be carryover from the preceding activity. For example, the child who has been scrubbing with a crayon may have been moved into block play. Here the back-and-forth scrubbing continues on the floor, with the child using a block rather than a crayon to make the back-and-forth motions.

8. Deficit Social Skills

Children who appear to have the potential for later learning disabilities tend to have more than their share of social difficulties. They may be bullying or aggressive, withdrawn, or overly dependent. Their behaviour often confuses other children and so they have trouble making friends. When they do succeed in forming a friendship, they tend to have difficulty keeping it. Sometimes the child puts too many demands on the friend, or has such inadequate play skills that the friend loses interest. Also, their impulsiveness may cause them to say and do inappropriate things. They may not foresee the possibility of negative consequences, such as hurt feelings or the unintentional destruction of a friend's favourite toy. When a child loses two or three friends (for reasons the child neither understands nor seems able to change), feelings of rejection are likely to follow. Rejection increases frustration, a sense of incompetence, and low self-esteem. These feelings, in turn, lead to a tendency to break into tears at the slightest provocation, to strike out for what seems to be little or no reason, or to withdraw even more.

PROGRAM CONSIDERATIONS

In concluding this section on possible learning disabilities in young children, one concept bears repeating. Characteristics associated with learning disabilities can be observed in all young children, at one time or another. Many preschool teachers have watched a child do a lovely painting only to see it overlaid from edge to edge and top to bottom with endless coats of paint. The teacher may mourn the loss of the painting (having mentally earmarked it for display at the parent meeting) but this once-in-a-while behaviour is no cause for concern and should not (because it is an isolated event) be considered perseveration. As noted before, in connection with all developmental differences, teachers must look for clusters of behaviours and note the degree to which a behaviour occurs. Questions that are appropriate to ask are these: Are the behaviours happening excessively? Do they interfere with the child's development and general well-being? Age, too, must be a consideration. It is always a warning sign when a behaviour is extreme and persists significantly beyond appropriate age levels.

Perseveration
repeating the same act over and over with no discernible intention (in an obsessive, ritualistic manner)

In working with children whose behaviours seem predictive of future learning disabilities, careful reexamination of the learning environment is essential (see Chapter 14), as is a thorough review of effective teaching strategies. These strategies have been described throughout the text in regard to various developmental issues. Many of the strategies have special relevance in work with preschool children whose behaviour disorders put them at risk of future failure at school.

Here are some strategies for teachers of preschool children with behaviour disorders to consider:

- Be consistent in the use of positive reinforcement to increase behaviours that facilitate the child's development, thereby decreasing behaviours that interfere with development.
- Provide the child with encouragement and descriptive praise for each step forward, regardless of how small.
- Provide learning activities that support the child's home language and culture.
- Remember that every child has strengths and does positive things; concentrate attention on these rather than on the child's needs and misbehaviours (Photo 10–16).
- Use task analysis (see Chapter 11) to teach whatever skills the child is having trouble with, whether learning to imitate, to focus attention, to say "No" instead of hitting, or any other skill or behaviour.
- Give directions one at a time and allow adequate time for the child to comply. Verify the child's understanding of the request; rehearse (walk the child through) the required response as often as necessary.
- Teach new concepts and skills in short sessions with concrete materials that allow a child to use several sensory modalities: seeing, hearing, moving, and manipulating.
- Be patient. Children with learning disabilities may have to be told or shown many times in many different ways how to accomplish a simple task. Do not expect learning to generalize from one situation to another. Each situation seems new to the child.
- Help parents understand that their child is not being difficult or inattentive on purpose. Tell them of their child's accomplishments, no matter how small. To enhance the child's self-esteem, describe his or her accomplishments to the parent in the presence of the child, whenever possible.

Photo 10–16
Be patient. Provide a lot of support and encouragement.

Summary

Teachers of young children with social and adaptive disorders may encounter a number of behavioural difficulties:

- excessive dependency on adults or general withdrawal from social contacts
- fears that result in excessive and unrealistic anxiety about everyday happenings
- withdrawal problems
- eating problems—the most serious of which is pica, the eating of inedible substances (lead-based paint flakes are likely to pose the greatest risk: intellectual impairment, even death, may follow excessive eating of this toxic substance)
- soiling and wetting that continues past the expected age for toilet-training

Social learning/adaptation disorders include

- autism spectrum disorder, otherwise known as pervasive developmental disorders (PDD), the most severe form of which is autism
- childhood schizophrenia
- attention deficit hyperactive disorders (ADHD)

These are all conditions that require diagnostic assessment and specialized program support.

Learning disabilities are classified under a variety of headings, depending on the researcher's, the clinician's, or the teacher's theoretical background. Confusion arises at times because some definitions of learning disabilities refer to them as being specific to reading, writing, or math. For early childhood educators, this raises a number of questions. For example, is it ever appropriate to diagnose a preschool-aged child as having a learning disability? If not, what about the many behaviours (distractibility, short attention span, visual-perception problems, and many others) that are excessive in some preschool children and that resemble the behaviours of older children who have serious problems with academic tasks? Is it not important to deal with these nonacademic behaviour disorders in the early years, before they become greater problems that are likely to have a negative impact on subsequent academic learning? The answer seems to be "Yes," and the question then becomes "How?" Strategies for teaching young children with all kinds of behaviour disorders and potential learning disabilities are found throughout this chapter and the other chapters in Section II.

Throughout this chapter, there is a cautionary theme: behavioural difficulties of every type are common among young children. Every child exhibits a number of them during the developmental years. It is only when certain behaviours begin to become so excessive that they interfere with a child's developmental progress that they are of great concern. Even then, to label or classify prematurely a young child who has so much development yet to come often does the child a grave injustice. It is not how a child is classified but how the child is cared for and taught—as an individual—that is the important issue in working with young children who are demonstrating a range of behavioural and learning difficulties.

RESOURCES

The following organizations provide useful information for parents and early childhood educators. Canadian resources are identified with an asterisk (*).

AUTISM NATIONAL COMMITTEE
http://www.autcom.org

AUTISM SOCIETY OF AMERICA
http://www.autism-society.org

INDIANA RESOURCE CENTER FOR AUTISM
http://www.iidc.indiana.edu/~irca

AUTISM SOCIETY CANADA*
http://www.autismsocietycanada.ca

AUTISM SOCIETY ONTARIO*
http://www.autismsociety.on.ca

AUTISM SOCIETY OF BRITISH COLUMBIA*
http://www.autismbc.ca

AUTISM SOCIETY NEW BRUNSWICK*
http://www.sjfn.nb.ca/community_hall/A/auti3200.html

CHILDREN AND ADULTS WITH ATTENTION-DEFICIT/HYPERACTIVITY
DISORDERS (CHADD)
http://www.chadd.org

FAMILIES FOR EARLY AUTISM TREATMENT (FEAT)
http://www.feat.org

GENEVA CENTRE FOR AUTISM*
http://www.autism.net

LEARNING DISABILITIES ASSOCIATION OF CANADA*
http://www.ldac-taac.ca

LEARNING DISABILITIES ASSOCIATION OF ONTARIO*
http://www.ldao.ca

NATIONAL CENTER FOR LEARNING DISABILITIES
http://www.ncld.org

STUDENT ACTIVITIES

1. Observe an early childhood classroom for one hour. Make brief anecdotal notes related to episodes of children showing short attention spans (cite examples) or poor motor coordination. Discuss these with the teacher to see whether the recorded behaviours are characteristic of the children you observed.
2. Analyze the preceding record to see whether there are recurring patterns or particular behaviours that were repeated frequently. Assume you are the child's teacher. Draw up a set of guidelines that you might present to the other classroom teachers as possible ways to work with the child.
3. Select any one of the visual-perception difficulties described in the text. Design a learning activity for a one-to-one tutorial situation that would give the child with the potential problem practice in developing the skill or in overcoming the difficulty. Adapt the same activity to a classroom game format that would be fun for all the children while giving the child with the potential difficulty the opportunity to learn as part of the group.
4. Wear a watch (preferably one with a second hand) and observe an early childhood program during an entire free-play period (30 to 45 minutes). Consult with the teacher first to identify which child might be considered overly active. During the first half of your observation, record the types of activities that the child is engaged in and the amount of time spent in each (also record time spent wandering about). Make the same recordings on another active child for the second half of the observation. Compare the observations and try to analyze the differences or similarities in the two children.

REFERENCES

American Psychiatric Association (APA). 2000. *Diagnostic and statistical manual of mental disorders* (4th ed., text rev.). Washington, DC: Author.

Autism Society of Canada. (2005). *Research into prevalance.* Retrieved August 17, 2005, from http://www.autismsocietycanada.ca/asd_research/research_prevalence/index_e.html.

Baker, B., & Brightman, B. 1997. *Steps to independence: Teaching everyday skills to children with disabilities.* Baltimore, MD: Brookes.

Barkley, R. A. (1998). *Attention deficit hyperactivity disorders: A handbook for diagnosis and treatment.* New York: Guilford Press.

Bee, H. (1999). *The developing child* (9th ed.). New York: HarperCollins.

Beers, M. H. (Ed.). (2005). Children's health issues [Electronic version]. *The Merck manual of medical information* (2nd home ed., section 23). Rahway, NJ: Merck.

Coleman, M. (1989). Young children with autism or autistic-like behavior. *Infants and Young Children, 1*(4), 22–31.

Conners, C. K. (1980). *Food additives and hyperactive children.* New York: Plenum Press.

Dawson, G., & Osterling, J. (1997). Early intervention in autism. In M. J. Guralnick (Ed.), *Effectiveness of early intervention* (pp. 307–326). Baltimore, MD: Brookes.

Deutsch, C. K., & Kinsbourne, M. (1990). Genetics and biochemistry in attention deficit disorder. In M. Lewis & S. M. Miller (Eds.), *Handbook of developmental psychopathology* (pp. 93–108). New York: Plenum.

Feingold, B. F. (1975). *Why your child is hyperactive.* New York: Random House.

Fombonne, E. (2003a). Modern views of autism. *Canadian Journal of Psychiatry, 48,* 503–505.

Fombonne, E. (2003b). Epidemiology of autism and other pervasive developmental disorders: An update. *Journal of Autism and Developmental Disorders, 33,* 365–381.

Haring, N. G., & McCormick, L. (1990). *Exceptional children and youth.* Columbus, OH: Merrill.

Harter, S. (1990). Processes underlying adolescent self-concept formation. In R. Montemeyer, G. R. Adams, & T. P. Gullota (Eds.), *From childhood to adolescence: A transition period?* (pp. 205–239). Newbury Park, CA: Sage.

Kopelwicz, H. S. (1996). *It's nobody's fault: New hope and help for difficult children and their parents.* New York: Times Books.

Landau, S., & McAninch, C. (1993). Young children with attention deficits. *Young Children,* May, 49–58.

Learning Disabilities Association of Canada. (2005). *Official definition of learning disabilities.* Ottawa: Author. Retrieved July 29, 2005, from http://www.ldac-taac.ca/Defined/defined_new-e.asp.

Murphy, K. R., & Barkley, R. A. (1996). The prevalence of *DSM-IV* symptoms of AD/HD in adult licensed drivers: Implications for clinical diagnosis. *Comprehensive Psychiatry, 37,* 393–401.

Swanson, J. M., & McBurnett, K. (1993). Effect of stimulant medication on children with attention deficit disorder: "A review of reviews." *Exceptional Children, 60,* 154–163.

Wolraich, M. L., Hannah, J. N., Pinnock, T. Y., Baumgaertal, A., & Brown, J. (1996). Comparison of diagnostic criteria for attention-deficit hyperactivity disorder in a countywide sample. *Journal of the American Academy of Child and Adolescent Psychiatry, 35,* 319–324.

NOTES

1. Characteristics of autism: reprinted with permission from the Diagnostic and Statistical Manual of Mental Disorders, Fourth Edition, Text Revision. Copyright 2000 American Psychiatric Association.
2. Characteristics of Asperger's disorder: reprinted with permission from the Diagnostic and Statistical Manual of Mental Disorders, Fourth Edition, Text Revision. Copyright 2000 American Psychiatric Association.
3. Characteristics of ADHD: reprinted with permission from the Diagnostic and Statistical Manual of Mental Disorders, Fourth Edition, Text Revision. Copyright 2000 American Psychiatric Association.
4. Definition of a learning disability: Learning Disabilities Association of Canada, adopted on January 30, 2002.

Section III

Planning for Inclusion

CHAPTER 11

The Developmental Behavioural Approach

KEY CONCEPTS

backward chaining
behaviour modification
descriptive praise
didactic materials
forward chaining
intrinsic motivation
learning theory
manual prompts

maturation
modelling
nonambulatory
operant conditioning
preventive discipline
reinforcement
renewal time
task analysis

OBJECTIVES

After studying the material in this chapter, the student will be able to

- Describe some early education practices that are a blend of developmental and behavioural principles.
- Define positive reinforcement and describe how skilled early childhood teachers use it in working with young children.
- Identify behavioural approaches used with young children within a variety of situations.
- Define preventive discipline and punishment and state how these do or do not support developmentally appropriate practices with young children.
- Explain task analysis and its importance in working with all children, especially children with developmental differences.
- Explain how task analysis can be applied in the learning of self-help/care skills for all children.
- Demonstrate forward and backward chaining in teaching a self-help/care skill.

Introduction

The developing child is in a state of continual behaviour change. Developmental or behavioural changes range from the simple to the complex. They come about because of physical growth, **maturation,** experience, and observational learning of peers and adults **(modelling)** within diverse social and cultural environments.

Basic developmental principles have been discussed specifically, in Chapter 7 and elsewhere throughout this text. This chapter will provide a brief analysis of behavioural principles, especially those that have particular relevance for teachers of young children. It will focus on reinforcement procedures, discipline and punishment, modelling, and task analysis, with emphasis on the role of adult social reinforcement. Positive reinforcement practices are emphasized as the first and preferred approach to effective discipline. This chapter will apply the concept of task analysis to the development of self-help/care skills.

The terms *self-care* and *self-help skills* are used interchangeably; therefore, we use the term *self-help/care skills* in this text. Self-help/care is the ability of individuals to manage personal needs and to adapt their behaviours to social expectations. The specific skills and adaptive behaviours that children are required to learn are determined by the culture in which they live. Though patterns differ, all cultures prescribe ways of eating, toileting, dressing, behaving sexually, sleeping, resting, and keeping public places orderly. The chapter also includes the application of the concepts of forward and backward chaining in teaching a self-help/care skill.

Maturation
developmentally, maturation is often defined as an internal process that governs the natural unfolding of innate ("preprogrammed") skills and abilities

Modelling
learning by watching and imitating another's actions; also called observational learning

Early Education: Developmental and Behavioural Principles—A Blend

Effective early childhood teachers rely on developmental principles and show an awareness of behavioural principles when deciding how to program for young children. They know that one of the best measures of the effectiveness of their teaching is a change in children's behaviour.

HISTORICAL INFLUENCES

A developmental-behavioural approach to teaching has been evolving for at least 40 years. By the middle of the twentieth century, developmentalists were in the majority. Researchers, such as Gesell et al. (1940), believed that development was independent of experience, a natural *unfolding* of innate or inborn abilities. The role of teachers (and parents) was neither to unduly restrict nor to push the child. Then came theorists like Hunt (1961), who argued that development was *not* independent of external influences. Rather, it was controlled to some unknown extent by environmental experiences. Hunt was greatly influenced by Piaget (1952). Piaget had theorized that though there was a natural progression that was developmentally based, changes in a child's thinking (cognitive structure) were direct results of exploration of the environment. Hunt went one step further. He suggested that learning depended on a good *match* between the child and the experiences available to the child.

The Problem of the Match

In early childhood education *the problem of the match* became a central issue. Teachers were trained to provide play materials and learning opportunities that attracted and held children's attention. At the same time, the materials were to

Photo 11–1
Activities should match the child's skill level.

Intrinsic motivation
feelings of pleasure and personal satisfaction derived from working on or accomplishing a task, discovering something new, or solving a problem

include new and intriguing elements (Photo 11–1). These were to be just a bit beyond the child's current skill level. Providing exactly the right match was the way to produce pleasure and continuing eagerness (motivation) to learn. There was no need for teachers or parents to push. The *joy of learning,* often referred to as **intrinsic motivation,** would take over. Children would seek out additional learning of their own accord, simply because they wanted to.

Learning from Success

The role of environmental influences was also central to the developmental ideas of Bijou (1959). He believed that the results (consequences) of a child's behaviour were the crucial element. According to Bijou, children tend to learn the behaviours that result in success and positive consequences. They avoid those that result in failure or negative consequences. Teachers were trained to present tasks step by small step and to provide positive consequences for each successful step. The result: a learning environment in which children had frequent success and were motivated to learn more.

Environmental Arrangements

Arranging the learning environment so as to help a child take the next step in skill development is a long-established and fundamental principle in early childhood education. The following are three examples from different periods in the history of early childhood education:

- Friedrich Froebel (1782–1852), hailed as the founder of the Kindergarten movement, is likely to have been the first to propose that early learning experiences be broken down into their smallest components. Froebel also argued that young children need hands-on experiences: materials to enjoy, examine, and manipulate (Froebel, 1911).

- Maria Montessori (1870–1952), a gifted physician, was a champion of the educational potentials of children with developmental delays and differences. She spent her life designing and demonstrating systematic and sequential learning activities based on what she called **didactic materials** (Montessori, 1912). Many of these materials, as well as her ideas about a prepared environment, are central to today's early education practices.

- John Dewey (1859–1952) is often given the title of founder of the *progressive education* movement. He, too, put major emphasis on the learning environment, especially as represented by the teacher, who was to respond, support, and guide children's exploration of everyday materials (Dewey, 1950).

Didactic materials
manipulative materials in which the child's errors and successes are self-evident—the material, not the teacher, provides the information; Montessori was the originator of many such materials

Photo 11–2
Materials and activities should be sequenced to provide both success and challenge.

In each of these approaches to early education, the route to sound learning reflects similar principles, a developmental and behavioural blend that includes these elements:

- a prepared learning environment matched to children's current skill levels (in behavioural terms, preparing the environment is referred to as the *arrangement of antecedent events,* a topic yet to be discussed)
- materials and activities sequenced in small enough segments so as to provide both success and challenge (Photo 11–2)
- emphasis on learning through play and active involvement with appropriate materials
- responsive teachers who serve as guides and facilitators

Behavioural Principles and Practices

Misinformation, faulty implementation, and abuse of behavioural practices have led to a knee-jerk reaction in many early childhood educators whenever the behavioural approach is mentioned, according to Wolery (1994), who goes on to say: "The behavioral perspective, although often seen as stressing the impact of the environment, in fact proposes that learning occurs from dynamic interactions between children and their environment" (p. 98). He then adds, "Particularly beneficial are those child-environment interactions that are initiated and directed by children and in which they are highly engaged" (p. 99).

The behavioural approach to early intervention is based on arranging the environment and implementing teaching strategies in ways that enhance children's learning experiences. Although this approach is important when working with all children, it has been particularly effective in facilitating learning among children with special needs.

Photo 11–3
Start with what the child can do.

ALL CHILDREN CAN LEARN

In an inclusive classroom, the most significant and useful behavioural principle for teachers is one that emphasizes the point that *every child can learn*. Some children learn faster than others. Some children learn more than others. Some children learn some things easily, other things only with great effort or not at all. Some children learn from one type of approach; others from a different approach. But all children can learn.

To make the *teachability* of all children a day-by-day reality, teachers need to understand and practise basic behavioural principles. In the inclusive classroom, these procedures are especially important. Each child can be provided with a responsive and reinforcing learning environment matched to his or her developmental level and special interests. Children who are gifted can be provided with learning opportunities that neither push nor hold them back but instead foster their interests and talents. Children with developmental differences, though they may learn more slowly or with greater effort, need to be provided with a responsive and reinforcing learning environment matched to their developmental skill levels. The essence of the approach is to start where the child is, developmentally, and build from there (Photo 11–3).

Children who have severe disabilities may have few observable behaviours to build on. Skilled observation is important here. Teachers need to be able to pick up on subtle cues that indicate a child's possible interest and awareness. For example, a child's eyes may widen as the caregiver approaches the crib, even though the child cannot raise or turn his or her head in the caregiver's direction. In some instances, teachers, parents, and caregivers themselves may have to decide what should be the starting point for learning. An example might be a child with multiple impairments who displays few behaviours of any kind. Simply getting the child to look in a given direction may be a first priority. Even to accomplish this, a teacher often has to structure the environment so as to evoke (trigger) an attending response from the child: the sight or fragrance of a favourite food or the sound of a loud bell—whatever will attract the child's attention and give the teacher a behaviour to reinforce and expand on.

REINFORCEMENT PROCEDURES

Operant conditioning
a teaching strategy in which the child's behaviour is shaped as the result of a planned response designed to reinforce a specific behaviour

Behaviour modification
a system by which particular environmental events are systematically arranged to produce specified behaviour changes

Learning theory
emphasizes the dominant role of environment and reinforcing experiences in all learning; social learning theory adds other dimensions—that learning also occurs through observing and imitating and that individuals can generate their own satisfactions (intrinsic reinforcement)

Reinforcement procedures come from research related to **operant conditioning, behaviour modification,** and **learning theory.** Volumes of studies demonstrate that behaviour is triggered by antecedent events and then increases or decreases according to its consequences (reinforcers). The principles can be put into a simple ABC format:

A: *Antecedent event* (that which precedes or comes before a behaviour—see Photo 11–4)
B: *Behaviour* (response of the individual)
C: *Consequence* (that which follows a behaviour)

A and C are environmental events, planned and unplanned, that both precede and follow a behaviour.

Example:

A	*B*	*C*
Teacher slices apples	*Child looks and says, "I want apple"*	*Teacher hands child a slice of apple*

The child's request (B) was triggered by seeing the teacher slicing the apple (A). It is likely the child will ask for an apple (B) every time the teacher is cutting apples (A), because the request resulted in a piece of apple being given to the child (C).

If specific learning (B) is to occur (or not to occur as in the case of inappropriate behaviours) then A and C must be decided on and systematically arranged. In simple terms, A is what teachers do *before* they want a child to respond. This includes the selection, arrangement, and presentation of activities and materials (and playmates, in some instances). Then, C (consequence) is what teachers do immediately following a child's behavioural response, such as providing or withholding reinforcers (the next topic to be discussed). Whatever adults do in A and C (or fail to do) will have some kind of an effect on the child's behaviour and learning (Allen, 1974; Chance, 1998).

Reinforcement is a response to a behaviour that increases the likelihood that the behaviour will occur again. Reinforcement takes two main forms: *positive* and *negative*. Reinforcement, as we will see, may also be both *external* and *intrinsic*. In this text, the focus will be mainly on positive reinforcement because of its effectiveness in supporting young children's learning and development.

Photo 11–4
Antecedents are what the adult does before expecting the child to perform.

Reinforcement
a general term for a consequence, an event, or procedure that increases or maintains the behaviour it follows; high grades are reinforcement for good academic performance

Positive Reinforcement

In simple terms, a positive reinforcer is a pleasant consequence of a behaviour; therefore, it has a high probability of increasing whatever behaviour preceded it. (Note: In the following example, A refers to *antecedent*, B refers to child's *behaviour*, and C refers to social *consequences*.)

Example:

A: *Teacher announces it's time to tidy up so children can go outside.*
B: *Ari runs over and begins to put toys away.*
C: *Teacher praises Ari for working with everyone to clean up quickly.*

Reinforcers that are usually successful with young children are

- toys, play, and other favourite activities
- the attention of certain adults

Different children like different things. A reinforcer for one child may be of little value to another. Hugging is a good example. It is generally assumed that all children like to be hugged. Not true: Some children may be selective as to whom they like to be hugged by. Therefore, hugging may not be an effective reinforcer for these children.

Negative Reinforcement

The strengthening of a behaviour by the removal of an unpleasant consequence is called negative reinforcement. Negative reinforcement is a confusing concept that has been explained in a variety of ways. Bee (1999, p. 289) gives one of the more easily understood definitions:

> Negative reinforcement occurs when something *unpleasant* is stopped. Suppose your child is whining and whining at you to be picked up. What happens? He stops whining. So your picking up behaviour has been *negatively reinforced* by the cessation (stopping) of the child's whining and you will be *more* likely to pick him up the next time he whines. At the same time, his whining has been *positively reinforced* by your attention and picking up, so he will be more likely to whine on other occasions.

Chance (1998, p. 102) defines negative reinforcers even more simply: "Negative reinforcers: A reinforcing event in which something is removed following a behaviour." (Note: Negative reinforcement is not the same as punishment, which will be discussed later.)

Example:

A: *Teacher asks children to tidy up.*
B: *Patrick continues to play.*
C: *Teacher says, "When you have tidied up you can go outside to play."*

In the example above, the teacher wants Patrick to tidy up. Her statement indicates the removal of something the child likes if he doesn't comply. Because Patrick wants the thing that the teacher states she will remove, he complies with the behaviour she desires. It should be noted that overuse of negative reinforcement as a child-management technique places the teacher in a power role that may lead to fear in the child, and for this reason should be avoided.

Intrinsic Reinforcement

Positive inner feelings of pleasure and personal satisfaction describe intrinsic reinforcement. This form of reinforcement comes from working on or accomplishing a task, discovering something new, or solving a problem (Photo 11–5). For those who love to play with water, playing with water is always intrinsically reinforcing; that is, the very act of playing with water provides hour after hour of pleasure, stimulation, and satisfaction. For children who fear getting wet, there is little or no intrinsic reinforcement; water play is taxing, something to be avoided. The same holds true whether it is riding a tricycle, building with blocks, or working with puzzles.

External Reinforcement

One reinforcer that is both powerful and universally appealing to young children of every culture is adult social reinforcement. Adult social reinforcement is made up of the attention of significant adults: parents, teachers, grandparents, other family members, and nurturing caregivers. Generally, adult attention is readily available and potentially plentiful. More than 30 years of research provides conclusive evidence that adult attention is likely to increase those behaviours that it immediately and consistently follows. The opposite is also true: When adult attention is consistently and immediately withheld (ignoring the behaviour) or withdrawn, the child's behaviour decreases. The following excerpt from a case study points out the appropriate and systematic use of teachers' attention in helping a child acquire a needed behaviour—improved attention span (Allen, 1974):

> Concerns about James's lack of attention span led teachers to make a series of observations. It was obvious that James was getting a great deal of attention

Photo 11–5
Intrinsic reinforcement: a sense of pleasure, satisfaction, and self-esteem

from teachers, yet there was no increase in his attention span. Teachers agreed, therefore, to focus their attention on James only on those moments, no matter how brief, when he was engaged with a material or activity. They agreed, further, not to interact with him just as he was leaving an activity or when he was flitting about. That is, they refrained from doing what they usually did at those times, which was to attempt to steer the child into an activity. Teachers consistently held to their plan as to when they would provide attention and when they would withhold it. James's span of attention soon began to increase.

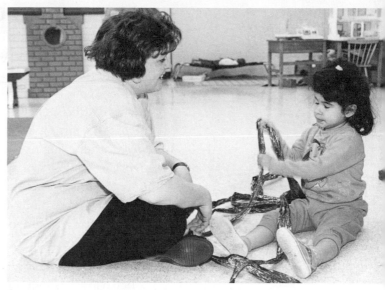

Photo 11–6
The essence of a reinforcement procedure is responding to children in positive and encouraging ways.

Many research studies demonstrate how powerful teachers are as sources of reinforcement for young children. Most important, the studies indicate how simple reinforcement procedures may bring out the best in each child. All that has to be done is what good teachers do so well: respond to children in encouraging and positive ways and provide materials and activities matched to children's interests and skill levels (Photo 11–6). The following are brief descriptions of everyday teacher behaviours that serve as powerful reinforcers for almost any young child:

- *Verbal responsiveness.* Example: producing relevant comments, interested questions, answers to children's questions, exclamations of approval (such as "Great!"), and **descriptive praise** or encouragement that focuses on some aspect of what the child is accomplishing, such as "Paula, you laced your shoe all by yourself!"

- *Physical proximity.* Example: quietly standing or sitting close to a child and showing genuine interest by watching, nodding, smiling, or listening.

- *Physical contact.* Example: touching, hugging, holding a child's hand, tussling, rocking, or otherwise physically comforting a child. (Teachers must note and discuss the occasional child who avoids or shrinks from adults' touch.)

- *Physical assistance.* Example: providing support on the climbing frame, pushing a swing, helping a child achieve balance on a walking beam, and so on.

- *Providing things that children want.* Example: providing a favourite nutritional snack, play materials, activities, or mini-excursions, such as riding in the elevator or crossing the road to watch the carpenter.

Descriptive praise
feedback that lets children know specifically what it is they are doing well

COMPETITION IS INAPPROPRIATE

Descriptive statements carry no implications that any one child is better than another. Promoting competition among young children establishes an uneasy learning environment. Children cannot appreciate the process of learning, or their own uniqueness, if adults imply that they should try to be better than someone else. The only competition that enhances development occurs when a child's progress is approvingly measured against that child's own earlier performance (Brophy, 1981): for example, "You are really learning colours. Now you know all the colour names of all the blocks."

WITHHOLDING OR WITHDRAWING REINFORCERS

Another form of adult social reinforcement, much less pleasant to practise, is taking away (withdrawing or withholding) something that is important to a child—a favourite toy, activity, playmate, or the attention of an important adult. Withholding reinforcement is used when an inappropriate behaviour is not decreasing in spite of teachers' efforts. (Recall the staff's first efforts to redirect James, with the resulting increase in flitting about.) Though punishment itself will not be discussed until later, withdrawing or withholding reinforcement, in one sense, is a form of punishment. It has less damaging side effects than does physical or verbal punishment, however. It is also more effective. Equally important, it cuts down on the emotional conflict between adult and child that so often accompanies other forms of punishment. In early childhood settings, withholding attention and other reinforcers can be accomplished in several ways:

- Teachers may ignore an incident and act as if they do not see the undesirable behaviour (as long as the child is not endangering himself or others). Ignoring can be accomplished by turning away for the moment and showing interest in another child or activity.
- Teachers may remove materials or equipment if a child continues to misuse them.
- Teachers may remove the child from play with other children or from an activity.

It will be stressed again and again in this book that in a well-arranged and developmentally appropriate early learning environment, the need for any kind of negative procedure should be rare. Hence the rationale for including in this text an entire chapter (Chapter 15) on appropriate environmental arrangements and the consequent positive effect on children's behaviour.

INCOMPATIBLE BEHAVIOURS

Incompatible behaviours are two or more responses that cannot occur together. An inappropriate behaviour cannot occur at the same time that an appropriate behaviour is occurring. For example, it is impossible for children to walk and run at the same time. Therefore, if the rule is "Walking in the classroom," teachers should turn their attention (social reinforcement) to children who are remembering to walk. The child who runs, after a first reminder, receives no further teacher attention until the running stops (withholding attention). Rules should always be stated in a positive manner; that is, teachers should state the behaviour they want to see rather than the behaviour they are trying to eliminate. Here are some other examples: listening is incompatible with talking; making a neutral comment is incompatible with teasing; waiting for the cookie basket to be passed is incompatible with snatching cookies. In other words, whenever a child is not behaving inappropriately, he or she is engaging in some kind of appropriate behaviour (even if it is only standing and watching for a moment). Recognizing this gives teachers the opportunity to respond to something appropriate rather than wasting their time and emotional energy on behaviours that are inappropriate.

Withholding attention from behaviours that are maladaptive or inappropriate need not (and should not) result in a child getting appreciably less adult attention. Children who misbehave tend to be attention seekers; ignoring them along with their inappropriate behaviours often results in more varied and even greater inappropriateness as they increase their efforts to get attention. The strategy is for teachers to attend to other, more appropriate (or at least, less objectionable) behaviours in which the child engages. The best behaviours for teachers to reinforce are those that are incompatible with the inappropriate behaviours. James, once again, will be the example:

James's constant flitting about the classroom prevented him from focusing on any one activity. In other words, flitting and focusing are incompatible behaviours. Teachers therefore stopped attending to his flitting and instead paid attention to those moments, brief as they might be, when he became engaged in an activity. The teacher in charge of the activity provided interest and support as long as James was engaged. When he left, that teacher and the others immediately turned their attention elsewhere, until such time as he lingered again, even briefly, with another activity. As noted earlier, James's attention span soon began to show rapid and marked improvement.

Support the Child When the Child Is Doing Something Positive

One problem that often occurs in early childhood settings is that the focus on punishment is too strong. Adults tend to remain fairly neutral until a child does something the adult considers inappropriate. *Then* the child is likely to get a great deal of attention, but of a punishing kind that will do little to eliminate the unacceptable behaviour. It is important to respond positively to a child who is engaged in positive or appropriate behaviours. An important phrase to remember is "Catch the child being good" (Harris, Wolf, & Baer, 1964). Adults should freely and spontaneously respond to (reinforce) the many appropriate things that children do all day long. It is almost impossible for a child to be good and bad at the same time. Appropriate behaviours, therefore, have the potential of crowding out inappropriate behaviours. The strategy is to focus very little attention on what adults have agreed are inappropriate acts. The same amount of attention is directed instead to almost anything else the child does. Adults need spend no additional time on the child. They simply spend the time in ways that are more effective and certainly more pleasant for all (Photo 11–7).

DISCIPLINE VERSUS PUNISHMENT

The goal of discipline is self-discipline. Discipline techniques used by teachers should support the child in developing control of his or her own behaviour. As children mature, they become more aware of the range of consequences that may result from their actions, enabling them to adapt their behaviour on their own.

Discipline is most effective when it is based on anticipation. Through their

Photo 11–7

It is important to respond positively when children are engaged in positive behaviours.

observations of children and their knowledge of child development, teachers can anticipate potential trouble spots and deal with them *before* they occur. In other words, adults prevent mishaps; hence the term **preventive discipline** (Harris & Allen, 1966).

Preventive discipline
a child management procedure for arranging the environment in ways that reduce the occurrence of maladaptive behaviours and increase the occurrence of appropriate behaviours

Preventive discipline depends on what teachers do and say to forestall trouble (in behavioural terms, this is referred to as *arranging antecedents*). How the learning environment is arranged can be one form of preventive discipline (see Chapter 15). By placing the drying rack next to the easel, for example, teachers help children avoid the many problems (and tension-provoking reminders) associated with carrying a dripping painting across the floor. By providing a parking place for wheel toys (instead of letting children abandon them "mid-road"), teachers help children avoid injuring others or getting into angry exchanges as to which child really owns a piece of equipment. The point to be underscored is this: *Environmental arrangements are a major determinant of children's behaviour and of children's learning* (Photo 11–8). Preventive discipline accomplishes the following:

- It communicates to children how to behave according to developmentally appropriate expectations, and then facilitates children's efforts to do so.
- It makes it easy for children to learn the vast number of behaviours and skills necessary to grow up to be confident and competent in a world that expects so much of young children and the adults who care for them.
- It helps children avoid unnecessary and ego-deflating errors that squander children's time and self-esteem.
- It ensures a positive environment in which teachers enjoy teaching and children enjoy learning.

Punishment, in terms of its common definition, consists of those adult behaviours that emotionally or physically hurt children—scolding, nagging, yelling, ridiculing, criticizing, isolating, slapping, shaking, and spanking. As noted earlier, punishing children is *not* an effective way of managing them. True, punishment often stops an undesirable behaviour at the moment. However, it usually is a short-lived victory for the adult and one that tends to backfire. Yelling at children is an example. Most children will stop, for the time being, whatever they are doing that is causing them to be yelled at. That behaviour, however, is almost sure to return again and again under various circumstances and often as soon as the adult who was yelling at them leaves the scene.

In many instances, punishment has undesirable side effects. In the yelling example, the behaviour that the adult does not like is stopped at the time. This reinforces the adult for yelling at the child. The result? The adult yells at the

Photo 11–8
By placing a learning centre away from other areas of activity, children can focus more easily.

child all the more. In addition, the adult is modelling yelling, literally teaching inappropriate yelling behaviour to the child: "Children who are yelled at yell back on other occasions. So, to a considerable degree, you get back what you give" (Bee, 1999, p. 499).

The same holds true of spanking or other forms of physical punishment. Some children who are spanked frequently, or otherwise physically punished, become highly aggressive (Bandura, 1973). Other children react very differently. Some behave as though they were tightly coiled springs. They often behave well at home or school but once out from under adults' eyes they seem to explode into a range of forbidden behaviours. Still other children appear troubled, turn inward, hold back, and become passive. It is as if they fear that whatever they do will result in ridicule, criticism, or some form of physical punishment. In general, punishment leads to loss of self-confidence and self-esteem. Children who are frequently punished (either verbally or physically punished) do not feel good about themselves or their world. Such feelings have a negative effect on all aspects of their development.

STOPPING A HARMFUL BEHAVIOUR

All children must be stopped (that is, have limits set) on occasion. A child who is endangering himself or herself or others, or causing serious disruptions at home or in the classroom, must be controlled. For many children, a reminder or a mild verbal reprimand is enough. This is especially effective in classrooms and homes where preventive discipline is practised, where children receive adequate amounts of positive attention for the good things they do all day long. When a child does not respond to ordinary reminders, the teacher may need to use a firmer tone of voice and more definitive words.

Example:

"No! Janis, I can't let you push Tammy off the tricycle. That can hurt Tammy."

When none of this works, the child may have to be removed from this activity—a form of discipline *that seldom needs to happen.*

WITHDRAWING THE CHILD

Clare Cherry (1983, p. 137) uses the term **renewal time.** She states that "time out is a widely used term, but it tends to be overused, as it can be applied to many different kinds of situations. It often characterizes punitive isolation." Cherry goes on to say: "I prefer the term renewal time. It is easy to say and it means what I really want—a chance for the inner self to become renewed, as opposed to the whole self being 'out.'"

In this form of discipline, the message given to the child is that he or she needs some time to calm down and to gain some inner control. Examples of renewal time are contained in these statements:

Renewal time
a discipline technique that gives a child the message that he or she needs some time to calm down and to gain some inner control

- "Playing alone for a little while will help you settle down."
- "You may read a book quietly or play quietly, but you need time by yourself because you were hurting (disturbing, etc.) other children."
- "You need some time to calm down. You were getting too wild and excited. You need to play quietly on your own for a while until you are calmer."

Giving choices also empowers a child:

- "You need to sit and watch, or you can play quietly somewhere."

The goal is (as it should be with all forms of discipline) to help children become self-managing. The process to follow in positive discipline is this:

1. Tell the child what is problematic about the child's behaviour, explaining why he or she is being asked to change what he or she is doing.
2. If the child does not respond, the teacher needs to tell the child again, this time explaining the consequences to the child if the inappropriate behaviour continues.

Example:

A child is throwing sand at another child. The teacher says, "Please keep the sand in the sandbox, Tony. If you throw the sand it could get in someone's eyes and hurt them." Tony continues to throw the sand. The teacher then says, "Tony, the sand needs to stay in the sandbox. If you keep on throwing sand, I am going to have to ask you to leave the sandbox. I don't want any of your friends to get hurt."

The teacher clearly explains to Tony *what* is inappropriate about his behaviour, *why* she feels that this behaviour cannot continue, and the *limit* she will have to place if he does not stop the behaviour on his own. Children often realize that they have made a mistake in self-management but may not yet have developed the inner control needed to change their behaviour. When they are asked to leave a play situation, the adult is letting them know that it is important to work on developing this control if they want to remain in their chosen play situations. To help children remember, the teacher can talk with the children about what happened and how they could have handled the situation more effectively.

Basic guidelines for withdrawing a child include the following:

- The behaviour is harmful to the child himself or herself (this includes physical hurt as well as situations in which a child may be becoming overly stimulated emotionally).
- The behaviour is likely to be harmful to another child.
- The behaviour is likely to harm property.

Time-out should be used only as a last resort. It is the extreme form of withdrawing reinforcement. *Time-out* means removing the child from all reinforcement, including teacher attention, other children, materials, and equipment. *Time-out should be used only with the permission of the parent and the consultants.* It should be reserved for seriously inappropriate behaviours (habitual antisocial behaviours, extreme temper tantrums, etc.) that have not responded to less severe forms of behaviour management. Children who do not comprehend verbal and problem-solving strategies for changing behaviour may need time-out to define the limits being set. (Note: Many provinces and territories have specific guidelines that must be followed for use of specific behavioural practices, including time-out.)

On those occasions when time-out has to be used, the time-out period should be short. After the child has begun to self-regulate, the amount of minutes for time-out should not exceed the child's age (e.g., for three-year-olds, three minutes would be the maximum). During the time-out process, adults in the room do not respond to the child. The child should be in a safe area with minimal stimulation and in clear view of the teacher. Other children should be reassured that the child will rejoin the group when he or she is calm. *A written plan that monitors the frequency and duration of time-out should be maintained.*

Photo 11–9
It is in the classroom, *not in time out,* that teachers help children learn appropriate ways of behaving.

An important reminder: Children do not learn *what to do* in time out; they learn only *what not to do.* If children are to learn how to work and play with each other and with materials, they need to be involved (Schickedanz, Schickedanz, & Forsyth, 1982). It is in the classroom, *not in time-out,* that teachers can help children learn appropriate ways of responding (Photo 11–9). Good teachers seldom need to use time-out or any other punishment procedure when preventive discipline is the practice and all children receive adequate amounts of positive attention. It must be remembered, however, that what is an *adequate amount* will vary from child to child, depending on individual differences.

Task analysis
the process of breaking down a complex task into smaller units so that learning can occur more easily

Task Analysis

Task analysis is a teaching procedure that grew out of the behavioural concept of *shaping* new responses (Photo 11–10). It is a particularly important teaching strategy to use when a child is unable to accomplish a task within a time period that is considered appropriate for the child's development. Shaping of behaviour is the process of reinforcing *successive approximations* (a series of small steps) toward the eventual mastery of a complex behaviour. In analyzing any kind of a task—tying shoes, counting bears, printing letters, defending possessions, making friends—the first requirement is to break the task down into its step-by-step components. The steps must be small and logical. They also must be in sequence, progressing from the known, simple, and easy to the more difficult and complex. Small steps provide frequent opportunities for success. Many small steps, and therefore many small successes, help the child avoid unnecessary frustrations. Too many frustrations are defeating to young learners and even more defeating for children who have special needs.

Photo 11–10
In task analysis (identifying the step-by-step procedure), teachers should watch the performance of an accomplished child.

OBSERVATION AND TASK ANALYSIS

In preparing to analyze a task, early childhood teachers often find it helpful first to watch a young child perform the task. It is especially instructive to watch a child who has only recently mastered a particular skill. The child's motor coordination and general approach to the problem are likely to be more finely sequenced and developmentally appropriate than are those of an older child or an adult performing the same task. When adapting a procedure to an individual child, the starting point is determined by observing that child. The rule is to start where the child is, with what the child can do. This provides the child with a successful experience at the start. It also enables the teacher to make positive comments immediately, thus getting the new learning off to a good start.

It is true that the first step may be far removed from what is seen as the end behaviour. Many times it is nothing more than a child standing and watching an activity that has been targeted as a developmentally necessary skill for that child; this, however, is but a first step, an opportunity for a teacher to reinforce a first approximation to a more complex skill. A teacher can stand companionably close, watch with the child, and comment briefly on some aspect of the activity. The following case study describes the application of the task analysis process.

Task Analysis: Ladder-Climbing Sequence

Planning process.

1. **Assess child's abilities and needs.**

   Before a task can be selected for a child to perform, a careful assessment of the child's current abilities and skills must be completed.

   Case History

   Matthew would soon be four years old. He was a pale, slow-moving child who seldom played with other children. He rarely engaged in the vigorous outdoor play activities typical of the rest of the group. Teachers agreed, based on a series of observations, that it would help Matthew's overall development if he were to learn to use the climbing equipment. However, he resisted all of their efforts to involve him in climbing activities. Below is a condensed account of the step-by-step procedures that resulted in Matthew's becoming not only an active climber but a more sociable four-year-old.

2. **Set a goal, objectives, and the task.**

   a. *Set a goal.* Set a goal and then identify the task to be performed by the child. The goal in the above example might be developing motor skills for outdoor play.

   b. *Identify objectives.* For example, the child will independently climb up to the top of the slide in the playground.

   c. *Set the task.* The task in this case is climbing a ladder.

3. **Determine the sequential steps necessary for performing the task.**

   The child follows this sequence of steps when climbing a ladder:

   a. looks at ladder

   b. approaches ladder

   c. places hands on rails of ladder

    d. places dominant foot on lower rung

    e. pulls body up with arms while at the same time pressing down with the dominant foot

    f. places other foot on bottom rung

    g. moves dominant hand up one rung

    h. moves dominant foot up to the next rung

    i. repeats above steps

4. Decide on an implementation plan.

Develop a plan and decide on how this plan will be carried out. Teachers need to agree on the following:

    a. the step in the sequence with which to begin

    b. the teaching strategies that are most appropriate for this child

    c. the type of reinforcement to be provided

    d. when and where the task will be performed

5. Implement the plan.

A short ladder with broad steps was set up against play equipment that Matthew often wandered past. A teacher was stationed near the ladder, supervising children playing in the area.

    a. Whenever Matthew wandered by, the teacher spoke to him and chatted with him. Often he drew closer, watching the children climbing about. When he stopped watching the children and looked as if he were about to move away, the teacher became busy with the other children.

    b. As Matthew stopped to chat more frequently and for longer periods of time, he sometimes leaned against or put his hand on the ladder. Soon the teacher began to chat with Matthew only when he was touching the ladder.

    c. Next, whenever Matthew was leaning on the ladder, the teacher made up a game, placing one of Matthew's feet on the lowest rung and then taking it off. Matthew delighted in the game. Soon he was putting his own foot on the ladder.

    d. Before long, Matthew himself was putting both feet on the bottom rung of the ladder. The teacher then changed the game to feet on and off the second rung.

    e. In this game-like atmosphere, where the teacher provided both physical and verbal reinforcement, Matthew was soon climbing up and down the ladder.

    f. The ladder was later moved to different locations. Matthew continued to climb on it with only occasional attention from teachers. It appeared that the activity itself had become fun for Matthew and therefore self-reinforcing.

    g. The next step was to place the ladder against another big piece of climbing equipment. As Matthew began to make the transition from the familiar ladder to the big piece of equipment, teachers once again provided an abundance of physical and verbal support.

By the ninth day of the program, Matthew was spending more than half of the outdoor play time in a variety of climbing activities. At mid-year he was as active and involved outdoors as any child in the group. Presumably, vigorous outdoor play with other children had become a pleasurable activity that would continue to be self-reinforcing.

USING TASK ANALYSIS FOR TOILET TRAINING

As noted at the outset, all self-help/care skills are learned. It follows, then, that all self-help/care skills can be taught. Success depends, in part, on physiological maturity, especially of the sphincter muscles, when toilet training a child.

Toilet training, once thought to be totally dependent on maturation, can be *task analyzed* and taught in its component parts. With some children, *each part,* in turn, may need to be task analyzed and taught step by step. Ordinary toilet training includes many steps. It starts with getting into the bathroom, pulling the pants down, and getting up onto the toilet. It concludes with getting off the toilet, pulling clothes up, and flushing. What could be simpler? Yet, for many young children, one or more of the steps may present great difficulty. Even the seemingly simple task of getting on and off the toilet may need to be broken down into smaller steps. For sure, using toilet tissue effectively is a challenge for all young children! Teachers may need to require additional information on toilet training children who are **nonambulatory** or have other special concerns.

Nonambulatory
unable to walk

STEP-BY-STEP PLANNING

In teaching any self-help/care skill, the teacher must know exactly where each child is in that particular skill sequence. This can be accomplished by asking a simple question about each step: can the child do it? If yes, the teacher can proceed to the next step; if no, the teacher figures out the substeps appropriate for that child at that point in the sequence. Figure 11–1 shows the procedure for the first two or three steps in the toilet-training tasks listed above.

Figure 11–1 SKILL SEQUENCE FOR INDEPENDENT TOILETING

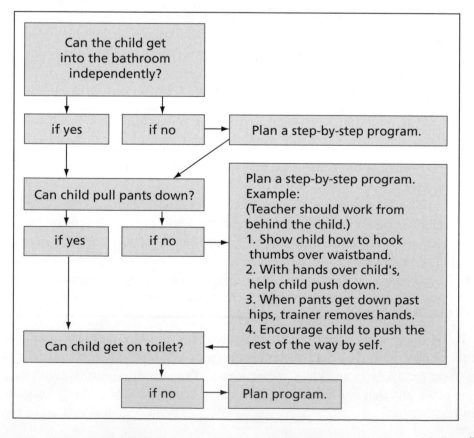

CHAINING IN TASK ANALYSIS

Self-help/care tasks, such as toileting, shoe lacing, and feeding oneself, are all examples of tasks comprising a set of smaller behaviours (skills), chained (sequenced) together and organized into what seems to be a single task. When the chaining concept is adapted to teaching self-help/care skills, the child is helped to learn one response, one link of the skill chain at a time. Once the child is performing the first component in the chain, the next step (or link) is introduced. Single components of the chain are added one by one until the child can perform all of them, in order, from start to finish. Step-by-step learning can be made easier if the child can see the entire chain being performed (see Chapters 13 and 20 for learning through observation and modelling).

On many tasks, forward chaining and backward chaining are equally successful. The choice depends on the particular task and level of skill the child displays. In **forward chaining,** the teacher helps the child learn the first step in the chain, then the second, and so on. In **backward chaining,** instruction begins with the last step and progresses in reverse to the first component.

The child in the following example of zipping has fairly well-developed fine motor skills; the teacher, therefore, has broken the task into only six component parts (a six-step task analysis). The steps are suitable for teaching the task with either a forward or a backward chaining approach. Throughout both forward and backward chaining, the teacher will demonstrate or provide **manual prompts** as needed.

Step 1. With both hands, the bottom front edges of the coat are brought together at the bottom.

Step 2. The zipper foot is inserted into the zipper catch.

Step 3. The zipper foot is seated in the catch by pushing up and down with opposing movements of each hand.

Step 4. The tab on the zipper is grasped between thumb and forefinger.

Step 5. The bottom of the coat at the zipper catch is held with one hand while the zipper tab is pulled to the top, with the other hand holding the zipper tab (Photo 11–11).

Step 6. The zipper tab is pushed down firmly into locked position.

In backward chaining, the child would first master step 6, then 5, and so on, back to step 1. The major advantage of backward chaining is that the child is always reinforced by task completion, even in the first lesson. Accomplishing the last step sends a reinforcing message to the child that the time has come to get on to something more interesting. At some point, for most children, the chain becomes one integrated skill they scarcely need to think about.

Forward chaining
breaking a task down into a series of small steps and teaching the first step first

Backward chaining
teaching starts with the last step of a learning sequence

Manual prompts
when the teacher's hand is around the learner's and actually putting the learner through the motions (may also be referred to as "hand over hand")

Photo 11–11
Step 5 in backward chaining for learning how to zipper.

PRACTICAL CONSIDERATIONS WHEN USING TASK ANALYSIS IN TEACHING SELF-HELP/CARE SKILLS

In many other dressing and self-help/care tasks, it is important that the adult work from behind the child. This ensures that the teacher's hands are performing the hand and finger movements in the same way that the child will be expected to reproduce them. Young children do not have a well-developed sense of spatial orientation or a concept of reversibility. Teachers' demonstrations, therefore, must be conducted from the child's perspective. For this reason and others, the use of lacing, buttoning, and zipping boards for children to practise on has been questioned. It is too confusing for many children to try to reverse and transfer the motions learned in practice sessions to their own bodies (Cook, Tessier, & Klein, 2004).

A word about the importance of suitable clothing when learning self-help/care skills: Children who are being toilet trained need underpants (and outer pants) with elastic at the top so that they can be pulled down easily. Children who are learning to dress themselves can learn more easily if their clothing has big, sturdy zippers that work, large buttons and unrestricted buttonholes, and simple fastenings, such as Velcro on belts, shoes, and overalls. When children are having prolonged difficulty in learning to dress themselves, temporarily providing clothing a size or two too big is sometimes a help. Obviously, teachers should never presume to tell parents how to dress their children. However, parents often welcome suggestions that help their children learn more easily.

PROMPTING, CUEING, AND FADING

Task analysis often needs to be accompanied by, and reinforced with, physical and verbal assistance referred to as *prompting and cueing*. Prompts and cues help all children, and especially children with developmental differences, acquire a skill they may be having trouble with. *Fading* is the process of gradually and systematically reducing assistance (the prompting and cueing) as much and as soon as possible without interfering with the child's progress. The goal is for the child to learn to perform the task as independently as is feasible. To illustrate these procedures, the task of learning to hang up a coat is described here:

1. The teacher accompanies the child to the cubby or locker and gives verbal cues: "Here is your locker. Here is the hook for your coat."
2. The teacher explains and demonstrates: "This is the loop that keeps your coat on the hook. It goes over the hook like this."
3. Taking the coat off the hook but holding it open, the teacher prompts, "Can you find the loop?"
4. When the child finds the loop, the teacher says, "Right. Now you can put your finger into it, just as I did."
5. The teacher continues, "Now, slip the loop over the hook." If the child cannot yet coordinate the necessary movements, the teacher guides the child's hand (provides a manual prompt).
6. After a few tries the teacher is able to withdraw physical assistance the instant before the loop goes over the hook and so can say to the child, "Look at that! You hung up your coat. Good for you."

In this example, physical assistance was gradually reduced while verbal prompts and cues and positive comments were continued. As the child got better at the task, verbal help was also reduced but only as the child showed near mastery of each step. Some tasks and some children need even smaller, more specific steps and special kinds of assistance.

Manual prompting is a common form of special assistance leading to skill mastery. Manual prompting (Photo 11–12), sometimes referred to as *hand over hand*, consists of positioning the adult's hand around the child's and actually putting the child through the motions. Once the child has the feel of the movements, manual prompting is gradually reduced.

Teachers must guard against overwhelming children with directions when helping them learn a complex task. Directions, like rules, should be kept to a minimum. They

Photo 11–12
In manual prompting, the teacher places a hand around the child's to guide the child's movements.

should be given only if the teacher is prepared to help the child carry through with additional prompting, cueing, and physical assistance. As with rules, *directions are more effective if worded positively*. It is more informative and helpful to say, "Hold tight with both hands" than it is to say, "Be careful. Don't fall." The latter statements provide children with no information about what they *should* be doing. In all cases, the primary goal is to encourage children's independence, especially in children with special needs. Therefore, teachers provide just enough assistance to ensure children's success but not so much as to promote overdependence.

And now a few words of caution: Slow down. Be patient. Adults best promote children's independence by waiting, allowing children adequate time to figure out what they are going to do next and how they will do it. This is in contrast to what happens all too often: The adult says "Put on your sock." The young child is still trying to figure out which is the open end of the sock when the adult grabs it and expertly puts it on the child's foot. What message does this convey to the child?

AMOUNT AND TIMING OF REINFORCEMENT

How much reinforcement is enough? The answer varies from child to child and task to task. Almost continual reinforcement—feedback—may be needed when a child is beginning to learn something new. Every time the new behaviour (or an approximation to the new behaviour) occurs, the adult tries to respond in some way. At times, smiling and nodding may be all a teacher can take the time to do (Photo 11–13, p. 238). As in the shaping and prompting examples, adult attention is gradually reduced as the child becomes more able. The goal, as always, is that the child's success (intrinsic motivation) takes over, keeping the child eager to continue learning. To accomplish this, a balance must be achieved: not so much adult attention that the child becomes dependent but enough so learning continues until the skill is well established and intrinsically reinforcing.

Photo 11–13
There are many instances when the teacher provides a nod or a smile.

Summary

Developmental concepts, such as the "problem of the match" and "learning from success," as well as behavioural principles, have blended into today's well-articulated early childhood teaching practices. The effectiveness of an early education program is demonstrated by changes in children's behaviour. To have healthy development, ongoing changes in behaviour must occur. The blend of developmental and behavioural principles and practices is good for all children and particularly important in inclusive environments where the range of skill levels is extensive. The blend of practices demonstrates that all children can learn; if a child is not learning, the responsibility is placed squarely on the program, not on the child.

In the behavioural perspective, systematic reinforcement procedures—if imposed within an appropriate structure—account for children's learning (or failure to learn). The principles can be put into an ABC format (A stands for antecedents; B stands for the child's behaviour; C stands for consequences). Reinforcements (consequences) are negative or positive. Positive reinforcement is the teacher's best tool. It is readily available through teachers' assistance, genuine interest, and positive reactions to each child and each child's activities. Positive reinforcement also resides in the interesting and appropriate materials and activities provided by teachers.

In some instances, reinforcers must be withheld or withdrawn so that a child does not get attention for behaviours that are detrimental to his or her development. When teachers must withhold reinforcement for an inappropriate behaviour, it is important that they double their efforts to give the child positive attention for useful behaviours. When they do so, inappropriate behaviours are likely to be *crowded out* by more appropriate ones.

Preventive discipline supports appropriate behaviour by guiding children before problems occur.

Renewal time involves removing a child from a situation that he or she is not able to cope with and directing him or her to a quiet area to play alone until he or she is able to rejoin the group. This is the preferred form of withdrawal. Time-out is used only in those infrequent situations where systematic positive practices have failed to produce necessary behaviour changes.

Punishment is the least desirable and least effective of all forms of child management. Though the punished behaviour may stop for the moment, it usually returns again and again. Frequent punishment has many undesirable side effects, including heightened aggressiveness and diminishing self-esteem.

Other educational practices related to reinforcement procedures include task analysis and learning through observation (modelling), a principle derived from social learning theory. Task analysis is the process of breaking a learning task into small sequential steps for those children who need special help in the form of reduced frustration and more frequent successes. Step-by-step learning is further facilitated with prompting and cueing, which can be reduced gradually as the child gains mastery of a task. Self-help/care skills can be taught effectively through task analysis using either forward or backward chaining. In every kind of learning situation, teachers provide encouragement and descriptive praise to the degree that is appropriate for individual children, rather than foster competitiveness.

RESOURCES

CHILD AND FAMILY CANADA
http://www.cfc-efc.ca
This site provides information about child care, child development, parenting, health, safety, literacy, nutrition, physical activities, play, family life, adolescence, learning activities, social issues, and special needs. Information is in English and French.

CHILDREN, YOUTH AND FAMILY CONSORTIUM
http://www.cyfc.umn.cdu
The Children, Youth and Family Consortium's electronic clearinghouse is a forum for sharing information and exchanging ideas. The wide range of topics include resources for children and families; youth; violence; children's health; chemical dependency, ADHD; disabilities; family economics; gay, lesbian, transgender, and bisexual issues; child care; statistics on children; and government resources.

MEDBROADCAST CORPORATION
http://www.medbroadcast.com
This Vancouver organization specializes in providing online medical information and services. It covers a wide range of topics relevant to families.

STUDENT ACTIVITIES

1. Observe for one hour in an early childhood classroom. Write down every example of adult social reinforcement that you see and hear.
2. Imagine a child engrossed in painting at the easel or at a table. List ten positive statements you might make that recognize the child's worth and efforts.
3. Discuss with several of your classmates how they felt as little children when they were punished and what they believe might be the long-term effects, if any. What experiences did they have with preventive discipline?
4. For several days, watch an older child brush his or her teeth. Do a task analysis of the activity, starting with the child's approach to the sink.
5. Talk with the parents of a preschool child. Ask what behaviours, both positive and negative, they feel their child may have learned through imitation or modelling from family or television or at school. (If you have a preschool child of your own, examine your own reactions.)

6. Observe a preschool or child care centre during arrival or departure time, a toileting period, or a meal or snack time. Select one situation and describe how a teacher might use task analysis to further a child's skill development. Outline the specific steps involved in the task analysis.

7. Select the one best match for each item in column I from column II and place that letter in the appropriate space in column I.

	I		**II**
___	1. Gesell	A.	modelling
___	2. intrinsic motivation	B.	didactic materials
___	3. Montessori	C.	hand over hand
___	4. positive reinforcement	D.	joy of learning
___	5. incompatible behaviours	E.	shaping
___	6. manual prompts	F.	standing and sitting
___	7. successive approximations	G.	developmentalist
___	8. observation learning	H.	pleasurable consequences

REFERENCES

Allen, K. E. (1974). Behavior modification principles." In J. C. Cull & R. F. Hardy (Eds.), *Behavior modification in rehabilitation settings.* Springfield, IL: Thomas.

Bandura, A. (1973). *Aggression: A social learning analysis.* Englewood Cliffs, NJ: Prentice-Hall.

Bee, H. (1999). *The developing child* (9th ed.). New York: Longman.

Bijou, S. W. (1959). Learning in children. *Monographs of the Society for Research in Child Development, 24*(5).

Brophy, J. E. (1981). Teacher praise: A functional analysis. *Review of Educational Research, 51*(1), 5–32.

Chance, P. (1998). *First course in applied behavior analysis.* Pacific Grove, CA: Brooks/Cole.

Cherry, C. (1983). *Please don't sit on the kids.* Belmont, CA: Pitman.

Cook, R. E., Tessier, A., & Klein, M. D. (2004). *Adapting early childhood curricula for children with special needs.* Columbus, OH: Merrill.

Dewey, J. (1950). *Experience and education.* New York: Macmillan.

Froebel, F. W. (1911). *The education of man* (Trans. W. N. Hailmann). New York: Appleton.

Gesell, A., Halverson, H. M., Thompson, B., Ilg, F. L., Castner, B. M., Ames, L. B., & Amatruda, C. S. (1940). *The first five years of life. A guide to the study of the preschool child.* New York: Harper and Row.

Harris, F. R., & Allen, R. E. (1966). *Undersix: Children in preschool KCTS television series and viewer's guide.* Seattle, WA: University of Washington.

Harris, F. R., Wolf, M. M., & Baer, D. M. (1964). Effects of adult social reinforcement on child behavior. *Young Children, 1,* 8–17.

Hunt, J. McV. (1961). *Intelligence and experience.* New York: Ronald Press.

Montessori, M. (1912). *The Montessori method: Scientific pedagogy as applied to child education in "children's houses"* (Trans. A. F. George). New York: Stokes.

Piaget, J. (1952). *The origins of intelligence in children.* New York: International Universities Press.

Schickedanz, J. A., Schickedanz, D. I., & Forsyth, P. D. (1982). *Toward understanding children.* Boston: Little, Brown.

Wolery, M. (1994). *Designing inclusive environments for children with special needs in early childhood programs.* Washington, DC: National Association for the Education of Young Children.

CHAPTER 12

Identification and the Individual Program Plan (IPP)

KEY CONCEPTS

bias-free screening and assessment

criterion-referenced tests

individual program plan (IPP)

interdisciplinary

norm-referenced tests

portfolio

reliable and valid tests

transdisciplinary

OBJECTIVES

After studying the material in this chapter, the student will be able to

- Explain this statement: "Scores obtained on IQ tests given to young children must be viewed with caution, even skepticism."
- Discuss the role of the early childhood teacher in the identification of developmental differences and in the IPP process.
- Identify different observational recording techniques and give appropriate examples for application.
- Summarize each of the major components of an IPP.

Introduction

The identification of developmental differences is a responsibility of everyone associated with infants and young children and their families. Though some provinces and territories in Canada provide screening of newborn babies and follow-up home visits by public health nurses, no federal legislation requires early screening and assessment of an infant's development. Recent brain studies give us powerful new evidence that the early years of development from conception to age six, particularly for the first three years of life, set the competence and coping skills that will affect future learning, behaviour, and health (McCain & Mustard, 1999). Early identification of special needs is critical in order to access early intervention and specialized programming.

The focus of this chapter is on these two issues: early identification of developmental differences and the delivery of special services through the individual program plan (IPP).

The Process of Early Identification

Identification of developmental differences can take place any time from a few weeks after conception to adulthood (age 18). These years are formally recognized as the developmental period. Early identification of differences is not limited to the first five to eight years of life. A child may be perfectly healthy up to age 12 or 15, and then show first-time symptoms of a "disability" that has an impact on development (juvenile rheumatoid arthritis, for example). The older child is as much in need of early identification of an emerging condition as is a two-year-old showing first-time symptoms of any kind. In both cases, early identification should lead to prompt treatment. In turn, prompt treatment can reduce the level of involvement and prevent the condition from affecting other areas of development.

The identification of developmental differences or potential developmental differences involves several steps: screening, assessment, diagnosis, and evaluation. The first two of these steps in the identification process will be discussed in this chapter.

EARLY IDENTIFICATION

In Canada, because of the universal health-care program, the identification of children who have developmental differences falls mainly on the shoulders of the medical profession:

- the doctor or midwife who delivers the baby
- the nurses who observe the baby directly after birth
- the family physician and pediatrician who usually sees the child at regular intervals

Programs and services available through community public health departments, medical centres, and community early intervention services seek to identify those children who may require further assessment to ensure early identification of developmental differences.

Screening is the process of identifying *possible* differences in a child's development that may indicate the need for a more thorough assessment or specific support (Photo 12–1, p. 244). Screening can be carried out by people without highly specialized training and is based on various observation techniques and screening tools. *Assessment* is the process used to measure a child's performance or development,

Photo 12–1
Screening often involves direct observation of the child in the play environment.

which may be based on observations, tests, or the child's behaviour. Specially trained early childhood resource teachers/early interventionists are often able to conduct informal functional assessments that can provide information to support appropriate programming. However, the use of standardized assessment techniques to obtain a more definitive diagnosis requires a licensed clinician.

SCREENING

Screening is important in the identification of developmental differences (or potential differences). Screening tests describe a child's level of performance, but *only at that point in time* (Allen & Marotz, 2003). Comprehensive screening evaluates the child's current abilities and needs in all areas of development. If areas of concern are identified during routine developmental screening, clinical assessments are indicated. Several points should be emphasized:

- Results from screening tests should not be confused with assessment. They do not constitute a diagnosis and should never be used as a basis for planning an intervention program.
- *Follow-through is essential.* "Identifying children with potential problems is only the first step; encouraging families to seek further assessment for their child is the next" (Hanson & Lynch, 1998, p. 95).
- Accurate results can be achieved only with **reliable and valid tests** developed specifically for use with young children. There is a scarcity of such tests. In the absence of a valid instrument, testing is of no value (National Association for the Education of Young Children, 1988, p. 12).

Reliable and valid tests
reliability relates to consistency—how accurate, dependable, and predictable a test is; validity refers to how accurately a test measures that which it purports to measure

Parents as Partners in Screening

Parents have a wealth of firsthand knowledge about their children (Photo 12–2). They know what their child can and cannot do in everyday life. Often, they are the first to suspect a problem even if unable to specify its nature clearly. It is estimated that 65 percent to 75 percent of hearing impairments in young children were noted first by their parents. The parents knew *something* was different (Harris, 1994). They did not necessarily recognize it as a hearing loss, but they did report to the health-care provider that their child acted strange or "talked funny."

A hearing loss, as well as a number of other subtle differences, may not show up during a routine medical checkup. When a developmental difference cannot be pinpointed by the clinician, parents sometimes are led to believe that "nothing is wrong with their child." They are often advised to go home and relax, to get over being so anxious. Ignoring parents' observations, however, is not in the best interest of the child. Failing to recognize a parent's concern in its early stages may result in a long-range negative impact on the child's development.

Photo 12–2
Parents have a wealth of knowledge about their child.

Cultural, Ethnic, and Linguistic Differences

Family customs, beliefs, and language influence a child's performance on screening tests (Banks, 1994). A child's responses may be scored as wrong even when they are right according to the family's values. The result may be an invalid (false) evaluation, suggesting that there is cause to be concerned about the child's development when none exists. Invalid assessment results became dismayingly apparent in the early days of special education reform, and they continue to be apparent in the over-representation of minority students in special education. These were the children who functioned perfectly well in their own communities and in their own language but had few skills and little background for functioning in schools designed to accommodate only the majority culture. As stated in the *Checklist for Quality Inclusive Education* (Langford, 1997):

> Age guidelines must also be looked at from a cultural perspective. Age guidelines suggest what is normal development during an age range. For example, a developmental checklist may state that children are expected to drink from a cup with on hand, unassisted between the ages of 13 and 24 months. However, in some cultures, children receive assistance with drinking until the middle years because interdependency between a mother/father and child is expected and encouraged. In this case, a developmental checklist item has not been sensitive to a wide range of child-rearing practices that influence the behaviour of a child. An educator may interpret a child's inability to drink from a cup independently as a problem rather than as a reflection of a cultural norm. As well, educators need to know that all children progress at vastly different rates of development or may lack experience with particular activities.

To avoid similar errors, safeguards must be built into every step of the screening and assessment process. Dotsch (1992) suggests the following:

- Conduct assessments in the child's dominant language or in the first *and* second language.
- Rely on nonbiased observations and anecdotal information, as well as on formal modes.
- Adapt assessment methods for the specific diverse child/family from family input.

Examples of these safeguards are evident in the Nipissing District Developmental Screen (NDDS), in which some of the developmental outcomes are rated as not common to all cultures (see Figure 12–1).

Figure 12–1 DEVELOPMENTAL SCREEN "30 MONTHS"

Child's Name ________________________

Birth Date ___________ Today's Date _______

The Nipissing District Developmental Screen is a checklist designed to help monitor your child's development.

✓ ✓

By ***30 Months*** of Age, does your child ...

Yes	No		
☐	☐	1.	Usually have healthy ears and seem to hear well?
☐	☐	2.	Put a toy *in* and put a toy *under* when asked?
☐	☐	3.	Join three words together, like "Me want ball"?
☐	☐	4.	Recognize the names and pictures of most common items (i.e., "Show me the ball")?
☐	☐	5.	Use pronouns I, you, me, and mine?
☐	☐	6.	Lift and drink from a cup and replace it on the table?*
☐	☐	7.	Imitate drawing vertical and horizontal lines? (Picture A)
☐	☐	8.	Remove clothing already unzipped or unbuttoned?
☐	☐	9.	Run without falling most of the time?
☐	☐	10.	Kick a ball forward?
☐	☐	11.	Jump off the floor with both feet? (Picture B)
☐	☐	12.	Try to join in songs and rhymes with you?
☐	☐	13.	Listen to simple stories?
☐	☐	14.	Act out daily routines with toys (e.g., feed doll, sweep floor)?
☐	☐	15.	Wait briefly for needs to be met (e.g., when placed in high chair at meal time)?
☐	☐	16.	Recognize self in mirror or picture?

* Item may not be common to all cultures.

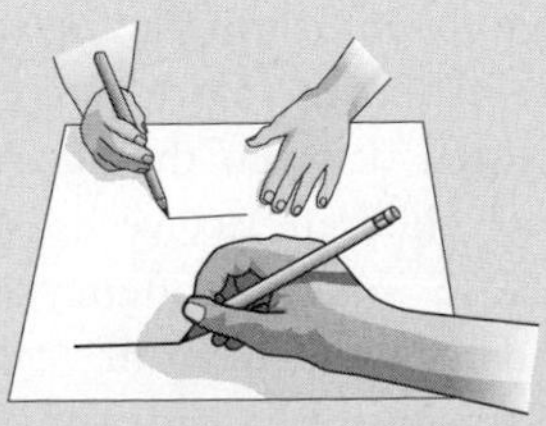

A

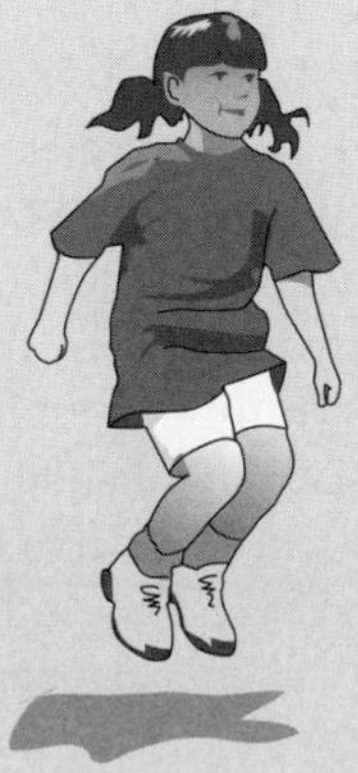

B

Always talk to your health care or child care professional if you have questions about your child's development or well being.

SOURCE: From *Observing Young Children, A Guide for Early Childhood Educators,* Second Edition by WYLIE © 2004. Reprinted with permission of Nelson, a division of Thomson Learning: www.thomsonrights.com. Fax 800-730-2215.

Types of Screening and Assessment Instruments

Early childhood screening tests take many forms (see Figure 12–2). Some, like the Peabody Picture Vocabulary Test, focus on only one aspect of development and must be administered by a professionally trained speech pathologist. Others tests, such as the Denver Developmental Screening Test II (DDST), Diagnostic Inventory for Screening Children (DISC), and the NDDS attempt to assess all developmental areas.

Screening tests also are available that assess newborns and older infants (Photo 12–3, p. 248), such as the APGAR (which assesses a newborn's colour, heart

Figure 12–2   Developmental preschool screen

Materials	Starting Point by Month	Does the Child . . . . .?			
Crayon, paper	36 & 37 months	Imitate both vertical and horizontal lines. Demonstrate 1/3 trials	YES	NO	REFUSE
	38 months	Repeat phrases. "little boy" _____ "big red truck" _____ "nice warm coat" _____ 2/3 phrases	YES	NO	REFUSE
6 cubes	39 months	Match colours. "Find another one like this one—the same colour." blue _____ red _____ green _____ 2/3 matches	YES	NO	REFUSE
Picture book p.1	40 & 41 months	Answer questions using related words. "What is the boy/girl doing?" girl crying _____ boy swinging _____ girl sleeping _____ girl skipping _____ boy sitting _____ boy reading _____ 3/6 answers	YES	NO	REFUSE
	42 months	Stand on one foot for at least three seconds. Demonstrate. 1/3 trials	YES	NO	REFUSE
Picture book pp. 2–3	43 months	Discriminate pictures apple _____ cup _____ doll _____ baby _____ 3/4 pictures	YES	NO	REFUSE
Crayon, paper	44 months	Imitate a cross (+). Demonstrate. 1/3 trials	YES	NO	REFUSE

Source: Reprinted by permission of Marian Mainland. President, Mainland Consulting.

Photo 12–3
Several screening tests are available for assessing older infants as well as newborns.

Criterion-referenced tests assessments that describe a child's developmental level and progress according to a prescribed set of skills, tasks, and activities

Norm-referenced tests instruments that compare a child's developmental level with a normative sample of same-age peers

rate, reflex, muscle tone, and respiratory effort) and the Baley Scales of Infant Development. Other tests assess vision (Snellen Illiterate E), hearing (Pure Tone Audiometry), and cognitive skills (the Wechsler Preschool and Primary Scale of Intelligence, or WPPSI).

A screening instrument noted for its interdisciplinary capabilities is the DIAL-3 (Developmental Indicators for the Assessment of Learning, third edition). DIAL makes the classroom teacher central to the screening process. The advantage is obvious: Except for parents, no one knows a child, or can interpret a child's responses, better.

Although there is no single test that identifies children who may be gifted, teachers play a major role in screening for giftedness. Several measures must be used. IQ scores, level of motivation, and creativity (which is difficult to define and measure) may be useful when backed up by a teacher's observations and insights into a child's developmental skills (see Chapter 3).

Criterion-referenced tests. Some screening instruments are **criterion-referenced tests;** that is, a child's performance on each task is compared with a preselected standard (*criterion*). A child's performance is not compared with the performance of other children. Criterion-referenced test items might ask, for example, "Can the child lace and tie his or her own shoes? walk seven consecutive steps on a balance beam? match five shapes and colours in one minute?" The Brigance Diagnostic Inventory of Early Development is one example of a criterion-referenced test. It is used to assess children (birth to age seven) in 11 developmental domains. This test is developed to assist teachers in program planning rather than determining a child's eligibility or diagnostic category. The DASI (Developmental Assessment Screening Inventory) is useful for testing nonverbal children because it strictly focuses on evaluating performance.

Norm-referenced tests. With **norm-referenced tests** the question becomes: How well does the child do, *compared with other children of the same age,* on tasks such as counting pennies, naming letters of the alphabet, or stacking six small cubes? Norm-referenced tests provide standardized information intended to relate to children's abilities at various ages. In other words, the norm-referenced test provides scales that compare the performance of one child with the averaged performance of other children of approximately the same age. It must be recognized, however, that these tests tend to be less than reliable with young children (Cohen & Spenciner, 1994), and some are culturally biased (Dotsch, 1998). The Battelle Developmental Inventory is an example of a norm-referenced assessment tool. It is useful because it is curriculum based. In other words, we can test a child, find the areas where the child lacks knowledge or ability, teach to that gap, and then retest to see if the missing information or skill has been acquired.

IQ tests. Most intelligence tests (IQ tests) are norm referenced. Tests such as the Wechsler Intelligence Scale for Children (WISC) and the Stanford-Binet Intelligence Scales are sometimes given to young children. The purpose is to attempt to determine

- how much the child knows
- how well the child solves problems
- how quickly the child can perform a variety of cognitive tasks

Photo 12–4
It is often difficult to determine IQ scores of young children with special needs. Furthermore, IQ scores do not predict later intellectual performance.

The scores from IQ tests must be viewed with caution, even skepticism. A number of factors may lead to poor performance on an IQ test (or any other test, for that matter). The child may be tired, hungry, or unwell at the time. He or she may be anxious about the unfamiliar testing situation and the unfamiliar person giving the test. The child also may be answering in ways appropriate to his or her own language or culture but inappropriate in terms of standardized test responses (recall the earlier discussion on cultural differences). Furthermore, some children are hampered by an unidentified developmental or sensory impairment. A partial vision or hearing loss, for example, can interfere with a child's ability to respond appropriately; thus, the child's IQ score may falsely indicate an impairment of intellectual functioning.

IQ scores of young children *do not predict future intellectual performance* (Photo 12–4). In fact, they are not even good at assessing a young child's current intellectual capabilities. The major problem with IQ scores is that they do not account for the child's learning opportunities (or lack of learning opportunities). Neither do they reflect the quality of the learning experiences a child may have had. The use of a single test score to determine a child's intellectual competence must always be challenged. In fact, *more than one instrument* should be used in any screening program to ensure a valid picture of the child's development. As Perrone (1990, p. 13) points out, "Teachers and parents have been told that tests have meaning, that they point out what children know and understand, that they can help give direction to instruction. The tests *don't* match the promise."

The Teacher's Role in Early Identification

The teacher's role is critical in the identification of developmental differences in infants and young children (Photo 12–5, p. 250). It is teachers' recorded observations of children in many situations, over time, that provides a valid picture of each child's

Photo 12–5
Systematically recorded observations are extremely useful in identifying children with possible developmental differences.

skills, capabilities, and special needs. All children in a group should be observed and informally screened to ensure that the activities provided are developmentally appropriate. It is through this observation and comparison of all members of a group that the range of individual differences becomes evident and developmentally appropriate programs are planned (Hughes, Paasche, & Greer, 1992).

TEACHERS' QUALIFICATIONS

Teachers have special qualifications and opportunities for experience in identifying children with diverse abilities. They should have knowledge of early development and understand its regularities and irregularities, enabling them to recognize developmental differences. Teachers also should have had sufficient training to allow them to provide infants and young children with sound developmental activities that bring out the best in each child during the assessment process.

Teachers are further advantaged in that they see children in a natural environment. In the classroom, a child is likely to be comfortable and spontaneous. Furthermore, teachers can observe children of similar ages and interests; this enables them to evaluate each child's development in the context of an expected developmental range. Teachers also have extended periods and many situations and activities in which to informally observe children. Contrast this with clinicians, such as the doctor, the audiologist, and the psychologist, who usually see the child only on brief and tightly scheduled visits. At these times the child may be ill at ease and behave quite differently from when they are in a familiar home or school environment.

The Teacher as Observer

According to Wylie (2004), "observing young children and recording their behaviour is considered essential practice in every quality childcare setting in Canada." The search for developmental differences should always begin with systematic observation of children as they work and play in the preschool or child care centre.

Observers must be *objective*—that is, they should write down only what a child actually does and says. *Subjective* recording, by contrast, occurs when teachers put their own interpretations on children's behaviour. Note the differences in the following statements:

- *Objective:* Susie smiled and laughed frequently throughout the morning; she cried only once.
- *Subjective:* Susie was happy and carefree today.
- *Objective:* Mark stamped his feet and screamed "No" each time he was asked to change activities.
- *Subjective:* Mark gets angry all the time.

Photo 12–6
Observation notes may focus on identifying preferred activities and playmates.

Systematic Observations

Most teachers are used to observing children; few, however, record their observations in an organized way. Systematically recorded observations are extremely helpful for programming (Hughes, Paasche, & Greer, 1992) and are often the key to effective identification of developmental differences (Photo 12–6). Each observation should start with these four parts:

1. child's name or initials (confidentiality of information is essential)
2. date and time of day
3. setting (and, in some instances, names or number of children and teachers present)
4. name or initials of the observer

Teachers' observations take many forms. The questions teachers need to have answered determine the observation strategy they will select. In most cases, it is best if more than one person observes the child, especially if there is a hint of a serious problem. When two people agree they are seeing the same thing, personal bias and misinterpretation of a child's behaviour is reduced.

OBSERVATIONAL RECORDING TECHNIQUES

Here we discuss a sampling of the many kinds of observation tools that are useful in working with all young children, including those with special needs. For a comprehensive overview of observation strategies, see Martin (2004) and Wylie (2004).

Checklists

"Checklists record the presence or absence of particular predetermined behaviours such as skills, attributes, competencies, traits, reactions, achievements, or stages of development" (Martin, 2004, p. 159).

- Checklists are a quick and effective way of collecting systematic information on one or many children.
- They can be used by teachers, aides, parents, volunteers, and children.
- They can be relatively simple or designed to give much more information (as in the teacher observation form and checklist shown in Figure 12–3).
- They are most useful when teachers design them to answer their own questions about children and the program.

Figure 12–3   TEACHER OBSERVATION FORM AND CHECKLIST FOR IDENTIFYING CHILDREN WHO MAY REQUIRE ADDITIONAL SERVICES

TEACHER OBSERVATION FORM AND CHECKLIST FOR IDENTIFYING CHILDREN WHO MAY REQUIRE ADDITIONAL SERVICES

Child's Name: _____   Birth Date: _____

Date: _____   Recording Teacher's Name: _____

LANGUAGE	YES	NO	SOMETIMES
Does the child:			
1. use two- and three-word phrases to ask for what he or she wants?	_____	_____	_____
2. use complete sentences to tell you what happened?	_____	_____	_____
3. when asked to describe something, use at least two or more sentences to talk about it?	_____	_____	_____
4. ask questions?	_____	_____	_____
5. seem to have difficulty following directions?	_____	_____	_____
6. respond to questions with appropriate answers?	_____	_____	_____
7. seem to talk too softly or too loudly?	_____	_____	_____
8. Are you able to understand the child?	_____	_____	_____

PREACADEMICS	YES	NO	SOMETIMES
Does the child:			
9. seem to take at least twice as long as the other children to learn preacademic concepts?	_____	_____	_____
10. seem to take the time needed by other children to learn preacademic concepts?	_____	_____	_____
11. have difficulty attending to group activities for more than five minutes at a time?	_____	_____	_____
12. appear extremely shy in group activities; for instance, not volunteering answers or answering questions when asked, even though you think the child knows the answers?	_____	_____	_____

Figure 12–3 (CONT.)

MOTOR	YES	NO	SOMETIMES

Does the child:

13. continually switch a crayon back and forth from one hand to the other when colouring?

14. appear clumsy or shaky when using one or both hands?

15. when colouring with a crayon, appear to tense the hand not being used (for instance, clench it into a fist)?

16. when walking or running, appear to move one side of the body differently from the other side? For instance, does the child seem to have better control of the leg and arm on one side than on the other?

17. lean or tilt to one side when walking or running?

18. seem to fear or not be able to use stairs, climbing equipment, or tricycles?

19. stumble often or appear awkward when moving about?

20. appear capable of dressing self, except for tying shoes?

SOCIAL	YES	NO	SOMETIMES

Does the child:

21. engage in more than two disruptive behaviours a day (tantrums, fighting, screaming, etc.)?

22. appear withdrawn from the outside world (fiddling with pieces of string, staring into space, rocking)?

23. play alone and seldom talk to the other children?

24. spend most of the time trying to get attention from adults?

25. have toileting problems (wet or soiled) once a week or more often?

(Continued)

Figure 12–3   (CONT.)

VISUAL OR HEARING	YES	NO	SOMETIMES

Does the child:

26. appear to have eye movements that are jerky or uncoordinated?

27. seem to have difficulty seeing objects? For instance, does the child:
    - tilt head to look at things?
    - hold objects close to eyes?
    - squint?
    - show sensitivity to bright lights?
    - have uncontrolled eye-rolling?
    - complain that eyes hurt?

28. appear awkward in tasks requiring eye–hand coordination such as pegs, puzzles, colouring, etc.?

29. seem to have difficulty hearing? For instance, does the child:
    - consistently favour one ear by turning the same side of the head in the direction of the sound?
    - ignore, confuse, or not follow directions?
    - pull on ears or rub ears frequently, or complain of earaches?
    - complain of head noises or dizziness?
    - have a very high, very low, or monotonous tone of voice?

GENERAL HEALTH	YES	NO	SOMETIMES

Does the child:

30. seem to have an excessive number of colds?

31. have frequent absences because of illness?

32. have eyes that water?

33. have frequent discharge from:
    - eyes?
    - ears?
    - nose?

34. have sores on body or head?

Figure 12–3 (CONT.)

GENERAL HEALTH	YES	NO	SOMETIMES
35. have periods of unusual movements (such as eye blinking) or "blank spells" that seem to appear and disappear without relationship to the social situation?	___	___	___
36. have hives or rashes?	___	___	___
37. wheeze?	___	___	___
38. have a persistent cough?	___	___	___
39. seem to be excessively thirsty?	___	___	___
40. seem to be ravenously hungry?	___	___	___
41. Have you noticed any of the following conditions:	___	___	___
•constant fatigue?	___	___	___
•irritability?	___	___	___
•restlessness?	___	___	___
•tenseness?	___	___	___
•feverish cheeks or forehead?	___	___	___
42. Is the child overweight?	___	___	___
43. Is the child physically or mentally lethargic?	___	___	___
44. Has the child lost noticeable weight without being on a diet?	___	___	___

Narratives

The narrative or running record observations are presented chronologically. They consist of "a series of observations in a sequence: minutes, hours, days, or weeks" (Wylie, 2004, p. 116). Narrative observations include anecdotal records, running records, and logs, journals, and diaries.

Anecdotal records

- Anecdotal records are brief written objective observations, each recorded individually.
- They allow observers to choose what is significant to record.
- They may focus on an individual child or group of children.
- They can form useful information regarding significant behaviours and development.

Running records

- Running records are objective narrative recordings
- They are written observations that capture everything the child does and says during a specific time.

- They can produce a well-rounded picture of a child's overall behaviour and development.
- They are a very useful form of observation, as well as the most time consuming of the narrative records.

Logs, journals, and diaries

- Logs, journals, and diaries are similar to running records but are less comprehensive.
- They may be kept in a loose-leaf notebook with a section for each child.
- They are notes jotted down during class time or immediately after children leave for the day.
- They may be general notes about a child or focused notes on some aspect of the child's behaviour and development.
- They may contain contextual information that could help explain certain behaviours.

Samplings

Sampling observations are those in which (a) examples of behaviour are recorded as they occur or (b) behaviours are recorded as they are demonstrated at previously decided intervals or (c) "work" samples are gathered (Martin, 2004, p. 125).

Photo 12–7
The familiar classroom is a good place to obtain language samplings.

Time samples

- Time samples are periodic and momentary observations to determine the presence or absence of behaviour.
- They focus on the behaviour of one child.
- They identify behavioural patterns.
- They record behaviours on a chart that can be analyzed to determine the needs of the child. For example, information may show that a child was engaged with materials in only 3 out of the 15 samples. This could mean that the child needs different materials or help in expanding his or her attention span.

Language samples

- Language samples are verbatim recordings (word for word, or sound for sound) of exactly what the child says or what sounds the child makes (Photo 12–7).
- They should be recorded phonetically (e.g., if a child says "du gul," it is written "du gul" even if the recorder knows the child is referring to "the girl").
- They should include physical gestures a child makes while communicating (e.g., pointing to the juice while squealing "Eeeeee").

Frequency counts

- Frequency counts keep track of how often a certain behaviour occurs.
- They assist educators in establishing how often a behaviour occurs:
  - excessively?
  - infrequently?
  - only under certain circumstances?
- They provide significant information as to whether a given behaviour is actually a problem, as well as how significant the problem is. For example, every time a behaviour occurs, a tally mark is made on a piece of paper. Over several days, the tally marks will show the frequency of behaviour.

Example:

One teacher was concerned about John's safety because of what she thought were his frequent attempts to climb over the fence during outdoor play. The other teacher thought it seldom happened. An actual frequency count showed that the fence-climbing attempts occurred four or five times each play period. Teachers now could agree that there was a problem. They assessed the play yard and realized that there was not much for John to climb on. They began to set up climbing activities several days a week. John's fence-climbing dropped to one or no episodes per day. On days when no climbing activities were set up, John's fence-climbing was again high. The frequency counts gave teachers clues to the extent of the problem as well as to their success in reducing the unsafe behaviour.

Duration measures

- Duration measures indicate how long an event or a behaviour lasts.
- They note the start and stop time of a child's activities.
- They show how long a child's attention span is or how much time the child spends in either appropriate or inappropriate behaviours.

Example:

Teachers were concerned about Omar's poor attention span. They decided to find out how many minutes at a time he spent at various activities. Several days' observations indicated that he spent many minutes (15 to 20) with hands-on activities (painting, block-building, puzzles). In contrast, he had a short attention span—only a minute or two—for activities that required listening (music, stories, conversation). These duration measures were invaluable as teachers planned Omar's program, conferred with his parents, and participated in the team meetings.

Charts

A chart is developed from observed information that is recorded onto a prepared format.

- Charts allow observers to record behaviours quickly and efficiently.
- They may be recorded during or after observation.
- They include routine information as well as behaviours like feeding and diapering.
- They may identify behavioural patterns (as in Figure 12–4, which shows a social skills chart).

www   **Figure 12–4**   SOCIAL SKILLS CHART

Social Skills Chart			
Child's Name _____ D.O.B. _____ Age: _____			
Observer(s) _____ Date(s): _____ Time: _____			
Behaviour	Frequency	Duration	Comment

Pictorial Representations

A pictorial representation is any visual interpretation of recorded observations. Mapping is one example of pictorial representations.

- Mappings can focus on one child or a group of children.
- They are efficient and easy to use.
- They can identify traffic patterns, safety concerns, and use of space.

Media Techniques

According to Martin (2004, p. 213), "a media technique is any method of recording or storing observational data that is achieved by mechanical, electronic, or technical means." Photography, videotaping, and audiotaping are examples of media techniques used to observe children. All these techniques can be used to support any traditionally recorded observations, as well as to become part of a child's development portfolio.

Photography can be used in many ways to enable educators to learn more about children. Photography can be useful in

- demonstrating evidence of changes in a child's physical appearance and growth
- helping a child remember situations
- recording specific aspects of a child's activity

Videotaping a child's activities or environment can be used for several purposes, such as,

- to use as a review when time permits for greater analysis
- to provide information to parents regarding their child's development
- to use for research purposes
- to assist in assessing the child's environment

Audio recording may be used for any of the following purposes:

- to share recordings with parents
- to record and keep records of a child's language, music, or reading skills
- to record a child's expressive language for analysis

Portfolios and Child Studies

A **portfolio** is a record-keeping device in which observations, health and social information, test results, work samples, and other significant information about an individual child are stored. This system enables child care professionals to keep records over time, add items as necessary, evaluate the child's performance, evolve plans to meet the child's needs, and review progress (Martin, 2004).

A child study is a thorough analytical document. It contains observations and collected information about a child, and it may include a variety of other information collected over time.

Portfolio
a carefully selected collection of a child's work that is used to document growth and development

EARLY IDENTIFICATION: CAUTIONARY NOTES FOR TEACHERS

Observation is a useful and important tool in providing high-quality education and care for all children. It is important to remember, however, that if teachers or other caregivers have a concern about a possible developmental difference in a child in their care, they must demonstrate caution, sensitivity, and respect in how these concerns are shared with families. Teachers should not keep concerns to themselves, but they should be careful not to raise concerns based on inference rather than actual observation. Some issues for teachers to consider are listed here.

Teachers should avoid

- making diagnoses
- using labels to describe children (remembering that all children in their program are children first)
- raising parents' anxiety
- telling parents what to do
- jumping to conclusions without adequate observational data

Teachers should

- develop good working relationships with families
- voice concerns to parents about possible developmental differences in their child
- listen carefully and respectfully
- be knowledgeable about local resources and be able to make helpful and appropriate referrals
- be culturally sensitive and take cultural and linguistic differences into consideration when evaluating behaviour
- remember that development encompasses a broad spectrum of individual differences
- be aware of environmental factors (Photo 12–8)

Photo 12–8
Teachers should be aware of environmental factors that may affect children's behaviour

The Individual Program Plan (IPP)

Individual program plan (IPP)
an approach to providing services to individuals with special needs: the process involves developing a written plan based on the child's strength's, needs, and interests; implementation and evaluation are part of the IPP process

The **individual program plan (IPP)** is an approach to providing services to individuals with special needs. The written plan provides the structure and direction for the services and activities to be provided to the child and family by the early intervention program. (Note: *Individual education plan* [IEP] is sometimes used by service providers interchangeably with IPP.)

Teachers are essential throughout the IPP process: in their observations of children's behaviour, in their implementation of the classroom aspects of the individual programs, and in their evaluations. Teachers should be responsible for integrating classroom practice and program recommendations by the child's IPP team. Furthermore, the ongoing evaluation of the appropriateness of each child's daily program is largely dependent on the teacher. In other words, teachers are central to the entire IPP process. The written plan provides the structure and direction for the services and activities to be provided to the child and family by the early intervention program.

THE IPP TEAM

The IPP is developed by a team consisting of the child's parents or parent surrogates and professionals from the various disciplines involved with the child and family (such as resource teachers, early childhood teachers, physiotherapists, a speech and language pathologist, and/or the case coordinator). The types of teams and the disciplines involved are varied. Several models for IPP teams have emerged in the last few years:

Interdisciplinary
refers to several different professions working together on a common problem, sharing information and exchange roles, depending on the case

Transdisciplinary
professionals sharing expertise, modelling, and instructing other team members on how to implement specific practices within the group setting

Bias-free screening and assessment
selecting and administering screening and assessment tools that ensure a child is given the opportunity for optimum performance

- *Multidisciplinary.* Professionals work independently of one another in a parallel format; each professional is viewed as important but takes responsibility only for his or her own area of clinical expertise. Within this model, a child may be withdrawn for individual therapy.
- *Interdisciplinary.* Professionals and parents collaborate in decision making around the program and service needs of each child and family, with individual team members contributing in their area of expertise. In most instances, extra support for children is provided within the group environment.
- *Transdisciplinary.* Professionals share expertise, model, and instruct other team members on how to implement specific practices within the group setting. (The term *transdisciplinary* is being used in this text.)

COMPONENTS OF THE IPP

The IPP should be based on developmentally valid, **bias-free screening and assessment.** Program and placement decisions are to be formulated from information from multiple sources: test scores, observation in situations in which the child is comfortable and at ease, and input from significant persons in the child's life (parents, grandparents, teachers, out-of-home caregivers). For an example of one aspect of a child's IPP focusing on motor skills, see Figure 12–4 on page 258.

The components of an IPP are the following:

1. observation and assessment
2. identification of strengths, needs, and interests

3. setting of goals and objectives
4. creation of an implementation plan
5. evaluation

Observation and Assessment

Before an IPP is written, a child's developmental skills must be assessed. As described earlier, this is an information-gathering (nondiagnostic) process. It is not, however, a one-time operation; instead, it should be an ongoing process throughout the year so that the child's progress can be tracked and programs adjusted as needed. Ongoing observation and assessment provide a comprehensive description—a developmental profile—of a child at particular points in time.

Depending on the results of earlier screening tests, the child may need to receive specialized assessments from specific disciplines (audiologist, nutritionist, physiotherapist/occupational therapist, and others). The early childhood teacher is responsible for collecting the general information that often provides the "glue" to hold together the overall developmental picture of the child (Photo 12–9).

Numerous assessment instruments have been developed over the past 20 years. In addition, there are developmental profile forms that many teachers of young children find even more useful. A separate chart or profile should be kept for each child. Periodic observations should be made and recorded for each child in all developmental areas: gross and fine motor skills, cognitive abilities, self-help/care, social and play behaviours, and receptive and expressive language.

A child's developmental profile should be updated periodically on the basis of observations and notes made by teachers as they work with children. Emerging skills show up clearly on the preschool profile. Mastering a skill in a particular area of development often depends on specific achievements in other areas. For example, a child cannot perform certain self-help/care tasks, such as buttoning and unbuttoning, until the *pincer grasp* is well established (Photo 12–10). Developmental delays also show up clearly. Delays may accumulate because of unrecognized relationships among developmental areas. By keeping a child's profile up to date, teachers can pinpoint a delay in one area and so explain problems in other areas. Language difficulties, for example, often lead to poor play relationships because of the inability to express ideas and preferences adequately. Poor verbal skills also may delay cognitive development or have a negative effect on intellectual performance because inadequate language interferes with formulating and expressing thoughts.

The information about the child's performance in the early childhood setting is a valuable part in the overall assessment process. The early childhood teacher should be able to provide information about the child's current skill level, as well as information about activities in which the child has interest and preference.

Identification of Strengths, Needs, and Interests

Teachers can use information gathered from observations and assessments to identify a child's strengths, needs, and interests. Information gathering may be informal, from parents, psychologists, physiotherapists, speech and language pathologists, and so on, or obtained in a more formal method, as discussed earlier in this chapter. Once information has been compiled, it may be useful to summarize the child's strengths, needs, and interests in a child profile chart (see Figure 12–5). Information summarized in the child profile chart will lead to the development of goals and objectives.

Photo 12–9
Teachers provide the "glue" that holds together the overall developmental picture of each child.

Photo 12–10
The pincer grasp is prerequisite to many fine motor tasks.

Figure 12–5   CHILD PROFILE CHART

Developmental Area	Strengths	Needs	Interests
Child Profile Chart			
Child's Name _____ D.O.B: _____ Age:_____			
Setting: _____ Observer(s) _____ Date: _____			
Physical: Gross Motor Fine Motor			
Communication: Receptive Language Expressive Language			
Cognitive			
Social/Emotional			
Self-care: Toileting & Hygiene Dressing/Undressing Eating & Drinking			

Setting of Goals and Objectives

Long-term goals. The IPP should include written statements specifying expected learning outcomes for each child each program year. Long-term goals are usually presented as broad general statements about what can be expected of the child within six months to one year, depending on the child's age.

Example:

Erin will be able to

1. *move about the room independently throughout the day*
2. *play cooperatively with other children during small group activities*
3. *use verbal skills to communicate her needs*

Long-term goals centre on priorities essential to the child's overall development, as agreed on by the child's IPP team. These sometimes are referred to as functional goals (Notari-Syverson & Shuster, 1995). For every child, the number and kinds of goals will vary. Goals for a child should not be so numerous or so complex as to overwhelm the child and family; additional goals can always be added at a future date as required. Furthermore, self-sufficiency goals, as important as they are, should not rule out goals that help improve the child's self-esteem and enjoyment of life.

Example:

Melinda was a bright and lively child born with severely malformed hands. Even as an infant, it was obvious that she had a talent and love for music and rhythm. Although long-term goals for this child must include learning to use a prosthesis on each hand (a major priority), her musical development is important, too. At least one goal related to music should be written into Melinda's IPP.

Short-term objectives. Every IPP should include a list of short-term objectives. These are mini-programs—step-by-step learnings that enable the child to achieve the designated long-term goals. Short-term objectives usually focus on skills or behaviours that can be measured (counted or timed) and acquired within one week to one month. The data give objective evidence of a child's progress. Learning to wear and become adept at using her prostheses might be a long-term goal for the child mentioned above. Exactly how this is to be accomplished and how it is to be measured is spelled out in the short-term objectives. Enhancing the child's musical talents might also be worked into the goals and objectives.

Example:

Melinda will pick out tunes using single notes on the piano while wearing her prostheses, with encouragement from the teacher, for 15 minutes each day.

The amount of time spent playing the piano and the numbers of tunes learned might be the measurable aspects of this objective. Furthermore, learning to play tunes on the piano is likely to be reinforcing for Melinda in her efforts at wearing her prostheses.

Photo 12–11
Alternating feet is a step in the task analysis for stair climbing.

Objectives should answer the following questions:

- Who? (child's name)
- Will do what? (desired behaviour)
- Under what conditions? (Where, how, when, with what kinds of support?)
- To what degree of success? (defines measure that determines success)

Example:

May-lin is a three-year-old child who has a very severe visual impairment. She currently is able to climb stairs, but places both feet on one stair before proceeding to the next stair. The goal set for May-lin was that she be able to navigate her environment. After completing a task analysis (see Chapter 11) for stair climbing, it was determined that the next step in May-lin's program should be that she be able to climb stairs with alternating feet, using the railing for support (Photo 12–11).

The objective would be written as follows:

- Who? (May-lin)
- Will do what? (climb stairs)
- Under what conditions? (using alternating feet, while holding the banister)
- To what degree of success? (for a minimum of five consecutive steps)

Example:

Steven is a three-year-old child with a diagnosis of Down syndrome. When requested, he uses single words to label objects, but only in imitation of an adult. Steven's IPP team set the following goal for him: Steven will speak in simple sentences to express his needs

Figure 12–6   MAY-LIN'S STAIR-CLIMBING PROGRAM

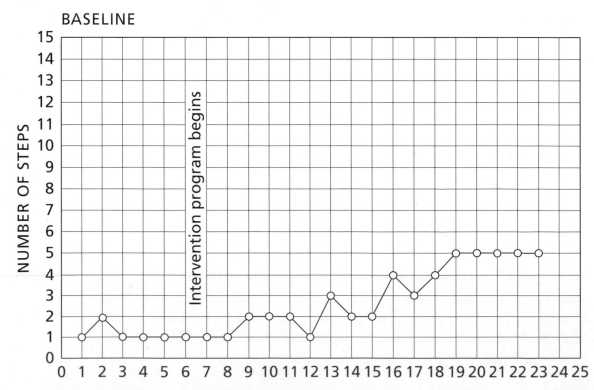

and wants. The task analysis for this goal identified the use of single words to express needs and wants as the first step in a program for Steven.

The objective would be written as follows:

- Who? (Steven)
- Will do what? (use single words spontaneously)
- Under what conditions? (to indicate his preference when offered choices)
- To what degree of success? (each time a choice is offered)

Graphing (transferring the measurements to a chart), as shown in Figures 12–6 and 12–7, brings progress into focus. Displaying children's progress in graphic form is beneficial because it provides a visual record of change over time. Behaviour changes, even when slow, appear more clearly on a graph. The visual display may also help both teacher and child be more aware of progress and so feel more successful. Success always leads to increased motivation. Lack of progress also is readily apparent on a graph. In such cases the program can be changed promptly so as to improve the child's performance and decrease frustration for teacher and child.

Creation of an Implementation Plan

A statement of the specific intervention services and support services for the family should be included in the IPP. Depending on the goals set for a child, the plan might contain recommendations for the following:

- The type of daily/weekly activities to be provided to the child in the early childhood program. For example, in the case of Jason (see Figure 12–8), the IPP team identified that Mrs. B. will provide daily opportunities for Jason to practise

Figure 12–7 STEVEN'S VERBAL RESPONSE PROGRAM

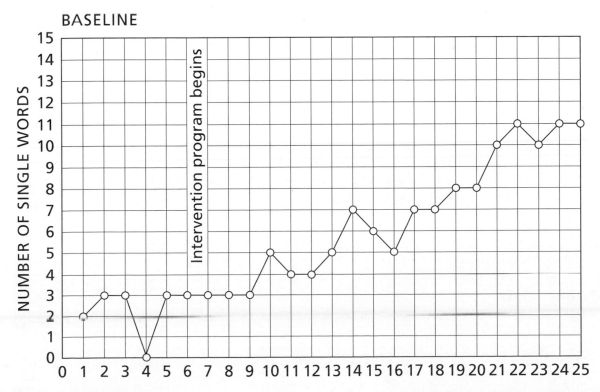

Figure 12–8   Individual program plan

Individual Program Plan

Child's Name: Jason   **Date of Birth:** _____   **Program:** ABC Preschool
 	
Conference Date: _____   **Team Members Present:**
            Mrs. M.—Parent
            Mrs. B.—Early Childhood Education
            Ms. G.—Resource Consultant

Area of Development: Gross Motor

Strengths (present level of functioning):
        1. pulls self to standing using furniture
        2. stands momentarily without support, lowering to sitting
        3. cruises around furniture
        4. will take 10 steps with both hands held

Child's interests in this area include: throwing balls, rolling balls across the floor, and being pushed in the big plastic car.
Long-Term Goal: Jason will walk independently.

Short-Term Objectives:
        1. Jason will walk 10 steps with one hand held by an adult.
        2. Jason will take 4 to 5 steps without support, walking between familiar adults.
        3. Jason will walk independently for a distance of 10 feet.

Implementation Plan (services to be provided):
        1. Ms. G. will provide specific written suggestions to encourage walking, which can be implemented in the preschool and home environments.
        2. Mrs. B. will provide daily opportunity for Jason to practise walking within the program routines.
        3. Mrs. B. will maintain weekly communication with the family, for the purpose of sharing observations.

Evaluation: Ms. G. will conduct biweekly observaitons, documenting Jason's progress.
Next Conference Date: _____

walking within the program routines. In her observation notes, Mrs. B. identifies two activities that are of high interest to Jason. Each day when Jason wants to participate in these activities, he will be supported in practising walking by the teacher to the areas in which his desired activities are taking place.

- Referral to a speech and language pathologist or a physiotherapist/occupational therapist (or both), as might be appropriate for Steven.
- Assistance to parents in obtaining funding for a specific piece of equipment, such as a keyboard for Melinda.

Projected starting dates should be specified for each service prescribed for the child, and the person responsible for carrying out the specific objective should be identified.

Example:

Josh will receive ongoing speech and language consultation services from the community speech pathologist beginning October 1.

The projected starting date assists the team members in implementing the plan. A reasonable length of time must be allowed for accomplishing the objectives and goals stated in the child's IPP. See Figure 12–8 for an example of an individual program plan.

The completed IPP includes statements about

- the child's present level of skill development and the quality of performance
- long-term (six months to one year) goals for the child and short-term objectives that will accomplish the long-term goals
- specific services to be provided, with target dates and team member responsible for carrying out the service
- accountability (evaluation) to determine whether objectives are being met

Evaluation (Statement of Accountability)

At least once a year (more frequently for younger children) the IPP should be evaluated to see whether the stated objectives are being met. Evaluations should be based on specifically described procedures, such as developmental assessment results and written observations. In actual practice, evaluations should be conducted more often. As mentioned earlier, an in-place system of ongoing assessments simplifies the procedure. The preschool developmental profile, for example, provides both ongoing assessment and program evaluation. Every item on the profile describes a specific child behaviour; its presence or absence can be noted by a teacher. Graphs also provide program accountability. By using the preschool developmental profile to assess a child periodically and by keeping graphs of a child's progress, a convincing evaluation process is always in operation.

Summary

The identification of developmental differences can take place any time, beginning with the first several weeks after conception. The earlier an area of concern is identified, the more likely it is that it can be treated effectively and that associated problems can be prevented. All young children (except those with obvious disabilities) should be screened; many differences are subtle and difficult to recognize.

Many kinds of screening instruments are available. Some are geared to overall development, some to specialized areas, such as hearing and vision, and some to particular ages or developmental domains. Whatever the test, for reliable results it must be given in the child's first language, with scrupulous regard for the customs of the child's family and the child's physical and biological state. More than one instrument should be used in the assessment process. Even then, the results of many tests must be viewed with extreme caution, especially IQ tests. Most early childhood educators view standardized IQ tests as being of little value when working with young children.

Teachers are major agents in the early identification process. Direct observation is a teacher's best tool in determining a child's developmental status and the suitability of specific classroom activities for the group and for individual children. Observation forms and checklists, especially those that teachers devise themselves, help teachers answer questions about children's behaviour and classroom practices. Teachers should always use their information with care and in the best interests of the child and family.

The individual program plan is a major and logical outcome of early identification and intervention procedures. A child's teacher and parent(s) are an essential part of the IPP planning process, along with other members of the transdisciplinary team. The IPP must be in written form. It should be based on bias-free tests and observations, and should specify long-term goals and short-term objectives. Services that will be provided and their starting dates should also be specified. Finally, the IPP should describe the accountability component: how the effectiveness of the implementation plan will be measured.

RESOURCES

CHILDCARE RESOURCE
http://www.childcare-resource.com/observe.htm
This site provides information on the importance of observing young children, including those with a variety of special needs.

ONTARIO MINISTRY OF EDUCATION, INDIVIDUAL EDUCATION PLANS
http://www.edu.gov.on.ca/eng/general/elemsec/speced/iep/iep.html
This site provides information on developing, implementing, and evaluating individual education plans.

STUDENT ACTIVITIES

1. Arrange a sheet of paper so that you can take a frequency count of how often a child initiates a conversation with another child. While observing during free play, select one particular child and tally how many times that child initiates conversation with another child. Do the same on another day with a different child. Compare the observations.

2. Select a partner. Each of you, independently of the other, will take a half-hour running record of the same child. Compare your observations to see whether you were seeing the same things. Critique each other's running record for objectivity.

3. Write to three early childhood centres in your province or territory that integrate children with developmental differences and ask for copies of their IPP forms. Compare and contrast these with the IPP components as given in the text.

4. Make a copy of the child profile chart (Figure 12–5 on page 262). Observe the same child for 20 to 30 minutes on three different days. List the child's strengths, needs, and interests in the appropriate box. When finished, discuss your findings with the teacher.

REFERENCES

Allen, K. E., & Marotz, L. R. (2003). *Developmental profiles: Birth through eight.* Albany, NY: Delmar.

Banks, J. A. (1994). *An introduction to multicultural education.* Boston: Allyn & Bacon.

Cohen, L. G., & Spenciner, L. J. (1994). *Assessment of young children.* New York: Longman.

Dotsch, J. (1992). Newcomer preschool children: Their cultural and linguistic adaptation to childcare settings. *Multiculturalism, 14*(2, 3), 24–26.

Dotsch, J. (1999). *Non-biased children's assessments.* Toronto: Bias-Free Early Childhood Services.

Hanson, M. J., & Lynch, E. W. (1998). *Early Intervention.* Austin, TX: PRO-ED.

Harris, S. R. (1994). Parents and caregivers perceptions of their children's development. *Developmental Medicine and Child Neurology, 36*(10), 918–923.

Hughes, A., Paasche, C., & Greer, M. (1992). *An early identification observation process in early childhood settings.* North York, ON: North York Interagency and Community Council.

Langford, R. (Ed.). (1997). *Checklist for quality inclusive education: A self-assessment tool and manual for early childhood settings.* London, ON: Early Childhood Resource Teacher Network of Ontario.

Martin, S. (2004). *Take a look: Observation and portfolio assessment in early childhood* (3rd ed.). Toronto: Addison-Wesley.

McCain, M., & Mustard, F. (1999). *Early years study final report.* Toronto: Publications Ontario.

National Association for the Education of Young Children. (1988). Position statement on standardized testing of young children 3 through 8 years of age. *Young Children, 43*(3), 42–47.

Notari-Syverson, A., & Shuster, S. L. (1995). Putting real-life skills into IEP/IFSPs for infants and young children. *Teaching Exceptional Children, 27*(2), 29–32.

Perrone, V. (1990). How did we get here? In C. Kamii (Ed.), *Achievement testing in the early grades: The games grown-ups play.* Washington, DC: National Association for the Education of Young Children.

Wylie, S. (2004). *Observing young children: A guide for early childhood educators in Canada* (2nd ed.). Toronto: Thomson Nelson.

CHAPTER 13 | Planning Transitions to Support Inclusion

KEY CONCEPTS

accommodations
inclusive
transition coordinator
transition plans

OBJECTIVES

After studying the material in this chapter, the student will be able to

- State the major goals of an early childhood transition planning process.
- Identify possible accommodations that need to be made by children, families, and service providers during the transition process.
- Describe a transition-planning format that includes program and personnel responsibilities.
- Discuss ways to ease a child with special needs into a new program.
- Suggest support services that could assist a child in adjusting to a new program.

Introduction

It is necessary to plan for the services required to assist young children with special needs as they move from one early childhood program to another or into an **inclusive** school-board setting. **Transition plans** should be an essential element of the child's individual program plan (IPP), ensuring that services to meet the specific needs identified by the family are addressed. To formulate such plans, early childhood educators need to develop specific skills and procedures for facilitating both the child's and the family's transition into a new program.

As children and families move from one type of program to another, whether it is a new preschool program or a Kindergarten program, they encounter new faces, new environments, and new procedures. Planning for these transitions into newness is critical. It is, however, an often-neglected component of early intervention programming, especially for children with special needs who are moving into inclusive environments. Each change may require numerous **accommodations** on the part of the child, the family, and the service providers (Rice & O'Brien, 1990). The child may need more time than his or her peers to adjust to the new environment, as well as learn how to play and work more independently. The family may need to alter their before-school child care arrangements to fit the schedule of the new program. The early childhood teacher may need to redesign small-group activities to accommodate a new child with a specific special need.

Planning for the changes required by the transition and developing ways to maintain the changes are critical components in ensuring a successful transition. If careful planning is not undertaken and followed through, the outcome may be an unsuccessful placement for the child and family.

There are three specific steps to take when trying to ensure that a successful transition will be achieved:

1. Identify possible challenges that may arise during transition.
2. Plan strategies for supporting the child, the family, and the receiving teacher or teachers.
3. Maintain ongoing support following the transition.

Transition Goals

The purpose of transition planning is to lay out a process that enables the family and the child to make a comfortable and positive change from one program to another. Ideally, the process produces a minimum of disruption in family routines, while supporting the child's developmental progress. The following is an example of the accommodations required of a child, a family, and a teacher during one transition program:

Abby, who was born with spina bifida, had gotten about in a wheelchair for most of her life. Psychological assessments indicated average to above-average intelligence. She has been in a private special education preschool and child care centre since infancy. Both parents work full-time. As Abby neared her fourth birthday, her parents decided she was ready to attend an inclusive community program. After four months of planning and working with their early intervention specialist, Abby began attending a full-day inclusive program.

Inclusive
equitable access is offered to all children, regardless of ability

Transition plans
the plans developed to ensure a comfortable and positive transition for the child and family as they move from one educational setting to a new educational setting

Accommodations
adjustments on the part of the child, family, or service providers that enable a successful transition to a new environment for the child

The community program teachers had concerns, too. They redesigned some of the materials and activities so that Abby would be able to participate during the first critical days of the transition. The teachers wondered, though, whether they would have the time or energy to continue to adapt materials and learning experiences. They wondered, too, whether they could consistently include Abby in large motor activities, given the demands on teachers' time made by a group of active four-year-olds.

The success of the transition into the community program ultimately would be measured by the extent to which Abby, her family, and her teachers were able to manage the many accommodations required of them. It is the ability to handle and adjust to a range of accommodations (the transition's *sustainability*) that determines the success of a transition (Rice & O'Brien, 1990).

Transitions in Perspective

The transition process requires systematic planning and evaluating (Photo 13–1). It also requires ongoing modification to keep it in tune with the needs of individual children, their families, and the service providers who are involved (Haines, Rosenkoetter, & Fowler, 1994). The perspectives of all must be considered in identifying the accommodations needed. A particular mother, for example, may believe that she should be consulted about every aspect of her child's education and that she should be the one to make the decisions about her child's transition to another program. In the same family, the father may believe it is best to leave such decisions to the teachers. The professionals involved in the transition may have ideas quite different from either parent's about the decision-making process and who should decide what. Respect for, awareness of, and responsiveness to these several perspectives are critical for a successful transition for the child and the family.

THE CHILD'S PERSPECTIVE

A child's developmental progress is the main reason for a transition from one program to another. The change in services may be agreed on because of the child's age (entering Kindergarten, for example, is usually based on chronological age). The change also may be called for on the basis of clinical evidence—an updated diagnosis or a change in diagnostic findings, as when an intermittent hearing loss is identified. Another factor may be that the child has acquired new and functionally significant skills. Whatever the reason, the child's ability to adapt to the next program is the central issue in determining the success of the transition (Haines, Rosenkoetter, & Fowler, 1994).

The accommodations required of a child during a transition will depend on the individual child and the *sending* and *receiving* programs. The child will need to make new friends, generalize old skills to new situations, and learn unfamiliar routines while attempting to explore a new environment. Children often have difficulty

Photo 13–1
The transition process requires systematic planning.

Photo 13–2
A child may have problems transferring well-established skills used at home to the new environment.

transferring even well-established skills to new situations (Photo 13–2). What looks like a similar set of expectations to professionals may not look at all the same to a child who has learned to respond to distinct cues or events that are not present in the new program. A child, for example, may be used to only one teacher or one particular type of instruction. That child may do well in a tightly structured, individualized program but have difficulty in a loosely structured program. Therefore, as professionals and parents prepare a child for a transition, they need to ask three questions:

1. What will be different for the child?
2. What skills does the child already have that will be useful in the new setting?
3. What skills does the child need to learn before a transition is attempted?

A child's strengths, needs, and interests should be identified before the transition plan is developed. Which accommodations will be easy for the child? Which will be difficult? To answer these questions, each child must be assessed in terms of

- his or her current skills
- the conditions under which the child demonstrates particular skills (e.g., does the child demonstrate them at home but not at school, or vice versa?)
- the skills the receiving program expects the child to have before entering the program

THE FAMILY'S PERSPECTIVE

Family involvement is a critical component of transition planning (Bruder & Chandler, 1996; Haines, Rosenkoetter, & Fowler, 1994; Johnson, Chandler, Kerns, & Fowler, 1986). A family must adjust to differences between programs by adapting to new schedules, finding new services, and accepting new responsibilities. Families may have to educate new school personnel about their child's special needs. They may be expected to set new goals for their child. They may need to adjust to fewer contacts with their child's teacher. Plans for the family component in a child's transition will vary, depending on family structure, personality traits, and other characteristics. Hazel and colleagues (1986) provide the following checklist:

Family Structure

- What is the family structure? (single parent/parents divorced, blended, etc.)
- How do family members define their family unit?
- How many other children are there in the family?
- What is the relationship of the extended family?
- What are the roles of the family members? (wage earner, unemployed, decision maker, caregiver, homemaker, etc.)

Family Characteristics

- What is the first language of the family?
- What is its cultural/ethnic background?
- What are the family's beliefs and value systems?
- To what extent is the family involved with the community?

Nature of the Child's Special Needs

- What effect do the child's special needs have on his or her ability to participate in family activities?

- How do the child's special needs affect family members' activities and needs?
- How do the child's special needs affect the financial, emotional, and physical needs of the family as a whole and as individual family members?
- Do the child's special needs pull the family together—make it stronger—as family members try to meet the needs of the child with special needs?

Personality Traits

- How do family members address their feelings and fears?
- Do they focus only on the present (or past or future)?
- Do they deal only with the facts of the situation?
- What appears to be the self-image of various family members?
- What seems to be their view of their lives compared with the lives of others? Do they face life with a sense of humour, a sense of resignation, a sense of getting even, or a sense of hope?

Developing successful transition activities depends on recognizing the diversity that each family brings to the planning process (Photo 13–3). Each family has its own misgivings. Each family has to decide on the accommodations they are willing and able to make. In general, families are concerned about questions such as these:

- What services and supports will be available in the next setting, and how can they obtain these services and supports?
- How will their child adjust to the new program, both academically and socially?
- How will the new teacher or teachers adjust to their child, and vice versa?
- What changes in daily routines will be required?

Families need adequate time to address these questions if they are to make logical decisions about their level of involvement in the transition planning. Some families choose to let professionals make the decisions, while others want to make the decisions themselves; most families fall somewhere in between.

Photo 13–3
Successful transition planning depends on recognizing and respecting the diversity that each family brings to the planning process.

Transition Planning

Planning is the key to successful transitions for the child, family, and teachers. As noted earlier, the accommodations required of everyone during a transition tend to be stressful. Careful planning reduces stress by putting the focus on specific issues related to the child's and the family's needs and preferences. When parents and professionals work as partners in developing a plan acceptable to all, it is likely that everyone will be more comfortable about what they are to do. It is likely, too, that everyone will find the time (or the help) necessary to accomplish the mutually agreed on tasks.

Successful transition planning should be an ongoing and integral part of every child's program. Planning an individual transition requires ongoing commitment. Time must be built into the regular program schedule for staff and parent meetings, for visits to the sending and receiving programs, and for exchange of child and program information. Ten basic steps (described in the following pages) are identified as central to the transition planning process.

STEP 1: COORDINATING THE TRANSITION

When several people work together to plan a child's transition, it is essential to appoint one person to coordinate efforts and take responsibility for getting things done. The **transition coordinator** may be the director of a program, a resource teacher/early interventionist, a consultant, an infant development worker, another member of the staff, or the case manager of the IPP or individual family service plan (IFSP; see Chapters 12 and 3). The professional background of the transition coordinator is likely to vary from child to child. A transdisciplinary team may rotate the coordinator's position among its members, depending on the child's and the family's special needs. Regardless of professional training, a major responsibility of the transition coordinator is to be familiar with

Transition coordinator
the team member who is responsible for coordinating the transition from one educational setting to a new educational setting

- the transition procedures of both the sending and the receiving programs
- the resources, placement, and service options available in the community

STEP 2: VISITING ALTERNATIVE PROGRAMS

Early childhood professionals within a community need to be familiar with one another's programs. Familiarity creates understanding and cooperation. For example, the infant development worker should be familiar with the preschool options available in the child's community. He or she should therefore be able to inform the parents of the choices available and support the parents in investigating the range of available settings. This provides parents with opportunities to become more knowledgeable and better able to make the most appropriate choice with respect to their child and family. Similarly, when the community early childhood staff know what social and academic skills are expected from five-year-olds by the local Kindergarten teacher, they are better able to develop successful transition strategies. Learning about the specific expectations of a program or classroom helps the current teacher and the family decide whether the child

- will be ready for the program under consideration
- needs additional skills
- is likely to need special help from the sending program before the transition
- will need certain changes in the receiving program in order to succeed

The transition coordinator (or individual teachers) should visit the programs where their children are most likely to be enrolled. If possible, visits should extend through a full session. Only by sitting in on a program in its entirety can the observer become familiar with the schedule in action, the range and tempo of activities, and teacher–child interactions.

Visits can be arranged by contacting the future program setting (Photo 13–4). An increasing number of school boards have an early childhood or Kindergarten specialist whose job it is to arrange meetings to discuss a program-to-program transition.

While observing, the coordinator and parents should make written notes. Features of the program that might create problems for the child or family should be underscored. Observation notes often are arranged under the following headings:

Photo 13–4
Coordinators can assist families in the transition process by arranging visits to new programs.

1. *Environment/physical setting:* the physical arrangement of the classroom (including accessibility for the specific child), the number of teachers and aides, and the daily schedule
2. *Staff–child interaction:* what children and teachers do and how they interact
3. *Program approach:* the learning opportunities provided for the children and the range of available supports
4. *Parent involvement:* the range of opportunities for involvement/participation by parents within the program (see Figure 13–1, which shows an example of a checklist that can be used by parents and professionals to plan for young children's transitions from one program to another)

STEP 3: HOLDING MEETINGS AMONG THE IPP TEAM

After the coordinator and family have visited several programs, the IPP team should meet and discuss the information obtained from the visits. Attention should be directed toward evaluating how each program may or may not be able to meet the priority needs of the child and his or her family.

Minor differences in approach are not likely to cause problems. However, when major differences exist, the staff of the child's current centre should consider adapting their program to reflect the expectations of the new setting.

STEP 4: DEVELOPING A TRANSITION PLAN

Ideally, the transition coordinator and the teacher meet with the family 9 to 12 months before the child's transition. This gives the family time to learn about and prepare for the transition. According to McDonald, Kysela, Siebert, McDonald, & Chambers (1989), "In a study from Alberta, Canada, on transition families participating in a home-based infant program, 64 percent indicated the need to begin transition planning 6 months to a year prior to the projected transition." A meeting

THE PROGRAM APPROACH	APPROPRIATE FOR MY CHILD AND FAMILY?		
	YES	NO	UNDECIDED

General:

1. Activities are planned to promote the child's growth and development in all areas, e.g., social/emotional, intellectual, physical communication, and self-help.
2. Daily activities are planned based on the needs of the group.
3. The children are provided with a choice of activities.
4. The children are interested and involved in the activities.
5. The staff are open to consultation from other agencies.

Specific:

1. There is an appropriate balance of child-directed exploratory play and teacher-directed activities.
2. The room is set up to promote social interaction between children.
3. Sensory play experiences are a daily part of the program, e.g., water play, music/rhythms, or sand play.
4. The daily activities take into account children's interests.
5. The selection of toys and activities are appropriate for my child.
6. There is a balance between small-group, large-group, and individual activities.
7. The program activities address the priority areas in which my child needs to learn and develop.
8. There are opportunities for the staff to meet for information sharing and planning on a regular basis.

Comments:

PARENT INVOLVEMENT

General:

1. Staff communicate with parents on a regular basis. I felt comfortable and welcomed by staff during my visit. The staff encourage full parent participation in their child's program.

Specific:

1. There are opportunities for parents to communicate with and get to know other parents.
2. Activities are planned that encourage parent involvement, e.g., meetings with guest speakers, social activities, etc.
3. The staff take into consideration the concerns of parents.
4. There is sufficient opportunity for parents to discuss their child's development with the staff.

Comments:

SOURCE: Community Living Toronto, 1992. "Choosing an Early Childhood Program: A Checklist for Parents."

should be held in advance of the IPP meeting so that transition-related goals may be identified. During the meeting the following should happen:

- The transition coordinator should introduce the topic of transition and explain the process.
- The family should identify their preferences, concerns, support needs, and other agenda items for their child.
- The teacher should summarize the child's progress and include suggestions for future goals.
- The family should begin to identify how much time they can devote to being involved, what they are able to do to prepare for the transition, and other issues they may want to address, such as hours of operation, program fees, and transportation arrangements.
- The minutes of this meeting should be circulated in a written report.

After the meeting, the teacher and family need to work together to develop ideas for specific goals related to the transition, and the family will need to begin to identify their strengths and needs, as well as the child's.

Two additional tasks of the transition coordinator are to (1) help the family determine the level of involvement best for them and (2) develop appropriate strategies with the families to achieve involvement goals.

Figure 13–2 provides specific suggestions as to the kinds of information families like to have regarding their child's transition. Information that families may want to share with new providers can be found in Figure 13–3. Figure 13–4 provides ideas that will help families prepare preschool children as they make the transition from one program to another.

Figure 13–2 WAYS THAT FAMILIES MAY BE INVOLVED IN THE TRANSITION PLANNING PROCESS

- Learn about the transition process.
  - How are children evaluated?
  - When will my child make the transition?
  - When will decisions be made?
  - What are the differences between early intervention and preschool?
  - What are my child's and family's legal rights related to special education?
- Be an active member of the transition-planning team.
- Participate in evaluating the child.
- Help amend the IFSP to include a transition plan.
- Work on goals to prepare the child and family for change.
- Help identify goals for the IEP.
- Visit potential programs.
- Participate in placement decisions.
- Share information about the child with new program staff.

Figure 13–3   INFORMATION THAT FAMILIES MAY WANT TO SHARE
WITH NEW PROVIDERS

- Types of things that the child enjoys doing.
- Things that are easy and difficult for the child to learn.
- The child's favourite toys and activities.
- How the child gets along with other children.
- Types of rewards that the child prefers (e.g., praise, hugs, stickers).
- Types of discipline that work best with the child.
- Kinds of support that the child needs during routine activities such as eating, dressing, toileting, etc.
- Things the child was working on in the previous program that families would like to see continued in the new program.
- Additional goals that the family would like to see addressed in the new program.

Figure 13–4   PREPARATION OF THE CHILD

- Talk with the child about the impending changes.
- Provide opportunities for the child to make new friends.
- Teach the child to care for personal belongings.
- Teach the child to share toys and materials.
- Teach the child to use toys and equipment appropriately.
- Help the child acquire as many self-care skills and as much independence as possible.
- Encourage the child to ask for help when needed.
- Allow the child to practise working independently.
- Teach the child to follow directions.
- Read with the child more frequently, encouraging increased attention and involvement in the stories.
- Help the child learn his or her full name, address, and phone number.
- Help the child learn his or her new teacher's name and the name of the school.
- Take the child to visit the new program and the new teacher.
- Talk with the child about rules and activities in the new program.

STEP 5: DETERMINING THE RESPONSIBILITIES OF THE SENDING PROGRAM

Classrooms in different programs vary greatly in their physical arrangements, the structure of learning opportunities, and the style, knowledge, and attitude of the teacher. To the best of their ability, teachers will want to prepare the child for the next environment, especially if it is quite different from the current one. For example, a child leaving a flexible preschool and entering a regimented classroom would be sure to benefit from learning some of the specific skills needed in the next classroom.

Once the transition goals have been identified, the sending program can create activities for working toward those goals. The specific activities will depend on the skills needed for the next program. For example, if the receiving setting is a kindergarten classroom, the early childhood program can incorporate the following ideas into its current curriculum:

Photo 13–5
Many receiving programs expect children to be able to raise their hands to attract the teacher's attention.

- Gradually give children more responsibility for their personal and classroom possessions.
- Teach children to ask for attention in nondisruptive ways (four-year-olds learning to raise their hands, for example; see Photo 13–5).
- Help children learn to follow directions given to the group in general.
- Teach children to care for their toileting needs independently.
- Teach children the difference between boys' and girls' toilet facilities (if this differentiation is made in the new setting).
- Gradually reduce the number of prompts from teachers to children during all kinds of tasks.
- Gradually increase the amount of time children work and play independently, without teachers' involvement.
- Teach children to line up and move in lines, if this is the practice in the new setting.
- Help children learn to complete one task before starting another.
- Teach children to recognize their printed name and to claim ownership of materials and possessions.
- Teach children to follow classroom routines and change-of-activity patterns (as much as possible, introduce the routines of the new program).
- Vary the length of activities.
- Vary the amount of help provided during and between tasks.
- Vary the type and number of instructions given to children.
- Teach everyday safety rules.
- Role-play meeting new children and ways of making new friends.

STEP 6: HOLDING PLACEMENT MEETINGS

Several meetings may be necessary to determine the appropriate placement for a child. It is important that the transition coordinator, the teacher, and any other professionals who worked with the child attend these meetings (Photo 13–6). Personnel from the receiving program may include the transition coordinator, a member of the program's special service staff, and a teacher representing the classroom program. The family also must be present and be encouraged to invite others involved with the child (a grandmother who frequently provides care for the child,

Photo 13–6
The transition coordinator and the child's teacher are but two of the key people at the placement meeting.

perhaps). Ideally, those from the receiving program would have observed the child in the current program before the placement meeting.

The group as a whole should discuss the child's overall performance and future needs. Information prepared by the sending teacher and the family regarding the child's abilities and progress toward transition goals should be circulated. This information provides the format for the discussion of what services the child needs and the potential sources of such services. There must be ample opportunity to ask questions, request further information, and receive clarification of particular issues. The service and placement decisions are based on the discussion at the meeting and on observations of the child. The child's parents should be equal partners in the decision-making process. When thinking about an appropriate placement, it is important to keep these considerations in mind:

- special services and supports available in the new program
- related services, such as transportation options between programs
- ratio of adults to children
- total size of group
- number of children in the group needing additional support
- availability of paraprofessionals, classroom aides, teacher assistants, or volunteers
- enrollment procedures and prerequisites
- date on which the child can enter the new program
- classroom requirements (e.g., special equipment)
- accessibility for children with physical disabilities
- medical or other clinical personnel available on the premises—if required

Once the appropriate placement has been determined, the parents, transition coordinator, and the teacher should meet with the new teacher, principal, or program director and the special service staff who will be involved with the child during and after the transition. The purpose of this meeting should be to review the child's current performance and special needs, as well as future goals for the child. Arrangements also should be made for the receiving teacher to visit the sending program and for the child and parents to visit the new program.

STEP 7: TRANSFERRING RECORDS

Transferring a child's records is essential to ensure that the staff members in the new learning environment receive relevant information. A clearly defined process for transferring records needs to be made between the transition coordinators. Written procedures for transferring records ensure that the right records are sent to the right persons in a timely manner. *Parental approval must be obtained before sending records of any kind to another person or program.* Parents must be informed about the records to be sent, whom they will be sent to, and when they will be sent. Ideally, parents should receive copies of any teacher reports that are to be sent to the receiving centre. The following questions can serve as a guide when planning the transfer of records:

- What method does each program use when getting parental consent for transfer of records?
- To what extent do the sending and receiving programs use the same types of records?

- What information collected by the sending program does the receiving program need?
- When and how will additional information be obtained?
- Who is responsible for sending the records?
- Who in the receiving program will accept and be responsible for the records?
- When and how will the records be sent?

STEP 8: HAVING THE CHILD AND FAMILY VISIT THE NEW PROGRAM

Photo 13–7
The child should visit the new program and be given time to explore the environment.

A visit to the new program by the child and parents should be planned as early as possible, so that they can see what the new program is like. The transition coordinator can make the appointment. The visit should include a tour of the building, time to explore the classroom, and time for the child to play in the play yard (Photo 13–7). It is of great value if the new teacher can arrange to spend a few minutes with the child and family. This kind of informal visit should help both the child and the family experience the new program and possibly reduce anxieties about the impending change. *The purpose of this visit is not for parents or teachers to discuss the child's abilities or specific needs.* A meeting without the child must be scheduled when such issues can be discussed.

STEP 9: MOVING INTO THE NEW PROGRAM

For some children, especially those with a developmental delay or other special need, a full session in the new setting may be too much at first. Scheduling arrangements should vary, depending on each child. Program flexibility is critical when young children, with or without developmental differences, are starting a new program. The following are three suggestions for children who are not ready to start out independently or with a full session:

1. The child might attend the new program for only one hour a day for the first week or so; the time then can be extended. How quickly it is extended depends on how quickly the child adjusts.
2. The sending teacher, transition coordinator, or parent might accompany the child for the first few days. As the child becomes comfortable in the new classroom, adult support can gradually be withdrawn.
3. The child might continue to attend the old program part-time while starting to attend the new program the rest of the time.

With systematic planning and cooperation among staff and family, the new experience can be made comfortable for all children as they make the transition from one program to another. Some ideas to help receiving children are as follows:

- Talk with the children about the new program, how the children are growing up, and how the new program is different (and even a little scary, perhaps—but that it will be fun, too).

- Initially, provide additional time for self-directed play so that children can become familiar with one another.
- Give simple one- and two-step instructions; gradually get children used to longer and more complex instructions.
- Vary the duration and type of activities more frequently at first.
- Vary the amount of teacher help during academic tasks, but always be available for a child who needs help.
- Throughout the transition period, review classroom rules and routines each day (more often for some children).
- Assign experienced children as *buddies* for new children.

STEP 10: OFFERING SUPPORT SERVICES

During the first weeks—even months—of a new program, the child may need extra assistance. This may be in the form of support services offered by the transition coordinator, the previous teacher, or the special service staff. Many receiving teachers welcome such offers. Others are not interested. Whether the support services are provided depends on individual teachers. If a teacher is interested, the coordinator should plan to maintain communication. Four services that might be made available to the receiving teacher are described below.

1. Teacher Conferences

Regularly scheduled meetings can be a critical part of the support services. They provide an opportunity for teachers to follow the child's progress. Suggestions can be offered as needed. During the first days of school in the new setting, the transition coordinator, who is familiar with the child's special needs and problems, can help. If trouble develops, the coordinator can suggest solutions based on the child's former program experiences. It is important that the coordinator also be available by phone, as problems can come up without warning.

Teachers sometimes want to schedule a few meetings with the transition coordinator after school, or they may want the coordinator to come and observe after the new child is enrolled. Sometimes the coordinator can provide the most help by simply listening quietly to a teacher describe the program day. Talking about a problem often leads to a solution (Photo 13–8). These meetings also can provide opportunities for teachers to express their feelings—both the challenges and the pleasures of working with children who have special needs.

Photo 13–8
Meetings between the IPP coordinator, resource teacher, and classroom teacher often lead to solutions to problems.

2. Family Input

The child's family is a prime resource. Regular contact between the teacher and the parents allows for the sharing of a child's progress, opportunities to express concerns, and identification of solutions.

3. Sharing of Materials and Activity Ideas

Transitions can be eased if the new classroom offers experiences familiar to the child. The sending program might lend a favourite learning or play material to the receiving program. Something familiar to use or hang on to tends to promote a child's sense of security. With familiar objects and activities readily available during the first weeks of the transition, the classroom, the teachers, and classmates seem less strange.

4. Teaching Assistants

Providing a teaching assistant for short periods several times a week often helps both the receiving teacher and the child during the transition period. The teaching assistant can supplement the regular teaching activities in the classroom (which is especially useful when a child needs intensive instruction or supervision during the adjustment period, however long that may be). A teaching assistant can work individually with the specific child or work with a small group that includes the child. Teaching assistants may be regular classroom aides, or they may be older children whose own learning will be enhanced by working with younger children. Teaching assistants also may be arranged through parent groups, community volunteer agencies, and community college or university early childhood programs.

Maintaining a Positive Placement Experience

The process of successful inclusion of a child with a special need may not always be a consistently smooth experience. Problems may arise if the early childhood teachers have not been part of the planning process. They may become unsure of the objectives or threatened by the developmental needs of the child as well as by the expectations placed on them with respect to the child. This can make teachers feel inadequate or frustrated, and it may lead to a certain amount of resistance. It is important at this point to get support for the teachers. Early childhood teachers should be encouraged to obtain help in overcoming difficulties of this type when they occur. The case manager, transition coordinator, or resource teacher/early interventionist should be contacted for support and help in resolving any problems that arise.

It is important to involve all of those working with the child in developing an effective team problem-solving approach. Here are six steps to include in effective team problem solving:

1. Identify the specific issues that are of concern and state them.
2. Gather all information that has a bearing on the situation.
3. Identify and state all possible options for resolution (brainstorm).
4. Agree on the most appropriate option.
5. Agree on a specific plan of action.
6. Set up a schedule for an ongoing group review of the process.

Summary

For children with special needs and their families, a successful transition from one program to another is critical to the child's long-range progress. The number and type of accommodations made by children, families, and service providers during periods of transition, and the sustainability of these accommodations, are critical factors in a successful transition. Transition planning should involve a minimum number of disruptions for the child, the family, and the teacher, and yet sustain the child's progress.

The various perspectives of the child, family, and professionals must be considered if the accommodations that each must make are to be recognized and planned for. To increase the likelihood of successful transfer from one program to another, systematic transition planning should be a component of all inclusive early childhood programs. Planning should begin within a few weeks of a child's enrollment in the sending program and continue throughout the year and into the next program for as long as necessary. Transition planning requires a number of steps. As a starting point, representatives—one each from the sending program and the receiving program—are appointed to serve as transition coordinators. Once selected, the coordinators are responsible for visiting other programs and becoming acquainted with classroom practices and staff. The coordinators need to learn the expectations of the other programs and how they differ from their own. Next the coordinators work with their own classroom staff to help minimize the differences between programs for the child who will be in transition.

Parents need to be included throughout the transition process. The parents and transition coordinators must discuss how to make the transition and together write up a specific transition plan. The plan should meet with the approval of everyone: parents, administrators, and teachers. At the time the child is actually transferred, careful pacing is required. Moving through changes too rapidly tends to be upsetting for any young child and especially for a young child with special needs. One recommendation is that the child's time in the new program be increased gradually.

As the child enters the new program, the receiving teacher needs to know what support services are available if needed (and wanted). Possibilities for support services include consultations with the staff from the sending program, from special service staff members in the current program, and from the family. There also may be loans of materials from the sending program and supplementary teaching in the form of teacher assistant services. It is the rare child, even one with a severe disability, who cannot be helped to succeed in a carefully selected new program. Changing from one program to another can and should be a positive experience for the child, family, and teachers. Careful, individualized planning and sufficient time are required.

RESOURCES

SpeciaLink Canada

http://www.specialinkcanada.org

This is the site for a Canada-wide mainstream network whose goal is to promote high-quality daycare for every child in the country, regardless of abilities.

Provincial and Territorial Associations for Community Living

http://www.cacl.ca/english/provteracls

The Canadian Association for Community Living is dedicated to promoting the participation of people with disabilities in all aspects of community living. This site lists all the provincial and territorial sites. Information can be accessed in English or French.

STUDENT ACTIVITIES

1. Interview a centre supervisor who has an inclusive setting that supports children with special needs. Find out what steps were taken and who was involved throughout the transition planning process.
2. Write a summary report on a preschool child with an identified special need who will soon be entering kindergarten. Include what you believe the student's strengths and needs are regarding transition.
3. Interview the family of a Kindergarten child with special needs. Ask them to describe the issues they faced during their child's transition into an out-of-home program (family daycare or a full- or half-day program in a centre).
4. Talk with an early childhood teacher who has had children with special needs included in his or her group. Find out what adjustments he or she had to make and what supports were provided.

REFERENCES

Bruder, M. B., & Chandler, L. K. (1996). Transition. In S. L. Odom & M. E. McLean (Eds.), *Early intervention/early childhood special education: Recommended practices* (pp. 287–307). Austin, TX: Pro-Ed.

Community Living Toronto (1992). *Choosing an early childhood program: A checklist for parents.* Toronto: Author.

Haines, A. H., Rosenkoetter, S. E., & Fowler, S. A. (1994). Transitional planning with families in early intervention programs. *Infants and Young Children, 3,* 38–47.

Hazel, R. A., Barber, P. A., Roberts, S., Behr, S. K., Helmstetter, E., & Guess, P. (1986). *A community approach to an integrated system for children with special needs.* Baltimore, MD: Brookes.

Johnson, T. E., Chandler, L. K., Kerns, G. M., & Fowler, S. A. (1986). What are parents saying about family involvement in transitions? A retrospective transition interview. *Journal of the Division for Early Childhood, 11*(1), 10–17.

McDonald, L., Kysela, G., Siebert, S., McDonald, S., & Chambers, J. (1989). Transition to preschool. *Teaching Exceptional Children, 22*(1), 4–8.

Rice, M. L., & O'Brien, M. (1990). Transitions: Times of change and accommodation. *Topics in Early Childhood, 9*(4), 12–14.

Section **IV**

Implementing Inclusive Early Childhood Programs

CHAPTER 14

Intervention with Specific Age Groups:

Infants, Toddlers, and School-Aged Children

KEY CONCEPTS

differentiated responses

enabling environment

in-home support services

psychological balance

responsive environment

school age care

sensorimotor profile

sensory stimulation

OBJECTIVES

After studying the material in this chapter, the student will be able to

- Describe the benefits of early intervention for infants and toddlers with special needs.
- Define the term "enabling environment" as related to infant and toddler caregiving.
- Explain the family's and the teacher/caregiver's roles in promoting infant learning through sensory stimulation.
- Discuss special considerations related to working with infants and toddlers with sensory impairments.
- Discuss links between the developmental characteristics of school-aged children and effective programming.
- Identify behavioural concerns that may arise in school age programs.
- Describe adaptations to school age programs that promote inclusion.

Introduction

This chapter focuses on intervention with and programming for very young children (birth to two-and-a-half years of age) and children (5 to 12 years old) attending school age child care programs. Within these specific age groupings, children have great variations in developmental skill levels. Therefore, an educator's responses to infant needs may differ from those required for toddlers. For example, during the toddler years, a child shows the improving language, mental representation, and memory skills necessary for engaging with the world. Mobile, energetic, and emotionally expressive toddlers need caregivers who can sensitively guide them in self-regulation without becoming overcontrolling and withdrawing support. Healthy infant and toddler development does not "just happen," even with babies who are born full-term and are developing within culturally appropriate expectations. Infants and toddlers are actively looking, listening, and learning through mutually responsive relationships with caregivers. Similarly, the developmental profile of 6-year-old children differs from that of 12-year-olds. It is important that those working with school-aged children recognize these developmental differences when planning intervention strategies and curriculum. This chapter also focuses on particular issues that arise in the inclusion of school-aged children with special needs in before and after school settings.

Infant and Toddler Programs: An Overview

The number of infants in need of special services is increasing (Photo 14–1). These services can be provided in an inclusive group setting, such as a child care centre, in a specialized clinic where families bring their infant or toddler for scheduled intervention sessions, or at home where a professional provides support to a family for an extensive period. Guralnick (2000, p. 28), after an extensive review of the early intervention system and out-of home child care in the United States, suggests that an inclusive child care program that offers early intervention services and child care is "ideal." He states, "the benefits that result in terms of continuity, quality and parental confidence of such an inclusive program cannot be overemphasized."

In the United States, federal legislation—PL 99-457—recognizes infant intervention as an important national option (Shonkoff & Meisels, 2000). Title I of the law authorizes services for infants who are at risk and those with developmental differences, from birth through two years of age. There is no comparable federal legislation on infant intervention in Canada at this time. However, in the early 1970s, responding to pressure from families, a few provinces began to fund programs that provided mainly **in-home support services** for infants with special needs. As suggested by Brynelsen (1990), the major difference between the development of infant services in the United States and in Canada was that in many Canadian communities,

In-home support services services, such as development assessments and parenting support, are provided for infants with special needs and their families in the home

Photo 14–1
The number of infants in need of special services is increasing.

programs were started on parents' initiative, in partnership with the professional community.

Over the years, infant development/early intervention programs have been established in most Canadian provinces and territories. However, the lack of sufficient ongoing research and coordination has meant that such services have developed mainly in isolation from one another (Brynelsen, 1990). In Nova Scotia, the Early Intervention Home Visit Program offers in-home support for children from birth to three years who are developmentally delayed in one or more areas or are at risk for developmental delay. The Babies Best Start Program in Ontario involves the training of parents in a community to carry out a home-visiting service to new parents who have similar ethnocultural backgrounds. In Alberta, the Lethbridge Parents as Teachers (PAT) Program is a home visitation program for families with children from birth to age five. Services provided during a home visit can include parenting support, referrals to other service agencies, and a yearly developmental assessment for early detection of delays. One of the underlying principles of home-based services is that the role played by families is of prime importance in infant and toddler development. Families are viewed as providing the most effective early intervention, although this intervention is most successful when professional support is available. Winzer (1997) identifies other benefits of early intervention:

- It relieves family stress and improves family functioning.
- It provides critical information about other services available.
- It prevents secondary disabilities, such as behaviour concerns.
- It provides a foundation for the early acquisition of developmental skills during a critical period in human development.
- It halts or prevents declines in development.

THE IMPORTANCE OF ENABLING AND RESPONSIVE CAREGIVING

In this section on infants and toddlers, the terms *teacher/caregiver, educator,* and *infant teacher* will be considered as interchangeable. When discussing infants and toddlers with special needs, the term *interventionist* will also be used.

Newborns are vulnerable to negative environmental influences. Inadequate nurturing, inappropriate stimulation, or insufficient medical and nutritional care can do great damage. Some infants are more vulnerable than others; all infants, however, are vulnerable to some degree, even those who are healthy and responsive at birth. Development is at its most critical stage when infants are most dependent on others to meet all their needs. The recent findings on brain research indicate that learning occurs within the context of supportive adult–child relationships. When adults fail in their caregiving responsibilities, an infant's development is put in jeopardy. Extremely low birthweight infants, as well as those who are medically fragile or at high risk, usually require intensive caregiving.

With infants and toddlers, the teacher/caregiver's responsibilities are similar. The focus should be on providing an environment in which daily routines, play activities, and the teacher/caregiver's responsiveness are geared to the behaviours, strengths, and developmental level of the infant or toddler. Such an environment is an **enabling environment.**

No matter how safe, sanitary, healthy, and well-supervised a learning environment may be, an infant or a toddler will not thrive developmentally unless the

Enabling environment
an environment that supports a child's optimal development

Responsive environment
adults actively engage with an individual infant and toddler and respond to his or her needs and sensorimotor and social exploration

caregiver actively engages and responds to the child (Photo 14–2). By its very nature, a **responsive environment** encourages and supports active exploration when adults provide individual infants and toddlers with opportunities and options for

- gaining access to what is happening in the environment
- making appropriate choices
- engaging in experiences that evolve from a simple to a more complex level
- creating an impact on their environment

Infant and Toddler Intervention

The goal of infant and toddler intervention is twofold: to enable infants and toddlers to explore and master their environment, and to encourage them to use their capacities and abilities in ways that are individually meaningful and productive.

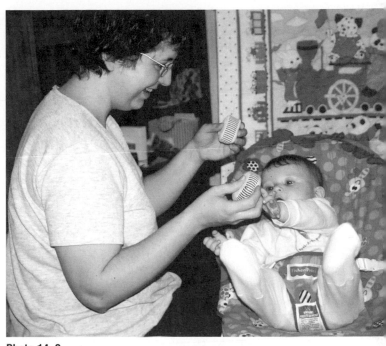

Photo 14–2
Caregivers need to actively engage with infants and toddlers.

SENSORY STIMULATION

Infants and toddlers usually respond to **sensory stimulation** and social stimulation. Caregivers choose different types of stimulation and increase the levels of stimulation that can be tolerated by the child. They identify through observation the individual differences in arousal and reactivity (Goulet, 1998). Caregivers share the child's attention to and interest and delight in exploring different stimulation. An

infant's or a toddler's actions are often contingent on their caregiver's responses. When the infant or toddler is overstimulated, the sensitive caregiver will reduce the stimulation and wait for the child to reorganize and refocus on other stimuli. A secure and trusting caregiver–child relationship is strengthened through the expression of positive emotions and mutual responsiveness.

Starting soon after birth, infants are learning to use their abilities to see, hear, taste, smell, and move about. These emerging skills enable them to be active participants in sharing a variety of experiences with others in their world. Toys and materials that stimulate the senses include those that encourage the infant's or toddler's developing abilities to see sights, hear sounds, touch and feel textures, and move the body in and through space (Photo 14–3).

Extensive research supports the conclusion that infants and toddlers who do not move about and explore their environment are less able to organize and

Sensory stimulation
objects and people that encourage infants and toddlers to explore their environment through seeing, hearing, touching, tasting, and smelling

Photo 14–3
Infants enjoy frequent tactile stimulation experiences.

Photo 14–4
Teachers/caregivers need to provide challenging but safe movement experiences.

represent their experiences internally. This is especially true of infants and toddlers with neuromuscular conditions affecting their balance and movement, and of infants and toddlers with visual or hearing impairments. These children, without special help, tend to engage in few exploratory moves. The family's and caregiver/teacher's task is to provide movement experiences that are challenging, yet result in relatively few frightening falls, bumps, or otherwise unpleasant experiences. As a teacher/caregiver helps an infant or a toddler build confidence in moving about and exploring the environment, the child is likely to show increasing interest in physical activity, and may even come to enjoy "rough-and-tumble" play. It must be remembered, however, that infants should never be rocked, shaken, or swung roughly, lifted rapidly and abruptly, or thrown into the air. Infants and toddlers cannot adjust posturally to quick extremes of motion. Serious injuries to the head, brain, neck, and back may result (Photo 14–4).

INTEGRATING SENSORY MODALITIES

Sensorimotor profile
an infant's preference for and use of one sensory modality over another for sensory exploration

Some infants and toddlers appear to enjoy all kinds of movement experiences; others may show a particular **sensorimotor profile** and be overly sensitive, sometimes in one sensory modality more than another. Still other infants or toddlers may be able to use comfortably only one sense at a time. An example is the child who likes to listen to a music box, but only if allowed to look away from the action. Great distress may occur if an adult tries to coerce such a child into listening and looking at the same time. It must be remembered, too, that how the caregiver/teacher perceives and responds to a sensation is not necessarily the way an infant or a toddler will react to the same sensation. It is best, therefore, for the family or teacher/caregiver to introduce a new experience when the child is in a calm state, in familiar surroundings. Experiences that cause distress should be modified or stopped and reintroduced under different circumstances or when the child is more developmentally advanced. Responsive caregivers protect infants and toddlers from overarousal or support the child's recovery from overarousal when it does occur (Goulet, 1998).

RESPONDING TO THE INFANT AND TODDLER'S DEVELOPMENT

Teacher/caregiver sensitivity is critical in recognizing the developmental accomplishments of the infant or toddler with special needs. Their achievements often seem so small when measured against those of healthy infants. However, the developmental gains of these infants must be viewed as "major victories and sources of pride and pleasure" (Provence, 1990, p. 2). To properly appreciate these victories, teachers/caregivers need to recognize that the potential for positive development exists in all developmental areas for every infant and toddler. Teachers/caregivers need to be aware, too, that the strengthening of one area, through appropriate intervention procedures, usually contributes to development in other areas.

A major responsibility of the infant caregiver/interventionist is to appreciate all aspects of development, both evident and emerging. Infants and toddlers with special needs exhibit a wide range of competencies and developmental needs. Developmental sequences follow the same pattern for children within the same social and cultural environment. However, anything that interferes with a young child's development may reduce his or her ability to utilize information.

Generally speaking, one sense cannot fully compensate for another. A child who has a visual impairment may become highly skilled at identifying objects and events through touch. That information, however, is never as complete as it would be if the child were also using vision. Even when the various sensory systems appear to be intact, sensory integration may be poor. For example, the infant may hear a teacher/caregiver's voice but be unable to orient his or her eyes or head movements in that direction. In these instances, the teacher/caregiver's role is to provide learning experiences and intervention activities based on the guidelines outlined earlier for responsive and enabling caregiving.

ENABLING THE INFANT TO RESPOND AND ADAPT

Infants with special needs may be less responsive and less vocal. Studying 15 mothers and their infants (including those with Down syndrome, brain injury, blindness, and various congenital disabilities), Stone and Chesney (1978) reported the following disturbances in behaviours commonly associated with attachment:

- delayed or infrequent smiling or vocalizing
- tenseness, limpness, or unresponsiveness when handled
- little effort to get the mother's attention

Similarly, premature and low-birthweight babies often have trouble forming attachments because of reduced physical strength or immature neurological development. It is important to recognize that lack of infant responsiveness contributes to less effective responding by others. Parents and teachers/caregivers, therefore, need to be available and ready to respond in kind when an infant initiates an interaction or responds to stimulation from the environment (Photo 14–5, p. 296). For example, if an infant or a toddler smiles spontaneously, the adult smiles back; if the infant or toddler smiles again in response to the adult's smile, the caregiver smiles once again and perhaps adds an affectionate pat or word.

Responding in kind may not be simple, especially when an infant's or a toddler's abilities are limited. For example, low-birthweight infants with medical complications usually are considerably less responsive than are healthy infants. Some parents of these infants may try to compensate by providing more physical and playful contacts than do parents of full-term, healthy infants (Brachfield, Goldberg, & Sloman, 1980). Parents may need to lower the number and the tempo of their reactions to match the infant's activity level, to avoid overstimulating the infant to the point that he or she may shut down.

Photo 14–5
Teachers/caregivers need to be available to support the child's initiations.

Clearly, adults need to find a middle ground. In some instances, it is best to wait for the infant to make an overture and then respond at a matching level of activity. In other instances, it may be better if the teacher/caregiver watches for signs of receptiveness and then initiates a simple activity, such as smiling and gently clapping the infant's hand against his or her own hand. More often than not, infants will signal "enough is enough" by averting their gaze and then looking back when they are ready for further activity (Curry & Johnson, 1990). To meet the needs of the infant or toddler, teachers/caregivers should develop the following skills:

- general sensitivity to the infant's or toddler's need for stimulation as well as for quiet
- responsiveness to specific signals, such as fussing and turning away
- talking and playing with the infant or toddler in ways that actively encourage development

ENABLING THE INFANT TO MAINTAIN PSYCHOLOGICAL BALANCE

Weak reflexes or the absence of muscle tone may interfere with an infant's or a toddler's ability to control his or her responses to the environment. Some infants and toddlers have difficulty becoming aroused, while others become too easily over-aroused. For example, the predisposition to respond to the parent or teacher/caregiver's face with matching facial expressions may overflow and engage the infant's entire body—the head, arms, legs, fingers, and toes. The infant is not able to dampen the intensity, so the response to stimulation involves the whole body in an undifferentiated way.

Such activity "overflow" often characterizes the behaviour of infants with special needs. Other examples include the following:

- extreme sensitivity, or marked lack of sensitivity, to everyday occurrences
- early reflexes and behaviour patterns that persist, making it difficult for the child to initiate, stop, or redirect his or her own behaviour
- exhaustion as a result of having to spend disproportionate amounts of energy in trying to control or direct neuromuscular activity (as in the child with cerebral palsy), or having to expend excessive energy in trying to seek out and process new learning

Among the jobs of the teacher/caregiver is assisting the child in becoming an active participant in appropriate learning opportunities in the immediate environment (Photo 14–6). Another is communicating with the infant or toddler in ways that let the child know that his or her messages and being heard and respected.

Some caregiving strategies may enable an infant or a toddler to maintain a **psychological balance:**

- Observe frequency patterns in arousal to and recovery from stimulation.
- Reduce situations that provoke extreme sensitivity.
- Introduce new activities when the child is most calm or alert (after a nap).
- Provide a stimulus shelter or comfort zone (an area with minimal stimulation) within the playroom.

Photo 14–6
The toddler is learning to become an active participant.

Psychological balance
an infant or a toddler's ability to maintain a balance between approaching and avoiding environmental events (stimuli)

ENABLING THE INFANT AND TODDLER TO DIFFERENTIATE RESPONSES

An infant or a toddler with special needs may retain undifferentiated social, cognitive, and communication responses longer. In social development, for example, the infant may not show the selective interest in parents or caregivers that is seen in most two-month-olds. Unable to receive information through one or more of the senses, this infant may withdraw from his or her immediate world or overreact to it. Either response can prevent the infant from becoming actively interested in what is going on. In turn, this prevents the infant from attaining a sense of self and from forming effective relationships with others. As a result, the infant or the toddler may

- respond in a global, all-or-nothing way
- resist changes and transitions to other activities or settings
- resist adaptations, extensions, and opportunities to interrelate or to combine elements and experiences

It takes skill and insight for a teacher/caregiver to help an infant or a toddler learn to modify what he or she is able to do and to accomplish **differentiated responses.** As a first step, the teacher/caregiver can help the child process incoming stimuli. For example, a puppet or toy that looks, feels, and sounds unusual might elicit a total approach or a total withdrawal reaction. If the infant can experience first the touch and then the sound of the object, the experience may become a manageable one. With some infants, an effort to touch the puppet still may spread throughout the child's entire body. When the child is therapeutically positioned in a manner that inhibits much of the overflow, the infant's energy can

Differentiated responses
infants' and toddlers' ability to differentiate simpler and more specific responses among global undifferentiated responses to stimuli

Photo 14–7
Provide opportunities for the infant to explore objects of interest.

be directed at making controlled arm movements that allow the infant to successfully reach for and touch the puppet. By helping the infant inhibit some responses so that others can be functional, the teacher/caregiver has enabled the infant to differentiate and effectively use an appropriate response from among his or her outgoing responses.

Once infants and toddlers develop some strategies for controlling their responses, parents and teachers/caregivers can help them develop a greater and more varied range of behaviours. Parents and teachers/caregivers can do this by creating opportunities for the infants to seek out, explore, and manipulate whatever interests them (Photo 14–7). The best learning opportunities occur when the new experience is a natural outgrowth of an old and familiar one. Extensions of earlier experiences need to be gradually introduced while remaining rooted in what the infant or toddler already knows. Parents and teachers/caregivers can assist in several ways:

- Provide many slightly different opportunities for the infant or toddler to do the same thing. For example, there can be balls and blocks of many sizes, plastic cups of different shapes, chairs of different designs, and mechanical switches that are activated in different ways. If the child already walks confidently on a smooth, flat surface, this ability can be challenged by putting out a bumpy mattress to walk on. If a child with seizure disorder has to adjust to wearing a helmet for head protection, happier experiences can be offered as starters, perhaps wearing different kinds of hats in preparation for adapting to the helmet.

- Offer new experiences similar to previous experiences and using familiar materials to ease transitions. An infant or a toddler may find bath time pleasant when sitting in a special seat in the bathtub. Using the same seat when introducing the child to the pool is likely to help the child adapt to being in water in a different setting.

- Change one dimension of an experience. When infants or toddlers are going outdoors to play on the grass, a teacher/caregiver can take along familiar play materials—balls, for example. As a toddler starts to play with the toys "in the same old way," the toys are likely to respond differently by not moving as freely on the grass. As a result, the toddler must internalize this new information about the toys and how differently they react in different settings. Such experiences motivate a child to explore the newly exhibited properties of balls (and other play materials) as teachers/caregivers transfer the toys from one situation to another.

ENABLING INFANTS AND TODDLERS TO INITIATE NEW RESPONSES

An infant or a toddler with special needs often uses energy to maintain internal equilibrium, making it more difficult to acknowledge external events. Or, if the child should become aware of external stimuli, the awareness tends to be

Photo 14–8
All infants and toddlers need to integrate experiences across several areas of development.

one-dimensional—that is, the infant or toddler addresses only one source of input while ignoring the others. Conversely, an infant or a toddler may use only one sense, such as vision or hearing, to experience an object. For example, the child may be so engrossed in watching an activity that any sounds or speech accompanying the action do not register (Photo 14–8). Also, an infant or a toddler may respond with one sense but not integrate the response with other sensory input. The child may look or touch, but not put the two behaviours together so as to gain more complete information. Infants and toddlers with perceptual motor difficulties, for example, may follow the movement of an object with their eyes. They may not, however, try to reach for or grasp the object as it moves out of visual range—indicating, perhaps, an inability to integrate and coordinate looking with touching.

Caregivers need to support and encourage all areas of sensory learning. They can observe infants and toddlers for a new response to stimulation and then provide opportunities for repeated practice of a skill by using similar materials. When a caregiver and a child jointly focus on stimulation, a skill may be extended and reinforced. The caregiver may move toys, particularly those desired, closer to the child to heighten his or her awareness of them. High-contrast materials (such as black-and-white combinations) help infants and toddlers with visual impairments use their residual vision. Prompting strategies that increase play behaviours include changing the presentation of a toy (e.g., turning it another way), placing a toy in the child's hands, and activating a toy and letting the child complete the task (Blasco, 2001). Ringing a bell near an object helps some infants attend to stimulation. With

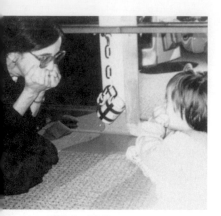

Photo 14–9
Teachers make materials accessible so that all children can explore and manipulate.

toddlers, frequent pairing of words and actions (e.g., "up" with the action of going up the stairs) helps them integrate different sensory stimulation.

ADAPTING PLAY AND LEARNING MATERIALS

Active contact with play materials allows infants and toddlers to experience some control over their environment. Hearing the chiming of a musical rattle when it is shaken or seeing a rubber toy that had been held under water float to the surface teaches the child the effects of his or her actions on the environment. All infants and toddlers, including those with special needs, need to have opportunities to manipulate objects and experience control. Remember, it is much more interesting and motivating for a child to bat a mobile or ring a bell than it is to watch as someone else bats a mobile or rings a bell.

As noted earlier, all children benefit from manipulative materials that enable them to produce some change or effect on the environment. The task of the teacher/caregiver is to make materials accessible and to figure out adaptations so that all children can explore, manipulate, and control play materials and everyday objects (Photo 14–9). Possible adaptations of materials and equipment for children with poorly developed motor skills are as follows:

- Suspend toys from activity frames.
- Place foam hair curlers over paint brushes or crayons for an easier hold.
- Attach toys to playboards or wall surfaces.
- Place toys on a tray.
- Attach objects to blankets or mats with Velcro loops (especially good for children who are not mobile).
- Deflate beach balls for easier grasping, throwing, and catching.
- Fit the child with a Velcro mitt and attach strips of Velcro to toys to make them more accessible.

Once play materials are accessible to the child, adaptive play goals should focus on these aims:

- increasing the duration of the child's play
- encouraging various kinds of manipulation of play materials
- introducing a wider range of toys and manipulative materials
- reducing a child's dependence on prompting from the caregiver

TIMES FOR SHARING AND LEARNING

The daily routines of feeding, diapering, bathing, dressing, and helping an infant or a toddler relax or go to sleep are prime times for a teacher/caregiver to interact calmly and playfully with the child (Photo 14–10). When an infant cries, for example, it usually is a signal that the infant needs something: food, diapering, comforting, company. Crying is usually the infant's or toddler's way of both losing control and attempting to gain control. Trust develops when the child's cries are answered in a prompt and caring way. Some infants sleep for short periods, wake often, and cry and scream (high pitched) for prolonged periods. These behaviours are hard for the caregiver to interpret and respond to, so caregivers need to be flexible and often creative in finding ways to soothe a child.

When comforting an infant or a toddler, the adult may be able to soothe with movement, sounds, sights, or touching. Rocking (gentle movement), soft singing (sounds), a favourite toy (sight and texture), or a gentle rubbing or patting (touch) will often successfully calm a baby. Sometimes an infant is signalling the need for warmth, security, or food. The appropriate caregiving response, then, may be gentle swaddling, loosely wrapping the infant in a soft blanket for a short time, being careful that circulation to limbs is not restricted. For infants with neuromuscular problems, swaddling often provides additional comfort by relieving the discomforting effect of twitching or jerking limbs or muscles. In the event that the baby is hungry, it is important that the feeding activity be made a happy and sociable time.

Photo 14–10
The daily routines are prime times for teachers/caregivers to interact playfully with an infant.

Feeding times may be difficult for infants with particular types of special needs. Mealtimes are likely to be less stressful if a relaxed attitude is maintained. This can be accomplished through appropriate positioning in a specially adapted chair or by seating the infant or toddler securely in the adult's lap. Certain conditions, such as cleft palate or lip, may require special feeding equipment. Children should be fed in the company of others, making mealtimes important social times (Photo 14–11).

INFANT AND TODDLER INTERVENTION: AN ONGOING CHALLENGE

As previously indicated, teachers/caregivers who work with infants and toddlers with special needs are challenged with providing a day-by-day learning environment that supports interactions between each infant and toddler and his or her world. To develop individual strengths and reduce the impact of the developmental disability or delay, teachers/caregivers should provide a variety of situations and activities that engage the child as a participant. Infants and toddlers especially need to integrate experiences across several areas of development. For this reason they often seem compelled to look at, touch, and suck on an object. Such achievements need to be viewed not as ends in themselves, but as abilities that enable the child to recognize the functions of objects and to participate in daily experiences.

Photo 14–11
Mealtime should be a social time.

Intervention for School-Aged Children

Musson (1999, p. 3) defines "**school age care** as an interrelated collection of adult-sponsored care structures, play environments, and program activities that are set up on a regular basis for school-aged children for the periods of time when school is not in session and parents are not at home." When educators work in these environments with school-aged children, especially those who have special needs, many components of the program must be considered. Couture and Jacobs (2001) investigated the quality of 20 Montreal school age care programs that integrated children with special needs. They found that less than half of educators were aware that a child with special needs was joining their program and "only six of the educators were involved in the planning process" (p. 32). This section highlights elements of a high-quality school age care program that are necessary for the successful inclusion of children with special needs:

- an understanding of the development of school-aged children
- effective transitions from the elementary school to the school age program
- intervention plans for challenging behaviours
- communication between programming staff and families
- programming for inclusion
- adaptations to promote inclusion

THE DEVELOPMENT OF SCHOOL-AGED CHILDREN

The development of school-aged children differs from that of preschool children in many ways. School-aged children generally have increased language and literacy skills, improved memory, and the ability to engage in more critical thinking. Children of this age are very "rule-bound," often spending more time deciding and debating the rules than playing the game (Photo 14–12). They have lots of energy that can put their more developed motor skills to good use by participating in physical challenges.

One of the key characteristics of this developmental period is the formation of strong peer relations. School-aged children need to be valued as individuals and accepted as part of a group. They need to gain self-confidence through successful completion of concrete tasks and products. They will gain self-esteem by being "good" at something and therefore need to develop a variety of skills. Teachers in school age child care programs need to be aware of these developmental characteristics when creating an individual program plan for a school-aged child with special needs. For example, although a school-aged child with a learning disability may require additional support in learning to read and write, he or she may excel in other school-age activities.

Photo 14–12
School-aged children are very "rule-bound," often spending more time deciding and debating the rules than playing the game.

TRANSITION FROM SCHOOL TO A SCHOOL AGE CHILD CARE PROGRAM

The transition from elementary school to a school age child care program may present particular challenges for some children. At the end of the day, children often come from a structured school environment in which certain expectations are established to a less structured school-age setting. A child may have difficulty adjusting to different environments and sets of expectations. Since they share responsibility for the individual child, it is essential that teachers in both the school and the school age child care programs have a collaborative relationship that provides for consistent communication of information about the child's strengths and needs and for greater consistency in expectations.

Some Canadian school districts have developed new innovations in partnerships between schools and early childhood education programs. For example, the First Duty Project in Toronto is a universal early learning and care program. It brings together three programs—Kindergarten, child care, and parenting supports—into a single program designed to meet the learning needs of children and the child care needs of parents. Within this unified program, the Kindergarten teacher and the early childhood educator work together to provide a seamless day for the children. This model is especially effective for a child with special needs as it significantly reduces the number of transitions that the child must navigate.

The transition from an elementary school to a school age program may necessitate another accommodation for the child. Schools typically have more support services for children with identified special needs. Indeed, some children with special needs have one-on-one support in their school environment and then have to function completely independently in their after-school program. Directors and families of children in school age programs often have to strongly advocate for additional supports for a child with special needs.

BEHAVIOUR ISSUES IN SCHOOL AGE PROGRAMS

A number of situations can contribute to increased child behaviour challenges in a school age program. As previously noted, the demands of a transition from a preschool to a school-age environment can make it difficult for a child to cope with and manage his or her emotions, resulting, in some cases, in serious behaviour concerns that teachers feel unable to handle. Couture and Jacobs (2001, p. 33) concluded, "programs of lower quality excluded children with behavioural problems more often than those of higher quality." Staff in a school age program then will need to thoughtfully consider ways to help a child settle in, reduce stress and cope with the transition. A school-aged child (and other family members) can be involved in different ways in developing strategies for coping, thus helping the child gain insight into his or her reactions to transitions. Strategies for coping may include making a change to the schedule (e.g., snack time or physical activity first), providing choices for activities, or giving opportunities to work and play alone, with one other child, or in a small group rather than a large group (e.g., circle time) (Photo 14–13, p. 304).

School-aged children are often more aware of physical, social, and intellectual differences. Although this presents opportunities to talk more about human differences, exclusionary behaviours among school-aged children also arise. In addition, school-aged children are forming specific peer groups that include and exclude children.

Photo 14–13
A strategy for coping with transitions can include opportunities for playing with one other child.

Children with special needs are particularly vulnerable to the exclusionary behaviours of their peers and may react to exclusion by seeking attention in negative ways or by withdrawing. It is important for teachers of school-aged children to intervene when they observe exclusionary behaviours and work with the whole group in developing skills in empathy, problem solving, and conflict resolution. With their growing cognitive abilities, school-aged children can become advocates for others and can learn to intervene and advocate when they observe situations of bias and exclusion (Photo 14–14). School-aged children can also learn that advocating for a child with special needs is more positive than is overprotecting the child, which reduces independence and a sense of competency.

COMMUNICATION BETWEEN SCHOOL AGE PROGRAM STAFF AND FAMILIES

In school age programs, teachers and families have fewer opportunities to talk about the child's challenges and to develop intervention plans. Couture and Jacobs (2001) discovered that only 12 percent of the educators of school-aged children in their study had met the parents of a child with special needs before the child had been included in the program. Contact and communication with parents in a school age program can be more difficult because older siblings in the same school may pick up children or parents may be rushed at the end of day when picking up their child. A concerted effort by staff in school age programs that includes a variety of communication strategies (see Chapter 5) needs to be made in order to build to consistent communication with families of school-aged children.

PROGRAMMING FOR INCLUSION

Curriculum in a school age care environment should be developed based on the strengths, needs, and interests of all children. It should be focused on a choice of play, creative arts, science, and recreational activities and not exclusively on

Photo 14–14
School-aged children can learn to intervene and advocate when they observe situations of peer exclusion.

homework. Space for doing homework should be set up, but completing homework should be an option not an expectation of the program. When planning the program, it is important to incorporate some games and activities that are cooperative and not competitive in nature. As school-aged children can sustain attention for longer periods, long-term projects can be planned for and implemented. Drama or dance productions, doing creative art, making videos, and writing plays are just a few examples of long-term projects in which many school-aged children enthusiastically participate. These projects should involve access to community resources that expand the school-aged child's world beyond the school and child care centre. It is essential to recognize the importance of social interactions in school age programs and develop activities that involve working in small groups that include all children.

ADAPTATIONS TO PROMOTE INCLUSION

It is essential to consistently consider adaptations for the child with special needs in order to develop programs that enable total participation. Teachers in school age care environments need to actively promote inclusion. Inclusion doesn't just happen. It needs to be fostered. For example, when selecting teams for games, teachers may need to develop guidelines for team formation to ensure that the child with special needs is fully included. This can be done through a variety of ways:

- numbering off class participants
- organizing teams on the basis of specific colours of children's clothes, socks, shoes, and so on
- having group discussions on finding novel ways to form inclusive teams

When planning cognitive games and experiences, some children may need more visual cues, others more tactile ones, and still others may need verbal or written cues to maximize their participation in an activity. Playing games frequently for repeated

Photo 14–15
To include children who have a range of special needs, adaptations to outdoor activities need to be made.

practice and providing the child who has difficulty following rules with an individual cue sheet that outlines those rules are ways this can be achieved.

Outdoor play is an essential component of a quality school age program (Photo 14–15). Adaptations will need to be made to include children who have a range of special needs. For example, a child in a wheelchair may need the support of a friend in such games as tag. Allowing the child to choose whether or not they need physical assistance will help to promote the child's sense of competency, which is a key school-age developmental task.

SCHOOL AGE INTERVENTION: AN ONGOING CHALLENGE

A major concern is that there is little acknowledgement and support for children with special needs in before and after school age programs. In addition, teachers in these programs may not have enough information and strategies to effectively support the school-aged child with special needs (Couture & Jacobs, 2001). Though there is growing support for children of Kindergarten age, many programs serving older children with special needs (ages 6 to 12) have limited funding and resources. What is needed to ensure the successful participation and inclusion of school-aged children with special needs are the following:

- more program resources (e.g., staff, consultants, materials, equipment, and access to on-going professional development)
- increased communication among the elementary school, school age programs, and families
- greater advocacy for quality inclusive school age programs

Summary

Social and economic factors, as well as legislation related to early intervention services, are resulting in increased numbers of infants and toddlers being cared for by individuals other than their parents. This shift away from parents' full-time care of their own infants and toddlers is generating a need for an increased number of infant and toddler teachers/caregivers/interventionists—trained individuals who are able to provide a responsive and enabling learning environment.

Providing appropriate care and promoting sound learning experiences are based on a teacher/caregiver's knowledge of infant and toddler development. They are based also on a teacher/caregiver's ability to implement this knowledge by providing responsive caregiving in an enabling and engaging environment.

Responsive teaching and caregiving means that each infant's or toddler's unique ways of responding are recognized, respected, and nurtured. Only by observing what an infant or a toddler is doing and how the child responds to overtures from others can parents and teachers/caregivers decide how best to respond to individual abilities and needs. Experiences should not be imposed on infants or toddlers; the adult should patiently try to engage the child's active participation, as an initiator as well as a responder.

All infants and toddlers need a safe, healthy, well-supervised, and engaging environment. However, even in such an environment, developmental differences, such as sensory impairments, motor or neurological dysfunctions, and severe health conditions, can affect the child's efforts to engage positively with their world. The infant or toddler may experience few consistent outcomes or results to promote a sense of accomplishment and confidence. For these infants and toddlers it is especially important that parents and teachers/caregivers respond in enabling ways. Families and teachers/caregivers who delight and share in very young children's discoveries, ideas, and perspectives of the world are likely to promote the emotional well-being of children who need extra support.

Emotional support, warmth, and caring are also essential ingredients of an effective, inclusive school age program. Educators need to recognize and value the unique developmental profiles of school-aged children. When working with school-aged children with special needs, particular issues may arise: the transition from the elementary school program to the school age program; peer relations; and communication between those involved in the care and education of the child. Strategies for working through these issues include seeking additional resources, creating consistent intervention plans, developing interdisciplinary partnerships, and advocating for the child and family. Program adaptations that promote inclusion are necessary for quality in school age programs.

RESOURCES

w w w

ZERO TO THREE: THE NATIONAL CENTER FOR INFANTS, TODDLERS AND FAMILIES
http://www.zerotothree.org
This website provides online articles, a resource list, and publications on children from birth to age three.

INFANT MENTAL HEALTH PROMOTION

http://www.sickkids.on.ca/imp/

This site includes the newsletter *IMPrint,* which often focuses on supporting infants with special needs.

CENTER FOR EVIDENCE-BASED PRACTICE: YOUNG CHILDREN
WITH CHALLENGING BEHAVIORS

http://www.challengingbehavior.org

This site promotes the awareness and implementation of positive evidence-based practices in dealing with young children who have behavioural problems.

SCHOOL-AGE NOTES

http://www.schoolagenotes.com

This site provides a newsletter focusing on the latest resources and curriculum ideas for school age programs.

STUDENT ACTIVITIES

1. Observe a wide-awake infant between three and eight months of age for 20 minutes in a setting where there is at least one adult. (This may require more than one observation session.) Record the following:
   - what behaviours the infant engages in
   - which behaviours are directed to others in the environment
   - how many of the infant's overtures were responded to
   - how the infant's behaviours were responded to
2. Based on your written observation, write a simulated report for the caregivers. Commend them specifically on what they were doing that was enabling; describe observed situations in which they might have responded or been more appropriately responsive.
3. Think about a caregiving/teaching routine—diapering, feeding, bathing—and list the kinds of infant learning experiences that a teacher/caregiver can weave into the routine.
4. Gather a variety of toys for infants and toddlers. How would these materials promote experiences with sensory stimulation? How could some of the toys be adapted for an infant with poor muscle control?
5. Think back to when you were eight years old. List some of your favourite things you did. How does it match to what you know about school-aged children?
6. With a partner, list as many competitive school-age games as you can. For each game, develop a way in which it may be adapted into a cooperative and inclusive game.

REFERENCES

Blasco, P. M. (2001). *Early intervention services for infants, toddlers and their families.* Needham Heights, MA: Allyn and Bacon.

Brachfield, S., Goldberg, S., & Sloman, J. (1980). Parent–infant interaction in free play at 8 and 12 months: Effects of prematurity and immaturity. *Infant Behavior and Development, 3,* 289–305.

Brynelsen, D. (1990, May). *Historical perspective on infant development programs in Canada.* Paper prepared for presentation to the Atlantic Conference, Halifax, NS.

Couture, M., & Jacobs, E. (2001). Integrating children with special needs in school-age care programs. *Interaction, 15*(1), 32–33.

Curry, N. E., & Johnson, C. N. (1990). *Beyond self-esteem: Developing a genuine sense of human value.* Washington, DC: National Center for Education of Young Children.

Goulet, M. (1998). *How caring relationships support self-regulation: Video guide.* Toronto: George Brown College.

Guralnick, M. J. (2000) The early intervention system and out-of-home child care. In D. Cryer & T. Harms (Eds.), *Infants and toddlers in out-of-home care* (pp. 207–234). Baltimore, MD: Brookes.

Musson, S. (1999). *School-age care, theory and practice.* Toronto: Addison-Wesley.

Provence, S. (1990). Interactional issues: Infants, parents, professionals. *Infants and Young Children, 3,* 1–7.

Shonkoff, J., & Meisels, S. (Eds.), (2000). *Handbook of early childhood intervention* (2nd ed.). New York: Cambridge University Press.

Stone, N., & Chesney, B. (1978). Attachment behaviors in handicapped infants. *Mental Retardation, 16*(1), 8–12.

Winzer, M. (1997). *Special education in early childhood: An inclusive approach.* Toronto: Prentice-Hall.

CHAPTER 15

Arranging the Inclusive Learning Environment

KEY CONCEPTS

anti-bias materials
emergent curriculum
induced incompetence
orderly sequences

self-help/care
structured flexibility
teacher-guided learning
   opportunities

OBJECTIVES

After studying the material in this chapter, the student will be able to

- Explain how indoor and outdoor learning environments and program scheduling influence children's learning in an inclusive setting.
- List a number of things that teachers can do to enhance awareness of developmental differences within a learning environment.
- Describe how an emergent curriculum approach can benefit all children.
- Discuss the major issues involved in planning a program schedule for children in an inclusive setting.
- Describe how to adapt routines and transitions to ensure the full and successful participation of all children.

Introduction

The learning environments provided by early childhood programs will influence, even determine, the development of countless numbers of children. Those environments and the way they are arranged will also determine how effectively teachers will teach and the kinds of messages children will get about themselves and others. According to Harms (1989, p. 232):

> The environment that adults create for children is a powerful tool for teaching. Through the way we structure children's surroundings, we communicate our values, provide guidance about how children are to behave in the environment, and influence the quality of their learning. Teachers of young children need to become aware of the constant influence the environment has on the children in their care.

The Inclusive Environment

In an inclusive setting, environmental arrangements assume special importance because of the range of differences among children.

Teachers should arrange play spaces and activities, both indoors and out of doors, so that children with special needs are included easily and naturally (Photo 15–1). By doing so teachers convey a powerful message about human values: *All kinds of children can play together and have fun.* Having fun together promotes genuine inclusion of all children. Many children in wheelchairs can join in the exuberant activity of a lively beanbag toss and other group games. Therapeutic equipment is

Photo 15–1
Indoor and outdoor play space should be arranged so that children with developmental differences can be included easily in all activities.

Photo 15–2
Minimizing clutter and confusion enhances the ability of all young children to concentrate on the task at hand.

available that is fun for all children: huge medicine balls, tumble tubs, balance beams, portable stair-climbing apparatuses, trampolines, and the like. (Specialized equipment and specific environmental adaptations will be discussed in subsequent chapters.)

Inclusive early education is based on the principle that children with special needs are first and foremost children. Their basic needs are essentially no different from those of all children, just more pronounced, as the following examples show:

- Loud and distracting noises are difficult for most children; for children with hearing impairments, such noises may be intolerable.
- Moving about safely, in an environment free of clutter, slippery floors, or rumpled rugs, contributes to the safety and security of every child; for children with limited vision or orthopedic problems, an environment free of obstacles protects against serious injury.
- Minimizing clutter and confusion enhances the ability of all young children to concentrate on the task at hand; for children with attention or learning disorders, reducing distractions may be the only way to promote learning (Photo 15–2).

A well-planned learning environment is a necessary context for meeting the developmental needs of all children. It is unacceptable to provide one kind of environment for "typical" children and a different kind for children with special needs. All children need to experience a range of equipment and materials and to engage in risk-taking for their development.

Teachers also need to use guidance procedures (discipline) that will reduce prejudice and promote positive outcomes in children with developmental differences. Helping children with special needs learn appropriate social skills reduces the behavioural differences that often set them apart and produce negative attitudes toward them. The most efficient way to accomplish this is by arranging the learning environment in ways that prompt acceptable behaviour in all children. Such arrangements are one aspect of preventive discipline.

Arrangements for Learning

A program setting, even the newest and most lavish, does not guarantee quality learning experiences. The physical plant may contribute to quality, but it does not ensure it. As Gordon and Browne (2000) point out, the environment is more than a plant; it is the physical and human qualities that combine to create a space in which children and adults work and play together.

Teachers must recognize that when a child is experiencing difficulties, the first move is to step back and take a look, observing the child in the context of the daily program. Necessary changes in the environment then can be made. Almost always, it is the environment that needs fixing, not the child. Rearranging the location of learning centres, for example, changes the way children "orbit" in a room. This, in turn, changes children's interaction patterns, stimulating involvement in new areas and often bringing about positive changes in group or individual behaviour patterns.

PLANNING THE ENVIRONMENT FOR LEARNING

The first step in planning an early learning environment is specifying the kinds of learning opportunities that will be offered. Most programs, including inclusive settings, plan three broad types of experiences: (1) learning through self-help/ care routines, (2) learning through teacher-guided learning opportunities, and (3) learning through play-discovery learning opportunities.

Self-Help/Care Routines

Competence in **self-help/care** leads to greater independence. Therefore, helping young children develop a full range of self-help/care skills is a major curriculum goal in early childhood programs. These are skills related to socially prescribed routines within early childhood settings, such as toileting, dressing, eating, cleaning up, and doing one's share of classroom chores. The goal of learning self-help/care skills holds for all children, including (and perhaps, especially) for children with special needs. Children with developmental concerns need to learn to live as independently as possible with their disability. The more proficient they become in caring for their personal needs, the more likely it is they will be able to be included in integrated/inclusive settings.

> **Self-help/care**
> skills related to socially proscribed routines in early childhood settings, such as toileting, dressing, eating, cleaning up, and doing one's share of classroom chores.

Self-help/care skills are learned behaviours, which means that they can be taught. An early childhood program can be a comfortable place for children to learn self-help/care skills. Teachers are trained to help children carry out these tasks. It is an established part of the teacher's job and time commitment. For many families, already overburdened with responsibilities and stresses, teaching self-help/care skills may be just one more frustrating and time-consuming task. If their child has a developmental disability, the demands may be overwhelming. Furthermore, the resistance and stress often associated with teaching certain self-help/care skills (toileting, for example) can lead to emotional conflict between the parent and the child. It is almost as if the parent's own self-esteem is damaged if the child is not acquiring all the socially approved self-help/care skills. Teachers do not have that kind of personal involvement in the child's early mastery of self-help/care skills. They do not feel pressured to push for early achievement. Instead, whether a child has a disabling condition or not, most early childhood educators know that time and effort are saved by slowing the pace and setting realistic expectations when teaching any new skill.

Building independence. During toddlerhood and the early preschool years, teachers need to systematically guide children through each step of each routine until the various skills become *automatic* and independent. Most children are striving for independence during the preschool years. They constantly watch and attempt to imitate the self-help/care efforts of older children and adults. Furthermore, they are willing to practise; in fact, they insist on practising, practising, and practising.

Photo 15–3
Walking with a walker increases independence.

All children should be able to experience the joy and self-esteem that come from mastering self-help/care skills. Children, regardless of ability, feel positive about themselves when they complete a self-help/care task independently. Some children with disabling conditions are not able to verbalize their accomplishments. They may not able to say, "Look what I did!" but their facial expressions leave little doubt as to their feelings of satisfaction.

It is true that getting about in a wheelchair, with leg braces, or with a walker can be challenging (Photo 15–3). However, use of such adaptive equipment need not prevent independence. What does interfere with independence is a lack of opportunities to learn how to manage routine matters, such as toileting, dressing, and eating.

Children with disabilities often try to do things for themselves, and these efforts often go unrecognized. Adults tend not to expect children with developmental and physical disabilities to even try to learn self-help/care skills. Also, well-meaning family members and caregivers who cannot bear to watch the child struggle may have snuffed out the earliest strivings for independence. In many instances, children with special needs become increasingly dependent because of learned dependence.

Individualizing self-help/care programs. In the North America culture, children are encouraged to do for themselves as much as possible; nevertheless, teachers must be prepared to make exceptions. Some children learn self-help/care tasks early and with ease; others have varying degrees of difficulty. In addition, a child may ask for help with a task that he or she has already mastered. Children, too, have their "off" days. Like adults, they become tired or upset, or feel unwell. A child may need assistance if routines in larger groups result in overstimulation and loss of self-regulation. In addition, teachers need to take into account each family's cultural attitudes toward independence in self-help/care skills. Cultural continuity can be maintained by providing children with support while at the same time gradually reducing the amount of adult assistance.

All children can be expected to be dependent at times. They need to know that it is okay to ask for help, to say, "This is too hard. I can't do it by myself." A child should never be ridiculed or belittled for asking for help, no matter how simple the task. Children who have been helped to feel competent most of time rarely seek help unnecessarily. Usually, they will ask for assistance only when they truly feel, at the moment, that a task is too much for them to do by themselves.

Supports provided by the teacher will vary and depend on the individual child and family. These include verbal and visual reminders, periodic or partial assistance, and assistance and close supervision. The following examples illustrate teachers knowing when to help, how to help, and how much to help:

- Guide a child's arm and hand so that he or she can reach all the way down into his or her wrong-side-out coat sleeve. This demonstrates how to grasp the edge of the cuff, and is helping the child learn that he or she can pull the cuff through, discovering that he or she can make a coat sleeve come right-side out.
- Put a rubber suction cup under the plate of a child with cerebral palsy so that the plate stays in place while he or works at feeding himself or herself.
- Lay clothes out within easy reach of a child who is just learning to walk with crutches. When everything he or she needs for dressing is at his or her fingertips, the child is more likely to manage happily and well alone.

Arranging an environment to support independence. Other environmental arrangements that promote self-help/care skills, particularly for children with special needs, are appropriately sized furnishings and accessories (Photo 15–4). Hooks, washbasins, toilets, and drinking facilities that can be reached and operated by children allow children to help themselves. Children with special needs can learn to take care of many of their own needs through various environmental arrangements. Consider the following examples:

Photo 15–4
The learning environment can be arranged so that children of every skill level can work and play. Modifications to housekeeping furniture provide a more realistic, concrete experience.

- Cork or raised tape placed along certain walls and pieces of furniture will help a child with a severe visual impairment independently find his or her way around a room.
- A prearranged comfortable and secure place to go to remove leg braces, as needed, frees a child of having to wait for an available adult.
- Large knobs or rungs on children's furniture facilitate the opening of drawers and doors.
- A child who knows how to adjust the volume on his or her hearing aid can reduce the amount of time the child is uncomfortable or not "tuned in."
- Equipment and materials in the classroom and play yard that are in good working order reduce frustrations and increase children's initiative and independence.

The last point is especially important. Few situations make a child with special needs—or anyone else, for that matter—feel more incompetent than a doorknob that spins aimlessly, a faucet that will not turn off, or a drawer that will not open. These experiences are especially devastating for children with developmental differences; they have to do more than their share of coping as it is. When something cannot be made to work, children often do not realize that it is the equipment and not themselves that is at fault. For the child, it may add one more frustration to accomplishing an everyday task. **Induced incompetence** is the term used to describe the effects of poorly functioning equipment on children with developmental differences.

Induced incompetence
the effects of poorly functioning equipment on children with special needs.

Washroom facilities. Learning to use a toilet independently is a developmental goal for most children during the early years. In designing a washroom, the following should be taken into consideration:

- Toilets and sinks should be of appropriate size and height.
- Adequate space should be provided for manoeuvring crutches or a walker, or for pulling a wheelchair parallel to the toilet or up to the sink.
- A handrail should be installed that will enable the child to steady himself or herself.
- A hollow block or small footstool should be provided for a child's feet to rest on, thereby reducing insecurity and fear of falling off the toilet.

Photo 15–5
Names on children's cubbies should be indicated clearly.

All children should be guided in developing self-help/care skills in going to the toilet and washing and drying their hands afterward.

In programs for toddlers or children needing help with toileting, teachers need to be immediately available to the children's washroom. For preschoolers who have become fairly trustworthy in handling their toileting needs, it is best if the washroom is accessible to all activity areas. Accessibility from the outdoor play area is especially important so that children can get to the washroom in a hurry as they often need to do. School-aged children can be expected to use a washroom out of sight of teachers, even down the hall. A teacher, nevertheless, needs to be available near the door where children leave and return.

Cubby areas. Cubbies or coathook areas (Photo 15–5) in early childhood centres should be as near as possible to the outdoor exit and the washroom. This location helps children keep track of coats and mittens as they come in to use the toileting facility. If there are no distractions en route, many children can be responsible for toileting themselves during outside play periods. This arrangement may put the cubbies at some distance from the door through which children arrive and depart for home. However, this distance need not be a problem if the traffic lane from the entry door to the cubbies is free of obstacles and clutter. A child's cubby can be identified in a number of ways: a child's first language, photographs, or Braille.

Sleeping areas. The sleeping area in all-day programs must be carefully planned and free of distractions. Placement of cots should

- be consistent—in the same spot every day to provide a sense of security for the child
- take into consideration an awareness of the specific needs of individual children; for example, a space to manoeuvre walkers or crutches independently, or a quiet corner without distractions for an overly active child

Teachers can assist children in settling down for a nap in a variety of ways, depending on home experiences, including choice of sleep toy, soft music, back rub, or being rocked to sleep. Alternatives, such as quiet activities, should be provided for children who usually do not nap and for early risers.

Teacher-Guided Learning Opportunities

Teacher-guided learning opportunities
the teacher directly supports the learning of skills during large- and small-group activities

Teacher-guided learning opportunities (also referred to as large- and small-group activities and one-on-one teaching or instruction periods) should be available throughout the program day (Photo 15–6). The teacher's intent is to support learning of skills that children need but cannot learn solely from a self-guided exploration of the environment. A teacher-guided activity might involve stories, songs,

Photo 15–6
Teacher-guided activities are interspersed throughout the program day.

fingerplays, discussions on care of materials, demonstrations of gentleness with animals, opportunities for children to learn names of objects, basic directionality and number concepts, and so on. These activities may be formally planned learning experiences or they may arise spontaneously out of a child's immediate interest or need (see Chapter 4 for more on incidental teaching opportunities).

Children with special needs sometimes need more teacher support in approaching and maintaining involvement in activities. They may have trouble initiating their own play idea or getting into the play of others. What they may need most is brief but frequent teacher guidance on how to join and participate in play activities. (Such methods will be discussed in Chapter 16.) They also may need teacher-guided activities related to skills that other children seem to acquire almost spontaneously. Pointing at objects might be an example. Most children need no help in learning to point; usually they have to be taught *not* to point. Children with perceptual motor problems or cognitive delays often need direct instruction in learning to point.

In arranging the location for teacher-guided activities, such as story reading or music and movement group time, a first consideration is ease of transition to and from other activity areas. Children can change activities more readily if teacher-planned interest centres and activities can be approached (and seen) from all other play areas. Furthermore, seeing that an attractive activity is starting up often serves as a cue. When a teacher wants to draw the children together for a group activity, children should be warned a few minutes ahead of time that they will need to be tidying up "in five minutes." A warning of a change can involve different communication modes, such as pictures, gestures, signs, objects, and music.

Children still in the process of tidying up a play area may need some teacher support in completing the task before moving on to the group activity. The teacher supporting the group activity can find subtle ways to involve a child who has a shorter attention span. During music and movement large-group times, some children are not able to attend the whole time. It is then appropriate to provide the child with an alternative activity.

Discovery Learning

Discovery learning includes child-initiated activities, a free choice of activities, and other opportunities to explore a range of learning centres set up by teachers. These should be given uninterrupted blocks of time in a well-planned play environment, both indoors and outdoors. The processes of exploration and experimentation are fundamental to early learning. It is through play that children discover their world and themselves. Play provides opportunities for children to apply their own ideas as well as the learning they have acquired in teacher-supported activities. At every developmental level, children need opportunities to play and to have access to play materials. Children with special needs, many of whom do not play of their own accord or even know how to play, must be helped to learn play skills. (Teaching children to play will be discussed in Chapter 16.)

Very young children and some children with developmental differences do not always benefit from *large* blocks of unstructured time. They may spend too much of their valuable time unengaged or inappropriately engaged because of their limited skills or short span of attention. For these children, brief teacher-structured activities are easily interspersed during free-play learning periods. Learning to point, mentioned earlier, will be used as an example:

Baillie needed to learn to point. During a play period, the teacher in the immediate area noticed Baillie standing about, seeming not to know what to do with herself. The teacher took her companionably by the hand, and said, "Let's go pointing" (an improvised game that Baillie enjoyed). While keeping her eye on the other children, the teacher walked around the area with Baillie for a minute or so, having her point to well-known objects. The teacher then helped Baillie point to what she would like to do next and followed up by having the teacher in that area help her settle in.

Discovery learning areas work well when they radiate from the location of teacher-supported learning centres and activities. Where these activity centres are placed is determined by furniture, storage, and the cleanup requirements of each area. Each centre should have sufficient space to allow a group of children to play comfortably together—including a child using a wheelchair, crutches, or a walker (Photo 15–7). Teachers' selection and grouping of materials in learning centres indicate clearly how each area is to be used. Children, and especially very young children and children with developmental differences, should not be given mixed signals. For example, some children are likely to think that it must be all right to colour in the library books if crayons are left on the bookshelves. The display of materials tells the child what to expect of the material and how to use it. This is particularly important in groups in which there are children with attention deficits or lower cognitive functioning. A broken or incomplete set of play materials should never be put out for children. (For example, it is better to have no puzzles than puzzles with even one missing piece.)

Photo 15–7
Each learning centre should have sufficient space.

Materials may need to be placed at different levels—on the floor, a wheelchair table tray, a raised table top—to allow each child access to materials independently or with assistance. Equipment and materials used and rotated should reflect the diverse needs of each child. Visual clues used to indicate play areas and expectations for behaviour should be varied: a picture, photograph, signed version, or the child's first language. Visual displays should represent human diversity; for example, photographs and posters should show all children (boys and girls and those with and without special needs) engaged in active play.

Including **anti-bias materials** that reflect developmental differences in learning centres benefits all children (Hall & Rhomberg, 1995). When children are exposed naturally to diversity through their play environment, they will more readily respect and accept human differences (Langford, 1997).

Anti-bias materials
learning materials (for example, adaptive scissors, dolls with leg braces) that reflect developmental differences

Photo 15–8
Diverse materials should be integrated into learning centres.

Example:

Karen's father was surprised when his daughter did not mention that her new friend, Lien, used a wheelchair. Karen's teachers explained that she was familiar with wheelchairs, having used one placed in the dramatic play area.

Show children appropriate uses of materials, such as crutches and Braille mats, and explain their purposes. Intervene when children are using materials inappropriately and model appropriate use. Some examples of materials to include in learning centres that foster awareness of diversity (Photo 15–8) include the following:

Creative art centre

- adaptive scissors
- left-handed scissors
- built-up handles of paintbrushes, crayons, and markers for an easier grip

Dramatic play centre

- dolls with varying abilities (with wheelchair, leg braces, crutches, eye glasses, etc.)
- communication materials, such as puppets, telephones, tape recorders, mirrors, computer, Braille writer, and picture boards

Outdoor area

- wheelchair route
- bells inside balls
- brightly painted ladder steps

EMERGENT CURRICULUM

Emergent curriculum
curriculum that is developed from a variety of sources, including children's play activities and questions, and that is personally meaningful, intellectually engaging, and socially relevant

Emergent curriculum is one approach to engage children in discovery learning. Emergent curriculum is described by Gestwicki (1998, p. 53) as a kind of curriculum that develops when exploring what is "socially relevant, intellectually engaging and personally meaningful to children." In theme-based teaching, adults decide what children will learn during a defined learning period. Sources for emergent curriculum, in contrast, can be children's play and questions, adult interests, events in the environment, developmental tasks, and cultural and spontaneous events. Interests and ideas are extended into long-term projects (Chard & Katz, 1989) or until the children begin to show an interest in a new subject or developmental task. In the emergent curriculum approach, children are viewed as competent learners and as producers of knowledge rather than as receivers of knowledge. Collaboration between teachers and children and between children during the process of learning about a topic or gaining new skills is considered an important feature of emergent curriculum.

Is emergent curriculum appropriate for children with special needs? Educators using the Reggio Emilia approach (a type of emergent curriculum) in Italy believe that a special curriculum should not be developed for children with special needs (Fraser, 2000). All children in a Reggio Emilia program participate at a level that is comfortable for them and express themselves using the "hundred languages of children." Fraser (p. 30) writes that educators in Reggio Emilia "believe that the image of the child as rich, strong, and powerful encompasses all children, including children with special rights, and that all children deserve to be given the support they need to reach their full potential."

Other educators view emergent curriculum as a way to fully motivate and engage learners. Pelo (1998) describes how a group of preschool children undertook a long-term project of getting a ramp built when a child's parent could not visit the centre because it lacked wheelchair accessibility. Julovich (1998, p. 128) describes the change in Chad, a school-aged child who used a computer (a chin switch to pick the letters) to communicate. Julovich shifted from setting writing activities to allowing learner choices for writing:

Chad experienced a new power in his daily efforts to tell what he knew or thought. From then on, he wrote every day about topics of his choice. He communicated ideas that were difficult or impossible for him to express any other way.

Teachers can practise emergent curriculum in other ways, such as these:

- Observe a child's play interests and integrate individual program plan (IPP) goals during extensions of the play interest.
- Use a problem to solve as the basis of a project. For example, a child has difficulty stepping into a swimming pool, so the child and his peers dig a hole in the sand, line it with plastic, and fill it with water. The children practised problem-solving, prosocial, and motor skills during the process of creating an alternative swimming pool. This example can be viewed in the video series *Making Friends* (Carr, 1997).
- Begin with a child's interest and create a topic or activity web.

  Example:

  Rao, a child with cerebral palsy, arrives at the centre with a small, fuzzy caterpillar in his hand. He wants to know what kind of caterpillar it is, what kind of cocoon it will make, what it eats, and what it will turn into. The other children crowd around to look at and admire Rao's find and ask questions of their own. The teacher puts aside her plans and quickly webs the questions. She asks the children where they might look for answers to their questions. The children brainstorm sources for information. They also discuss how they will care for Rao's caterpillar.

- Document learning processes through language samples, charts and graphs, creative art samples, photographs (depicting various stages of the children's activities), and videotaping. A documentation panel on activities or a project is posted so that the children and their families can view the learning process and the children's competencies and accomplishments.

Principles of Planning Early Learning Environments

Cutting across all aspects of environmental planning are certain basic principles. These include safety, visibility, ease of movement, teachers' availability, and structured flexibility.

SAFETY

Safety in early childhood settings and play yards is a major consideration in preventing accidents and fostering independence. Independence comes about only in a safe and secure environment where children know that adults can be depended on to protect them from harm and from harming themselves. Teachers should make sure that area rugs have nonskid backing or are glued or fastened down. A skidding rug is a hazard for all children and teachers and is especially hazardous for children who have visual or orthopedic impairments. Teachers also should make sure that materials and equipment are nontoxic, free of cracks and splinters, and in good working order. It is frustrating for any child to try to steer a wheel toy that has a bent axle; for a child with poor motor skills, it may lead to a serious accident. This can discourage the child from making further efforts to join in outdoor play. If the accident involved other children, avoidance of the child with special needs may follow. The children who were hurt (and their parents) usually do not understand that it was the equipment—not the child—that was at fault.

Order and Organization

Clutter and disorganization are incompatible with safety. Teachers must make sure that *everything has a place* and, when not in use, *everything is in its place*. A child with a visual impairment needs to know that the dough and cookie cutters and rolling pins (with no potentially hurtful things mixed in) are always to be found, for example, in the lower left corner of the dramatic play cupboards. Logical arrangements contribute to the child's independence; they enable the child to put materials away when finished with them, a responsibility of every child. The ongoing *restoration* of play areas is especially important in inclusive classrooms. The child mentioned above, who is visually impaired, needs to be confident that a rolling pin that rolled off the table earlier will not be left there for him or her to fall over later.

Teachers who routinely help children restore play areas after each use provide children with valuable lessons in common courtesy as well as regard for the physical safety of children with impairments (Photo 15–9). By the same token, regard for others also must be the concern of the child who uses special equipment. The child with an orthopedic impairment needs to learn how to position his or her crutches when they are not in use so they do not fall about, endangering others. A child who uses a wheelchair only part of the time must learn to park it in an agreed on place, not abandon it haphazardly.

Matching Children and Equipment

A critical aspect of safety has to do with matching equipment and materials to the skill levels of the children in the group. Wheel toys, all oversized, for example, pose a safety hazard for younger, smaller children. They also are a hazard for children with developmental differences, who may not be able to exercise good judgment in selecting suitable equipment. In many instances, the poor judgment is simply lack of experience. Children with special needs may be overprotected by well-meaning adults concerned about their safety. These children, if they are to develop independence, must learn to take risks. Learning to take risks, however, can be accomplished only where children are protected from becoming too frightened or seriously harmed.

The type of equipment and toys can also encourage or discourage play and engagement levels of children. If a particular child is frequently observed to engage in low levels of play, the teachers should take a look at the available activities. Are

Photo 15–9
Teachers help children restore play areas.

there materials at the child's play ability and level? Does the child need individual instruction to learn how to use the materials?

One final note about matching play materials with children has to do with the number of play materials available. If a classroom has only one of a very popular toy, the teachers can be sure that there will be problems with sharing. Although sharing is a critical skill for young children, teachers must find a balance between the amount of time they must intervene in "toy battles" and the best way to teach sharing. Teachers must determine that the room has an adequate number of materials so that children can use a desired toy within a reasonable amount of time. At the same time, be sure there are not so many toys and materials that the room is cluttered or that children do not have the opportunity to learn to share or wait their turn.

Safe Outdoor Environments

Outdoor play in a safe and carefully arranged play yard is an essential aspect of a quality program for young children. It is here that children practise physical skills, such as running, jumping, ducking, pumping, climbing, and kicking. They learn to throw, catch, and bat and to combine these skills into games. The outdoors also provides opportunities for children to learn voice and tone modulations—shouting, chanting, whistling, imitating a siren—all without causing discomfort for others.

Outdoor equipment (as well as indoor gym equipment) needs to be simple yet versatile. It should include ladders, planks, jumping boards, and simple climbing frames. There should be walking boards of various widths placed at different heights and combined with small portable climbing frames, ladders, and gangplanks with side rails. Equipment of this type can be arranged and rearranged to meet the needs of children with poor motor skills as well as those children with advanced skills. The arrangement in the outdoor area can be elaborate yet simple at the same time. Children just beginning to try out their gross motor coordination can be as well served as daring children in need of constant challenge.

VISIBILITY

A major function of early childhood education is encouraging children to explore and experiment with materials and equipment. This means that children are going to be taking risks as they try out new skills; therefore, they need to be visible to teachers at all times. Some of children's experiments will work; others will not. They all provide teachers with opportunities to teach. A six-year-old who decides to try jumping off a swing in motion, for example, presents a teaching opportunity. A teacher may make suggestions concerning speed and a jumping-off point suitable for a first attempt. Also, the teacher is alerted, ready to catch the child who does not heed suggestions or whose timing goes awry.

Visibility is especially critical in working with children with developmental differences who cannot always gauge the outcomes of their actions. At the first indication that a child is about to attempt something dangerously beyond his or her capabilities, the observant teacher can intervene immediately. The child's efforts can be redirected to provide encouragement for continued work on the skill, but in ways more suited to the child's skill level.

EASE OF MOVEMENT

Children and teachers need to be able to move about freely (Photo 15–10). Unobstructed traffic lanes and adequate space to manoeuvre trucks and doll carriages or wheelchairs and crutches enhance movement. Traffic lanes free of obstructions and

Photo 15–10
Teachers can support children's efforts in developing new skills.

unpleasant surprises (unmopped puddles of water on the floor, an abandoned doll carriage, or an upturned rug edge) are critical, especially for children with limited vision, as well as for those on crutches or in wheelchairs. Ease of movement within interest centres is important, too. Crowded activity areas, where children's movements are restricted, inevitably lead to conflict and aggression, as well as overstimulation for children with attention deficit hyperactivity disorders. Providing additional attractive interest centres prevents problems from arising. Small groups, of varying developmental levels, then have space to play together comfortably or side by side.

TEACHERS' AVAILABILITY

Teachers who are readily available are the key to a safe and comfortable early learning environment. Young children are learning *something* each of their waking moments. Teachers, therefore, must be available where they are most needed throughout the program day to facilitate learning. When children can move independently between activities, undistracted by inappropriate or unsafe activities, teachers can teach rather than police.

STRUCTURED FLEXIBILITY

To meet the range of developmental levels found within a group of young children, the learning environment must be well structured. At the same time it must be flexible and adaptable (Photo 15–11). Hence, **structured flexibility** is the ideal. A well-arranged environment, where rules and expectations are consistent, provides a secure yet freeing framework. Children can explore and test limits, and teachers can react spontaneously to the infinite variations in children's learning.

> **Structured flexibility**
> a well-structured early learning environment that also is adaptable to children's individual needs and preferences

Systematic planning and logical revision of arrangements are essential to both program structure and program flexibility. Both are based on teachers' periodic assessments of their programs. One instrument, the "Preschool Assessment of the Classroom Environment" (PACE) (McWilliam & Dunst, 1985) is useful and has been tested in inclusive environments.

Scheduling

In the inclusive setting, learning opportunities based on appropriate arrangements of space, material, and equipment are further enhanced by an organized schedule. Specific principles must be addressed when planning daily, weekly, seasonal, and year-long activity schedules for both children and teachers in an inclusive setting. Schedules vary. They are determined by the type of program, number of teachers, and the diverse needs of the children. The big hand of the clock should not rule programs. It is sequence of activities and allocations of ample time for children's learning needs

Photo 15–11
Learning environments must be well set up, flexible, and adaptive.

Photo 15–12
Child-directed activity periods can be extended as children become more experienced.

and interests that are the critical elements. The actual number of minutes spent in stories or transitions or snack time is irrelevant.

Two major scheduling factors are individual differences among children and their changing skill levels over time.

ACCOMMODATING INDIVIDUAL DIFFERENCES

To determine the sequence of activities, teachers must be sensitive to individual differences among children and to their special needs and preferences. Teachers should strive to maintain a global outlook of the overall plan of the day, the room setup, and the specific opportunities for learning. This view should vary during the year as teachers get to know children better and as children become more skilled in all areas of development (Photo 15–12). The length and type of activities and amount of outdoor time often differ from fall to winter, winter to spring, and spring to summer. In the fall, for example, children may need longer active play periods outdoors as they adapt to new children, new adults, and a group experience. In the winter, the colder weather and bulkier outdoor clothing may limit the range of activities available to some children with special needs, such as those with cerebral palsy, spina bifida, and other conditions that may affect physical coordination.

Many activities can be brought outdoors in warm weather. Easel painting and work with clay, for example, take on entirely different dimensions when done out in the fresh air. When basic components of the program are moved out of the indoor classroom and onto permanent outdoor tables, they give teachers and children a refreshing change of pace.

Depending on the developmental skills of children in a particular setting, the following strategies can be used to adapt large-group experiences indoors and outdoors (Gould & Sullivan, 1999, p. 22):

- shorten group time
- divide children into smaller groups
- provide chairs for children to sit on
- make group time optional
- provide alternative activities for children who need to leave the group time earlier

VARYING ACTIVITY LEVELS

Periods of high physical activity should alternate with periods of quiet activities. Most children are subject to a kind of *energy spillover* from active play periods. Therefore, learning experiences that require children's concentration should not be scheduled immediately following vigorous free play. A way around this is to insert a brief "cooling down" period, perhaps by spacing books at regular intervals on the circle area where a group music activity will be held. Books should always be available to children, even during free-play periods. If children are taught proper care of books from the start, their misuse during this transition activity is unlikely. As children assemble by ones and twos, they can look at books until the rest of the children have assembled and the music activity begins.

Children can be grouped in a variety of ways throughout the day: large group, small groups, multi-age groups, and siblings together. Multi-age groups, which consist of children of varying ages and abilities, give children natural opportunities to learn a variety of skills from younger or older children. In these groups, a child with special needs can assist a younger child in learning a new skill.

ENSURING ORDERLY SEQUENCES

Activity periods should generally follow predictable and **orderly sequences.** Most young children have trouble accepting any departure from what they are used to. Change in routines may be even more difficult for very young children and children with developmental differences. Children with pervasive developmental disorders (PDD) and attention deficit hyperactivity disorders (ADHD) frequently become overly attached to the daily schedule. Commonplace routines become rituals and must be held constant. Change is intolerable for some children; the unexpected may make the children extremely unsettled. All children (and most adults) feel more secure knowing what comes next.

Orderly sequences
events during an activity period follow a predicable pattern

GIVING ADVANCE NOTICE

Children do not give up on activities easily; teachers, therefore, should give advance notice or warning well ahead of an activity change (Photo 15–13). As stated earlier, several minutes before a transition, the teacher should advise the children: "Soon it will be time to put away the blocks and get ready for snack." It comes as no shock, then, when the teacher announces a few minutes later: "Time to get the blocks on the shelf; I'll help you get started." Ample time must be allowed for children to finish each activity and accomplish each routine. All children need the satisfaction that comes with task completion. Very young children and those who move slowly or with difficulty often need additional time. Therefore, activities and transitions should be scheduled so that all children can move at their own pace, whether fast or slow. A child who has a physical disability may require additional time to get from one place to another. This need should be recognized and the child should be appropriately cued when transitions are about to occur. It is demeaning to a child's efforts, even insulting, to carry a child who, given enough time, could walk from snack to music.

EMBEDDING LEARNING OPPORTUNITIES IN THE SCHEDULE

The challenge to teachers in a quality early childhood setting is to ensure that the children are always engaged in learning. Learning goals for children with developmental disabilities will include their IPP goals. Teaching to meet goals can happen any time a teaching occasion presents itself, but care should also be given to ensure that goals are regularly focused on by embedding these teaching opportunities throughout the day. For example, if a child has an IPP goal of greeting familiar adults, the teacher assigned to the greeting area will be sure to focus on that goal on a daily basis. Likewise, the teacher in the dramatic play area will

Photo 15–13
Teachers should give advance warning to prepare children for a change in activity.

Figure 15–1   SAMPLE SCHEDULE ILLUSTRATING THE INTEGRATION OF IPP GOALS
FOR PART OF AN EARLY CHILDHOOD PROGRAM DAY

Time	Activity	Teacher Location	Goals
8:30–9:15	Arrival	Teacher 1—Check-in Area	Sam—coat removal Belinda—greeting Anna—hang up belongings
8:30–9:45	Discovery Learning	Teacher 2—Blocks/Cars Teacher 3—Art Area	Fred—sharing Sarah Lynne—block building Tess—cutting Henry—expressive colour identification
9:15		Teacher 1—Manipulatives	Sam—six-piece puzzle Tess—bead stringing Anna—sorting by colour
9:45–10:00	Transition	Teacher 1—Wipe snack tables Teacher 2—Clean up block area Teacher 3—Clean up manipulatives	Fred—assisting teacher with snack prep Belinda—assist with cleanup Sam—hold containers for peers
10:00–10:20	Snack	Teacher 1—Break Teacher 2—Group A Teacher 3—Group B	Sam—communication board Belinda—pointing Henry—drink from cup Tess—picture exchange

work on individualized play skills with the children who have those goals in their IPP. By actually targeting times in the day during which ways to reach IPP goals are to be taught, teachers can provide children with regular opportunities to practise and strengthen these skills. See Figure 15–1 for a sample schedule showing this strategy.

Scheduled Time for Teachers

Teachers need scheduled times to carry out their own responsibilities and to have planned breaks during each session. Such time is not a luxury; it is essential. When children are present, the teacher's focus *must* be on teaching, *not* on preparing materials, *not* on cleaning up, *not* on discussing children's learning needs. A block of paid preparation time should be part of a teacher's schedule. Scheduled time for frequent, even though brief, staff meetings is also important. This can be most difficult to arrange in full-day programs, but it is not impossible. Here teachers discuss the events of immediate concern and the needs of individual children. Even the best of teachers are significantly less effective if they do not have scheduled, uninterrupted times to talk together about children's needs, staff–child relationships, and alterations in the physical setting or daily schedule. Daniel (1990) identified the failure to recognize the need for paid staff time for planning and preparation as one aspect of the current child care staffing crisis.

Transitions

In a quality program, a smooth transition appears effortless. The effortlessness is deceptive, however. It is the result of considerable planning, knowledge of each child, and attention to a multitude of details. Transitions should be used for teaching and for helping children learn about their own capabilities. At no time should children be waiting about idly or in rigidly enforced silence (Photo 15–14).

The underlying principle of smooth transitions is that each child moves individually, at his or her own pace, from one activity to the next. The individual differences among children provide the gradual movement between activities for the group as a whole. Children, because they use materials with different levels of involvement, will finish cleanup at varying times. Other children, because of different levels of self-help skills, will move through the cubby area routine and into discovery learning at different times. Some children may need to take a "transition toy" when moving from one transition to another. Other children may benefit from using transition cards or tickets that have a picture on them of the next activity (Gould & Sullivan, 1999).

Photo 15–14
Smooth transitions allow each child to move at his or her own pace from one activity to the next.

An appropriate curriculum cannot be carried out unless there is an adequate ratio of teachers to children. This is especially true in an inclusive early childhood program: The ratio of children to teachers must be increased as the number of children with special needs increases.

There may be a problem in some provinces and territories in which the size of the groups for young children is not legislated. In many of those provinces and territories where legislation does exist, group size may be too large for successful inclusion of children with special needs. The range of differences in group size for four- and five-year-olds varies, depending on the province or territory, from a maximum of 6 to a maximum of 30 children per group (Friendly, Beach, & Turiano, 2002).

Summary

Early childhood environments determine how well children learn and how well teachers teach. For children with developmental differences, an inclusive environment is the most suitable, with adaptations made for special needs. Teachers who provide a well-arranged learning environment communicate to children what it is that children can do in any given area. Children are less likely to transgress or behave inappropriately if the environment is well prepared.

The environment should be planned in terms of the types of learning that go on throughout the program day: self-help/care skills, teacher-guided activities, and discovery learning. Discovery learning that occurs within the emergent curriculum approach benefits all children because it focuses at a deeper level on children's competencies and interests. Teachers can arrange for activity areas that support the various kinds of learning in terms of five basic principles: safety, visibility, ease of movement, teachers' availability, and structured flexibility. Periodic assessment of all aspects of the environment is critical to advancing each child's development.

A daily schedule that is based on children's individual needs and differences furthers the benefits of the well-arranged classroom and play yard. Each segment of the daily schedule (in planned and predictable sequence) provides valuable opportunities for teaching and learning throughout the program day. All children are given advance notice when activity changes are scheduled; children with special needs often need extra advance warning and special help in dealing with departures from established routines. Regularly scheduled staff meetings, brief though they may be, allow teachers to teach more effectively.

Transitions are designed to enable each individual child to move at his or her own pace between program activities. Transitions characterized by large groups, idle waiting about, or rigidly enforced quiet create more misbehaviour and are detrimental to children's learning and self-esteem.

RESOURCES

THE PROJECT APPROACH
http://www.project-approach.com
This site describes how to implement the Project Approach, with specific examples of projects.

THE REGGIO EMILIA APPROACH
http://ceep.crc.uiuc.edu/poptopics/reggio.html
Information about the Reggio Emilia curriculum approach is available at this site.

WESTCOAST CHILD CARE RESOURCES CENTRE
http://www.wstcoast.org
This site provides access through its Marketplace link to multicultural/anti-bias resources.

STUDENT ACTIVITIES

1. Observe one child during free-play time in a preschool classroom. Track the pattern of the child's movement through activities over a 20-minute period. Indicate the activity areas in which the child was involved and the length of time spent in each, and list the areas the child did not approach.
2. Observe a preschool classroom and draw a rough sketch of the floor plan; indicate the location of furnishings, activity areas, doors, and windows. Which areas will accommodate a child who uses a wheelchair, crutches, or a walker? Which will not? Resketch the floor plan showing possible modifications that might better accommodate a child in a wheelchair.
3. Select any five activity areas in an early childhood program for three- and four-year-olds (e.g., music, easel painting, or water play). With three or four other students working with you as a teaching team, draw a basic plan for presenting these activities. Now decide among you what changes might be introduced into each structure to better serve both children who have developmental delays and children who are gifted.

4. Observe three different self-help routines in a child care centre. Describe the strengths and weaknesses of each for children with special needs according to the guidelines discussed in this chapter.
5. Draw up a daily schedule for a group of 16 four- and five-year-olds who are in an inclusive full-day child care program. Assuming three or four of these children need support with motor skills and cognitive skills, indicate special schedule adaptations that might be needed.

REFERENCES

Carr, A. (1997). Play and relationships: Programming for inclusion. *Interaction, 10*(4), 23–24.

Chard, S. & Katz, L. (1989). *Engaging children's minds: The project approach.* Norwood, NJ: Ablex.

Daniel, J. (1990). Child care: An endangered industry. *Young Children, 45*(4), 23–26.

Fraser, S. (2000). *Authentic childhood: Experiencing Reggio Emilia in the classroom.* Toronto: Nelson Thomson Learning.

Friendly, M., Beach, J., & Turiano, M. (2002). *Early childhood education and care in Canada 2001.* Toronto: University of Toronto, Childcare Resource and Research Unit, Centre for Urban and Community Studies.

Gestwicki, C. (1998). *Developmentally appropriate practice. Curriculum and development in early education.* Albany, NY: Delmar.

Gordon, A. M., & Browne, K. W. (2000). *Beginnings and beyond. Foundations in early childhood education* (4th ed.). Albany, NY. Delmar.

Gould, P., & Sullivan, J. (1999). *The inclusive classroom: Easy ways to adapt learning centers for all children.* Beltsville, MD: Gryphon House.

Hall, N. S., & Rhomberg, V. (1995). *The affective curriculum: Teaching the anti-bias approach to young children.* Toronto: Nelson Thomson Learning.

Harms, T. (1989). Creating environments for growing and learning. In A. M. Gordon & K. W. Browne, *Beginnings & beyond: Foundations in early childhood education* (2nd ed.). Albany, NY: Delmar.

Julovich, B. (1998). Emergent curriculum. In E. A. Tertell, S. M. Klein, and J. L. Jewett (Eds.), *When teachers reflect: Journeys toward effective, inclusive practice* (pp. 121–129). Washington, DC: National Association for the Education of Young Children.

Langford, R. (Ed.). (1997). *The checklist for quality inclusive education: A self-assessment tool and manual for early childhood settings.* London, ON: Early Childhood Resource Teacher Network of Ontario.

McWilliam, R. A., & Dunst, C. J. (1985). *Preschool assessment of the classroom environment. Unpublished scale.* Family, Infant, and Preschool Program, Western Carolina Center, Morganton, NC.

Pelo, A. 1996. Our school's not fair: A story about emergent curriculum. In D. Curtis & M. Carter (Eds.), *Reflecting young children's lives: A handbook for planning child-centered curriculum* (pp. 101–106). St. Paul, MN: Redleaf Press.

CHAPTER 16 | Facilitating Social Development

KEY CONCEPTS

affection or friendship training
contingent stimulation
environmental structuring
incidental social learning

self-assertion
social reinforcement
teacher-mediated interventions

OBJECTIVES

After studying the material in this chapter, the student will be able to

- Define social skills and explain their importance in the overall development of young children, especially children with developmental differences.
- Defend this statement: *The degree to which parents and caregivers respond appropriately to an infant's cues may be a major factor in determining that child's social development.*
- Describe the possible impact of developmental differences on early social development.
- Describe ways in which a teacher can structure an early childhood setting to foster social interactions.
- List at least 10 ways a teacher can help children with special needs learn appropriate play and social skills.
- Identify strategies teachers can use to structure peer-mediated social interactions.

Introduction

Social development occurs through each individual acquiring a wide range of skills that help people live together in a family, in a culture, and in a society. Gordon and Browne (2004) suggest four categories (called the Four Hows) for the wide range of skills children learn in the early years: (1) *how to approach*, to get in and be included; (2) *how to interact*, through sharing and cooperating; (3) *how to deal with difference*, such as teasing, bullying, including, and helping others; and (4) *how to manage conflict* by problem solving and handling aggression. All children must learn these skills. How well they are learned depends on the quality of the interpersonal relationships in the child's everyday life. Only through interacting with others can infants and young children learn the social skills (as well as the accompanying language and intellectual skills) necessary for optimal development. Only through interacting with others can young children get feedback about their social competence.

Photo 16–1
Taking turns is an important early learning skill.

Interpersonal relationships are reciprocal; that is, there is mutual responding or *turn-taking* (Photo 16–1). During the early months and years, social interactions depend on the child's ability to give and receive social messages. Children with special needs may fail to respond to social signals, or they may give too few appropriate signals. Either situation reduces feedback and may lead to negative responses; both situations will interfere with emerging social development. It is not unusual for the social delays in children with special needs to become a greater concern than those associated with their primary disability (McLean, Bailey, & Wolery, 1996).

No child should be excused from learning acceptable social skills. To exempt the child from this type of learning does the child a grave injustice. Many children seem to acquire social skills spontaneously or with only brief episodes of informal coaching. Children with developmental differences often need systematic help; appropriate social behaviours may have to be taught directly, over a considerable time. How teachers can help young children who acquire such a repertoire of social behaviours is the focus of this chapter. First, however, social skills will be examined from a developmental perspective.

Social Skills and Overall Development

Though discussed as an independent topic, social skills are never truly separate from other areas of development. Each influences all others. The following example illustrates the close interrelatedness of skills:

John ran to Aaron, who was sitting on the edge of the sandbox filling cake tins with sand.

John began, "Let's decorate cakes. Here are some decorations," and he poured small plastic rings into Aaron's cupped hands. Aaron replied: "Too many," handing a few back. "That's plenty."

John smiled at Aaron and began alternating rings around the edge of his sand cake while singing, "Now a blue one, now a yellow one."

Aaron stuck twigs into his sand cake and pulled a ring down over the top of each twig. Then he sang "Happy Birthday" several times, each time naming a different classmate.

A number of developmental skills can be identified in this play interaction. Both large and small motor skills are evident: running, pouring, catching, picking, and placing. Cognitive skills include arithmetic concepts of some, too many, and plenty, as well as colour recognition, naming colours, and understanding such concepts as *decorate* and *alternate* ("now a blue one, now a yellow one"). Memory was obvious, too, with Aaron singing "Happy Birthday" and recalling several classmates' names. Both children demonstrated good communication skills in the form of verbal exchanges, listening to each other, and smiling.

These developmental skills were in addition to, and blended with, high-level social skills:

- each child initiating his own ideas
- following suggestions from each other
- sharing materials
- role-playing as cake decorators

This exchange shows the developmental complexities that work for some children but *against* others. In the John and Aaron episode, each child was helping the other to learn and each was spontaneously reinforcing the other for a variety of skills and responses. *Spontaneous* peer reinforcement may not always happen for children with developmental differences; instead, their poorly developed play skills often lead to rejection. A negative cycle can then be set in motion. A continuing lack of skills shuts out further opportunities to learn. The lack of learning opportunities results in little positive feedback. The combination sometimes sets up emotional reactions that, as noted earlier, may cause as much developmental interference as the disability itself. It is important, therefore, that young children with (and without) developmental differences be helped to learn *appropriate* social skills (Photo 16–2).

Photo 16–2
It is important that all children be helped to learn social skills.

Appropriate Social Skills: What Are They?

One definition of *appropriate social skills* is that they are prescribed ways of behaving: They are the expectations of particular social groups as to how group members will conduct themselves in private and in public. Prescriptions for what is socially appropriate vary from community to community, culture to culture, and society to society. Variations exist even within the tight circle of home, early childhood centre, and neighbourhood. Confusing choices often result, especially for young children.

Examples:

As the youngest, five-year-old Doug is given anything he wants by his parents and teenage brother when he demands something. The same demands in the neighbourhood and preschool did not pay off. Children refused to give in and ran off, leaving him shrieking.

Rebecca painted with obvious enjoyment during the first week of school. One day she began to cry, pointing to a small paint smudge on her sleeve. The teacher assured her it would wash out and that the apron protected most of her dress. Rebecca would not return to the easel, even on subsequent days. What emerged were confusing social expectations between home and school. Teachers had assured Rebecca that it was all right if paint got on clothing; at home, her parents were concerned when "good school clothes got all dirty."

Lynn spent much of her time playing in the streets with older children. There she learned to hit, run, dodge, grab, and kick, all social skills necessary to that particular street setting. In the preschool, these same behaviours were considered socially unacceptable. Lynn had to learn to restrain the behaviours at school but to keep them ever ready when playing in the street.

These examples, described by teachers, are from real life. They point out how difficult it is to specify what is appropriate. In each instance, children were exhibiting social skills relevant to given situations in their lives; yet they were also receiving contradictory signals about the inappropriateness of those same behaviours in another context. Most children learn to deal with such contradictions. They find ways to adapt their behaviour to the expectations of various situations (a social skill necessary, for all of us, at every life stage). Such adaptations tend to be more difficult for children with special needs. They are likely to have trouble learning to discriminate when behaviour is appropriate and when it is inappropriate.

Rather than attempting to define a term like *social skills,* it may be of greater value to list the various aspects of these skills. The major social skills to be learned during the early years relate to getting along with others:

- interacting with children and adults, in a variety of ways, at home and away from home
- trusting and enjoying known adults outside the immediate family (Photo 16–3)
- recognizing and protesting inappropriate advances from known or unknown adults within or outside the family
- attending to self-help/care needs at home and in public places with consideration for others
- sometimes initiating play ideas with children and at other times following other children's lead
- participating in group activities through listening, taking turns, and contributing to group effort
- sometimes putting aside individual needs and interests so the needs and interests of the group may be met
- working and playing independently as well as cooperatively; learning to be alone without feeling isolated or rejected
- using language as the powerful social tool it is for persuading, defending, reasoning, explaining, solving problems, and getting needs and preferences attended to

Learning social skills is a complex task involving a wide range of values, knowledge, and skills. Kostelnik, Whiren, Soderman, Stein, and Gregory (2002) describe the necessary ingredients:

- *Cultural competence:* having knowledge of, comfort with, and respect for people of varying ethnic or racial backgrounds

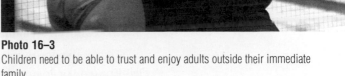

Photo 16–3
Children need to be able to trust and enjoy adults outside their immediate family.

- *Planning and decision-making skills:* making choices, solving problems, and planning ahead
- *Self-regulation:* having the ability to monitor ourselves, reflect on feelings, and resist temptation and peer pressure
- *Interpersonal skills:* maintaining friendly relationships and communicating needs, ideas, and feelings
- *Positive self-identity:* demonstrating sense of competence, purpose, and worth
- *Social values:* exhibiting caring and demonstrating responsibility, honesty, and flexibility

Acquiring Social Skills

Social skills are learned behaviours. Children's learning of a full range of social skills—*the socializing process*—cannot be forced or hurried. Mastering such skills is a major occupation of the developing child. Refinement of previously learned social skills and the learning of new ones continues throughout life.

TEMPERAMENT AND EMOTIONS

The development of social skills, as noted earlier, is influenced by home, school, community, and cultural expectations, and by the interpersonal relations within these environments. A child's emotional reactions, or more precisely, temperament, also exert influence (Photo 16–4). Based on differing behavioural patterns and ways of responding, Thomas and Chess (1977) described three types of infants: *easy*, *difficult*, and *slow to warm up*.

These personality or temperament traits may have genetic linkage. However, this is difficult to demonstrate and also relatively unimportant. What is important is that babies respond differently to what may be similar circumstances (as when they are in the same infant care program). These personal behaviour patterns appear to persist into childhood, affecting how others respond to a child. Parents and caregivers play a role in the persistence of personality traits. Behaviours that one caregiver reacts to as constituting a difficult temperament might not be perceived as at all difficult by another caregiver. That person might describe the child as eager, active, and happy-go-lucky.

Although every child's social responses are influenced by temperament, the fact remains that all social behaviours are learned. They can be seen and heard and sometimes felt, as when one child pats or strikes another. Social skills are observable ways of behaving (Photo 16–5). Like all behaviours, they can be eliminated, strengthened, or modified. This is true even of those responses labelled *emotional*. These, too, can be eliminated, strengthened, and modified. It is through their behaviours that we know children's emotional state—that we know whether they are feeling good about themselves, sympathetic toward others, hostile, generous, or fearful.

Picture the following:

- three children jumping on a jumping board, smiling, and talking
- two children laughing while they divide cookies
- a five-year-old running from a snarling dog
- two children walking together with arms entwined

Such behaviours provide specific clues as to which children are feeling happy, frightened, or loving. They provide clues, too, as to how well the children's social

Photo 16–4
A child's temperament influences social development.

skills are developing. Each of the responses was *learned* through social interactions with the child's physical and interpersonal environment. By carefully observing children's behaviours (facial expressions, bodily postures, gestures, verbalizations), children's emotions can be recognized and dealt with in ways that strengthen both their emotional development and their social skills.

SOCIAL REINFORCEMENT

The development of appropriate social skills begins with infant bonding, attachment, and the establishment of basic trust. As the child matures, the further development of social skills depends

Photo 16–5
Social skills are made up of observable behaviours.

almost entirely on the amount and type of **social reinforcement** available to the child when still young. All children need opportunities to interact with others in a give-and-take fashion. Most newborns *come equipped* with social behaviours that attract and hold the attention of significant adults. In the typical situation, the baby cries and someone comes and provides comfort. The baby is soothed and stops crying. The caregiver is pleased. This puts in motion a reciprocal system that is socially and mutually reinforcing for both infant and adult. Even the newborn is highly skilled at taking turns. Bee (1999) puts it this way:

Social reinforcement
the positive and negative feedback that children receive from adults and peers that leads to further learning, either appropriate or inappropriate

> As early as the first days of life, the baby sucks in a "burst-pause" fashion. He sucks for awhile, pauses, sucks for awhile, pauses, and so on. Mother enters into this "conversation," too, often by jiggling the baby during the pauses. The conversation looks like this, suck, pause, jiggle, pause, suck, pause, jiggle, pause. The rhythm of the interaction is really very much like a conversation and seems to underlie many of the social encounters among people of all ages. The fascinating thing is that this rhythm, this turn-taking, can be seen in an infant one day old.

Adult Responsiveness

Social reinforcement, in the form of adult responsiveness, is a crucial factor in determining how well a child's social skills will develop (Photo 16–6). When an adult responds to something an infant does by giving attention, a smile, or a kind word, or by fondling, the infant

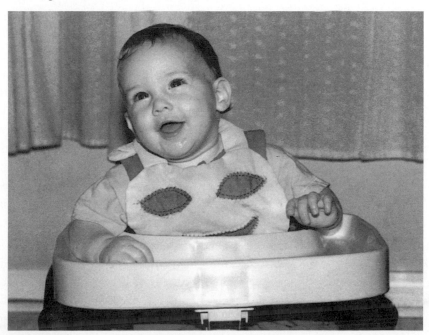

Photo 16–6
Infants soon learn that smiling makes good things happen.

will repeat that behaviour more and more frequently. If an adult ignores the behaviour, it will happen less and less.

The process of adult reinforcement is sometimes referred to as **contingent stimulation.** The degree to which parents, caregivers, and family members respond appropriately to the infant's cues may be a major factor in determining a child's social development.

Contingent stimulation responding to a child in a way that prompts further learning

As noted in Chapter 4, when there is at least partially contingent stimulation (responding) from significant adults, infants and young children develop better. Language skills develop earlier and children have more advanced cognitive abilities, greater self-esteem, and more durable attachments.

THE IMPACT OF DEVELOPMENTAL DIFFERENCES

A potentially responsive early environment cannot guarantee that a child will develop necessary and appropriate social skills. Through no fault of parents or care-givers, children with developmental differences often are deprived of stimulation and reinforcement. Consider these examples:

- An infant who is deaf cannot hear the crooning, loving sounds that his or her parents make during bathing, dressing, and feeding routines. Thus, the infant does not make lively responses. The lack of responsiveness reduces the parent's efforts to interact. To further compound the situation, an infant's hearing loss often goes undetected during the developmentally crucial early months. Not realizing that their infant has a hearing impairment, parents may take the infant's lack of interest in their conversation as rejection; unwittingly, they may respond less positively to the child, as well as less often. Social reciprocity, the give-and-take of the system, goes awry. This puts the child's social development, as well as cognitive and language development, at risk.

- Infants who are blind also are at high risk for poorly developed social skills. According to Fraiberg (1974), they do not engage in the mutual gaze interactions that appear to be crucial to the attachment process between parent and child. Mothers of babies who are blind often report that they feel rejected when their infants do not look at them. Interestingly enough, Fraiberg noted that four-week-old babies who are blind did begin to smile just as the babies who are sighted did. But then, something happened. At about two months, when the sighted babies were smiling with increasing delight at their mother's face, the babies with visual impairment were smiling less frequently and more tentatively. Gradually, the mothers in Fraiberg's studies on infant blindness seemed to withdraw psychologically from their babies, even though they continued to give physical care.

These examples do not imply that children with developmental differences cannot learn appropriate social skills. Quite the contrary—they can and do. With the help of relevant members of the interdisciplinary team, parents learn to recognize in their infants alternative kinds of signalling and responding behaviours. An infant who is blind, for example, may begin to thrash about at the sound of the parent's approaching footsteps. The child's parent comes to value this response in the same way they would value a welcoming smile from an infant who is sighted. Another example is that the infant who is deaf may snuggle in when picked up. The parent learns to respond by stroking the child rhythmically—better yet, by stroking *and* singing or crooning. Though the baby does not hear the singing, it usually gives pleasure to the parent. The singing may also transmit subtle vibrations from the parent's chest or throat that further stimulate the infant's responsiveness.

Overstimulation and overresponding may also interfere with an infant's ability to make use of a responsive environment. Overstimulation often occurs among fragile infants—those who are premature or of very low birthweight. They are easily over-loaded with (what are for them) too many signals coming in from the environment. Their underdeveloped nervous systems simply cannot handle the *rush* and so the infant *shuts down*, withdraws, and may become rigid or even rejecting of loving pats and cuddling. In a sense, the infant is "unavailable to its environment, becoming unable to obtain information or give feedback and, in turn, causing the parents and other caregivers to feel less competent and effective" (Bennett, 1990, p. 36). The opposite is true of the overresponding infant. In some instances, an infant with a central nervous system (CNS) disorder, for example, may have an involuntary but rigid arm extension when attempting to turn its head into a nursing position. The infant's strong-arming may be perceived by the parent or caregiver as rejec-tion or obstinacy, a reaction that interferes with establishing a warm relationship (Taft, 1981).

These illustrations point out, once again, the need to identify special needs as early in infancy as possible. Early identification, followed by interdisciplinary intervention for infant and family, is a key factor in preventing other behaviours (insecure attachment, for example) that invariably compound the special needs of the child.

Guralnick (1996) has developed an assessment tool called the Assessment of Peer Relations (APR) for evaluating social competence in preschoolers. This researcher identifies three social tasks important to young children: (1) peer group entry, (2) conflict resolution, and (3) the maintenance of play. Teachers can use this assess-ment tool to determine a child's use of social strategies specific to each task. Underlying emotional, social, and cognitive processes (such as emotional regulation and shared understanding) used by the child when selecting a social strategy are then assessed. Guralnick's work points out how complex peer interactions are and the importance of frequent adult intervention and support.

Promoting the Development of Social Skills

A number of strategies can be used to promote social interactions among children and the development of social skills in early childhood settings. The two main categories of strategies are

1. **Environmental structuring:** Teachers arrange features of the physical environment (e.g., materials, equipment, and interest areas) to foster social interaction.
2. **Teacher-mediated interventions:** Teachers provide direct support. For example, they may prompt children to engage in social interactions.

Environmental structuring
teachers arrange features of the physical environment to foster social interaction

Teacher-mediated interventions
teachers provide direct support to encourage children to engage in social interactions

STRUCTURING THE ENVIRONMENT

The materials and equipment available to children greatly influence their learning of social skills. Paints, crayons, and scissors, for example, are most commonly used in nonsocial but constructive play activities (Rubin & Howe, 1985). Materials that have proven to be good socializers include the following:

- housekeeping and dress-up play materials
- mural-painting and collage-pasting materials (several children work on the same piece of long paper)
- unit blocks and large hollow blocks
- trucks, cars, and airplanes
- lotto and other simple board games
- musical instruments
- puppets

When small groups gather, there need to be sufficient materials to go around, thus inviting each child's participation. It is also a good idea to have some duplicate materials. A child with a developmental difference then has the opportunity to use the same material as another child and so learn appropriate usage through imitation. Conversely, having too many different materials tends to promote solitary play. For example, a wheel toy for every child defeats a major goal of most programs—that of promoting sharing and turn-taking. A practical ratio is about one wheel toy to every three or four children; all kinds of inventive doubling-up games and cooperative ventures can be the result, such as wagon and tricycle trains.

Social interaction is more likely to occur when the environmental barriers among interest areas (e.g., blocks, dramatic play, and cognitive area) are reduced. Interest areas, such as sand, clay, and blocks, promote social interaction among children that ranges from early parallel and associative play to the most advanced cooperative play.

TEACHER-MEDIATED INTERVENTION

Play is the major avenue for early learning of every kind. Even in infancy, most children seem to play spontaneously and apparently effortlessly. In play-oriented early childhood programs, children appear to be self-propelled as they move through the curriculum. They learn new skills and practise them in the course of self-initiated play activities. They participate in group activities and join eagerly in teacher-initiated play opportunities. Almost every skill that children master is mastered through play.

Children with special needs may need more adult support in learning how to play. The play of children with hearing impairments is less social and more solitary than that of children who are hearing (Anita & Kreimeyer, 1992). However, children with a severe hearing loss, even those with serious language deficits, have been reported as having imaginary playmates. As for children with severe visual impairments, Skellenger, Hill, and Hill (1992) report significant delays in their symbolic play (make-believe, pretend, using one object to represent another—as when a doll blanket becomes a magic cape). Children with autistic behaviours or limited cognitive skills also tend to be lacking in symbolic play skills. This may lead to inappropriate use of materials, such as hammering the cookie cutters with the rolling pin or breaking the crayons into little pieces.

In general, children with developmental differences have fewer play skills (Photo 16–7). Often they hang back, not knowing how to get into other children's play. Or, they try to gain entry in inappropriate ways—for example, crashing a truck into housekeeping play—which leads to rejection. It is essential, therefore, that children who do not know how to play be taught. Teaching children to play may seem contrary to tradition. Yet no child should be deprived of this powerful avenue for learning and the many enjoyable experiences that come with it.

Strategies for teaching and supporting the development of play skills include the following:

- Physically guiding the child to a play activity and helping him or her to settle in.
- Orienting the child toward the material or equipment and handing the material to the child to establish physical contact.
- Putting a clothespin (or some other object) into the child's hand, and moving the hand so that it is directly above the container into which the object is to be placed.

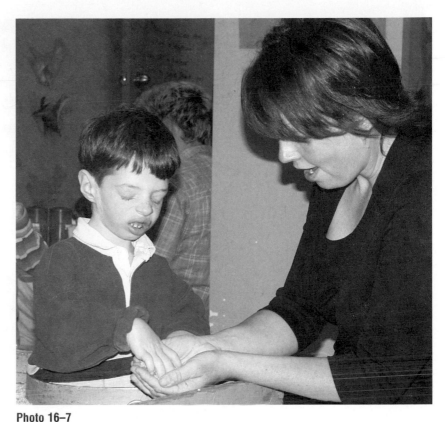

Photo 16–7
Children with developmental differences may have fewer play skills.

- Verbalizing to the child what he or she is doing: "You have a clothespin in your hand. You can drop it in the can."
- Rejoicing over the smallest accomplishments: "Look at that!" or "Did you hear that! You dropped the clothespin in the can." (In the beginning it does not matter that the child is involved only because the teacher's hand is around the child's hand, manually shaping the child's response.)
- Arranging for the child to be near other children in a given activity, thereby enabling the teacher to point out and describe what other children are doing and so begin to promote imitation (Photo 16–8, p. 342).
- Gradually helping other children join in activities, once the child has acquired a semblance of a play skill (e.g., two children might drop clothespins into the same can).
- Providing social reinforcement for the play: "It looks as if you two are going to fill that can full of clothespins!"
- Moving the child slowly but steadily toward group play by building small groups of two, then choosing three nonthreatening children who participate with the child with special needs in simple play activities, such as tossing beanbags into a box.
- Providing specific words if the child experiences a conflict with another child. Avoid the pat phrase, "use your words," as children often need adults to guide them verbally through the process of conflict resolution.

As a child with special needs begins to play more spontaneously, teachers should continue their assistance but in a less directive fashion. For example, when helping

Photo 16–8
Arranging for a child to work or play near another child facilitates social development.

a group of children decide where to play after music time, the teacher reviews the options for each child. The child with special needs is helped to choose after several other children have made their choices. Because the child has heard the choices reviewed several times and has heard several children choosing, making a choice becomes easier. It is helpful, too, for the teacher to pair the child who has a special need with another child who has chosen the same activity. This provides a good model for the child who is learning new skills both in locating the activity and in getting off to a good start.

Activities must be planned carefully so that children with developmental differences can experience maximum success. When a child with a severe visual impairment is participating in an art activity, the teacher might describe and physically help the child locate materials by guiding his or her hand:

"Here is the big circle to paste the little circles on. The little circles are here in the basket. Here is the paste, by your right hand. The sponge to wipe your fingers on is next to it. Corliss is working across the table from you." (This promotes the activity's social aspect.)

Along with helping the child who has developmental differences, teachers also need to help all children learn to be explicit about what they are doing in certain situations. For example, it can be disconcerting for a child who cannot see to have materials moved from the rehearsed location. Yet telling the other children not to touch his or her materials may cast a negative shadow on the child who has a special need. Instead, children can be taught the simple social skill, the courtesy (due all children) of stating what they are doing whenever they use or change another person's materials: "Kelly, I need some of your paste. I'm going to move it over here [guiding Kelly's hand] so we can share."

Gentle Insistence

Not all children with developmental differences are eager to play, nor do they want to be taught to play; they may even avoid play materials and would-be playmates (Photo 16–9). These are the children who sometimes need to be gently "pushed" just to get them to try a play activity that teachers know will be of developmental benefit to them.

Example:

Jolene was a somewhat solitary three-year-old with cerebral palsy. An instructional objective written into her individual program plan (IPP) by the interdisciplinary team was that Jolene learn to ride a tricycle. The physical therapist adapted a tricycle by adding a trunk support and stirrups. Jolene, however, would not get on. Teachers' coaxing intensified her resistance until just the sight of the tricycle set her to crying. The teachers were ready to give up—but not the physical therapist, who impressed on them the therapeutic value of tricycle riding for this particular child. The therapist maintained that this preschool treatment would promote more general development, as well as motor coordination, than any number of clinic sessions.

After talking it over with Jolene's parents, a plan was agreed on: One teacher would lift Jolene onto the tricycle and support (and comfort) her while the therapist put Jolene's feet in the stirrups and pulled the vehicle from the front. This they did, with Jolene crying louder and louder at first. The teacher continued to support her physically and to comfort her while the therapist moved the tricycle gently forward. Gradually, Jolene quieted.

Photo 16–9
Teachers may need to gently "insist" that a child try a play activity that will be of developmental benefit.

Within a few days she stopped resisting the riding sessions. Furthermore, and much to the teachers' relief, she appeared to be enjoying the sessions. Six weeks later, Jolene was riding her specially fitted tricycle independently, in the company of other children. Giving in to Jolene's anxieties (as well as the teachers') would have meant depriving Jolene of learning a play skill central to both her mobility and her social development.

Incidental Social Learning

As in the above instance, there are times when it is not only appropriate but even urgent to teach play skills directly. Most of the time, however, teachers can promote **incidental social learning** fairly easily by being alert to what goes on naturally among children. More frequently than we tend to realize, brief, positive interactions occur between children with and without special needs: smiling, handing materials, moving aside, helping to pick up the pieces of a dropped puzzle, and so on. Teachers can quietly comment about these commonplace interactions: "Martin, when you held the door open for Corey it was easy for him to get his wheelchair through. See how he is smiling at you?" When the teacher makes similar comments to Corey, both children are introduced to a higher level of socialization. The result may be interaction between the two.

Children's concern or anxiety about another child's developmental differences also offers opportunities for incidental social learning. A teacher may notice a child

Incidental social learning
the teacher promotes social interactions as they arise naturally and spontaneously

Photo 16–10
Teachers should acknowledge a child's concern over another child's eye patch.

looking obliquely at the black patch over another child's eye, or witness one child showing reluctance to hold another child's malformed hand, or overhear a child expressing fear about catching the paralysis of the child in a wheelchair. The children's concerns are genuine and not to be shushed or ignored. They provide opportunities for teachers to promote social learning and interactions. Often the teacher and the child with a developmental difference can respond together. Using the eye patch case as an example, the teacher might first acknowledge the one child's concern and then help the second child explain. If the child with the eye patch is not communicating verbally, the teacher can explain and ask for the child's corroboration (Photo 16–10): "The doctor put the patch on one eye so your other eye can learn to see better, right?" The explanation can be expanded further, depending on the interest and comfort level of both children. The teacher should always work to explain to the concerned child that "catching" developmental differences will not occur and that there are many, many things the other child can do. Often the two children can be guided into a joint activity at that point.

A child's first tentative steps toward joining a play situation are another form of incidental social learning that teachers need to note and reinforce. The child who stands and watches may be nearly ready to interact. A teacher might watch with the child for a moment or two at a time, while commenting on the activity: "It looks as if Bart is making cookies and Cami's making a pie." Another time, sensing the child's readiness, the teacher might help the child actually get into play: "Matt is bringing more cookie cutters for everybody to use." The teacher also can prompt the other children directly or indirectly.

Example:

Josh, a child with Down syndrome, had a drum in his hand but was standing apart from a small group of children who were experimenting with rhythm instruments. Teacher: "It sounds as though you need a drummer in your band." (pause) Teacher: "You could ask Josh. He has a drum." If Josh joined in, the teacher could then provide reinforcement to all, as a group: "What a good band! Mary and Meg and Fouad and Josh and Karen, your music sounds really good." (It is best not to make specific mention of the children having invited Josh into the group; this could make Josh stand out unnecessarily as being so different as to need special treatment.)

Incidental social learning can be expanded even further through play activities already in progress. Teachers need to reinforce the interaction, but subtly, to avoid distracting either child. Depending on the situation the teacher might

- move closer, kneel down, watch with interest, but avoid eye contact to keep from interrupting the children's mutual focus.
- smile and nod if either child turns toward the teacher, but keep the focus on the activity, not the child.
- bring additional materials to extend the play, placing them close to the activity (with or without comment, depending on the situation).
- make encouraging comments that further promote joint effort: for example, "Missy and Sam, you are building a long, long road. It looks as if it's going to go all the way to the gate!"

Frequent episodes of social interaction among children with and without special needs characterize quality inclusion programs. Such intermixing is most likely to occur, according to Wolery (1994, p. 115), "when children with special needs are in small groups, when competent peers are in the group, when the group includes mixed ages, and when teachers encourage and support exchanges and imitation."

Facilitating Affection and Friendship

Teachers can promote positive social interactions between children with and without special needs through **affection or friendship training** (McEvoy, Twardosz, & Bishop, 1990). These researchers suggest that group games, songs, and rhythmic activities can be adapted to promote interaction. In such activities as the Hokey Pokey, If You're Happy and You Know It, or The Farmer in the Dell, teachers can readily change the words to promote both physical and verbal exchanges as when the mother hugs the child and the child hugs the dog (Brown, Raglund, & Bishop, 1989).

Twardosz, Norquist, Simon, & Botkin (1983) offer three reasons to explain the effectiveness of the affection procedure in promoting social interactions between children with special needs and those without. One is the pairing of two children of differing abilities in a pleasurable experience. A second has to do with desensitization—children getting used to each other and inevitably less wary of differences. And third, children are given opportunities to practise affectionate behaviours in a nonthreatening and supportive situation.

There are a number of curriculum packages that can help educators teach social skills (see the Resources section at the end of this chapter) to children who are struggling with social development. These resources are most successful when the concepts and skills are transferred and practised by adults and children within a natural context.

> **Affection or friendship training**
> specific programs that promote positive social interactions between children with and without special needs

Sharing and Taking Turns

Sharing and taking turns are the foundation for good play exchanges among children (Photo 16–11). Yet these skills are the most difficult to learn because they involve *giving up something;* giving up anything is contrary to the young child's egocentric view of the world. "Mine! Mine! Mine!" is the clarion call of most children at some point in their development (at least in our country). With adult support, patience, and many unpressured opportunities to learn, most children eventually cooperate when a teacher says: "Mary, two more turns around the driveway and then its Sara's turn." The teacher can say this in many different ways to each child, over the weeks and months: "Sara, watch. Mary is going around the driveway two more times; then it will be your turn. Let's count." Or, "Mary, Sara has waited a long, long time for the tricycle you were riding, so she gets a long turn, too. I'll call you when she's through."

Photo 16–11
Sharing and turn-taking are the foundations for good play exchanges among children.

Gradually reducing the amount of available material is another way to teach sharing. Once again, it is the teacher who orchestrates opportunities that facilitate social interaction. Conflict among children is avoided when the teacher structures sharing experiences carefully, monitors the situation, and helps children manage the process.

Examples:

A teacher might put out fewer but larger portions of play dough to encourage children to divide their dough with latecomers to the activity. With the teacher's help, some children (certainly not all) will be able to break off a part of their dough; when two or three children do this, and the newcomer has an adequate amount to work with, the teacher can then reinforce the act of sharing. A spinoff is that children who did the sharing have provided good models for the children not yet able to share.

Several individual baskets of coloured wooden cubes might be poured into one larger basket. The children must then share common but plentiful material. Again, the teacher must be there to guide, partly by assuring the children there is plenty for all. If one child is accused of taking more than his or her share, the teacher might suggest that each child take no more than five cubes at a time (thus teaching counting, concurrently).

A child who has great difficulty sharing may be put in charge of a plentiful but uncontested material, perhaps tickets for snacks, or for a "train ride" (chairs lined up), or tickets "just because." The tickets may be nothing more than a quantity of small squares of coloured paper—irresistible, nonetheless, to most young children. As the child passes out the tickets, the teacher can comment on how well the child is sharing his or her tickets and also might point out, "You have a lot of tickets left too."

It is the responsibility of the teacher to promote and respond to friendly interactions between two children, thereby making spontaneous sharing somewhat easier. When two children decide to work on a puzzle together, the teacher can reinforce the friendly interaction by sitting down briefly and watching the children work. When two children are using a wagon together, the teacher may spend some time pulling them around. Teachers can also point out situations that involve friendly interactions: "Martha and Jay, you really have a long train now that you have hitched all your cars together." In addition, teachers can help children wait for a turn or a material by offering the child alternatives until the preferred material is available.

Self-Assertion

Self-assertion
a person standing up for his or her rights and possessions

Some children may give up too easily or fail to defend themselves or their possessions. All children need to learn to stand up for their rights and show **self-assertion.** It is especially important that teachers find ways to help children who have special needs to fend for themselves; otherwise, some may resort to using their disability to get what they want, such as by saying, "You shouldn't take my doll because I can't walk as good as you."

The following is an example of how a teacher might help a child with severely limited vision assert her rights:

Five-year-old Lisa, blind since birth, was playing with an interlocking floor train. Bart took one of her cars. Lisa, touching her train, realized a car was missing. She began to rock back and forth, whining and poking at her eyes. The teacher said, "Lisa, Bart has your car. Tell him to give it back." The teacher turned to Bart: "That car is Lisa's. Be

Photo 16–12
Young children learn many things by watching other children and adults.

*sure to hand it back when she asks you for it." By not retrieving the car, the teacher
helped both children: Lisa, to learn about the rights of possession; Bart, to recognize that
all children have rights that are to be respected.*

Imitation and Modelling

Young children learn many behaviours and skills by watching other children and
adults (Photo 16–12). Using these observations, they imitate what they have seen.
For this reason, adult behaviour in interacting with, and in the presence of, children
is very influential in determining the behaviours and attitudes a child will develop.
Teachers of young children who model acceptance of children with special needs are
helping to shape patterns of acceptance within their early childhood group.
Furthermore, providing children who have developmental differences with models
for appropriate behaviours, especially social behaviours, supports a major argument
in favour of inclusion. It must be stressed, however, that the inclusion of all children
does not automatically lead to their learning appropriate play behaviours and social
skills. From the start of the inclusion movement it has been apparent that *spontaneous* social interactions among young children, with and without developmental
differences, occur infrequently (Schwartz, Billingsley, & McBride, 1998). Teachers
play a major role in promoting and supporting social interaction by

- arranging the environment so as to ensure interactions among all children
- reinforcing the children, in general, for playing together
- reinforcing the children with developmental differences when they imitate
  appropriate behaviours

Each of these practices is discussed in detail in various sections of the text. Here we stress that if children with special needs are to learn from other children, they must be involved in a wide range of play activities. Once again, the teachers—through *modelling, guiding, responding,* and *developing activities* designed specifically to facilitate play interactions through small-group experiences—play a major role in supporting the development of social skills. Such activities might include the following:

- pasting projects (collage) in which children, perhaps, decorate a big carton for storing sand toys
- a giant-size pegboard, with children taking turns putting in pegs from their own baskets
- a big picture book to look at together, each child pointing to a preselected character when it appears (more verbal children can tell what their character is doing)

Teacher-Structured Peer Interactions

At times, teachers may decide which children should play together in which activities. This ensures the inclusion of a child with special needs in an activity with children best suited to that child's skill levels. The grouping can be done on the basis of mutual interests, temperament, or abilities. Wagon trains (several wagons and tricycles hitched together in separate pairs), as mentioned earlier, can be introduced. This wagon-riding game (and many others that teachers can devise) allows a child who cannot walk the excitement and enjoyment of being involved—perhaps sharing a wagon ride with another child who can walk. The child with special needs is an integral part of a spirited outdoor social activity. A rocking boat also promotes closeness and interaction as children synchronize their efforts to make it rock. A note of caution: Children who are just beginning to interact with other children should usually be paired with children who are not overly rambunctious.

Free-play and discovery learning periods are especially good times for promoting social learning through imitation and modelling (Photo 16–13). Teachers need to provide several interest centres and several attractive activities in which interaction is almost automatic: the water table, the dough table, the dramatic play area, a simple cooking experience. Easily conducted science and math experiences promote interactions, too, such as when a few children go into the yard together to pick up leaves to sort by size, type, or colour. The key issue is that social *interactions occur frequently and are pleasurable for all children.* Play experiences that are fun and enjoyable are likely to lead to happier and more satisfying peer relationships.

Peer mediating and peer tutoring. According to Wolery (1994), peer-mediated strategies take a variety of forms, yet all have certain elements in common:

- Children who demonstrate competent social skills are taught specific ways of engaging less competent children in social interactions.
- Children who mediate are taught to keep trying to engage the less competent children in social interactions.
- Children with special needs and the other children have ongoing opportunities to play together and practise skills together.
- Teachers provide children with support and reinforcement for working and playing together.

Photo 16–13
Discovery learning activities provide social learning experiences.

As discussed in Chapter 1, other children also may act occasionally as teachers for children with special needs. Sometimes these peer tutoring episodes occur spontaneously:

- one child helps another to rearrange and separate his or her fingers when putting on gloves
- a child indicates which cube goes where when two children happen to be involved in sorting colour cubes for storage
- another child at the table shows the child pouring from a pitcher how to steady it with the other hand so as to pour slowly and prevent the juice from overflowing the cup

Teachers also can plan child-teaching-child events. Such peer-teaching episodes are appropriate to any part of the program:

- At music, two similar instruments might be provided, with the child who can hear the music designated to help the child who is deaf recognize when and with what force to join in.
- During cognitive learning activities, the teacher could have two children work together, asking the child who is sighted to help the child who is visually impaired learn to put the wooden shapes into a form board.
- During free play–discovery learning, a teacher might ask a child with language delays to show a child wearing a prosthesis how to make a tunnel "just like yours."

In every instance, teachers should pair children carefully so as to ensure an appropriate match of skills and temperament. It is important that both children enjoy and benefit from the interaction. Never should either child feel burdened; never should either child's learning opportunities in any other area be curtailed. When carefully managed, peer tutoring should be of benefit to both children. The child with developmental differences has the opportunity to learn through play from someone who is a master at play—another child. The peer-tutor model practises and refines his or her own developing skills and learns a new and higher-order social skill, that of teaching or imparting knowledge. Hartup (1983) suggests even greater gains: The tutor gains in self-esteem because of the increased status that comes with being a teacher. The tutor also gains in sensitivity in that a certain amount of nurturing is required when teaching a peer who is less able in certain areas. Furthermore, it appears that child tutors undergo positive behavioural and attitudinal changes toward the children with special needs who are being tutored (Franca, Kerr, Reitz, & Lambert, 1990).

OPTIMAL STANDARDS FOR PLAY

Children who are learning appropriate social skills have the ability to be good models for the simple, everyday, fair play behaviours expected of children in an early childhood program. Appropriate use of materials and equipment is one example. *All children* need to learn to use community property responsibly. *No child* can be allowed to paint on the walls, crash a tricycle repeatedly (Photo 16–14), deface books, or waste materials. It is especially important for children with special needs to learn respect for materials and equipment—and to learn it in the company of other children, whenever possible. Otherwise, they may be viewed as unwanted playmates, disrupters of play activities, or people to be disliked or avoided. Let it be stressed, once again, that classroom rules (whatever they may be) apply to *all* children. There should be no double standards. To allow any child to repeatedly and unduly disturb or distress other children does the disturbing child a grave injustice.

Photo 16–14
The rules apply to all children: No child is allowed to crash wheel toys into others.

He or she is likely to be shunned, disliked, and excluded from play activities. Exclusion from play activities and play models closes the major avenue a teacher has for helping children learn appropriate social skills.

Summary

Children with developmental differences, like all young children, need to learn how to get along with others. To do this, they must learn appropriate social skills, which may be more difficult for children with special needs. Like all other skills, social skills are dependent on every other area of development. Nevertheless, children of all developmental levels can and do master basic social skills as prescribed by their respective families, schools, communities, and cultures.

All social skills are learned behaviours even though they are affected by individual temperament. Social development depends largely on reciprocal responsiveness between the child and significant adults, starting with the first hours and days of life. However, children with particular special needs may not be able to engage in the give-and-take typical of social interactions. For them, the entire socialization process may be difficult unless relevant members of the child's IPP team provide extra support for them and their family. Enrollment in an inclusive early childhood program can also help to advance social skills learning for children who require extra support.

Play is a major medium in early learning, especially in learning social skills. Not all children know how to play; some may even be reluctant to try. In these instances, children should be taught—using firm but gentle insistence if need be. This ensures that all children have both the fun and the incidental learning opportunities that are available only through play.

Learning social skills through imitating children who display a range of social skills is a major argument in favour of inclusion. For modelling to take place, children with and without special needs must interact. Effective social interaction often requires teacher intervention. Teachers should promote interactions among all types of children by arranging both physical and social environments. Teachers also should encourage peer tutoring (modelling and helping), which is sometimes planned but more often is incidental in occurrence. All children can benefit from peer tutoring and various kinds of peer mediation.

RESOURCES

SECOND STEP: A VIOLENCE PREVENTION CURRICULUM
http://www.cfchildren.org/ssf/ssf/ssindex/
Second Step is a social skills program that teaches children to change attitudes and behaviours that can lead to violence.

LEARNING DISABILITIES ASSOCIATION OF CANADA
http://www.ldac-taac.ca
This comprehensive website provides articles on social skills development and other issues relating to learning disabilities.

CLASSWIDE SOCIAL SKILLS PROGRAM: EARLY CHILDHOOD
AND KINDERGARTEN PROGRAM
http://vaxxine.com/socialskill/programdescription.html
This Canadian site provides a series of school-based programs to promote the social competence of children.

STUDENT ACTIVITIES

1. Observe in a child care centre that is a multi-age setting. Record anecdotal notes on three different children at three different age levels, displaying three different but developmentally appropriate social skills. During your observation, note any play skills the each child appears to still be learning. Could cultural factors account for these?

2. Visit a preschool, public school, or child care centre that includes children with developmental differences. Observe for 30 minutes one of the children who requires extra support in his or her social skills. Record the social skills the child displays, analyze your observations, and list some strategies the teachers use to support social interaction.

3. While making either of the above observations, list the indoor and outdoor play materials and equipment that seem to promote frequent cooperative play. Note in particular if children with special needs are using the equipment. If not, try to decide why not.

4. Work with another student or two as a teaching team and make plans as to the kinds of activities or materials you might present to promote sharing among three-year-olds, some of whom have developmental delays.

5. Assume you are working with a four-year-old with a cognitive delay and few play skills. You feel it is important that this child learn to play with blocks. How might you go about teaching block play to this child? Be specific. Select a classmate to be the child and demonstrate your teaching strategies in class. How might you include another child to help in teaching block play? Demonstrate.

REFERENCES

Anita, S. D., & Kreimeyer, K. H. (1992). Social competence intervention for young children with hearing impairments. In S. Odom, S. McConnell, & M. McEvoy (Eds.), *Social competence of young children with disabilities* (pp. 135–164). Baltimore: MD: Brookes.

Bee, H. (1999). *The developing child.* New York: Holt, Rinehart &Winston.

Bennett, E. C. (1990). Recent advances in developmental intervention for biologically vulnerable infants. *Infants and Young Children, 3*(1), 33–40.

Brown, W. H., Raglund, E. U, & Bishop, N. (1989). *A socialization curriculum for preschool programs that integrate children with handicaps.* Nashville, TN: Vanderbilt University.

Fraiberg, S. (1974). Blind infants and their mothers: An examination of the sign system. In M. L. Lewis & L. A. Rosenblum (Eds.), *The effect of the infant on its caregiver* (pp. 215–232). New York: Wiley.

Franca, V. M., Kerr, M. M., Reitz, A. L., & Lambert, D. (1990). Peer tutoring among behaviorally disordered students: Academic and social benefits to the tutor and tutee. *Education and Treatment of Children, 13*(2), 109–128.

Gordon, A. M., & Browne, K. W. (2004). *Beginnings and beyond: Foundations in early childhood education.* Clifton Park, NY: Delmar Learning.

Guralnick, M. (1996). *Assessment of peer relations.* Seattle, WA: University of Washington: Child Development and Mental Retardation Center.

Hartup, W. W. (1983). Peer relations. In P. H. Mussen & E. M. Hetherington (Eds.), *Carmichael's manual of child psychology* (4th ed., pp. 103–196). New York: Wiley.

Kostelnik, M. J., Whiren, A. P., Soderman, A. K., Stein, L. C., & Gregory, K. (2002). *Guiding children's social development: Theory to practice.* Clifton Park, NY: Delmar Learning.

McEvoy, M. S., Twardosz, S., & Bishop, N. (1990). Affection activities procedures for encouraging young children with handicaps to interact with their peers. *Education and Treatment of Children, 13,* 297–273.

McLean, M., Bailey, D. B., & Wolery, M. (1996). *Assessing infants and preschoolers with handicaps.* Columbus, OH: Merrill.

Rubin, K. H., & Howe, N. (1985). Toys and play behaviors: An overview. *Topics in Early Childhood Special Education, 5*(3), 1–9.

Schwartz, I. S., Billingsley, F. F., & McBride, B. (1998). Including children with autism in inclusive preschools: Strategies that work. *Young Exceptional Children, 2*(1), 19–26.

Skellenger, A. C., Hill, M., & Hill, E. (1992). The social functioning of children with visual impairments. In S. Odom, S. McConnell, & M. McEvoy (Eds.), *Social competence of young children with disabilities* (pp. 165–188). Baltimore: MD: Brookes.

Taft, L. T. (1981). Intervention program for infants with cerebral palsy: A clinician's view. In C. C. Brown (Ed.), *Infants at risk, assessment and intervention: An update for health-care professionals and parents.* Skillman, NJ: Johnson and Johnson.

Thomas, A., & Chess, S. (1977). *Temperament and development.* New York: Bruner/Mazel.

Twardosz, S., Norquist, V. M., Simon, R., & Botkin, D. (1983). The effect of group affection activities on the interaction of socially isolated children. *Analysis and Intervention in Developmental Disabilities, 13,* 311–338.

Wolery, M. (1994). Designing inclusive environments for young children with special needs. In M. Wolery & J. S. Wilbers (Eds.), *Including children with special needs in early childhood programs* (pp. 151–166). Washington, DC: National Association for the Education of Young Children.

CHAPTER 17

Facilitating Positive Behaviours (Managing Challenging Behaviours)

KEY CONCEPTS

aggressiveness

antecedents and consequences

baseline

behaviour disorder (BD)

conduct disorder

data collection

difficult behaviour/challenging behaviour

duration

fading

frequency

functional approach

goodness-of-fit

interval

oppositional defiant
    disorder (ODD)

replacement behaviour

temperament

OBJECTIVES

After studying the material in this chapter, the student will be able to

- Identify possible causes of behaviour disorders.
- Identify inappropriate behaviours that are within developmental and cultural norms.
- Explain what factors determine when an inappropriate or challenging behaviour requires special attention.
- List positive strategies for preventing (and reducing) difficult behaviours in the early childhood classroom.
- Outline a plan for behavioural change for an individual child in a group setting.

Introduction

All young children engage in challenging and inappropriate behaviours at least once in a while (Photo 17–1). Children learn the difference between appropriate and inappropriate ways of behaving by trying out new behaviours. It is a way of learning what to do (and not do), where, and when. Almost every child has had a tantrum or an irrational fear, or has balked at being separated from a parent. Most children are sometimes moody or withdrawn, aggressive or antisocial, argumentative or oppositional. Most young children retreat or respond negatively or aggressively to situations that are new, frightening, or beyond their understanding. It is the way in which the adult responds to this behaviour that helps the child to recognize the difference between appropriate and inappropriate ways of behaving—to begin to learn new coping skills and find more effective ways of dealing with difficult emotions. Kaiser and Rasminsky (1999) summarize some findings on the importance of the early years of life. They discuss how recent research by neuroscientists has uncovered the extreme importance of experience in the first three years of life on the development of the brain. The experiences of the young child in this formative period create specific connections in the brain. Citing Shore (1997), they indicate that "The more we help children refrain from their challenging behaviour, the less they're learning to use it—and the less likely that it's embedding itself in their brains. If you can anticipate when and where the child will have trouble, prevent the situation from occurring, and remind him of what to do instead of waiting for him to make a mistake, you can build a new pattern" (Kaiser & Rasminsky, 1999, pp. 15–16). Therefore, the more we help children refrain from their challenging behaviour and help them to establish viable alternatives, the less likely it is that this difficult behaviour will become a permanent mode of coping and interacting.

In this text, the term **"behaviour disorder" (BD)** is used to describe a child who is unable to conform to the expectations of his or her age, social, and cultural group; who seems to lack the ability or opportunity to learn or control appropriate behaviours; and who is unable to understand routine expectations. A behaviour disorder may also be the cause of secondary behaviour problems. The terms **"difficult behaviour"** and **"challenging behaviour"** are used to designate the impact a behaviour has on the people with whom the child is interacting.

Children with behavioural developmental disabilities are of major concern because they may get little positive feedback from parents, caregivers, and teachers. The frustration these children experience when they are unable to perform everyday developmental tasks often has a negative impact on their social interactions. This can result in such behaviours as tantrums or aggressive striking out at people or objects. Other children may withdraw and stop trying to relate. Adult reactions to these behaviours often unintentionally reinforce them, thus increasing the undesired behaviour, which in turn blocks the acquisition of more appropriate behaviour patterns.

What Makes a Behaviour Challenging or Difficult?

At what point does an inappropriate, challenging behaviour become a problem behaviour? a behaviour disorder? There are no easy answers to these questions because so many factors influence a child's development. Cultural norms, parental expectations and reactions to behaviour, and environmental arrangements, such as

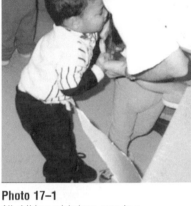

Photo 17–1
All children misbehave once in a while.

Behaviour disorder (BD)
describes a child who is unable to conform to appropriate expectations, who lacks the ability to learn appropriate behaviours, and who is unable to understand routine expectations

Difficult or challenging behaviour
describes the impact a behaviour has on the people with whom the child is interacting

Photo 17–2
A child may exhibit inappropriate behaviours once in a while.

too many distractions or too few, are some of the factors that influence a child's difficult behaviours. The range of congenital differences among children further complicates matters.

COPING WITH CHANGE

Another consideration is that coping with change can be extremely difficult for some young children. Many children need adult support and understanding when they are coping with change—whether it is the birth of a new sibling, the loss of a beloved caretaker, or the initial days of attending a new school program.

For example, replacing a longtime favourite caregiver with a stranger may trigger a response of acting out or withdrawal behaviours. The reactions usually are temporary (assuming that the new caregiver is a good one). The child's difficult behaviours usually disappear once he or she gains understanding and confidence. A child may also exhibit inappropriate behaviours when overly tired or hungry, or when coming down with an illness (Photo 17–2). These minor disruptions are not likely to develop into fixed patterns of difficult behaviour unless they are the only way a child can be sure of getting adult attention.

TEMPERAMENT

Temperament
an individual's psychological makeup or personality traits; of interest to the caregiver is how temperament influences an individual's responses to different situations

Goodness-of-fit
when the learning opportunities are appropriate to the child's developmental status

Another factor influencing behaviour is the **temperament** of the child. How the child's temperament does or does not blend with the temperaments of the other people with whom the child interacts may affect his or her development.

Behaviours that sometimes are viewed as inappropriate may be a reflection of the child's basic personality. Some children seem to be born with a temperament that makes them easy to manage, others with a temperament that makes them more difficult. An interesting aspect of this proposition is what Thomas and Chess (1986) call **goodness-of-fit.** These authors suggest that it is not the child's temperament itself that determines a behavioural outcome. Instead, it is how the child's personality characteristics match the demands of the environment, especially the expectations, as well as the temperament, of parents and caregivers. Consider, for example, a child who is active, independent, constantly curious, and into everything. This child may be seen as troublesome, a "behaviour problem," and a candidate for frequent punishment by overworked parents who hold high standards for order and routine. Conversely, energetic, creative parents might view the temperament of this active, into-everything child as highly desirable. They might go out of their way to reinforce, nurture, and respect the child's efforts at exploration and experimentation.

Young children who exhibit difficult behaviours are all too often labelled as "intellectually impaired" or "emotionally disturbed," or as having "behaviour problems." A common tendency is for adults to excuse these behaviours, explaining that the child "can't help it" or "doesn't know any better." Making such excuses is neither fair to the child nor sensible. All young children, regardless of their developmental level, should be supported in learning basic social requirements. Early childhood programs that fail to provide such learning opportunities do these children a serious injustice. Other children may come to dislike and reject them. This may result in an increased number of acting-out episodes or lead to excesses of aggression or withdrawal.

When Is Intervention Necessary?

Occasional episodes of challenging behaviours are rarely a cause for concern. However, when a behaviour or a pattern of behaviours becomes excessive, it is a problem. This raises the question: how much is too much? For classroom purposes, it is useful to define excessive behaviour as behaviour that interferes seriously with a child's (or other children's) ability to engage in normal, everyday activities (Photo 17–3). The four-year-old who has a brief tantrum once or twice a month is not likely to be a worry. The four-year-old who has a tantrum several times every day over minor frustrations is cause for concern.

DESIGNING INTERVENTIONS

Teachers, family members, and other interdisciplinary team members must work together to identify the challenging behaviour, identify the settings in which it occurs, and use this information to design interventions that all team members are comfortable with and able to implement. In their 1999 position paper, the Division for Early Childhood in the United States lists five features critical to the identification and intervention of challenging behaviours.

1. *Comprehensive:* Team members examine a comprehensive approach that includes teaching new skills, examining the environment, and developing appropriate consequences.
2. *Individualized:* As with all areas of intervention programs, individualization is the key to success.
3. *Positive programming:* This includes teaching appropriate skills, teaching children to self monitor, and teaching specific communication alternatives to the inappropriate behaviours.
4. *Multidisciplinary:* Extremely challenging behaviours need the input of the entire team—including the family, teachers, speech therapists, and often pediatricians and psychologists.
5. *Data-based:* Collection of data is vital to evaluating the effectiveness of any intervention plan. This is especially true because of the emotional response that challenging behaviours can trigger. Emotional responses make it hard to view changes in behaviour objectively. Data collection can also help determine environmental factors that could be influencing behaviour.

A FUNCTIONAL APPROACH TO MANAGING DIFFICULT BEHAVIOURS

The best way to deal with problems or challenging behaviours—those that cause concern to teachers and families—is to prevent them (Walker, Stiller, & Golly, 1998). For there to be effective prevention, teachers and caregivers must examine their own behaviour and identify factors that might be contributing to the child's behaviour. The early childhood environment can be arranged to decrease opportunities for acting out challenging behaviours. Therefore, when teachers have a child with challenging behaviours in the class, teachers should first examine their environment to determine whether changing something could alleviate a child's problematic behaviour.

Photo 17–3
Thumb sucking need seldom be considered a problem unless it seriously interferes with a child's participation in learning activities.

According to Koegel, Koegel, and Dunlap (1996), challenging behaviours have a communicative function. The task of parents and educators is to figure out what the child is attempting to communicate and to teach him or her a more appropriate way to get the message across.

A **functional approach** to behaviour management includes the following steps:

1. *Identifying the problem situation.* Observe, identify, and describe the challenging behaviour. Identifying and documenting the behaviour in a designated manner will also be useful when teachers begin to gather specific information about the challenging behaviour.

2. *Assessing the child and the environment (finding out how long or how often the child demonstrates the challenging behaviour).* It is also important to which events in the environment are contributing to the behaviour. These are known as **antecedents and consequences,** and every behaviour has them (see Chapter 11). By recording antecedents and consequences, teachers can identify patterns and gain information about why behaviour is occurring.

3. *Specifying an objective for the intervention.* What is the desired behaviour at home or in the classroom? Parents, teachers, and other members of the intervention team must decide what the child should be able to do. In some cases this may be a redirection of existing play behaviours or ways of interacting with peers.

4. *Assessing the function of the behaviour.* By carefully observing the child's behaviour and identifying antecedents and consequences, the teacher can often identify the function of the behaviour. Research suggests that the function of a child's behaviour can be broken down into (a) behaviour that occurs to gain attention or a desired item from an adult or peer, (b) behaviour that allows a child to escape or get out of a less than desirable task or activity, or (c) behaviour that occurs for self-pleasure, such as object spinning (Iwatta, Dorsey, Slifer, Bauman, & Richman, 1982).

5. *Identifying a replacement behaviour.* When developing a strategy to decrease a behaviour, it is critical for teachers to teach the child an appropriate behaviour that serves the same function as the problem behaviour. This new skill or behaviour is called a **replacement behaviour.**

6. *Planning the intervention.* Ensure that meaningful curriculum activities, frequent positive attention, choice, and a predictable schedule are in place. This step of the process focuses on prevention. The first changes that are implemented are those that facilitate the appropriate behaviour.

7. *Implementing the plan and ensuring that it is carried out as planned.* This is the step that puts the plan into action. Make sure that everyone in the environment understands the plan and knows how to implement it. If the plan is not implemented correctly and consistently, it will not work. Teachers need to be patient. It is difficult to change behaviour, and it may take two weeks or more before significant changes can be detected in a child's behaviour.

8. *Monitoring the child's progress and continuing to monitor implementation.* The purpose of this step is to make sure the plan is working. Teachers need to collect data about the child's behaviour to determine whether the goal has been achieved. The **data collection** in this chapter focuses on monitoring the child's behaviour and determining whether a specific intervention strategy is effective. If progress has been observed, teachers may start **fading** (i.e., slowly discontinuing) some components of the intervention.

Functional approach
examining and assessing the environment and teacher behaviour to determine in what ways they might affect a child's behaviour, then planning and carrying out an intervention, and monitoring the child's progress

Antecedents and consequences
antecedents are events that come before a behaviour (in behavioural psychology, the antecedent is the stimulus that causes a response); consequences are the events that follow a behaviour

Replacement behaviour
a behaviour that is taught to a child to replace an inappropriate one—a replacement behaviour should serve the same function as the inappropriate behaviour

Data collection
monitoring a child's behaviour and gathering information on it; data collection is used to evaluate the success of any intervention plan and is helpful only when it is easy to do and provides an accurate picture of the child's behaviour

Fading
gradually reducing prompts, cues, and physical assistance when teaching a particular skill

Data Collection and Monitoring Progress

A reliable and easy-to-use data collection system is essential to monitoring the success of any intervention plan (Kaiser & Rasminksy, 1999). Data determine whether the intervention plan is working. Data can provide information about the environment and what influences the child's behaviour. Data collection systems are helpful only when they are easy to use and provide an accurate picture of the child's behaviour.

TYPES OF DATA COLLECTION

Three types of behaviour data are most commonly collected in an early childhood setting: frequency, duration, and interval. **Frequency** refers to the number of times during the day, or a specific time, the behaviour occurs (Figure 17–1). This type of data collection is used to measure behaviours that have a distinct beginning and end. Hitting and biting are two examples of behaviours that can be effectively measured using a frequency count. **Duration** is the measure of how long each episode occurs (Figure 17–2). This measure would be used for behaviours that have a distinct beginning and end but last for at least a minute. Tantrums are typically measured this way. **Interval** measurement can often be an easier way to track behaviours and can be used for behaviours both long and short in duration. During interval measurement, a specific time of day or the entire day is broken into equal segments. The length of these intervals is determined by both the behaviour and how frequently adults can record the data. For example, teachers who want to measure a child's ability to share might divide the free-play period into five-minute segments. At the

Frequency
in research, it refers to the number of times during a specified period that a designated behaviour occurred

Duration
measures how long an event or behaviour lasts

Interval
a specified period of the day that is broken into segments to record the occurrence, frequency, and duration of a behaviour

Figure 17–1 AN EXAMPLE OF FREQUENCY DATA SHEET

	Monday	Tuesday	Wednesday	Thursday	Friday
Frequency of Hitting Peers	HHT IIII	HHT I	III	HHT II	IIII

Figure 17–2 AN EXAMPLE OF A DURATION DATA SHEET

	Monday	Tuesday	Wednesday	Thursday	Friday
Begin Time	930	1105	830	936	
End Time	940	1108	836	938	
Begin Time	1005				
End Time	1007				
Begin Time					
End Time					

Figure 17–3   AN EXAMPLE OF AN INTERVAL DATA SHEET

	Monday	Tuesday	Wednesday	Thursday	Friday
9:00–9:15	+	–	+	–	+
9:15–9:30	–	–	–	–	–
9:30–10:00	–	–	–	–	–
10:00–10:15	+	+	+	+	+

conclusion of segment, a plus sign (+) would be placed in the interval if the child was able to share for the entire time, or a minus sign (−) would be recorded if there was any occurrence of inability to share (Figure 17–3).

Before establishing any data collection method, a mutually agreed on definition of behaviour must be written (See step 1 on page 358). This will help to increase the likelihood that all individuals recording the data are recording the same behaviour.

COLLECTING DATA

Baseline
data that are collected on a behaviour before a systematic plan is introduced; these data provide a base against which later behaviour can be compared

Once the behaviour has been identified and defined, data are collected for at least three to five days before any systematic plan is made to reduce the target behaviour. This period of data collection is used to create as **baseline.** Baseline data provide a picture of how often or how long the behaviour is occurring. This information can be used later to compare behaviour changes when evaluating the effectiveness of the intervention. A vertical line should be drawn on the data graph to indicate the end of the baseline and the introduction of the behaviour intervention plan. Once the intervention plan is determined to be effective, data collection can be reduced or eliminated.

Some data collection methods can be time-consuming and impractical for a teacher to use. It is best to find a simple yet accurate way to measure the behaviour (see Figures 17–4 and 17–5, p. 361).

Data should be graphed and reviewed on a frequent basis. Decisions about changes in the behaviour plan should be made only after looking at the data. Data records should be saved; they can be useful in parent conferences and individual program plan meetings.

For each of the following behaviours, strategies have been suggested for ways in which teachers might reduce or prevent the behaviour. When deciding on a strategy, teachers should consider the function of the behaviour as discussed earlier in this chapter.

Conduct Disorders

Conduct disorder
a pattern of behaviour that involves extreme aggressiveness, destruction of property, disruptive behaviours, tantrums, or oppositional behaviours that violate the rights of others, social norms, or rules

Specific patterns of behaviour that call for special intervention often fall under the heading of conduct disorders.

Conduct disorders have been described in the American Psychiatric Association's *DSM-IV-TR* as "a repetitive pattern of behavior in which the basic rights of others or major age-appropriate societal norms or rules are violated"

Figure 17–4 SELF-GRAPHING DATA SHEET

An X is placed on the chart at each occurrence of the behaviour. Changes in behaviour from day to day are easily viewed using this method.

20													
19													
18													
17													
16													
15													
14													
13													
12													
11													
10													
9													
8		X											
7		X											
6	X	X											
5	X	X	X										
4	X	X	X	X									
3	X	X	X	X	X								
2	X	X	X	X	X	X	X						
1	X	X	X	X	X	X	X						

Figure 17–5 SAMPLE GRAPH FOR INTERVALS, FREQUENCY, AND DURATION MEASURES

Measurement can be changed to match need (for example, number of minutes of tantrums).

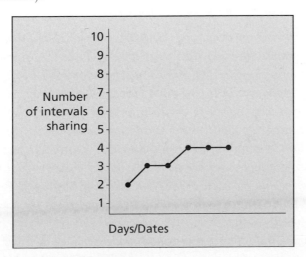

(American Psychiatric Association [APA], 2000, p. 68). In young children, conduct disorders may include

aggressiveness (physical fighting, bullying), physical cruelty
　　to people or animals
destruction of property
disruptive behaviours
tantrums
oppositional behaviours

In an early childhood program, these behaviours seem to be fairly evenly distributed among children who have and those who do not have handicapping conditions.

AGGRESSIVENESS

Aggressiveness, like so many other terms that we apply to children, is difficult to define. What is considered aggressive by one group of people, one parent, or one teacher may not seem noteworthy to another group, another parent, or another member of the teaching team.

Almost any child displaying continuing aggressiveness creates conflict among teachers, among parents, and among children. Often the child's problem spreads into conflict between teachers and parents, with the child caught in the middle. Ethical issues are always at stake. Teachers have to be concerned for the safety of all the children in the group, as well as the well-being of the individual child who is displaying the aggressive behaviour.

Example:

Peter, an only child whose parents worked long hours, had spent his first few years being cared for by a baby-sitter. He was the only child at this sitter's home. At age four, Peter's parents put him into a neighbourhood daycare centre. Peter had very little spoken language when he entered the daycare. He often became frustrated when he couldn't express his needs and feelings with words. He began to hit, kick, head-butt, and pinch when other children didn't do what he wanted. The children began to avoid him and not want to play with him. This led to an increase in the aggressive behaviour. The supervisor of the centre was worried that a child would be badly hurt, as Peter's kicking and head-butting were at times endangering children. Peter's mother was becoming concerned because he was beginning to hit and head-butt her. An early childhood interventionist was brought in to the daycare.

After observing the situation, the interventionist talked together with the teachers and Peter's parents. She concluded that a lot of Peter's behaviour stemmed not only from frustration because he was unable to express himself verbally, but also from his lack of previous experience in interacting with children in group situations. The teachers and the parents were urged to try to intervene whenever they perceived that Peter was becoming upset, to model using words, and to help Peter find simple words that would enable him to communicate his needs and feelings. It was decided that when Peter demonstrated aggressive behaviour, he should be removed from the situation and that attention would be given to the child who had been hurt. Peter would have to play on his own (something he really didn't like to do) until the teacher, through observation, felt Peter was ready to rejoin the group and play cooperatively. Before he was allowed to rejoin the group, the teacher would model for him what he could say if he was upset

Aggressiveness
acting-out behaviour in which a child may hurt other children, cause disruptions by intentionally throwing objects, or behave in ways that disrupt the group

about something with another child, letting him know that if he was having trouble with someone he could come to her for help. She would then help him settle into a new play area. At home, a parallel process would be followed. If he struck out at his mother, he would be sent to his room to play alone (for a maximum of five minutes) until she told him he could come out.

The importance of consistency between how the home and the daycare centre handled Peter's aggressive behaviour was also stressed. Furthermore, when Peter was acting appropriately, adults worked cooperatively to focus positive attention on Peter. The parents and teachers, by sharing their concern with regard to Peter's behaviour, were able to work together to help Peter develop more appropriate behaviour. The staff had to keep in mind the safety and needs of all the children. Reducing aggressive behaviour in a group is not easy. However, with early intervention and the cooperation of a home and a daycare centre, it can be successfully accomplished, as it was in the case of Peter. Within a month, Peter's aggressive behaviour had been reduced to only infrequent outbursts. His language was improving and, with the support of both the teachers and his parents, he was beginning to be able to use language to express his frustration and anger. He was also beginning to develop some friendships. Within three months, there were only very rare acts of aggression evident.

Young children often behave aggressively because they feel left out or do not know acceptable ways of getting into play. Children with developmental disabilities may lack the play skills or the verbal niceties that would make them desirable playmates (Photo 17–4). The teacher's responsibility is twofold. The first responsibility is to take the initiative in helping the child acquire the necessary play and social skills. The second is to watch for the child to show approximations to more appropriate play and interact with the child pleasantly and positively at those times. When a child with a history of aggression hurts another child, it is important that the teacher turn his or her full attention to the child who has been hurt or attacked. *The child who did the hurting should receive no adult attention at that time; however, that child may need to be prevented from further aggressive behaviour.*

If a child continues to be frequently and severely aggressive, a qualified interventionist should be brought in to help develop an individual program plan (IPP). No child can be allowed to repeatedly hurt other children or to create disruption by intentionally throwing or destroying toys and equipment. With the support of the interventionist, when more positive methods have failed, time-out may need to be implemented. Time-out is a nonaggressive way to help a child learn that he or she absolutely cannot attack other children. It should be used only with children who have been identified as having an ongoing, significant behaviour problem. *The use of time-out is a decision that should only be made jointly, among teachers, a behavioural interventionist from the transdisciplinary team, and the child's parents.*

Provincial or territorial regulations need to be reviewed in this context. In Ontario, for example, the Ministry of Community and Social Services has regulated the use of behaviour management practices, including the use of time-out. (See the Ontario Child and Family Services Act, 1992.) The regulation states that with extreme behaviour problems, when it is decided that a form of time-out is to be used, it should be done in consultation with the resource teacher, or a special consultant, and the parents. The procedure and process should be decided on, documented, and then clearly explained to the child (see Chapter 11).

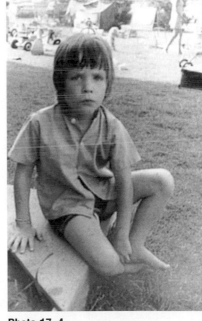

Photo 17–4
A child may lack play skills.

DISRUPTIVE AND DESTRUCTIVE BEHAVIOURS

Every early childhood classroom, at one time or another, has a child who seems bent on upsetting the program. These children interfere with teacher-directed activities and with other children's projects. Music periods are interrupted by the child making inappropriate noises, faces, and comments, or running aimlessly about the room. Books are tossed around recklessly and toys are unnecessarily damaged. The child tramples other children's sand structures, topples their block towers, soaks their clothes and hair at the water table, swears at them, or calls them names. The list of possible misdeeds is long. What early childhood teacher has not seen them all at one time or another?

Need for Attention

Photo 17–5
Give attention to children when they are behaving appropriately.

Many children who behave in these ways have learned that this behaviour is a sure way of getting adult attention. These children often have low self-esteem and other stresses in their lives. Like the overly active child, they are greatly in need of large amounts of attention from important adults. These children appear to feel that when they are behaving appropriately, they are ignored (which is often the case) and when they are misbehaving, they get immediate attention (which also is often the case). Research indicates that young children are seven times more likely to get teachers' attention when they are behaving inappropriately than when they are behaving well (Strain, Lambert, Kerr, Stagg, & Jenker, 1983). Therefore, the refrain that has been heard, and will be heard again and again in this chapter and elsewhere in this text, is *give attention to children when they are behaving appropriately* (Photo 17–5). We also must not forget the point made by Kaiser and Rasminsky (1999) with regard to how important positive teacher intervention is—that through consistently supporting the young child's positive behaviour, guiding him or her, and modelling appropriate responses when he or she is having trouble knowing how to cope effectively, we can have a direct impact on the neural connections that are made in the brain, resulting in permanent and positive influences on the child's future behaviour.

We need to eliminate or at least limit the amount of unproductive time, attention, and energy that teachers and parents spend when the child is acting out. *Half as much of that time directed toward the child when not misbehaving would go twice as far toward producing a more constructive environment* (Photo 17–6). Through

Photo 17–6
Teachers should recognize and support children's positive play.

structured observations of the child, parents and teachers are almost always amazed when they see how much of the time the child's behaviour is appropriate and how rarely this draws adult attention. This is the first step in identifying positive behaviours and developing ways of supporting the child when he or she is acting in socially acceptable ways. It is also the time to examine problematic behaviours and developing strategies for dealing with these so that they are not reinforced.

Mastering Routines

Many children who are disruptive have never understood or mastered classroom routines and expectations. They need to be *walked through* routines, one step at a time. For example, at the easel a child may need to be shown, and then asked to practise, how to return each paintbrush to the paint pot of its own colour. A first step may be for the teacher to remove all paint containers but two. This makes it easy for the child to "do it right." It also allows the teacher to give specific, descriptive feedback: "Great! You remembered to put the red paintbrush back in the red paint pot." Lengthy verbalizations must be avoided, or the important message will get lost. For example, teachers must not yield to the temptation to follow up with explanations about keeping the colours nice and clear for other children and so on. Such expectations can be discussed in small-group sessions, when necessary. As the child paints, the teacher can make appreciative comments, when appropriate, about the brightness of the colours or how successfully the child combined red and blue on the paper to make a new colour.

Need for Redirection

Disruptive acts that damage the classroom, equipment, or other children's learning experiences cannot be allowed. With most young children, simple, positive redirection is best. Statements, such as "Paint stays on the *paper*," "Walk *around* Mark and Judi's block tower," or "Tricycles stay *on the path*," are all that is required. Other children, especially those with a history of disruptive behaviours, may pay little attention to subtle redirection. When the child ignores redirection, what is often needed is a clear and firm statement about limits and expectations: "I cannot let you paint on the walls. The paintbrushes stay at the easel." If the child persists, either the material or the child should be removed, depending on the situation.

In summary, teachers should begin by observing and recording a child's behaviour and the adults' responses; then they should do everything possible to modify both the classroom environment and their own responses to the child's behaviour.

NONCOMPLIANCE

Refusing to do what an adult asks, or ignoring an adult request, is a frequent and typical behaviour of many young children (Photo 17–7). This is seldom a serious or unmanageable problem unless it becomes a child's habitual way of responding to adults. In those instances the child often is labelled *noncompliant* or *oppositional*. The following three episodes, recorded in less than an hour, are characteristic of one four-year-old's habitual noncompliance, which was not being effectively dealt with:

1. *Father: Michael, hang up your coat.*
   Michael: No, you do it.

   Father: All right, but you pick it up off the floor and hand it to me.

   Michael: You pick it up. (Michael started playing with a truck in the cubby next to his. Father hung up the coat, said goodbye, and left.)

Photo 17–7
Refusing to follow an adult's request is typical behaviour of many young children.

Photo 17–8
Teacher: "I cannot let you kick your ball into the sandbox when children are playing there."

2. *Teacher: Michael, let's pick up the blocks.*

   (Michael ran to his locker and sat in it, looking at a book he had brought from home.)

   Teacher: OK, Rachel, you pick up the blocks.

3. *Teacher: Michael, it's time to come in.*

   Michael: Not coming in (while continuing his climb to the top of the climber).

The first step in dealing with noncompliance (or any other problem behaviour) is collecting specific information through several systematic observations. The second step is consultation with parents and appropriate team members. It must be determined that the child does not have a hearing loss or a problem with receptive language (Photo 17–8). Innumerable children with these kinds of undiagnosed problems have been labelled noncompliant or disobedient (and have received undeserved punishments as a consequence). Others have been inappropriately labelled as "mentally retarded" or "emotionally disturbed" because they failed to do what they were told. The injustice is that it is often impossible for these children to follow directions without special intervention. Only after physical causes of noncompliance have been eliminated can a plan to promote more positive social behaviour be implemented.

OPPOSITIONAL DEFIANT DISORDER (ODD)

Oppositional defiant disorder (ODD)
a pattern of negativistic, hostile, and defiant behaviour—lasting at least six months—which interferes with social or academic functioning or both

Oppositional defiant disorder (ODD) is defined in the *DMS-IV-TR* (APA, 2000, p. 68) as follows:

> A pattern of negativistic, hostile, and defiant behavior lasting at least 6 months, during which four (or more) of the following are present:
>
> (1) often loses temper
> (2) often argues with adults
> (3) often actively defies or refuses to comply with adults' requests or rules
> (4) often deliberately annoys people
> (5) often blames others for his or her mistakes or misbehavior
> (6) is often touchy or easily annoyed by others
> (7) is often angry and resentful
> (8) is often spiteful or vindictive

A child is only considered to have ODD if the behaviour occurs more frequently than is typical in others of the same age and developmental level.

To be considered as having ODD, the level of acting-out behaviour must interfere with the social or academic functioning of the child. ODD is found more frequently in boys than in girls, typically beginning before the age of eight.

The majority of people who have worked with children with ODD seem to feel that reward and punishment is the only way in which to successfully treat this condition. Others, such as Ross Greene (1998), indicate that the cause is a combination of environmental and "brain-based" issues and that a more effective treatment is intervention. Explosions should be prevented by creating a less frustrating environment and by trying to anticipate the situations most likely to trigger an explosion so that the adults move in before it occurs. Greene points out that these children do not blow up purposefully; they are simply not able to express their frustrations in other ways. Greene advocates helping children to develop communication and collaborative problem-solving skills (Green, 1998).

One important thing to be aware of is that children with ODD tend to blame others for their behaviour and often create problems between their parents or between parents and teachers because they convince one of the parties that the other is mistreating them. It is important to have a child suspected of having ODD referred for a complete assessment and then, with the help of specialists, develop a plan to enable the inclusion of this child within the preschool environment.

Temper Tantrums

Young children who have frequent, full-blown temper tantrums require special help. The advice often given is for adults to ignore the tantrum. Although that is good advice, parents and teachers may find it nearly impossible to carry it out. They report that they repeatedly tried ignoring the child's tantrums and "it didn't work." The reason it did not work is that most adults give in long before the child gives in.

A child with a history of tantrums whose outbursts are suddenly ignored may go to even greater extremes of behaviour—having tantrums of increasing fury and duration. Some children accelerate their tantrums to the point of holding their breath until they turn blue or appear to stop breathing. As a tantrum becomes more violent, the adults who are trying to ignore the tantrum get increasingly anxious; finally, they can no longer restrain their concern for the child. They go to the child and provide attention in one way or another. As this pattern is repeated, the tantrums become worse.

The child learns two damaging lessons from such experiences: (1) that it takes ever greater and more prolonged fury to break down the adults' defences, and (2) that the defences invariably do break down and the adult eventually will provide some kind of attention. This leads to deepening trouble for both the child and the adults who are involved. Therefore, although ignoring tantrums is the surest way of ridding the child of such behaviour, most adults need help and support in carrying out such a program. Any one of several professionals on the transdisciplinary team is usually qualified and willing to work with parents and teachers in managing a child's tantrums.

MANAGEMENT OF TANTRUMS

Difficult as it may be, tantrums can be handled at school. It takes careful planning among teachers, parents, and a psychologist, an interventionist, a nurse, or other member of the child's IPP team. All the teachers in a room should be trained by a specialist on how to handle a child's tantrums. At the start of a tantrum, one teacher should take responsibility for the child who is having the tantrum. The child may need to be removed to a separate place where injury is not likely to occur and where the child is unable to break or destroy anything. Though not always available, a small, bare, carpeted room is best. The teacher should withhold all attention while the child is having the tantrum. However, the teacher (or another adult) must stay close by (immediately outside the door is preferable, unless there is a legal requirement that an adult remain in the room). When the tantrum has stopped, the teacher should wait a moment and then return the child to a play activity *with no lecturing or moralizing*. Later, the child should be complimented on how successfully he or she recovered and rejoined the group. Studies indicate that tantrums first get worse but then disappear within a week or less if adults can be totally consistent in carrying out these procedures.

The teachers in the classroom often can handle lesser tantrums without needing the help of a specialist. Like major tantrums, lesser ones will probably accelerate briefly when attention is first withheld. It is best if all the teachers have an agreed on process for managing a child's tantrums, so as to provide consistency of procedures. The teacher(s) not involved in the management of a tantrum should focus on the rest of the children, who may become uneasy as the tantrum escalates. Teachers should reassure the rest of the class that the child having the tantrum is upset, that the teacher with him or her is caring for the child and helping him or her to calm down, and that the child will soon be all right. The teachers should then attempt to refocus the group by, for example, reading a special story or setting up an activity that will keep the other children occupied and diverted. If there is no place in which to remove the child who is having a temper tantrum, and it is evident that he or she is distracting the rest of the group, a good strategy is to take the rest of the children on a walk around the building, to the gym or library, until the tantrum is over.

Teachers and parents must recognize that tantrums always are an indication that the child is experiencing stress, anxiety, frustration, or other upset. Underlying causes must be sought and the preschool or child care program studied for changes that might be made to help the child. In the meantime, and along with the other efforts, the tantrums must be brought under control. Otherwise, the tantrums themselves prevent the child from benefiting from the changes being made on his or her behalf.

Summary of General Strategies for Supporting Positive Behaviour

Photo 17–9
Teachers should provide children with advance warning and clear instruction.

The following strategies should be used to help to create changes in a child's behaviour:

- *Give advance warning.* Giving advanced warning is especially important for children who may have a lower threshold for managing change. A few minutes before a transition is to occur, let the child know that "we are going inside in five minutes," or he or she has "only five more minutes before cleanup."
- *Reduce overload.* Check frequently to make sure the child is not overloaded with directions, expectations, and picky rules.
- *Give clear directions.* Make requests and give directions clearly and briefly (Photo 17–9).
- *Allow choices.* All children, and particularly non-compliant children, need to be offered, as often as possible, opportunities to make choices (e.g., "Would you like to put the cups or the napkins on the table?"). Choosing and making decisions helps a child develop a sense of responsibility and independence. It also reduces the child's feelings that he or she is always being told what to do. Adults must be careful what kinds of choices

they offer young children. Whenever an adult offers a choice, the adult must be prepared to honour it.

- *Focus the child's attention.* Teachers can reduce confusion for all young children by making sure that children are paying attention before giving instructions. To capture a child's attention, follow these steps:

  1. Precede every request by speaking the child's name: "Gail, the pegs go in the basket."
  2. Get down to the child's level (the half-kneel, an almost automatic posture among preschool teachers, works well; see Photo 17–10).
  3. Look into the child's face and speak directly to the child. In some cases it is necessary to check the child's understanding by getting verification: "Where does the puzzle go?"
  4. Demonstrate, as needed, and hold a rehearsal: "John, turn the pages like this. Now you try it."

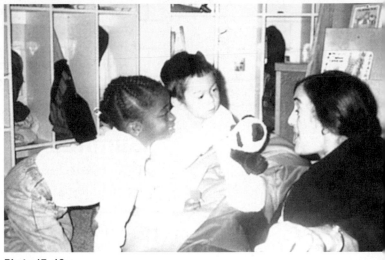

Photo 17–10
Getting down to the child's level and looking directly into his or her eyes helps to focus a child's attention.

- *Give adequate time to comply.* An instruction should not be repeated until the child has had ample time to comply. Teachers often give the instruction a second time (even a third time) while the child is gearing up, getting ready to comply with the initial request. When enough time has been given and it becomes obvious that the child is not going to comply, the direction should be offered a second time. The teacher's voice quietly conveys the expectation that the child will do it this time. The child should not be coaxed or nagged, bribed or offered a reward. Following the second request, when there is no compliance after a reasonable period, the teacher should turn away to do whatever else needs doing. The child should not be permitted to go on to another activity until the coat is picked up, the book is put away, or whatever else was requested. (See the example that follows.)

- *Show consistency and firmness.* When giving directions to children who are noncompliant, teachers need to be matter-of-fact, firm, and consistent. They also must be quietly confident of their own authority. If a teacher says, "Raoul, you may go to the woodworking table as soon as your blocks are picked up," then Raoul must do just that—pick up blocks before going to woodworking. The teacher who gives this direction to Raoul should then alert the other teachers that Raoul has a job to do in the block corner before he can play elsewhere. If other children are busy putting blocks away, the teacher should push a fair share aside for Raoul to take care of. At this point, the contingency can be restated clearly and simply: "Raoul, this is your share of the blocks to put away. You can go to woodworking as soon as you finish." It is appropriate for the teacher to offer to help the child: "As soon as you get started, I will help you put the blocks away."

- *Demonstrate sound judgment.* Teachers must always remember that their behaviour serves as a model for the children in their care. The teacher who shouts at the children "Be quiet!" or who handles the children roughly is modelling the very behaviours that teachers do not want children to use. Furthermore, because consistency is important, teachers must not set a requirement that children may not be able to carry out.

When these general strategies are not enough to create changes in a child's behaviour, a functional approach should be implemented.

Summary

This chapter has focused on a range of difficult and maladaptive behaviours that are manifested by young children. It has also provided a number of ways for teachers to work with children who have difficult behaviour. The importance of experiences and positive adult intervention on brain development during the early years has been stressed. Functional approaches to problem solving have been provided to help teachers develop some systematic ways of dealing with challenging behaviours. Emphasis has been placed on recognizing the importance of consistency between the way teachers and parents respond to a child's behaviour. It is important to remember that many of these problems experienced by young children are communicative in nature and that one of our goals is to help children to communicate and deal with their needs more effectively. Furthermore, many of the behaviours discussed are disruptive but are mainly a part of children's efforts at learning to discriminate between acceptable and unacceptable ways of responding to the expectations of their own home, school, and community. Seldom are acting-out behaviours cause for serious concern, unless they become excessive to the point of threatening the child's well-being or the rights and safety of others.

Most behaviour problems can be managed through careful arrangement of the environment: materials, activities, space, routines, expectations, and adult attention—especially when adult attention is focused on all the good things each child does each day. When a child's behaviour causes damage or injury, the child must be stopped; it is unethical to do otherwise. In extreme cases, where the child has not responded to careful rearrangement of the environment, temporary use of brief time-out periods may be needed. Brief time-out periods must always be used in conjunction with other procedures, including acceptance and understanding of the child's stresses and special attention to the child's appropriate behaviours.

RESOURCES

Pediatric Psychiatry Pamphlets
http://www.klis.com/chandler
This site contains a wide range of case histories and reports on child behaviour by Dr. Jim Chandler.

NOAH (New York Online Access to Health)
http://www.noah-health.org
This comprehensive American site includes information on children's health, behaviour, and social issues.

THE COUNCIL OF CHILDREN WITH BEHAVIORAL DISORDERS (CCBD)
http://www.ccbd.net

STUDENT ACTIVITIES

1. Select two or three fellow students and form a classroom teaching staff whose concern is a four-year-old overly aggressive child. Work together to formulate an intervention plan for this child. Prioritize the steps in your plan, beginning with the steps you will take before undertaking direct intervention with the child.

2. Select a partner; one of you plays the role of the teacher, and the other, a noncompliant child. Demonstrate several ways the teacher might work with this child to obtain compliance *before* the child balks at a request. Reverse the roles and play out several ways of helping a child share a wagon.

3. Divide a sheet of paper into five columns. Head each column with terms commonly used to describe children's acting-out behaviours: aggressive, destructive, disruptive, noncompliant, tantrum. Observe during a free-play period and put a mark in the appropriate column each time one of the behaviours occurs. Circle the mark if a teacher responds in any way. Figure out the ratio of teacher responses to child behaviours. Analyze to see whether certain behaviours draw more teacher attention than others.

REFERENCES

American Psychiatric Association (APA). (2000). *Diagnostic and statistical manual of mental health disorders (DSM-IV-TR)*. Washington, DC: Author.

Division for Early Childhood. (1999). *Concept paper on the identification of and intervention with challenging behaviour.* Retrieved August 17, 2005, from http://www.dec-sped.org/positionpapers.html#challengingbehavior.

Green, R. (1998). *The explosive child*. New York: HarperCollins.

Iwata, B. A., Dorsey, M. F., Slifer, K. J., Bauman, K. E., & Richman, G. S. (1982). Toward a functional analysis of self-injury. *Analysis and Intervention in Developmental Disabilities, 2,* 3–20.

Kaiser, B., & Rasminsky, J. S. (1999). *Meeting the challenge, effective strategies for challenging behaviours in early childhood environments.* Ottawa: Canadian Child Care Federation.

Koegel, R., Koegel, L., & Dunlap, G. (1996). *Positive behavioral support: Including people with difficult behaviors in the community.* Baltimore, MD: Brookes.

Ontario Child and Family Services Act. (1989). Toronto: Ministry of the Attorney General, Queen's Printer for Ontario.

Strain, P. S., Lambert, D. L., Kerr, M. M., Stagg, V., & Jenker, D. (1983). Naturalistic assessment of children's compliance to teachers' requests and consequences for compliance. *Journal of Applied Behavior Analysis, 16*(2), 243–249.

Thomas, A., & Chess, S. (1986). The New York longitudinal study: From infancy to early adult life. In R. Plomin & J. Dunn (Eds.), *The study of the temperament: changes, continuities, and challenges.* Hillsdale, NJ: Erlbaum.

Walker, H., Stiller, B., & Golly, A. (1998). First steps to success. *Young Exceptional Children, 1*(2), 2–7.

CHAPTER 18

Facilitating Language, Speech, and the Development of Communication

KEY CONCEPTS

articulation	motherese
articulation errors	overregularization
augmentative communication systems	prelingual communication
dysfluency	receptive language
expressive language	syntax
holophrastic speech	telegraphic speech

OBJECTIVES

After studying the material in this chapter, the student will be able to

- Define language and explain how it develops.
- Outline in developmental order the major steps in language development and give examples of each step.
- Explain the difference between receptive and expressive language and discuss the developmental significance of each.
- List a number of ways (including augmentative communication systems) in which teachers can help children with language delays expand their communication.
- Discuss dysfluency among young children and describe appropriate responses from teachers and parents.

Introduction

Learning language is a complex developmental task, yet most children accomplish it easily. In fact, children seem to have fewer problems learning language than researchers do defining it. *Language* is a system that enables individuals to express ideas and communicate them to others who use the same code. *Speech* is the sounds of a language, the ability to communicate verbally. Speech depends on articulation, the ability to produce sounds distinctly and correctly.

Language—whether written, spoken, or body language—is a complicated symbol system used for communication. The *symbols* used in language are words, signs, gestures, and body movements that stand for something other than the movements themselves (that is, the symbols represent ideas). It is the mutually agreed on meaning of symbols that enables group members to communicate with one another.

Communication is the exchange of thoughts and ideas, feelings and emotions, likes and dislikes. Although language is the major form of communication, there are other forms:

1. *Gestures and body language.* These may be used alone or with speech. Holding up a hand with fingers upright and palm facing another individual almost universally indicates "Stop."
2. *Printed words.* Books, letters, and directives allow communication without speech or one-to-one contact.
3. *Art forms.* Creative acts and products, such as music, dance, paintings, and the like, are also powerful forms of communication.

The code of every language is based on informally transmitted *rules* about grammar (word order) and word meaning (semantics).

In spite of its complexity, most children acquire language with relative ease (Photo 18–1).

Communicating with others is the essential purpose of language, and communication functions as both a social and a cognitive activity. Allen and Hart (1984) describe the interrelationship: Language serves as a social skill for interacting with others, for expressing needs and ideas, and for getting help, opinions, and the cooperation of others. It serves also as a cognitive skill for understanding, inquiring, and telling about ourselves and our world. It is for these reasons that children who have difficulty acquiring speech and language require early intervention.

Language Acquisition

Theories about language acquisition change or become more elaborate as research reveals more about environmental input and the complex connections between the brain and language (Pinker, 1996). Here we will take a brief look at current theories about language acquisition in the very young.

Photo 18–1
Imitating sounds is an early step in learning to talk.

THE ENVIRONMENTAL PERSPECTIVE

Until a few years ago, a popular theory of language development in the young focused almost exclusively on the environment: The child learned to talk by imitating words and then receiving feedback or reinforcement (Skinner, 1957). Today, most psycholinguists dismiss the explanation as simplistic. However, we cannot discount the role of environment and the input it provides. Children have to hear—or see—the language they learn. They learn very early that language has *function:* Words help them get what they want and need. Words also promote social interactions and provide explanations and conversations about things a child is interested in (Hart & Risley, 1999).

Infant-Directed Speech

Infant-directed speech, popularly called **motherese,** refers to the unique speech patterns that adults use with the very young. Many parents and caregivers speak more slowly and in higher-pitched voices when talking to infants. They use short sentences and a simplified, repetitious vocabulary that usually refers to something in the immediate environment. Cooper and Aslin (1994) note that babies only a few days old prefer to listen to motherese. In summary, the environment has adapted itself to respond to the needs of the language-learning infant.

Motherese
unique infant-directed speech patterns that adults use with the very young

THE IMITATION AND REINFORCEMENT EXPLANATION

Children learn by imitating the speech and language habits of others (Photo 18–2). In turn, they receive feedback (reinforcement).

THE MATURATION OR INNATENESS EXPLANATION

According to this viewpoint, language is said to unfold or emerge as a part of the developmental process, with the environment playing a far less dominant role. Similarly, *constructivists* (theorists who believe that children construct their own knowledge through engagement with the environment) propose that the words a child hears will be learned if they connect with what the child is thinking and feeling (Bloom, 1993).

Photo 18–2
Language acquisition depends on a combination of factors, including the ability to imitate.

THE INTEGRATED EXPLANATION

Bee (1999) points out that efforts to explain how children learn language is one of the most difficult challenges that face developmental psychologists. What seems most likely and more readily understood is the three-part concept suggested by Kaczmarek (1982). Language acquisition is

1. the maturationally determined mechanism for learning language (innateness)
2. the input, or quality and timing, of the child's early language experiences
3. the use the child makes of input and the strategies the child devises for processing spoken language and then reproducing it

There now is general agreement that healthy newborns arrive with a potential for language. They come equipped to learn to talk, and the environment shows them how. There is no dispute that language skills are developed through participation in language activities. Early language activities, for the most part, are informal and spontaneous, occurring during daily routines, casual play, and impromptu social

Photo 18–3
Language development begins long before the infant's first words.

Prelingual communication
body movements, facial expressions, and vocalizations used by infants before the first words are learned

exchanges. Such interactions *in the everyday world* are the main ingredients of language development. When language is not developing, the child is put at great developmental risk. Failure to acquire functional communication can have long-term educational and social consequences.

Sequences in Language Acquisition

Language and speech acquisition, as in all areas of development, occur in a sequential order. They follow a step-by-step pattern from children's early primitive sounds and movements to the complex expression and fluent speech characteristics of their home language.

PRELINGUAL COMMUNICATION

Language development begins in early infancy, long before the first words appear (Photo 18–3). Known as the preverbal, or more accurately, *prelingual* stage, the infant's language is characterized by body movements, facial grimaces, and vocalizations. During this period of **prelingual communication,** the foundations for communicative language are established. The earliest efforts take the form of crying, then cooing, then babbling.

Self-Echoing

Infants who have been babbling for a while begin to sound as if they are having conversations with themselves. They repeat a sound several times, pause as though listening to what they have to say, and then repeat the sound again.

Intonation

Babbling soon begins to be marked by *intonation,* rising and falling variations in the pitch that resembles adults' speech.

FIRST WORDS AND SENTENCES

Major accomplishments for the child are found in making first words and then sentences. Once these are mastered, language development progresses with giant strides.

Vocabulary

As babbling increases, first "words" begin to emerge. Parents often miss out on these first words because they are hard to recognize. In the beginning, infants tend to vary the sounds. They appear to be unsure, at first, which combination of vowels and consonants to settle on when referring to a particular object or action. After the milestone of the first recognizable word, somewhere around the first birthday, new words follow slowly. Months may go by before there is a real burst in vocabulary growth.

Receptive and Expressive Language

Language is described as having two dimensions: *receptiveness* and *expressiveness.* These dimensions are interrelated but are evaluated separately.

Receptive language refers to the words an individual understands or recognizes. Throughout life, we understand more words than we use

Receptive language
language that is understood; it precedes expressive language

when speaking. Although six-year-olds know approximately 14 000 words, they are likely to have many fewer words (about 2500) in their expressive vocabulary.

Expressive language. Words and sentences that an individual speaks or signs come under the heading of **expressive language.** Gestures, grimaces, body movements, written words, and various art forms are included under the same heading. Expressive language takes two forms:

1. *Initiative*—the individual starts a communicative interaction with another
2. *Responsive*—the individual answers or behaves in some way in response to another's verbal initiation

A child's expressive vocabulary seems also to contain a subset of receptive vocabulary related to the materials and activities the child is engaged in at the time. The more interesting the materials and the more children are encouraged to talk about them with someone, the larger their vocabularies become.

Expressive language
spoken words or signs that individuals use in communicating with others

EARLY SENTENCES

Children's progress in putting words together to form sentences is as rapid as vocabulary growth during the early years. Learning to combine words in a particular order pays off. It enables the child to convey more complex thoughts. This aspect of language acquisition is known as the development of **syntax.** It has several stages, beginning with the holophrastic language.

Syntax
the way in which words are put together to form phrases, clauses, or sentences

Holophrastic Speech

At the stage of **holophrastic speech,** the child uses a single word to convey an entire thought. The intended meaning is as unmistakable as a complete sentence. Holophrases usually occur in reference to something the child sees, hears, smells, tastes, or touches. The child's intonation or voice inflection also contributes to the meaning, as do gestures, such as pointing or looking up. The single word "doggie," depending on context, inflection, and gesture, can be readily understood to mean

Holophrastic speech
a state of speech development where a child conveys meaning with a one-word utterance

- "I want to play with this dog." (while toddling after the dog)
- "See the dog." (while pointing at a dog)
- "Where did the dog go?" (while looking outside)

During this period the child may use the same word for several objects or events. For example, *doggie* may mean *all* furry four-legged creatures; *bye-bye* often means both the absence of someone as well as someone leaving. Often, however, parents and caregivers have to work hard to figure out what the child wants. The say, "Show me," or they offer various objects until they select the "right" one.

Telegraphic Speech

Toward the end of the second year, the child begins to speak in simple two-word sentences. These sentences convey grammatical meaning even though many words are left out. Hence the term **telegraphic speech** because of the similarity to the way telegrams are written. Few parents or caregivers mistake the intent of abbreviated sentences, such as "Mama's purse?" "Daddy bye-bye," "Me want," or "All done!"

Telegraphic speech
the stage in language acquisition in which children's utterances are generally longer than two words, phrases convey grammatical meaning even though many words are left out

These abbreviated two-word phrases are an important milestone in language acquisition. They indicate that the child is learning the word order (syntax or

Photo 18–4
Language learning is rapid between the ages of two and five years.

grammar) of the language. Without appropriate word order, words cannot convey meaning, especially as sentences get longer. Most of us would agree that without conventional word order it would take a while to figure out what the child wants.

THE DEVELOPMENT OF LANGUAGE COMPLEXITY

Language acquisition progresses rapidly in children between two and five years of age (Photo 18–4). Children learn to

- use all forms of questions (e.g., *who? where? what? when? how?* and the seemingly never-ending *why?*)
- transform positives to negatives (e.g., *can/cannot, will/won't, is/isn't*)
- change verb forms, as required, to convey particular meanings (e.g., *run/ran, I will go/I went, It is raining/It has rained*)
- classify objects or animals (e.g., at first all dogs were just "dog"; now *this* dog is a collie-type of dog while *the other one* is a poodle-type of dog)
- indicate "more than one" through the use of plurals (e.g., *boy/boys, kitty/kitties, toy/lots of toys*)
- convey ownership (e.g., *mine, hers, ours, theirs, Daddy's*) (See Allen & Marotz, 1992, for more detailed age-by-age analysis.)

Overregularizations

Overregularization
language irregularities that occur because the child is applying previously learned rules of grammar; for example, "The mouses runned"

The years of rapid language development are characterized by several kinds of errors. Developmentally, these should be thought of as misconstructions, rather than as errors. They represent children's *best efforts* to apply the complex rules of the language to the situation at hand. Often the misconstructions occur because children are trying to regularize the irregular. This leads to **overregularization** (Rathus, 1988). Many children will say *digged* instead of *dug* for a while. When they say *digged*, they are relying on an earlier learning that called for adding *–ed* to a verb to indicate action in the past. These children, as yet, have no understanding of such things as irregular verbs. In a sense, *digged* is right. The child is applying the rule correctly. The child still must learn when not to apply it.

Young children also mix up and overgeneralize various forms of plurals. They may say *feets* instead of *feet, mouses* or *mices* rather than *mice, gooses* rather than *geese*. According to Rathus (1988, p. 277), such *errors* aid rather than hinder language learning:

> *Overregularization does represent an advance in the development of syntax.* Over-regularization stems from accurate knowledge of grammatical rules—not from faulty language acquisition. In another year or two, mouses will become boringly transformed into mice, and Mommy will no longer have sitted down. [italics in original]

When such *errors* occur, adults should, without emphasis or comment, simply use the correct form—"Yes, the mice ran away." The child should not be criticized or corrected directly. Children should not be made to feel self-conscious or cute, regardless of how charming or amusing an adult may find the misconstructions. Unless undue attention is focused on the situation, these perfectly normal irregularities will self-correct in good time.

By the end of the fifth year, the development of syntax is nearly complete. Most children will be using all but one or two of the conventional grammatical structures. They will be adept at creating and using compound and complex sentences and will have a minimum of 2500 words in their expressive vocabulary.

Teachers can expect five- and six-year-olds to understand most of what is said to them, *but only if they have had exposure to the vocabulary being used*. The range and type of vocabulary is influenced by the language environment in which a child is raised. For example, a child who knows colour names may be unable to follow the directions in a colour-matching activity. Why? Because the word *match* (or the concept *match* in a task-related context) is not in the child's vocabulary.

Photo 18–5
An essential skill for teachers is recognizing what children communicate nonverbally as well as verbally.

NONVERBAL COMMUNICATION

Though the primary focus of this chapter has been on verbal skills, children's efforts to communicate nonverbally are important, too. Adults need to be aware of what children do, as well as what they say (Photo 18–5). This is especially important with children who have language difficulties or delays. A child who shrugs, scowls, smiles, flinches, or looks off into space is communicating. Teachers and parents should try to respond to such efforts as often as possible. A responsive language environment is crucial to the development of communication skills.

EARLY WARNING SIGNS

As in all areas of development, the rate at which children develop language varies from child to child. Children who have hearing problems will almost always demonstrate a delay in language development, as well as some mispronunciation of sounds and words once they do begin to speak. (When the model for speech is heard inaccurately or unclearly, the child's speech will reflect what he or she hears.) Children with poor muscular control of the tongue and jaw (commonly occurring in children with cerebral palsy), or who have physiological problems in the hard or soft palate in the mouth, will also have difficulties in speaking. Early childhood teachers should be alert if they notice a cluster of any of the following symptoms. The list, from the Middlesex-London Health Unit (1990), was provided by the

Thames Valley Children's Centre:

- Child never makes attempts to vocalize sound.
- Child does not make any sounds.
- Child is embarrassed and disturbed by his speech at any age.
- There is concern about a child's dysfluency (stuttering).
- Child's voice is monotone, too loud or too soft, too high or too low for his age and gender, or has a poor quality.
- Child sounds as if he is talking through his nose or as if he has a cold.

As an infant:

- Child babbles normally until eight months of age and then stops.

As a toddler:

- Child uses mostly vowel sounds in his or her speech at any age after one year.
- Child does not recognize any familiar objects or does not follow any simple commands by 12 months of age.
- Child is not talking by 18 months of age.
- Child is not combining two or more words to express ideas by 22 months of age.

As a preschooler:

- Child is difficult to understand after age three.
- Child is still not using a variety of three- to four-word sentences by age three.
- Child uses sentence structure that is noticeably faulty at age four.

At school age (age five and up):

- Child has language that is disordered and irrelevant.
- Child cannot tell stories in sequence.
- Child has naming difficulties.
- Child does not appear to comprehend discussion.

If an early childhood teacher feels that there is some concern about how a child's speech is developing, he or she should seek the advice of a consultant. Regardless of the cause of a speech or language delay, it is important that a child not be made to feel self-conscious in any way about his or her speech. Teachers need to develop programs that encourage and enhance opportunities for verbal interaction.

The Teacher's Role in Facilitating Language Development

Teachers have a major role in facilitating language development in infants and young children. The foundation for building children's language and communication skills, according to Schwartz, McBride, Pepler, Grant, and Carter (1993), is the social communicative context of the environment. This means that in the inclusive classroom, teachers will engineer a social context in which people are sensitive to children's attempts to interact with others and in which the physical environment and the people in it make communication easy and enjoyable for children. In this context, teachers and children become partners who share responsibility for selecting and maintaining communicative interaction. It is most important to make sure that the environment is arranged so as to prompt both children's language and an appropriate degree of teacher responsiveness (not too much and not too little).

Photo 18–6
Teachers should make sure that there is plenty to talk about.

CREATING AN INCLUSIVE LANGUAGE-LEARNING ENVIRONMENT

To promote language development, teachers should arrange the learning environment so that every child has many opportunities to communicate. Teachers should also make sure that there is plenty to talk about (Photo 18 6). Activities should be arranged so that both materials and teachers are responsive to children's language efforts. The basics of arranging an effective early learning environment are covered in Chapter 15.

Teachers' skills and attitudes are discussed in Chapter 4. A brief review of a few of these concepts as they relate specifically to language acquisition appears in the following sections.

Teachers' Role

In creating an inclusive language learning environment, teachers should

- provide a relaxed atmosphere in which children are allowed plenty of time to say what they want to say
- be involved in authentic and meaningful conversations with children
- encourage highly verbal children to learn to listen so that less assertive or verbal children have a chance to talk
- work at being good listeners and responders
- answer children in ways that indicate that they really are interested and genuinely want to hear more
- respond with open-ended questions
- facilitate many opportunities for children to communicate with their peers
- provide duplication of complex materials so more than one child can use the same material at the same time
- encourage children to speak for themselves rather than have their peers speak for them

Photo 18–7
Some children may need more adult input, prompting, and encouragement.

In summary, children learn language by engaging in conversation, by using interactive communication with peers and adults. *Teachers do not need practice in talking;* children do. In an effective early learning program, talking is going on all the time, but it is the children who are doing most of the talking. Teachers are serving as facilitators, sometimes prompting, sometimes questioning, sometimes reflecting a child's thoughts back to the child (a sure signal to the child that the teacher is really listening). Children with language delays may need more adult input, prompting, and encouragement (Photo 18–7).

The Role of Questions

Questions, asked or answered, are an important part of language acquisition. A child who turns away without responding when someone says, "Hi, how are you today?" quite effectively ends the exchange. If this happens frequently, teachers, family, and playmates may stop trying to communicate. The child loses out on two important sources of learning:

1. Language play and practice that facilitates language acquisition (Photo 18–8)
2. Necessary information that most children get through everyday verbal exchanges

Teachers should ask questions *only* if they expect (and are willing to wait for) answers. If an answer is not forthcoming, the child should be helped to formulate one. It may be a simple verbalization or gesture originated by the child, or a response modelled after one the teacher provides. In any event, the child is expected to respond. All children, regardless of their speech and language skills, will soon fall quite naturally into the routine of responding, if teachers' expectations are realistic and consistent.

Activities That Promote Communication

Children need to have many things to talk about. They need novel materials to ask questions about. They need excursions, preferably simple ones, such as a visit to the house under construction across the street, so as to practise verbal recall. They need easily managed picture books that enable them to "read" the story. They also need active play for prompting language of every kind. For children in need of special help with language skills, the importance of materials and equipment that require physical activity, as well as activities that stimulate social interactive play, cannot be overemphasized. The following suggestions may be helpful in promoting communication skills with children:

Photo 18–8
Children need activities that prompt language.

- Puppets, manipulative, dramatic play props.
- Homemade instruments. Try paper plate tambourines filled with rice or beans.
- Fingerplays. These incorporate rhythm and children's inclination to move.
- "Stop and go" games. Try these with music or singing.
- Homemade puzzles. Take calendar pictures, body shapes, and so on, and cut them into pieces; then have children put them together while labelling and talking about them.
- "What's missing?" On a tray place several items, and have the children look at them. Then cover up the

tray, or ask the children to close their eyes, and take one item away. Then ask the children "What's missing?"

- Matching games. These can help reinforce the concepts of same and different.
- Weather charts. Have children cut pictures of various types of weather conditions to use at small-group times to discuss the day's weather.
- Photograph albums. Create albums with children focusing on children and the environment.
- Flannel board stories. Using pictures from a book, create a flannel board story by cutting out the pieces of the story and backing them with flannel. Have duplicate copies of the story for children to follow along or tell the story with the flannel pieces.

Incidental Learning and Teaching

Hart and Risley (1982) have demonstrated conclusively that incidental teaching is an effective strategy for improving language. Their research focused on developing children with and without developmental delays. Incidental teaching is defined as a child-initiated interaction between an adult and an individual child. This should occur when the child is engaged in free play or some other child-initiated activity. The child may be seeking information, assistance, materials, feedback, or reassurance. The adult can make use of this naturally occurring interaction to promote a brief but immediate and meaningful learning situation.

The whole point of incidental learning is to have the child find the encounters so pleasant, and so rewarding, that he or she will return to the teacher again and again to request help and share ideas and experiences.

Example:

Emily, a four-year-old with a language delay, held a paint apron up to the teacher. The teacher knelt down, smiled, and waited, giving Emily time to make a request. Emily remained silent. After a moment the teacher said, "Emily, what do you need?" (The teacher did not anticipate Emily's need by putting the apron on for her.) When Emily did not answer, the teacher asked, "Emily, do you want help with your apron?" Emily nodded. "Tell me 'apron,'" prompted the teacher. Emily made a sound somewhat similar to apron and the teacher said, "Yes, apron. Here, let me put it over your head. Now, I'll tie it." The teacher's last sentence modelled tie, the next word that would be expected once Emily had learned to say apron.

Had Emily not said apron, the teacher should still have put the apron on Emily, verbalizing a description of the procedure in simple language at the time.

A child should never be scolded, nagged, or coaxed. If teachers introduce pressure into incidental learning opportunities, many children stop making the contacts. Some children turn to communicating their needs less appropriately through whining, crying, or sulking. Children who are most in need of the highly individualized help that makes incidental teaching so effective are usually the first to be put off at any sign of pressure.

Speech Irregularities

Speech irregularities are common and even normal in speech development. Most children, 80 percent or more, will show some kind of articulation errors during their early years. These irregularities may not necessarily be predictive of future concerns.

Photo 18–9
Articulation refers to the production of speech sounds.

Articulation
refers to the production of speech sounds

Articulation errors
speech sounds that are inconsistent with the native language (usually a temporary developmental irregularity)

For a time, the ability to formulate thoughts and ideas is greater than the child's ability to pronounce words correctly or to organize the words into sentences that make sense. The irregularities that early childhood teachers are most likely to encounter are discussed in the following sections.

ARTICULATION ERRORS

Articulation refers to the production of speech sounds (Photo 18–9). **Articulation errors** are part of language development and are likely to occur as young children work at mastering the complex sounds that make up everyday speech. Misarticulations usually are classified as omissions, substitutions, additions, or distortions:

- *Omissions.* Sounds are left out, often at the beginning or end of words: "That's my 'agon (wagon)," "Here's the broo' (broom)."

- *Substitutions.* Interchanging sounds, such as *b* and *v*, as in "Put the balentines on the vack seat," or replacing one sound with another: "wabbit" for "rabbit."

- *Additions.* Inserting sounds not part of a word: "warsh" (wash) or "notta now" (not now).

- *Distortions.* Deviations in speech sounds usually occur because of tongue misplacement or missing teeth, as is the case with many six-year-olds: "schwim" for "swim" or "tink" for "think."

Lisping

Rarely is lisping (pronouncing *s* as *th*) considered a worrisome problem in preschool children. Seldom does it persist. Exceptions may be those few cases where the child's lisp has been showcased by adults who think it is cute. If lisping should continue into the primary grades, parents usually are encouraged to seek consultation.

Dysfluency

Dysfluency
hesitations, repetitions, or omitted or extra sounds in speech patterns

Stuttering is a common word for **dysfluency** or fluency disorders. *Cluttering* is another term also used to label a fluency problem. (Both terms are losing favour among developmentalists and speech and language clinicians.) *Dysfluency* better describes children's excessive repetition of particular sounds or words, noticeable hesitations between words, extra sounds, or the undue prolonging of a sound. Such speech irregularities are common. To label a young child as a *stutterer* is unwise, in part because of the self-fulfilling consequences. However, there are those few children who develop abnormal dsyfluencies during the preschool or primary school years. According to Zebrowski (1995), specific features of a common dysfluency, such as stuttering, distinguish it from a developmentally typical dysfluency:

- frequency
- type and proportion
- duration
- associated nonspeech behaviours, like excessive frustration or grimacing

STRATEGIES FOR SUPPORTING CHILDREN WITH SPEECH IRREGULARITIES

A developmentally common speech irregularity seldom needs to turn into a major problem. Teachers and parents can help to forestall such a consequence by practising preventive do's and don'ts:

- Make sure the child is getting good nutrition, adequate rest, and many more hours of active play than of television each day.
- Provide comfort, care, and support; reduce tensions as much as possible (difficult, but not impossible, even in this hurried world).
- Have fun with the child and with language; inject humour, simple rhyming activities, and simple riddles into everyday routines; music activities are also effective (such as repeating beats, echoing sounds, and filling in words in verses).
- Discipline with calmness, firmness, and consistency; avoid harshness, ridicule, or teasing.
- Offer activities in which the child can be successful and develop positive self-esteem.
- Become aware of local family literacy programs.
- Avoid correcting or nagging the child (avoid saying, "Slow down," "Take it easy," or "Think before you speak").
- Do not call attention to dysfluencies directly or indirectly; the child could become all the more tense when an adult focuses intently with exaggerated patience, a forced smile, or a rigid body, waiting for the child to "get it out."
- Avoid interrupting a child or acting hurried, as young children need plenty of time when trying to put their ideas into spoken language.
- Never compare a child's speech with another child's, especially if the comparison is unfavourable to either.

To correct a child unnecessarily undermines the child's confidence as a speaker. If children are to improve their language skills, they must keep talking. Children who fear that they will be criticized each time they speak will speak less and less; therefore, adults should avoid asking a child to repeat anything that they have understood.

REFERRAL

It is important to remember that speech and language irregularities are part of development. Adults working with young children should be aware of developmental patterns and not overreact to common speech and language irregularities. However, if a genuine concern exists, it needs to be identified as early as possible and an intervention program put into effect immediately. The early childhood teacher may be the first to perceive a possible communication difficulty. (See Chapter 12 on the teacher's role in early identification.) Whenever a teacher is in doubt as to whether a child has a difficulty with communication, parents should be consulted and assisted to seek help, if needed. Parents often have the feeling that *something* may be wrong. Conversely, it is common for parents to become so accustomed to their child's speech that they do not realize that their child is having difficulty communicating with others. Speech, language, and hearing (audiology) clinicians who specialize in young children provide the most reliable testing and consultation.

Photo 18–10
Speech therapy is sometimes necessary.

THE REFERRAL PROCESS

Consulting Figure 18–1 (pp. 388–389) may determine the necessity of referral to a speech pathologist for consultation, assessment, or therapy.

INTERVENTION

Young children who are diagnosed as having specific speech and language difficulties need an individualized intervention program (Photo 18–10). For best results, the early childhood teacher and the speech and language therapist must work together. In some cases, short therapy sessions in which the child works exclusively with a speech and language therapist are provided. Therapists can promote classroom cooperation by informing teachers regularly about the goals and strategies used in the child's treatment. The particular skills the therapist is working on and the progress the child is making should also be discussed. Within a transdisciplinary approach, the therapist works with a child who is experiencing communication difficulties and with small groups of children. This provides opportunities for the child to have ongoing practice in the use of new skills and to interact with peers, who serve as language models.

The foregoing does not imply that teachers or parents are expected to become language specialists. They can, however, readily learn simple procedures for facilitating individual children's speech and language development. This means that the teacher needs to develop a program in which all children are involved and that provides opportunities for the child with speech problems to practise the necessary sounds. The teacher should model correct pronunciation and support the efforts of all children. Programs such as the Hanan Early Language Parent Training Program (Grolametto, Greenberg, & Manoloson, 1986) may be useful.

Manoloson, Ward, and Dodington (1995, pp. 238–252) encourage parents to respond to and play interactively with their children. They state that parents and teachers should "allow your child to lead" (be able to drop their own agenda in favour of the child's), "adapt to the moment" (be able to enter into the child's play), and "add new experiences and words" (expand on what the child is doing or saying). They also discourage the parent or teacher from taking on the role solely of an "entertainer," "director," "reporter," or "watcher," stressing that when a teacher takes on these roles, the child is not given adequate opportunity to practise language (pp. 40–41). Teachers should sustain conversations, talking and encouraging many conversational turns.

Augmentative Communication Systems

Augmentative communication systems
communication systems used to supplement a child's verbal language; the systems may be sign language, picture symbols, or sophisticated computer systems, such as a voice synthesizer

Some children with severe disabilities do not acquire speech easily; others use some words but have such poor articulation that their speech is largely unintelligible. For these children, an augmentative communication system may enhance their ability to communicate. **Augmentative communication systems** include gestures, signs, symbols, prerecorded words and phrases, pictures, and, under special circumstances, voice synthesis. For preschool children, most augmentative systems use either sign language (Zeece & Wolda, 1995) or a picture/symbol exchange (Bondy & Frost, 1994). *Before* introducing an augmentative system as a primary communication method, a speech and language pathologist should be consulted. When selecting an augmentative communication system, the issue of *intelligibility* is important: Will the people in the child's environment be able to understand and communicate with the child using the system? Many young children with severe disabilities do not have the fine motor skills necessary to use sign language effectively. For these children, a picture- or symbol-based system may be a better choice.

Children using augmentative communication systems should be encouraged to use their systems in all different environments and activities, including at snack time, on the playground, during circle-time activities, and during free play. Using the system across activities will promote generalization and improve communication skills (Photo 18–11).

In inclusive programs, a simple sign system whose complexity can be geared up or down offers a tremendous boost to language and communication development for all children. Signing is both *functional* and *fun* for children who are preverbal or nonverbal, learning a second language, gifted and in need of ongoing challenge, or shy about speaking up. Signing also is successful with children with cognitive and behavioural disorders.

Photo 18–11
Communication boards may be activated by a pointer attached to a headband.

Summary

Learning to speak and use the native language is the most complex developmental task mastered by infants and young children. Explaining how children do it has been the subject of thousands of research studies as well as major, and often conflicting, theoretical formulations. In spite of disagreements about how children accomplish this difficult task, most children do, and with little apparent effort. Without specific instruction, children move through the developmental sequences in speech and language acquisition, from crying, cooing, and babbling to producing complex sentences and multisyllabic words in their first five or six years. Most speech and language irregularities come and go, and most appear to be self-correcting unless the child is pressured.

A number of young children have difficulties speaking or learning the language; some children have trouble with both. Differences may range from developmentally normal delays and dysfluencies to serious concerns requiring the services of a speech and language specialist or early interventionist. An undiagnosed hearing loss is always a possibility and needs to be ruled out first before diagnosing a language delay or impairment in a young child. A stimulating classroom environment with interesting materials and activities and support for social interaction among children, coupled with incidental teaching, has proven effective in enhancing the speech and language skills of all children at all levels of language development.

Teachers' knowledge of speech and language development and their skill in observing children are essential to identifying children with language differences.

RESOURCES

THE HANEN CENTRE
http://www.hanen.org
The Hanen Centre is a Canadian charitable organization with an international outreach. It is committed to helping young children with (or at risk of developing) language delays learn to communicate and interact effectively.

NORTH WORDS
http://www.northwords.com
North Words is a partnership of district agencies that provide speech, language, and hearing services to preschool children (birth to age five). This is the site for one of

Figure 18-1 COMMUNICATION CHECKLIST FOR CHILDREN FROM BIRTH TO AGE FIVE

REFER ANY CHILD...

- If you are concerned about her/his speech/language/hearing* development.
- If her/his speech and language skills have not improved over the past six months.
- Who often repeats sounds and/or words (stuttering).
- Whose voice sounds different/odd to you.
- Whose play or social interactions seems inappropriate.
- With a diagnosis such as cleft lip/palate, hearing loss, PDD/Autism, developmental delay (who is not already receiving services).

***Please refer to an audiologist for any concerns about hearing.**

Early Intervention is Crucial.
Call Toronto Preschool Speech and Language Services at
416-338-8255 TTY 416-338-0025

www.tpsls.on.ca

Date Completed: _____

Child's Name: _____

Child's Date of Birth: _____

Person Completing From: _____

Contact Address: _____ Postal Code: _____

City: _____ Phone No.: _____

TORONTO Public Health • Community Partners
Ontario

265S021

SOURCE: Toronto Preschool Speech and Language Services Infant Hearing Program.

Communication Checklist
For Children from Birth to Age Five

Toronto Preschool
Speech & Language
Services

**Infant Hearing Program
Speech & Language Program**

If the answer is **NO** to any of the following questions, call Toronto Preschool Speech and Language Services at **416-338-8255.**

Yes No

BY THREE MONTHS
Does the child:
- startle to a sudden sound? .... ☐ ☐
- make sounds? (*oo, ah*) .... ☐ ☐
- look at you with interest when you talk to her/him? .... ☐ ☐
- smile in response to you? .... ☐ ☐

BY SIX MONTHS
Does the child:
- turn to where a sound is coming from? .... ☐ ☐
- make several different sounds? .... ☐ ☐
- try to get your attention by looking at your face and/or making sounds? .... ☐ ☐
- make sounds and smile in response to your facial expressions and sounds? .... ☐ ☐

BY NINE MONTHS
Does the child:
- reach out to be picked up? .... ☐ ☐
- respond to her/his name? .... ☐ ☐
- make *speech-like* sounds? (*baba, gaga*) ...... ☐ ☐
- babble tunefully (sing-song voice) while playing alone? .... ☐ ☐
- turn to where a voice (spoken words) is coming from? .... ☐ ☐
- enjoy being played with and does he/she take turns making sounds back and forth? .... ☐ ☐
- understand *no*? .... ☐ ☐

NEL

BY TWELVE MONTHS

Does the child:

- use a finger to point out things to you in the environment? .... ☐ ☐
- imitate or use gestures like waving bye-bye? .... ☐ ☐
- let you know what he/she wants by using a combination of sounds and actions? .... ☐ ☐
- bring you toys he/she wants to show you and/or play with? .... ☐ ☐
- enjoy playing games like Peek-a-boo and Pat-a-cake and will he/she sometimes start the game? .... ☐ ☐
- understand some simple phrases? .... ☐ ☐
  (*Come here. Don't touch.*)

BY FIFTEEN MONTHS

Does the child:

- usually look at you when communicating? .... ☐ ☐
- repeat words he/she hears? .... ☐ ☐
- seem to be talking in sentences but not using real words? .... ☐ ☐
- say one or two words? .... ☐ ☐
- understand some simple questions and commands? .... ☐ ☐
  (*Go get a diaper. Where's the ball?*)

BY EIGHTEEN MONTHS

Does the child:

- point, look at you, and then at what what he/she is talking about? .... ☐ ☐
- use the word *no*? .... ☐ ☐
- say about ten or more words? .... ☐ ☐
- understand and use the names of familiar objects? (ball, light, bed, car) .... ☐ ☐
- sometimes answer the question: *What's this*? .... ☐ ☐
- take turns when playing with a partner? .... ☐ ☐
- use toys for pretend play? .... ☐ ☐

BY TWO YEARS

Does the child:

- point to some body parts? .... ☐ ☐
- use descriptive words? (hungry, big, hot) .... ☐ ☐

BY THREE YEARS

Does the child:

- follow two-part directions? (*Go to the kitchen and get your cup*) .... ☐ ☐
- participate in short conversations? .... ☐ ☐
- use sentences of three words or more to communicate? .... ☐ ☐
- talk about something that happened in the past? .... ☐ ☐
- ask *why* questions? .... ☐ ☐
- Do people outside the family understand 1/2 of what he/she says? .... ☐ ☐

BY FOUR YEARS

Does the child:

- talk in whole sentences using adult-like grammar? .... ☐ ☐
- tell a story that is easy to follow? .... ☐ ☐
- ask many questions? .... ☐ ☐
- answer *who, how, how many* questions? .... ☐ ☐
- use *I, me, you, he* and *she* properly? .... ☐ ☐
- start a conversation and continue it, staying on the same topic? .... ☐ ☐
- use language to create pretend situations when playing with others? .... ☐ ☐
- Do people outside the family understand more than 3/4 of what he/she says? .... ☐ ☐

BY FIVE YEARS

Does the child:

- explain how an object can be used? .... ☐ ☐
- answer *when* and *why* questions? .... ☐ ☐
- talk about past, future, and imaginary events? .... ☐ ☐
- participate in long, detailed conversations? .... ☐ ☐
- Do people outside the family understand most of what he/she says? .... ☐ ☐

SOURCE: Toronto Preschool Speech and Language Services.

the 32 preschool speech/language programs being implemented across Ontario in a joint venture with the Ministries of Health, Community and Social Services, Citizenship and Culture, and Education and Training.

THE CANADIAN HEARING SOCIETY
http://www.chs.ca
The Canadian Hearing Society provides a wide range of services to meet the needs of five consumer groups. Services are offered in a fully accessible and supportive environment by professionals experienced in meeting the needs of deaf, deafened, and hard-of-hearing people.

AMERICAN SPEECH-LANGUAGE-HEARING ASSOCIATION (ASHA)
http://www.asha.org
ASHA is the professional, scientific, and credentialing association for more than 99 000 speech-language pathologists, audiologists, and speech, language, and hearing scientists in the United States and throughout the world.

STUDENT ACTIVITIES

1. Listen to a child between three and six years of age. Record 25 spontaneous language samples in the child's home or classroom. (Review language sampling techniques in Chapter 12.) Discuss the child's language skills with your classmates.
2. Write down or tape-record at least 15 verbal responses of adults while they are caring for a child or children between one and three years of age. Is there evidence of motherese? Give examples.
3. How would you increase the language skills of a child who came up to you with a sweater in hand and said, "My sweater"? List ways to do this.
4. Work in small groups of four or five. Appoint a recorder. Generate as many ways as possible, including nonverbal ways, to let a child know you are interested in his or her new shoes and want to hear more about them.
5. Select a partner to act as a parent of a child who says to you, the teacher, "I'm really concerned. Ryan has been stuttering the last two weeks." Discuss with your partner what you would say to this parent.
6. Create four activities to promote communication skills for children who are using telegraphic speech.
7. Rearrange the following in appropriate sequence (from earliest to most complex normal language development):
   a) telegraphic speech
   b) grammatical overregularizations
   c) crying
   d) vocal intonation
   e) holophrastic speech
   f) complex sentences
   g) babbling
   h) first words
   i) cooing

REFERENCES

Allen, K. E., & Hart, B. (1984). *The early years: Arrangements for learning.* Englewood Cliffs, NJ: Prentice-Hall.

Allen, K. E., & Marotz, L. R. (1992). *Development profiles: Prebirth to eight.* Albany, NY: Delmar.

Bee, H. (1999). *The developing child* (9th ed.). New York: Longman.

Bloom, L. (1993). *The transition from infancy to language: Acquiring the power of expression.* Cambridge (UK): Cambridge University Press.

Bondy, A., & Frost, L. (1994). The picture exchange communication system. *Focus on Autistic Behavior, 9*(3), 1–19.

Cooper, R. P., & Aslin, R. N. (1994). Developmental differences in infant attention to spectral properties of infant-directed speech. *Child Development, 65,* 1663–1667.

Grolametto, L., Greenberg, J., & Manoloson, H. A. (1986). Developing dialogue skills: The Hanan Early Language Parent Program. *Seminars in Speech and Language, 7*(4), 367–382.

Hart, B., & Risley, T. (1982). *How to use incidental teaching for elaborating language.* Lawrence, KS: H & H Enterprises.

Hart, B., & Risley, T. R. (1999). *The social world of children learning to talk.* Baltimore, MD: Brookes.

Kaczmarek, L. A. (1982). Motor activities: A context for language/communication intervention. *Journal of the Division for Early Childhood, 6,* 21–36.

Manoloson, A., Ward, B., & Dodington, N. (1995). *You make the difference in helping your child learn.* Toronto: The Hanen Centre.

Middlesex-London Health Unit. (1990). *Safe healthy children: A health and safety manual for childcare providers.* London, ON: Author.

Pinker, S. (1996). *The language instinct: How the mind creates language.* New York: Morrow.

Rathus, S. A. (1988). *Understanding child development.* New York: Holt, Rinehart, & Winston.

Schwartz, T. S., McBride, B., Pepler, I., Grant, S., & Carter, J. J. (1993, December). *A classroom-based curriculum for facilitating communicative independence in young children with special needs.* Paper presented at the Division of Early Childhood Conference, San Diego, CA.

Skinner, B. F. (1957). *Verbal behaviour.* New York: Prentice Hall.

Zebrowski, P. M. (1995). The topography of beginning stuttering. *Journal of Communication Disorders, 28*(2), 75–91.

Zeece, P. D., & Wolda, M. K. (1995). Let me see what you can say; let me see what you feel! *Teaching Exceptional Children, 27*(2), 4–10.

CHAPTER 19

Facilitating Cognitive Learning

KEY CONCEPTS

assistive technology
attention span
brain development
classification
discrimination
embedded learning
perceptual motor skills

readiness as a learning theory
rote memorization
sensory integration
seriation
spatial and temporal (time)
    concepts

OBJECTIVES

After studying the material in this chapter, the student will be able to

- Explain the concept of readiness and how to relate this to maturation and learning theories.
- Make a case against prescribed paper-and-pencil tasks in preschool programs, and describe, instead, the learning activities that should be emphasized.
- Suggest ways that teachers can help young children with developmental differences learn to focus their attention on cognitive activities.
- Describe basic cognitive functions needed by all young children.
- Identify ways that teachers can help children, including those with special needs, become involved in group cognitive learning activities.

Introduction

The way in which children develop is influenced by congenital factors, as well as by the postnatal environment they experience as they mature. In other words, both heredity and environment affect the process of maturation. Recent research on the way in which the brain develops provides us with further insights on how **brain development** affects cognitive growth and learning. Readiness, as a concept, attributes changes in children's skills to experience and the step-by-step learning of developmental tasks. For example, if a child has learned to recognize food, find his or her own mouth, and hold a spoon right side up most of the time, that child is in all likelihood *ready* to begin the more complex behaviour of self-feeding. In other words, children are ready to learn a new and more complex skill when they can perform and synchronize the necessary, though less difficult, skills that precede the more complex skill.

The concept of **readiness as a learning theory** is useful when planning an inclusive program for young children. Because all children develop at different rates in different areas of development, an effective inclusive early childhood environment must be able to meet the needs of all children, regardless of how uneven their individual development may be.

An inclusive early childhood program should have at its foundation child-initiated play, supported by an enriched environment that offers many opportunities for active language development and hands-on learning experiences. Learning experiences presented in the form of workbooks, prescribed paper-and-pencil tasks, and **rote memorization** (the memorizing of numbers or letters without any comprehension as to what they stand for) do not enrich learning, and they are not appropriate in any pre-academic curriculum or for any young child. However, most early childhood educators now accept that pre-academic activities and spontaneous play are compatible. Quality early childhood programs should include cognitive experiences, sensorimotor activities, and intellectual experiences in their daily programs.

All children, those with disabilities and those without, vary greatly in how their cognitive abilities develop. Because the process of becoming literate begins in early infancy and continues throughout the developmental years, early exposure to a range of learning, language, and communication experiences in a safe, warm, and caring environment is most conducive to the stimulation of early cognitive functioning. This chapter covers approaches and ideas appropriate for supporting cognitive development in an inclusive early childhood program.

Brain development
affects cognitive growth and learning; children's brains need to be stimulated for the network of connections to grow and be protected from elimination

Readiness as a learning theory
recognizes the importance of being aware of the point at which a child has all of the necessary prerequisite skills to engage in specific new learning

Rote memorization
the act of memorizing numbers or letters without understanding them; being able to recite something that has little or no meaning for the one who has memorized it

Implications of Brain Development for Teachers of Young Children

Children's brains need to be stimulated in order for the network of connections to grow and be protected from elimination (see Chapter 5). This knowledge is of great importance to early childhood teachers and caregivers, and to parents of young children. As the research implies, young children are biologically ready to learn. The question that arises, however, is what best supports early brain development?

Shore (1997) writes that a decade or more of brain research has given us some answers to these questions. She cites five major points to consider:

1. There is a complex interplay between nature (genes) and nurture (environment) in the development of the brain. *Implication:* What children experience in the first few years may influence their future intellectual functioning as much as their genetic makeup does.

2. Early care (both positive and negative) has a "decisive and long-lasting impact" on a child's ability to learn. *Implication:* A daily helping of warm and responsive care by parents and caregivers helps a child's emotional and social development and self-control.

3. The brain has a great capacity to change, but there are some critical periods (such as when developing vision, language, emotional controls) that are more crucial than others. *Implication:* Teachers and parents can learn to take advantage of the appropriate period for teaching certain intellectual tasks.

4. Negative experiences or lack of stimulation are likely to have serious and sustained effects; the parts of the brain associated with emotion (affect) seem to show the most effect. Stress has an impact on the brain's function in memory and critical thinking. *Implication:* Parents, teachers, and caregivers should nurture young children to lessen the effects of poverty and neglect on children's lives.

5. The value of timely, well-designed, and intensive intervention is of utmost importance in brain development. *Implication:* Research provides proof that early intervention reduces developmental delays and the number of children who will require special education.

Jensen (1995) summarizes some additional principles of brain-based research:

- Each brain is unique; each age-level or grade-level learner should not be held to the same standards.
- Emotions run the brain; good ones create an excitement for and love of learning. Bad ones affect all attempts at learning.
- The brain is run by patterns, not by facts. We learn best with themes, patterns, and contextual experiences. The brain is poorly designed for formal instruction or rote memorization.
- Each of us learns through simultaneous styles, such as visual, auditory, and kinesthetic. We do not learn as well when tasks are linear or when information is presented out of context.
- All learning is mind-body. Posture and breathing affect learning.
- The brain is stimulated by challenge, novelty, and feedback in our learning environments.

Brain research has also had an impact on those who work with children who have developmental delays or neurological impairments. Greenspan's work (1992; Greenspan & Wider, 1997) focused on children with autism and other children with developmental delays or disabilities. Through specifically designed experiences, children developed new capacities in verbal, emotional, and social functions. Benasich and Tallal (1996) worked with infants and toddlers who had a specific language disorder. Through brain imaging studies, early detection of an auditory-processing problem allowed the researchers to intervene at a much earlier age.

Clearly then, information about brain research is of critical importance to parents and educations of all children, no matter their abilities or disabilities.

The question arises as to whether "academic work" is appropriate at preschool age. The answer is that pure academics—rote learning, use of workbooks, prescribed paper-and-pencil tasks—are totally inappropriate with preschool aged children. However, many cognitive and intellectual activities are embedded in spontaneous play and learning opportunities. It is up to early childhood teachers to

- support children's cognitive learning and emerging literacy
- develop play and learning opportunities that build on children's interests and stimulate new ones
- help children to find answers to questions
- support readiness for further information, guiding and prompting children to use the skills and information they already have in seeking answers to new questions
- use music and musical activities to enrich brain development in this area

In summary, children of all developmental levels, from the most delayed to the most gifted, need activities that support their level of awareness, stimulate curiosity, and foster the urge to ask and find answers to questions. Activities that involve sensory experiences, touching, seeing, hearing, tasting, and smelling, are essential. Early childhood teachers need to create and then maintain a developmentally appropriate environment in which children are free to explore and experience materials and activities through their senses in their own way and at their own pace.

Implications and Strategies for Supporting Active Learning in the Education of Young Children

ACTIVE LEARNING OPPORTUNITIES SHOULD BE EMBEDDED IN THE EARLY CHILDHOOD CURRICULUM

Preschools and early childhood centres are often pressured to demonstrate that children are doing more than playing, that they are learning "something worthwhile." This pressure has led to some early childhood programs emphasizing paper-and-pencil tasks and workbook exercises. *Such activities, however, represent an inappropriate and ineffectual teaching format for young children.* As Bredekamp (1987) points out, "Children need years of play with real objects and events before they are able to understand the meaning of symbols, such as letters and numbers. Throughout early childhood, children's concepts and language gradually develop to enable them to understand more abstract and symbolic information" (see Photo 19–1). Bredekamp and Copple (1997, p. 23), in their discussion of developmentally appropriate practice (DAP), indicate that children benefit from engaging in self-initiated spontaneous play from teacher-planned and structured projects and experiences.

Schickedanz et al. (1990; Schickedanz, 1999) suggest that "preschoolers are ready for academic content—lots of it," and draw on their research for evidence.

Photo 19–1
Children need years of play with tangible objects.

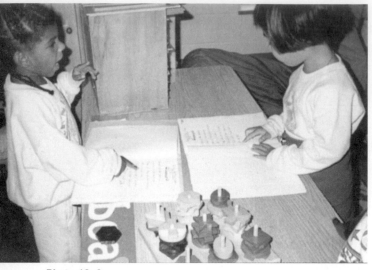

Photo 19–2
Cognitive activities are a part of most preschool activities.

Embedded learning
the intentional incorporation of specific learning objectives into play and routine classroom activities

Their conclusion is that cognitive skills learning *can be embedded* and are inherent in many experiences that are appropriate for young children (Photo 19–2).

COGNITIVE EXPERIENCES SHOULD SUPPORT EMERGING LITERACY IN YOUNG CHILDREN

The focus of early learning experiences should always be on enjoyable activities that promote children's effective use of language and the development of their social interaction skills, their emerging abilities to formulate concepts, and their interest in (and curiosity about) the world around them. The teacher's role in facilitating cognitive development is to first set the scene and then, by observing and listening, to follow the children's lead.

In this text we have referred, in some detail, to an "emergent curriculum" approach that creates an ever-changing, enriched learning environment built on the interests of the children (Gestwicki, 1999). This environment should develop experiences that provide for hands-on, child-initiated, and teacher-facilitated opportunities for learning. Early childhood teachers can play an important role by guiding, encouraging, and supporting children in individual and group projects and problem-solving situations, and by helping to structure the environment to allow for expansion of children's learning.

To further support readiness and emerging literacy, early childhood teachers can advance, *indirectly* but significantly, children's anticipation of learning to read, write, and do math by writing out a child's observations, stories, or questions and reading them back to the child, helping the child to find the answers to questions, and making and then recording measurements. They can also help children keep a log by writing down what each child dictates about observed changes—for example, in a plant's growth. With these kinds of cognitive readiness activities, most children, when they reach the primary grades, are ready and eager to learn to read about, tell about, write about, and to record their experiences. This type of programming reinforces the child's development in all areas and is particularly appropriate for inclusion because it enables each child, regardless of individual ability, to respond to the environment at his or her own level of development (see Chapter 15).

Skills related to concept development can be observed from infancy on, even in children with severe developmental disabilities. Children with special needs may be placed anywhere along the developmental continuum in cognitive functioning. A child who has severe motor disabilities may be advanced in some areas of cognitive development. A child with limited speech may be more cognitively advanced but not able to demonstrate his or her ability. Many children with disabilities never realize their cognitive potential; others excel far beyond their peers who have no special needs. What is important in early childhood programs is that expectations must start where the child is and work from there, step by step, focusing on planning cognitive activities that will benefit each child as an individual and the group as a whole (Photo 19–3).

Photo 19–3
Teachers should respond to children's questions and signs for further information.

This starting point is somewhat more difficult to find in an inclusive setting, in which teachers must be aware of a broader range of individual differences and needs in their group. Children with certain special needs, such as those with visual and hearing impairments, often need specialized guidance and encouragement in learning to use and develop all their senses and abilities to the best possible advantage. Support from a child interventionist or specialist trained in the education of children with vision or hearing deficits is recommended.

Children with cognitive delays may need more direct teaching, such as hand-over-hand guidance, when learning new concepts. For example, as the teacher is helping a child to button a coat, the teacher might gently guide the child's hand and start to count the buttons as the task is being completed. Counting can then be expanded to other things in which the child is involved (Photo 19–4).

In cases where a child's major disability is an intellectual impairment, it is important to identify the child's current level and rate of learning in deciding what type of tasks are an appropriate match, and then to proceed with a task analysis (see Chapter 11). The length of time and number of steps into which a task is broken down depends on the individual child. It may take one child several weeks to learn what another child can learn in a day.

Photo 19–4
Teachers should arrange the environment to support children's innate interests.

ASSISTIVE TECHNOLOGY SHOULD SUPPORT ACTIVE LEARNING

For children with significant special needs, computers and other types of **assistive technology** can foster independence by providing help with communication and mobility. When technical support is provided in the classroom, teachers, with the help of specially trained assistants, can work together to plan and implement the program for a given child.

Assistive technology various kinds of equipment, such as a computerized Braille system or voice synthesizer, designed to facilitate learning and communications for individuals with disabilities

Computers have tremendous potential as teaching tools for all children if their interactions with them are monitored and supported by adults (Davidson, 1990; Deiner, Dyck, & Hardacre, 1999). The value of computers in the classroom is directly related to the quality and appropriateness of the software that is used. The software market for children's programs is enormous and changes constantly (see the Children's Technology Review website listed in the Resources section at the end of this chapter). The computer is useful in supporting a child's learning when it is used as a resource for information and for finding answers to questions that develop from the children's play and exploration. It is also useful in helping to develop eye–hand coordination and may encourage practice and provide help for children who are delayed in this area of development. For children who have difficulty in expressing themselves, the computer may be able to act as an aid in helping with communication. At no time should the computer become the primary focus of the curriculum in an early childhood program. It should be treated as a useful resource in much the same way as a tape recorder might be used to collect information, record children's songs and conversations, or play music to support ongoing activities.

NECESSARY SKILLS FOR COGNITIVE LEARNING

Children with special needs often have difficulty acquiring readiness skills on their own. Teachers need to identify the missing skills in each child and then find ways to teach these skills, step by step.

Children may also have behaviours that will delay or interfere with learning, including the following:

- a short attention span
- a limited ability to imitate
- perceptual motor inefficiency (Photo 19–5)
- inadequate fine motor controls (eye–hand–wrist coordination)
- a limited ability to formulate concepts
- poorly developed short-term and long-term memory
- an inability to follow instructions

All cognitive skills are intertwined with one another and with all other areas of development. This interrelatedness is the essence of the *whole child* concept of development. For example, when children are recalling their trip to the zoo, all skills come into play, and even overlap, as the teacher helps the children to discuss and act out what they saw, heard, and did. This interrelatedness of developmental skills also makes a convincing argument against an academic, subject-matter approach in the education of young children.

Photo 19–5
Teacher support is often needed when children have perceptual motor inefficiencies.

Attention Span

Attention span is the length of time an individual is able to concentrate on an activity or event. The ability to simultaneously *focus* on certain aspects of the environment and *ignore* others is essential. When working with a puzzle, a child needs to be able to focus on the frame board and the puzzle pieces while ignoring other children's play activities. As stressed in Chapter 15, children's ability (or inability) to focus their attention is strongly influenced by classroom arrangements.

Attention span
the length of time an individual is able to concentrate on an activity or event

Example:

Three-year-old Jeri picked up a completed puzzle from the table, dumped it out, looked at it briefly, and tried to put in a piece. She then picked up a second puzzle and dumped it out also. Next, she picked up a nearby truck and ran it through the puzzle. Leaving the area with the truck, she went to the sand table. There she picked up some sifters, sifted for two minutes, and then went over to look at the fish.

Jeri's "short" attention span can be related to activities that may have been developmentally too advanced (the puzzle she chose), an environment that was too stimulating for her (she just couldn't focus in on any one thing), and perhaps how the room was arranged, as well as the fact that no teacher stepped in to support her interest in any one area.

A child cannot be successful (or even interested) when materials are overly difficult or poorly arranged (the puzzle and the truck on the same table). Many children have the potential for longer periods of attention, yet they do not stay with activities because the materials are developmentally inappropriate or set up in inappropriate ways (Photo 19–6).

It is true that attractiveness of materials and the ways in which they are presented are important factors in determining how involved a child will become with an activity. Even so, there are children who have trouble becoming involved on their own, regardless of the attractiveness of the setting. They need help from teachers in getting started. Once their attention is engaged, however, they too learn to focus. Bailey and Wolery (1984, p. 133) suggest several ways in which teachers can help children, especially those who are delayed, focus their attention:

- Provide materials that are appealing and colourful, can be manipulated, and have built-in feedback (true of many Montessori materials).
- Offer participation as a privilege rather than a responsibility.
- Give children an immediate role: "Julie has the punch to punch the train tickets."
- Instruct or prompt an activity: "I'll help you start a fence at this end. Where shall I put my first block?"
- Identify children's preferences for materials; preferred materials result in longer involvement.

Imitation and Modelling

The ability to imitate is essential to all learning (Photo 19–7, p. 400). Children who do not imitate spontaneously must be taught if they are to learn other

Photo 19–6
The child's ability to focus attention is strongly influenced by classroom arrangements.

Photo 19–7
The ability to imitate is essential to all learning.

developmental skills. However, the inability to imitate often goes unrecognized and so becomes the cause of continuing learning difficulties. When a child with developmental differences is enrolled in a group, an informal assessment of imitation skills should be a priority. (A simplified version of a game, such as Simon Says, can tell a teacher a great deal about a child's ability to imitate.) If imitation skills are lacking, initial teaching priorities should be concentrated in that area. Bailey and Wolery (1984) make the following suggestions for teaching children how to imitate:

- Imitate the child. Imitating the child's vocalizations and gestures often stimulates the child and also reinforces the child's further efforts.
- Provide models appropriate for the child's level of development.
- Provide whatever assistance is needed to help the child learn to imitate. Placing a mirror in front of the child, for example, allows the child to judge the accuracy of his or her imitations.
- If necessary, be directive in teaching the child to imitate. Physically put the child through an imitative response. For example, the teacher points to the child and says, "Marla, point to the circle," while stretching out the child's index finger and placing it on the "point to" object. An encouraging and descriptive comment follows: "Marla, look at that! You're pointing to the circle!"
- Make imitating a rewarding and playful experience; learning to imitate should be fun.
- Provide positive feedback and encouragement for approximations (first efforts) to an imitative response. When a child finally points to an object, even though it may not be the one requested, respond positively: "You're pointing to a blue truck. Good for you. Now let's find the red one and you can point to it too."

Perceptual Motor Skills

Perceptual motor skills
movement generated by sensory messages, by what is seen, heard, touched, tasted, or smelled

Sensory integration
the process of more than one sense working together to understand a sensory message and to translate the message into appropriate action

Perceptual motor skills are made up of two closely related processes (Photo 19–8). One has to do with *understanding* sensory messages: what is seen, heard, touched, tasted, or smelled. The second is the translation of the messages into appropriate actions. Generally, more than one sense is involved in a response; this is referred to as **sensory integration.** The following are three examples of perceptual motor skills coupled with sensory integration:

- A two-year-old stops her play and turns at the sound of an engine. She looks up, moves her eyes back and forth, and then points to an airplane. This child is exhibiting integrated visual (seeing) and auditory (hearing) skills, resulting in appropriately matched motor responses of turning, scanning, and pointing.
- A four-year-old picks up a bar of cocoa butter, smells it, bites off a corner, and then spits it out while making a wry face. The child is expressing appropriate smell and taste perceptions and responding with relevant perceptual motor responses: The cocoa butter smelled like candy, and she took a bite. It tasted more like soap than candy, however, and so she spit it out while making a face indicating an unpleasant taste.

Photo 19–8
Perceptual motor skills are made up of understanding sensory messages and translating them into appropriate action.

- A five-year-old, during group time, reaches into the Mystery Bag and verbally identifies unseen objects by touch.

Every preschool activity involves various forms of perceptual motor skills: climbing, jumping, riding wheel toys, watching a caterpillar creep, splashing in puddles, building with blocks, playing with table toys, painting, working with clay, colouring, cutting, and pasting. Music, stories, and dramatic play provide opportunities to pantomime, pretend, and practise the perceptual motor skills essential to everyday life.

Children with delayed perceptual motor skills often receive incomplete or distorted sensory messages. In some instances, children have become nearly immobilized because they are so distrustful of moving about; for example, children with poor depth perception are sometimes hurt and badly frightened by stepping off into unanticipated space. Children with poor directionality or who lack the ability to retain "position in space" may fear becoming lost or disoriented. Thus, children with sensory difficulties often need special activities, adapted materials, and additional support in using their intact senses.

Fine Motor Skills

Fine motor skills (eye–hand coordination; use of fingers, hands, and wrists) are closely related to perceptual motor skills. Both are important in learning self-help/care skills, as well as in learning to use all kinds of tools: paintbrushes, hammers, crayons, markers, and eventually pencils for printing and then writing. Practice in fine motor control is embedded in early childhood activities. The same activities that enable practice of fine motor skills have important cognitive, social, and language components:

- water-play: pouring, squeezing, measuring
- block-building: stacking, bridging, balancing, putting away
- art activities: painting, hammering, woodworking, clay modelling, cutting, pasting, crayoning, and so forth (Photo 19–9)
- housekeeping: dressing dolls, pouring "tea," stirring "soup," and setting the table

Manipulative materials, sometimes referred to as *table toys,* are especially good for promoting fine motor control and perceptual motor skills simultaneously (Photo 19–10). Among the most useful are these:

- wooden beads and strings with metal or plastic tips
- puzzles and parquetry blocks
- picture dominoes and lotto games
- nesting and stacking cups, kitty-in-the-keg, form boxes
- pegs and pegboards, hammer-and-nail sets
- Montessori graduated cylinders and colour boards

When appropriately matched to children's skill levels, manipulative materials ensure practice sessions that are informal and fun for all children. They also can be used successfully by children with developmental delays, because they are so readily adaptable. The following examples demonstrate how manipulative materials can be adapted by teachers to support a child with special needs:

Photo 19–9
Fine motor skills are a readiness skill.

- For fine motor skill development, wooden beads are especially useful. Offer only the largest wooden beads with a stiff wire on which to string them; a straightened coat hanger with its ends wrapped in tape works well. Also, peg handles can be attached to puzzle pieces in order to make lifting of puzzle pieces easier.
- For a child who has delays in cognitive as well as fine motor development, select puzzles that have few pieces. Each piece should be a recognizable object.
- Adaptation of materials is also important. For example, when a child has mastered the simple puzzles but the next ones seem too complex, teachers need to be inventive. Here is one suggestion. Several of the inside pieces of more difficult puzzles can be taped down from underneath with a strip of clear tape doubled back on itself. These pieces remain in the frame when the child turns the puzzle out. Less is required of the child; fewer pieces have to be replaced to complete the task and the job is simplified because finding the fit for border pieces is usually easier. The task gradually can be made more difficult by taping down fewer and fewer puzzle pieces. The advantage to this procedure is that each time the child completes the task there is always the reward of seeing the completed puzzle.

Photo 19–10
Many activities simultaneously promote fine motor control and perceptual motor skills.

- Nesting cups can be presented, beginning with only four or five of the larger cups, handing these cups to the child in order, one at a time. Once the child has the concept of the cups fitting into each other, the cups can be placed on the table for the child to pick up. As the child becomes more proficient in nesting cups, more cups can be added to the sequence.

Concept Formation

Concepts and *concept formation* are difficult terms to define without becoming overly technical. In this text, concepts will be defined as internal images or ideas (mental activities) that organize thinking. Concepts enable us to make sense out of our world. By continuously formulating new concepts, children impose order on the many things they must learn during their early years. Concepts developing in preschool-aged children include

- colour
- texture
- size
- shape
- weight
- same versus different
- directionality and position in space, such as *up, down, inside, outside, on top of, under,* and *over*

By continually formulating new concepts, young children impose order on all of the many things they must learn.

Skills related to concept formation include discrimination, classification, seriation, understanding of spatial and temporal relationships, memory, and the ability to follow directions.

Discrimination. Concept development depends on the ability to *discriminate*. **Discrimination** is the ability to perceive likenesses and differences among related objects and events. Put even more simply, it is the ability to "tell things apart"; to specify "same or different"; and to match objects, sounds, or ideas in terms of one or more attributes (characteristics). Opportunities to practise making both simple and complex discriminations are found throughout the preschool day:

Discrimination
the ability to perceive likeness and differences among related objects and events; to specify same versus different; to match objects, sounds, or ideas in terms of one or more attribute

- At music time the teacher introduces a song that asks: "Who is wearing sandals? boots? running shoes? blue socks? striped socks? no socks?"
- A variety of sorting tasks are usually available, such as putting the yellow pegs in one compartment and the blue pegs in another.
- Unit blocks often are put away according to the size and shape drawn on the shelf.
- A patterned string of wooden beads may be presented for children to copy— a small round blue bead, a big square red bead, and then a long green bead. This is repeated several times. This task is complex in that the beads vary on three dimensions: shape, size, and colour.

It should be noted, too, that the fine motor and perceptual motor skills are demanding. It might be that a child could make the necessary discriminations but not have the fine motor skills for stringing the beads. This is an instance in which the teacher would need to make an adaptation in materials, perhaps providing a wire rather than a string for threading the beads. A child with more severe physical

Photo 19–11
Concept development includes the ability to perceive likenesses and differences.

Classification
part of concept formation in which an order is imposed on objects or events into specific categories

Seriation
the process of arranging objects and events along orderly and related dimensions, for example, beginning, middle, end or small, bigger, biggest

limitations might participate by identifying the next bead, and another child or adult can place it on the wire.

Discrimination tasks can be adapted to fit any developmental level. For children who are functioning at a higher level, the bead-stringing task can be made more complex by introducing number concepts as well as colour, space, and shape: for example, repetitions of three small round blue beads, two large square red beads, and one long green bead. Or it can be made very simple for a child who has a developmental delay, such as alternating a square red bead with a square blue bead; or simpler yet, by having the child select and string only large blue beads (with large red beads in the basket as distracters). Adaptations for individual differences are unlimited (Photo 19–11).

Classification. The process of imposing order on objects and events is another major characteristic of concept formation. This skill is sometimes described as the ability to classify. **Classification** involves the formation of categories. In other words, children learn that cats, dogs, and squirrels have certain characteristics in common: fur, four legs, a tail, and so on. On the basis of these shared attributes, the creatures all fall into the category of *animal*. Each category is then subject to further breakdown as the child's experiences broaden. *Dog* becomes a category by itself when the child learns to discriminate among different kinds of dogs—poodles, collies, Airedales, and so on. Learning to classify, like learning to discriminate, can be taught.

Seriation. **Seriation** is the process of arranging objects and events along orderly and related dimensions (a prerequisite skill is the ability to make fine discriminations). Examples of seriation include the following:

- tall, middle-sized, shortest; and eventually, "These tall ones are taller than those tall ones"
- first, last; next-to-last
- happy, sad; "saddest one of all"

Seriation experiences like those in the preceding list help children learn to make comparisons about quantities, time and space, and affect (feelings). Learning to tell about what happened in the order of occurrence is another seriation skill that many older preschoolers begin to master (Photo 19–12).

Example:

"Yesterday we went to Grandma's. We got to play in the attic. Then we had dinner but first Grandma made us wash our hands and faces 'cause we got so dirty. After dinner Grandpa read to us and then it was time to go home and I slept in the car."

Many early childhood activities lend themselves to seriation practice and to endless adaptations for children

Photo 19–12
The arranging of objects in a prescribed order is an example of seriation.

with cognitive delays. For example, children can retell a story that has just been read, or teachers can ask, "What comes next?" when reading a familiar story. Sequenced picture cards (commercial or teacher-made) are also useful. The cards tell a story when arranged in proper order: The first card may show a child digging a hole in the ground, the second shows planting a seed, and the third shows the child pulling up a carrot. For more advanced children, the series can be longer and more complex, including pictures related to watering, weeding, and sprouting. For the child with very limited seriation skills, the teacher might use just two pictures, a child climbing up on a stool and then jumping down. At first, the teacher and child can alternate placing the cards, with the teacher stating what comes first and what happens next.

Spatial and temporal relationships. Learning how objects and events are related to space, to time, and to the child is another aspect of concept formation. **Spatial and temporal (time) concepts** include this grouping:

- on, in, under
- in front of, behind, next to
- in between, in the middle, second from the end
- yesterday, today, tomorrow
- soon, after a while, later, not yet

Spatial and temporal (time) concepts
how objects are related to space and time and to the child

Many children seem to learn such concepts automatically. However, there are children with and without developmental differences who need direct instruction. Spatial and temporal concepts are best taught as children themselves are moving about in space and time. For example, each child must learn to recognize his or her body-occupying-space in relationship to the body-space of others. This may not come easily and certainly it does not come early. Toddlers may literally "plow through" other toddlers as if they did not exist.

Active play is especially helpful in developing children's spatial awareness (Photo 19–13). Outdoors, a teacher might comment, "Hamid, you climbed so high. You are on top of the ladder box." If the child is having difficulty forming spatial concepts, the teacher should do an immediate follow-up: "Where are you, Hamid?" and wait for the child to respond. If the child does not respond, the teacher models the words "high, on top." When the child repeats the statement, the teacher corroborates: "That's right, Hamid. You are high; you are on top."

Learning to understand time is more difficult for most children. As with spatial concepts, time concepts are most effectively learned in relationship to play and everyday activities. Children understand short and more immediate time intervals most easily.

- "Time to come in *after* you run around the track two more times."
- "Snack comes *when* we finish this story."
- "We will get back *in time for* lunch."

Photo 19–13
Active play is especially helpful in children's development of spatial awareness.

Memory. The ability to remember what previously has been experienced and learned is a skill necessary to all new learning. Two kinds of memory are required: long-term and short-term (being able to remember what took place some time earlier as well as what happened in the immediate past). Tasks requiring rote memorization are inappropriate for young children. Activities that encourage children to practise remembering within their everyday work and play activities are the kinds that foster learning. Developmentally appropriate activities might include

- Conversational questions *of interest to the child* (with teacher prompts, after a suitable pause):
  - What did you have for breakfast? . . . (orange juice? cereal? anything else?)
  - Where does your kitten sleep? . . . (in a basket?)
  - What was the caterpillar doing on the leaf? . . . (crawling? chewing on the leaf?)
- Remembering one another's names and teachers' names, and using these names appropriately
- Remembering where materials are stored so as to get them out and put them away properly
- Telling what object or objects have been removed in games, such as "cover the tray"
- Story- and picture-reading activities, as mentioned in the discussion of seriation
- Leaving the bathroom in prescribed order for the children who will be using it next

For children with cognitive, neurological, or related impairments, the teacher often can begin memory training by telling the child what comes next: "The paper towel goes in the basket." The teacher should then follow up immediately: "Where does the paper towel go?" The child has to remember only long enough to repeat the information (or comply). A child's memory system may be activated more slowly if he or she has a delay; therefore, it is important to give adequate time to respond. In teaching paper towel disposal, for example, the teacher must allow adequate time for the child's memory to become charged and produce action.

Ability to follow instructions. The ability to follow instructions and carry out requests is important. Children with language, cognitive, or neurological impairments often have trouble with such tasks. Whenever a child has repeated difficulty, teachers should ask themselves the following five questions:

1. Does the child hear (or see) well enough to know what is expected?
2. Does the child have the vocabulary necessary to understand the request?
3. Does the child understand the concepts? For example, does the child understand *match* when the teacher says, "Match circles of the same colour"?
4. Is the child able to imitate the behaviours expected, as when the teacher demonstrates how to fold a piece of paper in half?
5. Are the instructions too complicated or given too rapidly? too many at one time?

Three- and four-step directions, spoken in rapid sequence, are more than most young children (let alone children who have a developmental delay) can manage. It is true that a few older preschoolers might be able to carry through on "Would you be so good as to go to the sink and wet a sponge—I think there's one under the sink or in the bathroom—and then wipe up all that messy paint on the floor and halfway up the table legs?" Many others would be completely lost. A few might try to carry out the last step in the direction (the only thing they remember) by rubbing at the paint on the table leg with their hand, perhaps.

The younger the child in age, experience, or developmental level, the simpler the directions should be. *It is important that teachers take nothing for granted about what children understand.* For very young children and for children with developmental delays, directions should be given one at a time. The process works best when the teacher gets down to a child's eye level and speaks directly to the child (Photo 19–14), and the language used is clear and free of unnecessary words or explanations.

Example:

"Marty, we're going to have to get this paint wiped up. Would you go to the sink (enough of a pause to let the child start moving toward the sink) and find a sponge?"

When Marty has the sponge in his hand, the teacher gives the next direction: "Now, wet the sponge." If the teacher wants to make sure that the child does not cross the room dripping water all the way, an intermediate instruction should be given: "Squeeze some water out of it."

Some children might not know what the teacher expects, so the teacher says, "Like this," pantomiming how to squeeze a sponge. "Now, let's go over and wipe up the paint on the floor."

When that is accomplished, the teacher can draw the child's attention to the paint on the table legs.

Instructions should be accompanied by gestures—for example, pointing when asking a child to put the car on the shelf.

Most children who are developmentally ready can learn to follow instructions if they are allowed to begin with one-step directions, like those in the example above. When the child has mastered one-step directions, it is logical to move to two- and then, perhaps, three-step directions. In an inclusive setting, when teaching how to follow complex directions or instructions, it is often a good idea to pair a child without a disability with a child who has a disability.

Photo 19–14
When giving directions to young children, teachers should get down to the child's eye level.

Prerequisites for Reading, Writing, and Math

Other cognitive skills and activities are more closely associated with reading, writing, and math. The following is a list of a few skills appropriate for promoting reading, writing, and math readiness in early childhood programs:

- "Reading" a series of pictures on a page from left to right and top to bottom. (Many picture books and board games are set up to promote this kind of pre-reading visual organization in children.)
- Pencil or crayon activities that begin to show some degree of eye–hand control (scribbling large swirling circles upon circles; making the marks that children often describe as "writing"; experiencing occasional success at writing his or her own name).
- Freestyle cutting with scissors (Photo 19–15, p. 408). Some children spontaneously try to "cut on the line."

Photo 19–15
Freestyle cutting is a prewriting skill.

- Counting a row of objects from left to right (or top to bottom, as in coat buttoning) by touching each in turn (one-to-one correspondence).
- Grouping objects in sets of two, three, or four.
- Identifying groups of objects as the *same, more,* or *less.*
- Recognizing that different but similar sounds are not the same. (Numerous
  songs, fingerplays, poems, and teacher-improvised games contribute to this
  learning.)
- Certain matching, ordering, and spatial relationship games and activities found
  in computer programs for young children.

None of these tasks is easily accomplished. They require at least minimal competence in the underlying skills discussed earlier in this chapter. However, all of them
can be taught, to some degree. All can be sequenced so as to facilitate children's
learning. Learning to cut on the lines is used below as an example:

*Julio was a seven-year-old who was highly distractible and had poorly coordinated fine
motor skills. Using a pair of specially designed scissors that allowed him to put his hand
over Julio's, the teacher helped Julio learn to hold the scissors and then to "cut" the air with
them. Next, the teacher prepared strips of paper about 1.5 cm wide with heavy lines
drawn across them at 2 cm intervals. The teacher held up a strip and instructed Julio to
open his scissors. The teacher then inserted the strip between the scissor blades, in contact
with one of the black lines, and said, "Cut." It was a simple matter for Julio to close the
scissors. Success was immediate and evident—a cleanly cut piece of paper came off with
each contact. To add interest to the task, the teacher soon switched to strips of brightly
coloured paper, feeling that Julio would not now be distracted from his cutting task by the
variations in colour. Julio's cuttings were put into an envelope to either take home to play
with or paste into a "picture" at school.*

SUPPORTING EMERGING LITERACY

It is important to support a child's emerging literacy. "One of the first indications of an emerging interest in learning how to read and write is children's recognition of environmental print, in letters such as the *M* for McDonald's restaurants or words such as STOP on traffic signs" (Fraser, 2000, p. 203). Initial attempts at "writing" occur at about the same time. Children make scribbling notations on their pictures and assume that they represent a message. Sometimes their meaning becomes evident to adults.

Example:

Denise, at the age of three, began making a series of six circles in the corner of all of her pictures. She told everyone that this was her name. In fact, because she was the only child "signing" her work in this way, it became unnecessary to put her name on pictures. She had created her own unique signature, and it communicated who had painted this picture.

Adult attitudes to children's first attempts at "writing" are critical in reinforcing the child's future attempts at communicating through symbols. Children whose initial responses are greeted with enthusiasm by adults are more likely to continue to understand, practise, keep developing, and learn conventional symbols.

It can never be stressed enough how important it is to read frequently to young children. It is through early and enjoyable experiences of being read to that children become motivated to learn how to read by themselves.

Planning and Presenting Learning Opportunities

A successful early childhood program depends on careful planning, whether the learning opportunities are informal and incidental or teacher-initiated. How the materials are presented, what child-initiated opportunities are made available, and how children are grouped also determine the success of cognitive learning activities for a child who may have special needs.

GROUPING CHILDREN

An early childhood group with as many as 15 to 20 children will function most effectively if divided into three or four small groups for teacher-supported activities. The number of teachers or assistants that are available usually determines the number of groups. Group size can be increased as children become more skilled and more experienced. The closer children with developmental disabilities get to their Kindergarten year, the greater is the benefit of having opportunities to work in groups, as long as the specific tasks are appropriate for the developmental level of the child. Younger children and children with developmental disabilities continue to need more support and attention from teachers.

GROUP COGNITIVE AND INTERACTIVE ACTIVITIES

An overall goal for early childhood settings is to help children be interested, comfortable, and appropriately challenged. To ensure that children do participate actively in all activities, the following arrangements are suggested. These are especially important with children who have a developmental delay, are overly active, or have trouble staying on task.

Short Periods

Teacher-directed activities should be limited to short periods: three, four, or five minutes. This time can be lengthened if the interest and involvement of the participating children is maintained. Activities should always be concluded *before* children lose interest.

Nonthreatening Materials and Activities

Start with materials that children enjoy and are familiar with: crayons; simple puzzles and manipulative materials; pictures of everyday objects to talk about, match, and

Photo 19–16
Teachers should arrange materials before children arrive.

group. Such materials allow most children to feel comfortable and competent, right from the start.

Preferred Materials and Activities

Noting what materials and activities are preferred by which children is important. These can be presented several days in a row to firm up the child's comfort and competence. Preferred materials also are useful as takeoff points for increasing the complexity of learning tasks and expanding them when a child is ready.

Readiness to Expand Learning Opportunities

If a child has become inattentive or frustrated, the teacher needs to observe the child in the context of the learning situation. Often, the problem resides not in the child but in the learning environment. Changes may need to be made in the materials or activities so they more closely match the child's interests and ability level. It is best to have additional materials immediately at hand to expand activities and create new interest.

Preparation

Before children arrive, all materials for the daily program should be assembled and handy to the learning centres (Photo 19–16). However, teachers must remain flexible to change. If children arrive with new ideas and interests, teachers should put aside their planned ideas and pick up on the interests of the children, supporting the children's ideas on how they might explore (see Chapter 15).

Cognitive activities should be enjoyable for children and for teachers. When readiness activities are fun and developmentally appropriate, children will be eager to participate in the learning experiences. Eagerness to participate invariably promotes successful learning in children. Successful learning is also enjoyable and motivating for teachers in that it represents their effectiveness as teachers.

Summary

Stimulating learning for young children involves recognizing the children's interests and developmental levels—as well as the range of needs within the group. Programming for young children should pick up on the interests of the children and include a range of informal, pre-academic, cognitive, language, social, motor, and perceptual motor opportunities.

Readiness activities *should not* include drills and workbooks or paper-and-pencil tasks. Readiness is embedded in developmentally appropriate, child-focused activities and interactions. Promoting children's day-by-day integration of developmental skills and fostering their eagerness to learn is of prime importance in supporting cognitive activities that take place in the early childhood years.

A decade of research on the brain provides new insights into a child's early brain development. We now recognize that there is a high level of complex activity during the first few years of life. We recognize that early experiences, in partnership with the child's genes, shape the brain. Through repetition and use, the brain's network system retains early connections. By the teenage years, half of these connections are discarded. The brain's plasticity as well as the critical periods for learning have great implications with regard to the importance of appropriate and timely early intervention.

Readiness skills (sometimes referred to as pre-academic skills) can be taught to children if they do not occur spontaneously through the normal developmental processes. In other words, a child's short attention span or inability to imitate or follow instructions should be noted. Instead of a "wait-and-see" approach, many skills can be encouraged through step-by-step teaching. In addition to attention span, imitation skills, and following instructions, other specific readiness skills include perceptual motor and fine motor skills, memory, and the ability to formulate concepts. Readiness skills (or pre-academic learning) for reading, writing, and math skills should be inherent in an enriched early childhood program.

When learning opportunities are developmentally appropriate, interesting, provoke exploration and inquiry on the part of the children, and pick up on the children's interests, all children in the group, including children with developmental differences, should be able to participate and enjoy them, especially if teachers support the children's learning and help the children acquire whatever prerequisite skills they may lack. One of the most important aspects of all activities should be that they are enjoyable to both children and teachers. Enjoyment leads to participation, spontaneous learning, and feelings of success.

RESOURCES

The following websites offer useful resources on children's learning processes.

NATIONAL ASSOCIATION FOR THE EDUCATION OF YOUNG CHILDREN
http://www.naeyc.org

EDUCATION RESOURCES INFORMATION CENTER
http://www.eric.ed.gov

CHILD & FAMILY CANADA
http://www.cfc-efc.ca

CANADIAN CHILD CARE FEDERATION
http://www.cccf-fcsge.ca

CHILDREN'S TECHNOLOGY REVIEW
http://www.childrenssoftware.com

STUDENT ACTIVITIES

1. Observe an inclusive preschool or early childhood program. Describe some children's behaviours that are indications of pre-academic "readiness."
2. Observe one particular child in a group, preferably a child with a developmental disability or delay. Describe the kinds of adaptations that teachers make to enhance this child's learning. If you saw no such adaptations, suggest what might have been done.
3. Select three of the manipulative materials listed in the chapter (or materials of your own choosing). Demonstrate for the class ways the materials might be presented or adapted to match the skills of a child with a cognitive delay.
4. Observe a teacher for 20 minutes. Write down everything the teacher does that relates to facilitating children's cognitive learning.

REFERENCES

Bailey, D. B., & Wolery, M. (1984). *Teaching infants and preschoolers with handicaps.* Columbus, OH: Charles E. Merrill.

Benasich, A. A., & Tallal, P. (1996). Auditory temporal processing thresholds, habituation, and recognition memory over the 1st year. *Infant Behavior & Development, 19*(3), 339–357.

Bredekamp, S. (Ed.) 1987. *Developmentally appropriate practice in early childhood programs serving children from birth through age 8.* Washington, DC: National Association for the Education of Young Children.

Bredekamp, S., & Copple, C. (1997). *An activity-based approach to early intervention* (rev. ed.). Washington, DC: National Association for the Education of Young Children.

Davidson, J. L. (1990). *Children and computers together in the early childhood classroom.* Clifton Park, NY: Delmar Learning.

Deiner, P. L., Dyck, L., & Hardcare, L. (1999). *Resources for educating young children with diverse abilities: Birth through 12.* Toronto: Harcourt Brace.

Fraser, S. (2000). *Authentic childhood.* Scarborough, ON: Nelson Thomson Learning.

Gestwicki, C. (1999). *Developmentally appropriate practice, curriculum in early education* (2nd ed.). Albany, NY: Delmar.

Greenspan, S. I. (1992). *Infancy and early childhood: The practice of clinical assessment and intervention with emotional and developmental challenges.* Madison, CT: International Universities Press.

Greenspan, S. I., & Wider, S. (1997). *Facilitating intellectual and emotional growth in children with special needs.* Reading, MA: Addison-Wesley.

Jensen, E. (1995). *Brain-based learning and teaching.* New York: Brain Store Incorporated.

Schickedanz, J. A. (1999). *Much more than the ABC's: The early stages of reading and writing* Washington, DC: National Association for the Education of Young Children.

Schickedanz, J., Chay, S., Gopin, P., Sheng, L., Song, S., & Wild, N. (1990). Preschoolers and academics. Some thoughts. *Young Children, 46*(1), 4–13.

Shore, R. (1997). *Rethinking the brain.* New York: Families and Work Institute.

CHAPTER 20

Bilingualism and Second-Language Development

KEY CONCEPTS

bilingual education

caretaker speech

code switch

heritage language

home language

minority language

other first language (OFL)

scaffolding

subtractive bilingualism

OBJECTIVES

After studying the material in this chapter, the student will be able to

- Identify current issues in Canada that relate to first- and second-language learning in young children.
- Discuss the importance of supporting first-language development within the context of an English- or French-speaking early childhood program.
- Describe the potential consequences to the young child and family of the loss of the child's first language.
- List ways in which teachers can support the growth of the child's home language, in both the preschool and the home environments.
- Describe programming that supports the learning of English as a second language.

Note: The authors want to acknowledge the significant contributions of Merylie Wade Houston (1992, 1995) to this chapter.

Introduction

Sao Chan refuses to speak Chinese to her parents at home. She gets upset if they address her in their native language when they pick her up at Kindergarten; if they speak Cantonese to her, she answers in English. Her teachers call her Susan.

Ebrahim's family members have been told that, if they want their son to do well in school, they must speak only English to him at home. His mother and grandmother try their best with the limited English they know.

Omi's behaviour is of concern to his teachers at his child care centre. The teachers don't know what to do with him. Omi won't do anything but ride the tricycles. When he is invited to paint or play with puzzles or join in group activities, he answers back very rudely. And, on top of that, many of the younger boys are now following him and doing everything he does.

Photo 20–1
Many children in Canada enter early childhood programs with their language development in a language other than English.

Increasing numbers of children in Canada are entering child care, nursery school, or Kindergarten with their early language development in a language other than English (Photo 20–1). Immigration projections (Statistics Canada, 2003) predict that these numbers will continue to increase, particularly in large urban centres. In these cities, children who are born outside Canada or who are born to families that have immigrated recently may soon represent a large portion or even a majority of the child population. Early childhood educators often cite children's lack of English as the single biggest language concern in their centres.

Speaking a **home language** other than English is *not* a "special need." But because many teachers see children struggling to communicate in English, because it is so prevalent, and because teachers are not sure how to assist these children, it is important to spend some time discussing it here.

Note that we are talking about children who have language: They think in a language, they speak in a language, and they understand concepts of a language. The language, however, does not happen to be English. "This is Mi Ryung. She speaks Korean," not "This is Mi Ryung. She doesn't speak English." Notice the difference?

The examples at the beginning of this chapter point out that the issue is not only one of spoken language. Body language, cross-cultural communication, self-image, and respect for cultural values are only a few of the areas we need to address (Gonzalez-Mena, 2001; Kilbride, 1997). This chapter discusses these and related issues, and describes ways in which teachers can support the learning of English as a second language as well as the growth of children's home language. Note: Although Canada has two official languages, most of the discussion in this chapter is about the use of English. Much of the information applies also to the French as a second language situation, in which French is the dominant language of the surrounding community as well as of the educational setting. The terms **heritage language** and **minority language** refer to languages other than English and French.

Home language
usually refers to the child's first language, the language a child hears in the home environment; often referred to as the "mother tongue"

Heritage language
in Canada, a language other than English or French that has been passed on from generation to generation

Minority language
in Canada, languages other than English or French

Learning and Teaching Language

WHY TEACHING ENGLISH AS A SECOND LANGUAGE IS SO IMPORTANT NOW

It is not new to have children who have English as a second language (ESL) in early childhood settings, but the recent steep increase in their numbers is changing the educational needs of all of the children and families involved. In fact, although families with a first language other than English or French may very soon be in the majority in many urban areas (Statistics Canada, 2003), the term *minority language* continues to be used to refer to the relationship to the dominant language—in most of Canada, English. The term **other first language (OFL)** is a more appropriate term to use.

At the same time as numbers of children who have an OFL are increasing, research is teaching us new things about the learning of first and second languages. It used to be thought that children "naturally" learn new languages and that if only the parents would speak English at home, their children would do just fine.

It is now being shown that such advice is not only wrong, but it can also be damaging to the children and families involved.

Other first language (OFL) in Canada, a person's first language that is other than English or French

THE IMPORTANCE OF LANGUAGE LEARNING

Much of the assessment done on children by classroom teachers is based on language ability (Dotsch, 1998). Certainly, the articulate child is instinctively thought to be intelligent and creative. Teachers, along with families and others, frequently are impressed by and pay attention to a verbal child. Chapter 18 discusses the interrelationship between cognitive development and the development of language. Because of the perceived connection between increasing cognitive structures and language maturity, it has always been assumed that it was important to help children develop skills in English as quickly as possible. The inability to speak English has been treated as a deficit by teachers. Skill in speaking another first language has seldom, or ever, been taken into consideration by the practitioner in evaluating a child.

Subtractive bilingualism developing a second language (English) that replaces the first language (home language), causing the first language to cease to develop

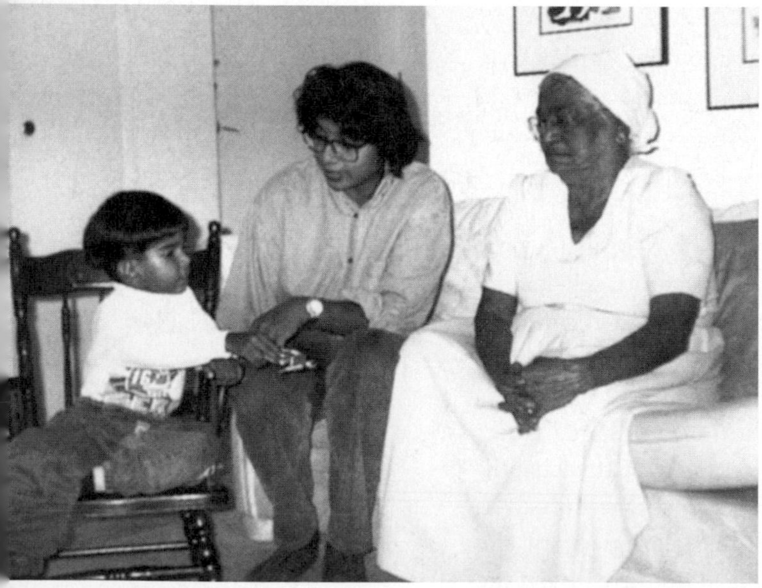

THE EFFECT OF PRESCHOOL SECOND-LANGUAGE TRAINING

When a child learns English in an early childhood setting after starting to learn a different language at home, the English usually develops *instead of* rather than *in addition* to the first language (Wong-Fillmore, 1991). This is referred to as **subtractive bilingualism,** and it leads to a loss of whatever skill the child already had in the first language. In a home with parents and other family members who may speak only the first language, the child quickly loses the ability to communicate. This is a high price for families to pay for sending their child to an early childhood setting—loss of the ability to talk to their child. If parents and older family members cannot use their traditional language to transmit their culture and values, they have (to a large degree) lost the ability to raise their child and may therefore lose the connection

Photo 20–2
Use of the home language enables generations within the family to communicate with one another.

between generations (Photo 20–2). These social reasons alone seem to require that the child continue to learn and use the family's language (Gonzalez-Mena, 2001). There are other good reasons, too.

It is important to support the use of the home language because of evidence (Cummins, 1984) that the more children speak their first language, the better they learn English. The reason for this is that learning a language teaches the brain what language is: what it is for, how it works, and how it is structured. That skill can then be applied to the learning of another language. The more highly developed the child's skill is in the first language (L1), the more skill he or she has available to use in learning the second (L2). So continuing to speak the first language actually helps the child to learn

Photo 20–3
Social language can be picked up quickly through mimicking.

English. The later the introduction of English, the stronger the knowledge of and practice in the first language will be. Remember the difference between the two-year-old's telegraphic speech and the six-year-old's compound and complex sentences, as outlined in Chapter 18.

Another reason for maintaining the development of the first language is that we need language in order to think (Cummins, 1981). Cognitive learning is closely linked to both receptive and expressive language. Children's ability to think in their L2 will not catch up to the same ability in their L1 for five to seven years, although their fluent social language may sometimes mislead us. Social language is surface language, and it can be picked up quickly, through mimicking (Photo 20–3). Teachers often protest, "Language isn't the problem; he can talk all right," because they have noticed the child's relatively fluent surface language. This will not reflect the child's ability to express concepts for many years, however. Box 20–1 lists some suggestions for ways parents can help their children retain their first language.

Box 20–1   IN-THE-HOME SUGGESTIONS FOR FAMILIES

What Can Families Do to Help?
- Read and tell stories to your child in your first language. Stories include your own family saga, where you are from, and funny things that people have said and done.
- Borrow books from the child care centre or the public library. Take your child to get his or her own library card. Even infants and toddlers can have a library card. It's free. Ask the librarian about books in your first language.
- If you still have relatives or friends in your first-language country, ask them if they can send books for your child. After they are outgrown, consider donating them to the child care centre. If you travel, remember to look for books.
- Talk to your child in your first language and point out interesting things to them. Also read signs, labels, and posters to them when you are out.
- Offer to translate simple books into your family's first language for the preschool or child care centre, either in print, on tape, or by telling a story to the other children.
- When your child is old enough to register for elementary school, ask the school for information on heritage language or international language classes in your first language.

SOURCE: Houston (1995).

How Bilingual Education Works

With what we know at present, probably the best way to educate young children who have first languages other than English is in a bilingual setting. In these settings, concepts are presented in the first (or home) language, thus developing the child's cognitive strengths, and then are reinforced in English. In this way, comprehension and English language development are combined.

Bilingual education
concepts are presented in the first (or home) language and then are reinforced in English

Note: **Bilingual education** should not be confused with *French immersion*. Francophone teachers teach children in French immersion programs in French. The children's home and community language is usually English, and they are learning French as an additional language.

In an optimal setting for bilingual education, the teacher shares the children's language and culture. There are a number of communities across Canada in which the population shares a common language, culture, or religion, where such bilingual programs are thriving. There, children are able to become truly bilingual and reap the additional cognitive benefits of being able to think in two languages.

Code switch
moving from one language and its cultural expression to another, depending on the situation

Children who learn two languages in this way learn to **code switch**—to move from one language to the other depending on the situation they are in. Children who speak an English dialect also code switch—for example, from Jamaican patois to standard English. Teachers and parents often worry that the children will become confused, but if both languages are taught well and valued, this doesn't seem to happen. Although Bee (1999) admits that there may be a drop in IQ during the period of initial introduction of the second language, this quickly corrects itself. Hakuta and Garcia (1991) find that the higher the degree of bilingualism, the higher the level of cognitive development.

There are two major difficulties that stand in the way of delivering bilingual education: (1) the expectations of parents and (2) the reality that many schools have children who speak a number of different home languages.

CAN BILINGUAL EDUCATION BE DONE WITH YOUNG CHILDREN?

Many parents are hesitant to register their children in a bilingual program before they start elementary school. They know that, to be successful in "big school," their children will need a good command of English, and they want them to start to learn it now. Parents are prepared to try to switch to the use of English in the home if it means that their children will do better at school. And both the parents and the children quickly recognize the connection between language and power. The "power" language in many parts of Canada is English. So children themselves will sometimes refuse to speak their home language after they have started school. If the parents speak an English that is not as "good" as the teacher's, the children may lose respect for their parents, for their heritage, and ultimately for themselves. It is essential that the teacher do some good parent education, so that the parents understand why learning only English at a preschool age will be harmful both to their children's learning of English and to their future use of the first language.

The second reason that explains why there are not many successful bilingual programs for young children is that most communities and schools in Canadian cities reflect a number of different language groups (Photo 20–4). The Mount Pleasant Neighbourhood House preschool in Vancouver has 15 different languages among the 30 families involved (McMurter, 1992). It is, of course, unreasonable to expect one teacher to be able to speak and teach in several languages.

In spite of this challenge, we must find ways to

- support the growth, not just the maintenance, of the children's first languages
- show that we support and value the families' cultures and languages, in order to build the self-esteem of the children and to have other children recognize their value
- teach new concepts in the children's first language(s) in order to continue to develop their critical thinking skills as well as to support the learning of English
- prioritize the delivery of a first-rate early childhood education program to all children, including children who are learning English as a second language

SUPPORTING THE CHILD'S FIRST LANGUAGE

The unilingual teacher can do much to encourage a child in the learning of his or her first language:

- Strongly encourage the family to continue to use their first language at home.
- Work toward hiring staff who reflect the language, cultural, racial, religious, and economic backgrounds of the children and their families (Photo 20–5, p. 420).
- Introduce new concepts in the child's first language wherever possible.
- Involve families in curriculum planning so that they can reinforce concepts in the home language.
- Help the families to help their children make the leap from home to school by letting them know the learning skills needed to "make it" in the classroom, such as speaking up, answering questions, and waiting their turn.
- Show respect for the families' values by adjusting expectations to reflect those of the home—for example, helping children wait until the teacher is free to listen if interrupting adults is frowned on by the community (Hendrick, 1992) or honouring the request of parents that their child not have ice-cold drinks in the winter or play in water.
- Show respect for the families' backgrounds by reflecting them in the toys, books, dramatic play materials, posters, music, food, and so on, in *daily* use in the classroom.
- Don't just allow—*encourage* the children to use their home language in play, especially "pretend" play.

Photo 20–4
Languages from around the world are found in today's schools and child care centres.

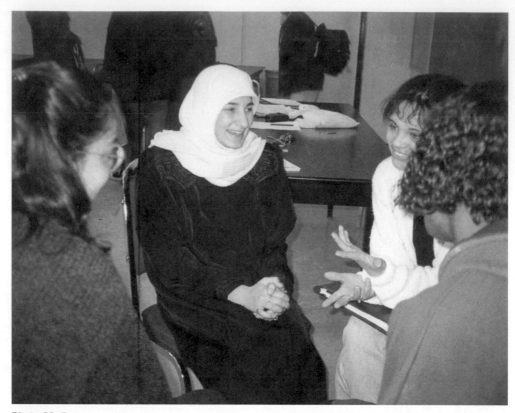

Photo 20–5
Work toward hiring staff who reflect the language and culture of the community.

USING FAMILIES FOR INFORMATION AND ASSISTANCE

Language, as we learned in Chapter 18, is nonverbal as well as verbal. Body language and gestures vary in meaning from group to group. Most of us are aware of the teaching of some groups, including some West Indian and Chinese families, to show respect to a teacher by avoiding eye contact. This can be more than confusing to a teacher who uses eye contact as a measure of social development. The common hand gesture used to beckon a child may be insulting to some. It could be their gesture for calling a dog. The "okay sign"—a circle made with forefinger and thumb—commonly used in Canadian dominant culture, may be extremely rude to others. Teachers should be encouraged to take any available courses on cultural knowledge (York, 1991). Because there is variation among any group of people on any given subject, and in order to avoid stereotyping, *the best source of information is the family of the child* (Photo 20–6). A good way to ask is: "How do you do it in your family?"

A lot can be learned by visiting the child in the home. For example, during these visits different cultural expectations of behaviour for boys and girls can become clearer. Boys may be expected to be more aggressive than girls, never to cry, and to belong to a group. Sometimes the oldest child is expected to be a group leader and have direct authority for the others and be responsible for their behaviour. Omi, described at the beginning of this chapter, clearly was playing this role within the group. Recognizing that these cultural factors affect the children's behaviour and learning may lead to changes in the program's curriculum.

Photo 20–6
The best source of information is the child's family.

ADDITIONAL MEASURES TO SUPPORT FIRST-LANGUAGE DEVELOPMENT

The following additional measures can help you support students' first-language development.

- Learn the correct pronunciation of the child's name. We have no right at any time to change or Anglicize a child's name, unless the parent initiates a request. Some names may be difficult to pronounce at first, but learning to pronounce them phonetically with the family's help opens the first door to a good working relationship. It is critical to learn both the child's and the adults' names and correct forms of address. This is especially true of children from other countries, whose names and manner of addressing others are different from Western traditions.

- Children need to see their families become part of this new child care world (Photo 20–7). Find out the family's interests and abilities and invite them to participate in the program, not for "culture days" but just as any other parent would be invited. Remember that this will be hard at first since the culture of the classroom, as well as the language, is likely to be different. Plan a specific job to be done. If no family member is available during the day, ask if parents could serve on the advisory board, sew bookbags, help with bookkeeping, or contribute snacks. Be careful not to ask families with OFLs only when there are menial or housekeeping tasks to be done.

- Fill the classroom with books, tapes, and records in the children's heritage languages. They are available at some bookstores and at children's libraries. Families, community associations, churches, synagogues, or mosques will often donate books outgrown by older children. Visitors to the native country, or a relative there, may also be sources for purchases or donations. Even if no one in the classroom can read the books, the families can. That is

Photo 20–7
Parent involvement in the centre is important for all children.

a special talent that must be acknowledged. If parents are willing to tape-record a reading of the book, ask them to ring a bell when it is time to turn the pages. It is important to use the same standards always used in selecting the books to read: choosing for age appropriateness, good illustrations, and other usual criteria.

- Learn a few basic words and phrases in the child's first language (*hello, drink, Mommy will be back soon, Daddy, Grandma, do you need to go to the toilet?* etc.). With the families' help, display some phrases on the bulletin board and in a newsletter, and incorporate them into children's songs.

- Ask the families to save boxes and cans for the housekeeping corner that reflect the foods, language, and calligraphy of the home country.

- At New Year's, which may be in September (Rosh Hashanah), October (Diwali), March (Nowruz), January/February (Chinese New Year), or many other times of the year, ask all the families to find a calendar that they can obtain free that reflects their language, culture, or religion. Put up the calendars and use them.

- Don't assume how much and what the children know—what their previous experience and body of knowledge are. Ask the families. They are the best resource.

- Find translators ("graduated" parents, or people from local school, church, community, or government organizations) and use them for parent meetings, interviews, and messages. This is the teacher's responsibility. Be careful if using older children to translate for their parents. This may violate the natural order of authority between the generations. Families often take great pride in the linguistic abilities of their children, but be careful to check, especially when dealing with guidance and educational issues. The interpreter must be acceptable to the family, both for confidentiality and for professional status. All families have a right to understand and be understood when their children's well-being is at stake.

PROGRAMMING TO SUPPORT THE LEARNING OF ENGLISH

Now that we have built-in protection for the child's first language, we need to look at ways to support the learning of English. (Note, however, that the following programming guidelines are equally pertinent to the learning of French as a second language.)

The first question that teachers often ask is "How long does it take for a child to learn English?" The answer depends on several variables: the child's opportunity and willingness to interact with competent English speakers, how similar the first language is to English, and the child's age. Dotsch (1992, pp. 24–26) has shown that, for immigrant and refugee children, both previous positive experience in a child care setting and the lack of a serious traumatic event help speed up language acquisition. In general, it takes at least three months before children begin to under-stand what is said to them, two years before they can carry on a conversation, and a full five to seven years before they can think in a second language (Cummins, 1981).

During the first three or four months, when the child is unable to understand what is being said, remember that words without understanding are just noise.

Terrifying noise. Remember how important it is to use gestures and hugs to reassure a new child while gradually introducing words (Photo 20–8).

There are several factors that can help facilitate language learning:

- *Scaffolding language.* It is important, at first, to support words with gestures, actions, facial expressions, objects, or pictures to reinforce meaning. Without the context of meaning, the child hears only noise; he or she cannot isolate and identify the sound of the word and remember it. As the child acquires more receptive language, the gestures and actions can be slowly reduced so that the child becomes more dependent on the sound of the word rather than the gesture. Any early childhood teacher knows how to "perform" for children. An ESL teacher must be even more of a "performer." Exaggerate and keep the language very simple; but get carried away with the silliness. If teachers are lucky, the children will giggle. That brings us to the second point in second-language learning.

- *Using the affective component.* Simply put, this means that if teachers show the children that they like them, the children are more likely to like the teacher too. And if they like the teacher, there is more motivation to try to communicate, so they will acquire a second language more quickly. It helps if staff members develop a special relationship with each child, right from the beginning. As each new child joins the group, one staff member can become the child's special friend to help with this transition.

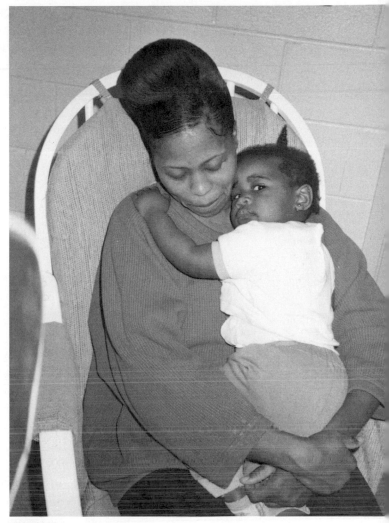

Photo 20–8
Use gestures and hugs to reassure children.

Scaffolding
a teaching and learning process in which the teacher provides decreasing levels of support while placing higher demands as the child progresses toward the goal of independent problem solving

- *Planning good programming.* Finding out where children's interests lie and developing exciting, interesting programming promotes speech. If nothing of interest is going on in the room, what is the children's motivation to talk? We don't teach English to young children, we provide an enriched language-learning environment and then motivate children to want to communicate. For more ideas, see *Multicultural Early Childhood Education—A Resource Kit* (Kilbride, 1990) and Freire & Bernhard (1997).

- *Taking the necessary time.* Remember, it can take months before children begin to understand meaning, and years before they may feel comfortable talking to teachers. But when they do speak, respond with warm reinforcement.

The Enriched Language-Learning Environment

Keeping in mind our goals to support the first language and to introduce the second language, how does this all come together in early childhood education programs?

The ideal language-learning classroom is well staffed, busy, messy, bright, and stimulating, just like any other ideal classroom. With a slight change of emphasis, the classroom can meet all the needs of the child who speaks a first language other than English. Consider the following ideas:

- *Plan time for one-to-one and small-group work.* Try to organize the staff so that one or two adults establish a warm, personal relationship with each child, and can spend some time each day in one-on-one interaction with that child (Chud & Fahlman, 1985). Small-group work often gives the child who is learning a second language the encouragement and opportunity to speak without the competition of children who have English as a first language and who always know the words first. Take advantage of any opportunity to relate directly to the child during washroom and other caregiving times.

- *Turn off the tape player and other background noise.* Turn off the CD player or tape recorder during time when children are working on building language. Save tapes and records for small-group time when they can be listened to and concentrated on. Consult with the parents to select music from the child's own cultural background that can be played, when appropriate, during unstructured time.

Caretaker speech
Used in second-language learning to direct the child's attention to the immediate environment, labelling everything, speaking simply, and repeating and expanding on the child's words

- *Use caretaker speech.* Caretaker speech directs the child's attention to the immediate environment, labelling everything, speaking simply and slowly, asking rhetorical questions, repeating and expanding on the child's words. "What's that? It's a ball. Ball. Can you throw me the ball? It's a red ball." The level of caretaker speech matures as the child's command of the language increases.

- *Use sensory activities for talking and interacting.* Join the child at the sand or water table, or model together with play dough or clay. The soothing, open-ended nature of these activities makes it possible to participate fully without language, while helping the child relax and be receptive to new words about feelings, textures, and temperatures. This is often a good time to encourage the child to label in their first language, thus teaching the teacher (Photo 20–9).

- *Allow "non-teaching" quiet time.* Learning a new language is exhausting. All children need time to be alone with their own thoughts. They need relaxing creative play time without teacher interference when they can speak their home language alone or with others, or, if they choose, play with English-speaking classmates. Culture shock can leave a child in such a state of stress that the new language can make a teacher seem even more alien and the environment even more threatening. Allow silence.

- *Encourage peer play with English-speaking children.* It's important for children with an OFL to play with children who speak English. As children, they need to hear native English-speaking children speaking "child talk." Saville-Troike (1976) has shown how English use expands as soon as a fluently English-speaking child joins the group. It is also important that the children hear the teacher speaking to children in English.

Research also shows that the number of English interactions in dramatic play increases when a teacher supports the play. This more intense involvement by the teacher in dramatic play is one of the few areas where the role of the teacher should be different with children who speak a first language other than English (Fraser, 1992).

Photo 20–9
Use sensory activities for talking and interacting.

- *Set a good example.* Be a good language model. Speak good, correct, if simple, English. Dotsch (1992, pp. 24–26) tells us to slow down a little, but not to talk louder, or the children might think that they did something wrong. Remember that the children's receptive English (what they can understand) is always more advanced than their expressive language (the language they speak).
- *Use songs for transition times and routines.* Be consistent in the language used for routines. Avoid saying "Tidy up, please," one day, "It's time to tidy up now" the next, and "Put the toys away" the third day. Songs provide an easy way to use the same words, rhythm, and tone each time. A simple song for tidy-up time, for snack time, or for washing hands, sung by all the staff, provides the child with an aural (heard) cue that immediately connects words and action.
- *Sing lots of songs and use fingerplays with actions.* During large-group or circle time, establish a set of "old favourites," simple fingerplays, songs, and games with gestures to support the meaning of the words. Children find this repetition comforting. Children will often sing before they speak. Remember singing a song in another language, such as "Frère Jacques," years before knowing any French? (Even your accent was probably pretty good.) Singing in a large group is less threatening, especially to a child who is shy or one whose culture doesn't encourage drawing attention to oneself. And singing provides practice in the rhythms of a language.

    This is another good area in which to involve the families. Ask a family member to teach everyone—the teacher, too!—a new song in another language. Sometimes children's songs in other languages can be found on tapes or

Photo 20–10
While building language skills, remember the child's other needs.

CDs. If no one can handle the whole song, try to get help to translate the chorus of a favourite song into several languages that represent the group. Songs that include counting are particularly easy to use (or adapt) for this purpose. (Paul Fralick's *Make It Multicultural—Musical Activities for Early Childhood Education,* 1989, can help teachers get started.)

- *Program for language.* Most children like technology and can use a simple calculator or adding machine even without words. Let children operate the tape recorder themselves. If a computer is available, try writing books; Polaroid or digital camera pictures of a field trip are great material (remember to bring a tape recorder). Invest in an inexpensive set of walkie-talkies. Even though they never push the right button, many kids will talk into a walkie-talkie or will listen. Don't interfere too much; just let them go. Old microphones or a TV console are terrific language-stimulating additions to the dramatic play area.

  Making old-fashioned tin-can telephones is a great fine motor activity. Get a child to hold one end to their ear and listen to a friend saying silly things. Enough cans and string for everyone are required, of course. If the classroom ends up looking like a spider's web, what a good challenge to talk as we try to get untangled!

  Some programs have asked Bell Canada for old telephones. If the teacher or a parent is handy, telephones can be hooked up to each other so that children can actually hear through the earpiece. But it doesn't matter—the children will still pretend.

  Attitudes change quickly in all children when language and related technology are added to the programming. Children whose first language is English need language stimulation, too.

- *Plan easily followed activities.* Plan lots of activities in science (planting, magnets) or cooking. These subjects require materials and procedures that can be labelled and demonstrated but also followed visually. While building vocabulary, the participatory nature of these activities builds feelings of success and increased self-esteem.

- *Read out loud.* Read books, read instructions, read calendars, and read street signs. Read to the children at every chance. Making the connection between written symbols and words is the basic emergent literacy skill needed for reading. Read in natural situations; don't overwhelm the children.

- *Continue to provide for other needs* (Photo 20–10). While building language skills, remember that the child's other needs—social, emotional, physical—are the same as those of any other child. Of course, language and other needs go together: "What a big jump!" "Where's my hug?"

Aboriginal Language Issues

Most of the discussion in this chapter also applies to children and families who speak Native languages in Canada, but there are some issues that are special to this group. Socially and economically, for complex historical reasons, and as a result of racist attitudes, Aboriginal people are frequently disadvantaged within the larger society. It is important that all early childhood educators pay special attention to the education needs of the founding peoples of our country. The terms *Aboriginal people, First Peoples,* and *Native people,* as used here, refer to status Indians, non-status Indians, and Inuit people.

BACKGROUND

There are 50 different Native languages in Canada, belonging to 11 ancestral language groups: the Algonquian, Athapaskan, Iroquoian, Salishan, Eskimo-Aleut, Wakashan, Tsimshian, Siouan, Haidan, Tlingit, and Kutenaian families of languages. Some of these language families contain only one language, while others contain a number of distinct languages: One Algonquian language, for example, is Cree, which is spoken by 22 percent of Native-language speakers in Canada. Cree itself has a number of dialects. Kutenaian and Tlingit, conversely, each contain a single language with fewer than 500 speakers.

The number of speakers of Aboriginal languages as a first language is diminishing. On some reserves, 100 percent of the population are Native-language speakers. But among Aboriginal people in Vancouver, for example, only a small number speak their Native language in their homes (Frideres, 1993). And the average age of these speakers is over 40. If only the older generation speaks a language, the language dies as the last speaker dies. Huron was last spoken early in the twentieth century. Once a Canadian Aboriginal language is lost, there is nowhere else in the world to go to get it back.

It is a common pattern to have elders who speak only the Native language, a middle-aged group who speak both the Native language and an official language (English or French), and a younger generation who speak only the official language. It is obviously difficult for elders to pass on oral traditions and cultural values to children if they do not share a language.

Most families feel that their children must be able to speak, read, and write English or French to survive in Canada. Education is seen as the key to doing well. But it must be admitted that education has not done its job for Aboriginal children in the past. Educators are now looking at language issues as being part of the key to making changes that will enable children to be more successful in school while maintaining traditional values and identity.

EARLY CHILDHOOD RESPONSE

Aboriginal groups and early childhood educators across Canada are beginning to develop early childhood programs designed to meet the needs of the children and families in their communities (Photo 20–11, p. 428). The vision statement in the Meadow Lake Tribal Council's early childhood program (Ball & Pence, 2001, p. 20) states:

> It will be the children who inherit the struggle to retain and enhance the people's culture, language and history; who continue the quest for economic progress for a better quality of life; and who move forward with a strengthened resolve to plan their own destiny.

Photo 20–11
Provide stimulating program activities designed to meet the needs of the children and families in their community.

Child care centres such as Winnipeg's Nee Gawn Ah Kai (Children of Our Tomorrows) more than meet these objectives. Aboriginal staff members are able to speak Cree to support children who have recently arrived from the North speaking Cree. Staff are working to develop a bilingual program to teach the language to children whose families have lost it. Meals include bannock and other traditional foods. Traditional values are an integral part of the curriculum because the staff are members of the community.

There are few curriculum materials available to support such teaching. Families and communities must work together to develop materials and the training to use them. Early childhood education training programs are beginning to change to reflect these needs.

One such program is at the Arctic College of Iqaluit, which has recently developed and taught the first early childhood education program in Nunavut and the Northwest Territories. The skill of the students as well as of the elders in the community of Nunatta has been used to design a program that supports language and literacy in both Inuktitut and English (McNaughton & Stenton, 1992, pp. 20–21). The early childhood values of cooperation, noncompetitiveness, teaching by example, and respect for the child's freedom mesh very well with Inuit traditional child-rearing practices (Colwell & Wright, 1992, pp. 18–19). However, another value, the prohibition on expression of feelings, has made children susceptible to substance abuse and has contributed to a high suicide rate. Working through these conflicts between early childhood and cultural practices is a challenge to all culturally sensitive programs. The Meadow Lake Tribal Council of northern Saskatchewan and the School of Child and Youth Care of the University of Victoria are working together to develop an early childhood education training program that recognizes that both the Aboriginal and the traditional educational system have important contributions to make (Ball & Pence, 2001).

Whether in a northern community, a small town, or an inner-city early childhood setting, programming must support the children's development of their identity as Aboriginal people. The family's traditional language forms an essential part of that identity.

Summary

Children do not just "pick up" a new language, so our school systems are full of children with no real, solid language base. It takes a relaxed child with high self-esteem, a good language modeller with a lot of appropriate animation, and an environment that fosters first-language retention to make acquisition of the new language possible.

By supporting first-language development, by building in family involvement, and by using good second-language teaching strategies, early childhood educators can help make sure that the children in their care not only retain their first language, but also mature in its use; not only learn English as a second language, but also achieve total command. It all starts in early childhood.

RESOURCES

FIRST NATIONS PARTNERSHIP PROGRAMS

http://www.uvic.ca/fnpp

This site provides information about the partnership between the School of Child and Youth Studies at the University of Victoria and a number of First Nations communities.

WESTCOAST CHILD CARE RESOURCE CENTRE (BRITISH COLUMBIA)

http://www.wstcoast.org

Westcoast Multicultural and Diversity Services provide resources, information, and training to promote multicultural, anti-racist, and anti-bias child care programs. Westcoast Multilingual Child Care Resources provide translated information for families in a number of languages.

ABORIGINAL CHILDREN'S CIRCLE OF EARLY LEARNING

http://www.accel-capea.ca

The Aboriginal Children's Circle of Early Learning (ACCEL) is a fully functioning bilingual web portal clearinghouse on Aboriginal early childhood development (ECD). This site can be used to review, research, and discuss best and promising practices; to exchange information with a highly engaged network of Aboriginal ECD practitioners and researchers; and to keep in touch with the emerging needs of communities across Canada.

STUDENT ACTIVITIES

In reference to the case examples at the beginning of this chapter, complete the following exercises.

1. Explain why Sao Chan refuses to speak Cantonese to her parents at home (see page 415). Discuss the implications of her attitude. List five things that you could do to help. What advice would you give to her family?

2. Ebrahim's family wants him to learn English as soon as possible (see page 415). In a small group of three or four, role-play a family interview in which the teacher discusses first- and second-language learning. What support people should be present at such an interview?

3. Work in small groups of four or five. Generate as many examples as possible of children's behaviour that is affected by cultural expectations. Start with Omi's situation (see pages 415 and 420). Pass your group's list of examples to another group. Using the new list passed to you, identify the issues involved in each behaviour and discuss how you would handle it as a teacher. If you

cannot identify the cultural issues involved in each behaviour, indicate the resources that would help you.

4. Arrange to do an observation in a child care centre that has some children who speak a home language other than English. Using one room as your source, list examples of (a) programming that supports home language maintenance, and (b) programming that supports the learning of English as a second language. List five program activities that would enrich the language-learning opportunities in the room.

REFERENCES

Ball, J., & Pence, A. (2001). Training in First Nations communities: Five "secrets" of success. *Ideas in Interaction, 15*(1), 19–24.

Bee, H. (1999). *The developing child*. New York: Holt, Rinehart & Winston.

Chud, G., & Fahlman, R. (1985). *Early childhood education for a multicultural society: A handbook for educators*. Vancouver: WEDGE Publishing, University of British Columbia.

Colwell, K., & Wright, P. (1992). Arctic realities: Developing early childhood training for Inuit students. *Multiculturalism, 14*(2, 3), 18–19.

Cummins, J. (1981). *Bilingualism and minority-language children*. Language and Literacy Series, Ontario Institute for Studies in Education. Toronto: Ontario Institute for Studies in Education.

Cummins, J. (1984). *Bilingualism and special education: Issues in assessment and pedagogy*. Clevedon, Avon (UK): Multilingual Matters.

Dotsch, J. (1992). Newcomer preschool children: Their cultural and linguistic adaptation to childcare settings. *Multiculturalism, 14*(2, 3), 24–26.

Dotsch, J. (1998). *Non-biased children's assessment*. Toronto: Bias Free Early Childhood Services.

Fralick, P. (1989). *Make it multicultural—Musical activities for early childhood education*. Hamilton, ON: Mohawk College.

Fraser, S. (1992). Talk to play and play to talk: A multicultural initiative. *Multiculturalism, 14*(2, 3), 27–30.

Freire, M., & Bernard, J. (1997). Caring for and teaching children who speak other languages. In K. Kilbride (Ed.), *Include me too! Human diversity in early childhood* (pp. 177–196). Toronto: Harcourt Brace.

Frideres, J. (1993). *Native peoples in Canada: Contemporary conflicts* (6th ed.). Scarborough, ON: Prentice-Hall Canada.

Gonzalez-Mena, J. (2001). *Multicultural issues in child care* (3rd ed.). Mountain View, CA: Mayfield.

Hakuta, K., & Garcia, E. E. (1991). Bilingualism and education. *American Psychologist, 44*(2), 374–379.

Hendrick, J. (1992). *The whole child* (2nd Can. ed.). Toronto: Maxwell Macmillan.

Houston, M. W. (1992). First things first: Why early childhood educators must support children's home language while promoting second language development." *Multiculturalism, 14*(2, 3), 47–50.

Houston, M. W. (1995). Tell me a story (then tell it again): Supporting literacy for preschool children from bilingual families. *Interaction*, Spring, 32–35.

Kilbride, K. M. (1990). *Multicultural early childhood education—A resource kit.* Toronto: Ryerson Polytechnic Institute.

Kilbride, K. M. (1997). (Ed.), *Include me too! Human diversity in early childhood.* Toronto: Harcourt Brace.

McMurter, J. (1992). Thirty preschoolers—Fifteen languages. *Multiculturalism, 14*(2, 3), 79.

McNaughton, K., & Stenton, D. (1992). Literacy, leadership, and practice: One formula for effective early childhood education training. *Multiculturalism, 14*(2, 3), 20–21.

Saville-Troike, M. (1976). *Foundations for teaching English as a second language.* Englewood Cliffs, NJ: Prentice-Hall.

Statistics Canada. (2003). *Analysis series: 2001 census. Canada's ethnocultural portrait: The changing mosaic, 2001 census* (Catalogue number 96F0030XIE2001008). Retrieved April 20, 2005, from http://www12.statcan.ca/english/census01/products/analytic/companion/etoimm/contents.cfm.

Wong-Fillmore, L. (1991). When learning a second language means losing the first. *Early Childhood Research Quarterly, 6,* 323–346.

York, S. (1991). *Roots and wings: Affirming culture in early childhood programs.* St. Paul, MN: Redleaf Press.

Glossary

The numbers in parentheses are the page numbers in the text where the discussion of the term can be found.

Accommodations:
adjustments on the part of the child, family, or service providers that enable a successful transition to a new environment for the child (272)

Adaptive equipment:
mobility devices, prostheses, and prescribed alterations of standard furnishings to meet the needs of children with special needs (165)

Advanced psychomotor ability:
eye–hand or eye–foot coordination is at the level of a much older child, as found in some children who are gifted (124)

Adventitious deafness:
deafness acquired through injury or disease after birth (101)

Advocacy:
speaking and acting in support or on behalf of people or ideas (39)

Advocacy group:
a group of individuals who work together for a particular cause; the Epilepsy Association works to ensure equal access, opportunity, and acceptance within society for persons with epilepsy (6)

Affection or friendship training:
specific programs that promote positive social interactions between children with and without special needs (345)

Aggressiveness:
acting-out behaviour in which a child may hurt other children, cause disruptions by intentionally throwing objects, or behave in ways that disrupt the group (362)

Amino acids:
one of the chief components of proteins; amino acids are obtained from the individual's diet or are manufactured by living cells (112)

Amniocentesis:
a medical procedure to determine if genetic abnormalities are present in the developing fetus; can be done about the 16th week of pregnancy (gestation) (38)

Amplification device:
devices, such as hearing aids, that make sound louder and clearer for a child with a hearing impairment (136)

Anaphylactic shock:
a rapid allergic reaction that can be life-threatening if not treated immediately; it is caused by an intense overreaction of the body's immune system to a trigger (180)

Anemia:
a reduced number of red blood cells usually resulting from inadequate nutrition; often characterized by listlessness and pale appearance of the skin (116)

Anoxia:
a shortage of oxygen to the brain that can cause physical damage to the brain before, during, or at any time after birth; anoxia is one of the major causes of physical and cognitive dysfunction (114, 161)

Anti-bias materials:
learning materials (for example, adaptive scissors, dolls with leg braces) that reflect developmental differences (319)

Antecedents and consequences:
antecedents are events that come before a behaviour (in behavioural psychology, the antecedent is the stimulus that causes a response); consequences are the events that follow a behaviour (358)

Anxiety disorder:
an extreme and lasting concern and fearfulness in certain situations, which other children their age do not experience; these commonly include separation problems, overdependence, withdrawal from social interactions, and so on (191)

Articulation:
refers to the production of speech sounds (384)

Articulation errors:
speech sounds that are inconsistent with the native language (usually a temporary developmental irregularity) (384)

Asperger's disorder:
a neurological disorder with many of the same characteristics as autism; the exception is that children with Asperger's disorder are intellectually high functioning (197)

Assistive technology:
various kinds of equipment, such as a computerized Braille system or voice synthesizer, designed to facilitate learning and communications for individuals with disabilities (397)

Asymptomatic:
showing no signs of a disease or impairment, which nevertheless may be present (112)

At risk/high risk:
indications (either physical or environmental) that an infant or child may develop serious problems (110)

Ataxia:
a lack of motor coordination, ataxia is characterized by poor balance and a lurching kind of walk, reflecting a lack of voluntary muscle control (162)

Athetosis:
fluctuating or uneven muscle tone; muscle control that goes from one extreme to the other (either too low or too high) is typical (162)

Attention deficit hyperactivity disorder (ADHD):
behaviour that is characterized by consistently short attention span, inattentiveness, distractibility, impulsivity, and heightened levels of movement and physical activity (hyperactivity) (198)

Attention span:
the length of time an individual is able to concentrate on an activity or event (399)

Auditory:
refers to what is experienced through hearing (102)

Auditory brainstem response (ABR):
a procedure that measures the brain's response to high-frequency sound (137)

Auditory nerve:
the nerve along which the sensory cells (the hair cells) of the inner ear transmit information to the brain (1)

Augmentative communication systems:
communication systems used to supplement a child's verbal language; the systems may be sign language, picture symbols, or sophisticated computer systems, such as a voice synthesizer (388)

Autism:
a pervasive developmental disorder, a social-communicative problem that emerges before a child is three years old (195)

Autism spectrum disorder:
see pervasive developmental disorder (194)

Autosomal recessive disorder:
a gene carried by healthy parents on any one chromosome except the sex chromosomes that, if inherited from both parents, results in a child with a medical condition not present in the parents (112)

Backward chaining:
the opposite of forward chaining; teaching starts with the last step of a learning sequence (235)

Baseline:
data that are collected on a behaviour before a systematic plan is introduced; these data provide a base against which later behaviour can be compared (360)

Behaviour disorder (BD):
a chronic or pervasive challenging behaviour (187, 355)

Behaviour modification:
a system by which particular environmental events are systematically arranged to produce specified behaviour changes (222)

Bias-free screening and assessment:
selecting and administering screening and assessment tools that ensure a child is given the opportunity for optimum performance (260)

Bilingual education:
concepts are presented in the first (or home) language and then are reinforced in English (418)

Biological insult:
interference with or damage to an individual's physical structure or functioning (110)

Biological risk:
infants and children whose systems have undergone some kind of biological insult, such as an accident, injury, or severe stress, are at risk for developmental disabilities (94)

Blindness:
vision loss severe enough that it is not possible to read print, requiring the child to be educated through the use of Braille and other tactile and auditory materials (102)

Brain development:
affects cognitive growth and learning; children's brains need to be stimulated for the network of connections to grow and be protected from elimination (393)

Caretaker speech:
used in second-language learning to direct the child's attention to the immediate environment, labelling everything, speaking simply, and repeating and expanding on the child's words (424)

Case manager:
the member of the IPP team who assumes responsibility for coordination of the program and services for the child (55)

Cerebral palsy:
a condition that affects muscular control; it is caused by damage to various parts of the brain. Its effects range from very mild (nonincapacitating) to moderate (involving fine or gross motor skills, or both), to pervasive (involving almost all areas of the body's physical activity) (160)

Challenging behaviour:
see difficult behaviour (355)

Chemotherapy:
the treatment of cancer by using drug therapy used to kill cancer cells (173)

Chorionic villus sampling (CVS):
a test for genetic abnormalities that can be done between the 9th and 11th week of gestation; at this time, amniocentesis is considered the safer procedure, resulting in fewer miscarriages

Chronic:
in reference to a health problem of long duration and frequent recurrence (101)

Classification:
part of concept formation in which an order is imposed on objects or events into specific categories (404)

Cochlea:
a snail-shaped structure in the inner ear that allows hearing to occur (134)

Cochlear implant:
a device, surgically placed by opening the mastoid structure of the skull, that allows electrical impulses (sound) to be carried directly to the brain (143)

Code switch:
moving from one language and its cultural expression to another, depending on the situation (418)

Cognitive delay
intellectual growth that does not follow the expected rate of development due to genetic or environmental conditions or a combination of both (107)

Communication and language disorders:
difficulties with speaking or learning language, which can lead to serious disruptions in cognitive and social development (98)

Conduct disorder:
a pattern of behaviour that involves extreme aggressiveness, destruction of property, disruptive behaviours, tantrums, or oppositional behaviours that violate the rights of others, social norms, or rules (360)

Conductive hearing loss:
refers to problems in the mechanical transmission of sounds through the outer or middle ear, which in turn reduce the intensity of sound vibrations reaching the auditory nerve in the inner ear (134)

Congenital:
refers to a physical condition that originates during the prenatal period (109)

Congenital deafness:
deafness present at the time of birth (101)

Contingent stimulation:
responding to a child in a way that prompts further learning (76, 338)

Contractures:
permanent tightening of muscles and joints (160)

Coordinated teaching:
when a child with special needs is in dual placements, staff from the specialized program and those from the inclusive early childhood setting provide coordinated programming for the child (73)

Cortical/cerebral visual impairment:
visual impairments originating in the brain (144)

Criterion-referenced tests:
assessments that describe a child's developmental level and progress according to a prescribed set of skills, tasks, and activities (248)

Culturally sensitive:
classroom activities, materials, and curricula that acknowledge and respect the different ethnicities that are represented in the classroom and community (50)

Data collection:
monitoring a child's behaviour and gathering information on it; data collection is used to evaluate the success of any intervention plan and is helpful only when it is easy to do and provides an accurate picture of the child's behaviour (358)

Deaf:
having a hearing loss so severe that the individual cannot process spoken language even with amplification (134)

Descriptive praise:
feedback that lets children know specifically what it is they are doing well (225)

Developmental delay:
development of a skill progresses at a slower rate so that a child demonstrates the skill as a younger child would (93)

Developmental deviation:
some aspect of a child's development is different from what is seen in other developing children (93)

Developmental disabilities:
a range of conditions that interfere with any aspect of the normal development of the child (93)

Developmental disequilibrium:
a period of inconsistent behaviour, which often follows a spurt of rapid development (75)

Developmental milestones:
points at which specific skills are acquired in a fairly predictable order (92)

Developmental sequences:
an ongoing process of moving step by step toward mastery of each developmental skill in every area of development (91)

Didactic materials:
manipulative materials in which the child's errors and successes are self-evident—the material, not the teacher, provides the information; Montessori was the originator of many such materials (220)

Differentiated responses:
infants' and toddlers' ability to differentiate simpler and more specific responses among global undifferentiated responses to stimuli (297)

Difficult behaviour:
describes the impact a behaviour has on the people with whom the child is interacting (355)

Discrimination:
the ability to perceive likeness and differences among related objects and events; to specify same versus different; to match objects, sounds, or ideas in terms of one or more attribute (403)

Dual placements:
when children with special needs spend a part of the day in a specialized program and part in an inclusive child care setting (73)

Duration:
measures how long an event or behaviour lasts (359)

Dysfluency:
hesitations, repetitions, or omitted or extra sounds in speech patterns (384)

Dysgraphia:
difficulty with or inability to express thoughts in writing, and/or to identify the written symbols of language (98)

Dyslexia:
an impaired ability to read and understand written language (98)

Earmould:
that part of an amplification device (hearing aid) that is fitted to the individual's ear (141)

Echolalic:
describes a condition in which language is characterized by repetition of words and sentences that do not convey meaning; this condition is often associated with autism (195)

Embedded learning:
the intentional incorporation of specific learning objectives into play and routine classroom activities (396)

Emergent curriculum:
curriculum that is developed from a variety of sources, including children's play activities and questions, and that is personally meaningful, intellectually engaging, and socially relevant (129, 320)

Emotional disturbances:
characterized by behavioural or emotional responses so different from appropriate age, cultural, and community norms that the responses adversely affect educational performance (100, 187)

Empowerment:
planning and carrying out intervention activities in ways that pass as much control and decision making as possible on to the family (49)

Enabling environment (infancy):
an environment that supports a child's optimal development (292)

Encopresis:
chronic soiling problem (193)

Enuresis:
chronic wetting problem (193)

Environmental influences:
the impact of environment on the development of the child (121)

Environmental risk:
factors in a child's environment, such as poverty, child abuse, family beliefs, and inaccessibility of medical care, that put the child at risk for developmental disabilities (94)

Environmental structuring:
teachers arrange features of the physical environment to foster social interaction (339)

Expressive language:
spoken words or signs that individuals use in communicating with others (377)

Facilitative teacher:
a teacher who makes things happen by planning, implementing, and evaluating a range of teaching strategies (82)

Fading:
gradually reducing prompts, cues, and physical assistance when teaching a particular skill (358)

Failure to thrive:
refers to undersized infants whose bodies, for various reasons (organic, genetic, or environmental) either do not receive or cannot use the nurturance necessary for proper growth and development (56)

Family uniqueness:
perspective that recognizes that every family is different (50)

First trimester:
the first three months of prenatal development (110)

Forward chaining:
breaking a task down into a series of small steps and teaching the first step first, in contrast to backward chaining (where the final step is taught first) (235)

Frequency:
in research, it refers to the number of times during a specified period that a designated behaviour occurred (359)

Functional approach:
examining and assessing the environment and teacher behaviour to determine in what ways they might affect a child's behaviour, then planning and carrying out an intervention, and monitoring the child's progress (358)

Genetic mutation:
an alteration in the chromosomal materials (genes) that control inherited characteristics (173)

Genetic predisposition:
a child is born with a genetic makeup that will enable him or her to function at an intellectually high level (121)

Gifted and have ADHD:
unlike most children who are gifted, these children have trouble effectively using the strategies and skills they, have and their giftedness is not recognized (126)

Giftedness:
evidence of superior or unusual ability in areas such as intellect, creativity, artistic talent, physical agility, or leadership (121)

Goodness-of-fit:
when the learning opportunities are appropriate to the child's developmental status (356)

Handicap:
relates to environmental or functional demands that, when placed on an individual with a disability, cannot be met (93)

Handicappism:
assumptions and practices based on physical, mental, or behavioural differences that foster differential and unequal treatment of people (5)

Health conditions:
refers to the range of health problems a child might have and how these affect their growth, development, and everyday lives (160)

Health impairments:
chronic or acute disorders, such as heart problems, leukemia, and asthma, that threaten a child's overall development (101)

Hearing impairment:
a hearing loss that can have a delaying effect on a child's cognitive, social, and language development (101)

Heritage language:
in Canada, a language other than English or French that has been passed on from generation to generation (415)

High risk:
a high probability of developing serious problems (113)

Holophrastic speech:
a state of speech development where a child conveys meaning with a one-word utterance (377)

Home language:
usually refers to the child's first language, the language a child hears in the home environment; often referred to as the "mother tongue" (415)

Hydrocephalus:
a condition that occurs as the result of a buildup of cranial spinal fluid in the head; if not corrected (shunted), can lead to an enlargement of the head and, ultimately, pressure on and deterioration of the brain (163)

Hyperactivity or hyperkinesis:
used to refer to children who are highly active, energetic, impulsive, and distractible and who have a hard time waiting their turn or listening to instructions (198)

Hypertonicity:
abnormally high muscle tone (161)

Hypotonicity:
too little muscle tone, "floppiness" (161)

Immune system:
that aspect of body functioning responsible for warding off diseases (176)

Incidental social learning:
the teacher promotes social interactions as they arise naturally and spontaneously (343)

Incidental teaching:
using a spontaneous teaching opportunity, which is always initiated by the child when he or she asks for help, materials, or information (77)

Inclusion:
children are included, with additional assistance and resources, regardless of ability in early childhood settings, educational environments, and community programs (3)

Inclusive:
equitable access is offered to all children, regardless of ability (272)

Incontinence:
a lack of bladder or bowel control (163)

Individual family service plan (IFSP):
similar to the IPP, the IFSP is a written plan that describes services for families with young children with special needs; it is written collaboratively with parents and describes the child's current strengths and needs (5, 54)

Individual program plan (IPP):
an approach to providing services to individuals with special needs: the process involves developing a written plan based on the child's strength's, needs, and interests; implementation and evaluation are part of the IPP process (5, 260)

Induced incompetence:
the effects of poorly functioning equipment on children with special needs (315)

In-home support services:
services, such as development assessments and parenting support, are provided for infants with special needs and their families in the home (291)

Integration:
children with special needs are given extra support so that they can be integrated into a regular setting and meet the existing expectations of the classroom (3)

Interdisciplinary:
refers to several different professions working together on a common problem, sharing information and exchange roles, depending on the case (260)

Intermittent hearing loss:
hearing comes and goes because of a build up of fluid caused by repeated ear infections (135)

Interval:
a specified period of the day that is broken into segments to record the occurrence, frequency, and duration of a behaviour (359)

Intrinsic motivation:
feelings of pleasure and personal satisfaction derived from working on or accomplishing a task, discovering something new, or solving a problem (220)

Learning disability:
one of a number of disorders that may affect the acquisition, organization, retention, understanding, or use of verbal or nonverbal information, even though the individual is of at least average intellectual ability (thinking or reasoning or both) (203)

Learning disorders:
the name given to a group of problems that can cause children who have average IQs and reasonable adaptive functioning to nevertheless have difficulty learning to read, write, do math (87)

Learning theory:
emphasizes the dominant role of environment and reinforcing experiences in all learning; social learning theory adds other dimensions—that learning also occurs through observing and imitating and that individuals can generate their own satisfactions (intrinsic reinforcement) (222)

Mainstreaming:
children with special needs have to "be ready" to be integrated into the mainstream (3)

Manual prompts:
when the teacher's hand is around the learner's and actually putting the learner through the motions (may also be referred to as "hand over hand") (235)

Maturation:
developmentally, maturation is often defined as an internal process that governs the natural unfolding of innate ("preprogrammed") skills and abilities (219)

Mediated learning model:
based on the teaching premise that cognitive and social processes are interdependent factors in all learning (83)

Medical model:
an approach to understanding disabilities that individualizes and pathologizes a disability as a biological impairment, a deficit, or a dysfunction residing within the person (28)

Meningocele:
a congenital protrusion of the spinal cord through the vertebrae; it is limited to the covering of the spinal cord and usually causes little or no neurological impairment (163)

Metabolic disorders:
single-gene defects that cause a breakdown somewhere in the complex chemical activities needed to metabolize food (111)

Metabolize:
the chemical process within living cells by which energy is manufactured so that the body systems can carry out their functions (174)

Minority language:
in Canada, languages other than English or French (415)

Modelling:
learning by watching and imitating another's actions; also called observational learning (219)

Motherese:
unique infant-directed speech patterns that adults use with the very young (375)

Multiple disabling conditions:
the condition of having more than one disability (99)

Multisensory deprived (MSD):
refers to a child who is both blind and deaf (133)

Muscle tone:
the interaction between the central nervous system and motor activity; the term does not mean the same thing as muscle strength; without muscle tone there is no voluntary movement (108)

Myelomeningocele:
a congenital protrusion of the spinal cord through the vertebrae; paralysis and lack of sensation below the protrusion (usually the lower trunk and legs) are often the result (163)

Neurological:
refers to the functioning of the nervous system (114)

Nonambulatory:
unable to walk (234)

Nonintrusive:
professionals respecting the privacy of families and not intruding into families' lives or lifestyles without an invitation to do so (55)

Norm-referenced tests:
instruments that compare a child's developmental level with a normative sample of same-age peers (248)

Occlusion:
an obstruction; as used here, something to prevent vision; an occluder is the object the examiner uses to prevent a child from seeing (usually one eye at a time) (146)

Operant conditioning:
a teaching strategy in which the child's behaviour is shaped as the result of a planned response designed to reinforce a specific behaviour (222)

Oppositional defiant disorder (ODD):
a pattern of negativistic, hostile, and defiant behaviour—lasting at least six months—which interferes with social or academic functioning or both (366)

Orderly sequences:
events during an activity period follow a predicable pattern (327)

Orthopedic conditions:
conditions involving the bones and joints (160)

Orthopedic impairments:
developmental differences that interfere with walking or other body movements (99)

Other first language (OFL):
in Canada, a person's first language that is other than English or French (416)

Overregularization:
language irregularities that occur because the child is applying previously learned rules of grammar; for example, "The mouses runned" (378)

Peer imitating:
young children with special needs observe and imitate more advanced skills modelled by peers (14)

Peer tutoring:
one child instructing or assisting another (19)

People-first language:
language that focuses on the person instead of the disability; for example, saying "a child with autism" rather than "an autistic child" emphasizes abilities rather than limitations (5)

Perceptual motor skills:
movement generated by sensory messages, by what is seen, heard, touched, tasted, or smelled (400)

Perinatally:
occurring or existing at the time of birth (109)

Peripheral vision:
that degree of vision available at the outer edges of the eyes (150)

Perseveration:
repeating the same act over and over with no discernible intention (in an obsessive, ritualistic manner) (210)

Pervasive developmental disorder (PDD):
a serious disturbance that affects a child's social-language interaction or ability to engage in imaginative play or both (194)

Phobias:
fears that result in excessive and unrealistic anxiety about everyday happenings (192)

Pica:
craving to eat nonfood substances (192)

Portfolio:
a carefully selected collection of a child's work that is used to document growth and development (259)

Postlingual hearing loss:
hearing loss occurring after the child has acquired speech (134)

Postnatally:
occurring or existing after birth (109)

Potentially gifted:
refers to a child who has advanced vocabulary and oral language ability, understands abstract concepts, uses play materials in creative ways, catches on quickly to new ideas and concepts, memorizes easily, and has a long attention span (122)

Prader-Willi syndrome:
a genetic disorder characterized by obesity, short stature, disorders in sexual development, and a tendency toward behavioural and cognitive disabilities (179)

Precocious:
the term used to describe young children who appear remarkably bright or unusually verbal and who may demonstrate outstanding talents in some specialized area, such as art, music, math (121)

Prelingual communication:
body movements, facial expressions, and vocalizations used by infants before the first words are learned (376)

Prelingual hearing loss:
hearing loss occurring before the child has acquired speech (134)

Prenatal:

before birth (40)

Prenatally:

occurring or existing before birth (109)

Preorientation and mobility skills:

the ability of a child who has a visual impairment to map out and travel in a room safely (149)

Preventive discipline:

a child management procedure for arranging the environment in ways that reduce the occurrence of maladaptive behaviours and increase the occurrence of appropriate behaviours (228)

Primitive reflexes:

the responses the infant is born with, such as grasping, stepping, rooting, and sucking. Most of these disappear around four months of age and are replaced by similar but voluntary behaviours, as in the sucking response (162)

Prostheses/prosthetic device:

artificial devices replacing body parts that are damaged or missing at birth or later removed (166, 167)

Protein deficiency:

a factor in maternal malnutrition when the mother's diet is lacking in milk, cheese, eggs, meats, and so on, which can result in premature or seriously low-birthweight babies (114)

Psychological balance:

an infant or a toddler's ability to maintain a balance between approaching and avoiding environmental events (stimuli) (297)

Radiation:

The use of high-energy penetrating rays to damage cancer cells, stopping them from growing and dividing (173)

Readiness:

the point when a child has all of the necessary prerequisite skills to engage in specific new learning (76)

Readiness as a learning theory:

recognizes the importance of being aware of the point at which a child has all of the necessary prerequisite skills to engage in specific new learning (393)

Receptive language:

language that is understood; it precedes expressive language (376)

Reciprocal relationships:

interactions between individuals in which each person gives and receives in response to the giving and receiving of the other (49)

Refractive errors:

problems, such as astigmatism, hyperopia, and myopia, are caused by a minor malformation of the eye that influences the bending of light rays (144)

Regeneration:

the regrowth, repair, or renewal of the spinal cord or other parts of the body (163)

Reinforcement:

a general term for a consequence, an event, or procedure that increases or maintains the behaviour it follows; high grades are reinforcement for good academic performance (223)

Reliable and valid tests:
reliability relates to consistency—how accurate, dependable, and predictable a test is, and validity refers to how accurately a test measures that which it purports to measure; for example, a score on a verbal IQ test for a child with an undiagnosed hearing impairment is not likely to be valid; the test does not measure the child's intelligence but rather how well the child's faulty hearing allows for interpretation of questions (244)

Renewal time:
a discipline technique that gives a child the message that he or she needs some time to calm down and to gain some inner control; a chance for the inner self to become renewed (229)

Replacement behaviour:
a behaviour that is taught to a child to replace an inappropriate one—a replacement behaviour should serve the same function as the inappropriate behaviour (358)

Residual hearing:
the degree of hearing of a person who is deaf or hearing impaired (135)

Residual vision:
vision remaining after disease or damage occurs to a person's visual system (147)

Resilience:
the ability to "come back" after a damaging or traumatic experience (95)

Resource teacher/early interventionist:
a professional with special training and expertise in planning and implementing developmentally appropriate programs for children who have developmental problems (56)

Respiratory distress syndrome (RDS):
a problem commonly found among premature infants because of the immature development of their lungs; it may also occur in about 1 percent of full-term infants during the first days of life (110)

Responsive environment:
adults actively engage with an individual infant and toddler and respond to his or her needs and sensorimotor and social exploration (292)

Reverse integration:
programs in which children without special needs participate in programs originally established for children with special needs (8)

Rote memorization:
the act of memorizing numbers or letters without understanding them; being able to recite something that has little or no meaning for the one who has memorized it (393)

Scaffolding:
a teaching and learning process in which the teacher provides decreasing levels of support while placing higher demands as the child progresses toward the goal of independent problem solving (83, 423)

School age care:
programs offered before and after school on a regular basis in a various settings for school-aged children (302)

Seizures:
bursts of electrical energy in the brain that cause uncontrolled muscular movement and reduced or total loss of consciousness, as in epilepsy (174)

Self-assertion:
a person standing up for his or her rights and possessions (346)

Self-help/care:
skills related to socially proscribed routines in early childhood settings, such as toileting, dressing, eating, cleaning up, and doing one's share of classroom chores (313)

Sensitive or critical periods:
a time when a child is especially responsive and able to learn a particular skill (12)

Sensorimotor profile:
an infant's preference for and use of one sensory modality over another for sensory exploration (294)

Sensorineural hearing loss:
a hearing loss that involves a malfunctioning of the cochlea or auditory nerve (134)

Sensory impairments:
difficulties in the ability to sense the environment through a specific sensory modality, such as hearing or sight (133)

Sensory integration:
the process of more than one sense working together to understand a sensory message and to translate the message into appropriate action (400)

Sensory stimulation:
objects and people that encourage infants and toddlers to explore their environment through seeing, hearing, touching, tasting, and smelling (293)

Seriation:
the process of arranging objects and events along orderly and related dimensions, for example, beginning, middle, end or small, bigger, biggest (404)

Service coordinator:
the member of the IPP team who assumes responsibility for coordination of the program and services for the child (56)

Shunting:
a process for implanting a tube (shunt) into the brain to allow proper circulation and drainage of fluids from within the skull into one of the body cavities (163)

Signing:
manual communication systems such as finger-spelling or ASL (American Sign Language) (140)

Social model:
an approach to understanding disabilities that identifies the barriers that prevent the social inclusion of people with disabilities and then focuses on the capacity of people with disabilities to change these barriers, with the help of others (28)

Social reinforcement:
the positive and negative feedback that children receive from adults and peers that leads to further learning, either appropriate or inappropriate (337)

Spasticity:
abnormal muscle tone—evident in taut muscle activity or too little muscle tone, both of which prevent fluid movements, as seen in cerebral palsy (161)

Spatial and temporal (time) concepts:
how objects are related to space and time and to the child (405)

Special ability in art:
an indication that a child may be potentially gifted in this area (124)

Special ability in music:
an indication that a child may be potentially gifted in this area (124)

Special needs:
challenges in learning and functioning in one or more areas of development and
increased vulnerability to environmental and non-environmental stresses (92)

Specific learning disabilities (SLD):
a difficulty in any of the following areas: attention, memory, reasoning, coordination,
communicating, reading, writing, spelling, calculation, social competence, and emotional maturation (98)

Speech reading:
the more accurate term for lip-reading (139)

Spina bifida:
the imperfect development of the spinal cord and spinal column that occurs during
the first 30 days of fetal development; it can cause severe disabilities (160)

Standardized IQ test:
a measure of intellectual performance based on averages that have been established by
testing large numbers of individuals of the same age (ideally of the same socioeconomic
background, too) (108)

Standardized tests:
assessment instruments that include precise directions for administration and
scoring (108)

Stigmata (stigma):
an identifying mark or characteristic; a diagnostic sign of a disease or disability (110)

Strabismus:
eye muscle imbalance problems, which are correctable with eyeglasses (145)

Structured flexibility:
a well-structured early learning environment that also is adaptable to children's
individual needs and preferences (325)

Subtractive bilingualism:
developing a second language (English) that replaces the first language (home
language), causing the first language to cease to develop (416)

Syndrome:
a grouping of similar physical characteristics (110)

Syntax:
the way in which words are put together to form phrases, clauses, or sentences (377)

Tactile:
refers to that which is learned or perceived through touch (102)

Tangible reinforcers:
material things that the individual likes; in children, favourite foods and drinks, toys,
stickers, and so on (older children usually like money) (196)

Task analysis:
the process of breaking down a complex task into smaller units so that learning can
occur more easily (231)

Teachable moments:
specific points when a child's level of readiness and interest come together to create the best milieu for new teaching (13, 77)

Teacher-guided learning opportunities:
the teacher directly supports the learning of skills during large and small group activities; also called one-on-one teaching or instruction periods (316)

Teacher-mediated interventions:
teachers provide direct support to encourage children to engage in social interactions (339)

Telegraphic speech:
the stage in language acquisition in which children's utterances are generally longer than two words; phrases convey grammatical meaning even though many words are left out (377)

Temperament:
an individual's psychological makeup or personality traits; of interest to the caregiver is how temperament influences an individual's responses to different situations (356)

Total communication:
a system for teaching children who have severe hearing impairments that combines speech reading and a sign system (139)

Transactional aspect of development:
the understanding that children and adults influence each other in their ongoing relationships and that both children and adults learn from these interactions (75)

Transdisciplinary:
professionals sharing expertise, modelling, and instructing other team members on how to implement specific practices within the group setting (55)

Transdisciplinary team:
team that shares the responsibilities for assessment, program planning, implementation, and evaluation across members (55)

Transition coordinator:
the team member who is responsible for coordinating the transition from one educational setting to a new educational setting (276)

Transition plans:
the plans developed to ensure a comfortable and positive transition for the child and family as they move from one educational setting to a new educational setting (272)

Traumatic brain injury:
includes injuries to the head that cause tearing of the nerve fibres, bruising of the brain against the skull, or bruising of the brain stem (103)

Visual acuity problems:
problems in how well an individual is able to see (144)

Visual impairment:
vision loss that include the following conditions: blind, partially sighted, blindness, and low vision (102)

Vulnerability:
lack of resistance to or ability to recover from a damaging or traumatic experience (95)

Wedges, bolsters, and prone-boards:
therapeutic positioning devices prescribed for use by physiotherapists and occupational therapists in treating children with impaired motor skills (167)

Zero reject:
no child is ever excluded for reasons of level or type of special need from full participation in a program or service (8)

Photo Credits

1 © Ariel Skelly/CORBIS.

3, 198, 209, 251, 349 Thomson Nelson.

6, 14, 128, 192, 194, 196, 202, 221, 228, 283, 337 Top, 342, 347, 381 Courtesy of Yes I Can! Nursery School.

8, 35, 126 Photodisc/Getty Images.

19, 137, 147, 227, 311, 312, 317, 323, 341, 379, 405 Courtesy of Play and Learn.

21, 281 Bottom, 314, 336, 426 Courtesy of Eglinton Public School.

49, 80, 91, 92, 206 Bottom, 238, 245, 293 Bottom, 294, 296, 299, 316, 335 Courtesy of George Brown College.

58, 63, 76, 162, 163, 164 Bottom, 167, 169, 178, 220, 224, 231 Top, 284, 345, 366, 368, 374, 384, 402 Top, 404 Top, 419 Used with permission of Thomson Delmar. From K. Eileen Allen and Glynnis E. Cowdery, *The Exceptional Child: Inclusion in Early Childhood Education* (Clifton Park, NY: Thomson Delmar, 2005).

73, 77, 87, 146 (both), 208, 249, 315 Courtesy of April Cornell, Executive Director, Ontario Foundation for Visually Impaired Children.

89 © Royalty-Free/Corbis.

123, 275, 319, 343, 410 Photo by Steven Savicky, courtesy of Bernice Cipparrone, Child Development Institute, Parkdale/High Park Ontario Early Years Centre.

171 Top Used with permission of Thomson Delmar. From Nicki Potts and Barbara Mandleco, *Pediatric Nursing: Caring for Children and Their Families,* First Edition. (Clifton Park, NY: Thomson Delmar Learning, 2002).

201, 293 Top, 298 Courtesy of Ingrid Crowther, *Introduction to Early Childhood Education: A Canadian Perspective* (Thomson Nelson: Toronto, 2005).

217 Stone/Getty Images.

289 © Michael Newman/PhotoEdit Inc.

306 Eyewire.

428 © Corel.

Index

Hurma

Hurma